Masterclass 01/ Getting to Know You

Introduction

Me and my "No Face" mask.

DOI: 10.1201/9781003324287-2

Welcome to the first of our 48 masterclasses together. These masterclass lessons are based on my own 2D ACADEMY's *"Tuesday Night Live"* online diploma classes, where I teach the foundations of animation and production. Hopefully you'll embrace this book as your *one-stop-shop* for learning animation – whether you're a home-based, self-teaching student; a student on a formal animation degree program; a professional trying to raise the bar of your work; or an instructor of a formal animation program seeking to teach your students the essential things they need to know. I've tried to make the material in this book definitive for both students and instructors alike. The studies will be intensive no doubt if you hopefully follow-through on everything – but they should be fun too. They are set up as they are however, to make you a *master animator* in the future.

As I have said already, we each stand on the shoulders of giants. In my honest opinion, the greatest character animation works created decades ago have never been bettered – not even today, with all the amazing technology we have at our disposal! By contrast to those far off Halcion days, the animation world – although it has a greater volume of production material than ever before – is depressingly low in terms of the quality of character animation coming out. It can be shown by the volume of "moving wallpaper" that is around on the TV networks, the internet and even (sadly) the mainstream cinemas (such as they are) that we live in an age of character animation mediocrity.

There are those rare exceptions of course, such as with the wonderful indie *Wolfwalkers* movie! © Cartoon Saloon Ltd., Melusine Productions.

If you at all care about the future of quality animation – especially quality traditional 2D animation – it may indeed fall upon your shoulders to be the new significant game changer of tomorrow. That is what this book is all about. I have tried to lay out the very best of foundations for you, in terms of animation knowledge and production know-how. In so doing, I have tried to be the *best*

NOT AN END – BUT A BEGINNING!

" If you place a fully-trained animator on a computer, they'll amaze you with how well they can bring inanimate characters to life. If you put an utrained animator on a computer however, all you'll get is moving shapes. The challenge of the digital age is not to learn software first and foremost, but to learn how to make things move well before touching a computer. That's the whole purpose and inspiration of this book! "

Tony White

" When buying from an artist/maker, you're buying more than an object. You are buying hundreds of hours of failures and experimentation. You are buying days, weeks and months of frustration and moments of pure joy. You aren't just buying a thing, you're buying a piece of heart, part of a soul, a moment in someone's life. Most importantly, you're buying the artist more time to do something they are passionate about. "

unknown author

" This book is all about tradition, and learning the great secrets of the past. But it is the future master animators yet to come that must continue that tradition, with their new vision, innovation and imagination. I sincerely hope that this book will help enable that process. "

Tony White

Author

Tony White, renowned animator, director, professor, mentor and author has been active at the highest level in the animation industry for over 50 years, and currently teaches 2D animation online at his 2D ACADEMY. White began his career working with legendary industry professionals like award-winning illustrator Ralph Steadman and animation gurus Ken Harris and Art Babbitt (original lead animator on *Pinocchio*, *Fantasia* and others at Disney). He also personally apprenticed with and then professionally directed/animated for the late, great Richard Williams (three-time Oscar winner and author of *The Animator's Survival Kit*). In addition to offering his live and online masterclasses at the online "2D ACADEMY", White is additionally the founder/director of the "DRAWTASTIC Animation Festival" and moderates for "2D ANIMAKERS", an online network and source of learning for the worldwide animation community. White is currently illustrating his first ever graphic novel, 'MADA and the Magic Tree", which is a mystical hero's journey adventure story based on an animated movie script he once wrote for the big screen.

Acknowledgements

Of all the people I would like to thank for this book being brought into existence, it is to those people who have bought, borrowed and read this book who I thank first and thank most earnestly. You are the **future** of this most wonderful of all artform we call *animation*, and I am honored that you chose my book at this moment in your life journey to learn your craft from me. Next, I wish to thank all those giants of the **past** who have gone before me, those who struggled and persevered for their knowledge that is extensively contained here and have, in one way or another, passed that inspiration on to me so that I might enjoy the successful and incredible career that I have had. Finally, I wish to thank all those of my **present**, who have supported me, encouraged me, and allowed me to use their work, words and examples to illustrate the pages of this book. You too are a great inspiration for which you have my greatest respect, which is precisely why your work appears here too. Not least of all these is my wife Saille, who has been the rock and the muse upon which all that is offered here has been built. Thank you for simply being you and enabling me to be the best "me" I can possible be.

Introduction

I have greatly enjoyed a 50+-year career in high-level character animation. Indeed, I have never stopped animating in all that time and feel I am only just now producing my most accomplished work. However, I still remain a product of a great tradition that went before me. Hand-drawn animation, as we know it, has been around for well over a century now – and the really scary thing for me is that I've actually been creatively active in almost half of that time! Yet those who went before me were the really great ones. They defined the industry and left a legacy we can barely dream of at its highest level. In all truth, we still cannot remotely match the great character animation of what the best of the best did long before this digital age – despite all the amazing technology we have at our fingertips. I have long recognized, and fully accept, that I stand on the shoulders of giants – a large number of whom I met, learned from and even apprenticed with at the beginning of my career. Animation giants, such as **Ken Harris**, **Art Babbitt**, **Chuck Jones**, **Frank Thomas**, **Grim Natwick** and many, many more, were huge influences on me as I venture forward in the early days. I was especially lucky enough to apprentice with the late, great **Richard Williams** too. I worked as his personal assistant for 2 years and then as an award-winning director/animator in his London studio for a further 5 years, prior to setting up my own! The very first project I assisted him on – and the first film credit I ever got – was "A Christmas Carol", which won an Academy Award.

But now the giants are gone and I am maybe the last of the next generation after those great masters to still be animating and teaching the secrets of an art form that I love and cherish so much. As the traditional hand-drawn character animation industry is now (shamefully) nonexistent in the USA, and with no signs of a reprieve, I have always felt a tremendous weight of responsibility on my shoulders to preserve and move forward again this incredible tradition. This book of masterclasses – born of all I know and all I have experienced over the years – is my way of gifting the younger generations all the material that they need to become master animators and filmmakers in their own right. I hope it will be seen as the definitive textbook I would have loved to have possessed at the beginning of my own career. It is somewhat inspired by the spirit of the Japanese culture – where, even far beyond their Anime tradition, they actively cherish and fight to preserve all their other great arts and crafts traditions. It is sad to say that now, here in the one country that once led the world so outstandingly in terms of traditional, hand-drawn animation, there is not the slightest interest in respecting or honoring the great legacy they once had. Consequently, I hope that this book will be a light in the darkness, and honor the knowledge of the great animators and animation of the past that has inspired generation after generation. I hope it will also be a clarion call for the young master animators of the future, who can perhaps bring about a renascence of traditional hand-drawn animation long after I have departed for that great lightbox in the sky. I therefore dedicate this book to anyone who dares to dream, and pick up a pencil in the hope of making that dream a reality.

About This Book

The online Zoom course upon which this whole book is based.

"Animation Masterclasses: From Pencils to Pixels" is a collection of masterclasses and guidelines for the teachers, animators and soon-to-be animators of the future. I hope everyone can learn from it – or teach from it – making it the ultimate and definitive textbook for all who want to make things move well!

As you can imagine, I have put my everything imaginable into these masterclasses. As a result, I suspect that this book could well be my last on the subject as I've little more to say on the subject, except for teaching or mentoring students one-on-one. For this reason, I've striven to make it my best. Everything you find here is based on the extensive discoveries I've gleaned throughout the career that has spanned over 50 years, as well as from some of the greatest character animators ever. At the heart of this learning and teaching has always been the *"core principles of movement"* – techniques that underpin all forms of animated expression – whether they be **2D**, **3D**, **Claymation**, **Stop-Frame** or whatever. Specifically with all this in mind, this book is fundamentally structured around my *"live"* 48-week course in animation and production that I teach through my own **2D ACADEMY**.

I have done this as the learning I share and the techniques I use have been honed in the cauldron of proven experience. In this way, I envisage this book as being a reliable companion for anyone who is either learning animation on their own; learning through a degree-level program of full-time education; learning as an existing professional who is wishing to raise the bar on their work; or even teaching as an instructor who is responsible for bringing knowledge and experience to the world the master animators of tomorrow.

I believe this is the very least I can do, if I am indeed to honor of the great master artists and animators who have taught or inspired me along the path of my own animation journey.

This Book's Structure

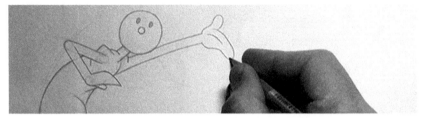

I'm drawing on a lot of experience here!

To achieve my stated objectives, I have structured my masterclasses into four distinct sections, based on the 48-week course I teach at my own **2D ACADEMY**.

Section I: This section communicates many *core principles of movement*, using traditional hand-drawn animation techniques.

Section II: This section communicates more *core principles of movement*, but taught in a digital environment, using *"Moho"* as my tool of choice.

Section III: This section develops a powerful film idea through structured *pre-production* processes, ready for production.

Section IV: This section applies tried and tested *production* techniques that make the completion of an animated film possible.

Each of these sections contains **12 specific masterclass lessons** related to the theme of each section, with each lesson establishing as specific objective. I would stress too that although many of the exercises are of a *"drawn"* nature, students **do not necessarily have to be able to draw well** to do them. So, whether students work with the most basic of *"stick-figures"* or perhaps draw with the dexterity of a *Rembrandt* or *Leonardo da Vinci*, they should find that they can ultimately animate equally well, as long as they study with due diligence, a passion to learn and the temerity to reach for the stars.

The Book's Curriculum

2021-22 Curriculum
MODULE 01: "TUESDAY NIGHT LIVE" *(Starting September 14th, 2021)*

Week no.	
01	Course Introduction / Flipbook Fun
02	Traditional 2D animation intro
03	Keys, breakdowns & inbetweens
04	Squash & Stretch
05	Slow-in/Slow out
06	Timing & placement
07	Generic walk action 01
08	Generic walk action 02
09	Generic walk action 03
10	Personality walk action 01
11	Personality walk action 02
12	Running action 01

2020-21 Curriculum
MODULE 02: "TUESDAY NIGHT LIVE" *(Starting November 10th, 2020)*

Week no.	1st Year Students	2nd Year Apprentices
01	Generic Run action	A-B-C Production work.
02	Generic Run with "MOHO"	A-B-C Production work.
03	Stylized Runs 02	A-B-C Production work.
04	Character Jump 01	A-B-C Production work.
05	Character Jump 02	A-B-C Production work.
06	Character Throw 01	A-B-C Production work.
07	Character Throw 02	A-B-C Production work.
08	Weight 01	A-B-C Production work.
09	Weight 02	A-B-C Production work.
10	Dialogue 01	A-B-C Production work.
11	Dialogue 02	A-B-C Production work.
12	Overlapping action	A-B-C Production work.

MODULE 03 & 04 CURRICULUM
(Starting February 9th, 2021)

Week no.	Module 03	Module 04
01	PROJECT PLANNING / STORY	ANIMATION BLOCKING (1)
02	CONCEPT ART	ANIMATION BLOCKING (2)
03	CHARACTER DESIGN	BREAKDOWN POSITIONS (1)
04	STORYBOARDING (1)	BREAKDOWN POSITIONS (2)
05	STORYBOARDING (2)	INBETWEENING (1)
06	AUDIO TRACK / BREAKDOWN	INBETWEENING (2)
07	STORYBOARD ANIMATIC	BACKGROUND ART (1)
08	CHARACTER RIG (1)	BACKGROUND ART (2)
09	CHARACTER RIG (2)	ANIMATION COLORING (1)
10	BACKGROUND LAYOUTS (1)	ANIMATION COLORING (2)
11	BACKGROUND LAYOUTS (2)	COMPOSITING & ADJUSTS
12	POSE TEST ANIMATIC	FINAL RENDER + PRESENT

MODULE 04 CURRICULUM
(Starting February 9th, 2021)

Week no.	Module 04
01	ANIMATION BLOCKING (1)
02	ANIMATION BLOCKING (2)
03	BREAKDOWN POSITIONS (1)
04	BREAKDOWN POSITIONS (2)
05	INBETWEENING (1)
06	INBETWEENING (2)
07	BACKGROUND ART (1)
08	BACKGROUND ART (2)
09	ANIMATION COLORING (1)
10	ANIMATION COLORING (2)
11	COMPOSITING & ADJUSTS
12	FINAL RENDER + PRESENT

This book's curriculum is structured around my first 48-week 2D Academy animation course.

To give the reader a more specific idea of how the four sections of this book are composed, I believe the following curriculum outline will explain. You should also be aware that all my "live" diploma classes at the **2D ACADEMY** begin with a specific *"observation gesture drawing"* warm-up exercise. These therefore are also included with each of the 48 masterclass lessons that lie before you:

Section I: *The Core Principles of Movement – Traditional Techniques*

Masterclass 01/**Getting to Know You**

Masterclass 02/**Squash, Stretch and Bouncing Balls**

Masterclass 03/**Keys, Breakdowns & Inbetweens**

Masterclass 04/**More on "Squash & Stretch"**

Masterclass 05/**More on Slow-In & Slow-Out**

Masterclass 06/**Timing & Placement**

Masterclass 07/**Generic Walk Action 01**

Masterclass 08/**Generic Walk Action 02**

Masterclass 09/**Generic Walk Action 03**

Masterclass 10/**Personality Walk Action 01 – "Double Bounce"**

Masterclass 11/**Personality Walk Action 02 – "Sneak"**

Masterclass 12/**Personality Walk Action 03 – "Front Walk"**

Course outcome: By the end of this module, students will understand many of the *essential principles of motion* and be able to demonstrate them through their *completed animation assignments*.

Section II: *More Core Principles of Movement – Digital Techniques*

Masterclass 13/**Introduction to Moho**

Masterclass 14/**The Full Rigged Character**

Masterclass 15/**Character Walk 1**

Masterclass 16/**Character Walk 2**

Masterclass 17/**"Arnie" Generic Walk**

Masterclass 18/**Generic Walk Variations**

Masterclass 19/**New Year Greeting**

Masterclass 20/**Double Jump**

Masterclass 21/**Slow Sneak Animation**

Masterclass 22/**Throwing Action**

Masterclass 23/**Digital Coloring**

Masterclass 24/**Working with Color**

Course outcome: By the end of this module, students will demonstrate an understanding of *all the necessary principles of motion* – including *anticipation*, *follow-through*, *fluidity* and *flexibility* – enabling them with sufficient skills to take on their own *animated short film project*.

Section III: *Personal Project – Pre-Production*

Masterclass 25/**Storytelling**

Masterclass 26/**Concept Art**

Masterclass 27/**Character Design**

Masterclass 28/**Storyboarding & Film Language**

Masterclass 29/**More on Storyboarding & Film Language**

Masterclass 30/**Audio Record & Breakdown**

Masterclass 31/**Storyboard Animatic**

Masterclass 32/**Character Rigging 1**

Masterclass 33/**Character Rigging 2**

Masterclass 34/**Layout 1**

Masterclass 35/**Anatomy of a Sequence**

Masterclass 36/**Final Pose Test Animatic**

Course outcome: By the end of this module, students will have **completed all the essential pre-production elements** in readiness to create their own animated short film project.

Section IV: *Personal Project – Production*

Masterclass 37/**Key Pose Animation 1**

Masterclass 38/**Key Pose Animation 2**

Masterclass 39/**Breakdown Positions 1**

Masterclass 40/**Breakdown Positions 2**

Masterclass 41/**Inbetweening 1**

Masterclass 42/**Inbetweening 2**

Masterclass 43/**Clean-Up 1**

Masterclass 44/**Clean-Up 2**

Masterclass 45/**Background Art**

Masterclass 46/**Inking**

Masterclass 47/**Coloring**

Masterclass 48/**Post-Production & Distribution**

Course outcome: By the end of Module 04, students will have successfully **completed their own animated short film project** – with successful students submitting their work into the dedicated category at the "**DRAWTASTIC Animation Festival**" will be presented with a **2D ACADEMY** *Diploma* if their film is accepted for screening at the event. The best of all entries at each event will be awarded one of the festival's coveted "**Golden Pencil Awards**".

Beyond This Book

The DRAWTASTIC Animation Festival's coveted "Golden Pencil Award".

I want you to understand that just doing the masterclass exercises in first two sections of this book – then making your own short film in the last two – need not end there.

If you complete everything, you have two additional options to take your reputation further. Additional details will be discovered at the back of this book, but for now let me just say that you can initially turn all your exercises into a personal **SHOWREEL** that can be shown online. We'll explain how you can do that at the end.

Then, if you want to enter your *Showreel* into a special book student category that will be set up for you at the "**DRAWTASTIC Animation Festival**", you'll also have an opportunity of winning one of their coveted "**Golden Pencil Awards**" in the foreseeable future!

Needless to say, both options will give you an amazing opportunity to further your career in animation. So it is surely worth you putting in the effort needed to get through every assignment in this book with these opportunities in mind.

As indicated, full details can be found at the end of your studies here. But hopefully these incentives will provide additional motivation, as well as potential exposure, for you as you work through the following 48 masterclasses!

Final Note to Course Instructors

Vive la hand-drawn animation.

We live in an age where the industry has minimal expectations and technology dominates technique in expectations. Therefore, so much of the material contained in this book might well be considered excessive – even "old school" – in the light of that. However, if you believe, like me, that a solid understanding of the core principles of movement using traditional hand-drawn techniques is the finest foundation any student can have, you'll want to hold the line a little and give your students the opportunity to learn in the best way possible. Remember that the groundbreaking 3D animated movie, "Toy Story", was made with the use of the finest, traditional, hand-drawn animators from Disney – and would have been nothing if CG technicians had made the film! This therefore set a precedent for the future of Pixar, and indeed the entire CG/3D animation industry at the highest level that respects traditional knowledge and skills. In reality, the world of animation is an unpredictable and infinitely innovative beast and amazing things with new and old techniques bubble to the surface – especially in terms of short or indie-based productions. So, it is really important to give your students every weapon possible at their disposal, including a firm foundation of knowledge using traditional techniques. You never know that one of them may ultimately become the new **Walt Disney** or **Hayao Miyazaki** or whoever and take traditional animation into the public arena once again too!

With this firmly in my mind, I have given students here all the core principles of traditional knowledge and techniques, personally upheld or uncovered in a career lasting over 50 years, both in animating and in teaching. With such knowledge at their disposal, they will undoubtedly have a better chance of succeeding in an ever-demanding digital industry out there. When all is said and done, sitting at the shoulder of a master – or just someone who really knows their stuff – is still the finest way of learning a skill. Unfortunately, these kinds of *"apprenticeships"* are long gone in the industry. However, if you can generate a state of competence and confidence within your classroom – using time-honored techniques that have been handed down for a century or more – then you will succeed like none other can. Perhaps the academic environment you work in is not ideal, and such high expectations are not there. However, if you can show your students through your own practical hands-on methods, then you'll have done something that all the books and all the Internet courses will fail to do.

Lastly, I wish you well with your classes and share with you here every tip and every trick I know to help you and help your students to become the *master animators* of the future. After the award-winning experience I have had and encountering so many great animators and teachers in the world of animation myself, it is the very least I can do!

THANK YOU!

THE CORE PRINCIPLES OF MOVEMENT – TRADITIONAL TECHNIQUES

Equipment Required for This Section

My studio.

DOI: 10.1201/9781003324287-1

For the work to be produced in "**Section I**", you'll need the following equipment. *(Note: I have primarily listed traditional hand-drawn "paper & pencil" animation equipment here. But digital 2D animators should be able to adapt and complete all these assignments, using their computers, iPads or other tablets, using suitable 2D animation software or apps. Indeed, for my next Module 01 online class, I intend to teach hand-drawn iPad/tablet-based animation, using the "Rough Animator" software.)*

Sketchbook: This is a standard sketchbook, used exclusively for the *"Observational Gesture Drawing"* warm-up sessions opening up each lesson in the book.

Pegged animation paper: *"Pegged animation paper"* means animation drawing paper that has registration peg holes punched in it. There have been several registration peg systems used in animation over the decades, but the primary one today for professionals is the *"**Acme**" peg system. However, students on a budget can just as easily use blank white photocopying or printing paper with three round holes punched in it. Both systems allow each animation drawing to be registered to a "Peg Bar", which is the next item of equipment required for Section I.*

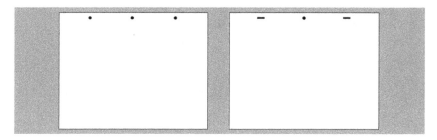

The "Round hole" and "Acme" paper options.

Peg bar: *"Peg Bars"* are registration devices, taped to a *"Lightbox"*, that stop the animation drawings from sliding around from drawing to drawing. It is important that animation drawings are registered, one with another, so there is no moving around when the drawings are filmed. The peg bar enables that punched drawing paper, with the appropriately shaped punch hole, will always remain in a fixed position on the screen. Peg bars are available for either the *"Acme"* style of punched paper or the *"Three Hole"* style. A good animation supplies company, like "**Lightfoot**" in California, should be able to supply students and professionals alike with one peg bar or the other.

The "Round hole" and "Acme" peg bar options.

Lightbox: Traditionally created animation is done by creating many drawings, many of which have to be drawn midway between other key drawings. Therefore, up to three sheets of paper can go together at any time. Bottom line, it is essential to have a *"Lightbox"* that will enable you to see through those several layers of drawings at once. Essentially, a Lightbox is a backlit drawing surface that you can switch on and off. These can range from the truly exotic – such as one of the origin, coveted tailor-made drawing desks they used during the "Golden Era" of the Disney studio – down to the very inexpensive LED light tablets that can be bought on Amazon. All will need a suitable peg bar taped to them.

The modern "LED tablet".

Pencils: In terms of "Pencils", pretty much anything you like drawing with will do. However, if you want to go quite *"pro"* about it, you'll find that the ***Col-erase*** ***"BLUE"*** pencils are a dream to work with (the "Blue" version, but not the "Photographic Blue", which is too light to work with). But bottom line, draw with whatever pencil you're most comfortable with.

The Col-erase "BLUE" pencil.

Eraser: Col-erase pencils have an eraser on the end of them, but this wears down very quickly when you do a lot of drawing. So, it is wise to have an additional eraser available too. Any soft eraser works fine. I also prefer to have a kneedable one to work with too – often known as a *"Putty Rubber"*.

A "regular" eraser and a "kneedable" eraser.

Pencil sharpener: If you're doing a lot of drawing and expect to do much more after you've worked your way through all the exercises in this book, I strongly recommend that you get an "Electric" pencil sharpener. If you're working on a budget, however, a regular hand-twist one will be OK, but not as fast and efficient to work with.

My battle-scared "Xacto" electric pencil sharpener.

Frame-by-frame drawing capture device: Animation requires that once you have drawn all the drawings you need to make something move, you then have to capture them on a frame-by-frame basis and render those captures to video. There are expensive ways to do this and inexpensive ones. The most expensive is to have a tailor-made camera device over your lightbox, so you easily capture your drawings into a computer for rendering to video in a suitable film program. I personally use a combined instructor lightbox/camera setup from the "Lightfoot" – but that is primarily because I do so much professional-level animation, as well as capturing demo material for my classes. So it really pays for itself in time.

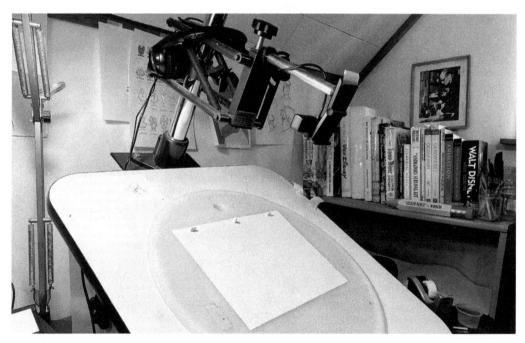

My instructor desk and camera setup from the "Lightfoot" company.

A second option here would be to scan your drawings individually into an animation or film editing program that can render them to video. Software such as Digicel's *"Flipbook"* for the former or *"Premiere"* or *"Final Cut Pro"* for the latter springs to mind here. However, if you are going to scan your drawings, it's important that you tape a peg bar to your scanning surface, to ensure consistent registration.

Other capture camera options plus a scanner with peg bar taped to it.

Finally, if you're really on a budget, one of my students created an inexpensive, yet ingenious, way of capturing her drawings by propping up her phone and capturing her drawings that were hung from a peg bar taped to the wall! The only thing you need to ensure is that (i) your phone has an app that captures single-frame images that can then be rendered to 24-frames-per-second video; (ii) you do not move the camera while you are capturing the pictures as the animation will jump all over the screen afterward; and (iii) you ensure the peg bar is fixed against the surface, so the drawings don't jump around while they are being captured.

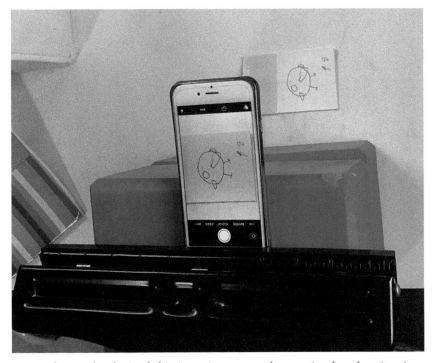

My student, Ada, devised this ingenious way of capturing her drawings!

Of course, if you're working *digitally*, then you don't really have to worry about any of the traditional equipment above. You will need a drawing tablet, a drawing pen and a computer, iPad or other tablet with 2D drawn animation software included in it. This is a much more expensive setup of course. But in the case of the drawing tablet option, you can be portable when you work. Indeed, from now onward, my "Module 1" online animation class is going to be taught on the iPAD and using "Rough Animator" software.

My iPad platform, using "RoughAnimator" software.

III PERSONAL PROJECT – PRE-PRODUCTION

II FURTHER CORE PRINCIPLES OF MOVEMENT – RIGGED DIGITAL TECHNIQUES

Contents

First Edition published 2023
by CRC Press
6000 Broken Sound Parkway NW, Suite 300, Boca Raton, FL 33487-2742

and by CRC Press
4 Park Square, Milton Park, Abingdon, Oxon, OX14 4RN

CRC Press is an imprint of Taylor & Francis Group, LLC

Library of Congress Cataloging-in-Publication Data
Names: White, Tony, 1947- author.
Title: Animation masterclasses : from pencils to pixels : a complete course in animation & production / Tony White.
Description: First edition. | Boca Raton : CRC Press, 2023.
Identifiers: LCCN 2022015633 (print) | LCCN 2022015634 (ebook) |
ISBN 9781032348841 (hardback) | ISBN 9781032345864 (paperback) |
ISBN 9781003324287 (ebook)
Subjects: LCSH: Animation (Cinematography) | Computer animation.
Classification: LCC NC1765 .W474 2023 (print) | LCC NC1765 (ebook) |
DDC 791.43/34—dc23/eng/20220715
LC record available at https://lccn.loc.gov/2022015633
LC ebook record available at https://lccn.loc.gov/2022015634

ISBN: 978-1-032-34884-1 (hbk)
ISBN: 978-1-032-34586-4 (pbk)
ISBN: 978-1-003-32428-7 (ebk)

DOI: 10.1201/9781003324287

Typeset in Myriad Pro
by codeMantra

TONY WHITE

ANIMATION MASTERCLASSES

FROM PENCILS TO PIXELS

A COMPLETE COURSE IN ANIMATION & PRODUCTION

CRC Press
Taylor & Francis Group
Boca Raton London New York

CRC Press is an imprint of the
Taylor & Francis Group, an **informa** business

ANIMATION MASTERCLASSES: FROM PENCILS TO PIXELS

Today, it is commonly believed that if you learn software, you can become an animator. Yet nothing could be further from the truth. Master animators are *trained* and not born. Software, as is the humble pencil, is merely yet another tool through which an animator can apply their knowledge. However, neither software nor pencils give you that knowledge, nor do they do the work for you. If you place a fully trained master animator on a computer, or give them a pencil, they'll astound you with their mastery. However, if you put a non-trained animator on a computer, all you will have is a technician creating moving objects – as you'll see all over YouTube and other video platforms.

This book teaches you exactly how to become a *Master Animator* – whether you ultimately plan to use pencils, computers, drawing tablets or rigged characters. It's a complete course in its own right, being a collection of 48 masterclasses gleaned from the author's 50 years of experience of top-level animating, teaching and filmmaking. It will also train you in the value and application of observational gesture drawing. This book of masterclasses by a master of the art, **Tony White**, is entirely designed to be *THE* definitive reference book for students learning how to make things move really well – as well as how to create films once you know how to do so.

A book for everyone:

For home-based, self-study students: It is a perfect manual to take you from raw beginner to proven animated filmmaker.

For full-time students: It is an ideal companion to supplement your full-time educational studies, which, no doubt, is overly based on software technology.

For current animation professionals: It is a comprehensive archive of animation tips and techniques that will enable you to take your work to the next level.

For current animation educators and instructors: It is a book that can be the ultimate curriculum and study program, enabling your own students to become the master animators of today and tomorrow.

instructor I can ever be, based on a lifetime of real knowledge and experience. You, on the other hand, have the responsibility of being the *best student* you can ever be. In all likelihood, I won't be around to see if you make it in the fullness of time. But at least I can be a humble planter of seeds, from which I hope great oak trees will grow. Viewed in that light, I have already placed a great weight of responsibility on your shoulders! Wear it well. I call it *"passing down the pencil"*!

All hail the humble pencil!

You may also be wondering why, in this digital, technologically driven age, you should take your first faltering steps into animation mastery by drawing your work when the rest of the world is using computers? Well, if you're made of the stuff that drawing is everything to you, then you probably won't even have that question in your mind. But if you believe that computers do everything better, then you'll need convincing! The real thing to understand here is that we all learn best by a "tactile" understanding of how things work. In any creative skill, it truly is through that "eye/mind/hand" process that we can fully learn and understand how animation works. By relying on software to do everything for us, we learn very little. Draw, modify it, polish it – even the most simple of chores, with the most limited of stick figure drawing, if drawing is a challenge to us – we will learn so much more than pushing a few digital buttons. Therefore, I urge you not to reject the practical drawing work found here. I can assure you, if you master the material using such pencil-driven methods, you will be so much further ahead of the competition when you take on the software part in the animation world. Never forget – it is not the *"software"* that creates great animation. It is the *"artist"* who drives that software. This course is designed to make you a far better driver than the technicians out there!

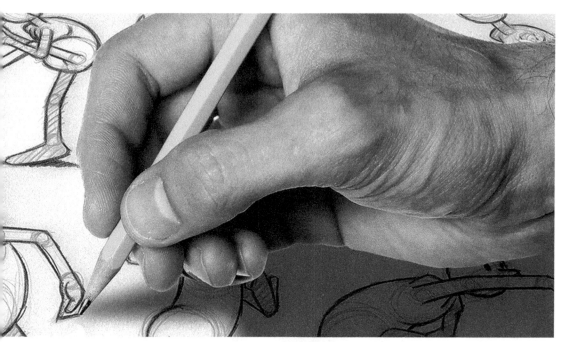

Never underestimate "Pencil Power"!

By venturing into this book of animation masterclasses, you are entering into an exclusive club. After 50 years in this industry, overlapping with 20 years of teaching at the highest levels in recent decades, I can assure you that everything you'll find here is both necessary and significantly tried and tested. And much of it not by me – but by the great master animators who evolved it before me! Some things may even seem trivial to you at first, and you may be tempted to jump ahead and move forward faster. But believe me, *"baby steps"* are essential if you're going to reap the benefits of the much larger strides you will make later. Nothing is wasted here, nothing superfluous, nothing without cause. Therefore, please accept the knowledge and experience I'm sharing with you. It's the stuff of legends – past, present and future. Hopefully you'll be one of those too, in time!

The good news for you right now is that you're required to do very little in this first animation masterclass lesson. It's more a question of reading and absorbing what is being shared – especially later, when we'll talk about "**Key**", "**Breakdown**" and "**Inbetween**" drawings, among other things. Before that I will throw an optional animation assignment at you. However, before we do any of that, let's get warmed up for the tasks ahead.

Embrace the poise of a master!

Warm-Up Drawing

Before we do anything else, I want you to do an *"observational gesture drawing"* exercise. Gesture drawings are the animator's version of the "five finger exercises" that concert pianists do. We will be doing one at the head of each masterclass lesson, so be prepared! I have based them on my far more expansive *"Drawing for Animation" online* course that can be found on the *"2D ANIMAKERS Network"*. But although I've scaled these exercises down for this masterclass book, they do not lose their potency by them being reduced in content. Quite the opposite, they are more specifically focused for the lessons you are about to learn. There will be more than enough here to really test and train your *"hand/ mind/eye"* coordination as an animator. For the record, my **"The Animator's Sketchbook"** (CRC Press; ISBN-10:1 1498774016) covers them too in a similar way, and as that book is effectively a sketchbook too, you might want to use it as your sketchbook of choice for this course. It will certainly look impressive if you have a completed version of that in addition to your showreel of animation!

"The Animator's Sketchbook" – just one of my previous books!

Now, you need to recognize at this point that these warm-up observational drawing sections, I'm not teaching you **how to draw**. That's something you need to pursue elsewhere, if you feel it's important to you. What I am going to do here, however, is to help you *"observe"*. Observation is a significant muscle you need to exercise if you're at all serious about being an animator. Observation is the cornerstone of animation knowledge. Ideas may come from the imagination, but when you want to put meat on those imaginative bones, you HAVE to go to the real world and observe people or things that are close to what you are planning to execute through animation. But to do that effectively, you have to train your eye first to see what is *actually* there, not what you *think* is there. That's why our warm-ups at the beginning of each lesson here are going to be entirely *observational*. It is a fundamental part of and animator's learning process.

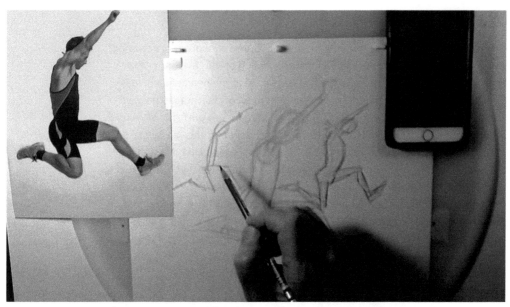

I often give an example of "speed gesture drawing" to my students.

If your "poses" in animation are not correct, no amount of inbetweens, glossing over, special effects, added music or even wishing on a star will ever make your animation work. Poses are sacrosanct. That's why learning strong gesture drawing at this stage is so important for every student and for every future master animator in creating better poses – whether they work in 2D, 3D or any other form of animation!

With regard to animation "gesture drawings", we are not talking about *photographic* or *realistic* drawing here. We are mainly concerned with core *shapes*, *angles* and *proportions*. In terms of the drawing time requested, I'm trusting you to respect the **time limits** I will be giving you too. It's only by working within strict time and other guidelines that you'll get the full benefit from what needs to be done and what needs to be experienced. Pretty pictures are not the order of the day here. Accurately observed *construction drawings* against the clock are, no matter how challenging they might be, the crucial thing here. So, no cheating!

And don't be afraid if your drawing skills are not high. They aren't for many top animators out there. What is important are your observational skills and your ability to interpret what you see **to the best of your ability**. Well-crafted stick figures, accurately interpreted and communicated, are FAR more valuable to the animator than beautiful, classical drawings that do not capture the pose or attitude of what is being observed at all!

 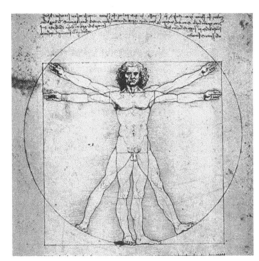

Drawing can be from the sublime to the ridiculous, or vice versa.

So, all that established, our first *observational gesture drawing* session is "Coffee Drinkers"

If I randomly ask to draw someone drinking coffee, you'd probably come up with a sketch that's pretty *generic* in your imagination. However, if I urge you to first turn to the real world for references, you'll find that there are an infinite variety of pose options. The two poses below are of people drinking coffee. They are very different, emphasizing the fact that you need to think carefully about the pose you would choose if you were going to draw, or animate, someone drinking coffee for real. So, look hard at the two images below and sketch them in just **3 minutes** each. Be very disciplined. The more disciplined you are, the more you'll learn – and the greater the advantage you'll get from the exercise.

Comments: If you study these two pictures above, you will see that they are not just physically different, but they are different in terms of *visual storytelling* too. Ask yourself, what mood, emotion or attitude are they expressing? Then decide which one best suits the scene that you are contemplating, where you animating this for a project.

These two drawings are just the tip of a huge iceberg of other possibilities of course. Type in *"coffee drinkers"* into Google Images and you'll see a whole host of options popping up. Better still, go out for a coffee with your sketchbook and capture the various poses and gestures that people in the coffee shop are presenting when drinking their coffee. Be aware of how you, yourself, are drinking coffee also! The world is a huge database of information like this for animators and artists. So go out with your sketchbook and take full advantage of it whenever you can. Most important of all, train your *"animator's eye"* to observe all the different people, poses or personalities – not just coffee drinkers, but all of life in its infinite variety.

NOTE

At first, "observational gesture drawing" won't be easy to do in the time given. But that's OK. Try your best to do it. In time you will learn to cope with the time limitations the more you do of it. So don't be put off if you struggle at first. Remember, these timed, observational gesture drawing sessions are designed to build your animation muscles, so don't neglect or ignore them. They are as important to you as is the factual stuff that's contained in this book. More in some ways! Both compliment each other in all reality and both will lead you to animation mastership.

Instruction

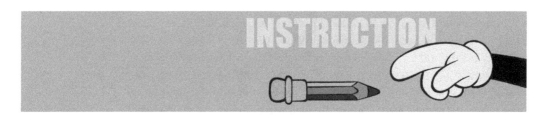

The previous warm-up drawing session is clearly more about *looking* and *analyzing* than the actual doing. You have to draw of course, that stands to reason, but you will learn so much by simply looking and analyzing what you are looking at when you draw than how well you draw. That's why I say that even people who struggle with drawing can do these sessions – and the masterclass exercises also. So, I want you to get familiar with the pattern of instruction we're going to follow beyond this first lesson – starting with a *warm-up drawing session* every time, then moving on to the animation *instruction*, which is also drawn – at least in this first section. These tiny steps of learning, along the path of animation discovery, will prepare you well to run a marathon on your own eventually.

Here, I must repeat again that the BEST way to learn animation is by going through a **hand-drawn approach** – yes, even for those who struggle with drawing.

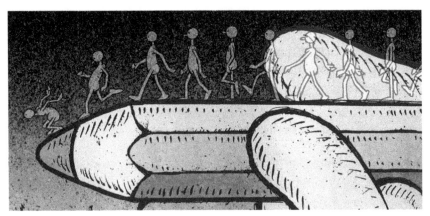

If you're struggling with drawing, it's sometimes best to just jump straight in there!

Now, I don't just say that because of my personal background in traditional animation. It is more a case that it is very important for any artist – especially an animator/artist – to develop a tactile understanding through their eye, brain, hand coordination when doing observational gesture drawing. Having skills in traditional hand-drawn animation anyway is also a great asset to have in this job market day and age – especially whenever a hand-drawn, 2D animation style is required and you're the only one in a studio team who can do it. Employers love employees with diversity like that and are more likely to hire you, with both 3D and 2D skills, than anyone else. They will probably have learnt too that the person who was trained traditionally excels with computer-based animation far more than anyone else! On a full-time educational level, you will probably find that once you have digested and completed all the assignments in this book too, you will probably have a greater understanding of the principles of movement than your instructor, who more and more are technology based only!

Whenever I teach a first lesson on a course, I tend to focus on my students getting to know me and my credentials to teach the course session, rarely about specific teaching. We're going to hit the ground running by talking about traditional animation skills in the next masterclass lesson. So for the time being, kick off your shoes and relax a little as I introduce myself to you. I believe that it's fundamentally important for students to have confidence in their instructor by meeting them and knowing a little of what they know and what they've done. So let me indulge myself

"If you can think something, you can draw it. If you can draw it, you can animate it!"

here for a minute. In a regular classroom, I would show you my archive show-reel and a number of award-winning and other animated productions I have created in the past. Unfortunately, this book doesn't allow me to do that. But in lieu of that, please check out my ArtStation page at *https://www.artstation.com/tonymation*.

Also check out other links to my work and career here. Then read a basic resume of my activities and qualifications beneath that.

My student work: http://www.tonywhiteanimation.com/my-students-work.html
My teaching school: http://www.2dacademy.com
My ANIMAKERS Network: https://www.animakers.club
My animation studio website: http://www.drawassic.com

Educational Qualifications

Current State of Washington Education Certificate (2013–2016): Required for my position at an Australian-owned college in the Seattle School District required that I obtained the following certification...:

CERT 1V (passed in Australia – 2011): Required by the Australian government for my teaching at an Australian-owned school in Seattle at that time.

Honorary MFA (2002): **Henry Cogswell College**, Everett, Washington, for exceptional achievements in animation techniques and production.

LSIA in Graphic Design, Typography and Illustration (1968): East Ham Technical College, London, England – with an additional 1-year, scholarship supported, independent study in "illustration" under the supervision of award-winning illustrator, Ralph Steadman.

Teaching Experience

2D ACADEMY (2017–present day) Founder/Senior Instructor: teaching traditional hand-drawn 2D animation skills, digital 2D animation skills and animation production skills, online and in the classroom (when possible).

Shoreline Community College (2018–present): adjunct instructor for "History of Animation" and "Drawing for Animation" online classes.

Academy of Interactive Entertainment (2011–2017): Program Director and Senior Instructor for AIE and Seattle Skills Center. *(Teaching: Drawing, Designing, Writing, Traditional and Tradigital 2D Animation. Software used: "Photoshop", DigiCel "Flipbook" and "ToonBoom Studio". Currently studying ToonBoom "Harmony Essentials".)*

DigiPen Institute of Technology (2005–2011): Dean of Art and Animation

Dean/Senior Lecturer/Program Advisor – teaching "Advanced Animation for Portfolio" classes and supervisor of senior 2D/3D film and game projects. Previously taught "Traditional 2D Animation" and "Sprite animation". *(Software used: "Maya" [animation only], "ToonBoom Studio", "Sketchbook Pro", "TV Paint", "Photoshop", "Premiere", "Final Cut Pro" and DigiCel's "Flipbook".)*

Henry Cogswell College (2001–2006): Senior instructor for *"Traditional 2D Animation"*, *"Directing"*, *"Character Design"*, *"Writing, Storyboarding & Animatics"* and *"History of Animation"* classes.

Author

My writers home page: https://www.amazon.com/Tony-White/e/ B000APQQN0%3Fref=dbs_a_mng_rwt_scns_share

"ANIMATOR'S SKETCHBOOK" (2015): Groundbreaking sketchbook publication, offering over 60 guided drawing assignments for animation students and professionals to *"see"*, *"interpret"* and *"record through drawing"* from observation to improve animation techniques and execution. Based on the author's years of classroom teaching and apprenticing talented young animators interested in improving their abilities.

"ANIMATED COLORING BOOKS/FLIPBOOKS" (2015): Series of various printed flipbooks to encourage an interest/knowledge of animation through coloring and drawing.

"DRAWN TOGETHER" (2014): Compilation of 222 various artists and animators, each donating a drawing in support of traditional hand-drawn animation. Self-published eBook – via iTunes/Amazon/Barnes and Noble for iPad, Kindle, Nook and Android devices.

"MOTION COMICS" (2013): Approaches to creating animated graphic novels, comic books and cartoons. eBook on iTunes.

"JUMPING THROUGH HOOPS: The Animation Job Coach" (2011): The most up-to-date book yet on the challenge of getting a job in today's animation industry. Researched in the summer of 2010 and written in the fall. All aspects of the industry were approached for feedback – that is, *large-to-small film and game studios, forensic animation studios, medical animation studios* and *online animation forums. (Note: An updated eBook version was published in 2013 via iTunes for the iPad.)*

"**THE ANIMATOR'S NOTEBOOK**" (2010): Definitive book on the key principles of animation. Specifically – *"Process and principles of animation", "Generic walks", "Stylized walks", "Personality walks", "Quadruped walks", "Runs", "Jumps", "Weight", "Arcs and anticipation", "Overlapping action", "Fluidity and flexibility" and "Basic dialogue"*.

"**HOW TO MAKE ANIMATED FILMS**" (2009): The first half of this book is a 10-stage course on the traditional principles of animation. The second half of the book defines the 22-stage production process of making animated films.

"**ANIMATION FROM PENCILS TO PIXELS ~ Classical Techniques for Digital Animators**" (2006): The ultimate book on traditional animation techniques, embracing over 30 years of award-winning experience in 2D animation. Translated into several languages.

"**THE ANIMATOR'S WORKBOOK**" (1986): Has become a classic textbook for schools and student animators worldwide, launching many careers and being translated into several languages. Has sold over 82,000 copies.

Professional Experience

Currently creating my first-ever graphic novel: A *"mystical hero's journey"* story, entitled *"MADA and the Magic Tree"*. Enabled by generous Patreon supporters at https://www.patreon.com/Muse2D.

Director/Writer/Animator/Producer (2012): *"Revenge of the Fly"* short animated film. Commissioned by the Seattle International Film Festival and selected for numerous festivals across the USA.

Director/Writer/Animator/Producer: *"Fire Gods"* short animated film commissioned by the "Museum of Glass" in Tacoma, WA. Created to tell the history of glass and glassmaking for screening in the museum and in schools. Created to offer valuable production learning experience for my students at the time.

Director/Writer/Animator/Producer: *"Endangered Species"* short animated film. Created to accompany my book, **"Pencils to Pixels: Classical Techniques for Digital Animators"**. The film is my personal homage to the rise and fall (and hopeful rise again) of traditional hand-drawn animation. Again, this film was conceived to offer a rare industry experience opportunity for my students at the time.

Owner/Director/Animator: "Animus Productions" (1978–1998): Producing over **200 animated TV commercials, two TV Specials**, and **several short films**. Winning a Blue Ribbon Award for 30-minute animated TV Special for PBS, "Cathedral" – shortly followed by "Pyramid", based on the success of "Cathedral". **Director** (1992) of a 10-part live-action/animation TV drama series, entitled "**The Ink Thief**". Starring *'Rocky Horror Show'* creator, **Richard O'Brien**.

British Academy Award (1978): For animated short film, "HOKUSAI ~ An Animated Sketchbook"

Apprentice/Director/Animator (1972–1978): At Richard Williams Studio, London. Responsible for numerous award-winning TV commercials, as well as being assistant to Director, **Richard Williams**, on the Oscar-winning TV Special by Charles Dickens, *"A Christmas Carol"*. **Designer/Writer/Director/Animator** of the prestigious **D&AD Silver Award**-winning animated titles for "The Pink Panther Strikes Again" movie.

Background Artist/Writer/Head of Design/Background Artist (1968–1972): At Halas & Batchelor, London – for the animated TV series, "Tom Foolery" and "Jackson Five".

Courses, Festivals and Professional Lectures

DRAWTASTIC Animation Festival (online 9th season to be screened in February 2022) **Founder/Director**: Celebrating everything *drawn*, *illustrated*, *sketched* or *animated* by hand or computer in animation.

WHAT'S UP DOC! (2015): Keynote speaker at EMP's opening of the Chuck Jones/ Looney Tunes exhibition of Warner Brothers animation in Seattle.

MASTERING 2D ANIMATION (2013): The first of three advanced online courses that teach traditional and tradigital approaches to 2D animation.

2D OR NOT 2D Animation Festival (later became the online "DRAWTASTIC Animation Festival): Creator/Founder. Started over 18 years ago – bringing top animation talents from all over America and Europe to Seattle. Inaugural festival opened by the late Roy E. Disney, nephew of the great Walt Disney.

Lecturer: To international audiences – including the Norwegian Film Institute – Oslo (1988), Swedish Film Institute – Stockholm (1989), Tri-be-ca Grill Guest Director – New York (1992), Israel Animation Guild – Tel Aviv (1994), etc. Featured in multiple television and print interviews. Keynote guest lecturer at the **Jilin Institute of Animation** in Changchun, China (2010), and the **ISA Conference** in Dublin, Ireland (2011). Several lectures and workshops at **CTN Animation Expo** in LA from 2011 thru 2013.

Recent Projects and in Development

"THE OLD MAN MAD ABOUT ANIMATION"/"THE HERMIT" (current): My personal *"animated memoirs"*, including *"animated meditations for the soul"* – a 100 autobiographical film relating the moments, people and events in my unique five-decade career in animation. Also drawing a graphic novel version of the project also.

WROTE & DEVELOPED: Several full-length animated movie projects/scripts – **"MADA and the Magic Tree"**, **"Spirit of the Game"**, **"W.H.R. and his Amazing Uncle Lubin"**, **"Dreamsinger"**, **"Spirit of the Game"** and **"Bad Penguin"**. (As ever… still seeking production finance!)

Awards

2015, **Award of Merit** at **IndieFest Film Awards** for *"Thank You Stan"*. Honorable mentions at various other international short film festivals. *(Writer/Designer/Director/Animator.)*

2013/14, **Honorable Mention** at **various short film festivals** for *"Revenge of the Fly"*. *(Writer/Director/Animator.)*

2008, **Park City Film Music Festival: Bronze Medal Award** for outstanding musical score on *"Fire Gods"*. *(Writer/Designer/Director/Animator.)*

2007, **Park City Film Music Festival: Gold Medal Award** for outstanding music score on *"Endangered Species"*. *(Writer/Designer/Director/Animator.)*

1999, **New York Film and Television Festival**: For *"A Seafarer's Tale 2"* presented to Tony White, Animus Entertainments Limited, London. *(Director/Animator.)*

1998, **New York Film and Television Festival**: For *"A Seafarer's Tale"* presented to Tony White, Animus Entertainments Limited, London. *(Director/Animator.)*

1991, **New York Festivals Finalist Award**: Presented to Tony White, Animus Productions for *"Hands On/Big Moments"*.

1990, **The Mobius Advertising Awards**: Certificate for outstanding creativity in international competition, for *"Build A Cat"*, presented to Tony White, Animus Productions Limited, London.

1988, **British Television Advertising Awards**: Silver Award for film title, *"Rousseau"*, presented to Animus Productions, Director: Tony White.

1988, **British Television Advertising Awards**: Silver Award for film title, **"Picasso"**, presented to Animus Productions, Director: Tony White.

1988, **British Television Advertising Awards**: Craft Award for film title, *"Rousseau"*, presented to Animus Productions, Director: Tony White.

1985, **Creative Circle Honours**: Silver Award, for best use of animation, *"Lamot Pils Lager* and *Volcano"*, presented to Tony White, Animation Partnership.

1985, **London Film Festival**: *"Potterton: This Ol' House"*, directed by Tony White and selected as an outstanding film of the year.

1984, **London Film Festival**: *"Lamot: Volcano"*, directed by Tony White and selected as an outstanding film of the year.

1983, **British Television Advertising Awards**: Bronze Award for film title, *"Swan Lake"*, presented to Animation Partnership, Director: Tony White.

1982, **CLIO Awards**: Certificate for creative excellence, for International TV/Cinema, Recognition: Animation, *"Boar"*, by Animus Productions, London, Director: Tony White.

1982, **CLIO Awards**: Certificate for creative excellence, for International TV/Cinema, Recognition: Dentifrice/Pharmaceuticals, *"Boar"*, by Animus Productions, London, Director: Tony White.

1982, **CLIO Awards**: Certificate for creative excellence, for International TV/Cinema, Recognition: Dentifrice/Pharmaceuticals, *"Bear"*, by Animus Productions, London, Director: Tony White.

1982, **U.S. Television Commercials Festival**: For outstanding creativity in the production of television commercials entered in international competition, awarded to *"Swan Lake"*, Director: Tony White.

1979, **International Film Exposition**: Los Angeles, Hollywood, U.S., for *"HOKUSAI~An Animated Sketchbook"*. *(Writer/Designer/Director/Animator.)*

1978, **British Academy Awards**: The Best Short Factual Film, *"HOKUSAI~An Animated Sketchbook"*. *(Writer/Designer/Director/Animator.)*

1977, **D&AD Award**: For *"The Pink Panther Strikes Again"* movie titles. *(Writer/Designer/Director/Animator.)*

1973, **Chicago Film Festival**: First place for *"Quartet"* animated short film. *(Writer/Designer/Director.)*

1970, **United Nations**: Writer/Director/Designer of *"A Short Tall Story"*, used by the organization to promote peace around the world. *(Writer/Designer/Director.)*

Animation Links

For more understanding of the lessons and assignments in the following masterclasses, I've set up a dedicated web page for students, containing samples of animation that I will refer to. They can be found at **http://www.2dacademy. com/masterclasses.html**. Tag this page as you'll be referring to it a great deal as you work through the assignments that follow. There you will find valuable references for specific assignments and exercises I will be setting you as you advance. They will give you an indication of how things move, as opposed to how I try to clearly explain things with words. Being a "visual and tactile" learner myself, I hope they will help many people understand the principles of movement we will be talking about.

Flipbooks

A flipbook.

OK, I lied when I said you could kick back and relax with this opening lesson! In a minute, I want to give you a flipbook assignment that you might like to do. I believe that this will be a fun assignment if you take it on – aimed as it is, to simply to get you in the mood for the more serious animation learning that's to come. You don't have to do it if you really don't want to. But I suggest you do it, to simply get some motivation and momentum going.

Maybe you know this already, but the most direct, inexpensive and yet often most fun way to explore animation is through the humble "**Flipbook**". These are obviously the cheapest and most direct approach to doing animation. All you need is a pencil and a small "flickable" sketchpad – or preferably – loose blank, small cards. You can simply draw on each page/card, one by one, making each drawing slightly different from the previous one – then flick them in order afterward. You'll be amazed at how versatile and imaginative flipbook animation can be!

Flipbook animation can come in all shapes and sizes, as my instructional book and this fun flipbook device show here.

I've even used "sticky" or "Post-It" notes to animate some things. Any of these, drawn on, one drawing per page or card, can produce some fabulous action when flipped from back to front, or front to back; however, you prefer to draw and flip them. Some amazing flipbooks have been created by professional animators in the past. Yet even drawing moving stick figures can be thrilling if you want to give it a go.

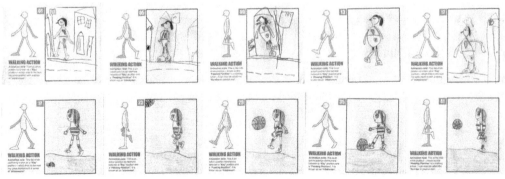

You are never too young to draw a flipbook – as my beautiful young granddaughters, Isla (top) and Abbie (bottom), show here!

TIP: *If you're using loose cards to do your flipbook, consider stapling them together if they're not too thick when you put them together. And if and when you staple them, don't forget to tape around and over the staples at one end, so you don't cut your fingers on the sharp ends of the staples. Alternatively, for a less treacherous approach, you can simply wrap rubber bands tightly around the end of your flipbook cards – or use a good old fashioned Bulldog Clip – which should hold them together when you flip them.*

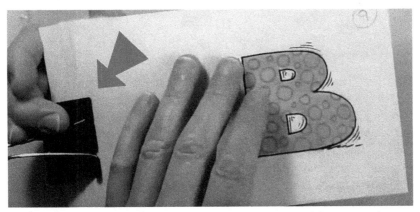

I have often used a Bulldog Clip to demonstrate the card flipping technique to students.

It may be of interest to mention here that I am writing this book during the worst of the COVID lockdown around the world. Because of this, my in-classroom animation classes have been forced online, meaning that my students had none of the usual physical equipment to do their animation work that a physical classroom would provide. As a result, I had decided to teach the entire course using a flipbook approach, via Zoom classes, on occasions. I was astounded to discover that this proved to one of the most productive and successful classes I've ever taught on the principles of animation!

I love working in all the different styles you can go with flipbooks.

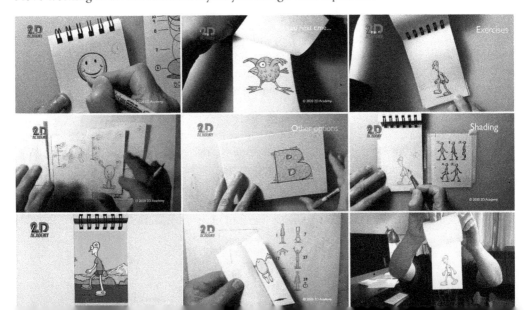

The students totally rose to the occasion and did some of the best *"principles of movement"* work, using just flipbooks, ever. So that confirmed to me that not only flipbook work can more than hold their ground in a classroom, but that remote teaching is effective too. Luckily, my "**2D ACADEMY**" classes were already geared to this, so we had made an excellent start before everyone else. So, this is just to say that no one should reject flipbooks as an acceptable way of learning animation – at least in the early stages. Luckily though, we have no such limitations with regard to the contents of these masterclasses. Your equipment will be what you make it for yourself.

Flipbook Assignment

OK, so let's now get you to maybe dip your toes into the animation water. To do that, I recommend you take on this simple flipbook exercise. I simply want you to animate a *"stick figure"* moving. Your stick figure can do anything you want it to. Run, jump, throw something, fall apart and turn into a butterfly. The decision is yours. Just make sure that you start with an establishing position and then draw on, page by page or card by card, with a slightly new position each time. At the end, you can flip it and see your stick figure move.

Stick figure movement on a sticky note flipbook.

Filming Your Flipbook

Flipbooks are quite simply fun as they are. In other words, you can carry them around in your pocket or bag and simply show your flipped animation to family, friends or whoever you like. No technology is necessary. However, if you're interested in posting your work to *social media*, or even want it as part of your *showreel* material we'll talk about at the end of this book – or even try to win a *"Golden Pencil Award"* – you might want to film what you've done. So let's talk about how you might do that.

For starters, your mobile phone camera is perfect for doing that. Have a friend film you as you flip your animation to the camera. Repeat the flipping three or four times in the same shot; however, as pages do tend to stick together, your audience will need to see it a few times to fully appreciate the movement. This is especially true if you're seeing it as part of your *showreel*!

Filming a flipbook.

Better still though, if you're drawn a card-based flipbook, why not scan your cards, one by one, and render them out to video using a film editing program. The quality will be incredibly high, giving you much better material for your showreel or social media content. If you repeat the action several times, you might even add a music track to it, to make it look even more professional.

NOTE

I've actually created a whole video course on flipbooks for young students. It contains a series of 27 videos that teach animation as a fun exercise in flipbooks and explain all the core principles at the same time. The course is available at a reasonable price to members via the 2D ACADEMY website

Keys, Breakdowns and Inbetweens

Now, it's time to share with you some of the main terminology of animation. Essentially, most animation is broken down into three specific kinds of drawings or poses – "**Keys**", "**Breakdowns**" and "**Inbetweens**". Each one of these is fundamental building brings of creating the illusion of living, breathing movement on a screen or monitor.

Key, breakdown and inbetween.

Looking at this illustration, you'll see key differences in the way these drawings are numbered. "**Key**" drawing numbers are *circled*, emphasizing that they are the *major* drawings in a sequence of movement, marking a distinct pose or change of direction in the action.

"**Breakdown**" drawings *(also known as "**Passing Positions**" in walks)* are numbered in *parentheses*. They are of secondary importance, being the first *midpoint* drawing linking two keys. They are the first *inbetween* if you like.

Lastly, the "**Inbetween**" drawings are numbered plainly, being that they are halfway positions that link between the key and breakdown drawings in a sequence. They vary in terms of the number of drawings that need to be placed between key and inbetween drawings. The number of inbetweens used depends on whether the action needs to be slow or fast.

NOTE

Having less inbetween drawings means faster movement. More inbetweens slow the action down.

Peg Bars

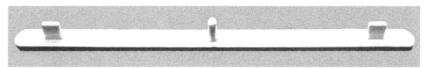

Acme peg bar.

To obtain accurate registration from drawing to drawing, an animator uses a **peg bar**. If drawings are not registered in this way, the animation will jump around frantically on the screen when played back. So peg bars are essential to work with at all times.

Capturing Animation

Don't forget also that if you're going to test or film your animation, you're going to require a fixed camera or scanner to shoot your drawings frame by frame. Whatever method you use to do it though, you're going to also need a peg bar taped to it for drawing registration.

Of course, we are talking about traditional, hand-drawn animation techniques here. Working digital is different. Indeed, there are a number of 2D animation software packages out there that will enable the drawings to be directly executed into the computer – such as DigiCel's *"Flipbook"* or the free art/animation *"Krita"* software for desktops and *"Rough Animator"* for iPads, etc. It all depends on how serious you are, or what your budget allows, when determining how you shoot or capture your animation material

Old-school rostrum camera.

Personally, I am very passionate about using an old-school, traditional hand-drawn approach when I animate. I believe it is a much more accurate and controlable process when inbetweening – and I just love the tactile feel that pencil on paper offers when you're working. But that said, I also love the way technology enables you to clean up, ink and color your rough pencil drawings when you have imported them into your software of choice. But I recognize also that other animators these days will draw straight into the computer without ever touching a pencil or paper. Even so, there's nothing like having a stack of hand-drawn animation drawing in your hand and flipping them to see how they move.

Flipping bottom-pegged animation drawings.

(And of course, if you become famous one day, your original drawings could be worth a fortune – which digital drawings never will be!)

The Basic Process of Animation

Whether you're working traditionally or digitally, let us briefly outline the process of creating a scene in animation. We'll elaborate further on it elsewhere in this book, but for now here is the simple version.

i) Create your "**Key**" animation positions, being the basic poses that will define your action without the inbetweens being put in.

ii) Shoot a "**Key Pose Animatic**" of your poses – meaning you film your drawings one after the other, holding them for as many frames as you imagine would cover the inbetweens to the next key. Continue this throughout the scene, then play back your video to see if the general pattern of the keys is working in a kind of "click, click, click" visual style.

iii) When you are happy with your key poses and feeling the general timing of the holds is good, add your "**Breakdown**" drawings – usually the first, mid-point inbetween drawing between two keys.

iv) When all your breakdowns are completed, shoot another "**Key Pose Animatic**", this time halving the holds you used for the keys, putting in the breakdown positions too.

v) Playback the video. It should still have a "click, click, click" staccato visual style to it, but with the breakdown drawings in, you should get a slightly smoother flow to the action.

vi) Adjust for any changes you feel are necessary and film again.

vii) When you are convinced that your keys and breakdowns are working well, add in the inbetween drawings in accordance with the number of frames you have chosen as holds. In other words, if we assume right now that we're going to animate on "2s" (meaning we hold each animation drawing for two frames each) and the hold you have between "Key 1" and "Breakdown 1" is eight frames, then you will need three inbetweens linking them to get a smooth action. Place in these inbetweens, and all the subsequent inbetweens, to complete your drawn action.

viii) Shoot all your drawings on 2s to complete your first "pencil test".

ix) Adjust and redraw your animation if necessary until it is exactly as you envisioned it.

Exposure Sheets

As you can imagine, animation that contains many characters, special effects and layers of props and background artwork can get pretty confusing as you work on it. This is especially true if you're working in a big studio, team situation. Then, it is really important that everyone, quite literally, has to be on the same page. This is where the "**exposure sheet**" (or "X sheet") comes in.

"Exposure sheets" are not seen so much – or at least, talked about – in this digital age. However, all animators should avoid them at their peril. They are essential to keeping your thinking and animation process logged on one place, for all to see. Essentially, an exposure sheet is just like a spreadsheet that allows you to plan out your animation in terms of **frames**, **layers** and **timings**. A simple exposure sheet will look like this.

PROD.	SEQ.	SCENE								SHEET

ACTION	DIAL	EXTRA	4	3	2	1	EXTRA	CAMERA INSTRUCTIONS

Blank exposure sheet.

The horizontal lines going across essentially represent the *frames* of film being covered, and the vertical lines more or less represent the *layers* of different animation you have to do. We can go into how to use layers in animation later, but let us focus on the *"frames"* aspect of an exposure sheet for now. If you know the length of your scene of animation up front, then you just mark off a start position at the top of the horizontal lines, and a bottom one, depending on how many frames your scene of action is going to cover. In the following example, we can see that this is a "1-second" scene, due to the fact that there are 24 horizontal frames from top to bottom. This therefore requires 12 drawings - "1" thru "23", to be shot on 2's and projected at 24 frames per second to achieve that 1-second screen time. The numbered column of drawings to the left - featuring the same drawings shot on 1's - illustrates that this would achieve half of the screen time.

As you "**Block out**" the key positions, the animator will put *circles* around the numbers of the drawings that represent the keys they will become.

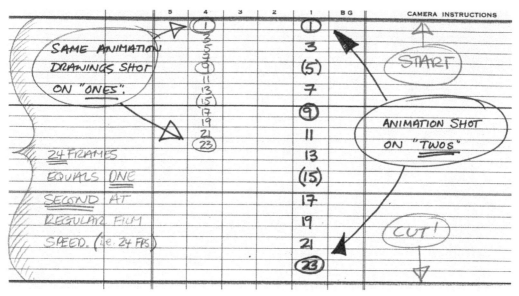

Filled-in exposure sheet, showing key drawings in circles.

By establishing this by shooting a *"pose test"* of just the key drawings held for the number of frames indicated, it reveals just how many inbetweens (the non-circled drawing numbers) will be needed to be needed to link one key to another. This then allows the animator to decide where the need the first of these inbetweens to be placed – that is, the **"Breakdown"** drawings – and they will mark these drawings with a parenthesis around it.

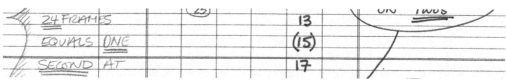

Breakdown drawings are indicated using parenthesis.

NOTE

The above suggests it is very easy to arrive at a simple calculation of where keys, breakdowns and inbetweens are placed. In reality, it is a process of trial and error, where the animator will make their first best guess, then film it to test it out, only to possibly find that they need to rework some of it to improve the timing and action. They then make the changes and test it all again. This indeed could be something that is done several times before a final decision on the correct timing and placement of keys, breakdowns and inbetweens are made.

We will be talking about all this in more depth later but, for now, it will help you understand just a little of the terminology and process of animation up front.

Clearly, this is all a lot for you to take in from the get-go if you've not done any animation before. However, don't worry as we'll return to it all in greater detail later as indicated. Just recognize that to be an animator of any kind, you'll need to have a pretty organized mind – especially up front at the planning stage. Eventually, you'll do it all instinctively in the end – when you have a great deal of experience under your belt. But, for now, if it is relevant to mention these things here, even if it runs the risk of it seeming confusing to you. Trust me, by the end of this book, it should all be second nature to you!

Final Comment

Remember finally that despite all this jargon and method, it's ultimately **what ends up on the screen** that's most important – not so much how you get there. Ultimately, you'll find your own best way of working and that means you'll probably break some of these rules when you do so. However, unless you understand the rules in the first place, you won't know how to break them most effectively. So, please bear with it as I go through all those terminologies and rules with you.

The bottom line here is that the evolution of the surest animation process has come to us as the result of a great deal of blood, sweat and tears by the industry's founders. So, let us proudly stand on the shoulders of those giants for a while longer, so that you at learn some good habits, before you discover your own better ones – based on the evolving requirements of new technology, plus the wisdom of your own bitter experience.

Masterclass 02/ Squash, Stretch and Bouncing Balls

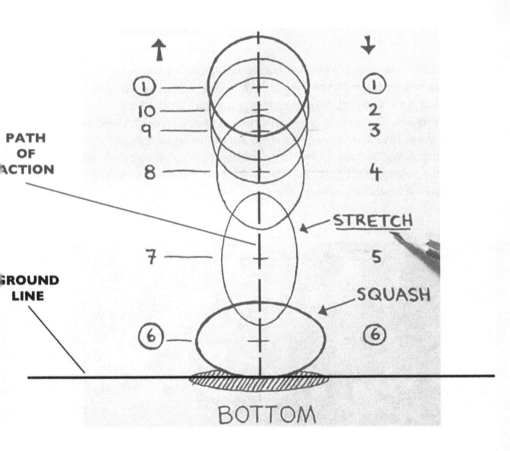

Introduction

In masterclass 02, we're going to dip our toe into the very simplest of exercises – the "**Bouncing Ball**" – using the very simplest of techniques – the "**Flipbook**". Now, don't be fooled by things that are labeled "simple". Here, you are beginning to lay down the foundations of very important, fundamental principles

DOI: 10.1201/9781003324287-3

with this lesson. So, definitely don't neglect it by being too impatient to move on to seemingly more ambitious things! (Yes, even if you're experienced at animation already!) None of us cease learning, whatever our age or wherever we are on the experience scale. Therefore, it might just surprise in what you can ultimately get out of doing a simple flipbook exercise.

Warm-Up Gesture Drawing

Everyone does some kind of physical exercise in one way or another. House chores alone are a major part of these activities – as is physical exercise in the gym or out in the backyard. We all tend to take the more menial things for granted. However, it pays animators well to look at them again with a fresh and analytical eye. The following single-image gesture drawing exercise will help you with that. My "Drawing for Animation" course uses four varied poses here. But for the purpose of this book, we'll focus on just one for now. You should allow yourself **3 minutes** to draw this pose.

Shutterstock photograph.

Comments: Notice the body angle, the angles of the shoulders, compared to the angles of the hips. There is a kind of counterpoise there. Notice how the elbow of the left arm relates to the knee of the left leg and the right leg. Notice the angle of the head and the angle of the right arm, and generally, the balance of the whole pose. Also, as a time saver for all these timed gesture drawing sessions, you might wish to sketch in the *"inner skeleton"* of the subject first – not the real skeleton but as a simple stick figure character. Make sure you get the **lengths**, **angles** and the **relationships** of the body and limbs, one to the other, first.

I am not the world's greatest figure artist. Therefore, I struggle every time I attempt one. However, I do find that in roughing out the basic inner angles and forms of the figure first, it gives me a better platform to flesh out the other shapes in the time I have left.

Then, when you're sure you've achieved accuracy there, start to build out the **flesh** – focusing solely on **volumes** and **form**.

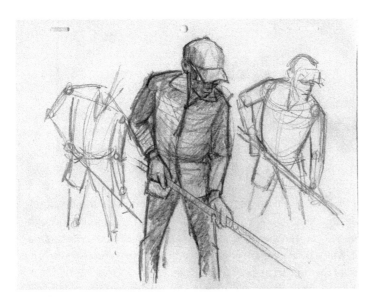

Remember always that in doing "observational gesture drawings", you are not seeking to achieve a photographic likeness of the subject – or something that will appear in a gallery later. You're simply seeking visual information that you can transfer into your animated character's key poses later. So, don't be afraid to get down rough and dirty with way you're doing!

Remember always that you're NOT trying to do *photographic representations* of what you're seeing here. Instead, you're sketching loosely drawn structures – solely as reference for animation poses you might need to create in the future.

Instruction

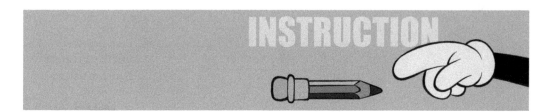

Now, in great contrast to the digital revolution we've all been in for some time now, let us return to the pure foundations of traditional hand-drawn animation – the humble "Flipbook" – in earnest. The flipbook is the simplest and most low-tech approach to animation there is, reportedly invented by the great artist and animator in the pioneering days of animation, **Winsor McCay**.

Winsor McCay and his iconic film "Gertie the Dinosaur".

Working with a flipbook at the very beginning of your animation mastery journey is a valuable foundation upon which everything else can be built. Through the humble flipbook you can quickly discover the essence of what good animation is all about, which is why we are going to begin with this simple lesson on a flipbook version of the *"Bouncing Ball"*.

The Bouncing Ball exercise is pretty much the first introduction to core movement principles that any animation instruction will contain. It is simple to draw, but contains within its simplicity such important principles as "**Squash & Stretch**", "**Weight**", "**Flexibility**" and "**Timing**". It is all too easy to dismiss the Bouncing Ball as being far too childish for a serious animation student. But it will be a major error if you ignore its principles and practice here.

The "Bouncing Ball" is still the best introduction to animation there is!

If you refer the demonstration "Bouncing Ball" video in our dedicated website page – http://www.2dacademy.com/masterclasses.html – you'll see what a standard Bouncing Ball action should look like. The thing to look for with a Bouncing Ball is the snap of the bounce on the ground and a distinct slowdown and hovering at the top of the bounce. We assume for this test that the Bouncing Ball is made of soft rubber, and therefore, it has a degree of bounce and flexibility about it. If it were a pingpong ball, or a bowling ball, it would behave very differently of course. However, for now, let's go with a standard rubber ball, bouncing on a solid surface.

The most important thing to feel with a Bouncing Ball sequence is the fact that it needs to feel like it is moving under the effects of gravity. Walt Disney had a great phrase to describe good animation – *"plausible implausibility"*. He meant by this that in order for an audience to buy into the animation they are watching, it had to be *plausible* for them to do so. In other words, it had to be part of the kind of experience they were familiar with in the real world – even though the world of animation is, in itself, often *implausible*. A well-animated Bouncing Ball should do that. It can bounce eternally if we want it to – unlike the real world – but as it does so it does need to display some of the real-world qualities we would expect of it. In this case, it is "gravity" and we'll explain how you can do that.

To create the gravity effect, we need to respect what happens when an object moves up against the force of gravity and moves downward under its influence. What we're essentially talking about here is *"deceleration"* on an upward path and *"acceleration"* on its return downward. Add to the mix the tensile nature, or flexibility, of the rubber ball, which pushes it straight back up again, and you have all the qualities of a good Bouncing Ball action. All we need now are the techniques to make it so when we animate it.

So, using "down and dirty" demo keys I created for my flipbook students recently, here are the two key pose positions of a bouncing ball.

The two key Bouncing Ball positions.

Position "A" is the ball in the air at the top of the bounce. Notice that it's perfectly round and not distorted in any way. Position "B" is where it is hitting the ground. Notice that it is very distorted, as a result of a soft shape hitting a hard surface. This is called a "**Squash**" position in animation, because it is deformed. Note that the volume of the ball does not change. If the vertical height is lessened, then the horizontal distortion is widened. In a simple, generic Bouncing Ball action, I would number these "**1**" and "**11**".

The "**breakdown**" positions of these would more or less be halfway up and halfway down. They would also be deformed, but this time it would be higher in the vertical and narrower in the horizontal. This is called "**Stretch**". The faster an object is moving, the more stretch there is. We give it a stretch position to simulate the kind of motion blur you would see if you film a fast moving circular ball and freeze just one frame at its fastest position. In film or CG animation, we would call that a *motion blur*. However, with line-drawn animation, it is hard to simulate a blur (except in digital animation, where a blur can be easily simulated) – so we draw a stretched oval shape to mimic the blur effect.

Compare the "normal" ball with the "stretch" version.

Now, the really interesting thing here is that we time these breakdown drawings and their actual positioning slightly differently when we consider the animated action. Remember that due to the effects of gravity, an object falling is **accelerating**, whereas an object rising is **decelerating**. So, to achieve that we first position the breakdown drawings to enable the effect we need. Therefore, with the falling action (from keys 1 to 11), we find that if we actually place the breakdown stretch position touching the ground, as it has a sense of real impact into the key position, 11.

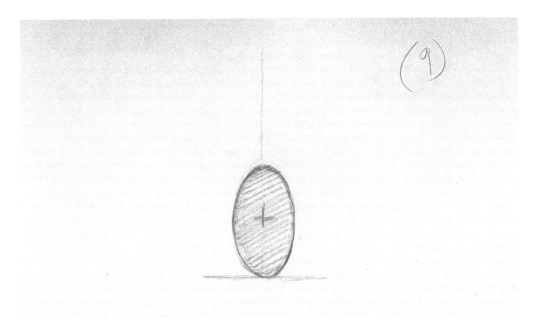

The "stretch" ball breakdown position as it hits the ground.

On the other hand, when the ball is rising (keys 11 back to 1) – because we are creating a looping action with the ball bouncing up and down continuously – we position the breakdown stretch position halfway up, giving a sense that it has really dramatically bounced off the ground after the stretch position, 11.

The upward "stretch" breakdown position immediately after the "squash".

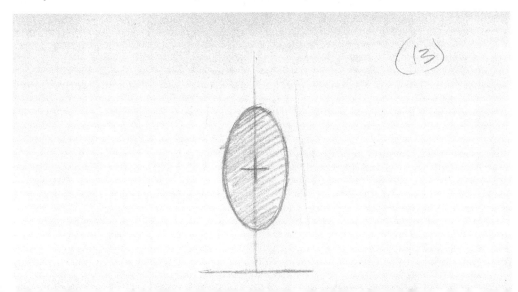

The final trick to give that decelerating/accelerating effect is to load the inbe-tweens tighter to the top of the bounce, both up and down. So, when the ball comes down from key position 1 to the breakdown position (which we'll call "9"), we will subdivide the halfway placement of the inbetween so they start close to-gether and widen apart on the way down. This is called "slowing-out". A chart an animator creates to indicate this would look like this.

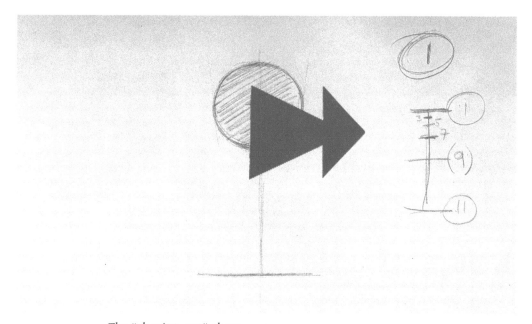

The "slowing-out" chart.

Note that the inbetween drawing 7 is halfway between 1 and 9. Then, when 7 is finished, inbetween 5 is halfway between 1 and 7. When 5 is completed, anoth-er inbetween is created (3), which is halfway between 1 and 5. This will create an acceleration effects as the closer together the drawing are, the slower the action will be. Conversely, the wider the drawings are apart, the fast the action is. So here with are starting slow at the top of the action, with each drawing progres-sively getting wider apart as the ball descends, ensuring that the ball is speeding up as it drops down.

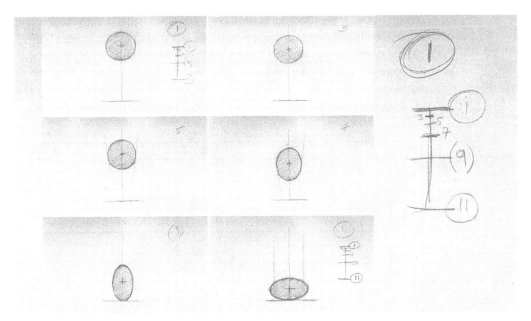

The "slowing-out" chart + plus animation frames.

The opposite of this is when the ball rises. If we have the same number of inbetweens used in the rising action to the falling action, then the rising breakdown drawing between 11 and 1 is number "13". With 13 created, we now add an inbetween halfway between it and number 1, calling it 15. Then, when we create the next inbetween, we call it 17. Once 17 is created, we add another inbetween, which is halfway between 17 and 1, called "19". Finally, a last inbetween drawing is created between 19 and 1, called "21". This action ensures that the drawings are getting closer together as they near the top, number 1 position – enabling the ball to appear as if it is slowing down as it rises to the apex (number 1 position). This is called "slowing-in" in animation terminology.

The "slowing-in" chart + plus sequencial ball drawings. (Note that the "stretch" breakdown position on the way up is further off the ground than on the way down!)

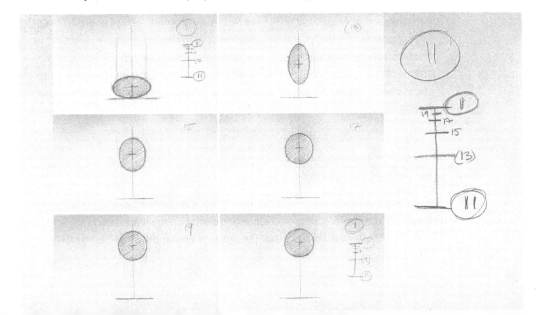

So with these simple procedures, we have created a ball that is both accelerating as it descends and decelerating as it rises. The fact that the action comes from 1 and returns to it means we can loop the action continuously for as long as we like. In an animator's exposure sheet, which was once used to record their animation thoughts clearly – but is still a great method for keeping their timing and key positions straight in their own minds – would look like this when filled in.

Action	Fr	Dialog						Aux 2 Pegs	Aux 1 Pegs	Top Pegs	Bot Pegs	Fr	Camera Instructions

The "Bouncing Ball" exposure sheet.

Remember that horizontal lines here represent "frames" of film and the vertical lines represent "layers" of animation. However, in this case, we are only talking about one layer, hence it being easy to understand. Blanks in the horizontal "frame" lines indicate that the preceding drawing needs to be carried on, into the frame too – meaning each drawing is to be held for two frames each. This timing of the drawings is known as "2s".

iPad Animation

To satisfy the digital animators out there, I have recorded a demo of the *"Bouncing Ball"* exercise created entirely independently on my iPad, using the "Rough Animator" software. I believe that the **iPad**, or similar drawing-based tablet, has huge potential for traditional animators with the knowledge I am sharing here. So I wanted to show an alternative way of animating a bouncing ball that will work well in a digital environment. I will do similar demos for some other exercise elsewhere in this book. They can be found on our dedicated website page too, http://www.2dacademy.com/masterclasses.html.

Suggested Assignment

Now, you have seen how a bouncing ball works in principle, it's time for you to have a go. However, whether you're approaching this using a conventional 2D "pencil & paper" style, or using a simple "flipbook", the following illustration will be useful to indicate all the recommended positions and timings. We'll demonstrate using a flipbook technique however.

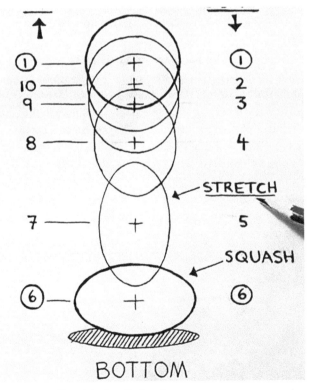

My Bouncing Ball guide for flipbook use.

Now, start with your first drawing of the ball at the top of the bounce on your first page. Decide, however, what is your first page. In other words, some flip-book animators like to flip from the back to the front, like a professional 2D animator does with full-size animation drawings. Others prefer to flip from the front to the back. Whatever your preference is, drawing your first bouncing ball there. Next, turn the next page over it and draw your second position, just a fraction different from the first position, as indicated on the chart above.

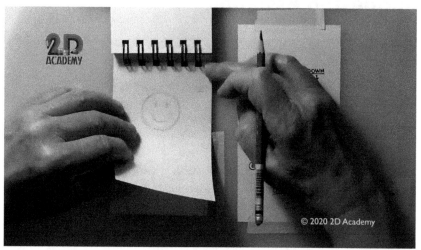

Drawing page 2 of my animation class flipbook demo. (Note: For more convenience, using loose blank cards, rather than a ringed sketchbook like this, might be better to work with when creating a flipbook.).

Then, turn down the next page and draw the next drawing – and so on until you have your ball dropping down and bouncing up to the top position again. You may be able to flip the action as it is, but I strongly recommend that you repeat the sequence two or three times to get more flow and meaning to the action. If you like, get a friend or partner to film your flipping action on a camera or their phone, so you can play it back and see it more completely in "real-time" video speed. If you're happy with the basic action, consider adding a design to the ball, turning it into a sun, a soccer ball, a beach ball – or even an eyeball with pupil, red veins and all, as a student of mine once did so successfully. Film it again and post it online if you want to share it. Congratulations! You have just animated your first sequence of movement!

Masterclass 03/ Keys, Breakdowns and Inbetweens

Equipment

I have preserved this old rostrum camera and early IBM computer control unit for years in my garage. I hope to find a museum that will publicly display it one day.

For this exercise, you will need the traditional animation equipment we described earlier – pencil, paper, peg bar, lightbox, eraser and pencil sharpener. You will also need a means of *capturing* your drawings, frame by frame and converting them to video. It is possible to do this exercise using just a flipbook – or better still, separate blank cards that will make a flipbook – but your learning will really be best served if you use traditional tools and equipment here.

> **NOTE**
> The 2D Academy has an "Equipment" link guide on its course web page at http://www.2dacademy.com/animation.html.

DOI: 10.1201/9781003324287-4

Warm-Up Gesture Drawing

This observational gesture drawing warm-up concerns "**Sporting Action**". Observing sporting action gives an animator some of the most valuable examples of strong physical action imaginable, although the warning is that with animation, we don't just copy real-world action, we have to *caricature* it, or *exaggerate* it at best. Therefore, the following two poses below give you an opportunity to observe, analyze and then emphasize them in a way that makes them even more dynamic than they are.

Your two sporting action poses.

As you can see, they involve a soccer player kicking a ball and a baseball player hitting one. We've probably all seen a million balls kicked and another million balls hit, but have we really looked at them to see how they are physically done. These two poses offer such an opportunity to train your *"animator's eye"* in just that. In my *"Drawing for Animation"* course, I go into more sporting poses for this exercise. But for now, these two poses will suffice. (Although I do strongly recommend that you do many more of these kinds of poses and many others, in your own time whenever you can – so you build a larger database of pose observations in your subconscious and your sketchbook!)

Here though, be disciplined with yourself and take just **3 minutes** to draw each one. Keep the following observations in mind when you sketch them.

Soccer kick observations: Again, we're looking at angles – angles of the shoulders and angles of the hips. Look how high the right is compared with the left hip, for example. So, just think of things like that and pay attention to the angles of the arms and the hands and the angles they make to the body and each other.

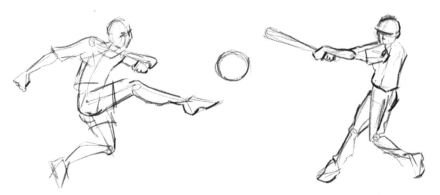

Sporting action gesture drawings by Tina Brun.

Baseball hit observations: Many people in America, as well as abroad, have played baseball as a major sport. So, we see a million of these hits all over the place, but do we ever analyze what actually goes into them and pose related to them. So this one will give you 3 minutes to study that. Note here the angle of the body lean. Also note that the weight of the hitter is basically on the back foot. There is some weight on the front foot of course, but it's not much compared to the back. Essentially, the center of gravity is much more over the back foot than the front. Be aware of the angles of the shoulders, the arms and the bat – which is effectively an extension of the arms. See also that the head is looking in an entirely different direction than you would imagine. Take all these factors into consideration as you draw.

Gesture drawings do not need to be large to be effective. Here, I drew a series of demonstration sketches on small sticky notes!

Instruction

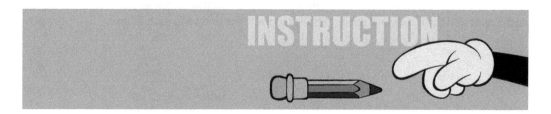

In the last lesson, you did what we call *"straight ahead animation"* using a flipbook. Straight ahead animation means that you start with an initial drawing and then add successively different drawings, one after the other. Ultimately, you have a sequence of movement that can be quite fluid, organic and spontaneous. However, the majority of commercial animation is not done that way, as greater disciplines need to be respected in the interest of continuity. Therefore, the industry uses a process that is referred to as *"Keys & Inbetweens"*, which is what we'll explore now. To do that, I'm referencing material I actually created for a series of flipbook videos – effectively producing an on-demand course for kids, containing 27 videos. However, I think they will more than well illustrate the principles we are about to deal with here.

Having flipbook fun on my video series. (Again, loose blank cards might be easier to work this than a ringed sketchbook when using a flipbook approach.)

Field guide: The first thing we do before animating a scene in conventional hand-drawn animation is creating what is called a "**Field Guide**". A *field guide* effectively shows us the area we will be working in, in addition to any location points within the scene that we need to animate too. In this case, we are going to be animating a letter "**A**" bouncing up and down (like our Bouncing Ball), so the obvious location point for that would be a ground line or surface upon which the A is bouncing. In addition to the ground line, I am going to draw a dotted line on the *field guide* – which represents the "**path of action**"; the A will be bouncing up and down along. With these two things on our field guide, we have everything we need to create our bouncing letter.

Demonstrating the field guide in my video class.

We keep the field guide on our animation pegs at all times, as it provides us with a permanent guide to what we're going to be doing. So, the first thing we do is we draw our letter A on the ground on a separate sheet of paper. This is in a position where it will prepare to bounce. This will be our first "**Key Drawing**" and so we'll call it number "**1**".

Showing the number "1" on the first drawing.

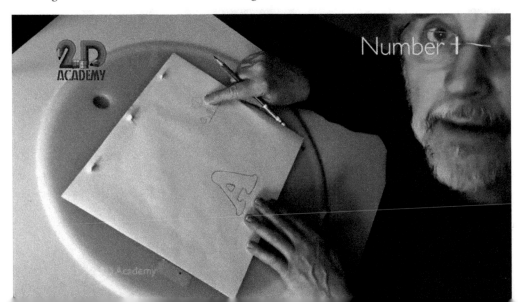

Traditionally, we number the drawing in the top right-hand corner of the paper. However, I have found that we can also place the number to the right of the action, so that it is visible when we film our drawings to test them. Having a visible number like that on screen means that if we need to make any action or timing changes later, we can see immediately what numbers have to be redrawn, or even renumbered. Now, if you switch your lightbox on, you'll see clearly that the A is sitting on the ground in its initial position.

Viewing the first drawing and field guide with the lightbox on.

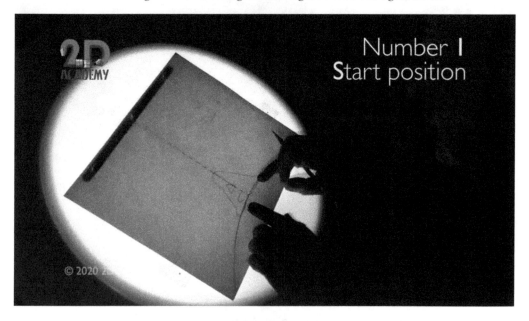

It should be comfortably on the ground area and lined up centrally with the vertical dotted line on the field guide. Indeed, you can see that I've actually drawn a small cross in the center of the A, which is accurately aligned with the dotter path of action behind it.

Showing the cross in the center of the "A".

Next we draw our second "key drawing". This time we're going to draw the A
at the top of it. And again, I'm going to add a little cross in its center, aligned
with the dotted path of action. This means that now we have the position
of the A at the top and the bottom of its bounce. We'll call that key drawing
number "19".

Showing the "A" at the top and bottom of the jump.

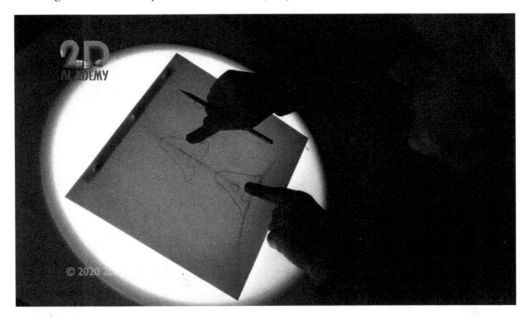

Next, we have to work out how they get from one to the other, both upward and
downward. To do that we'll create little "**animation chart**" that work it out for
us, including the number of inbetweens we'll need and the numbers we'll be
calling them.

Indicating the animation chart.

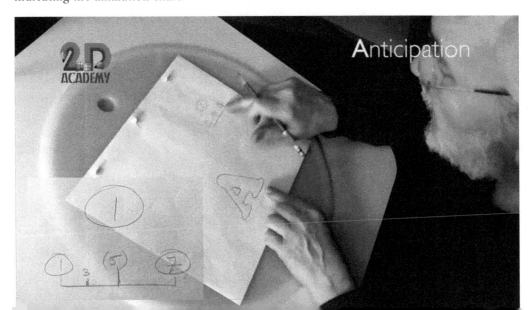

Now we're going to reference our previous *Bouncing Ball* assignment. Remember we said that to give the appearance of weight and gravity we need, the A to be *"slowing-in"* toward the top of the bounce and then *"slowing-out"* from the top to the bottom. Basing them on the notion that our animation will be shot on "**twos**" (i.e., each drawing will be held for two frames of film when with film them), these are the charts and drawing numbers we need to create. However, before we get into that, I want to add one more animation principle to your vocabulary – "**Anticipation**".

"Anticipation" is an action we create that precedes a major action. In other words, if a character is going to run off to the right of the screen from a standing start, we will move it to the left in some way before it goes. If it's going to run to the left with its main action, it will do a little move of some kind to the right to *"anticipate"* the run. Similarly, if a character is going to jump up into the air as its main action, then we have to do a little "squash down" before it leaves the ground. And that is exactly what we will do with our letter A here.

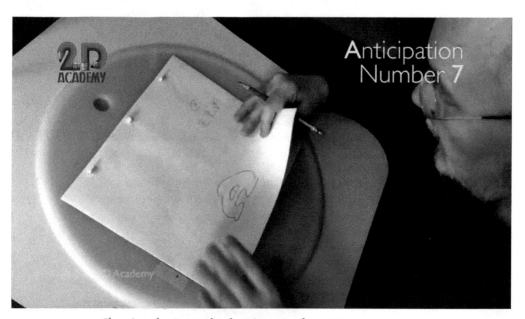

Showing the "squash" drawing, number "7".

So before we actually inbetween the A going up and down between the two keys we have created, let us first draw our *"anticipation key"* on another sheet of paper next and work that out. Basically, this key drawing will look like our key "1" drawing squashing down on the spot, shortening in height and widening in width. (Remember that with "squash" and "stretch" the volume inside the object has to remain consistent throughout.)

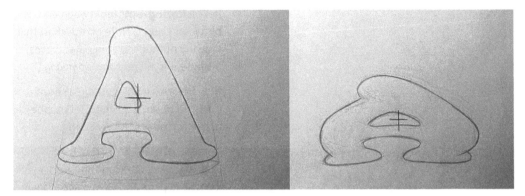

Compating key positions "1" and "7".

Incidentally, if you "flip" your drawings back and forth while they're on the pegs, you will get a rough preview of the action we're going to be attempting. But now, with our *anticipation* key duly created, we'll draw a little chart on drawing "1", to show us how many inbetweens we need to put from 1 and the anticipation key drawing, which we'll number as key "7". (And don't forget to add the little central cross mark on it too, lining up with the dotted path of action line on the field guide.)

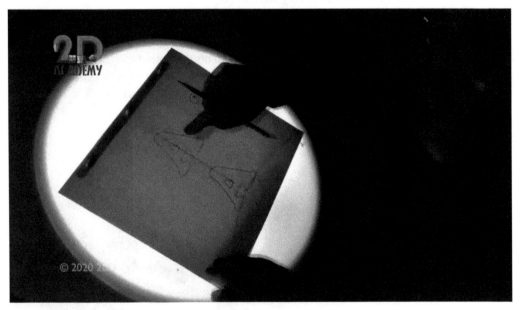

Indicating the crosses on each key drawing, lining up with the path of action on the field guide.

Working with two keys – 1 and 7 – and animating on 2s, it is clear that we'll need two inbetween drawings to link between them. Every animator will work that kind of thing out themselves through experience in time – that is, do I want that the anticipation to be slow or fast? However, for this example, I'm choosing to use two inbetweens and charting them out in a way that the first inbetween – the "**breakdown position**" – is halfway between them and the

Breakdown drawings are always written in parentheses.

next "**slowing-out**" inbetween – 3 – is between 1 and 5. Note on the chart that drawing number "5" is in parentheses, because it is a *"breakdown drawing"*.

Now before we do anything else with the main bouncing action, let us inbetween this anticipation action first, to see how it is done.

First, place key drawings numbers 1 and 7 onto the pegs and then place a clean sheet of paper over them. Number this drawing "5" – remembering to add the parentheses too! If you put the lightbox on behind them, you'll see their different shapes. Essentially, to create the inbetween you need to draw halfway between the two. Now, with something this simple, you can probably do it by eye, but let me show you something that – especially in other, more difficult challenges – will help you considerably. The process is called "**Superimposition**", and I've yet to see it demonstrated in any other books than mine, which is a pity as it often makes the big challenges of inbetweening so much easier. Of course, you can only use this technique when working with *pencils and paper* – it can't be done *digitally* yet, to my knowledge.

With the lightbox on, draw accurately (i.e., over the dotted line on the field guide) a small cross that is halfway between the crossed on key drawings 1 and 7. You might also lightly draw a line that represents the dotted path of action line too. (If you put one on each of the two key drawings, that will be even better – although the lines only need to be light enough so you can just see them.)

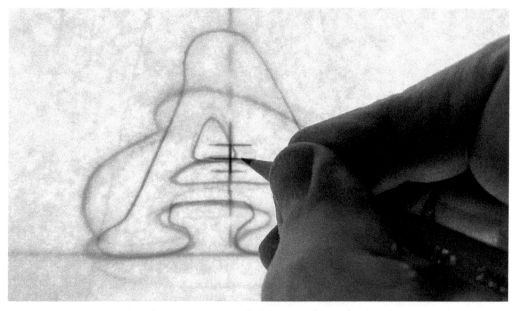

Drawing the center cross of "(5)" over the path of action.

Now, take drawings 5 and 7 off the pegs. Line up the crosses and the lightly drawn line of 7 with those of drawing 1. Now, place drawing 5 over those, lining up its cross and line with theirs. This will make them all "superimposed", one over the other, and therefore much easier to see where the inbetween lines of 5 need to go. LIGHTLY sketch the inbetween lines of 5 between those of 1 and 7.

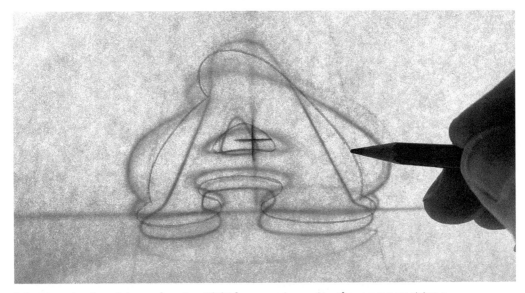

Inbetweening breakdown drawing "(5)" by superimposing the center positions using backlighting.

When you've done that, place them all back on the pegs. Now, you will see that you have an inbetween that is probably more perfect than if you'd drawn it by eye. Make sure, however, the feet of the letter A don't go any lower than the lowest part of those on drawings 1 and 5. If they do, then adjust them by redrawing them in the same place.

Showing the completed three drawings when placed on the pegs.

(Let me emphasize again here that the "Superimposition" technique I have just described is probably overkill for inbetweening your letter A anticipation at this stage. It really is meant for much more complicated inbetweening action with much more complex characters that are much further apart. However, I wanted you to see it in the most simplistic way possible, so you can learn it easily. I will return to more complex superimposition techniques in a minute and later, where we will go into other examples in much greater detail. You can see a video demo I did for "Superimposition" on this book's dedicated web page, previously mentioned.)

If you put your drawings on the pegs in the right order – that is, 1 on top, 5 in the middle and 7 on the bottom – you can "roll" or "flip" your drawings back and forth to test the inbetweened action. If it looks good, you can darken your lightly drawn lines on 5 and move on to the next stage. If not, then fix whatever is wrong with the 5 drawing, then thicken those line up when it's working as it should.

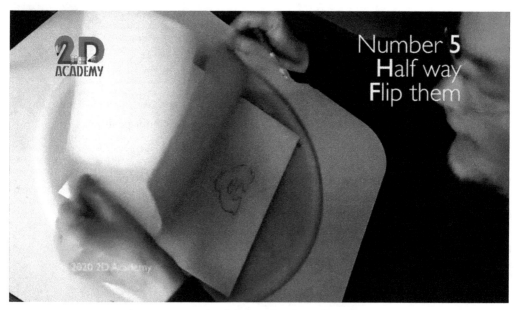

Test the movement by flipping the three drawings on the pegs.

Once your breakdown drawing 5 is finished, place it on the pegs with number 1. You can place drawing 7 to the side for the time being. Now, create your inbetween number "3" between 1 and 5 in exactly the same way as you did in between 5. This will then give you your first set on inbetweened drawings – 1–3–5–7.

The next inbetween, drawing "3".

You can place them on the pegs and with the lightbox off, flip or roll them as before to check that there are no glitches or misalignments. If there are, it is important to fix them at this stage as there is nothing worse than seeing great animation that has inaccurate inbetweens that spoil it's flow!

OK, with your anticipation action complete, it's now time to move on to the actual bouncing up and down of your letter A. This time we have to consider the inbetweening linking key drawing "7" and key drawing "19" – from the anticipation to the top of the bounce. For this, I have created another chart for you that represents that action. You'll see immediately that there are more drawings located together at the end of it, as that caters for the fact that that action needs to "slow-in" toward the top of the bounce.

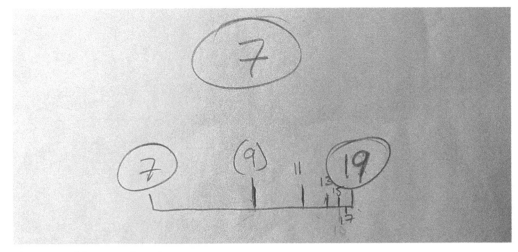

The upward bounce chart from "7" to "19".

This shows that our first, "breakdown", inbetween is number "9" followed by the ever closer drawings "11", "13", "15" and "17" as we reach the key drawing number "19". In other circumstances, I would say just inbetween these as we did the anticipation sequence before. But, remembering the previous Bouncing Ball exercise, we have to add the notion of "stretch" to our breakdown position. This effectively means that although the drawing number "9" is positioned more like an inbetween, its shape needs to be entirely different. So in that sense, it could almost be called a key drawing. This is what it looks like when placed over keys 7 and 19 with the lightbox on.

The backlit "stretch" drawing "9" between 7 and 11.

So, how do we best draw this one? Well, let's remind ourselves of how the Bouncing Ball behaved when it was going upward. Remember that on the upward path, the first breakdown inbetween was actually off the ground and halfway up. So, the simple way to do this is to put drawings 7 and 19 on the pegs, place a new sheet of paper over them, numbering it "9" and then draw in the little center cross halfway up the dotted path of action on the field guide beneath, just as we did before. You can even lightly draw a line, as before, to show the direction of the path of action too.

Now, take drawings 7 and 9 off the pegs and simply place the cross of drawing number 9 over the cross of drawing number 19. Make sure the path of actions line up too. (You might even want to lightly tape the drawing down in this position, so the new drawing doesn't slide around while you are working it out.) Then, with 9 superimposed over 19, lightly draw what you think a stretched version of the letter A might look like.

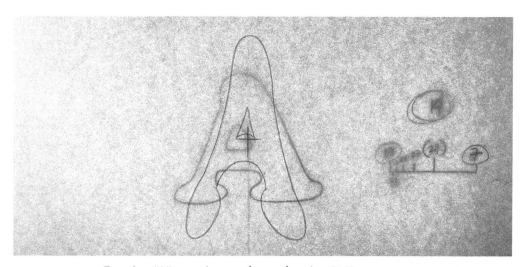

Drawing "9" superimposed over drawing "19".

Remember that it will be narrower in width but longer in length, with all the changes being symmetrical around the central cross. Draw everything lightly though, so you can easily make adjustments later. Now, place drawings 7, 9 and 19 onto the pegs in order and flip (or roll) the drawings to see if the general flow and direction is correct between them all. If it is, then darken up your lightly drawn lines on 9, or redraw until you get it right.

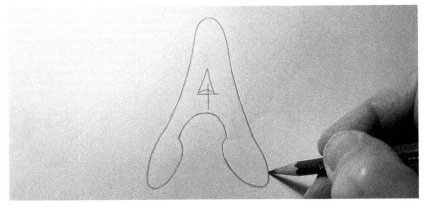

Darkening drawing "9".

Now, you have (hopefully) a perfect, stretch version of your letter A completed; you can add the next inbetween – which according to our chart is number "11". This again is best done by superimposition. So, place drawings 9 and 19 onto the pegs and place a fresh sheet of paper over them, numbering it "11". With the lightbox on, draw a small cross in the center of the other two crossed and lightly draw in a path of direction line. Next, take drawings 9 and 11 off the pegs and superimpose their center crosses over one another, as before, making sure all the path of action lines match up too.

Superimposing the center crosses to start the inbetween drawing "11".

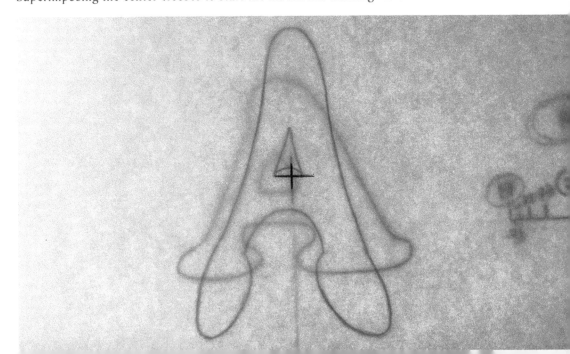

With them all in their correct positions, lightly draw what you think is an inbetween shape, between the lines of A in drawings 9 and 19. You will have to "eyeball" (i.e., judge is visually by eye) this to find the correct inbetween position, although if you get it into a reasonable halfway position it will work – as long as the central crosses and paths of action are lined up. Remember, although this inbetween drawing may look strange to you, as long as the general volume of the shape you draw is plausible, all will be good.

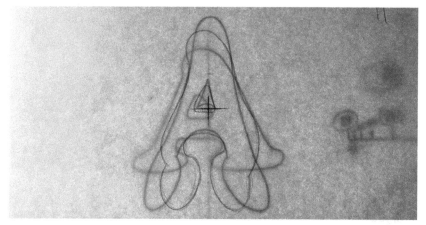

The final drawings 9, 11 and 19. Note that the "feet" drawing "11" is not in between 9 and 19 as I wanted them to shift in slightly on the way upward.

Place your drawings in order on the pegs and flip/roll them to check. Hopefully the transition in shape they require will work smoothly and perfectly. Redraw, if not.

With your inbetween number 11 successfully completed, continue to create the others. That is, inbetween "13" will be superimposed between 11 and 19, inbetween "15" will be between drawings 13 and 19, and finally inbetween "17" will be between drawings 15 and 19.

All the backlit inbetween drawings, from "9" to "19".

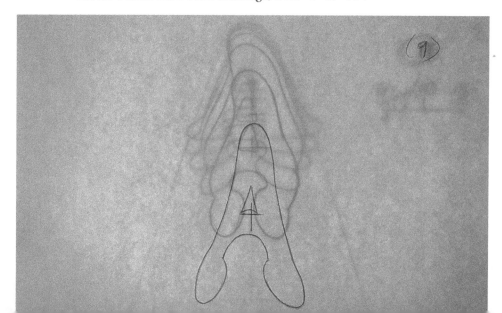

When they are all done, place them on the pegs and flip/roll them as best you can. You might even be able to flip them successfully of the pegs with so many drawing done – that is, place drawing 1 on the bottom, 3 on top of that, 5 on top of that and all the way through until 19 on the top. Then, hold them up in front of you and flip our drawings from back to front.

Flipping drawings from back to front.

It should show you your animation going down smoothly into the anticipation and up to the top of the bounce. (If you find flipping the drawings this way diffi-cult, fan them out slightly before you flip them and they will then to work better.)

Now, you have the A bouncing up, you now need to inbetween it going down – that is, from 19 to 7. (Note: we are not taking it down to key drawing number "1", as that is not a squash position. To get that feeling of squashing when it hits the ground, we'll use key drawing "7" as our bottom position.)

The process of inbetweening the A down is effectively the opposite of what we did going up. Now, if we want to take a *"cheap and nasty"* approach to this, we could simply reverse the drawings back to key drawing '7". It would work but it wouldn't work as well as what I'm now going to tell you, as I think my most respected students should always aspire to the *best* rather than the most con-veniently *quick*. (It might be that you have to do that from time to time in the industry, but for now, I want you to know how a master animator would think it through.) So, let's now look at my suggested *"animation chart"* for the num-ber and placement of inbetweens. You'll see that there is a new set of numbers with the closer ones being at the top and the *"breakdown position"* being at the bottom. This is to accommodate the *"slowing-out"* action we need here – that is, gravity causes the A to accelerate as it moves downward.

The slowing-out chart down.

But all is not as it seems on this occasion, with regard to the breakdown drawing. On the way up, the breakdown position was effectively halfway, although the shape of the breakdown drawing was not. On the way down, however, although the shape can be the same, the position of the breakdown is not halfway. Indeed, the feet of the A in this instance are almost contacting the ground where they are on key drawing "7".

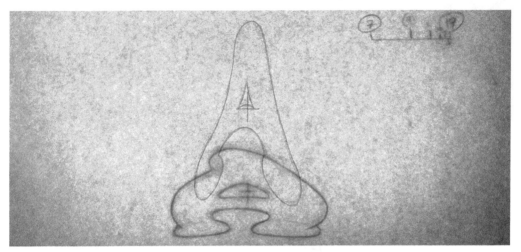

The feet on the breakdown drawing "(29)" stretch down for the ground.

Trial an error by animators over the decades found that we get a greater sense of contact with the ground if the base of the *"stretch"*-shaped contact drawing is in exactly the same place as the base of the *"squash"* key drawing. So, to achieve this, place key drawing "7" on the pegs and place a new sheet of paper over it, numbering it "29" – remembering to put it in parentheses because this is a "breakdown drawing". Mark out lightly on 29 the path of action and the base position of the letter A on 7.

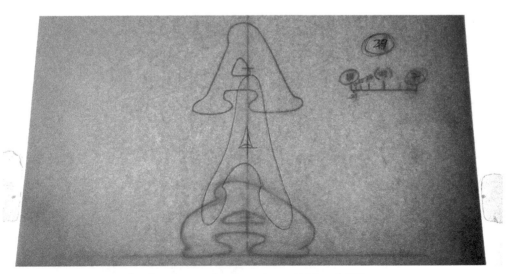

"Stretch" drawing 29, between keys "19" and "7".

Take these drawings off the pegs and now, with the lightbox on, take the previous breakdown drawing number "9" and trace it onto new breakdown drawing number "29" – making sure that the paths of action are accurately lined up and the foot of 29 is touching the base position you traced from drawing number 7. You can draw this much darker as you know it is an accurate breakdown drawing, as you created before.

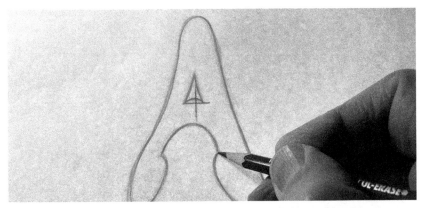

Breakdown drawing "29" being traced from breakdown drawing "9".

With the lightbox off, place drawings 29 and 7 on the pegs and flip the action between them. You should see a huge change in shape – from stretch to squash – but the base should be positioned consistently between them. If all this works fine, you can start inbetweening. Basically, the inbetweening here should be superimposed exactly as you did it before, except that your will be inbetweening in reverse. In other words, inbetween "27" will be halfway between 19 and 29. Inbetween "25" will be halfway between drawings 19 and 27. Inbetween "23" will be halfway between drawings 19 and 25, and inbetween "21" will be halfway between drawings 19 and 23.

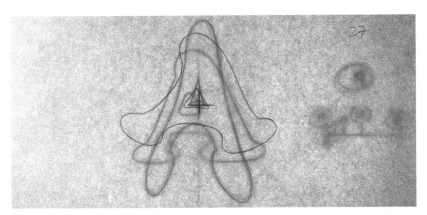

Inbetween "27" being superimposed between drawings 19 and 29. Note that I opened the legs on this drawing to give a sense of the legs reaching out before coming together.

When you've completed all those inbetweens and checked them by rolling them in order on the pegs – or putting them in reverse order and flipping them in front of you – then "congratulations"! You have created our first animated action traditionally!

Now, just to follow through on that, if we wanted to write this action down onto an animator's exposure sheet, repeating the bouncing three times, it would look like this.

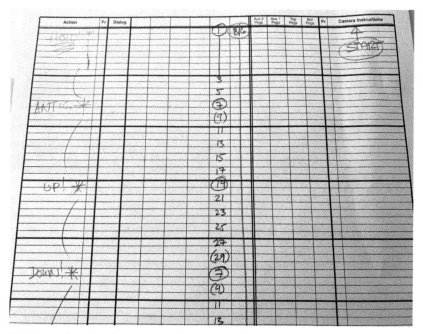

The bouncing "A" charted on an exposure sheet.

OK, the last thing you need to do now is capture it onto video. Now, we discussed earlier the various processes that you might use for this, so I don't want to pre-empt anything you might be doing by describing another method. However, I will just say that as long as you capture each drawing on "**2s**" at "**24 frames per second**" (fps) as indicated on the exposure sheet above, your action should look great. If it doesn't in any way, then we should consider perhaps the two most common mistakes. If your bouncing action seems a little staccato and stretched vertically, then you probably positioned the "up" key position of your letter A too high, meaning it is covering too much distance up and down. One tip on this is that every inbetween you create should have a tiny overlap with the preceding and following drawing. It may be just a line width with the breakdown positions, but if it's there, then your eye/brain coordination will be able to compute the link up for you and it will feel smooth. If there is space between drawings, then it will be harder for your brain to make the connection, and therefore, it will feel jumpy or staccato in terms of its up and down movement.

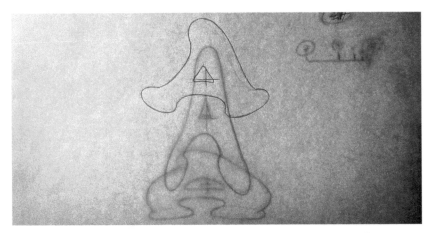

Note the overlapping of each drawing, ensuring that it will flow better than if they were not overlapping.

If, on the other hand, your action is jittery from side to side, then you didn't position your inbetweens on the path of action accurately enough, meaning that as the inbetweens move up and down, they're slightly moving from side to side also. Hopefully, however, your action is really smooth and convincing. So again – congratulations on creating your first complete, traditionally based animated action! You can see my version of this moving on our dedicated website page.

Suggested Assignment

Either recreate the bouncing A action we have just explained or take the first letter of your own name and have that bounce up and down in this way instead. I have done this exercise with my "live" course students. Having the first letter of your name bouncing up and down like a "bouncing ball" with the rest of the name beside it makes a great *"opening title"* for your own personal "**Showreel**" The rest of my student showreels contain all the pencil-drawn exercises in this course, plus the short color film they do at the end. If you're going to use this suggested exercise as the title for your own showreel, embelish your drawing by cleaning them up and coloring them in a design of your own.

The layout drawing for my own showreel titles. I first animated the circle as a "bouncing ball", then, when I saw it was moving correctly, I added the "T" for Tony within the circle drawings.

Masterclass 04/ More on "Squash & Stretch"

Gesture Drawing

Our observational gesture drawing here is about single person action. With animation, we usually concentrate on a single character moving, although some scenes can involve more than one of course. However, for the majority of time, we have just one character to think about. So today, we're going to focus on two poses that will make you look at just how people stand and how people pose their bodies when doing a single activity. Again, this is much less than my *"The Animator's Sketchbook"* is dealing with, or my *"Drawing for Animation"* course. But it is enough to train your hand/eye coordination, which is the most important reference method you have when constructing animation keys. Remember always, if your keys are not good, then your animation will never be good. So the sole purpose of these drawing warm-up sessions at the start of every masterclass lesson is to train you to see what is before your eyes in the real world and how to communicate that through good drawn poses in the animation world.

Remember always that, as animators, we need to become good *"people watchers"*. So much can be learned by watching people do everyday things – or not so everyday things. The following two poses will help you to focus on the kind of *"body language"* we're talking about here. You can see that we have two very different poses to consider – a construction worker and a rock star. You need to

DOI: 10.1201/9781003324287-5

give yourself just 3 minutes for each, capturing their essential visual message – exaggerating their poses to make them even more dynamic if you can.

Here are some thoughts to guide you as you draw.

Construction worker comments: Again, look at all the angles – the shoulders, hips and angle of the torso. Look at the positions and angles of the head and neck. Straight left arm and bent right one. The angle of the mechanical drill and the relation and positioning of the torso and shoulders above it. Notice also that there is a subtle forwarding position of the upper body, as the construction worker eases their body weight over the front/left foot more than the back – giving them more purchase to force the drill into the ground. These are all things your *"animator's eye"* should be aware of when you're sketching your character.

Rock star comments: This pose couldn't be more different than the previous one. Both are holding a *"prop"* – the first a heavy drill and this one a much lighter guitar. Consequently, their pose, balance and weight positioning are very different. Note here that the overall thrust of the pose is back and up, whereas with the previous one, it was forward and down. Because there is much less weight associated with the prop being held, the rock star can lean back more onto the back foot, arm held high. But again, note all the angles – the different angles of the shoulders and hips – the fact that the feet are wide apart, front to back. The head here is up too, whereas it was down on the construction worker. Play with all these things and exaggerate the pose as much as you like to get an iconic rock star pose. If you ever animate one, this position would make a great key drawing – especially if pushed forward through exaggeration.

Instruction

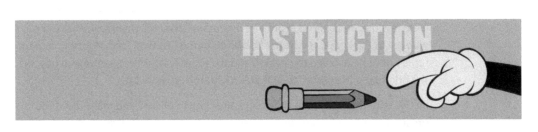

As you know, we've already mentioned "**Squash & Stretch**" in our two previous masterclass lessons, but today, we're going to dig a little deeper into these very important principles – and some more. It might be of interest to you that Squash & Stretch was one of the *12 principles of animation*, listed by the great Disney legend animators, **Frank Thomas** and **Ollie Johnston**, in their classic book on the Disney method, *"The Illusion of Life"*. There are actually more, which will be covered later here. In addition to *"Squash & Stretch"*, these are the ones that *"Frank and Ollie"* felt were the main priorities.

Anticipation

Straight ahead/pose to pose

Staging

Follow-through and overlapping action

Slow-in/Slow-out

Arcs

Secondary action

Timing

Solid drawing

Appeal

Exaggeration

Frank and Ollie were two of the famous *"Nine Old Men"* of Disney animation, and a study of all of their works will reward young animators greatly. They have had books devoted to them, and there is much material about them that can be found through Google and other search platforms.

NOTE

As I said, the "12 principles" were first mentioned in Frank and Ollie's wonderful book, "The Illusion of Life", and every animator today consider these like the 12 commandments of animation. Yet, a couple of them don't seem quite as relevant in our modern age of digital animation and video game application, but we'll move on from those for the time being. I personally would add many more, "**Weight**" and "**Balance**", which I'll deal with later in this book. Suffice it to say, in the book, you will learn pretty much all the "core principles of movement" that you'll ever need on your journey to becoming a "Master Animator".

But they were not by any means the only great artists or animators during the Disney studio *"Golden Age"* – not even the much quoted *"Nine Old Men"* were. There were so many other talents that shone at that time in the studio, but they were less reported. **"Fred Moore"** is legendary among Disney animation fans who are in the know, as was **Art Babbit** to name just two. Fred Moore's claim to fame is that he evolved the design and personality of *Mickey Mouse* well beyond the original *"rubber hose"* style that Mickey started out with.

Fred Moore brought more shape and anatomy to Mickey and really did some great animation with him. In my classrooms, I often screen a video of Fred Moore's YouTube *"showreel"*, which is packed with animation goodies throughout – especially with work representing his great ability in using *"Squash & Stretch"* in his character animation. Serious students should check it out to see how it worked so beautifully for him. In many cases, it is not easy to spot the subtle *"Squash & Stretch"* he applied to his animation, but it is quite visible in his animation of the *Seven Dwarfs* for example, especially on their faces.

Now, let me share what I do as a demo for my live classes. It illustrates further how to animate *"Squash & Stretch"*. *(See my demo version of it on the dedicated web page.)*

My simple animated demo that illustrates "squash" and "stretch".

With this exercise, we are going over old ground to some extent. But it doesn't hurt to replicate some of these things as familiarity breeds understanding, meaning the more you do of something in animation the better you'll get at it. It's not even that the old-fashioned style of *"rubbery"* Squash & Stretch is used in today's rigged and more anatomical style of CG animation. But under the surface, the principles are very valid in all animation, even if the rubbery look is removed and we just use solid anatomy to replace the more fantastic squashing and stretching of body parts.

So, what follows is the way I created the *"Squash & Stretch"* exercise for my students. It is deliberately very simple and mechanical in nature, simply to get the principle across. Hopefully, however, if the principle of "Squash & Stretch" is completed and understood, it will inevitably lead to be it being applied to a multitude of different and far more complicated expressions of it, later in the animator's career.

The first thing you need to do therefore, like the *"Bouncing Ball"* exercise, is to create a "**field guide**" which contains a horizontal ground line (that the character will stand on) and a central, vertical *"path of action"* line. This is the foundational reference that all your drawings will be based upon.

The "field guide".

Next, you need to create, on a new sheet of paper, your number "**1**" key position. You can see that mine is really simple, as we should keep drawing time to a minimum right now. It also has an animation chart indicated – a *slow-in* action that goes to key number "9". And with my lightbox on, you can see that it is standing on the *ground* line, and everything about the character is central to the *path of action* line behind it.

My number 1 drawing.

One you have your key drawing number "1" completed, it is now time to draw key pose number "9". This will be a *"squash"* position, like this.

Number 9 squash position.

You see that it is definitely squashing down – meaning that it is **lower in height** but **wider in width**, so ensure the *inner volume* remains consistent. (Meaning that the volume of the character must never change when you add squash or stretch to its form as that will effectively make it larger or smaller, which we do not want to do.) You can see that the legs are bending too, to emphasize the *"squash"*. You'll note also that I've lifted the arms up too and squashed the features of the face in accordance with the distortion on the body.

With key drawing number "9" established, we now need to draw our following *squash* position, we need to now create our last key – the high-up "stretch" position. We will eventually number this key drawing as "**21**", but we need to draw it first. See it below, you'll notice immediately that the deformation on the body is much longer **vertically** and a lot less wider **horizontally** – making this one a "portrait-shaped oval", with the features of the face distorting accordingly. You'll note also that the legs are elongated and the heels have risen, to emphasize the push up action. Similarly, the arms are now drawn down.

The "stretch" position - which could be even more extreme if required!

To ensure I maintain the inner volume of the character when deforming it, I superimposed it over drawing number "1" and carefully ensured that where I increased the height of it, I also made sure the reduction in width was compatible with that volume distortion.

Superimposing over drawing number "1" to ensure consistent distortion of inner volume.

TIP

Here is a quick method of arriving at your stretch shape; once you have created your squash shape earlier. When laying your new number 21 drawing paper onto the pegs, put your lightbox on and trace the vertical path of action line from underneath. Also have your number 1 key drawing on the pegs and mark the position of the bottom of the circular body. Now, turn your lightbox off and put a mark above the bottom of the body one, indicating how high you want it to rise in the stretch position.

So, now we have our **three main key positions** – the start and end position (1), the "squash" position (9) and the "stretch" position (21) – it is time to add the inbetweens.

The three key positions.

You can see from the "slow-in" chart, from 1 to 9 that the "breakdown position" of the inbetweens is going to be drawing number "3".

Slow-in chart, indicating that "3" is the breakdown position.

The inbetween is created by tracing the path of action from the field guide below, finding the center point of the proposed drawing (the center of the nose is a suitable point) then superimposing the noses of 1, 9 and 3 – drawing lightly the inbetween position on "3".

Superimposing the nose of drawing "3" over the noses of 1 and 9.

When a lightly drawn version of "3" is placed onto the pegs and checked with the other two keys, 1 and 9, the line can be strengthened and finished, in preparation for the "pose test" we will shoot later, when all the key and breakdown drawings are completed.

Strengthening up and darkening the line on drawing "3".

We now have our first completed breakdown drawing number "3".

Completed breakdown drawing "3".

Now, we have to create our second breakdown drawing, "**15**", which the "slow-out/slow-in" chart indicates is halfway between key drawings 9 and 21.

Slow-in/Slow-out chart from "9" to "21".

This can again be achieved by superimposing the nose of drawing "**15**" over those of key positions 9 and 21 and then drawing the inbetween lightly.

Superimposing "15" over 9 and 21.

Once the lightly drawn breakdown is checked with the keys on the pegs, it can then be drawn darker if all is OK. Notice however that instead of inbetweening the arms with everything else, I have lifted them up slightly, to give a somewhat *"overlapping action"* effect to their movement.

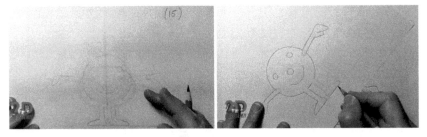

Lightly drawing and then darkening the breakdown "15" drawing.

Finally, we must now draw the final "breakdown drawing" required – from key "21" back down to key "9". This completes the cycled action. The midway break-down drawing is, therefore, drawing "**27**".

Slow-in/Slow-out chart, from 21 to 9.

This is again done by superimposing the drawings over one another, drawing the inbetween lightly, checking it by flipping the drawings on the pegs, and then darkening up the line for the "pose test".

Lightly drawing and then cleaning up the line of breakdown "27". Note though that, in the middle drawing, I have brought the arms in close to the body, to increase the "overlapping action" on them that I was after.

With all the keys and breakdown drawings completed, it is time to shoot a "pose test" of all the actions. The best way to do this is have them hold on the screen for the number of frames they and the next inbetweens would occupy in screen time. Therefore, an exposure sheet of the "pose test" would look like this.

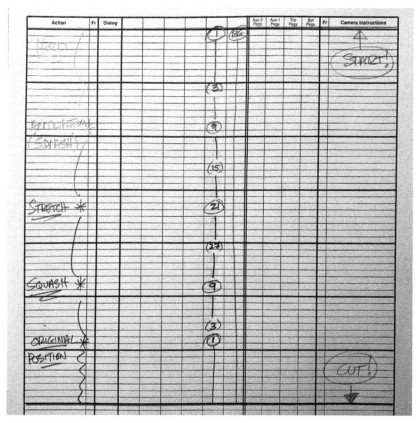

The keys and breakdowns timed out for the pose test on an exposure sheet.

The drawings would look like this.

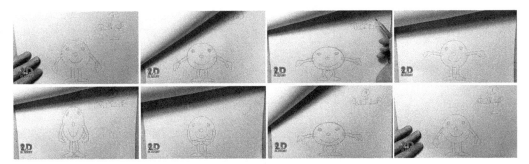

The final key and breakdown drawings to be filmed for the pose test.

If everything looks good with the pose test, then it's time to add the inbetweens. The process is to follow exactly the approach with also with the breakdown drawings. Find the nose midpoint, superimpose all three drawings over
the nose positions, draw the inbetween lightly, and then, when you have tested
the rough inbetween on the pegs, darken up the lines. So, with the first set of inbetweens, you need to create "**5**" between "3" and "9". Then, with 5 created, you
need to draw "**7**" between 5 and 9. That completes the first set. For the second
set – between 9 and 21 – you already have breakdown 15. So, the first inbetween
to do in this set is "**13**", between 9 and 15. Then "11' between 9 and 13 – and so
on, and so on.

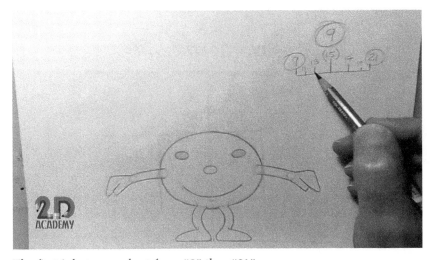

The first inbetween chart from "9" thru "21".

With all the inbetweens completed, I suggest you now film them on "2s" – that
is, each drawing held for 2 frames of film – with a "hold" on drawing "1" at the
beginning and end. The exposure sheet for this would be.

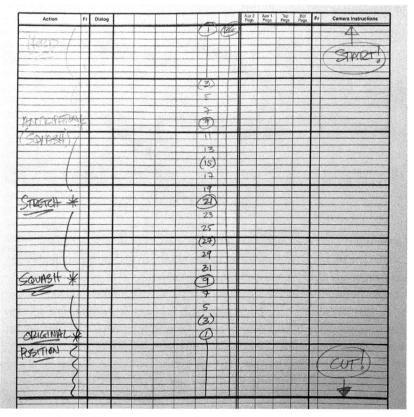

Exposure sheet of final animation, shot on 2s.

Suggested Assignment

I recommend that you pretty much follow this instruction and create your own version of the transitioning action from *"squash"* to *"stretch"*. However, why not either create your own (simple) character design to work with, or else – use this character given and add designs, decoration, clothing and anything else to embellish it when you are sure the roughed out pencil action is working fine. These amazing screencaptures from **Winsor McCay**'s 1911 film, "**Little Nemo**", might fire your imagination somewhat.

More detailed character design by Winsor McCay.

And definitely go for extended kind of "squash" and "stretch" he went for too.

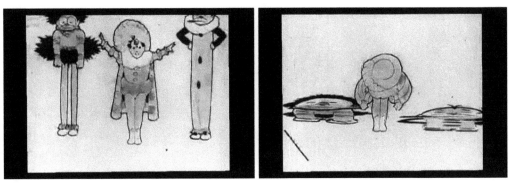

Greatly extended "squash and stretch" keys by Winsor McCay.

Masterclass 05/ More on Slow-In and Slow-Out

Warm-Up Drawing

This warm-up drawing exercise this time is entitled, "**two-person action**". A great deal of animation requires that one character interact with another. Therefore, it pays us to study the physical interaction of two characters from the real world, working or playing together. As mentioned before, in my *"The Animator's Sketchbook"* and *"Drawing for Animation"* online class, I require four separate interaction studies to be completed. But here, let us focus on just one of them, getting from it the essence of that which has to be seen and understood. You have **4 minutes** to observe, analyze and sketch out this picture of two people relating to each other. As ever, please be disciplined with yourself on time, to gain the greatest benefit from the exercise.

DOI: 10.1201/9781003324287-6

Pose observations: As you can see, you have two completely different story-telling poses occurring here. One can only imagine what has gone on here. The result of an argument? An intolerable ongoing situation? One man is clearly in the doghouse, while the woman looks to be in a place where she cannot forgive whatever it is. But without a doubt, the body language here is all-important. He is slumped forward, head in hands, staring at the ground. She is apart from him; arms folded resolutely, head turned away as if she wishes she were somewhere else. Remember also that , in the time you have, you can't really get into the facial expressions with your observational gesture drawings – unless you draw incredibly fast and meaningfully of course. But you can totally express these different moods and attitudes from body language alone. So work on that – the angles, proportions and relationship from one person to the other – exaggerating the pose as much as you dare. Clearly, this is a more challenging exercise than the ones before.

More outstanding class gesture drawing work by Tina Brun.

Remember also that it is necessary for you to push yourself at all times, as ultimately understanding relationships and the body language between two characters is of paramount importance. If you were animating this in a character sense professionally, such exaggerations of pose and attitudes would be entirely necessary to bring the required storytelling dynamic to your scene.

Instruction

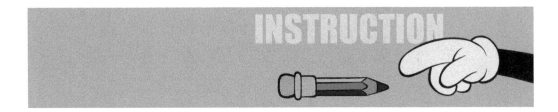

So now let's focus a little more on the principles of *"slowing-in"* and *"slowing-out"* – one for the Frank and Ollie *"12 principles of animation"*. We've already dealt with it earlier of course, but this is a very quick and simple exercise that will demonstrate to you just how important this core principle is. In fact, nothing in nature except the most mechanical of machines moves at a constant rate – it is either slowing down or speeding up. Even robots or android bipeds would move this way in many instances. So, an animator has to ask himself or herself, from key to key, is this particular action moving faster or slower, or even? Therefore, a complete appreciation of the principles of *"slowing-in"* and *"slowing-out"* is invaluable to any animator.

Pendulum Swing

The best way of learning how effective **"slow-in"** (deceleration) and **"slow-out"** (acceleration) is can be best demonstrated by a simple swinging pendulum. And to do that, we will explore two ways of achieving it – the wrong way and then the right way. We'll start with the wrong way and take it from there. But first, we need to set up our foundational material for both approaches.

Field guide: So, the first thing to do is create a field guide of the pendulum setup. Previously, we had to draw everything on the same paper layer. However, this time I want you to draw this on two layers.

Hand-drawn pendulum swing by one of my previous students, Emma.

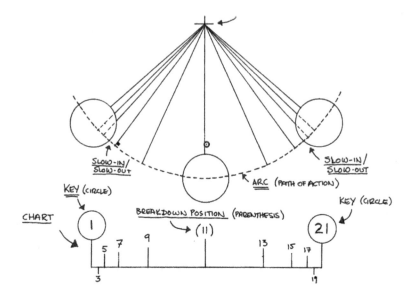

Field guide for students working on a pendulum swing.

The cross at the time and the box around the paper area is effectively your *"field guide"* layer. The vertical pendulum arm – the top of which is exactly matching the cross (pivot point) position – has a circular ball on the base of it. This pendulum is its own layer and is actually a "key" drawing. We will call this key drawing number "11".

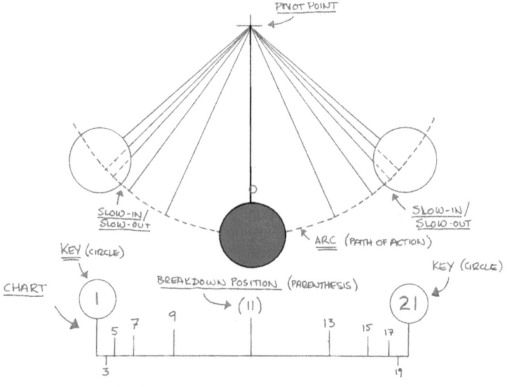

Key drawing 11.

Now, create two more key drawings on separate sheets of paper – one representing the pendulum at its highest point to the left (number "1") and another representing the pendulum at its highest point to the right (number "21"). Make sure that the top of the pendulum on both matches exactly the cross (pivot point) on the field guide beneath.

NOTE

The drawing numbers on this first "wrong" exercise may seem a little weird at first, but I am trying to avoid you actually drawing two sets of pendulum animation here. So, just go with what I'm saying on this one, as all will become clear on the next "right" version.

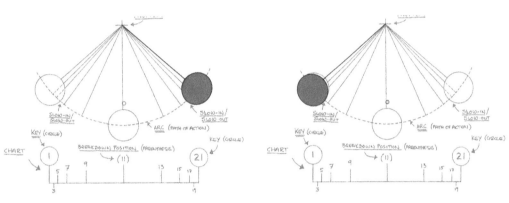

Key poses "1" and "21."

The inbetweens linking these three drawings are as such. Notice that each is an equal distance between the keys – called "**evens**", or "**even inbetweens**".

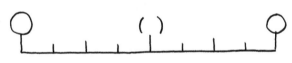

A typical "evens" pendulum chart.

Draw each of the inbetweens on separate sheets of paper, making sure at all times the top of the pendulum arm of each is matched to the cross in each case too. If not, the top of the pendulum arm will jiggle about as it swings.

With all your inbetweens complete, you now need to capture your drawings on "2s" (i.e., two frames of film per drawing). Capture the action going from left to right once and then immediately reverse the capture of drawings from right to left. Repeat this cycle twice more before rendering your capture to video. Play back at 24 frames per second, ideally. You will see your pendulum swinging backward and forward; however, it will not be convincing in terms of the pendulum having weight or responding to the forces of gravity upon it.

All the "even" inbetweens of the first half of the swing.

NOTE

You will be able to see both pencil-drawn versions of the pendulum swing – bad and good – on our special web page at http://www.2dacademy.com/masterclasses. html.

So, now we will do the second version, applying the principles of *"slow-in"* and *"slow-out"*, which will give it weight and will communicate that it is obeying the laws of gravity. (In that, as it swings upward, the swing will slow down and as it swings downward, the swing will speed up. It will be subtle, but effective! And this is the chart we will use to do our inbetweens.

The correct "slow-in/slow-out" pendulum chart.

This is where the numbering you used before will make much more sense. For example, you'll see that we actually removed two inbetweens – the even numbers, 10 and 12 – but have added more to the mix – inbetweens 3, 5, 17 and 19. To create these, you will do the following. On the left, you will draw inbetween "5" between 1 and 7. Then you will create inbetween "3" between drawings 1 and 5. On the right, you will draw inbetween "17" between drawings 15 and 21. Then, you will draw inbetween "19" between 17 and 21.

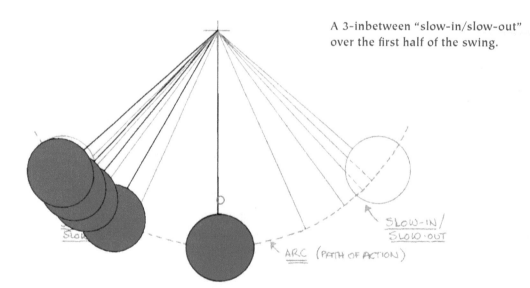

A 3-inbetween "slow-in/slow-out" over the first half of the swing.

Again, capture these drawings this time, also on 2s, following your number order to swing it to the right and reversing the numbers to bring the swing back from right to left. Repeat this action at least three times before you stop capturing and then render to video.

This time, as you play it back, you will notice that the pendulum tends to slow down a little to the end, and more slowly speed up from that position as it returns in the opposite direction. In this way, it is at its fastest in the middle and lowest at the top of the swings.

You can change the timing of the pendulum swing by adding (to slow it down) inbetweens, or re-moving (to speed it up) if you like. But the principle of *"slowing-in"* and *"slowing-out"* at the top of the swings should be applied accordingly.

NOTE

I again refer you to the pencil-drawn versions of both pendulum swings on our special web page at http:// www.2dacademy.com/masterclasses.html.

Hopefully this wrong/right comparison will convince you that the principle of *"slowing-in"* and *"slowing-out"* is a good asset to have in your animator's tool-box. Bearing the effects it offers in mind at all times as you animate any action from key to key, imagine how it might assist the timing of what you are trying to do with any action you are tackling. Sometimes "evens" is the way to go, as not all key-to-key actions require acceleration or deceleration. *"Slow-ins"* and *"slow-outs"* are usually applied to the beginning and ends of movements overall, varying each time. Therefore, it is always necessary to understand just **WHY** you are using a *"Slow-in"* or *"slow-out"* in your animation, remembering that to not use it at appropriate times will diminish what you are seeking to do.

Suggested Assignment

Just doing the above exercise should be sufficient for you to understand the principles involved here, but if you want to test it further, think of animating something else where a *"slow-in"* and *"slow-out"* will be really effective – such as a hand playing with a yo-yo spinning up and down, or a conductor's baton as he leads the orchestra.

Masterclass 06/ Timing and Placement

Warm-Up Drawing

Pose & Silhouette As an animator or artist, it is fundamentally important that everything you create is visually strong and readable. Animation keys especially need to be clearly seen and express the strongest *"storytelling poses"* they can. To do that, poses need to be "**silhouetted**" well. Silhouetting is creating a key position or pose in a way that there's no overlap of information and that the "negative space" around that key position or pose is strong. Therefore, the following pose will help illustrate that. It has a clear image of a person to the left, with a blackened silhouette version of it to the right. This is a "good" pose as you can see what's happening on both sides.

DOI: 10.1201/9781003324287-7

Action pose with its own blacked-out version.

Remember that strong silhouette poses should be able to tell a visual story better, even when blackened out like the above. Bad ones do not, as you'll find out in this next exercise. Here, the blackened silhouette is not visible on the right. You are required to draw it on the left-hand side of your sketchbook page in **3 minutes**. However, leave space clear on the right – as the next stage of this drawing assignment is for you to draw an outline of your left-hand drawing and fill it in. But first, draw the pose as you see it, now.

Once you have completed this observational gesture drawing, draw a blacked-in version of it on the right of your page. You will immediately see why this is a BAD pose for animation. With the regular character running toward us shot on the left, we can see all kinds of visual information. But when it is blackened in on the right, pretty much all the information is obliterated.

Indeed, we clearly have no idea of what's going on here; hence, it is a perfect example of *"bad silhouetting"*. Poses like this should be avoided accordingly. Of course, it is not always possible to have every animation key drawing silhouetted, especially when working in a fixed camera view environment, 2D animation world. But, within all the poses you create for an animated sequence, you should try at all times to make the most important key poses in that collection as well silhouetted as possible.

Obviously, if your character is placed against a white background with no other conflicting imagery behind it, the need for silhouetting is **not** so important. However, if you have a complex, fully colored character moving against a complex, fully colored background, then problems in clarity may ensue.

What your
previous exercise
should look like.

Sometimes clever coloring can save visual complexity, even if the
silhouette is bad. This is a development work for a personal project that is
based on the amazing works of the marvelous British artist, William Heath
Robinson.

This principle of course can apply to any single cartoons, comic strip frames, graphic novel or any other form of illustrations you do too!

It is at such times that silhouetting becomes fundamentally important to the reading of your action from the perspective of the audience – especially if your character is working with a prop. (In which case, it is better to have that prop positioned away from the body.) So, always try to get into the habit of considering *"Pose & Silhouette"* whenever you're creating animation key poses for a better reading of your action.

Instruction

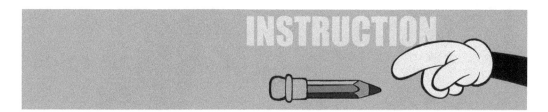

Timing and Placement

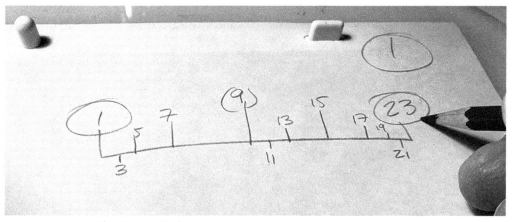

Charting out inbetweens.

In my live classes, I like to show this visual demonstration of *"timing and placement"*. It helps students understand how the placement of inbetweens works and how speed and intent change if you add or remove inbeweens. It also works as a follow-up demonstration of *"slowing-in and slowing-out"*. It is another exercise that can be done by drawing, or even faster by using a 2D animation software program of your choice. My choice has always been the now defunct, *"ToonBoom Studio"*.

The ToonBoom Studio interface.

Sadly, ToonBoom technologies removed this software from the marketplace some time ago, in favor of what was their supposedly *"new and improved"* program at the time – "**Harmony**". However, even at its basic *"Essentials"* level, *ToonBoom Harmony* is way too complicated to teach the core principles of movement at a basic beginner's level. It takes so long to learn the software that there is no time to teach the things that really matter in a classroom – the core principles of movement. So, I still prefer to use *ToonBoom Studio* for demonstrations like this, even though I know my students can no longer get access to it. I solved the problem for me however, by adopting "**Moho**" as my program of choice in the classroom – which is so much more accessible for beginners just starting out – and is on an upcurve in the industry IMHO, especially since the original designers of the program have bought it back and are developing it further. Needless to say, we will be using *"Moho"* in *"Section II"* of this book.

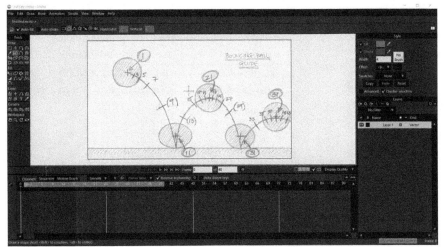

The Moho interface.

Now though, to help you understand the importance of "timing" in animation, here's a simple image of a car, about to move across the screen from left to right. We'll call it a "**fast**" action. Below it you will see a simple "evens" chart of three inbetweens.

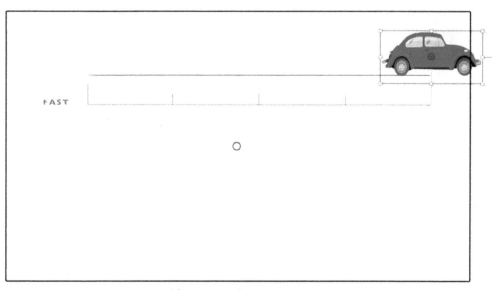

VW moving with "even" inbetweens.

Remember what I said earlier about there being a slight overlap between one object/character and the next – and how that helps the human brain accept the movement, fast though it is. Well, this demo does have a very slight overlap between the front fender and the back fender on each position, making it just on the bounds of comfort. If there is a space wider that doesn't allow for such an overlap, then the action will have a judder to it, because the brain doesn't process it well enough. So the tip is, even if you want a really fast action, try to still keep a little overlap from frame to frame. If you can't do that, consider stretching the object/character along the line of its trajectory – or even create motion blurs, frame by frame, enabling an even overlap

In my classroom, I show the speed that this simple action creates, so I recommend that you replicate this somehow and capture it on 1s (one position per frame of film), from one side to the other. When you do this, you'll see that the car (or whatever object/character you want to re-place the car with) moves across the screen very fast and even in pace. That may work for some scenes you are planning to an-imate, but now all. So what do we do to modify it to accom-modate that?

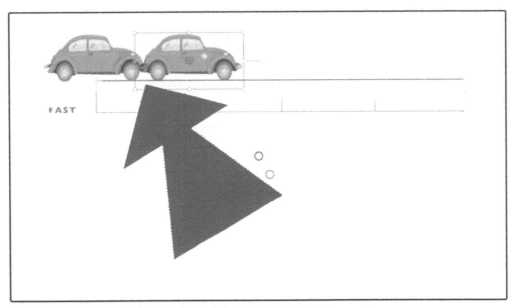

Even a small overlap helps the flow of the action.

The next demo frame shows a progression from our previous example. This shows how to slow down the movement of the same car action to create a "**medium**" speed action. This is done by keeping the inbetweens as "evens" but simply putting one more inbetween midway between our existing inbetweens.

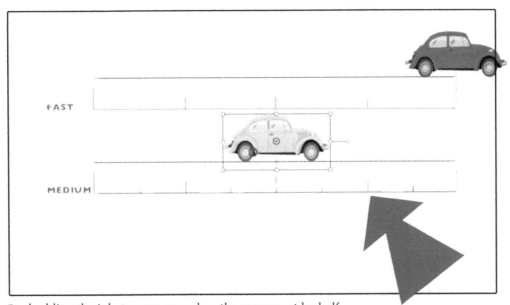

By doubling the inbetweens, you slow the movement by half.

Capture all these positions on 1s, and you'll see that the car has now slowed down half from the original version above. Actually, in the classroom version of this, I have both the top car and the bottom car running at the same time, so the difference is totally obvious. So, if you can set up your animation to show the two actions, side by side, you'll get a sense of what the extra inbetweens offer to the speed and smoothness of the action.

Finally, let's create a "**slow**" version of the action. Again, it is "even" timing but we have again added a new set of inbetweens halfway between the existing ones.

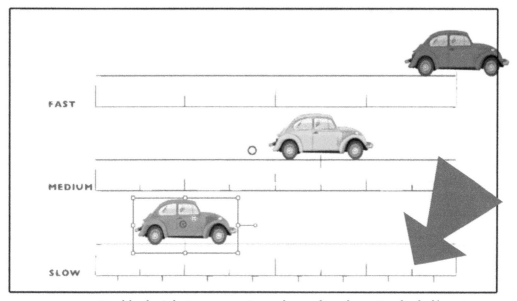

Double the inbetweens again, and you slow the action by half again.

Capture these on 1s and view the difference. Noticeably slower – giving you a sense on how many inbetweens create certain variations of speed. Realize also that if you show each position on 2s (one drawing for two frames of film), everything would be half the speed you've seen so far. All of this should give you a definite sense of what we are talking about when we are talking about "timing" and "placement" of inbetweens. It is not a definitive guide as other characters will require different timing approaches – even from different keys to other keys in the same sequence. But having a generic guide like this to work with, you at least have a sense of something that will take away the more challenging "time and error" approach that most beginners have.

A failure to understand timing can often be seen when reviewing inexperienced animator's work on YouTube or other video platforms. Quite often the keys, poses and ideas are great. But the animator has failed to put in enough inbetween drawings to get a maximum, flowing effect. This can often destroy great animation, something I personally notice on many Anime films for example – although the Anime industry is by no means not alone in all this.

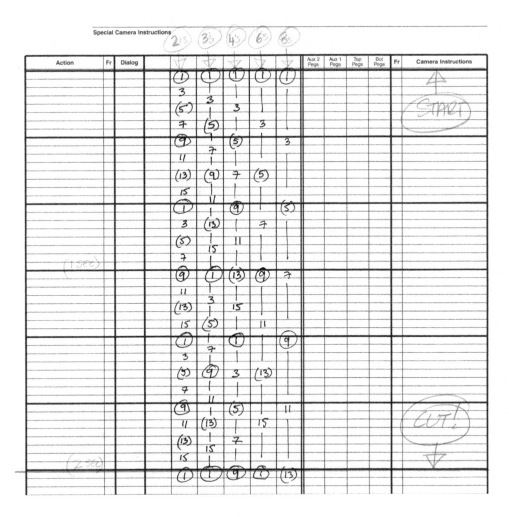

Poor animation is often created on "4s" (each drawing is held for 4 frames of film) – or even more, up to "6s" or "8s" and beyond. This exposure sheet shows the same 16-frame cycle, shot on 2s, 3s, 4s, 6s and 8s.

Now, I know Anime purists will throw their hands up at this and say that this is how Anime's meant to be. However, when I look and see the incredible artwork and the often very powerful key positions, my heart bleeds for the fact that the brain dismisses them as they are often too far apart, or often have too few in-betweens to help the audience's brain to connect the dots. I think this is a huge flaw in what is quite often a very admirable and impressive artform – and our legacy as animators is what we leave on the screen, and how well it performs, rather than just the abstract notion of moving designs, however well they are drawn.

Anyway, all this has been demonstrated a car movement that is even across the screen. What if the car is slowing to a stop however? Or what happens if the car hits a solid brick wall at speed? This is where the element of "placement" becomes very important. What might the latter look like for example? Well, let's start with our slowest, even inbetween example. The car is speeding along and hits a solid object. Clearly, like the squash on a bouncing ball hitting the ground, there will be a form of squash on the car when it hits the immovable object of a wall.

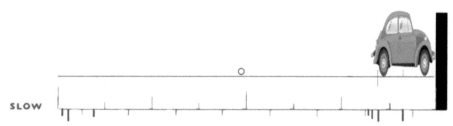

SLOW

The car will "squash" when it hits a wall.

As you can see, this version has a black vertical wall that the car will hit, plus a number of extra inbetweens that will add some variation to the action. You'll see some evidence of "slowing-out" and "slowing-in" too. For example, see the three extra inbetweens we have added to the left-hand side of the chart.

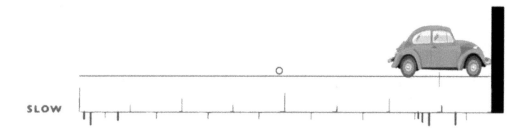

SLOW

When a solid object like a car hits another solid object like a wall, something has to give. The inbetween chart will be devised in accordance what gives first – or whether we are animating a "real" world or a "cartoon" one.

These represent the car accelerating from a static position. The car is heavy, carrying a lot of weight, so it will need to ease into top speed, rather than hit top speed from frame 1. So those three "slowing-out" inbetweens will ensure the car accelerates to top speed from frame 1. In reality, there would probably be more slowing-out inbetweens there, so that the acceleration is more naturally gradual. But for the point of illustration here, I have made them minimal and simple to do. At the other end of the chart, we have more extra inbetweens. But these do not relate to the going into the wall action. Instead, they are the "slowing-in" inbetweens that occur after the car has hit the wall and is bouncing back.

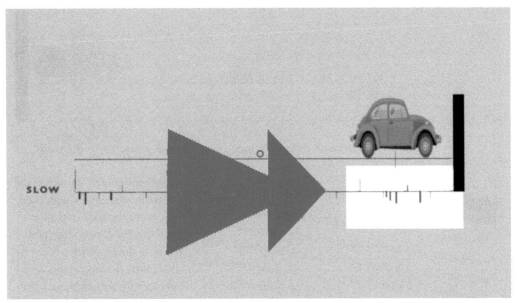

Here, the car bouncing back from hitting a wall slows-in to a halt – as indicated with this chart.

Naturally, like our *Bouncing Ball* action, there will be a big bounce back from the actual hit of the wall, and then, the speed of the car will decelerate to a stop after it happens. So those extra slowing-in inbetweens in red are for the car bouncing back from right to left.

One last thing we must consider in all this is what happens to the car when it actually hits the wall? Well, imagine it is the Bouncing Ball on its side and the wall is the ground line that the ball bounces on. At the point of contact, the car will "Squash" against the wall. As it bounces back – if that is the plan – then the breakdown position will have a degree of distortion too.

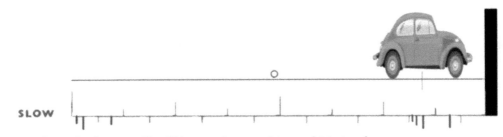

As it rebounds, the car will still have a degree of "squash" in its shape.

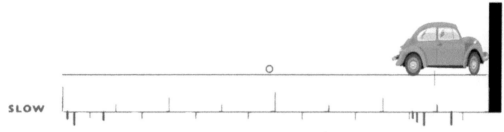

SLOW

The VW fender will deform before anything else when it hits the wall.

We are talking about a more rubbery "cartoon" car here, rather than a real-world metal one, which would probably just crumple up against the wall. Here, using the rubbery car example, we can better illustrate a more "plausible, implausible" solution. Therefore, instead of the car keeping its shape, as it did in the original evens/slow action we demonstrated, the squash effect would begin the moment the car's front fender hit the wall.

It would probably continue for one more frame against the wall, then immediately bounce back in a more *"stretch"* shape after it left the wall, slowing-in to a final normal shape position at the very end of those added slow-in in-betweens on the chart. Now, all this can probably be improved and polished by you if you want to devote more time to it. But these are the core principles you need to understand to get the broader action correct.

Suggested Assignment

I recommend that you tackle this action using a similar car, a ball or any other character or object of your own conception. But by doing it somehow – then capturing everything on both on 1s and 2s – I believe you will get a great sense of how this all works in real time, on a screen or monitor. Remember always that knowing about something abstractly is somewhat valuable. But actually doing it from personal experience will teach you so much more. So whether you hand-draw it or use 2D animation software to do a digital version, I strongly suggest you do something along these lines to really get a sense of how *"timing"* and *"spacing"* really work. Speed can be perfected by good *"timing"*, and effective action can be achieved through *"spacing"*.

Masterclass 07/ Generic Walk Action 01

Warm-Up Drawing

Pose Alternatives

When animating any action, an animator needs to understand the circumstances in which that action is taking place. For example, if a character is performing a walking action, then a number of factors need to be taken into consideration by the animator. What is the environment like that the character is walking through? What is the weather like in that environment? What is their age and health? What is their mood or sense of urgency?

DOI: 10.1201/9781003324287-8

Walking down steps will affect a person's posture.

All these factors influence the way that a character walks and the pose they adopt when they are walking. The following three poses offer some insights into the variants to be considered when animating a character. Time yourself with just **2 minutes** for each of them, to focus your understanding of the poses they are adopting.

Baby walk observations: We all know that when babies try to walk initially, they invariably fall flat on their faces. This is usually because they allow the center of gravity in their body to lean ahead of their feet, and their feet/coordination are not quick enough to stop them from falling forward. Walking aids like this help the child not to fall as much – unless they lean too much from side-to-side, in which case they'll probably fall sideward. Note still therefore that the body weight is still too far forward for their feet to hold the balance, but their hands on the walking aid prevent it from happening. This should all factor into the angles you choose to sketch your observational drawing, making a great exercise to remember for future possible animation reference.

Old man walking observations: The first thing to notice is that there are similarities between this and the baby pose. Again here, the body weight is far ahead of the feet on the ground and, due to age, the character will not be able to save him if unaided. However, the walking stick provides sufficient support to keep him up. Remove it and he too will fall forward onto the ground. Note also the curve on the torso and the lifting of the near shoulder, above the left shoulder, to accommodate his grip on the walking stick. All these things you have to train your eye to see, if you are to become an effective animator. These are the factors that you have to understand if you're animating an elderly person – are they frail, do they need assistance and if so, what kind of assistance do they need?

Uphill walk observations: Here, we have another forward lean on the character although this time it is nothing to do with age – it is about environment and weather in that environment. When we walk uphill or when we walk against a strong wind, we need to lean forward to get momentum. Conversely, when we walk downhill, or a strong wind is at our backs, we need to lean more backward in order for us not to be thrown flying forward. All these things are factors in this pose. So very much concern yourself with "angles" here. The angle of the path. The angle of the body. The angle of the legs that are reaching forward to the hips in a way more than a generic walk would require. Even the angle of the cart she is pulling, and the angles of her lower and upper right arm support the dynamic thrust forward feel that this pose has. Realize too that if we rotated this picture so that the path she is walking on were horizontal, her lean forward would be far too far forward to sustain without her falling on her face. It is the street angle, and the strength of wind that she is walking into that clearly sustains the pose she is making.

Gesture drawings sketches of all three Shutterstock poses.

In conclusion here, we only thought of three of the possible factors that can influence a way that a person walks – other than a basic *"generic walk"* that we could learn about now. All of these poses involved a character leaning forward more naturally than a generic walk would require. Imagine therefore if we were drawing a character that was walking downhill or had their back to a powerful wind or even if they were drunk and uncoordinated. There really are an infinite range of possibilities to consider here – which is why finding out the factors influencing the character you are going to animate walking beforehand is so vitally important. For example, if someone is eager to get where they are going, they will walk fast.

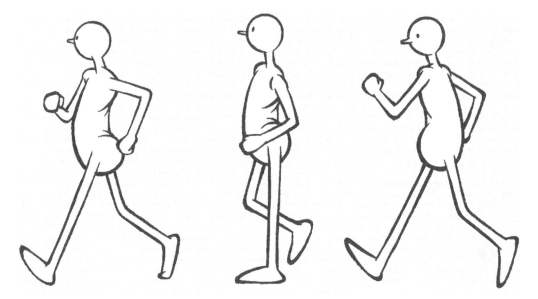

Fast walking pose.

Whereas if they are in no hurry to get where they want to get, the attitude of the pose will need to be adapted significantly.

A character that's in no hurry.

The faster the walk is, the shorter the strides and the faster the action is likely to be.

If they are happy with life, then they will tend to have a more bouncy, jaunty way of walking that is sprightlier.

Short strides can tell their own story.

Sprightly, striding walk.

Whereas if they are old, sad or depressed, they will more likely tend to appear bent and bowed, head down and walking with dragging feet.

Slower, more elderly character walk.

NOTE

If you feel you are not making much progress with your observational walks, or aren't consistent with how the good parts are going, do not stress. Just keep drawing. Always keep drawing! There is also a thing call "plateauing" that you need to know about. This is basically where for a few sessions you're really feeling into it; the drawings go well, when suddenly you think you can't draw at all. You have reached a plateau and can't seem to get beyond it. It may even feel to you that your drawing is getting worse. It is not. It's simply that you've raised your game a little but then it just stays where you are with what you are doing and you lose perspective on the progress you already have made. Just keep at it, keep pushing forward. It may take a while but then, suddenly, you get another breakthrough and seem to sail on again. But then, you hit another plateau, and all suddenly feels lost. It is not, it is just you adjusting to a new level of execution and you just need to hang in there, even if you feel you are not making progress any more, or are even slipping back. This is natural. So, again, just keep pushing forward. Keep drawing and you will eventually rise to another plateau. It's frustrating of course – or at least it feels that way – but in reality, you are moving ever forward with your work, no matter what you think. So the purpose of all these warm-up gesture drawing sessions is to train your "animator's eye", but it is also to give you a platform where your drawing skills can slowly evolve – whatever you think at any particular time. And remember that there is no such thing as competition in drawing. If you feel others are progressing faster than you, they are not. Each person is different and progresses in his or her own way and at their own time. Others may appear to be more talented than you or are moving forward faster than you. But they may be on a spurt from their last plateau and you are just hitting one. They may appear more talented than you, but you might be the person to make the next big animated success production that is known for its original style and approach. You can therefore only judge yourself against you, not others. And always keep drawing, despite everything! As the old saying says … When times get tough, the tough get going!

Age, as we have seen, plays a role too. Understanding of mood and purpose is important and observation is everything! So keep your mind enquiring and keep your mind open to the possibilities for your character in any scene that you are animating – a walk or otherwise.

But now it is time to learn how to animate a *"generic walk"*, the most important of all walks. That is because a generic walk is the basic, mechanically structured walk, from which so many other variations of walk – and many, many more – are derived from.

Instruction

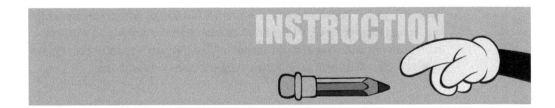

This particular lesson or two on the "**Generic Walk**" is closest to my heart. Being able to animate a convincing animated walk, let alone extensions from that into *"personality"* and *"eccentric"* walks are arguably the hardest things for an animator to pull off. It has long been acknowledged that someone who can convincingly animate a Generic Walk can pretty much tackle everything, as many of the principles involved in walking action apply to so many other animation tasks. For this reason, I have focused significantly on walks in my previous books and intend to do so here too. Over the years, I have found very easy and accessible ways for students to learn how to animate a walk, so hopefully the following will not be too painful for you. Here, I'm using traditional, pencil and paper techniques to create the perfect "generic walk", but if you're working digitally, I'm sure you can adjust these instructions to match the needs of your own particular 2D app.

DEFINITION: Before we go any further, it might help if we actually say what a "walk" is. A walk is defined as a biped form of movement where one leg is always on the ground at the same time. A "run", by definition, is a biped form of fast movement where both legs are off the ground at one point in the action. Knowing that helps us in the way we interpret and create both.

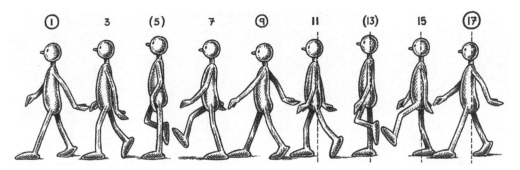

The standard "Generic walk".

Every one of us knows how to walk. We put one leg in front of the other and swing our arms. Right? Well yes, but until we actually go to think it through from an animation perspective, we take it for granted as we do what we do instinctively – no doubt after going through many bumps and scrapes to master it as young toddlers! Well, attempting animated walks could get you into similar mental bumps and scrapes if you are not guided through it sympathetically. And that's exactly what I plan to do in two-staged lessons here and now.

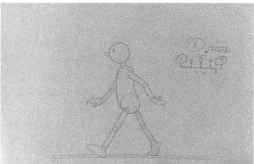

The two stages of working – "lower body" then "upper body".

But first we should ask, what exactly is a Generic Walk? Well, at this point in my classroom teaching, I would show a video of what a Generic Walk looks like. But I can't do that in a book. But I can show you if you go to the **dedicated webpage**. There you will find a pencil-drawn, "generic walk" action, shot on "2s" and repeated.

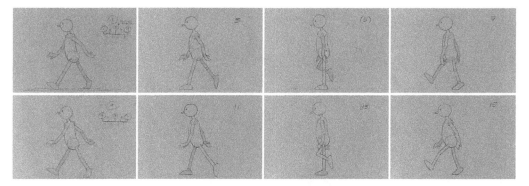

The major positions in the generic walk video.

If we analyze this in its most simplistic way, we can say that the legs alternate in going from back to front and back again, while the arms swing in opposition to the legs. What I mean by this is that when the *left leg is forward*, then the *right arm is forward* and when the *right leg is forward*, the *left arm is forward*.

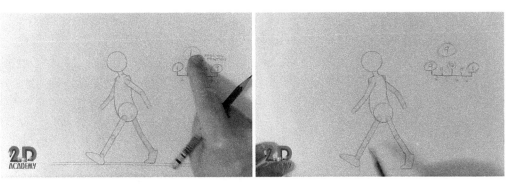

Although unfinished, these are the two definitive "key stride" positions.

Now this isn't the whole story of animating a good Generic Walk, but it is a start. Perhaps drawing out the start will help you process it better. So, why not draw your own character in a single stride position like this. You can use any character design you like of course, but I find that "simple is best", and therefore, something like this basic design will help you so much more in the early learning stages. Be aware of the fact that the character should not overstride or understride with the legs on this pose. To do so will make things so much more unconvincing. If you like, trace this image so that you're sure to get it right in the first instance. Later on, you can experiment as much as you like. Note too that the neck of the character bends forward toward the head and is not straight up from the body, and many people are drawing it. Make sure that the right leg is forward as is the left arm. The neck bending forward like this gives an ease of pose – whereas a straight upright neck angle gives a certain stiff look to the silhouette. An angled neck is also anatomically incorrect when considering human bipeds anyway. Just look at anyone around you from a profile view and you'll see it immediately. Note too that the hands are kept at a slight angle to that of the lower arm – but that's something we'll deal with specifically in the next lesson.

TIP

See that I have lightly shaded the far leg and the far arm on this drawing. This will help you later when you are inbetweening arms and legs and need to differentiate the front from the back when the lightbox is on particularly. It will also give you a better understanding of what is going one when you eventually capture a pencil test video to see if it's working OK. But don't shade too heavily or darkly however, as that will be difficult to see through in a backlit situation. Just shade it dark enough to note the difference between the limbs of the front and the limbs of the back.

To start, we're just going to concentrate on the legs and pelvis area of the body, as that is the most crucial part of the action to do correctly.

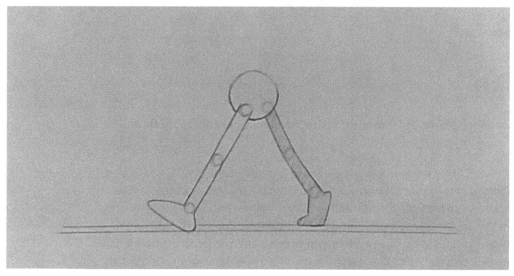

The first "key stride" position, number "1".

We'll add the upper body once the lower body is working well. But before this, let us build a "Field Guide" that will help the process we're about to do. It shows the extent of the "Field" that the camera or scanner should see, plus two ground line with the character, one for the near foot and one for the far foot.

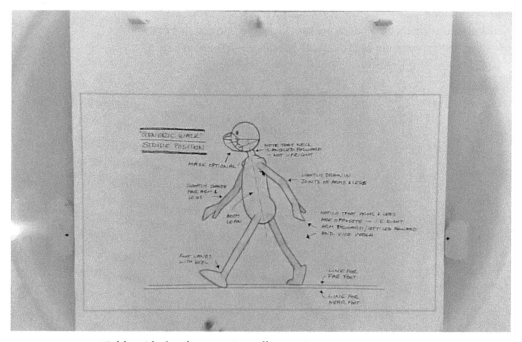

Field guide for the generic walk exercise.

Re the "**ground lines**": These represent the "paths of action" that the feet will take when sliding along in the walking action. One is above the other because, with perspective, things get smaller as they get further away from the view, meaning that the right leg is marginally smaller than the left leg. This would not be true if we're looking at the character from any other angle of course but is so from this particular profile viewpoint. Remember, therefore, that whenever the right foot touches the ground, it will always be on that upper line somewhere, and when the left leg touches the ground, it will always be on the lower line. You need to be always aware of this.

OK, with your "field guide" on the pegs, place a new sheet of paper over the top and trace the legs and a circle where the pelvic area is located. I tend to lightly trace the ground lines on all my walk drawings too, as it helps know where they are if you're working without the Field Guide behind to show where they are. Number this drawing – a "Key" drawing – as number "**1**" to the right-hand side of the paper. That done, your first key stride drawing should look like this.

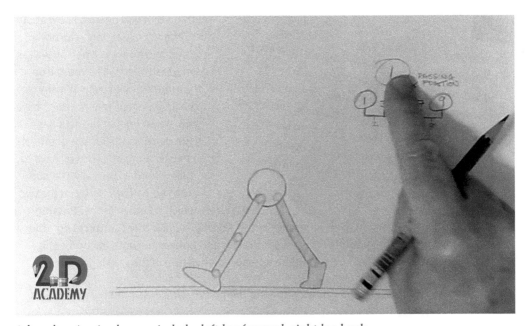

A key drawing is always circled – left leg forward, right leg back.

With that completed, now take a fresh sheet of paper and copy this first drawing – but this time **reverse** the legs so that the *right leg is left forward*. Don't forget however that the foot of the left leg needs to be on the bottom ground line, and the right foot on the upper ground line! Number this key stride drawing number "**9**". Now you should have two keys. Key drawing "**9**" looks like this.

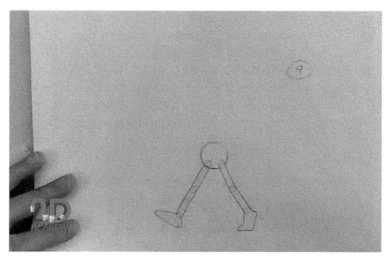

The opposite stride position, key stride number "9".

Numbering your key stride drawings "1" and "9" will produce a very fast walking action. However, I have chosen to do that as the division of inbetweens linking the two keys as easy to appreciate at this stage. Later, you will learn that walks will more often than not need more inbetweens to make them look natural and have certain qualities beyond the "generic". But for now, just be aware of that and we'll go with this faster version for the first exercise.

Now we come to another really important thing that you need to know about the Generic Walk action – the body rises up and down as a person walks! Many, many bad walks you see on the Internet – and even in many cheap animated shows – don't have this, meaning that the action is not convincing. But as a potential master animator, you will have to allow for this. Basically, the body rises up halfway between the two stride positions, which is known as the "**Passing Position**". This is because in the *"Passing Position"* the "**Contact Leg**" (the leg on the ground at the time) is straight and upright beneath the body. This forces the torso up, giving the up-and-down nature of the walking action.

The "Passing position", showing the body rising, with the left foot on the ground.

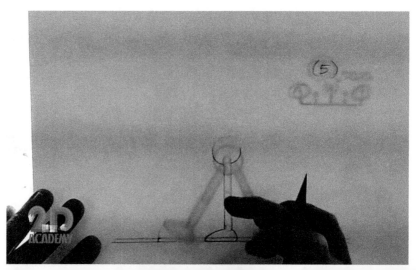

Now, to find out the midway passing position needs some concentration. So I'll go through it carefully here. In the classroom, it is so much easier to demonstrate over a lightbox but I'll do my best to explain it well here.

Remember that what we're doing is creating a looping walk, meaning that the character is actually walking on the spot and not covering ground across the screen. This is because to do otherwise will require you to do an excessive number of drawings that will not be necessary for what we have to learn here. Walking on the spot is a totally acceptable production approach too, as long as any background behind the character moves the same direction and distance that the feet slide throughout the action.

When you create a walk cycle on the spot, the background needs to pan past the character to give the illusion of progress – as indicated by this Warner Brothers style walk sequence I created for a talk I gave about Chuck Jones at Seattle's EMP.

The first thing to realize in creating a *"passing position"* here is that the front foot (i.e. the character's left leg) on key "1" remains on the ground and becomes the back foot on key number "9". The right foot does the same from key "9" back to "1" when we complete the repeating cycle. So, knowing that the *"passing position"* is halfway from 1 to 9 on the first stride, we have to work out exactly where the middle position is to put the contact (right) foot there. It doesn't help that on key 1 the heel is down on the foot but the toe is up, whereas on key 9, the toe is down and the foot up.

Drawing the "passing (vaguely a number 4) position".

Clearly accuracy of measurement is important here, so what I do is draw a dotted line down from the toe on key 1, showing where it would be if the foot were flat.

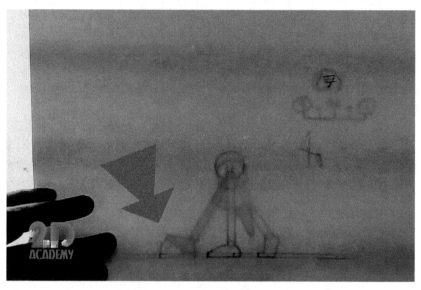

The toe of the "passing position" is located precisely halfway between the back toe and the toe on the front foot, assessed by angling it down flat.

Then I would place both key drawings onto the pegs, then add a fresh sheet of paper over the top of them – the passing position – numbering it number "5". (In parentheses please!) I would then trace the bottom ground line on "5" and measure a halfway point on it, starting from the imagined toe position on key 1, through to the toe position on key 9.

Note that "passing" and "breakdown" positions are always written in a parenthesis.

That shows me where the toe on passing position 5 will be, and knowing that the foot on 5 will be flat on the ground, I actually remove 5 from the pegs, super-impose it over one of the feet one drawing 1 or 9 (it doesn't matter which, but the consistency of foot size and shape does) and trace the foot – ensuring that the toe and the bottom of the foot being traced are lined up with the toe position mark and the lower ground line. Therefore, when I place the passing position 5 back onto the pegs, the midway foot position will be accurate.

Note that when drawing the free foot on inbetweens like this passing position, I tend to superimpose and trace it over the corresponding foot on a key drawing. This ensures that it maintains consistent size and shape from drawing to drawing.

You'll note by the way that in my original stride pose, I have drawn in small circles that represent the joints of the limbs – namely the shoulder, elbow, wrist, hip, knee and ankle joints.

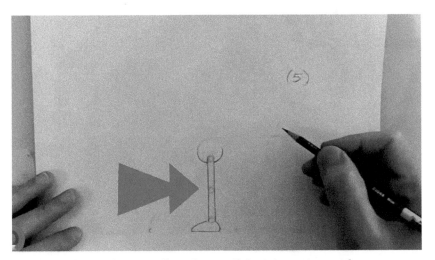

See that I always draw small circles at all the joint points with my animation, so it makes it more accurate while measuring out inbetween limb sizes when superimposing.

This we will use to good effect at the next stage. I told you just now that on the passing position the contact leg on the ground is **straight** beneath the body. This means that if you draw vertical lines from the width of the ankle joint of the contact foot, it will give you the angle of the leg the character is above in the passing position.

The leg beneath the body on a Generic Walk is always straight – ensuring that the body rises.

To know how long that leg is, superimpose the straight leg over (a) the lower part of the leg on 1 or 9, lining up the ankle circles and marking off the knee circle on our straight leg.

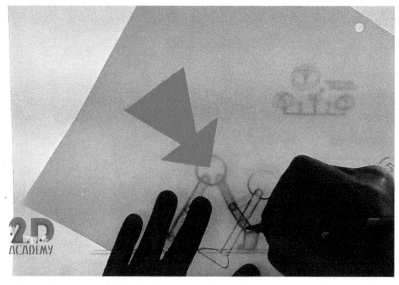

Superimposing and tracing the lower leg from the one on the key drawing, to keep the proportions accurate and consistent.

… then do the same for the upper leg, from the knee to the hip …

The upper leg was also superimposed and traced over the key drawing upper leg too.

Now with the hip position on the leg known, you can superimpose it over the pelvis of 1 or 9, remembering that the hip on key 1 is forward and the hip on key 9 is back. So when you trace the pelvis on the hip position of 5, it needs to be in the middle and low on the pelvic area. This should give you a passing position of the contact leg and pelvis like this.

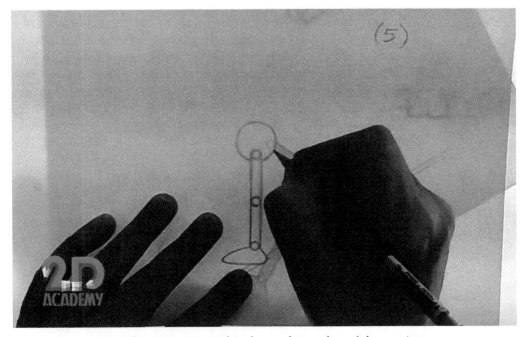

The pelvic area was also superimposed and traced over that of the previous key position, prior to the line being drawn darker and stronger.

Next, we need to consider the "free" leg – which is the back leg on key 1 and the front leg on key 9. This obviously needs to be positioned on the ground, halfway from front to the back – hence the pose being known as the *"passing position"*. I additionally tend to call this the *"number 4" position – not because of page numbering, but simply because its ideal bent-leg shape in the right position with the contact leg looks like a "number 4", numerically speaking.*

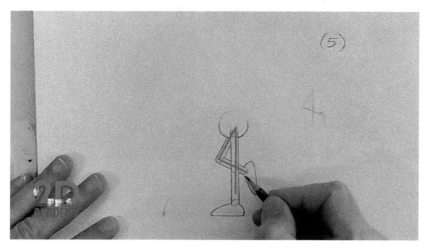

The free leg on the "passing position" is always like a number 4.

Note that I tend to point the toe back a little as it is coming through. Otherwise, this is generally a bent leg in the air. (We will talk about variations to this when we get to personality or eccentric walks however.)

Anyway, congratulations – you have now just finished your first passing position! Before you go forward, however, double-check that the pelvis is rising higher than the pelvis on 1 and 9. The straight leg beneath it should naturally push it up, but if you measured the lower and up leg sections wrongly, it might not do so. If it doesn't, fix it now as everything we do from now on will relate to that up-and-down action of the hips and pelvis.

Remember that the pelvis is always higher on the "passing position" than on the key stride positions.

So now you should have completed drawings 1, 5 and 9. Put them on the pegs in order and flip them from front to back. You should see the near leg coming from front to back and the body rising up and down, as indicated above. Now we need to create the transition inbetweens linking them, which apart from one really important aspect on both are pretty much literal inbetweens. So, let us deal with the exceptions in each case, as they will mark the difference between a great generic walk and a so-so one. First, the transitional inbetween from 1 to 5. Putting 1 and 5 on the pegs you will see that the back leg is going to be moving to the passing position bent leg.

The temptation here would be to just inbetween it, with the rest of the lower body. But, in actual fact, we want to give it the appearance of it **pushing off the ground** longer than a straight inbetween would suggest. So, we need to juggle a little to get this ideal position. My suggestion is to inbetween everything else first, except for the back leg. Now, I won't confuse you in various ways to get an accurate inbetween on the body here, as it is pretty straight forward, especially if you use superimposition on the pelvic area to work out the hip positions specifically. However, to help you know what you're aiming for, here's an illustration of what inbetween number "**3**" (i.e. halfway between 1 and 5) should look like, minus the back leg.

Inbetween 3 is all midway between 1 and 5 – except for the back leg.

Now to deal with the back leg. Remember I mentioned earlier that as long as the background movement behind a repeat walk cycle action matches the positions of the feet? Well now's the time to put that into practice. When we created the passing position, we found the halfway distance the foot moved from front to back. Indeed, the contact leg on 3 should be halfway between 1 and 5 in terms of foot placement, as it is sliding to the back of the ground line without lifting up. This tells us how far the background needs to move to match that foot, drawing-to-drawing.

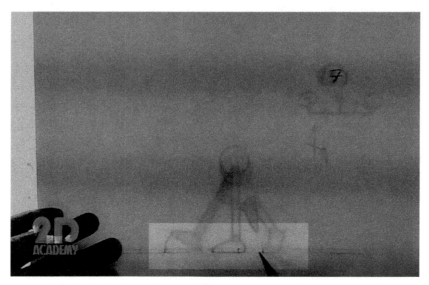

Remember that anything that touches the ground with a character has to slide the same distance every time – as does the background behind it.

Indeed, anything touching the ground on any walk cycle needs to move at the same speed as the feet, to match the speed of the moving background behind. So if the character were holding a walking stick next to one leg, then that walking stick would need to move the same distance as the foot while it was on the ground. And so it is with the back leg, in view of the fact that we need to keep it on the ground longer to give it the effect of pushing off. To give it the effect, the distance that the toe on 3 moves from the back toe on 1 needs to be the same distance the contact foot on 1 moves to the contact foot on 3. As long as it does that the push off will look authentic and nothing will slide strangely against a moving background behind it. (Which has moved the same distance as the walk foot slide each time.)

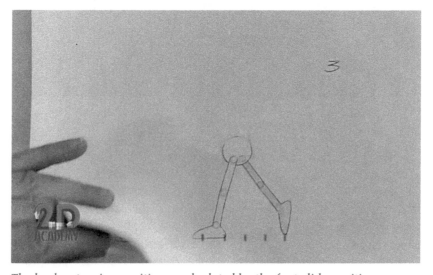

The back extension position – calculated by the foot slide positions.

Now we have transition inbetween 3 out of the way we need to focus on transition inbetween number "**7**". Again, the free leg is doing something that the rest of the lower body is not doing on this one. So start by inbetweening everything except the front leg on 7, halfway between drawings 5 and 9. This should give you something like this.

The inbetween of drawing "7", except for the front leg.

Now, the difference that the front leg on 7 makes with the rest being inbetweened is governed by the fact that when we walk, we actually swing our leg through – **above and beyond** – the final point where our lead heel comes down on the next stride. The correct action looks like this.

The completed inbetween number "7" – showing the heel is somewhat higher and further forward than the heel "hit" position on key number "9".

The temptation of most inexperienced animators is to inbetween the free leg on the passing position; straight down to where it is on the next key stride position. But this is wrong and would give a clipped, somewhat stuttering look to the walk action. So make sure that you draw the front, free leg on drawing 7 like that above. When you get to see all the drawings, flipped in order on your pegs, you'll get to appreciate the naturalness and the difference it makes. Indeed, although we haven't completed both strides to the walk cycle yet, I often capture the first stride on video, repeating it several times, to see if the flow of it is as it should be – a fast but naturally flowing action with the free leg somewhat following a path of an oval from back to front.

That achieved, it is now time to work on the second stride of the walk cycle, and because it is a walk *"cycle"*, we will be doing our inbetween positions from key 9 back to 1. Here are the charts that show what we are doing.

Basically, we repeat the process of creating the first stride inbetweens for the second stride. EXCEPT this time the contact leg is the front leg, on the lower ground line and the far (free) leg is coming from back to front in the transitions and number 4 position we did last time for the near leg. I won't repeat all the explanation again but here is what the passing position (number "13") should look like.

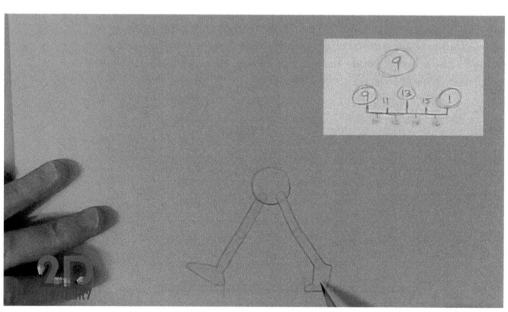

The linking chart from key "9" back to key "1" should be approached in exactly the same way as with the first stride – except that now it is the opposite arms and legs.

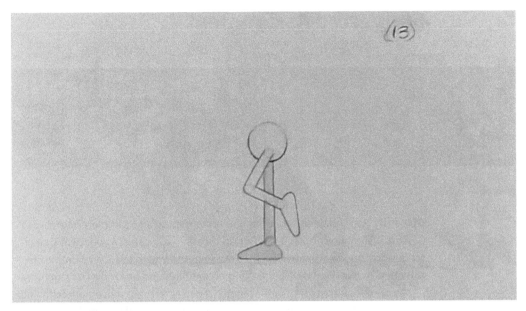

Passing position number "13".

The inbetweens linking 9 and 1, through breakdown "13", look like this.

The completed 2nd stride – "9" thru "1".

Once you have all your walk cycle completed in this way, capture your drawings and repeat the rendered action several times, on 2s, on video. This will show you a very fast – but hopefully very convincing – *"Generic Walk"*. Remember though, this is just the beginning of where you can ultimately take this knowledge of walk animation. It may be "generic" at this stage, but it is the foundation of walking action that can be developed in so many other ways, as we shall see.

Suggested Assignment

Obviously, you should attempt the above instruction and complete your own Generic Walk action yourself. As indicated earlier, you can use your own character design if you like, but I STRONGLY recommend you to use a very simple character design – with no details, clothing or anything else beyond a basic geometric structure – at least for now. Once you've perfected your movement with your simple character and proven it works by testing, you can always go back and add as much more detail to it later. If you do all that detail from the beginning and it doesn't work, you'll find that you have a heck of a lot more drawing to do again!

Also, when you're content that your *Generic Walk* is working in this way, I would also suggest you add in the *"even"* numbered inbetweens too, and film those with the *"odd"* numbers on 2s too. This will slow the same movement at half the speed and will also give it a much smoother appearance.

Masterclass 08/ Generic Walk Action 02

Warm-Up Drawing

Sad Emotions

In animation, it is always really important to focus on the *storytelling* power of individual poses when animating. Emotions, for example, can be expressed powerfully; simply by the way a pose is created. In this and subsequent drawing sessions, we are going to explore some of the important factors involved when trying to express emotion through poses. In this particular example, we are going to look at some examples of poses that represent "**sadness**". What follows therefore are two observational poses that show people in a state of sadness. You should give yourself **3 minutes** to sketch each.

DOI: 10.1201/9781003324287-9

Pose 1 comments: The main effect of any sadness pose is the fact that there seems to be a huge weight on the person – everything is being dragged *downwards*. Look at the angles going down here, especially the eyeline of the character as he stares at the ground. He is leaning forward too, with an overall slumped demeanor. Dropping the free hand down, the other hand supporting the head, which is also bent down. All these things suggest a resignation that what is being faced is too hard to hand. We have all been there, so we can empathize a great deal.

Pose 2 comments: Again, a very similar story. Everything has a downward feel to it. Body slouched. Note the arms and hands supporting the tilted head, with the arms being supported in turn by the knees. Gravity – in terms of the implied situation and the physical reality of the emotional weight being carried – is at work here too. The toes pointing inward, is also a body language clue of uncertainty or helplessness. The gaze is also down, indeed everything about this pose – like the last one – cries out "sadness" of one kind or another. Generally, there is just too much heaviness of emotion to bear here.

Hopefully, these exercises are not making you too sad yourself? If you can stand back in any situation and view things with the eyes of an artist/animator, you can experience compassion but with the detachment of capturing truth through observation. We can only repeat again that the overall expression of a sad pose is an overbearing downness of the attitude – emotionally and physically, one reflecting the other. Again, we've all been there at one time or another. Sometimes it's for a good reason but at other times we don't know why we feel the way we do, we just do. At such times, the head drops with the spirit and everything is all too much trouble.

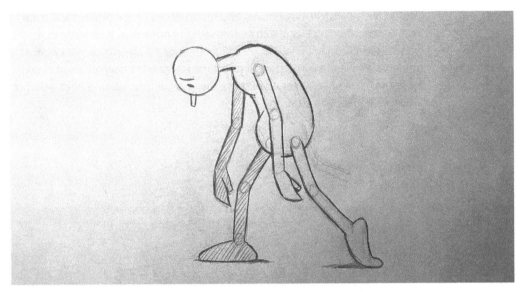

What I call my "sad zombie" pose.

Your sad poses need to express this, because if the pose suggests it the animation will totally reflect it too. And draw on your own experiences of sadness also.
If you feel it, you will be able to express it through your work better. I call that
the *"method school"* of animating. Imagine yourself into the character, whether it
is a cartoon character or otherwise, and imagine yourself to be inside that character, feeling what they're feeling. It is great to draw on personal experience as
much as possible, but never neglect researching the subject too – like drawing
these kinds of reference poses when you need to see what "sad" looks like.

Your own emotional moods should influence your reference drawings.
The mirror is your friend, not matter what it reflects.

"Sad" often means we move slower and more deliberately, which means in animation terms adding lots of extra inbetweens to make it so. Hopefully, that won't make it too sad for you to contemplate – but if it does, take that emotion, bottle it somewhere and express it next time you need to animate a sad character. In the meanwhile, cheer up because the next gesture drawings we'll attempt will involve "happy" poses!

Instruction

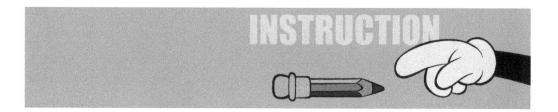

In this lesson, we're going to complete our Generic Walk. So, the first thing I want you to do is take your original Field Guide with the full body pose drawn on it, then place over it your key stride position, number "1". That done, I want you to trace just the torso, neck, outline of the head (but not eyes or nose), and arms (but not the hands yet).

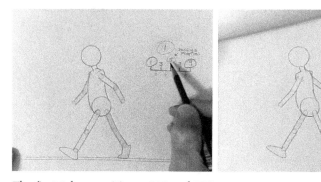

The first 2 key positions, "1" and "9".

Note especially the angle of the torso as you draw it. It is leaning slightly forward, which is something we all do when we walk. Walking is a process of movement where we're constantly out of balance, but once we learn how to handle it by using counter balancing arms and fast moving legs, we no longer fall flat on our faces – as we did as babies before we learnt how to do otherwise. Consequently, if your character's torso does not lean – in other words, you draw it straight up, or even leaning backwards – the audience won't so easily buy into this being a realistic walking action.

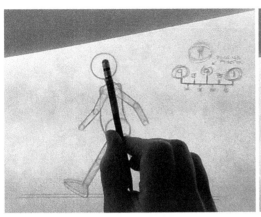

The correct (left) and incorrect (right) body leaning angles for a character walking from right to left.

Forward leaning generates momentum, and the further you lean forward the **faster** the action will be or should be if you're creating it in animation. So, bear all this in mind when you're tracing your torso, neck, head outline and arms. (And don't forget that the neck itself naturally leans forward in almost everyone. It is not upright from the top of the torso!) This will now give us an almost completed first key stride position, "1".

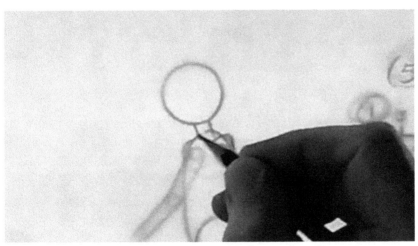

This is the natural angle for the neck – never straight upright!

That done, place key drawing "1" on the pegs and place key drawing "9" over the top of it. Also trace on the torso, neck, head outline on this one. However, REMEMBER, the arms will be **reversed** in their positions, like the legs are from 1 to 9.

NOTE

Whenever I trace one drawing through to the other, I always draw lightly when the backlighting is on. When the entire tracing is done, I turn the backlight off and thicken/darken the lightened lines so that they look stronger looking. Sometimes the backlighting can overpower your look of the line, so seeing it in natural light is the best way to strengthen it – or "clean it up" as we might say.

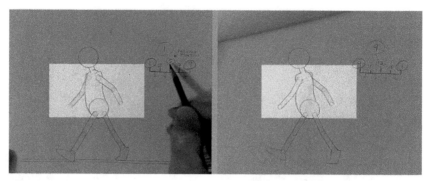

Note the different arm positions, key to key.

So here are the charts we were working on the previous lower body lesson.

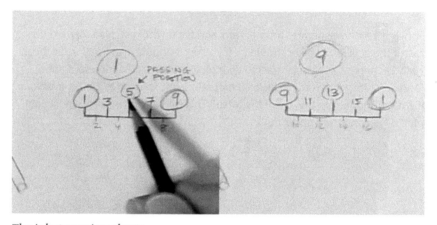

The inbetweening charts.

So, in view of the fact, we know to inbetween the arms from the keys 1 and 9, we must create the arm passing positions, numbers "5" and "13". The quickest way to do this is to superimpose the two key torsos, and then superimpose each passing position over them, to find the most accurate halfway position for the arms. The final arms on "5" will look like this.

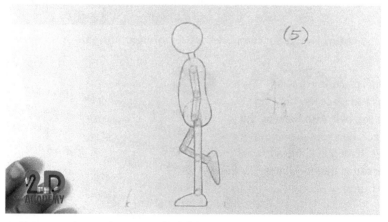

Halfway position of arms on breakdown "5".

To achieve this, I used this following process. First put all three drawings on the pegs, with the passing position drawing on time. Turn on the light box. Seeing the other positions beneath, draw the imagined top and bottom of the torso, as guidelines, like this.

Marking out the guidelines at the top and bottom of the torso.

Now the halfway position of the top and bottom on the torso is established, we can take drawings 1 and 5 off the pegs, leaving just drawing 9 on them. With the lightbox on, superimpose the torso of drawing number 9 over the torso of drawing number 1. Next, superimpose the top and bottom torso guide marks over the top and bottom of the torsos on drawings 1 and 9.

Superimposing drawings "1", "5" and "9".

Now lightly trace the torso onto drawing number 5, as well as sketching in the halfway point of the arms from one key to another. Effectively, the arms will be more or less straight down the torso – the back arm concealed by it – although I would put a slight bend in the near arm, as it is weak to drawing a limb with joints perfectly straight. That gives us a lightly drawn inbetween.

The lightly drawn inbetween.

Place all the drawing back onto the pegs, with drawing 5 on the top. Switch off the lightbox and proceed to strengthen up the arms and torso inbetween lines, so that it looks like the passing position drawing, indicated above.

Darkening-up the light drawing.

Now you have completed passing position 5, you need to complete passing position 13. This can be done so easily - simply by superimposing the torso of drawing 13 over the torso of drawing 5, then tracing it.

Note that passing position "13" looks pretty much the same, except that the legs are reversed.

When you get more into personality or eccentric walks, these arm positions may not be the same. However, on a Generic Walk it is fine to make them the same, as the movement we are creating is pretty robotic and mechanical all round. Therefore both passing position inbetweens will essentially have the same locations for the arms.

The hands added to the arms in both key positions.

Now we have keys and inbetweens for the torso and arms, we can use the same superimposition approach to inbetweening as we used to create the passing positions. However, now we can trace one set of arms from the first stride, as every remaining arm position will be different from the others – unlike the passing position. So, in order to create the first inbetween – drawing number "3", between 1 and 5 – you should do the following. Place drawings 1, 3 and 5 onto the pegs – with drawing 3 on the top. Put the lightbox on and lightly mark the inbetween positions for the top and the bottom of the torso, as we did with passing position 5.

Marking the reference points, top and bottom of the torso and neck.

Take the top two drawings off the peg and superimpose the torso of 5 over the torso of 1, then superimpose the top and bottom torso trace marks over the torso of the other two drawings.

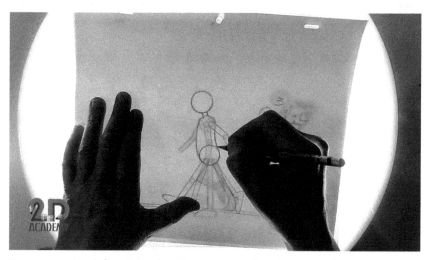

Superimposing inbetween drawing "3" over drawings 1 and 9.

Lightly trace the torso and the inbetween position of the arms. Place all three drawings back on the pegs and check that your inbetween 3 is accurate. If it is … turn the lightbox off and, with the drawing 3 off the pegs, clean up and darken the lines you lightly drew when inbetweening it. You should have the first three drawings of the torso and arms done and they should look like this.

Drawings "1", "3" and "5".

If all is good, create inbetween "7", between drawings 5 and 9, in the same way just described. If all goes well, your finished five first-stride drawings should look like this.

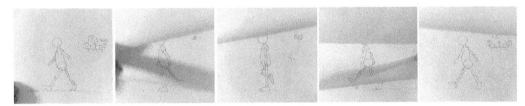

The five drawings of the first stride.

If they are and everything is correct, now you can apply the same process to the second stride, giving you the 5-second-stride drawings.

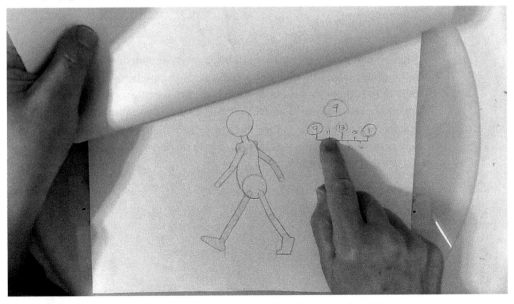

With the first stride completed, it is now time to do the second stride.

You can test this by capturing and repeating the same looping action several times on 2s if you like. This will completely reassure you that your work is fine so far. If it is not, then fix and/or adjust your drawings as best you can.

Having got the hardest part of the upper body action completed successfully, let us now focus on the "easier" things. First, we need to add the neck and head outline to our drawings. You should have the neck and head outlines drawing in on keys 1 and 9, which in actual fact are identical. So, now superimpose the torso on 9 over the torso of 1, lining up the torso of 5 with that too. Now it is simply a case of tracing the neck and head (not the eyes and nose yet however) onto drawing 5 from the other two drawings.

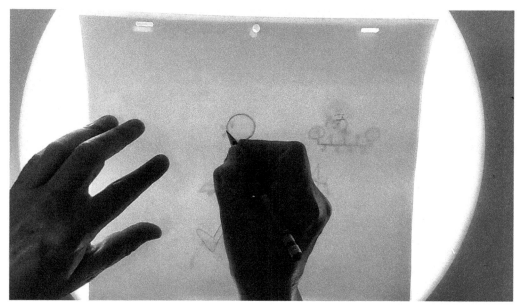

Superimposing to trace the head and neck.

There should be no movement or difficult inbetweening here as everything is in the same place. With the neck and head of 5 complete, next do the same process for the other inbetweens of the first stride – namely superimpose "3" over superimposed drawings 1 and 5, then trace. Next, superimpose "7" over superimposed drawings 5 and 9, then trace that too. With the first stride done in this way, complete the second stride drawings in the identical way, giving you a sequence that looks like this.

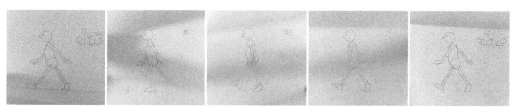

Flipping drawings to check the head movement.

Now we have everything but the hands and the features of the face to do, we must finally finish those to complete our walk. For this, we are going to encounter a thing called "overlapping action". Overlapping action is a technique that brings flexibility to what we're doing. Essentially, overlapping action (also termed as "follow-through animation" by some animators) means that if there is a primary action going on, then anything subordinate to that will tend to drag behind the main action and catch up later. Therefore, we apply that process to the hands; it means that as an arm moves forward, the hand will tend to drag behind it somewhat. Then, as the arm swings backward, the hand will appear to drag behind it in the opposite direction.

Notice that the hands drag behind the arms as they move forward and back.

So in our Generic Walk cycle, the first thing to do is trace key one from our Field Guide master pose. You can see that the hands are bent in a certain way in relation to the lower arm. With the hands on key 1 traced, place key 9 over the top and trace the same angle of hands onto the opposite arms – meaning that in key 1 the far hand is bent backwards, whereas on 9, it is bent forward. On key drawing 9, however, the hand on the far arm is bent forward, whereas the hand on the near arm is bent back. This is because they have all reached their dragging back positions at the end of each respective arm swing.

Hands dragging on key positions "1" and "9".

When we create the hands on the passing positions and inbetweens, however, we have to think it through and make sure we put the right angles to the arms throughout. So, in terms of passing position "5" – between 1 and 9 – the hand on the near arm will look like this. **(Note:** *We are only working with the near arm right now, as that's the one that's clearly visible in front of the torso.)* If we think this process (of the hand dragging behind the arm) through carefully, we will arrive at these positions for the first stride.

Front hand on first key stride – make sure you don't make the angles greater than this.

NOTE

That there is no inbetweening of the hands from drawing 1 and 3. The hand just immediately flips over to the opposite direction after 1, giving it a much more dynamic effect. If we inbetweened it to an effectively straight position on the hand in relation to the lower arm, it would give the action a soft or weak effect for the changeover of direction. By flipping it over immediately, from one drawing to the next, we get a "snap", which feels more natural or dynamic.

Follow the same process for the hand on drawings 9 thru 1 – the second stride action – making sure the near hand is drawing in the opposite direction to the first stride positions. This is because, remember, the hand is following and dragging behind the lower arm direction, which has changed.

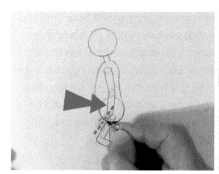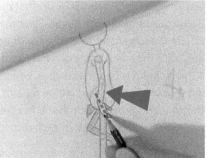

Angle of hands in relation to direction the arm is going.

OK. If you now want to work out the hand action on the far hand – effectively being in the opposite direction of the near hand – you will get this sequence for the first stride.

Back hands also drag behind the arms as they move forward and back.

Repeat the process for the second stride, using the same principles of the angled hand.

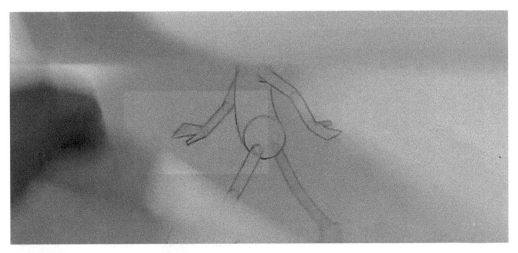

The back hand on a key stride pose.

Congratulations! You have almost completed your first Generic Walk action! All there is to do now is add the head features and you're done. However, you might want to capture your current drawings and loop it a few times on 2s, just to confirm all is good. If you have followed all these instructions, then it should be. The only real danger to look out for is an unnatural, overaggressive flapping of the hands on the lower arms. If you're getting that, then you've simply bent the hand angles too far in relation to the lower arms. Reduce that angle and all should be well. If there is hardly any overlapping action on the hands apparent, then increase the angle of the hands.

With regard to the features of the eyes and nose on the head, we deliberately left those till last, just having the circular outline of the head drawn for now. However, in order to get a little flexibility in this area, we need to apply some "overlapping action" to the head too. So, just as the hands dragged behind the lower arms in each direction above, so the head needs to give a similar appearance if we want to imply a natural flexibility there. So, bearing in mind that the neck and body move UP on the passing positions and DOWN on the key stride positions, we need to draw the head accordingly. So, on both keys trace the nose and eyes UP on the head outline, that is, just as it is on our Field Guide drawing. However, on the passing positions, draw the features looking DOWN on the head outline, giving the drawings a look like this.

Remember, the head is up on the key stride positions and down on the passing positions.

Now simply inbetween the features on the inbetweens – halfway between the up and down positions on the keys and passing positions for both strides.

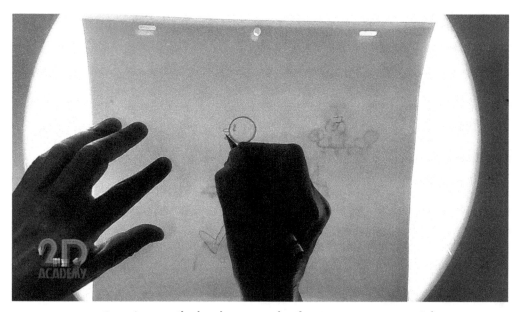

Superimpose the heads over each other to create accurate inbetweens.

Finally, capture and test your drawings again by rendering the cycle a few times on 2s. If the head is bouncing up and down too extremely, then reduce the down angle on the passing positions and re-inbetween the remaining drawings. If the up and down movement on the head is not enough, then increase the angle on the passing position drawings and, again, re-inbetween the other drawings. If all is good at this stage, you definitely need to be CONGRATULATED for creating your first successful Generic Walk action!

This has all been a challenge if it's the first time you've done it, I'm sure. But hopefully you've persevered to create something you can be proud of. We will advance your knowledge of walking further in the next lesson, but for now just focus on pulling off this exercise first, as well as maybe taking on the additional suggested assignment below. Remember, the more animation you do, the better you'll get at doing it. So, invest your time now in fully accomplishing this stage of Generic Walks before moving on to a more advanced approach.

Suggested Assignment

SUGGESTED ASSIGNMENT

First make sure you have followed and accomplished what is required for the basic Generic Walk. If you have, consider designing your own biped character and doing a Generic Walk for that character too. Don't add too much detail and don't overdress your character or elaborate on it too much. What you don't want is flowing robes or hair at this stage, as that will take you into more demanding territory – in terms of overlapping action or follow-through action.

These things we will go into much more detail later, so there's no need for you to stress and struggle with it now. You'd be much better advised to simply do a Generic Walk for a ball with legs and arms, or even a traditional "Flower Sack" character, which will give some new challenges but still keep you in the comfort zone of you still just working through a Generic Walk. For fun, I once animated a pencil walking, as you've seen on the cover of this book.

"Junior Arnie" is another simple character I use for working with students.

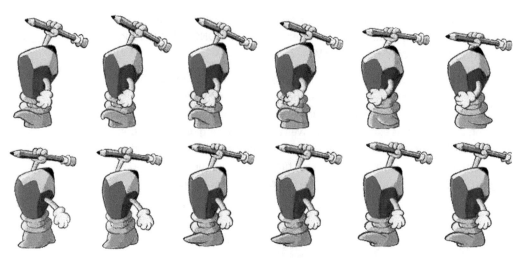

Once you know and understand the principles of the "Generic Walk", you can apply the action to all kind of objects and characters.

Masterclass 09/ Generic Walk Action 03

Warm-Up Drawing

Happy Emotions

In the last lesson, we focus on poses related to sadness. So, just to contrast and balance out in this lesson, we are going to focus on "**happy**" poses. In contrast to the rather emotionally down poses we drew last time, I want us now to study happy poses. Look at the following two examples of happy poses and note how the body language is so much different.

DOI: 10.1201/9781003324287-10

Pose 1 comments: There are lots of angles to consider here. Note the angles of the shoulders to the hips. Notice how the arms are angled, the legs and the head. It's very important when you are doing observation gesture drawing for animation that you recognize these things. We're not saying that you have to re-cord these realistically or photographically. Instead, we're looking at geometric shapes, dynamic angles and the power – or storytelling potential – of a pose like this. As ever, make them 3-minute poses.

Pose 2 comments: Well, I guess you can be happy at any age, and at this age, it would be great to be able to do what he's doing! That said, look at the angles here. Even though both arms are thrown upward, they're not exactly the same. So make sure your gesture drawing reflects this. In other words, they are not mirroring exactly, from left to right. The legs are very much closer to mirroring, but not quite. Remember with observational gesture drawing, it is important to draw what you see – not what you think you see! Even look at the angle the walking cane makes to the body and limbs and make sure you represent that accurately. Exaggerate if needs be.

I hope there's a contrasting feeling within you, comparing this exercise and the last? Today, there is a more exuberant expression in the visual than last week. We're getting into a positive and uplifting vibe here. Happiness is important to us all, even though that is not guaranteed in life. Personally, I find a great deal of happiness in just drawing, as well as doing hand-drawn animation. Indeed, it is my greatest therapy. I find that when I'm depressed, or angry or whatever, picking up a pencil and drawing gives me a sense of peace, and it gives me back energy that less positive emotions do not do.

Drawing - in my happy place!

So, my recommendation is that if you're in any way a creative person, yet subject to down times, always pick up a pencil and draw. It really is the best therapy there is for an artist. In the next lesson, we're going to deal with another emotion that we need to observe, so I hope you're happy enough now to approach that with confidence.

Instruction

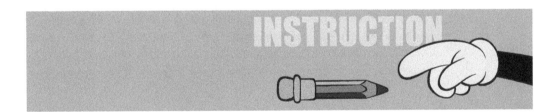

With a standard Generic Walk under our belt, we should briefly discuss how we might go beyond the generic and add a little more *personality* or *storytelling* to the action. In the next lesson, we're going to dig more deeply into "Personality Walks". But for now, I want to just open your eyes a little on how just small modifications to the generic walk approach can reap huge rewards in communicating a little more emotion or personality. The easy and most direct way of doing this is in altering the key positions a little or modifying the passing positions. Here, I will give you a few examples of this, which hopefully will make you more aware of the potential for innovation there is here. There are many, many ways of modifying a Generic Walk to get a significantly different feel to the action, but we will deal with just these ones for now – if nothing else, to motivate your thinking processes.

The Slow, Sad or Sloppy Walk

As indicated, even Generic Walks can be changed into simple personality walks, just by re-drawing the *"passing position"* or the *"key stride"* positions. For example, if you wish to have a walk of a sad, lazy or slack jaw person – or even just dragging their feet in a reluctant way to avoid something they don't relish – create a passing position that is not in the usual "number 4" position. Instead, keep the passing foot dragging on the ground, like this.

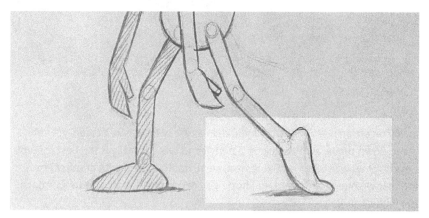

The main change for a sad or sloppy walk is the dragging foot on the passing position.

When this is done, you simply inbetween from key to passing position with the same foot dragging action on the ground, as with the passing position – then flipping the foot over, close to the ground, at the last minute. You are also advised to increase the number of inbetweens throughout the strides too. That will slow the action down. By its very nature, this really is a slow walking action, so needs many more inbetweens to take it from the fast, Generic Walk version.

Military Walk

In terms of changing the passing position to reflect more of a personality walk, here's the kind of simple pose adjustment that will turn the basic Generic Walk into more of a military/marching walk. Instead of the "number 4" position being as it was before, this time lift the passing knee up high and in front of the body, with the toe pointing down more. Again, more "slow-in/slow-out" inbetweens to and from the "passing position" need to be added to give the action increased definition.

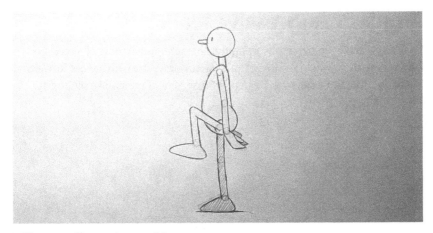

Military walk passing position.

Fussy or Nervy Walk

Shortening the stride length on the keys and restricting the swing of the arms also can achieve a "fussy", "twitchy" or "prissy" walk. Sometimes, even carrying the arms up in front of the body on the key and passing positions can accentuate the action too.

Fussy or nervous walk passing position.

It is likely that this action will not need many extra inbetweens to make it work, as fussy or nervous people tend to move in a fast, staccato and/or twitchy way. Experimenting with the number of inbetweens used should be considered, to get a perfect timing for the action you're going for.

Angry or Aggressive Walk

This can be achieved by simply giving the character much more of a forward lean to their torso, while swinging the arms strongly, and with a more forward inclination. The arms can even be bent with an almost punch-like silhouette.

Angry walk passing position.

Again, this should be one of the faster walks. Note above that a scowling expression on the face – achieved by drawing a "V" shape with the eyebrows – can bring additional ferocity to the motion.

Heavy and Bouncy Walks

Finally, you can get the effect of a character appearing "heavy" or "light" when they're walking by simply readjusting the inbetweening charts on a regular Generic Walk action. For example, if you put an emphasis on the passing position by adding more "slow-in/slow-out" inbetweens to and from the passing position, the character will tend to remain in the "up" position for a longer time. By contrast, it gives a bouncier effect to the key stride positions if you leave those inbetweens as they are.

Heavy walk passing position.

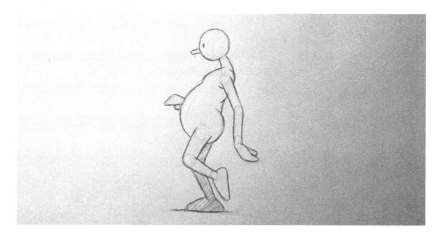

On the other hand, if you put the extra "slow-in/slow-out" inbetweens to and from the key stride positions, the tendency this time will be to give an appearance of the character dwelling longer on the ground and less with the "up" passing position. This should give it a greater sense of weight or heaviness.

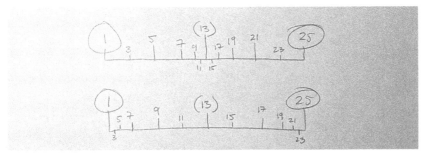

Two charts showing the slowing-in to the passing position option and the slowing-in to the key positions option.

Experimenting with "slow-ins" and "slow-outs" in Generic Walks – and with all other forms of animated, key-to-key action – can often bring surprising results if you experiment with your own ideas too.

Suggested Assignment

In an ideal world you should do ALL of the above, to experience how they work. However, if you are pressed for time, just **pick just one of the above** and perfect it's technique. Doing at least one of them will teach you how adapting the generic can bring surprising and often very satisfactory results from a little extra effort.

Masterclass 10/ Personality Walk Action 01 – "Double Bounce"

Warm-Up Drawing

Fear Emotions

Previously, we have observed emotional images relating to sad and happy emotions. In this exercise, we will look at **"fear"**. Fear is something we all experience in life, but how can we explore it from an animation pose perspective? The following two poses will give us some experience of doing so – although there are many other image examples for us to observe of course. As usual, limit yourself to 3 minutes for each pose.

DOI: 10.1201/9781003324287-11

Pose 1 comments: This is somewhat of a standard, fear-driven pose. Probably the first fear pose we would imagine in our minds would be this kind of recoiling back, the hands up for protection, attitude. And the look on the face says everything. Again, look at the angles involved, the fact that the character is leaning to one side but with his weight on his back foot rather than the front. The curve on the torso is important too. Everything he is doing is trying to keep himself as far away from the thing he fears as possible – while his feet seem frozen to the spot, not able to run away.

Pose 2 comments: So, here we have a very different image of fear. In this case, it's almost like burying your head in the sand, almost in denial of something you don't want to see and hoping it will go away. This kind of curled up fetal position pose is one to consider if you're animating a character who is frightened. It is different and it says so much more about the personality of the person than does the more generic previous pose. It suggests that they are a person that easily gives up, prefers to hide away, rather than confront things. Definitely look at the angles on the legs and how they overlap and complete a rough bodily circle with the arms, joined by the one elbow we can see. The curve of the spine contrasts to the straights of the upper and lower arms or legs. It is a complete withdrawal of functioning here.

They say there's no greater fear than fear itself. Fear is something that dominates artists and animators especially – quite apart from the regular fears of everyday life. This is the fear of expressing ourselves, fear of trying anything new and fear of rejection. Yet in reality, it's only by trying something new that we learn. Because, even if we fail, we learn something significant from that failure, and that in itself gives us a greater understanding for moving on with our work. They say a master in anything has become a master because they have "failed" more times than anyone else!

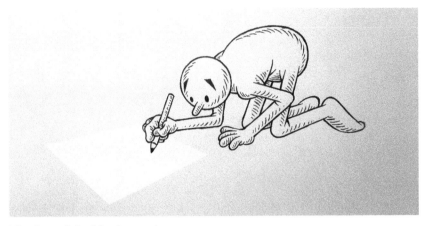

The fear of the blank page!

However, because of fear artists, writers and animators are painfully aware of the blank paper in front of them – more through fear of being criticized because we dare try something different. People like continuity and familiarity, so it is much easier for us as insecure artists to give them what they want rather than break the mold and try something new. So as artist/animators, we need to conquer the fear element within ourselves to overcome the uncertainties of covering new ground, learning new things – especially in the world animation, where the very meaning of the word is thought of as "cartoon films", yet in reality, it can be so, so much more than that. In the creative sense, fear leads to atrophy – which is why we see so much of the "same old, same old" in the animation world today.

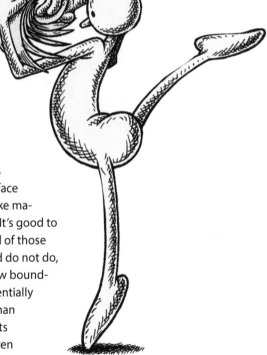

I am hoping that with the knowledge that this book can bring, a few of my readers will dare face the fear of doing something different and make major animation breakthroughs with their work. It's good to be challenged, exhilarated, even exposed – all of those things. But let not fear dictate what we do and do not do, for then you will never reach those unique new boundaries, or areas of expression, that you can potentially reach. Certainly, there are no limits to the human imagination – and therefore, there are no limits in expressing our ideas through animation. Even if you fail for the first and second times, you are still learning things that no one else has learned, which can propel you to even greater breakthrough success later!

It is to the contemporary 2D animators in the indie trenches that we must look to for original finesse and fresh imagination.

Instruction

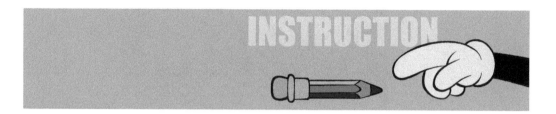

By now you should have completed, at the very least, a successful Generic Walk, plus at least one variation of it. Next, we must move the bar higher, by introducing you to a **"Personality Walk"**. Personality walks go beyond the purely generic, communicating to the audience either an aspect of a character's personality, their mood or their general attitude in the world they find themselves in. So for the next three lessons, we're going to complete a different one in each. These will give you a thorough understanding of how variations from the Generic Walk action can be very valuable to have in your toolkit.

There is no limit to where a crazy walk can go, as long as it is adapted from universal generic principles.

The Personality Walk we will be learning this time is the **"Double Bounce Walk"**. The Double Bounce is probably the most long-lived and recognizable of all the personality walks and was the one that the very early Mickey Mouse character used to adopt. As a result, it is a fun, jolly and happy walk. But instead of it being like a Generic Walk, with the character moving up and down every stride, with a double bounce walk the character goes up and down TWICE on every stride. This chart might show you what's going on during one stride of a double bounce walk.

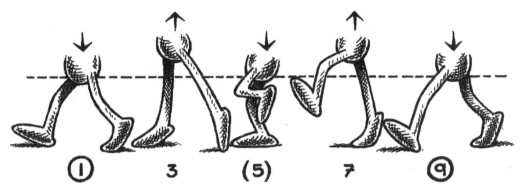

The key positions of a double bounce walk.

Now, the big benefit of starting personality walks with a double bounce walk, is that it is still very much based on many of the key factors of a Generic Walk. Therefore, it should be familiar territory for you to learn easily at this stage. The first thing to do is take the Field Guide

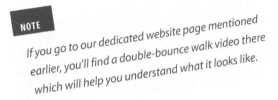

NOTE

If you go to our dedicated website page mentioned earlier, you'll find a double-bounce walk video there which will help you understand what it looks like.

from your Generic Walk exercise and trace it, on the pegs, onto a fresh sheet of paper. However, for now, only draw the lower part of the body first. As when you did the Generic Walk, you can add the upper body action later, when the lower half is working fine. This first lower body tracing will be the key stride Frame "1" of your Double Bounce walk. It actually makes it very convenient that both key stride positions can be used from the Generic Walk. So just trace the lower body of both keys "1" and "9" from your previous Generic Walk drawings, like this.

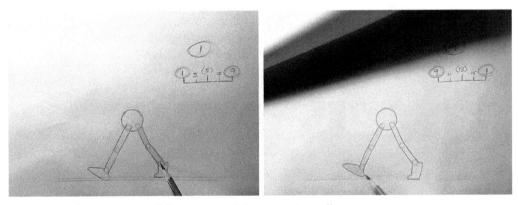

Keys "1" and "9" are traced from those of the Generic Walk.

From now on however, you will be creating all new drawings, yet based on the same inbetween charts as before. Remember that with a Generic Walk, the body rises in the passing position, due to the fact that the contact leg on the ground is straight beneath the torso, pushing it up. Well, as a Double Bounce walk requires two up and down bounces in a stride, rather than one, we actually have the body **down** on the *"passing position"*, bending the contact leg beneath the torso, like this.

With a double bounce walk, the body is bend down on the passing position.

However, on the two inbetweens, "3" and "5', we have to force the body **up** on those drawings, keeping the legs as straight as we can, even having the character up on the toes of their feet if possible.

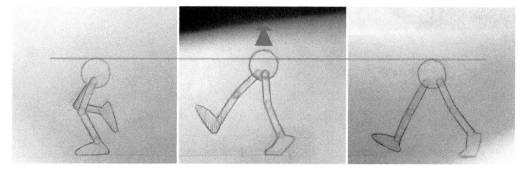

The body rises on the inbetween "7" is featured here.

Placing all five drawings on the pegs in order, flip them backwards and forwards and you'll see that the body goes up and down twice on the stride. Then, if all goes well, complete the second stride drawings in the same way.

Flip all five drawings to see the full "up and down" movement.

Now, in theory this will work fine, but it will be very fast. Nevertheless, if it is working OK, add the upper body the same way that you did for your Generic Walk. It needs no extra explanation other than that, so I'll leave to your own devices on this one.

Once the legs are working correctly, it is time to add the upper body, arms and head – plus mask, as it was drawing in isolation at a time of the worst of Covid!

Eventually you will have your Double Bounce walk completed, both the top and bottom halves of the character. These will be on "odd" numbers though, and very fast in its action. So, I would suggest to you that with this Double Bounce walk, you inbetween all the drawings – adding in all the even numbered drawings, in addition to the odd numbers that we have already.

All the key 'up and down" positions of the double bounce walk over two strides.

Then capture your drawings and view a repeat cycle of them several times over on 2s. This action will be much slower than with the Generic Walk, but much smoother and clearer to see. Extend the "up and down" movement for a stronger effect, if necessary.

Suggested Assignment

I suggest that if you are to fully appreciate how to do a Double Bounce walk, you should definitely do this preceding exercise, as advised. However, you might want to work on the arms in a different way. For that you need to do some research and work out the arm action for yourself. Originally, the Mickey Mouse walk didn't have his arms swinging backward and forward, as with a Generic Walk. With his original walk he did a kind of swimming action on oval arcs that looked much more effective. It looked a little like this.

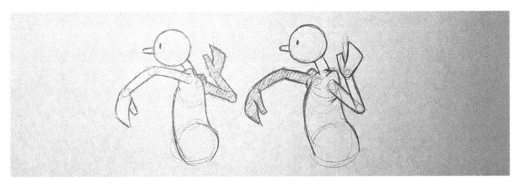

I once remember seeing Mickey Mouse doing a double bounce using a kind of swimming arm action. I don't know what the film was but here's a sketch of what I remember. The point is, that once you have the "up and down" movement you can try anything!

So, appreciate the original Mickey Mouse double bounce action and add those arm movements to your character. Doing so will really help you understand better, not only the action we have discussed but the process of observing, interpreting and then replicating an action that you've never done before. This is the essence of being and thinking like an animator, and the sooner you begin to train your eye and mind for this process the better. Good luck!

11

Masterclass 11/ Personality Walk Action 02 – "Sneak"

Warm-Up Drawing

Extreme Emotions

It seems we're putting a lot of emphasis on emotions right now, but they really do dominate our world, our lives and the way we interpret things in storytelling. So, in terms of animation, it is good to focus on the kind of visual imagery that exemplifies what a character is feeling or going through. Therefore, looking at "extreme" emotions here will not be out of place. The previous focus on three core emotions – sad, happy and fear – will cover a great deal of the human (or animated character) experience. However, now we should look at the kind of extreme emotions we understand and identify with too. Hopefully, the previous three exercises will have given you a small hint of the infinite options that such emotions can be portrayed through animation poses. This time, we'll concentrate on bringing extreme expression to our poses of emotion. We'll do that by adding a great deal of "forced perspective" to the mix.

DOI: 10.1201/9781003324287-12

Forced perspective drawn image.

Perspective is something we'll actually devote one or more of these observational drawing warm-ups to later. But for now, let's look at two wide-angled photographic images that will allow us to get more extreme with our gesture drawing. Feel free to fully push the perspective on both of them to even greater extremes if you like. Again, these are designed to be 3-minute poses and no more.

Pose 1 comments: It is probably quite difficult for you to overemphasize this pose because it is so extreme already. Nevertheless, do feel free to try, as all the best animation poses are an exaggeration, or caricature, of the real world. That is no different here. For example, that hand that is furthest away from us – make it even smaller than it is, which makes the huge near hand even larger. Similarly, you could make the size difference between the back and front foot. The bottom line is to exaggerate all you see here, making it bigger or smaller – such as the hips coming toward us being bigger and the head going away from us getting smaller. We will be dealing with something like this in animation "Masterclass 12", so this is all good practice to get your mind thinking along the lines of forced perspective.

Pose 2 comments: Now this one really is a forced perspective shot, so there is really very little you can do to emphasize it – although I would still try if you can. Make it more extreme by making those near feet even bigger in relation to the head and body, which you can make even smaller by proportion. Look carefully at those near feet too. One is nearer than the other, and both are seen from slightly different angles, so you can push those angles and proportions in relation to each

other too. Even the shoulders are at a slight angle, with his left one being marginally higher, so that is something to exaggerate more too. All this should give you ideas for when you're posing your future animation poses, and you need to make the action much more dramatic or surreal.

Now of course, you're most likely never going to come across a pose that is exactly like these. However, as I just said, these kinds of exercises will at least begin to open your mind as to what can be possible and what can be pushed through exaggeration. And this is the real point of doing these observational gesture drawings. They are not intended to give you poses you can use, but instead, we are giving you a vision of concepts that you can use, in order to create more dynamic poses when you're doing animation.

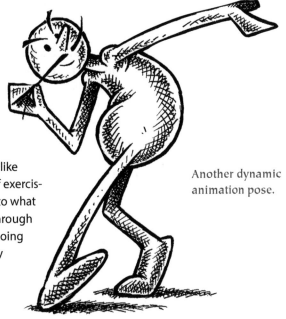

Another dynamic animation pose.

This will not be quite so possible when you're using rigged characters in 2D or 3D software, but it is certainly possible when you're drawing your keys from scratch, traditionally or digitally. In all honesty, I would say that I've used a forced perspective in animation for only a couple of times in my career, but when I have used it, it is really effective. We will certainly be looking at something like a forced perspective for the lesson 12 animation assignment, where a character is walking toward the camera, dramatically.

Using a forced perspective on a front walk can be quite dramatic.

You'll see that it has quite a dramatic effect on the movement of a character or object. Forced perspective should not be used all the time, just reserved for scenes of action that need great emphasis. For example, imagine a shot where a character is throwing a punch at the camera. For this, you would pull the hand back in anticipation of the punch forward that is coming – making it proportionately quite small. However, when the fist comes right up to the camera, you could exaggerate that too, so that the fist fills the entire screen, or comes even closer, for even one frame only – just showing part of the middle finger of the punching hand before the fist is withdrawn immediately backward to a more normal position beside the body. This would have a huge impact on the action if it were handled in this way.

Instruction

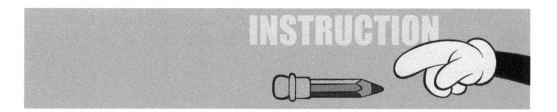

Now you should have some understanding of the mechanics of a Generic Walk, we're now going to push the envelope a little and talk about *"Personality Walks"* more specifically. Personality walks go beyond such basic mechanics and have an approach that is not just an adaptation of a Generic Walk. In this particular case, we're going to learn how to do a "**Slow Sneak**", which is another of those great animation traditions that is not much talked about anymore. However, it is another of those valuable skills that any master animator should have in their toolkit.

The key positions of a Slow Sneak action.

Over the years, animators have found their own way of animating sneaks, often in accordance with the scenes they are including the sneak walk action in. Additionally, the action of the arms during the sneaks can be many and various. However, here, let us just focus on a more basic and generic approach to the sneak action, with the arms simply held in front of the body for convenience. Once you have successfully animated a generic sneak, however, you might want to research how animators have moved beyond the generic in the past – or in fact, you might experiment on your own to see what you come up with.

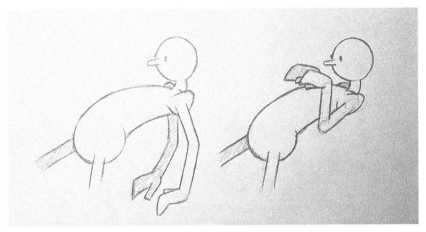

There are many options you can try for the arms in a sneak action. These are just two.

The first thing to realize, when we attempt to animate a generic "Sneak", is that unlike the Generic Walk – a stride of which is made up of two key stride positions – with the sneak there are **4 stride positions**! Explained in a nutshell, these are (i) the full stride position with the torso leaning back,

(ii) the same key stride position with the torso leaning forward, and

1st key stride position – leaning back.

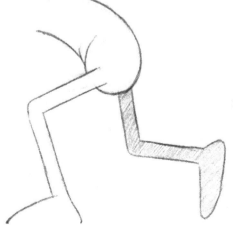

1st key stride position – leaning forward.

(iii) the opposite stride position with the torso leaning back again.

(iv) then the same stride position with the torso forward.

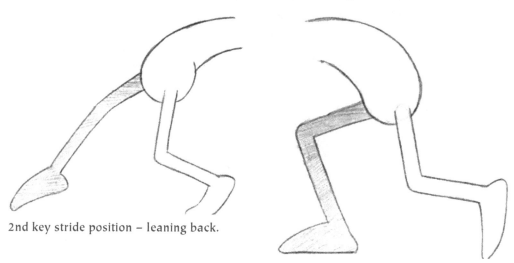

2nd key stride position – leaning back.

2nd key stride position – leaning forward.

The arms meanwhile are generally carried together in front of the torso, with a little overlapping action that is dictated by the body movement. The head works best if it is kept in a focused, looking forward position for now.

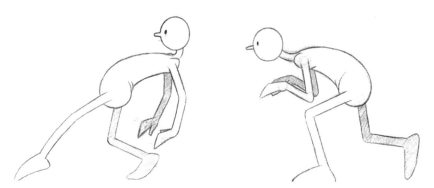

The head and arms forward and back on a sneak stride.

But of course you might consider having the character look back, over their shoulder, later if the feeling you want is that they're being pursued and stalked from behind. That aside, what is happening in the *"slow sneak"* action is that the first stride is made with the torso leaning back and away from the front foot, then the torso swings forward over the front foot, then it swings back again as the legs move to the opposite stride position. The same thing happens on the second stride that completes the walk cycle.

The final four key positions of the two sneak strides.

Beyond that, there are other core differences that we must factor in. For a start, when we are creating the *"passing positions"* between all of the key poses, we need to add more arched flexibility to the torso. In other words, for the passing position linking the first key to the second, the body will arch back in a "**convex**" way – whereas the passing position from the second key to the third it will flip to an arched "**concave**" shape. These will look like this.

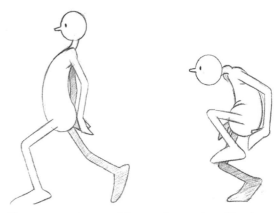

The final change we must make when comparing this action to the Generic Walk action is the fact that a sneak moves much slower. Therefore, we need to add a lot **more inbetweens** to pull it off and give it the more cautious, deliberate speed that a sneak needs. Remember, the use of a sneak is applied when a character is either trying to sneak away from a character or situation or else it is trying to sneak up on a character or situation. So, the need here is for the character to be unobserved either way and with a feel that everything they are doing is deliberate. Also, we must consider the placement and timing of the inbetweens. This is be-

The two passing positions – forward and back – on the 1st stride.

cause we need to put more emphasis on the end positions of the body moving forward and moving back. Consequently, we need a great deal of slowing-in and slowing-out around those positions. A suitable set of animation charts for the 1st stride look like this.

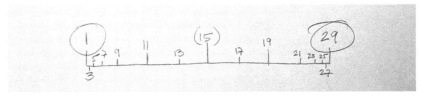

The 1st stride inbetween chart, showing the heavy slow-in and slow-out at the end of the action.

Note that now we have numbered our three key positions "1", "15" and "29", and the inbetweens are bunching up either side of them to create that slowing-in and slowing-out motion. Here are the charts for the second stride action, which links back to the first to create the cycle of movement.

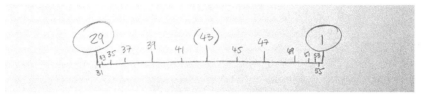

The 2nd stride inbetween chart, linking the cycled action back to key position "1" again.

For the inbetweens required between all of our keys, I recommend that you refer to the passing action on a Generic Walk for the legs. But with the body, keep the arch on the torso consistent when it is concave going forward or convex going back. Like the switchover on the hands of the Generic Walk however, do not in-between the torso changing it arched direction. Instead, simply flip it over on the first key in the opposite direction again, like you did with the Generic Walk hands.

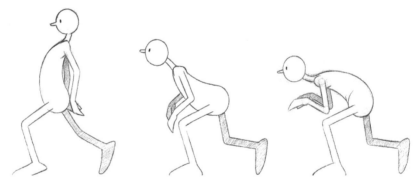

The action to the end of the stride positions – indicating the flop over from the convex to concave torso shapes as the stride ends.

Hopefully, this will give you a successful sneaking action on your first try.

Suggested Assignment

Again, I strongly recommend that you work through all of the previous suggestions and, first and foremost, create that first sneak for yourself. Once you have achieved that, I suggest you maybe play with the number of inbetweens you use between your key positions and/or play with the arm movement to see what variations you can get there. There is a huge amount of scope you have with a generic sneak action. The more you play with it, the more it will reward you.

 NOTE

Before we leave the subject of "sneaks", we might just mention the **"fast sneak"**. As you will have seen, the regular sneak is quite a slow action, but the fast sneak is, as it sounds, fast. It's used when a character is trying to escape quietly – or trying to sneak up on something quickly – and uses the minimum of frames to do so. A fast sneak cycle can in fact be done with a minimum of **6 frames**. These are as follows:

All of the poses in a fast sneak sequence.

Basically, these are broken down into two "key" down positions, "1" and "7". Two key up positions, "5" and "11". The inbetweens, "3" and "9", are not strictly inbetweens, as they are what we call "thirds" – meaning they are not in the middle but one third from the upper or lower key positions in an action. This the case or the fast sneak, they are kind of thirds that are slowing-in to the top position, charted like this.

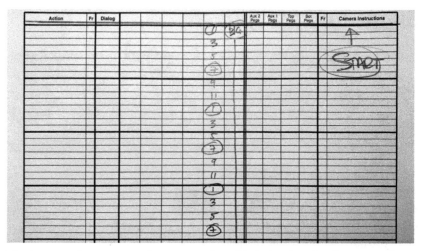

The fast sneak exposure sheet. Note that this is having the drawings shot on "two's". However, for a superfast, fast sneak, you could shoot them on "one's" also.

The secret is to not have the up and down keys too far apart. But shot on two's like this it can give a very credible fast sneaking action, if you need that.

12

Masterclass 12/ Personality Walk Action 03 – "Front Walk"

Warm-Up Drawing

GESTURE DRAWING

Transitions

For our last exercise in Section I, we're going to do something a little different. It should test your animator's eye and mind a little more! I'm calling it "**Transitions**". We're still doing observational drawing, but we're also going to add some imaginative drawing too. Below is an exercise that contains two outer action poses, with a blank space between them. You should give yourself 6 minutes to draw the outer poses as normal, but then you need to draw in the missing pose that links them in the middle. It's entirely like imagining a *"breakdown drawing"* between two key drawings when animating. But work fast, as this time you should only give yourself 2 minutes for each drawing – 1 minute less than normal! That alone should increase your speed and heighten your visual and spatial capabilities. Do all three sketches on the same sheet of paper.

DOI: 10.1201/9781003324287-13

(2)

3

Pose comments: As you can see, the two outer poses are well defined. The one to the left should be seen as starting position, Key "1", and the one to the right the end position, Key "3". The "breakdown drawing", in the blank area in the middle, will be Sketch "2" and should be halfway between the pose of 1 and 2. Consider well angles, volumes and proportions on each.

Fill in the blank. Draw what you think the "breakdown position" of these two key poses are?

Transitions are fundamentally important when doing animation. Key poses are always the most important thing you must do, but the transition pose (*"passing position"* in only walks, but the *"breakdown position"* everywhere else) is crucial to get right too.

It can vary significantly, depending on what you're trying to achieve in an action. Indeed, there are times when moving from one key to another that you have to be quite imaginative how you are going to make that transition. A transition drawing is not always logical inbetween. So, you need to need your observation of what is happening, then you have to feel how that transition can best happen.

When you are transitioning from one hand position to another when the swinging arm changes direction in a Generic Walk – or the torso arch changes in the Sneak action on the extreme stride poses – are often not literal inbetweens. So, you need to sense what would be right in every case. Often this decision can only be made with experience, when you have tried and tested all kinds of alternative options in the past. But at least try to make an educated guess at first, if you're new. The best thing to do is try two or more options for transitions from key to key, then test them all and see what's best. It's a longwinded way of approaching it, but in doing it, you will learn so much. In the meantime, this particular drawing exercise is just a taster of what you can expect when you get into more dynamic action later and the transitions from key to key need to be worked out carefully. Observing real-life actions and transitions will help you a great deal of course, which is why we are doing so many observational drawing exercises throughout this book.

FYI: Here are that actual transitions positions for the poses above. Realize though that with animation you have to exaggerate what the real world offers, not faithfully copy it.

This is the actual "breakdown position". How close was your drawing?

Instruction

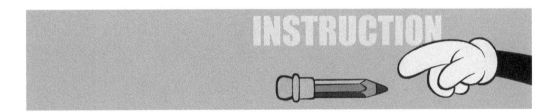

For the last traditionally animated lesson in Section I of the book, we're going to return to the Generic Walk. However, as we did that exercise totally from a profile point of view, I now want us to approach it from the front, where a whole new set of factors come into play. The "**Front Walk**" exercise should be valuable to 3D, Claymation and Puppet animators too, as with these disciplines we are looking at the more three dimensions aspects of a walk. We are not changing the timing, inbetweens or key positions, however, just enhancing them from this new point of view – as well as dealing with the issue of "balance" in a walk. From the front, the positions of two front stride positions should look something like this.

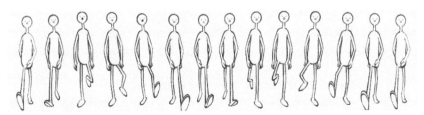

Two strides of a front walk, showing the balance shift from left to right.

Notice, however, how the perspective is exploited by exaggerating the elements of the character that are far and near. The near foot therefore is exponentially larger than the norm, as is the far foot exponentially smaller. The arms and hands go through a similar process of distortion too, making the both poses look far more dynamic. The most important thing to recognize here though, is the way the body balances over the contact feet, meaning there's a small side-to-side action going on.

"**Balance**" is something that I took many years to fully appreciate in my career. I would animate quite oblivious of the notion for most of the time for TV commercials and got away with it on the whole. However, when I was once commissioned to animate a dancing dragon – as animators are prone to do from time to time – I struggled to make the action convincing. I did my research and gesture drawings from real-world dancers, and although I analyzed my keys well and drew them accurately, I could never understand why the sequence just didn't seem convincing.

Bad balance for the dancing dragon – because the "center of gravity" of the dragon's body is left of the "point of contact" on the ground, the foot.

My client was OK with it, and it did go through all the appropriate dance positions. But for me, something was just not jelling, and I was far from satisfied with it. So I went back to my research material and studied again over and over. I seemed to have got all the angles and proportions right, so I was quite confused that it was not flowing convincingly as I was imagining it to do in my mind. Then, just as I was about to give it up as a bad job, I suddenly noticed that most of my key poses had bad balance. No one had taught me about balance in the past, so this was a sudden epiphany for me! Here's what I learned.

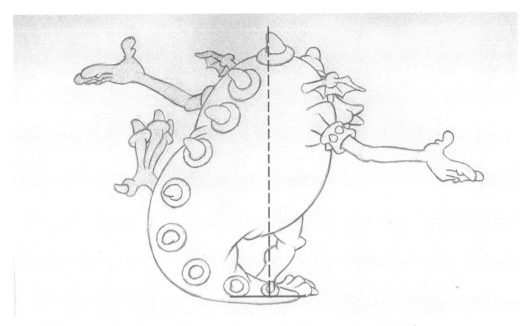

Good balance on the dancing dragon – because the "center of gravity" of the body is above the "point of contact" with the ground, the foot.

If a character is not in balance at any point of its movement, the action will not be as strong as it should be – unless the character deliberately needs to be out of balance – like a drunk or someone losing consciousness.

A drunk character, clearly out of balance.

Technically, with biped action, balance means that the center of gravity of the body has to be over one, or both, points of contact with the ground – in other words, the feet. If the character's body is balanced over two feet on the ground, then all well and good. However, if the character needs to lift one of their feet off the ground, it really doesn't look convincing unless you first shift their center of gravity over the contact foot before lifting the free on.

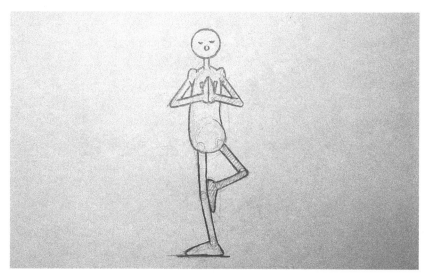

Balance awareness.

This was what was not happening with my dancing dragon. I was lifting a foot to make the next step or jump, but I wasn't shifting the weight over the contact foot to enable it to do that. As a result, I redrew all my keys, adjusting the balance accordingly, and then just inbetweened it using the same timing and placements as before. It worked perfectly! So, looking at our front run keys, see how the body weight is shifted over to the contact foot wherever possible BEFORE the free foot lifts up on the passing positions. Practically speaking, this can be done on the key stride positions, the center of gravity being more of over the front foot before the back foot lifts to come forward. The body shift is especially visible from the front view.

The main positions of a front run, showing the shift of body weight from side to side as the character changes contact feet.

Remember too, when you do your inbetweens, the minute the front foot hits the ground the body weight has to begin to shift towards it, so it enables the back foot to lift while appearing in balance.

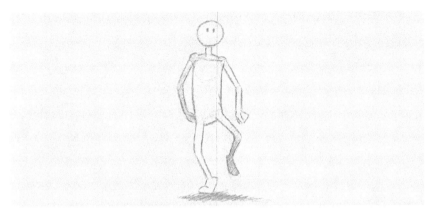

When a character is shifting from foot to foot – as in a running action for example – the body weight shift over towards the contact foot also.

The shift from side to side doesn't have to be too much or two wide. In essence, the momentum generated by a fast walk will mean that your shift doesn't need to be too dramatic. The same thing is true with a light, skinny character that has little weight to deal with.

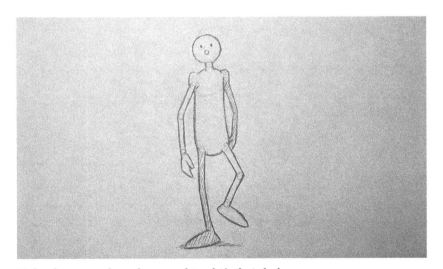

Light characters have less need to shift their balance.

But with a really heavy character – like my dancing dragon or Sumo wrestler – it definitely does need to be there.

Heavy characters however have more need to shift their balance.

"Balance" is fundamental to all animation, not just walks. If you watch people who are dancing around, ice skating, doing gymnastics or generally going through all forms of jumping, you will see that there are distinct shifts of weight, due to the need of balance in all things. Always bear this in mind when animating.

Suggested Assignment

It goes without saying that you should definitely do this exercise to learn the lessons of balance well. If you are really courageous and have the time, have a go at the **"Circular walk"** exercise on the ends of pencils that you can see on our dedicated web page. Because the character is walking around a circular path, they will naturally lean in to establish their balance – for the same reason that a motorcyclist leans in when going around a corner.

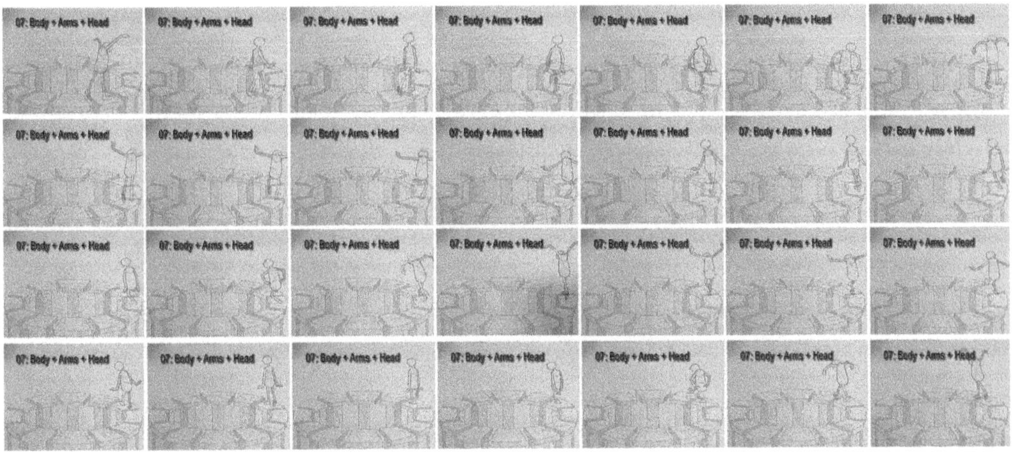

Note how the figure on the right of the frame leans into the curve of the walk, assuring a natural balance to the action.

I actually assigned my students this exercise when I was teaching on a degree course a few years ago. The students really muttered under their breath at the time, due to the severity of the challenge. But now, years later and with those same students successfully pursuing careers in the industry, they grudgingly thank me for pushing them that extra yard. It's a scary exercise to take on but I promise you'll learn so much from doing it!

OK, so now, let's go digital!

In this section, we learned really important principles of movement using *traditional, hand-drawn* techniques. In Section II, we will learn more core principles of movement, but this time in a digital 2D environment, primarily using Moho software.

FURTHER CORE PRINCIPLES OF MOVEMENT – RIGGED DIGITAL TECHNIQUES

Disclaimer: I am always wary of writing about animation software, as technology moves so fast that things can change in the blink of an eye. I am also not as much an expert at the inner (and outer) workings of Moho as I am a traditional hand-drawn animator. Therefore, I have to state that what follows is writing in good faith, and is as current as it can be at the time of writing in 2021. However, should time impose changes in any of the following Moho instructions, I encourage readers to reach out to the Moho website where they will find excellent current tutorials that may assist you and overcome or update anything that I write here. Just know that the following lessons are based on a series of 12 classes I taught, using Moho, and they are only recorded here because I can honestly say that they were 100% effective and productive at the time and version of the software we were using.

Equipment Required

MOHO software (*There are "Debut" or "Pro" options at the time of writing.*)

You will continue to use your existing "Section I" equipment from time to time too, yet not merely as much:

Pegged animation paper

Peg bar

Lightbox

DOI: 10.1201/9781003324287-14

Pencils

Eraser

Pencil sharpener

Means to capture your individual drawings from a fixed capture position.

Masterclass 13/ Introduction to Moho

So here we are in the "pixels" section of our masterclass book. Students can work with any 2D animation software that they prefer, as this section doesn't attempt to teach software but merely use software to explore further principles and technique of movement. We are using "**Moho**" to work with in this section but, truly, it is not a recommendation of purchase. I have said elsewhere that the old – and now non-available – *"ToonBoom Studio"* has always been my software of choice for working digitally and with students in the classroom but once upon a time. But although I still do use it for much of the time on my home studio computer, I cannot any longer use it for teaching, as students have no access to it. As a result, I have turned to the software that I most like to use instead – Moho – because I think it is much more accessible as a program than any of the others. It is never my intention to teach students using software alone, and so in that sense, using Moho is a necessary evil. But I think it's still a good evil as Moho is pretty easy and accessible for new students of animation; therefore, I will use it here.

There are two options with Moho, "Debut" and "Pro", and either will work at this stage. If you are serious about your animation journey and software appeals to you, then it will be better to invest in "Pro" for the long term. "Debut" however has most of the functions that most students will use when exploring digital software, so that will be more than fine for now. Also, as I am not an expert in Moho in terms of knowing the software inside out, I have co-opted Moho user to review this section for me who can correct anything that I may have got wrong or do not yet now about. Consequently, I thank Ruben Cabenda for kindly agreeing to help me with this section.

Of course, if you're a *"luddite"* when it comes to technology and your passion is solely for traditional, hand-drawn techniques, then you can adapt the masterclass lessons taught in this section and, wherever possible, use drawn techniques instead.

DOI: 10.1201/9781003324287-15

Warm-Up Drawing

All that said, and being that we're entering the digital zone, you still have to keep your pencils sharp at the beginning of each lesson, as it is necessary to keep our warm-up "observational gesture drawing" sessions going before we get into the instruction. So, here we go with the next one.

"**Balance**" is something vitally important that animators need to know about. For example, you can create a great sequence of movement with a character – but no matter how good it is, if the key positions are not in balance, then the action will not be convincing. Balance can work in many ways of course. But with a biped character, the important thing is that the character's *"center of gravity"* must always be over their two feet at all times. If the character lifts one of their feet, however, the center of gravity must first shift over to the remaining *"contact foot"* that is on the ground. That's why with a walking action, as we have said before, there should always be a certain degree of body shift from side-to-side – the greater shift often occurring with the heavier of walking characters. It is also emphasized when a character has weak leg muscles and they rely on balance, rather than strength, to keep them moving and upright. Of course, breaking the rules of balance can be valuable too – in the sense that if you're animating some-one who is intoxicated, or it's a baby trying to walk for the first time, of for some-one who is tripping over something – then the balance (or more accurately, the center of gravity) has to be away from the point or points of contact with the ground. Consider these two balance poses as example and give yourself **3 minutes** to do gesture poses of them.

Pose 1 comments: So this pose perfectly illustrates the fact that a heavier person has to shift their weight from one side to the other, in order that they can lift the free leg up and forward on each stride. This character is probably in the process of just putting their right foot down, but you can see the center of gravity has shifted over the left leg – their "contact leg/foot" – so that the other leg can lift up at the back and plant itself down at the front. Of course, the minute that right leg and foot touch the ground, the body mass will shift to the right and over it, in order that the left leg can next lift up and come forward.

Pose 2 comments: So balance isn't just a left-to-right shifting thing. It's a 360-correction around any point that is in contact with the ground. Here, you can see the balance is forward and back. In other words, the two points of contact with the ground are the hands in this case. So, in order to maintain perfect balance, this person has to adjust herself into such a position that there's an equal amount of their weight to the right, or to the left, to the front, or to the back before they achieve a perfect balance pose. In other words, the center of gravity, of all their combined weight, is directly over the hands on the ground.

So yes, balance is everywhere we look and move. The two examples you've just drawn are the more obvious examples, but just remember that everything you do is about balance. When you, yourself, were a baby and trying to walk, I'm sure you didn't get it. You had to teach yourself how to balance without falling on your face or butt. And you fell where you did because your balance was ahead, or behind, your feet on the ground and your legs weren't fast enough to adjust to this. The eventual secret you had to learn was to get your foot or feet under where your center of gravity was, to save you falling over. Now of course, we take this for granted with every step we take – not even needing to consciously think about it. (Unless of course, we're a little intoxicated – in which case even the unconscious side of our thinking may not save us!) So even if you are trying to balance the length of a pencil on your finger, you can't do it unless you find the precise balance point where the weight of the pencil on one side matches the weight on the other. And that reflects not only on how you animate but also on how your life is managed too. Life is all about balance. If we "go out on a limb" so to speak, emotionally or even philosophically, we have to be prepared to counterbalance, otherwise we become obsessive in any one direction and usually end up in a world of hurt. So I find that life in the animation world, as well as life in the real world, has to respect the rule of "balance" at all time and on all the layers of our being. If nothing else I hope that in doing these two quick exercises, you begin think about doing your future key poses with a strong sense of balance to them. Trust me, it will mean a world of difference to your animation!

Instruction

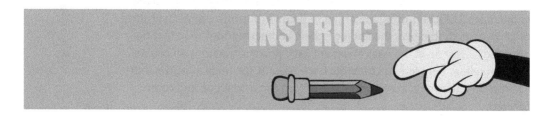

In preparation to getting really serious with Moho in the next masterclass lesson, I would like to offer a gentle introduction to the Moho software interface here, as well as give you a really simple exercise – a digital version of the "**Bouncing Ball**" to get you a little more familiar with how it works.

Remember, none of these masterclasses are about **teaching software**. Far from it! However, I am going to give you just enough basic information about the workings of Moho, so you have enough knowledge of it to do the principles of movement exercises we are going to cover in this section. If you want more, there are many software-specific tutorials outs there, not least on the Moho website itself. You'll see immediately that Moho has far more capabilities than we we'll cover here. However, the ones you're about to learn are all you need to do the 2D animation assignments here in this section. You can of course take all the principles covered in this Moho section and do them traditionally on paper if you like. But I think you'll see that for certain work, digital software does have a lot to offer the 2D animator. So, it would be good for your to tip your toes in the technology waters for a little while here, as I have done to teach it.

Finally, the overriding message I will offer you, no doubt again and again, is that as a well-trained character animator, you will have to **fight the software tooth and nail** along the way to get things right! What I mean by this is that animation software of any kind does make life easier, in the fact that it will do most of the inbetweening for you. But, quite often you don't want the animation to go the way that the software demands, rather than you are planning it. However, the more you're trained and experienced as a master animator, the more you'll realize that there's no such thing as a *mathematical* inbetween – which is what software is inclined to do, unless overridden. You have already learned that *timing* and *spacing* is not a mechanical process. Instead, it is more an art at its highest level! For example, things are often accelerating or decelerating from key to key, and indeed inbetweens are rarely logical inbetweens. So, you will have to learn here that what Moho offers may not be what a talented an experienced animator wants, unless they manually override what it offers. That said, in venturing into the Moho waters here, let's take advantages of its best capabilities.

The Moho Overview

Moho launched their v13.5 version in 2021 to great acclaim. © Lost Marble

Before we do anything, let us first look at the Moho interface and explore the few things that we need to know about it. Things may vary a very little here, depending on the version you are working – currently named *"Debut"* or *"Pro"* at the time of writing. Most of the time they are identical, so any discomfort you may experience by working with either should be minimal.

Now Moho is a really huge program, and I'm definitely not going to overwhelm you with lots of things here. But you do need to know what follows in order to start animating with it. We're only going to work with the animation tools in Moho here – and the very basic ones. It could be that when you reach *Sections 3 & 4* in this book, you might want to make your personal film project in Moho. In that case, you'll have to do further studies of it to utilize its greater production capabilities, and I will only mention the "must-know" when we need them here. So, for now let's keep it simple. I know some of you will instinctively want to rush forward with the software and discover everything you can about it, as I always do. However, I urge you to hold off and just learn the class material contained in this book first, as that will more than adequately teach you how to make things move well in Moho.

So, let's see the basics of setting up and executing a simple exercise. Let's start with the interface.

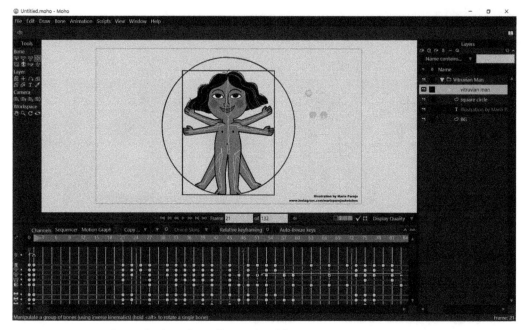

The Moho interface. © Lost Marble

Moho calls the working area the "**Stage**". This is where all your animation can be seen. This image in the stage is the default image they currently build into the program. So don't worry about it at all right now. When you start to animate, it will go away.

Close-up of the stage. © Lost Marble

Also, when you get to know Moho better, you can change it to whatever image you prefer. But for the time being, let's leave it as it is and go via the "File" tab to "**Project Settings**".

Project Settings

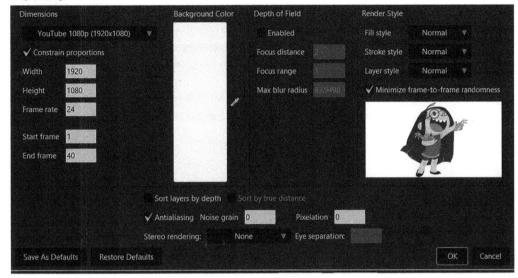

The new project settings drop-down menu.

In the interests of simplicity, I don't want you to worry about everything you see here. What I do want you to check however is your "**Constraint Proportions**" are **1920 × 1080** pixels, and your "**Frame Rate**" is **24 frames per second**. Your "**Start Frame**" will be **1**, and your "**End Frame**" can be **40** for now. (Note: This is easy to change later but for now the End Frame number is a token number to get us started.) You can leave the "**Background Color**" as **WHITE** for now although this can be changed if you want to. All those project settings are the only things to worry about for now. They should put you in a good place to start your animation proper. So, click "**Save as Defaults**", then "**OK**", and we'll move on.

Next open up "**File**" and "**New**" to start our first project, giving us a screen like this.

The new project screen.

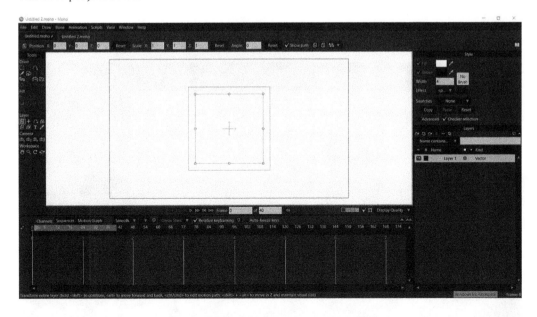

As indicated earlier, we are not going to create a digitally animated *"Bouncing Ball"*, as opposed to the drawn one we did before. It's a nice and easy exercise to learn at this stage, as it was at the beginning of your drawn animation section. However, to give it more interest this time, instead of the ball just bouncing straight up as we did before, I want us to animate it bouncing laterally – that is, from one side of the screen to the other. I also want to add gravity into the action, in the sense that as the ball bounces, it will get lower and lower. For this, I have drawn a "**Action Guide**" to demonstrate what I mean. You might want to create a drawn copy of this, so you can use it in the following exercise. Alternatively, you could "**Save Image As**" from the one supplied on our dedicated webpage.

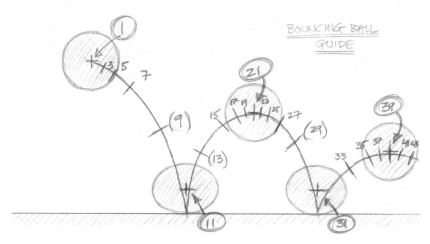

The Action Guide to work with.

Once you have your guide drawn, go to "**File**"/"**Import**"/"**Tracing Image**". Click on this and it will bring up a window of your computer's files and folders. Locate the drawing file you have created from mind, then click on it and "**Open**" to import it. This should make your Moho interface look like this.

The Moho interface Stage with the guide imported.

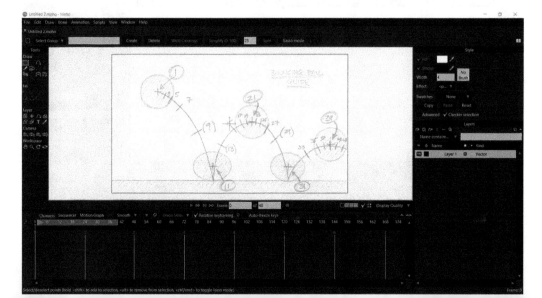

Note that is looks lighter than the original drawing you no-doubt created. That's because a *"tracing image"* will not be visible when you render out your animation to video. It is for guide purposes only; hence, it's background lightness. You'll note that it's highlighted on the *"Layers"* column to the right of the Stage, titled "**Layer 1**". You can rename this if you like or leave it as it is.

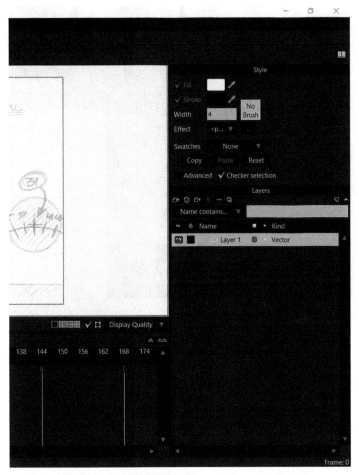

"Layer 1" is now highlighted on the Layers column.

So, now we have our action guide established we need to save our newly created Moho file, so you don't lose what you're done so far, just in case something goes wrong. Therefore, go to "**File**"/"**Save As**" and find a folder where you want to saved it to your computer. You may have found that when you set-up Moho on your computer, it selected a folder for you already. If that works for you, then go with it. If not, chose a folder of your choice for saving here. You can name it anything you like, but I called mine "**Bouncing Ball 01**". Now it is safe. And remember too,

NOTE

*If you ever want to lose your tracing image from the Stage, you can hit "**Control / U**" and it will go away. Hit the same again and it will return.*

every time you do something new to this file that you like, hit "**Control / S**" or "**Command / S**", whether you're on a Windows machine or Mac. That way you won't lose anything if there are mishaps.

Saving the file using Command/Control "S".

NOTE

In the digital world we are now in, you need to get into the habit of saving everything you do, as you do it. There will be many stages covered when animating it. There will be many stages covered when animating digitally, so I tend to "Save", then "Save As" a new file, every time I create a Stage I'm happy with and am ready to move on. So, it is not unusual for me to have anything from version "1" to version "41" of an animation scene if it goes through that many subtle stages – maybe even more on big or complicated scenes. The rationale for this is that if you drastically go wrong at a particular stage in the process, you can always go back to the previous file in the sequence, meaning you just lose the last thing you did, not everything

Preparing for the Bouncing Ball

Now let's actually get into creating our *Bouncing Ball* character. But before we do that however, let me explain a little more of the interface to you – at least the things you need to know for this assignment. For example, all the "**Tools**" you'll need are up at the top of the left-hand column.

Now be prepared for the accessibility of those tools visually changing as we do different processes within the program. But initially, we're just going to focus on two or three essential tools, which we'll get to in a minute. In the meantime, down along the bottom is our "**Timeline**".

Close-up of the Timeline.

You'll note that the frames are numbered across the Timeline from left to right, but the area we'll be animating in – Frames 1 to 40 for now – is highlighted in **turquoise**. And to see what frame number we are currently on, look to the white box on the left, beneath the Stage. The right-hand white box indicates the last frame in the scene – which can be changed later if we want to shorten or lengthen it. Currently, we made it **40**, as you know. The left-hand white box indicates the frame that our timeline "**cursor**" is currently standing at – "**1**" in this case.

Close-up of start and end frame windows.

If you move the vertical cursor along the Timeline, the number in the left-hand white box will show you what frame you are currently on. Here, we are at Frame "15".

Close-up of the Moho tools.

Close-up of the Timeline and cursor at Frame 15.

Now, the really important thing to know about Moho is that when you're setting up your scene or creating your character, the cursor on the Timeline needs to be at "**0**". This frame will never show in the final film render, but it is crucial for doing all the rigging or other preparation work, prior to you actually starting to animate. On Frame 0, for example, the Animation Tools **do not show up**. They only do so when you move to Frame 1 and beyond. Also, any rigged character you may be using to animate could well look strange and "exploded" on Frame "0".

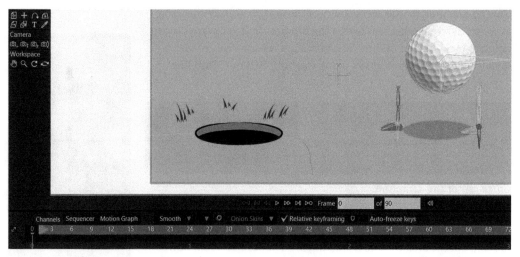

Close-up of cursor on Frame 0 and showing the character exploded.

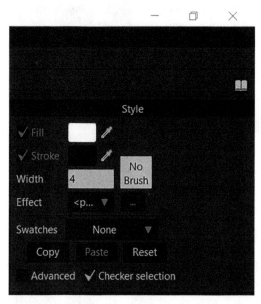

Close-up of color box window.

The last thing you need to know before we move on is that the creation line and color palette information is to be found at the top of the right-hand column.

Most important to know about this is that when you're actually drawing or creating a vector character in the program, the top box indicates the color of the "**Fill**" you are drawing, and the lower box indicates the color the "**Line**" ("Stroke") will be. So, if I were to randomly create a ball (circle) shape as it is now, the outer line is black and the inner fill is white. That is because the boxes in the top right are displaying that way.

Size windows and colored character matching tools.

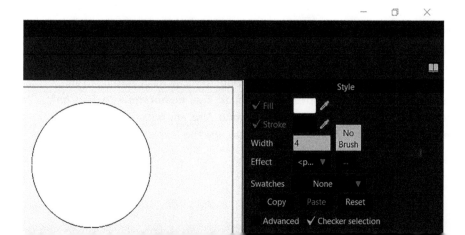

If I were to change the colors of each by using the respective box **dropper tool** to select different colors in the color swatch window below, the created ball shape would now reflect those colors instead.

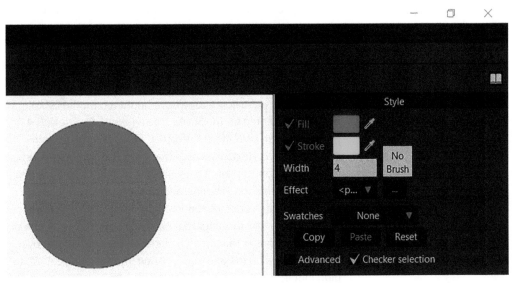

Color change as dropper is used.

Actually, another important box lies just beneath the dropper boxes. This is where the **thickness** of the Stroke line can be determined. If you change the number, you'll change the size of the Stroke line that you'll be drawing with. For example, here are two versions of the ball – one with the Stroke thickness at "**3**" and another with the thickness at "**10**".

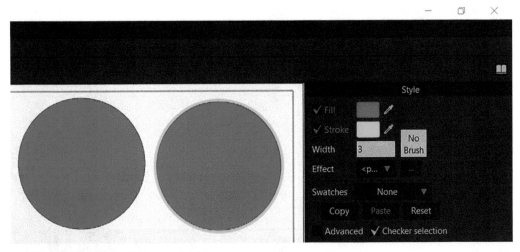

Ball line showing its different thicknesses.

Now, at last, we're ready to actually animate our Bouncing Ball. So, let's do it in the easiest way we can, remembering the *"Squash"* and *"Stretch"* principles we have already worked with. You can see these indicated by the plotting marks and numberings on the *"Path of Action"* that the center of our ball will take on the action guide. Again, these points are just guides of what we're planning to achieve, but as we work into it, we may find that our animation may not match them exactly. They are a starting point, but the actual work in Moho may modify them.

The draw shape tools.

So, the first thing to do is actually create a ball to bounce. For this example, we're going to select a bright red for the Fill color and a darker red for the Stroke. The width of the Stroke is **4** pixels. That can be done at the top of the right-hand column of the interface. Next, make sure that the Timeline cursor is set at Frame "**0**", bottom left. That will allow us to work outside of the actual animation Timeline, and all we do there will not factor on the screen once we render the final action to video. That done, and to draw the actual ball, we're going to go up to one of the Tool buttons at the top of the left-hand column. Hover over them and click on the one that is "**Draw Shape**" (shortcut "S") to highlight it.

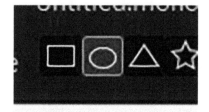

Close-up of Oval tool.

Once the Tool is highlighted, look above at a selection of shape buttons and select the "**Oval**" one.

That will now allow us on Frame 0 to create our ball by "**left click**" and "**dragging**" the cursor on the Stage. However, if you simple left click and drag, the shape will not be the perfect circle we need for the ball.

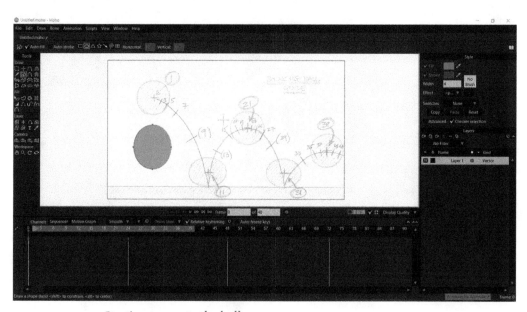

Starting to create the ball.

So, if we hit "**Control/Z**" to remove it again, then click on the outside circumference of the ball and "**left click**" and hold the "**Shift**" key down and drag, you'll see that on this occasion, you'll get a **perfect circular shape**.

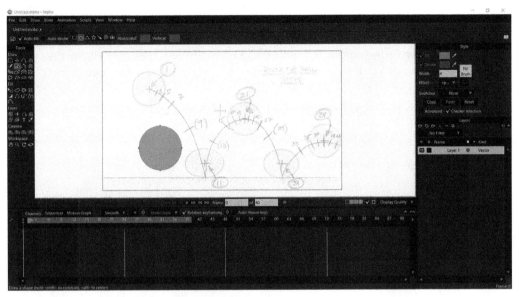

Second option for creating the ball.

The problem with this still, however, is that the circle is not quite in the right position and could well be not the right size we have indicated in our background guide. So, "**Control/Z**" again to remove our ball. Now, align the cursor to the center point of the ball on the Stage, click down on the mouse, and this time hold down "Shift" & "Alt" and drag from there. This time the circle will expand from the center, meaning that it will now match perfectly the size and location of the ball on the guide. We now have our perfect ball, where we want it, on Frame 0.

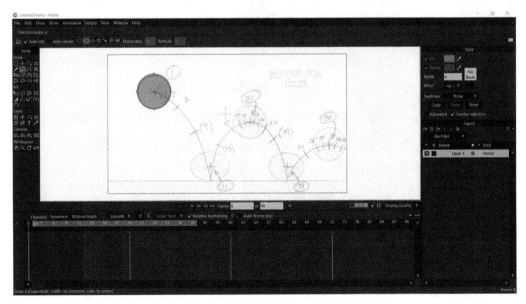

Third option for creating the ball.

The last thing we need to do before we begin the animation process is to place the "Origin Point" of our ball. The Origin Point is the point on the ball, around which everything moves if we try to deform the shape of the ball. (Which we will need to do when we add Squash & Stretch to the action.) So, to set the Origin Point to where we want it – that is, in the center of the ball. This will make it easier to rotate, squash or stretch the ball when we are animating. Click on the button in the Tool panel directly to the left of the ball shape. If you hover the cursor over it, you will see that it is named "**Set Origin Point**" – or "**Command/O**" as a shortcut. Now you'll be able to select where you want the new Origin Point to be, which is at the center of the ball, here…

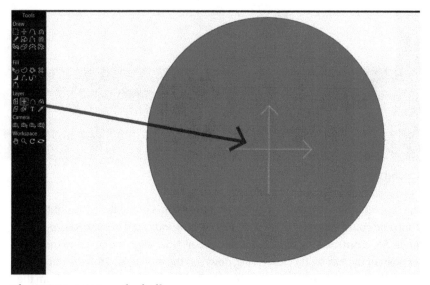

The Origin point on the ball.

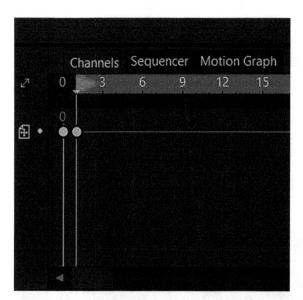

The key round dot symbol, indicated on Frame 1.

This means that if you change the shape of the ball in any way – known as "Deforming" – it will do so in any direction from the Origin Point.

So, to now create our first animation key position, we move the Timeline cursor to "**Frame 1**" on the Timeline, having once selected the transform layer tool to animate the ball. Then, if you just click with the cursor over the ball on the Stage, you will see a little round dot appear on Frame 1 on the Timeline. This signifies that a Key Position has been created.

Now, if you look at the guide on the *Stage* background, you will see that the next Key is to be positioned on Frame "**11**". So, drag the Timeline cursor along to Frame 11, and then drag the ball down from its first position, so its Origin Point touches the ground where the Squash key is on the guide. This means you'll see on the Timeline at Frame 11; we have created our second Key Position – although we don't have the Squash shape established for it yet.

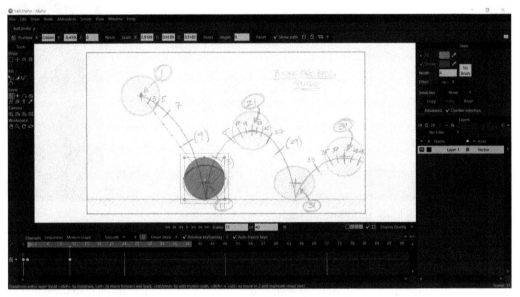

Second key position, on Frame 11.

Now just to test this out, if you hit the "**Play**" button beneath the Stage, you'll see the ball shape sliding from 1 to 11 in a straight line. If all is good with yours, then move the Timeline cursor to Frame 21, where the third Key Position is indicated. Move the ball to this position and a new round circle will appear on the Timeline at that frame. Test again if you doubt what you've done.

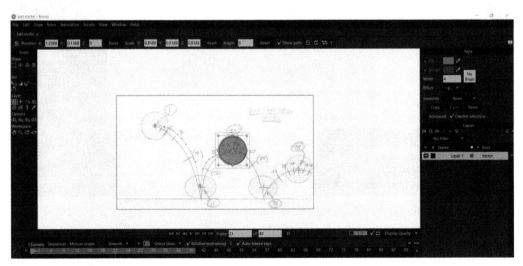

Next key position, on Frame 21.

So, if all is good, do the same thing from Key Frames "31" and "39". This should give you Key Positions in ever place we need them in accordance with our background guide.

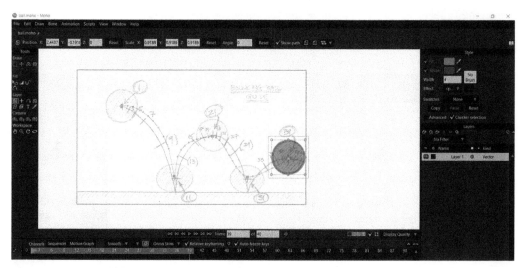

All keys up to and including Frame 39.

Now, so the ball does stop midair, you might want to create one more Key Position – not indicated on our Guide – at (say) Frame "**48**" beyond the edge of our Guide. That will create an additional flowing action that will take the ball out of the shot entirely eventually.

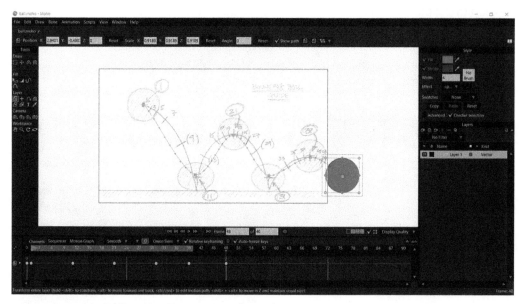

Adding Key Frame 48 to the action.

NOTE

Now that we have set a final frame that is beyond our original scene length of 40 frames. So, go to the second white frame box under the Stage and change that number from 40 to 48. Now, when we hit Play and run the keys action again, it will show the ball roughly bouncing out of the shot to the right – although it's clearly not very good yet, so we're far from finishing action as it should be yet! But at least the playback gives us a feeling about the timing and spacing we have imagined.

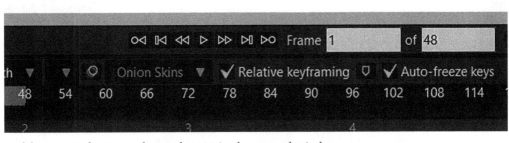

End frame number now changed to 48 in the second window.

Now, we're going to start refining things. Look at the light blue line that Moho has created, indicating the "**Path of Action**" the ball is taking so far. Obviously, this is no-where near the Path of Action we created for ourselves with the drawn guide. Notice too that the dots on the Moho Path of Action line represent every frame of film that has been created by establishing the keys. (These indicate the placements of the Points of Origin by the way, not the center of the ball, as our sketch guide does.) These points are a prime example of what I was saying about software creating its own logical inbetween positions, which are often nothing like the positions an experience master animator would use. So we have to fight the software to make it better.

NOTE

*If you are not seeing the Moho path of action on your Stage, go up to the button above the stage that says "**Show Path**", click on that and you should be able to see it.*

The Show Path window is checked.

To modify the Moho path of action, we need to go to a function in Moho called **"Motion Graph"**. To access it, you need to click and drag across all the keys in the Timeline – 1 through 40. Then release on your mouse button to highlight them. You'll know they're highlighted, as they will be circled in **RED**. (Make sure the key on Frame 0 is NOT highlighted however!)

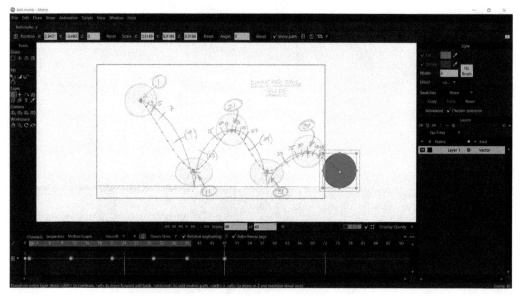

Note that all the keys are now highlighted in RED.

Next, right click on one of the keys to bring up a drop-down menu. Select the one called **"Bezier"** and left click on that. That will place a **tiny dot** in the center of your keys on the Timeline.

Note the Bezier dot in center of the keys.

Then go to the button just above your second key, named "**Motion Graph**".
Click on it to reveal a rather confusing arrangement of graph lines instead of
your key markers.

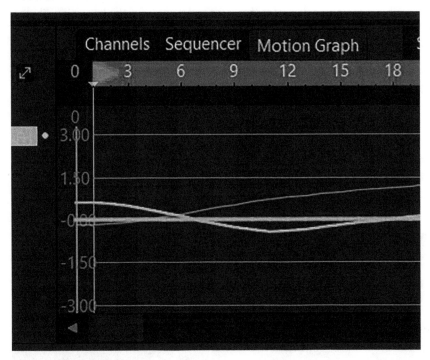

The Motion Graph.

Next, to highlight what we're going to be looking for, **double-click** on the small
button to the left of the Timeline, titled "**Layer Translation**". That will transform
the graph to reveal **colored dotted lines** and **circled key positions**. These lines
are called "**Curves**".

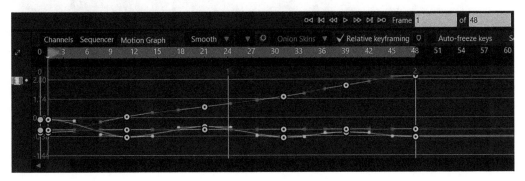

Showing the Curves.

The RED Curve is what is known at the "**X**" curve, the BLUE one is the "**Z**" curve and the GREEN one is the "**Y**" curve. This can be simply explained by saying that "X" is basically the movement from left to right – in other words, **horizontal** direction. The "Z" curve represents any movement **forward and back**. Finally, the "Y" curve represents movement that is up and down – **vertical** direction. Therefore, by moving the curve positions, we are essentially affecting the way the ball moves along the Stage.

Now, because we effectively want the ball to move across the Stage horizontally at an even pace for this exercise, we therefore have to make the **RED/X curve** look as straight as possible. So, adjust the keys to correct the X curve line. We don't have to be absolutely perfect with this, but the more "up and down" shape there is to the curve, the more varied the ball's velocity will be. So just gently manipulate the keys on the X curve to try and get the line as straight as you can. For subtle adjustments, use the "**Handles**" that are attached to the keys along the curve.

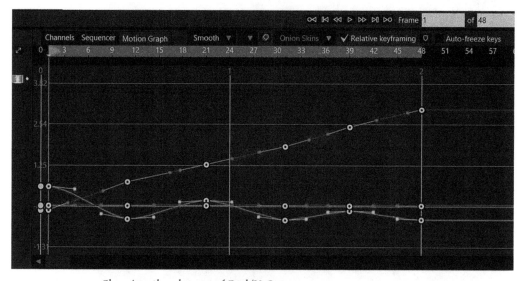

Showing the change of Red/X Curve.

Play back the action to ensure the velocity of the ball from one side to the other is pretty consistent. If it is, then now go to the Z curve for adjustments up and down. (Note: As the ball is not moving nearer to us, or further away, we don't have to adjust the Z curve at all.) On the Y axis (curve), we need to try and adjust it to the shape of the arced path of action curves we have on our drawn guide – which it is not doing right now.

Remember here that we are dealing with slow-ins and slow-outs on the book at the top of the bounces, so our Y-axis has to reflect this too. Essentially, to get a slower action along the path, we need to have the curve more horizontal, and to get a faster action along the curve, we need it more vertical. So, to achieve these two objectives, we work with the Bezier Curve Handles. To get the slower action, you need to pull the Handle more horizontally and the increase the speed you pull the relevant Handle to a more vertical position, like this.

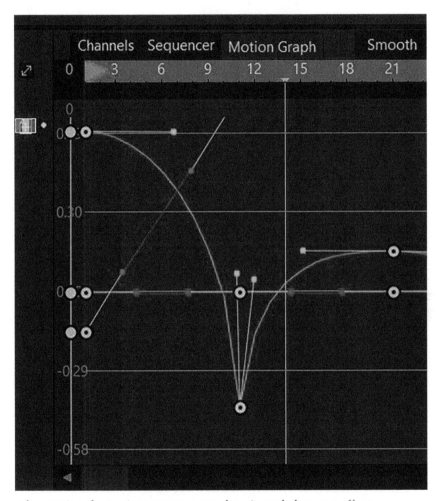

Adjust using the Bezier curves to get slow-in and slow-out effect.

You'll see that the curves are flatter at the top of the bounces and sharp and angled at the bottom. This will give us the acceleration and deceleration we're looking for, with the sharp angles giving us dramatic "snap" to the bounce.

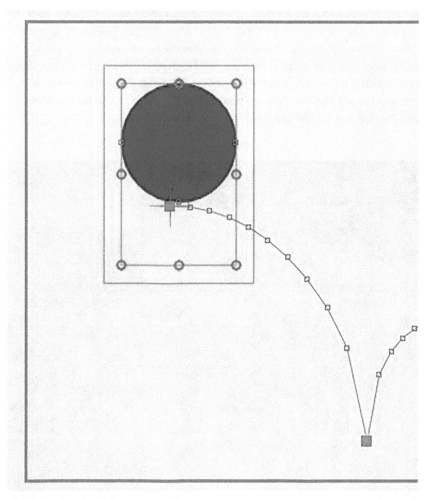

Showing the sharp bounce angles.

Do this for all the bounces along the Timeline, testing it by hitting "Play" as much as possible to see it moving in a way we hopefully want it to. You'll most likely find that it doesn't work as you imagine it at first, but the more you change and test what you're doing, you'll find that you'll eventually get to a bouncing ball that you can be proud of. And remember, as I said at the beginning, your final action may not match your original drawn guide as anticipated. But if it works on playback, then all is good. The original drawn guide was only that – a guide. By *"working the curves"*, you should ultimately arrive at a bouncing ball that is so much better than you originally envisioned it.

And never forget – you are running the software; it should not be running you! Software has its subtle ways of imposing its will on you, so you have to be ever vigilant. Don't accept what it does, unless it improves what you want. Rather, impose your will on what you're going for, even if it takes you longer to arrive at that. For example, here I improved the bouncing action by moving the apex of the bounces even higher on the second and third ones. This takes it further away from the original drawn guide, but it ultimately works better that way!

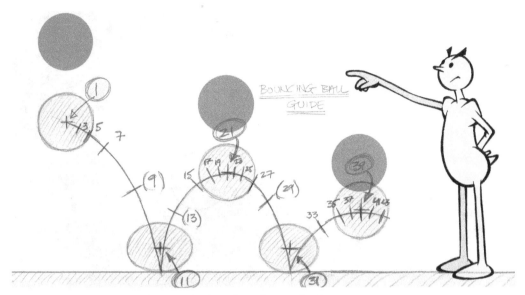

Don't be afraid to push the keys higher than the guide if you want a
greater effect with the action. Remember, the software is under your
control, not you it!

And don't forget either, technology is ultimately not always reliable – so don't
forget to **save a new version of all of this as you successfully complete it**. It
will most certainly save you having to start it all again if the unforeseen happens!

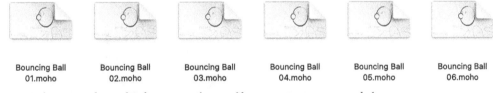

| Bouncing Ball 01.moho | Bouncing Ball 02.moho | Bouncing Ball 03.moho | Bouncing Ball 04.moho | Bouncing Ball 05.moho | Bouncing Ball 06.moho |

Don't forget to do multiple saves of your file to protect your work from
inevitable crashes!

Now, all this said, don't forget we're not finished yet! When the ball moves
through the air and hits the ground, it needs to be deformed into either a
Stretch or a **Squash**. However, before we consider that, we had to get the timing and placement right on the core animation, which we did. Now we need to
click back on the "**Channels**" button above the Timeline at the beginning, we
can work on our Squash & Stretch shaping of the ball. So, move the cursor to
Frame 11 to start this process by creating a Squash on it. So, grab the top point
of the ball on Frame 11 and hold down the shift key as you drag it down toward
the Origin Point.

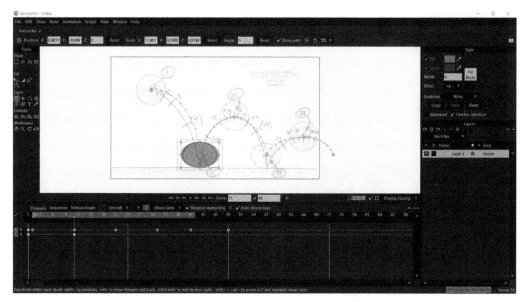

The Squash on Key Frame 11. Don't forget to adjust the dimensions so that the volumes remain consistent.

That done, we now need to widen the sides to ensure we keep the look of volume consistent with the downward Squash. So, grab the side and pull it out giving you a much more convincing volumetric shape overall, especially if you hold down shift while dragging.

Close-up of Squash shape.

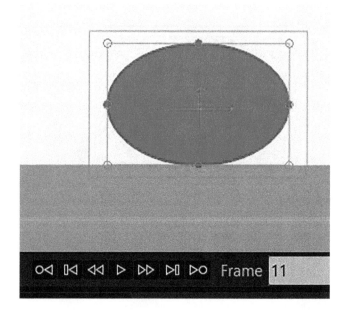

Now, if you "**Scrub**" backward and forward however – that is, drag the Timeline cursor to and from Keys 1 and 11 – you'll see that the ball is changing shape but it's not the shape we want on the accelerating descent. In other words, we want it to Stretch toward the end, not simply transform from a pure circle at the top of the Squash shape at the bottom. So, we need to go back to Frame "10", the one before the Key Frame 11. Using the "**Transform**" tool to the left of the Stage *("Command/M" for the shortcut)*, we need to click on the Frame 10 ball to highlight it, then shift while dragging until we have the perfect Stretch position. Remember again to keep the volume inside the ball consistent when doing this.

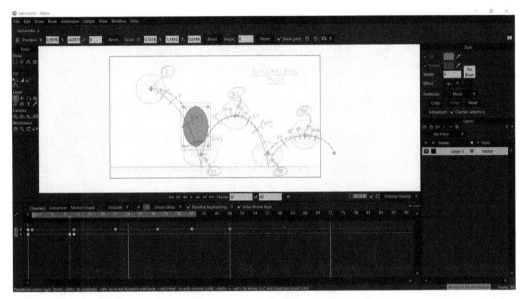

Creating the vertical stretch on Frame 10.

However, as the ball should not be vertical and is instead following a path of action, we need to take the side of the selection box around the ball and rotate it until it is angled in line with the path of action direction at that point.

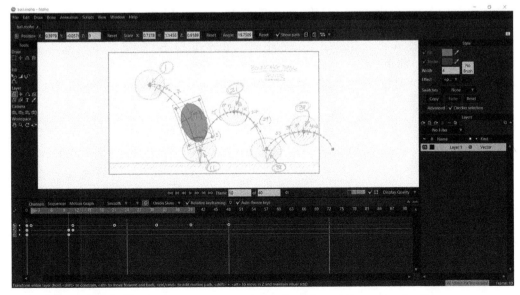

Rotate the stretch ball on Frame 10 to match the direction of the path of action.

Now Scrub between 1 and 11 on the Timeline again to check the action. It should have improved considerably. If all is OK with that, make sure you reset the rotation of the ball at Frame 11, as you will notice that the rotation is not what is. We now need to add the Stretch beyond the hit on the ground. So this time, go to Frame 12 on the Timeline and create the Stretch position in the same way as we created it on Frame 10 – remembering to rotate it this time the other way, so that the length of it reflects the path of action in that direction.

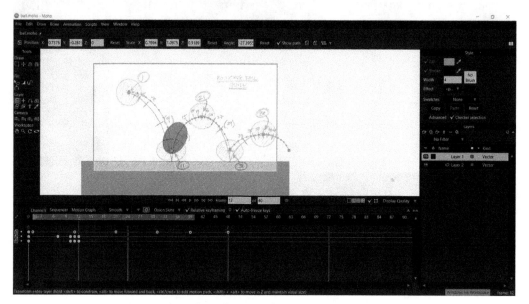

Creating and angling the stretch or Frame 12.

Scrubbing then from 1 to 21 should give you a really nice bouncing action with good Squash & Stretch. If not, adjust until it does. Remember also to reset the scale and rotation on Frame 21 and Frame 39 the same way, so that it will return to its original size. At Frame 7, 15, 27, and 36, reset the scale. This way you will have more control of where you want it to start stretching or where it needs to return to its original size. When all is good, continue to add Stretch and Squash to all the other keys and the inbetweens either side of the bounces, producing your completed bouncing ball action.

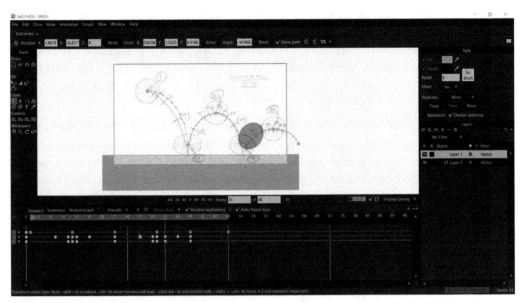

Completing the Squash/Stretch action along all the bounce frames.

When you are happy that your bouncing ball is moving as it should, then it's time to render it out as a video. So stage one of this is to hit "**Command/U**", to lose the drawn guide from the back and just have a white background instead. Then, if you Play that back, you'll get a much nicer profile silhouette of the action as it moves. Remember though, that the speed you see it in playback in the software program is never going to be precisely the real-time speed you'll see it in its video form. So, now it's time to render it out for a final check.

Finally, to create a video of your action from Moho, you need to export it as follows. Go to "**File**"/"**Export Animation**" *(shortcut: "Command E")* and click on it. This will bring up an export box. Double-check everything, especially the first and last frame numbers. Otherwise, everything is probably fine in its default stage. Moho has a convenient setting here that will name the video file the same as the Moho file name and place it in the same folder. That way you'll have no trouble finding it. When you're satisfied that all is good, hit the "**OK**" button and Moho will begin to render. (Note: If you have the "Debut" version of Moho, you may not have the same rendering to video options that Pro has, so you'll need to adapt accordingly.) Now, Moho will reveal a second window for you to see the render process. At the top of the window, you'll see a green progress line. When it travels all the way across to the right of the window, that window will disappear, as your video file will be complete. Once it is, it will pop up for you to view. Hopefully, all will be well, and you'll have created your very first digital animation in Moho. Congratulations!

Introduction to the "Generic Run"

Before we move on to the next Moho lesson, I want to introduce you here to animating a "**Generic Run**" using primarily drawing techniques. You don't have to do this exercise now if you don't want to. However, I strongly advise you to do so, as it will help you prior to doing the Moho version.

Now everything we've been talking about so far – apart from the initial flipbook assignment – has been using *"Key to Key Animation"*. That is, we have created keys, breakdown (or passing) positions, then inbetweens. Animating a Run, however, is more of a thing we call *"Straight Ahead Animation"*. Straight ahead animation means that instead of creating keys, you start with a first position then subsequently add a next one that is slightly different, and then another, and another, until your sequence is finished. I have to stress that 99% of animation today is done with the *Key Pose* system, but there are occasions where *"Straight ahead"* is preferable – such as with an animated run, or as I once did, fingers drumming on a desktop.

The next thing to realize – which is why we can use a key pose system here – is that a "Run" is **not just a fast walk**. It has a very different approach to it. This is best explained by the notion that with a walk one foot is on the ground through, whereas with a run, there is a point where both feet are off the ground at the same time. This will become evident as we discuss the stages of creating a run. However, for the time being, here's a diagram that illustrates the difference of them both. You can see that with the top walk stride action, one foot is on the ground at all times. Whereas with the two run strides beneath it, both feet are off the ground during the upper stride positions.

The differences between a walk and a run.

In my class, I usually show students what a human run looks like on video. The video I show is a beautiful, slow-motion shot of Usain Bolt, the fastest man on earth. If you can find this video, you'll notice that as he runs, both feet come off the ground midway through the stride. If you look at the other runners too, you'll see the same thing is happening also – confirming that with runs there are points were not feet are on the ground, as opposed to walks. Let's look at the outlines of some real sprinters in action.

Silhouetted stills of real sprinters.

If you go to our dedicated web page, you'll see a repeat "Generic Run" on video. The one I've used are where the eight stages are our odd numbered positions, inbetweened with even number drawings to make the action slower and smoother. So, the odd numbered drawings are numbered "1", "3", "5", "7", "9", "11", "13" and "15". The even numbered drawings are "2", "4", "6", "8", "10", "12", "14" and "16" – with inbetween "16" being halfway between 15 and 1 to complete the cycle. A spread of the generic, odd numbered positions look like this.

The eight major positions in a running action – the first and the last are identical.

So, now let us now go through these odd-numbered stages in more detail. Remember that this is best approached initially using *"straight ahead animation"*. So if you're going to attempt this, start with the first stage initially, then create your subsequent poses stage by stage. This would be a fun exercise to do as a flipbook incidentally – taking the following run poses and applying them to the ball (below) poses on a separate page or card of your flipbook. That way you can test it immediately, without the need of equipment. Alternatively, you could create a quick character in Moho too and modify the following flipbook instruction to match the digital approach. To create it from a hand-drawn perspective, however, I suggest you should probably use a really simple character for now in your flipbooks, like this ball with arms and legs.

A very simple character to work with – basically a ball with arms and legs.

For the actual poses to help you draw your ball character running, we'll refer to those indicated in "Fig. 02_050" above

Stage 1:

17 (1)

Drive off position.

Drive off position (Pose "1" on guide): This position is a bit like a stride position for a run – in the sense that the back leg is pushing off hard and the front leg is reaching forward. It is not like a walk stride, however, as the foot is way up in the air, creating a dynamic pushing forward position. With runs, the arms are more dynamic looking too, so you'll see they are more bent than with a walk, looking like the character is punching the air. This is especially true of really fast runs, like sprinting. It is less so with slow runs, like long-distance running, with the arms much straighter like walk arm action.

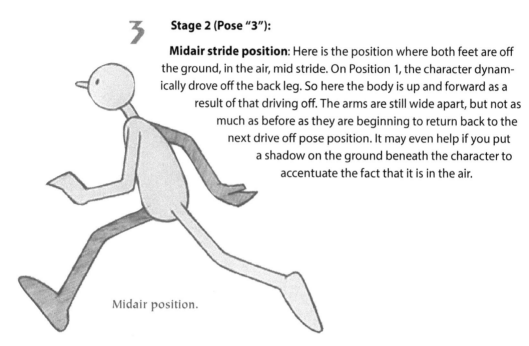

Stage 2 (Pose "3"):

Midair stride position: Here is the position where both feet are off the ground, in the air, mid stride. On Position 1, the character dynamically drove off the back leg. So here the body is up and forward as a result of that driving off. The arms are still wide apart, but not as much as before as they are beginning to return back to the next drive off pose position. It may even help if you put a shadow on the ground beneath the character to accentuate the fact that it is in the air.

Midair position.

Stage 3 (Pose "5"):

Contact position: This position is where the front leg, having been reaching forward, now makes contact with the ground. You'll notice that there's a slight bend in the leg, due to the impact and the fact of the body weight baring down on it. The back leg is not moving forward although it's not quite as far forward as the passing position on a walk. The arms are pretty much half way between the extreme front and back positions.

*(**Note**: If you plan to animate this action with the even numbers being added as inbetweens, you might want to push the lead foot forward a little in inbetween "4", in anticipation of it contacting the ground on 5. This is a little like the "7" position on the Generic Walk, just before it hits the ground in the "9" key stride position.)*

Contact position.

Stage 4 (Pose "7"):

Sink down position.

Sink down position: This position is halfway between the "7" position and the next drive off "9" position. It is a slight anticipation to the drive off – in the sense that the contact leg is bending a little more, in preparation for driving off in the next stride. This particular pose gives the action a little more weight as a result of that. The arms have moved on a little from the midway positions, in preparation for their drive off positions.

Stage 5 (Pose "9"):

2nd drive off position.

2nd Drive off position: This is pretty much an identical position to Position "1" – except now we have reversed arms and legs of course. On a Generic Run, this is pretty much the same for all the 2nd stride positions.

Stage 6 (Pose "11"):

2nd midair position.

2nd **Midair stride position**: This is also pretty much an identical position to Position "3" – except now we have reversed arms and legs of course.

Stage 7 (Pose "13"):

2nd contact position.

2nd Contact position: This is also pretty much an identical position to Position "5" – except now we have reversed arms and legs of course.

Stage 8 (Pose "15"):

2nd sink down position.

2ns Sink down position: This is also pretty much an identical position to Position "7" – except now we have reversed arms and legs of course.

Of course, as we're doing a cycled, Generic Run action here, we will now next return to the number "1" position again and repeat the action over and over again for as long as we need it.

Capture your drawings using whatever method you choose and play back the action on 2s at 24pfs. You should see the body's center of gravity somewhat moving through an oval forward and back action – due to the push off the drive off positions and the breaking on the contact position before sliding back to the next drive off position. If you character's body is just going vertically up and down on the spot, you are not doing it right and need to put more "up and forward" positioning with the character after the drive of poses.

Suggested Assignment

Whether you do this exercise using a flipbook or in Moho, I strongly advise you doing it in one way or another. We will be talking about doing it digitally in a minute, so maybe drawing it will be a good option for better understanding what is going on for the time being. Consider also doing it with a more recognizable biped character if you've already done it with a ball-shaped one – emphasizing rotations on the shoulders and hips as the arms and legs move dynamically forward and back. You might also want to experiment with stride lengths and the height you push the character off the ground after the drive off positions. Remember: The faster the run, the less of an "up and down" movement there will be – and the slower the run, the less the stride length will be.

Masterclass 14/
The Full Rigged Character

So far, I've tried to make your introduction to Moho simple and as minimal as possible. I will try at all times to not make this a course on learning software, but there is significant information that you'll need, in order to focus on the "principles of movement" side of animation, rather than the technology. However, we do need to push on with some Moho software imperatives now. Not making it too daunting, I'm going to add a little new material on Moho in each lesson as we go through Section II for the book, hopefully not overwhelming anyone in the process – especially the traditionally minded 2D animators, like myself!

So, after our even more important warm-up, observational drawing exercise, we'll start to explain the mysteries of a rigged biped character.

Warm-Up Drawing

In the previous drawing warm-up, we dealt with balance exercises. However, as "balance" is so important to the animator as far as I'm concerned, we're going to do another one here. Balance is what makes "so, so" animation really good animation, and really believable in the audience's mind. Therefore, it's always good to train our minds in looking for the balance in everything, so one more exercise here can do nothing but strengthen that discipline.

DOI: 10.1201/9781003324287-16

By the way, it is worth commenting here that in my "live" classes, I find that students do very quickly learn how to do solid balance gesture drawings. However, some tends to draw them at an angle to the sides of the paper they are using. Now, this might seem a nitpick to some, as the actual requirement of the challenge is met – it's just that being at an angle with the sides of the paper, it looks wrong of first inspection. This is probably just due to a student drawing their assignment with the paper askew from their particular point of view. However, nitpicking or not, I tend to ask them not to do this as, essentially, we're not only trying to develop their "animator's eye" here, but we're also training ourselves in the aesthetics of presentation. Remember, when you animate, you can't have the screen at an angle to the way you're drawing characters. So it is important that you draw your gesture drawings, respecting the confines of the space you're drawing in. So, always try to keep your paper upright when you're drawing your exercises, so that you learn to place – or "Stage" – them correctly within the area you are working in. This is all part of the extensive creative disciplines that animators need to adhere to. That said…

In this "**Balance 2**" assignment, we are continuing to explore something that is fundamentally important to animators. Pushing the extremes of balance in animation is really important, so hopefully these exercises in general will make it second nature for you to think about balance as you animate. What follows is one **3-minute pose**, plus another **4-minute pose** that should push you harder. Our first 3-minute pose is entitled "**Single Arm Balance**"…

Pose 1 comments: So, this pose is a much more dynamic balance pose than you've done before – more muscular and more compact. But again, the object of your drawing is to make sure you get the aggregate of the body weight equally massed either side of the point of contact with the ground. If the character did not do that themselves, then they would fall on their face, there side and/or their back legs. So, your drawing has to perfectly indicate that making it plausible to the view that this is indeed a perfectly balanced pose. In the real world, if he bent his straightened back leg inward toward the body – or even if he stretched his free, right arm beyond his head – he would indeed be pulled forward as the very delicate balance here would be breached. Your drawing needs to reflect this delicate balance too. Notice especially that there is a strong, "**dynamic line of force**" linking the right foot, the right leg, the curved spine and the extended neck and head. This invisible line gives great strength to the pose and is something that you will learn to develop when creating your more dynamic key poses when animating. All the great master animators of the past were able to do this.

The second, even more challenging, 4-minute balance pose now is called "**Duo Hip Balance**", for obvious reasons…

Pose 2 comments: There is not much balance to be displayed by the guy on the ground here, but there is a requirement that he keeps that upright leg firm and strong, so that she can balance stably on it. Notice that the contact point of his foot is perfectly aligned with her center of gravity, meaning that her body mass is equally spread around the point. So again, your drawing needs to reflect the very subtle, yet very powerful, balance exercise that is going on here. Remember that if she were to bring her left arm into her body, that delicate balance would be lost and she'd come tumbling down, and similarly, if she bend either of her legs at the knees. So, make sure your drawing communicates the delicacy of this balance yet again, using the *"dynamic line of action"* through her legs, torso and arm to reflect the balance that is occurring here. Note too that although he is flat, prone and solidly anchored to the ground, with his vertical leg at an almost right angle to his body, his down leg – although ostensibly flat on the ground too – is not actually perfectly straight and has a subtle bend at the knee, which makes it appear all the stronger.

As I've said before, there's probably never going to be a situation where you'll need to animate anything with these particular poses. Maybe there will be, which will be fortuitous. However, most likely you will never need these particular poses in your life as an animator. But, it's really important that when you create any pose in animation – specifically with biped characters – that you always make sure it's in balance. (Unless of course, it needs to be out of balance, in which case you exaggerate that imbalance within your pose by pushing the body weight far beyond the point of contact on the ground.) But anything that needs to be in balance to be convincing – walking, dancing, running, throwing, jumping, anything – you should always reflect on that as you're creating your poses. That's why these drawing exercises are extremely valuable in training your animator's eye in knowing what to look for. I wish I'd had something like this at the beginning of my career, as it took me a long, long while to discover how important balance was to creating strong and convincing movement. So time spent on these drawing exercises here can never be wasted time! It really is true that until you start recognizing and applying the principles of balance for example, that your animation can never aspire to the highest levels. The exciting this for me is that once your animator's eye is open to seeing principles such as balance, you can never see the world in the same way again because balance – or the lack of balance in some cases – is presenting itself everywhere!

Instruction

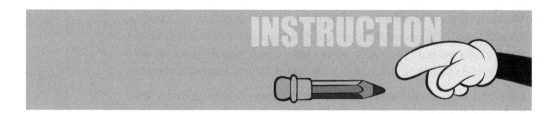

In terms of what we're dealing here, from a Moho perspective, I just want to give you a couple of quick things to be aware of. This is what we call a "**rigged character**" in Moho (or indeed any other animation program you may come across)…

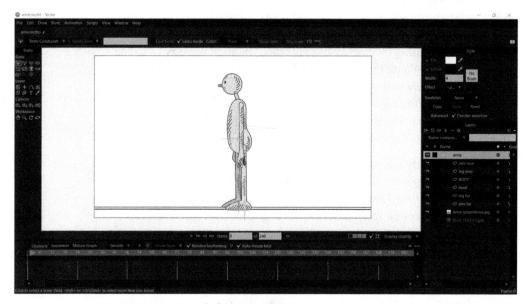

"Arnie", our rigged character design.

You can see the basic profile of the character's yellow silhouette and inside it a kind of skeleton. In fact, that's exactly what it is. All those blue structures within the torso and limbs are known as "**Bones**", and they are the means by which we articulate, or move, the character's body. Remember, with digital/computer animation, we are essentially acting like puppet masters, pulling the right invisible strings, to bring the character alive. The *"Bones"* are the strings in this case, and it is through those bones, and the joints that give the body parts movement and flexibility, that we bring our character to life.

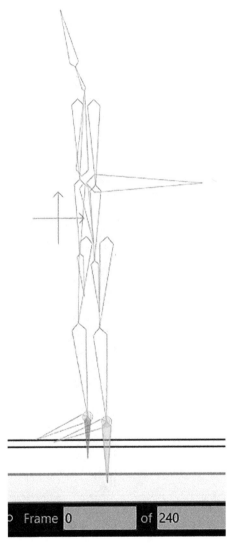

The character's "Bones".

"**Rigging**" is a process that we need to learn in order to turn our character designs into living, breathing characters on the screen, but we'll deal with that later as we don't want to overcomplicate things at this stage.

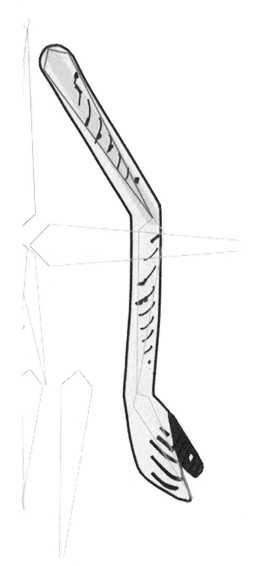

Close-up of rigged arm.

Essentially, you will use the "**Animation Tools**" in Moho to move the bones of the character. These are activated when your character is rigged – as can be seen here on the **highlighted layer** level to the right of the stage.

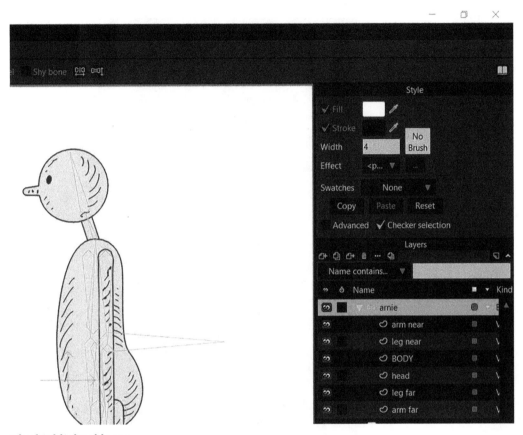

The highlighted layer.

With that particular layer highlighted, the **"Animation Tools window"** will appear at the top of the left-hand column.

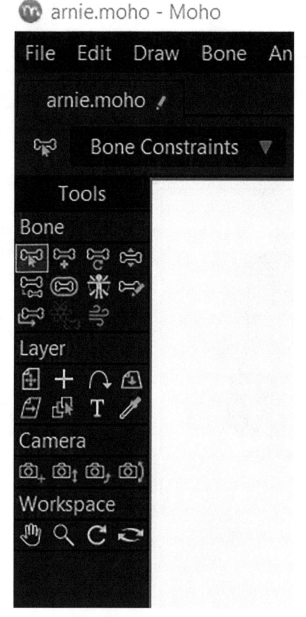

The Animation Tools window.

Now I don't want to overwhelm you with too much information here, but I do want you to try a little exercise. The character above is perhaps too much to handle in its entirety right now, so we're going to use a rig that just has an arm and a torso to play with. (Note: You can download this simplified character rig at out dedicated web page.)

Essentially, to move the arm, you use the "**Transform**" tool and click and drag the bones of the arm into the position you want. We're going to have the character move from a "**down arm**" position to a "**up armpointing**" position.

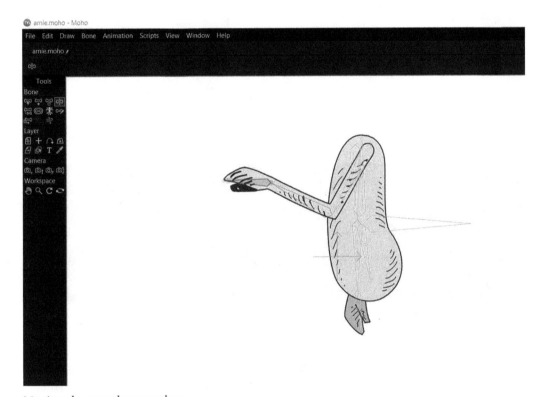

Moving the arm down and up.

Before you animate your arm however, I want to talk to you about a very important principle of animation that brings flexibility. It is called the "**successive breaking of joints**". So, if we're attempting to move the arm into a pointing position in Moho, the worst way of doing it is to set a key pose for the arm down, then a key pose to the pointing arm up, and simply in between them.

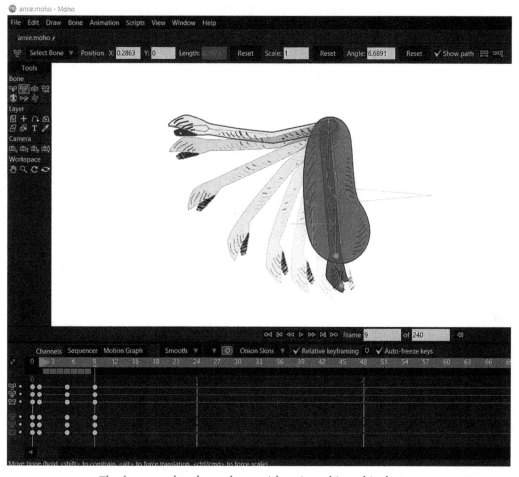

The front- and end-arm keys with onion-skinned in-betweens.

I know we see this all the time on TV animation, or on the web, but it is so unconvincing and mechanical that it needs to be addressed. Understanding the *"successive breaking of joints"* will help here.

Successive Breaking of Joints

Essentially, the *"successive breaking of joints"* principle recognizes that we do not use all of the joints in our bodies at the same time in a movement. There is a staged use that brings flexibility and believability to the action. The example I often give is a baseball pitcher. Instead of the ball being held back, then thrown forward, there is a series of movements that the pitcher goes through in order that the ball be thrown fast and accurately. Let us explore them…

Pitcher on the mount.

Step back: Note that before a pitcher throws forward, they take a step back. This is a real-life action that supports the animation notion of "**Anticipation**". Remember, if there is a main action, anticipation suggests that we first make a small action in the opposite direction to anticipate that. This makes the main action all the more dynamic. Consequently, the fact that a pitcher actually does that in a real-life throw is confirmation that the principle is correct…

Pitcher leans back.

Foot plant: Having leaned back, the pitcher then turns their head away, as part of the anticipation before the throw. This happens incredibly quickly of course.

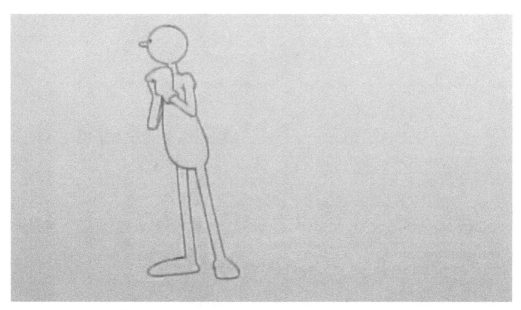

Pitcher looks away.

Transition: In preparation to the actual throw, the pitcher begins to transition to a lead foot position. He does this by bunching up his body and moving his center of gravity forward.

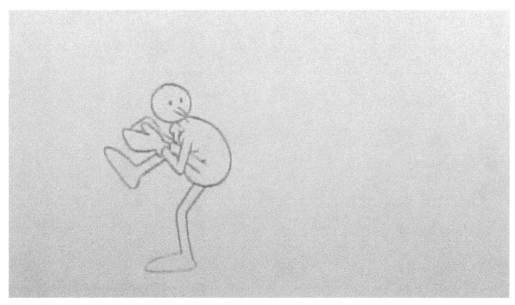

Pitcher transitions forward.

Plant front foot: Then to put down a solid foundation from which to throw from, the pitcher plants down a lead foot ahead of his body.

Pitcher plants his front foot.

Hips forward: With a solid base made with the lead foot, the body weight moves forward via the hips. Moving the hips forward in this way creates a fulcrum point for the rest of the throwing action to unfold.

Pitcher's hips forward.

Shoulder forward: After the hips, the lead shoulder moves forward over and beyond them, like an unfolding whipping action, preparing the arm to make its throw. However, the arm really doesn't do that until the shoulder is in place – a little further forward than the hips.

Pitcher's shoulder moves forward.

Elbow forward: Now we really see the "successive breaking of joints" occurring. Once the shoulder comes forward, the elbow immediately follows with the wrist still held back a little.

Pitcher's elbow forward.

Wrist forward: Next, with the elbow forward, the wrist flips forward too, in preparation for the ball release.

Pitcher's wrist forward.

Fingers release: Finally, with the wrist fully extended, the fingers whip through, catapulting the ball forward in to the throw.

Pitcher's fingers release.

Follow through: We must not forget also that with such a force being unleashed, the throwing arm and hand do not stop there. Indeed, the whip forward and through and almost – if not totally – wrap around the front of the body. The torso itself is either way over the front foot, attempting to keep its balance, or else it has overbalance with the effort, causing the pitcher to take a small step forward.

Pitcher follows through.

Recover: Finally, with balance catered for, the pitcher will begin to move their weight backward, to return to a final, standing, recovery position – watching the ball hopefully fly where it's required to go.

The pitcher recovers.

Clearly, there is more to throwing than meets the eye – unless it is an "animator's eye" which should see all these things automatically. So, with all this in mind, let's consider what could be involved in a simple "**pointing**" action...

Lean back: For an "Anticipation", you might have the shoulder move back slowly in preparation for the point.

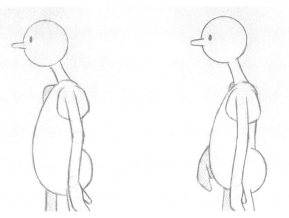

Pointing-arm shoulder moves back.

Shoulder forward: The shoulder might then move back forward as the arm begins to bend, ready for the pointing action.

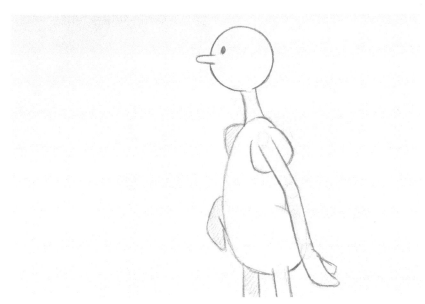

Shoulder comes forward.

Elbow forward: With the wrist and fingers still coiled, the elbow will begin to reach forward a little.

Elbow forward.

Wrist forward: Following the elbow, the wrist might follow through in preparation for the point, although the hand – and specifically the pointing finger – may well be held back a little and bent.

Wrist forward.

Finger point: Finally, as the wrist reaches its full extension, the hand will bend through carrying the unbending, pointing finger with it. The finger will be the last thing to reach a full extension.

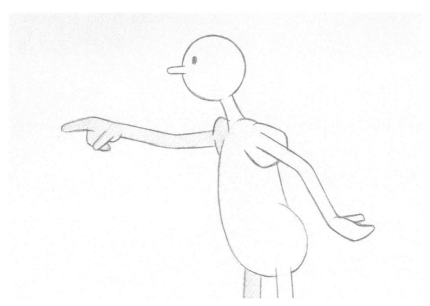

Extended finger point.

Slight recoil: It might be even more dramatic if the point goes a little beyond the position of most comfort during the pointed action, therefore settling back a little to a position that is more comforting. This will give an extra snap to the ultimate point.

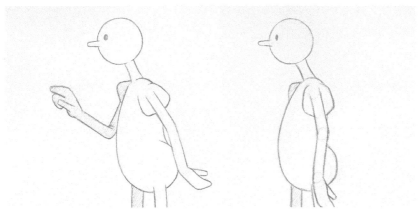

Recoil and recover.

Clearly, the point is somewhat similar to the pitcher's throw, but is not so dynamic as a sporting action. It is all very subtle and shouldn't be overplayed. However, even working minimally, this will bring much more flexibility and believability to the action – as opposed to just having starting and end positions for the arm and just in-betweening it! Therefore, consider any action you are preparing to animate and how an application of *"successive breaking of joints"* might make it more natural and therefore improve it.

Suggested Assignment

Download the simple "**Arm Rig**" and animate a sequence where the finger points. If you want to go one stage further, bring the arm back to the original down position, without simply in-betweening it. In other words, how would *"successive breaking of joints"* be applied in this situation?

Masterclass 15/ Character Walk 1

Although we talked a little about a full-biped character in the last master class, we are going to go simpler today by having a golf ball walk! It will still need you to draw on the knowledge we share in the first section of this book, but suffice it to say, this will be a little easier than having a full-biped character walk at this stage. However, before we get to any of that, we have an observational warm-up drawing to do…

Warm-Up Drawing

We're going to do something different this time. Although traditional animation is two-dimensional, in reality, you have to consider three dimensions if you're going to exploit the full potential that the principles of movement contained in this book promise. In other words, you need to be able to draw a character, consistently, from every angle. Big budget studio productions have a team of folks to create their films, and part of that production team is the "**Character Designer**". A good character designer has to be able to accurately draw their characters in all directions, in order to better inform the animation team how to best draw that character from many viewpoints. Consequently, they will create a "**Turnaround Model Sheet**" for the animators – which is an accurate analysis of a character from at least 4 distinct angles – front, right-side profile, back- and left-side profile. There is more to it than that of course, and we'll be dealing with it all in Section III. However, in terms of observational gesture drawing, it is not a bad

DOI: 10.1201/9781003324287-17

exercise to change students on this. What I did in one of my zoom classes therefore was to give students eight views of my head and shoulders and ask them to draw me from all those angles on one sheet of paper. It was a challenging assignment, but they all benefitted a great deal from it. So, here, I am just going to give you the four main views of that session and ask you to do the same in one page of your sketchbook. These are the four views…

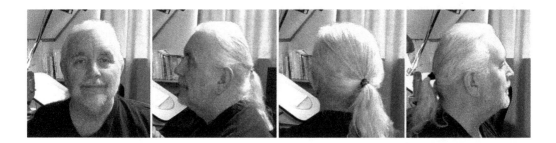

So, I want you to give yourself just **2 minutes** to draw **each viewpoint**. The crucial thing here – as always on observation gesture drawing – is not to create a photographic likeness. Instead, we are looking at consistent **volumes, structures,** and **proportions** of everything, from viewpoint to viewpoint. This means that you should attempt to make sure that on each of your drawings, the head remains the same size, the location of the features is consistent and you get a sense of recording all the important features to make that so. Construction lines are fine, as are projection lines from the first view all the way across for the other three views. That is how *"Turnaround Model Sheets"* are done, so you are following a precedent.

Instruction

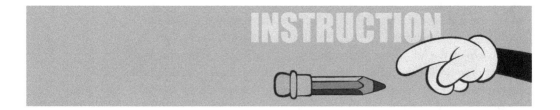

In this lesson, we're going to do a "**Golf Ball Walk**", and I'm going to break it down into four sections. But first, let's cover an overview of what this assignment is. This is what our rig and our background to the animation looks like…

Golf ball rig.

Hopefully, as we work through this, Moho will make a little more sense to you. For this reason – and tied into my approach of not giving you too much to think about each time – I've left the arms off the ball, just adding the legs only. There will be a trick later, when we have our ball jumping into the hole after walking up to it. However, we'll pass on that for the time being.

Immediately, let me just go over a few Moho things before we start. They will be important for you to know. Key things that I probably have said before now are that the left button on your mouse allows you to select and move highlighted objects and bones around on the stage, whereas the wheel in the middle of our mouse allows you to zoom in and out. The right mouse click and hold down allows you to grab the entire image on the stage and move it around.

And while we're on *"zoom in and out"*, you'll notice if you go really close in on any Moho object, there will be no breakup of the edges – as Moho is a "**Vector**" program and objects created in it will remain sharp, large or small.

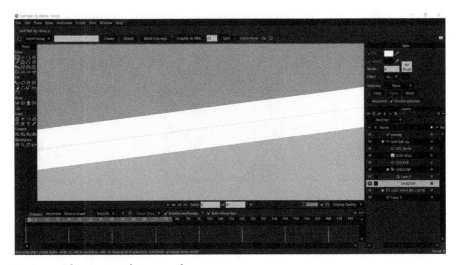

Vector wide view and vector close-up.

If your software is a "**Bitmap**" program however – like the otherwise wonderful "**TV Paint**" from France – you will notice the pixels that make up the images will break up or get fuzzy if you move in too far. The simple rule of thumb other than this is that a vector program is fast and contains low file sizes in general, whereas a bitmap program like *"TV Paint"* offers an infinite opportunity to traditional art techniques and textures – like **pencil grain**, **charcoal**, **watercolor paint**, **oil paint**, etc. – making it a much more creative proposition for the more *"artistic"* animator. Pixel and bitmap programs are great for what they do, and you just have to be smart when you choose to use them for a particular job.

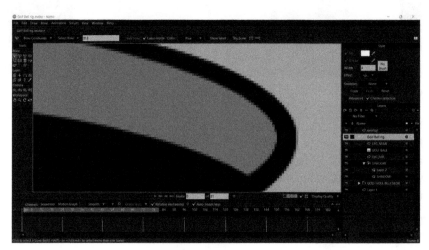

Difference between vector and bitmap in close-up.

The only real new Moho controls you're going to need to know for this particular lesson are some specific animation tools. So, if you look to the top left of the Moho interface, you will see the "**Tools**" menu window. Here, when you are in animation mode, you will need to use the "**Bone Manipulation**" tool *(Control/Command / "Z")*.

The other is the "**Transformation**" tool *(Control/Command / "T")*, which allows you to distort or change the bone lengths in the rig.

Close-up of Bone Manipulation tool.

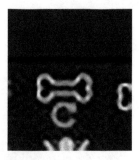

Close-up of Transformation tool.

And apart from reminding you of the "Stage", "Time line" and "Layers" aspects of the interface, we've already discussed, that this all your essentially need to know for this exercise. Remember also, you will not get the animation tools' buttons to show, unless this *"Bone"* layer is selected and highlighted.

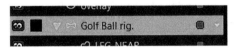

Highlighted bone layer.

And remember too, the *"Bones"* are the part of the rig that enables you to move its various parts. A bone appears **RED** when it is highlighted. Here we see the *"upper leg"*, *"lower leg"* and *"foot"*…

Highlighted bone on rig.

"Control/Command/Z" will undo what you previously did – and multiple uses of that can take you back a long, long way in Moho if you need to. So, let's look at a pose text sequence of the action we're going to animate. This **"Action Guide"** view is not the actual Moho action we're going to be doing, but instead it's a drawn background field guide that will block out our proposed action for you. You can download the full *"Golf Ball Rig"* file and the *"Action Guide"* file from the dedicated website.

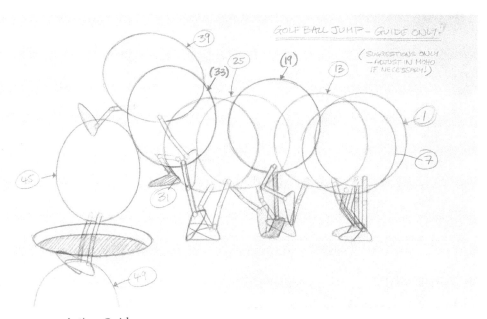

Action Guide.

TIP

As we're dealing with a 2D world here, not a 3D world, I want to show you a little tip for an illusion I set up for more easily getting the ball into the hole. It's something I used a lot in my old, traditional animation days as a background artist. Now, if the hole were part of the background art, as it appears here, we would have big problems matching the edge of the ball as it disappeared behind the near edge. This could really have slowed us down. However, the little trick I used was to have the grass in front of the hole, in addition to the near edge of the hole on a separate layer that is positioned above the animation layer.

Showing grass patch over the golf hole background.

*This means that I simply need to animate the ball dropping into the hole and down off the edge of the screen without matching anything, whereas the matching "**over-lay**" of the top level grass and near edge entirely covers the ball as it descends, giving the illusion that the ball is dropping into the hole! This is entirely digital "sleight of hand" but saves so much time and effort if you can plan things like this to help you.*

The golf ball drops behind the grass overlay patch, as if going into the hole.

Anyway, knowing all this, you're at last ready to go with "**Stage 1**" of the animation. This means that we're just going to complete part of this exercise in this lesson, and then reserve the second part for the next lesson, once you've mastered this part. Now, you'll see that the instruction for all this will appear quite long in terms of explanation, but the actual execution of it is quite quick as you do it. So don't be put off by the length of this chapter. Anyway, it's time to show you how to do this first part...

Now, having opened a "New" scene in Moho, I want you to go to "**File/Open**" to select the file "**GOLF BALL ANIMATION MASTER.moho**" I have provided for you. Your Moho interface should now look like this…

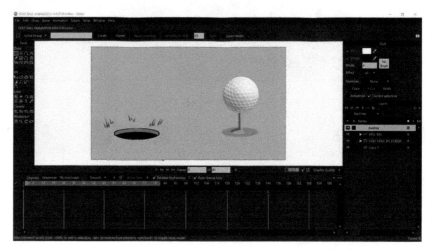

The opening frame.

As you'll see, there's nothing actually happening right now. It is just the golf ball rig, standing in its first position. If you scrub along the time line therefore, nothing will be moving, because we have not animated anything yet. If you go to frame "**0**" however, you'll see that the rig looks somewhat exploded.

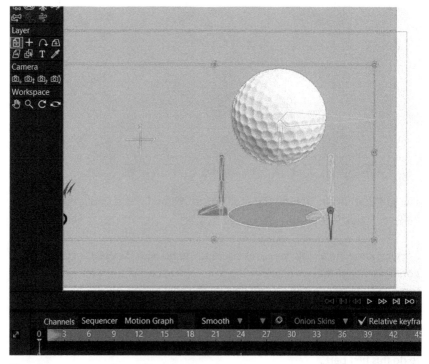

The rig as seen on frame 0.

That's fine here as it shows how it's put together. However, when we move to frame "1", it looks different and will be even more so when you move everything into place.

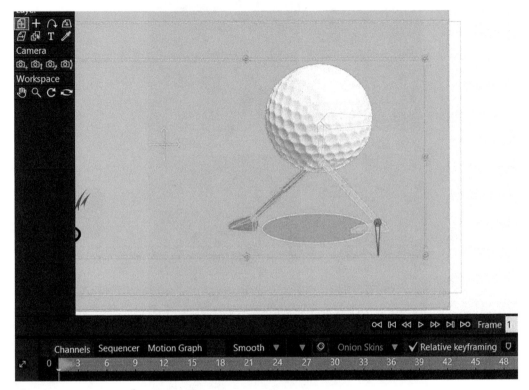

The rig now seen on frame 1.

Anyway, go to the "**Layers**" column to the right and select the bottom layer, "**Layer 1**". It should highlight in yellow...

Layer 1 highlighted in layers column.

Now, go to "**File/Import/Tracing Image**" and select "**ACTION GUIDE.jpg**" from the files I've provided for you, then hit "**Open**". After that, you should now see that a transparent-looking version of the Action Guide is displayed on the Stage...

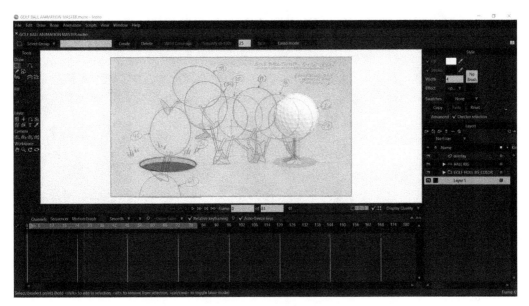

The Action Guide appearing in the background of the Stage.

You should find that *"frame 1"* indicated on the Action Guide drawing should pretty much line up with "frame 1" of the Gold Ball animation pose. If it's not absolutely perfect, but very close, that's fine. It is only a drawn guide to give you approximate positions. If it's not close at all, then you'll have to move the golf ball to that position on "frame 1" of the time line. But, the files are set up so they should match closely, so I doubt you'll need to do that.

Note too on the Action Guide that all your suggested keys are drawn in for you. Actually, there are both *"keys"* and *"breakdowns"* indicated – "**1**", "**7**", "**13**", "**19**", "**25**", "**33**", "**39**", "**45**", and "**49**". Again, they may not be accurate to the final animation you'll create in position or timing, but they will be good starting points for now.

Also at this stage, make sure you "**Save**" your file after doing this as you don't want to lose it later if something goes wrong or your computer crashes for one reason or another. (And do remember the advice I gave you earlier – always save a new version of your file, every time you successfully complete a new procedure. In emergencies, you'll always be able to go back to the previous version and just have to re-do the last thing you did only! If you don't do that, you could get into a long sequence of animating, only to find you have to do it all again if something goes wrong – which is likely to do with software and computers, trust me – and you lose your current working file.) In saving it therefore, you might start out by calling it "**Animation 01**" for example, and save it into the same folder you're currently working in. Then, every time you do save it after that, you simply add a number at the end – such as "**Animation 02**" and "**Animation 03**". If you look to the top left of your interface, you'll see that your file is indicated as being "**ANIMATION 01.moho**". (**Note**: *You'll probably see another titled file next to it – "**Untitled.moho**". That is the original file that set up when you opened Moho. It is safe to click that one off if you want, as you'll never use it.*)

OK, to be able to animate this rig you need to go to the right-hand *"Layers"* column and select the **"Bone/BALL"** layer to activate the appropriate tools…

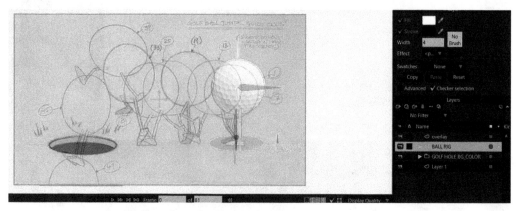

The "Ball" selected in layers level.

Next, go down to the time line and move the vertical cursor to **"frame 1"**. Remember, you can tell what frame your cursor is on by the **first of the two white boxes** beneath the stage…

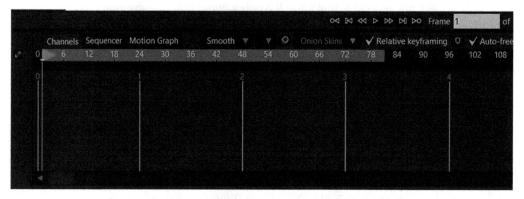

The time line cursor set at frame 1.

Then, with either your **"Manipulate Bone"** tool (Control/Command Z) or your **"Transform Bone"** tool (Control/Command T)…

Close-up of animation tools.

…you work on the next stage. And that next stage is to simple click on the ball – which will then show on frame 1 of the time line that small white dots have appeared, which is an indication that our first "**Key**" has been created. This is a great moment to hit "**Control/Command S**" to save it, as a precaution.)

Now, we're going to create our second key position, "**Key 7**". So, scrub (move the cursor along) the time line to "**frame 7**". Hit "**Control/Command Z**" and click on the "master bone" on the ball…

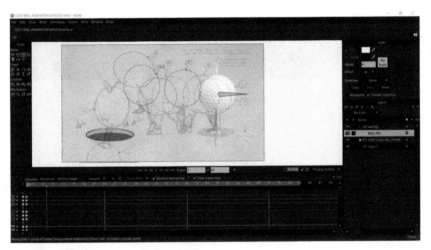

Highlighting the master bone on frame 7.

…and move the ball to match as close as you can the red "**7**" sketch on the *Action Guide*. (**Note**: *The feet won't move at this point – unless you choose to move them – as they have "**Root Bones**" attached to them. This means that they won't move, whatever you have done to the character.*) When you've done this, you'll see that the rig pretty much matches the guide and a new key will be established in the time line…

Final key on frame 7.

If you scrub the cursor on the time line backward and forward, you'll now see the ball and the legs moving. If all is good, move the time line cursor to frame "**13**", so we can create our next key. That done, with *"Control/Command Z"* selected, move the ball to the *"13"* guide position. Now, this time you'll see the legs are stretching weirdly. But that's OK as we're going to fix that next. The important thing is to get the ball positioned as close as you can to the 13 position on the guide. With that done, look to the time line and note that yet another key has been created…

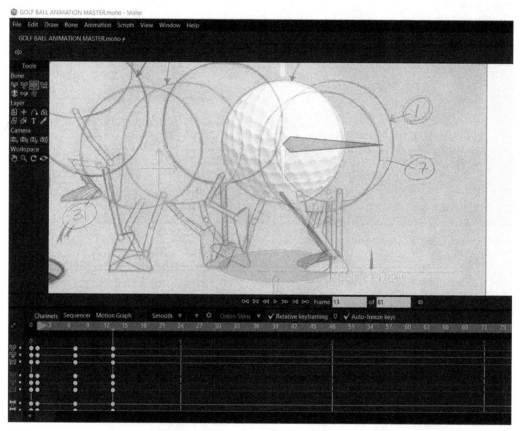

Key 13 – adjustment 1.

Remember that what we're doing is very much like moving a stringed puppet – with the bones being our strings to do that. This is good to know as now we need to move the leg foot forward into the position it's shown in on the guide drawing. So, click on the **far "root bone"** and lift it forward into the positions seen on the guide. Again, get it positioned as close as you can – especially the heel. Now, you'll immediately see that the toe is much lower than the toe of the drawing, so now select that foot bone and bend it up to as close to the same angle on the drawing as you can. (And again, don't worry if you can't precisely match the drawing. The drawing is merely an estimated guide, so get as close as you can.)

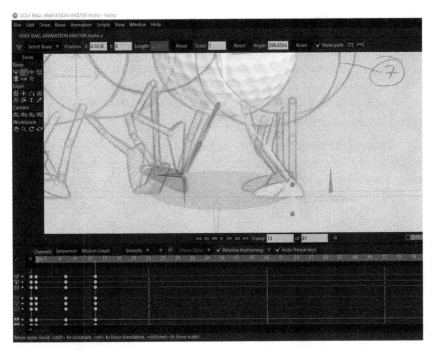

Key 13 – adjustment 2.

Now, the only thing that you'll notice at this point is that the back foot is on the ground, whereas on the guide drawing it's bent with the heel up. This gives us an ideal *"key 13"* position…

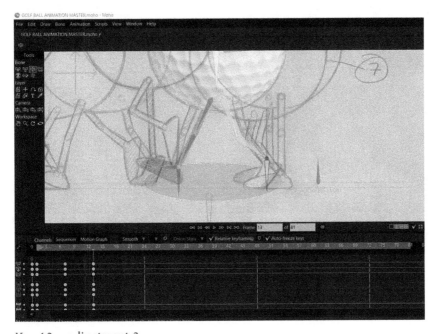

Key 13 – adjustment 3.

If you now scrub between all the 3 keys on the time line, you'll get to see the action building up too. If you want to see that action even clearer, go over to the *"Layer 1"* tab on the right, click on the eyeballs symbol to its left and the sketch will disappear, making the rig so much more visible. *(Shortcut "Control/Command U" will do this too of course.)* When you scrub this and are satisfied that all is fine, click the guide sketch back on and we'll continue. But first, hit *"Control/Command S"* to save what we've done, just in case!

So now we want to create key "**19**". To do that, move the time line cursor to *"frame 19"* and hit "**Control/Command Z**" to move the body to match the ball pencil guide position. Again, the contact leg will do weird stretchy things with the toe up. But that's OK; we'll fix it immediately.

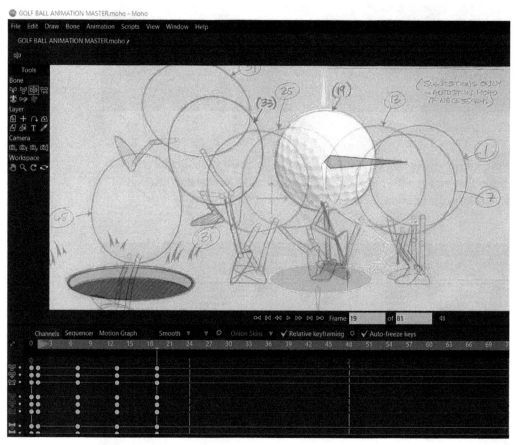

Key 19 – adjustment 1.

To fix the contact leg/foot issue, all you need to do is select the *"foot bone"* and move it down, so that the toe touches the ground. You'll notice that it still doesn't match the drawn toe position on 19, so select the "root bone" and slide the toe along the ground until it does match it.

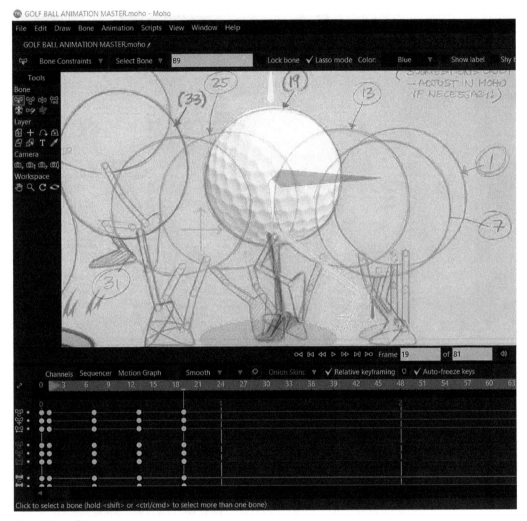

Key 19 – adjustment 2.

Finally, we need to move the back leg through to the "**number 4/passing position**" as indicated on the drawing. So, select the *"root bone"* for the back foot, lift it up, and forward and get it as close to the position of the passing leg on drawing 19 as you can…

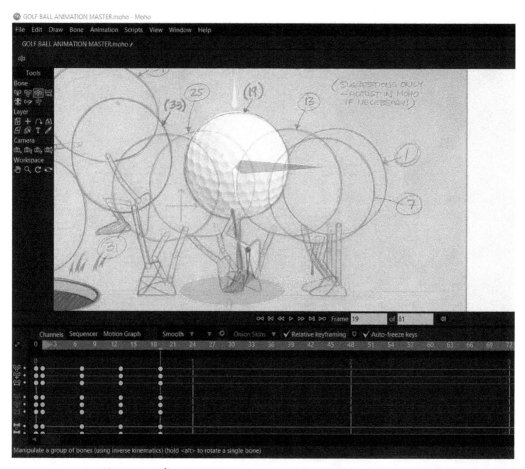

Key 19 – adjustment 3.

You have now successfully created your next key position. *(Although it is a "passing position" in reality, but it helps to call it a key here, while we're setting up the action.)* Scrub to test, and then save!

Now, having explained the process of creating keys for the previous four positions, I'm going to leave you to create the next two key positions – "**25**" and "**31**" – on your own. You simply follow the same process we've used so far and all will be fine.

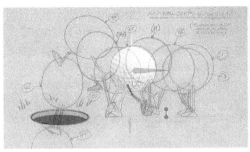

Key positions, 25 and 31.

The next key position we're going to is "**33**". Now, you'll notice that on this key position – and the next *"39"* position – I have indicated the ball going through a *"Squash"* & *"Stretch"* deformation. But, whereas I would do this kind of thing traditionally, for now we won't do it for our ball. So just make sure the ball, when you move it, is pretty much in the center of both *"Squash"* & *"Stretch"* positions. This is what *"33"* will look like…

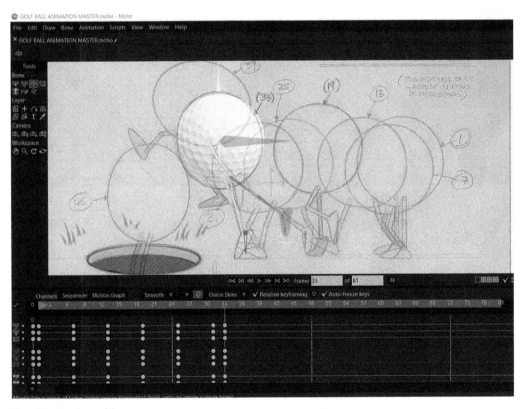

Key 33, start position.

So with that in mind, select the body bone and move the ball into the center of the *"stretch"* shape. You'll see that the leg stretches extremely long and the foot is remaining flat on the ground. So, as we did before, bend down the foot of the contact leg so that the toe is beneath the groundline, then move the *"root bone"* up until the toe of the contact leg matches the position of the toe on the drawn version. Then, grab the root bone of the free leg and move it up to match the drawn free leg position as best as possible, moving the foot angle with the free *"foot bone"* once you've done that…

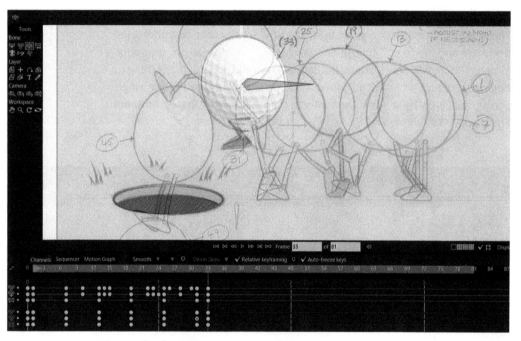

Key 33, final position.

Scrub to test, then "**Save**" of OK.

So, let's now move the cursor on the time line to "**39**" and create a key there. Again, select the ball and move it up into the center of the drawn *"squash"* position. You'll see the contact leg stretches more than ever and eventually follows the ball up. However, as it has just pushed off the ground, we want to give it a sense of effort, so we're going to bend it up and back a little, with the toe pointed abruptly downward. Then, selecting the free/far foot, lift it up by the "root bone" and move it into the drawn position, indicating a dynamic position, somewhat similar to the push-off position of an animated run. *(Note that it might now be possible to match the legs precisely with the drawing here, especially with the lead leg, but get it as close as you can.)* As long as it reflects the feel of the drawn version, all will be good…

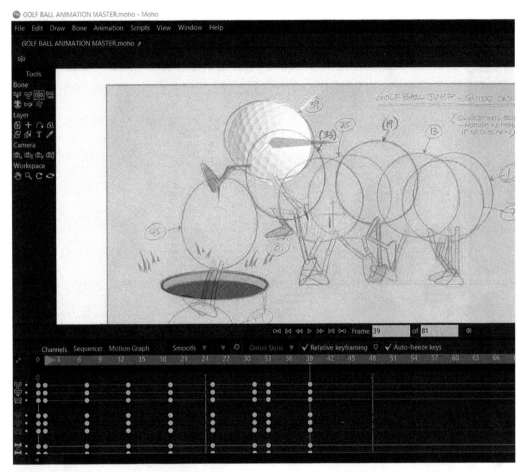

Final 39 key.

Scrub to test, then "**Save**" of OK.

Now, we just have two more key positions to do – "**45**" and "**49**". We pretty much follow the same process for both of them – starting by moving the ball and then adjusting the legs to match the drawn guide. However, you'll find that as you move the ball downward this time, it will cause the legs to scrunch up under the body, as both "root bones" are trying to keep the feet locked into the same positions of the previous key. So it might help if you half move the ball down first, then pull the feet down as far as you can toward where they need to be, then bring the ball down to reach its final drawing position, adjusting the feet afterward. This is what that two-stage process might look like for key "45"…

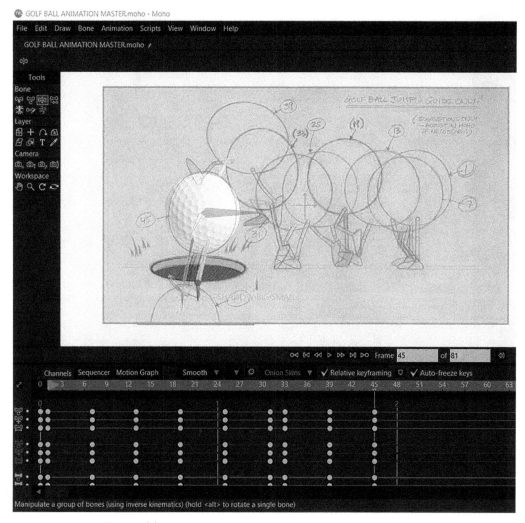

Key position, 45.

Scrub to test, then "**Save**" of OK.

And this is what it might look like for key *"49"*…

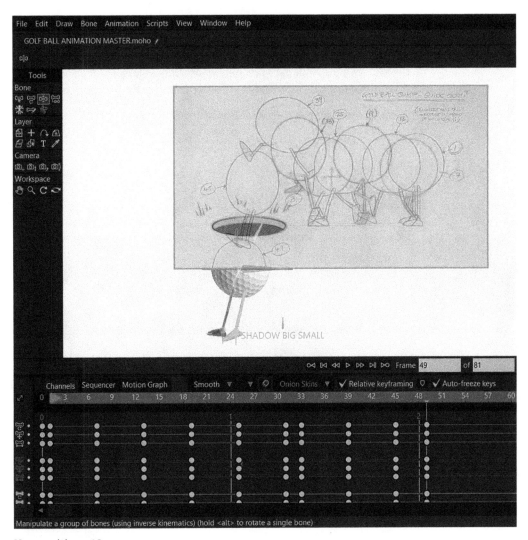

Key position, 49.

Scrub to test, then "**Save**" of OK.

OK, so that essentially gives us all our key positions, and if you "*scrub*" the action, it will be very much in the ballpark of where we want to be. Now if we didn't have the hole's "*grass/edge*" overlay in front of the rig, we would have to add another key off the bottom of the stage – so that it looks like the ball is dropping out of the screen if it wasn't meant to drop into a hole. But that "*overlay*" hides the ball from our sight, once it drops behind, so we don't have to worry about it.

Finally, let's hit "**Control/Command U**" to remove the sketch guide, then hit the "**Play**" button to see the action uncluttered. Make sure however that before you do that, the second white box under the stage is set to a number larger than "*49*", which is our last key. I defaulted that end number at "*50*", so all should be OK. But, if it has changed for any reason, you need to make sure that it's anywhere higher than the number of the last key, "*49*".

Now when it's playing, it's not going to show the smoothest or most fluid of actions. That's because Moho is doing logical in-betweens, linking all the keys. We rarely want that to happen, so we need to get in there and make modifications on the in-betweens. And that's precisely what our next lesson will be about. Congratulations, you've just created your first scene of character action in Moho!

And don't forget to "**Save**" before you shut down Moho ahead of the next lesson.

Suggested Assignment

I think in this case the above assignment is all you need to do for now. So, focus on it and complete it as far as is indicated, as it will give you a very strong foundation upon which you can build the next lesson.

Masterclass 16/ Character Walk 2

Having blocked-in our foundational action on the golf ball walk, we can now look at "polishing" it. Polishing our action is where we take over from Moho and don't let it do what it wants to do, at least in terms of in-betweening. However, before we get to that, let's do another warm-up, observational gesture drawing session.

Warm-Up Drawing

We're going back to our normal pattern of timed drawing poses right now. This time we're looking at the principles of "**Jumping**". I want you to do this hear as in the next class we're actually going to do an exercise in Moho on jumping, and I want you to be ready to think about the action ahead of time.

When animating characters' jumping, it is important to remember the original *"Bouncing Ball"* principles were learned before. Specifically, I am talking about *"Squash"*, *"Stretch"* and *"Slow-ins"/"Slow-outs"*. Here, we're going to add one more into the mix… *"Anticipation"*.

What follows however are 4 major poses to consider when animating any jump. The four we must consider are (i) the "**Start**" position, (ii) the "**Squash**" *(also judged as the "**Anticipation**")* position, (iii) the *"Apex"* position and (iv) the "**Landing**" or "**Cushion**" position. You could also add to that list a fifth position if you like – (v) the "**Resolve**" position. *(Which is effectively the 1st position again.)*

DOI: 10.1201/9781003324287-18

This timed, observation drawing exercise will focus entirely on the five key positions below. As these poses are in silhouette, you should give yourself some license in terms of clothing details, etc. Indeed, you could even exercise your imagination here but creating your own character for the positions. Limit yourself to just **2 minutes** for each pose...

Pose 1 comments: As you can see, this *"Start"* position has our skateboarder pretty much in an upright, balanced pose. Apart from his turned head, he is pretty much symmetrical overall, with his center of gravity pretty much centered between his feet. He is leaning forward a little, with knees somewhat bent, to help him cushion himself against the bumps in the road. Finally, note that he is on tiptoes at the same time, for the same reason. So your drawing should reflect this.

Pose 2 comments: So, now having established the skateboarder's starting position, we are not going into the jump preparation stage. It is called the "Cushion" or "Anticipation" position. *(Remember, the principle of an "anticipation" position is that before a major action happens, there is a smaller action added in the opposite direction first – in this case, a "down" before the "up".)* So, essentially, he is squatting down, ready to jump – a bit like winding a spring up before unleashing a mechanical device. Notice that he's still pretty much centrally balanced between his feet here – although the arms and legs are bent much more than before. He is also not so much up on his toes at this point.

Pose 3 comments: Here, the skateboarder is stretching up on his ascent. The body is opening up, but the back (driving) leg is delaying, so that the push can be down for as long as possible.

Pose 4 comments: Here, the skateboarder is in the *"apex"* position. He is fully up in the air. His body mass is at its highest position, and he is momentarily detached from board he is on. His arms are up, to assist the upward motion of his body, and his legs are coming up toward his body, with his torso somewhat upright. The feet are momentarily transitioning in the air. Notice too that his head is bent forward, so he can see more clearly where the board is beneath his feet.

Pose 5 comments: Notice now that he's down, with his feet reaching out for the board and the ground. His body is beginning to open up straighter again as he prepares for contact with the ground and the inevitable cushion action it will need when it gets there. He is not so symmetrical here however, with his left shoulder higher and rotated forward, whereas the other arm and shoulder is extended downward and back.

So, let's always remember that jumping is a very dynamic action – whether from two legs or one. We need to generate a great deal of energy, to push our body mass up against the forces of gravity. Consequently, a great number of balances are employed in a jump, in addition to a strong *"anticipation"* or *"squash"* first. It helps to imagine the legs of a jump are like springs and the anticipation/squash action is we, winding up those springs – that is, adding tension to them – before releasing them. Now in old-fashioned *"cartoon"* films, the characters did literally squash like rubber. However, today, with more anatomically rigged characters (in both 2D and 3D), we rarely squash them in a rubbery way. Instead, we use the anatomy – i.e., the extreme bending and extending of limbs, joints, etc., in a solid and realistic way – to achieve the same effect. And whether it's *"cartoon"* or not, when the character jumps up, there will be a deceleration toward the apex and an acceleration from the apex – *"slowing-in"* & *"slowing-out"* – due to the force of gravity. The power of a jump can be emphasized more if the legs are extended on the push-up, with the toes contacting the ground for as long as possible, despite the height the body is making. Also, in coming down, the character needs to extend their legs as far as possible, so their toes can contact the ground and act as stabilizers, before the body weight follows – putting pressure on the legs, which must bend to cushion that weights.

Hopefully, you can put all this into practice in the next Moho exercise, after this current walking one is complete – which we will attempt to do now.

Instruction

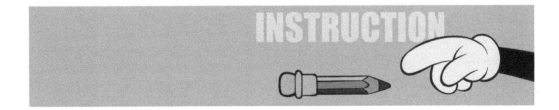

In this lesson, we're going to continue with the *"Golf Ball Walk"*. We have hopefully blocked out all the key positions in Moho now and have the rudiments of a walking action. However, to make it really convincing, we now need to "**polish**" the action. Polishing is a major part of an animator's process as hardly anything we create from the get-go is either right or perfect. Polishing hopefully allows that to occur. There are a million options on what might constitute polishing and every animator will have their own idea of what that means for them. However, if I give you an insight into how I would approach it with this walk, you'll have an inkling of what is required. Now, polishing to a professional level on a major production could have many stages to it. But, for here and now, let us work through just one polish, to see how the process works.

Now, as we're really doing something new to what we did before, I suggest that the first that you do, here and now, is to save your scene with a new title. So, hit "**Save as**" and rename your scene "**Animation 02**". That means if anything goes wrong with the one, then you still have the previous one to fall back on if necessary.

"Polishing" is all about finessing, or making better, what we already have. So, the first thing to look at is the foot on the far leg as it completes its first stride. It is rotating around a center point in the foot, rather than it feeling that foot is solidly on the ground. This is happening at the end of the next stride too, and beyond. So we need to do that. Also, the *"up & down"* movement on the ball as it moves is OK, but is still somewhat "**floaty**". *(Meaning that it has no snap or weight to it.)* That too needs to be fixed. I think the ball needs a bigger, sharper "anticipation" before it jumps up and down into the hole too. I'm sure also that there are a couple of more things you might find about yours as you work through it.

Start this *"polishing"* process by **scrubbing** the cursor slowly along the timeline. This will give you a much better appreciation of what's happening (or not happening) than playing the action at full speed. And doing this on the file I'm working with shows that, as the ball dips down in "anticipation" before the first stride, the near foot is slightly rotating down, so that the toe goes beneath the groundline.

TIP

You are about to embark in a whole series of small modifications to your existing walk and jump action. It is my **STRONG RECOMMENDATION** *that every time you satisfactorily do a new change, you immediately* **SAVE THE FILE WITH A NEW NAME EACH TIME** *– so as not to lose all your work if you make a mistake later and don't have a previous version to fall back on. So, as you're on file name "Animation 02", I would just change the numbering each time to "Animation 03", "Animation 04", "Animation 05", etc.*

NOTE

With the new and more advance rig file that will be released after the publication of this book, you don't encounter this problem. So, there should be no need to rotate or adjust the toes.

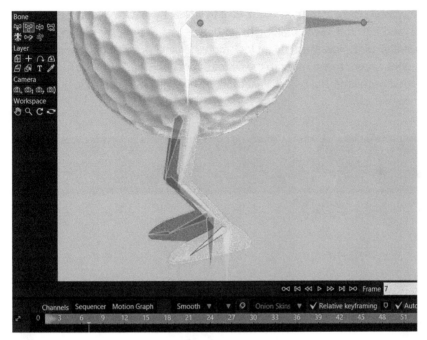

Bad foot position.

This is an easy fix. Place the cursor on key frame "7" on the timeline and using "Control/Command T", select the bone in the near foot and adjust the toe upward so it matched the position of key frame "1". Now if you scrub between them, the foot should stay in place and no longer dip down.

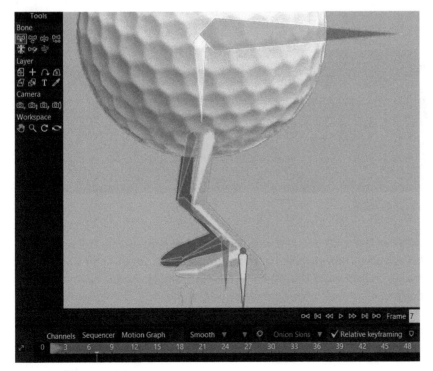

Corrected foot position.

Now, while we're at this, we might want to look at the back foot between keys "7" and "13". With Moho running the in-between show here, the foot moves in a straight line. However, it might look more elegant if we lift it upward on arc as it goes. So, on "frame 10", grab the far foot "root bone" and push the toe on the foot down a little. Now, scrub again and see how it looks. It should look a little more natural.

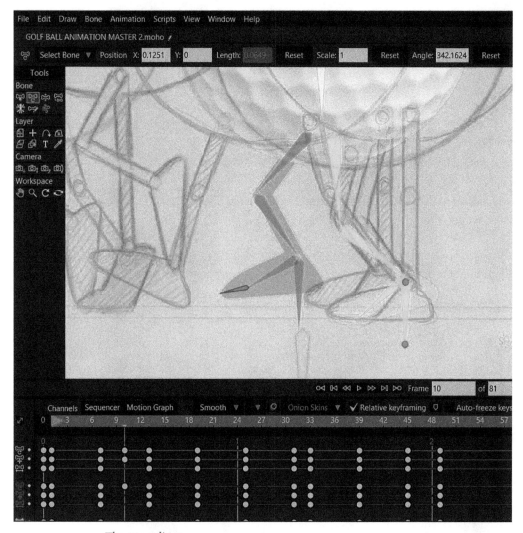

The toe adjust.

With that first stride polished, we can now deal with the rocking foot on the far leg as it plants down in preparation to the next stride. So, select the frame after the key stride position (13) – "14" – and select the foot bone and rotate the toe down so that it matches the toe on the next key position, "25". If you do that correctly and scrub the action from key to key, you should see the foot looking solid on the ground now, and not rocking as before.

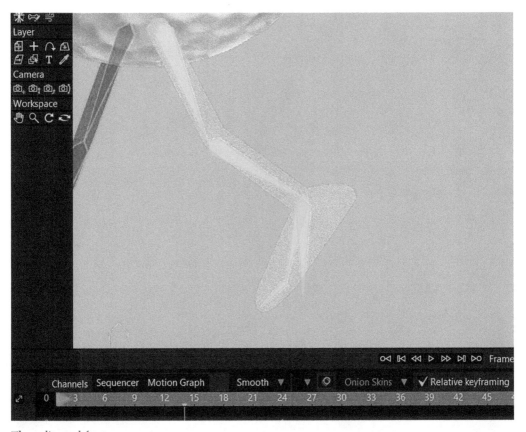

The adjusted foot.

However, you'll notice that on key "25" that far leg is pushing off the toe more dynamically. So, as Moho will have in-betweened the foot from "14" to "25", it will still do a kind of rotating action. We don't want that, especially on passing position "15". So, with "15" selected on the timeline, adjust the far foot to be flat on the ground. Now, you may need to juggle around your key positions around a bit here, but the big thing to achieve is that the foot remains flat on the ground from "14" to "19" and then rotates up onto the toe on key frame "25". The toe in every case should be in an identical position and not be sliding around in any way. You might also experiment a little more here also, by keeping the foot flat down up to and including frame "22" also, which will give the rotation up onto the toe on "25" even crisper. If you can achieve any, or all of this, then it will definitely look a lot better than before.

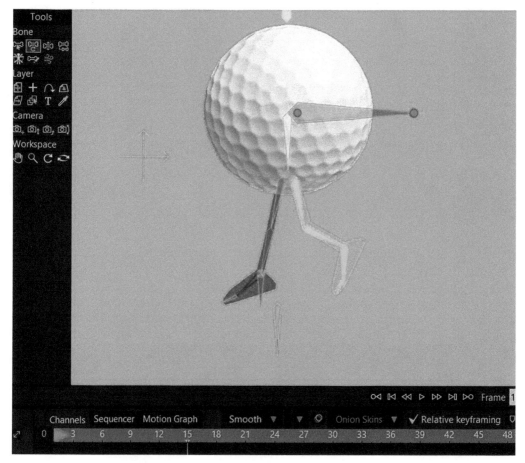

Be sure to experiment with the foot positions here, until you get something you feel works best.

In doing this much so far, you will hopefully begin to get an idea of what *"polishing"* is all about, and how it's done? So, let's continue.

You'll notice that when we make the next key stride positions – frame "33" – the back foot from "25" is just Moho in-betweening to its position on "33". So, like the back leg on a walk pushing off immediately after a key stride position, we want to delay it and keep it's toe down on the ground for as long as possible. So, on frame "28" force that back leg back, keeping the toe in the same position as it is on "25". Then, beyond frame 28, keep the foot back a little more in the air, pointing away from itself, before coming forward. This will all give it a much stronger pushing-off feel.

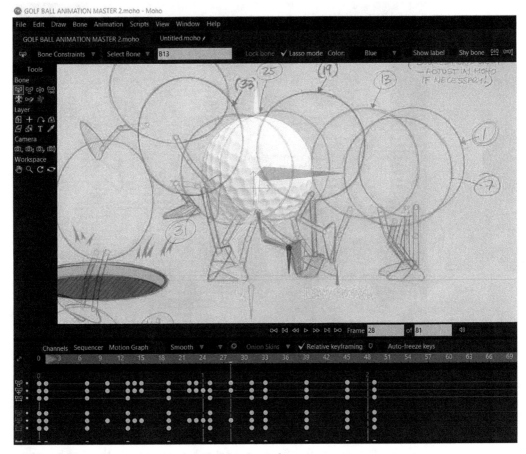

The back leg position on 28, extended backward.

Now, let's look at the lead (near) foot, to see what that's doing when it too hits the ground. Again, like the previous (far) lead foot, it is rotating round to key position "33", which we also don't want. So, on the frame after it hits the ground – frame "26" – flatten the foot so that it remains flat on the ground, through frame "33". This will also look more solid. Now again, you may have to juggle your key positions around a little here to keep everything fixed and consistent. But, the ultimate objective is to keep the toe position fixed in the same location – "25" through "33" – with the entire foot flat on the ground from frame "26" onward. Again, you might want to keep the foot flat on the ground until at least frame "30", after which it can do a final rotation around the toe on key position "33".

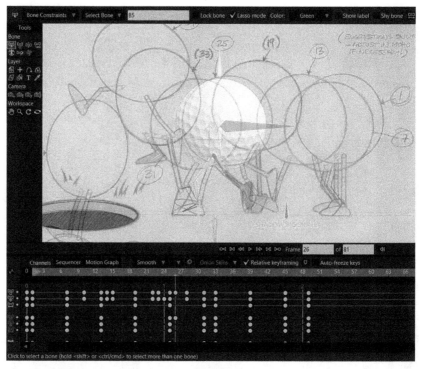

The front foot, flat on the ground through frames 25–33.

Now, beyond 33, it is jumping into the air. This all feels a little soft and weightless to me. So, the options we have here are making a much bigger squash position on frame "25" – pulling the ball down and bending the knees much more there – and speeding up the takeoff action, slowing-in much more to the apex key position on frame "39". This you can do using the "motion graph" option we used before on the bouncing ball exercise. The object of this exercise is for the ball to have a bigger anticipation down before taking off, and then to make the takeoff fast but slowing-in much more at the apex of the jump.

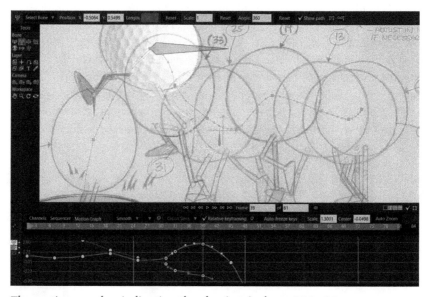

The motion graph – indicating the slowing-in from 33 to 39.

Another thing you can do to make the take of more dynamic is to move the far leg much faster up to a dynamic, leading, bent knee position, and have it there much sooner. Like this…

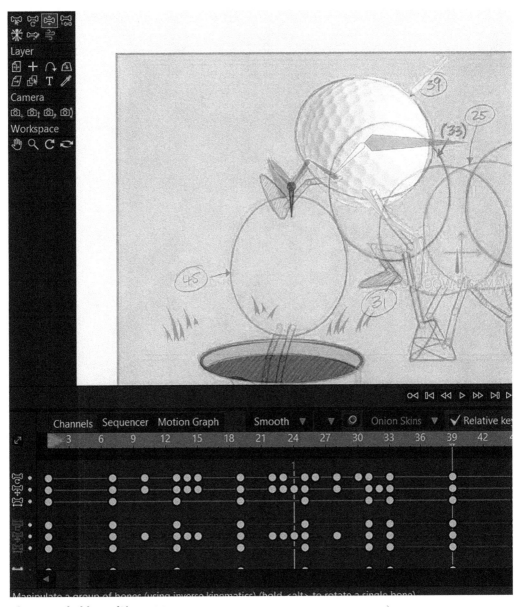

The extended knee lift on 39.

You might also delay the takeoff leg longer after the push off, as we did with the previous stride. The object here being that we want it to feel like it's really pushing off the ground for the takeoff – hence keeping the toe down in its original position as long as possible.

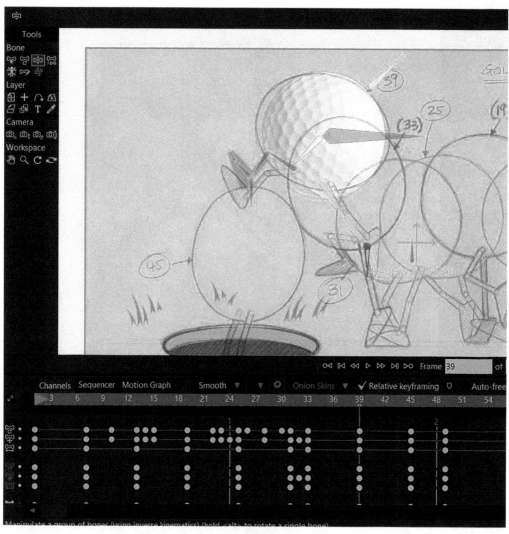

Extending toe down and straightening back leg on push off.

On the downward path from key frames "39" to "45", we can use the motion graph tool to have the ball hovering longer from the apex position, accelerating down to the "45" position. This will again help the sense of weight and gravity we need.

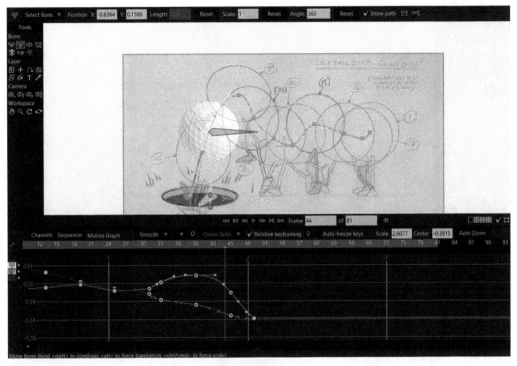

The motion graph – slowing out from 39 to 45.

Another thing to consider is working the jump-up and jump-down in-betweens on arcs, rather than the straight direction that Moho makes them take from "33", to "39", to "45". This will have a more natural flow to it, although you might have to manipulate almost every frame to make it really fluid.

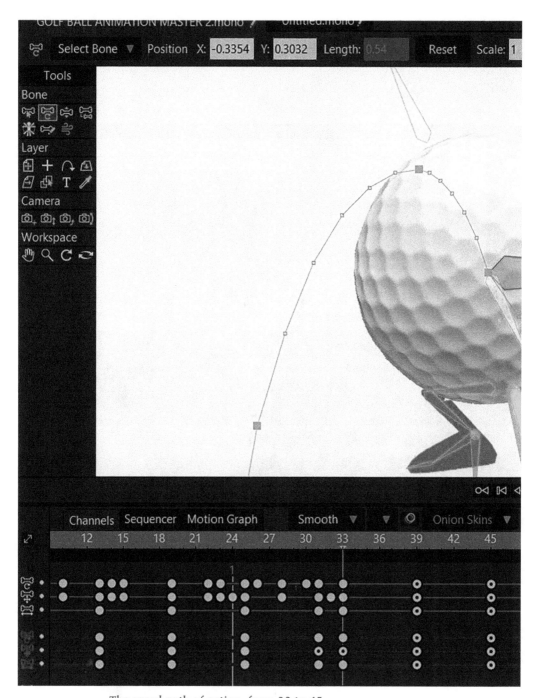

The arced path of action, from 33 to 45.

The final thing to consider in this "first-pass polish" exercise is to maybe have the legs circle more in their off-the-ground action. This will make them much more convincing than the straight in-betweens that Moho automatically wishes to impose on them. Again, it might be a frame-by-frame, trial-and-error way of doing it. But, if you follow this guide, I think you will be pleased with the result…

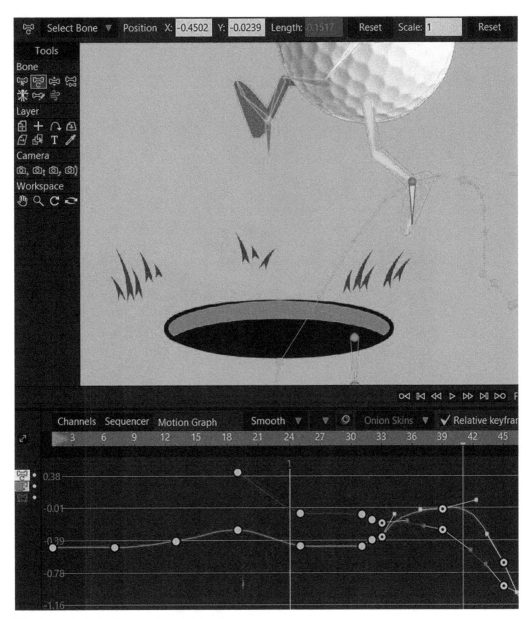

The legs circle in the air, from 33 to 45.

Anyway, these few polishing tips will give you an insight into the process. As beginners, it will be hard for you to know what to look for. But, these suggestions will get you started. There is so much more we can do with this scene, but for now, this will be enough to go on with I'm sure. Remember, animation is all about timing, so even moving keys to have more or less in-betweens is an option too. To do that, you simply "**right click/drag**" the cursor over all the white dots on a key frame – turning them red – then dragging them in one direction of other to increase or decrease the in-betweens. Just don't drag over existing key frames; otherwise, your animation will go crazy. Again, this is something to practice, using trial-and-error, do don't forget to **SAVE A NEW VERSION** of your existing file, as I'm sure things will go wrong if you're doing it for the first time!

Suggested Assignment

I think you will have enough on your plate just working through all this for yourself. So, I don't have any additional assignment suggestions for you here – other than encourage you to do lots of polishing and re-timing experiments with differently saved files. Ultimately, we all learn best through failure, then perseverance, then finally getting it right. That process is called "experience" – as it is through experience that you will actually learn the most!

Masterclass 17/ "Arnie" Generic Walk

Hopefully, you found the previous assignment not too challenging to do? In this lesson, we are on familiar *"Bouncing Ball"* territory – well, not exactly a *"Bouncing Ball"* in itself, but close. It is our Apple character, which is this time jumping using the same principles. But first, let's look at our observational gesture drawing warm-up challenge…

Warm-Up Drawing

Everyone walks, but everyone takes it for granted just how they walk. Essentially, we all put one leg in front of the other and go… right? Well, yes we do. But, however, there are several elements – five in fact – to a walk from an animation point of view that we need to be aware of, as you probably know by now. These are (i) "**Key stride poses**", (ii) "**Passing positions**", (iii) "**Back leg extensions**", (iv) "**Front leg extensions**" and (v) "**In-betweens**". The actual process of animating a walk has been dealt with extensively elsewhere in this book. However, below are five walk poses that will help you observe and remember them. Take **2 minutes** to sketch each one, drawing them all on one page of your sketchbook. Combined, they cover those five aspects of a complete walk cycle… a complete walking action.

DOI: 10.1201/9781003324287-19

Pose 1 comments: This is pretty much a *"Key pose stride"* walk position. He is pretty upright in his pose, so I would suggest you put a little more lean into the angle of his torso if you were animating this pose. We can assume that he is walking pretty slowly; as the more lean forward there is to a pose the more it implies a fast walking action. Yet, to give this pose a little *"off-generic"* personality, notice that the forward arm is much further away from the body than the back arm. That implies that he is someone laid-back and easy-going in the way he moves forward – unlike a military-type person who will swing their marching arms far from the body, front and back.

Pose 2 comments: So, in this one – a *"Passing position"* – we don't see any measurable swinging of arms at all. Indeed, the left arm is not swinging at all, as it is casually holding onto the strap of the bag, to stop it falling from her shoulder. Her lean forward is hardly visible at all, so we can assume that she is ambling along, rather than rushing for anything. The fact that her *"free foot"* is pretty low to the ground supports that understanding too. If she were rushing, that foot would be much higher. Note that the *"contact leg"* is always straight under the body on the *"Passing position"*, which is what causes us to move up and down when we walk.

Pose 3 comments: Although it is similar to the last pose, in the sense that the left hand is holding a bag strap, this one is far more dynamic as a pose. Pretty much with a *"Back leg extension"*, you can see that the body lean is increased and the front leg has a confident, striding-out air to it. When someone has a large stride length, it shows they are keen to cover as much ground as they can, to get to where they want to go quicker. We don't see much swing of the free arm however, as the weight of the skateboard is holding it down somewhat. But generally, this is the most energetic pose of them all, so far.

Pose 4 comments: Another shift is personality here, at least in terms of the last pose. The front free foot is just making contact with the ground, showing a little bit of a *"Front leg extension"* – although we can assume the foot has just come back down from a position that is just higher and further forward from this *"heel hit"* position. The lean is slight however, with the arms hanging loosely down by the sides of the body. Hanging arms can indicate tiredness, age or lethargy in the person. We can assume also that with the short stride length, this elderly person is not rushing to get anywhere – or doesn't have the energy to rush anywhere!

Pose 5 comments: OK, this one is a bit of a joke pose! However, it is a valuable pose for two reasons. Hands are hard to draw in any circumstance, so you're going to have to work hard to make this one convincing. However, being a *"Key stride pose"*, with both toes touching the ground, you could argue that this is a *"tippy toe"* stride position of someone doing a fast or slow *"Sneak"*. Toes contacting the ground at the front of the stride suggest a cushioning of the *"hit"* when the foot touches down – usually done to lessen the sound. On the toes of the back foot suggests a more bouncy or energetic drive off. So you could use this foot action for that of a springy, bouncy or sneaking person – despite the humor of that shot.

Although these exercises were pretty conventional in terms of *"walk"* poses, they did offer a number of insights that were useful. They do underline the fact that observation is fundamentally important to the animator, so it is good to look at pictures we would normally take for granted and analyze just why they are what they are. There are very subtle things we see in people walking that we can transfer to our animated walks all the time. It separates them from one another and gives them personality if we emphasize those things through caricature and extended action. We all fundamentally walk the same way of course, putting one leg in front of the other and our arms swinging in opposite directions as we do. However, it is just HOW we each do that differently that gives us clues in how we can take our animated walking action away from the *"generic"*. Like fingerprints, not two people have exactly the same walk, which is why we are all slightly different from one another.

Different walk styles.

An animator needs to notice this and transform it into unique actions, even though the walking action is essentially that *"one leg in front of the other"* thing. A way of walking can reveal many different things about a character. For example, what "mood" are they in? What is their intention – are they trying to get somewhere fast, or are they dragging their feet in dread or laziness? Are they happy, sad or apprehensive? This all factor in to the way a person walks. How are they physically – are they heavy, thin, nervy, injured or are they even somewhat slow on the uptake? The poses you put them in will suggest these things. Finally, what is the terrain they are walking on, or the weather conditions – or are they carrying something, or not? All these things affect the walking poses you create, and how you will go off the *"generic"* and into the more *"personality"* style of walk. Observing these things in the real world will give us many clues on how to approach the animated world – which is exactly why I have given you these five poses to study and interpret. There are a million more poses and walks to look at, out there, you just have to open your *"animator's eyes"* to see them!

Usually, to new students, I will teach them to animate a walk early on in their studies, because I believe that in doing a good walk you learn so much about animation, as to pull off a good walk is the hardest thing for any animator to do. But, when I teach a walk initially, I teach a *"generic walk"* – a mechanically sound walk. This means how leg and feet move, how much body lean, what is the head doing, is there a little *"overlapping action"* or not, and other basic things like that. These are the things that define how an average person walks. However, when looking at other people walking and we want to put their personality into the movement, we have to think of ways to vary the action from the "generic", to give them identity or personality. In other words – *"breaking the rules"*. However, you have to know the rules first to break them and that's where a well-understood "generic walk" will give you a solid platform on which to build. There are so many ways that you can change a walk from the generic – simply by doing such things and changing the *"passing position"*, the way the feet contact the ground, the arm movement and so on. Which is why observing, and drawing, people walking in the real world is so important. Animators should be constantly observing life anyway, but specifically when walking. There are an endless supply of people-walking reference out there, each with a slight difference to the way they walk. So, as an animator, you have to train your eye to see those differences.

Instruction

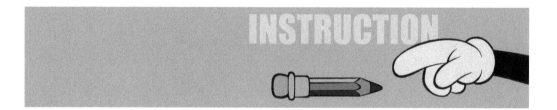

It makes perfect sense now to start talking about walks in Moho. We will naturally use a *"generic walk"* as our starting place. But as indicated above, that will give you a solid starting point or foundation upon which you can build variations that you may need to do in the future. We'll talk about how to do the latter, further on in this series of master classes. But for now, the *"generic walk"*. As with all the Moho rigs we are using in this section, you can download this particular **"Arnie"** rig from our dedicated website.

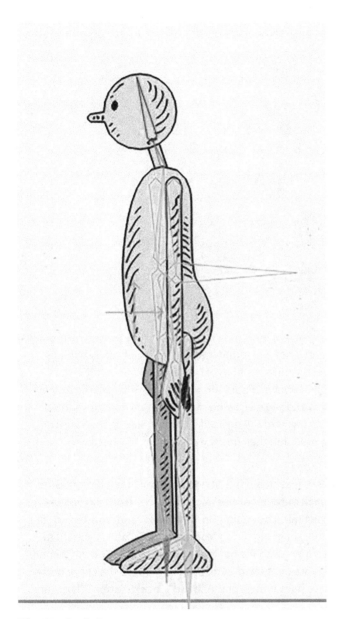

The "Arnie rig".

When you download it, it will be called "**ANIM 01.moho**". So, the very first thing I want you to do is save it as a new working file, "**ANIM 02.moho**". That means that if anything goes wrong with your assignment at this stage, you will always have the original at your disposal – as opposed to having go online and download it every time. Now, looking at this new *"Arnie"* rig, you can see that we're on familiar territory with this one. He's a biped character, with two arms, two legs, a torso, a neck and a head. I've added the stages of approach to creating our Moho-animated *"Arnie"*, which should be familiar to you from previous lessons. Nevertheless, I think it will be helpful to add them to the background here, as reminders.

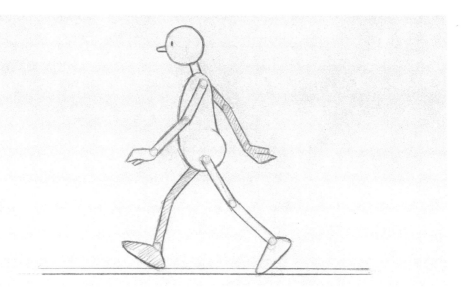

Generic walk guide sheet.

However, before we start, I need to introduce you to a couple of new things in this Moho rig – primarily because it has extra bones and a slightly different format. As mentioned above, I've set this one up very much in the form of a notebook or a ruled card design, allowing me to give you notes on-screen all the time. However, in terms of the rig itself, I'll first explain it, then we'll do some pose "**blocking out**", and then finally we'll work on "**in-betweens**" and "**timing**".

In short, this process is to first create the "**stride position**", then the "**passing position**", next the "**back extension**" positions, then the "**front extension**" and finally work out the timing by adding "**in-betweens**" and "**rendering**" the whole thing to video. So, I'm going to use "**command Z**" on the keyboard to highlight bones. That allows us to see our "**root bone**", which is the major one that all the other bones are generated from. Use this to move the entire body around. Beyond that, we have bones for the "**head**", "**neck**", "**arms**", "**legs**" and "**feet**".

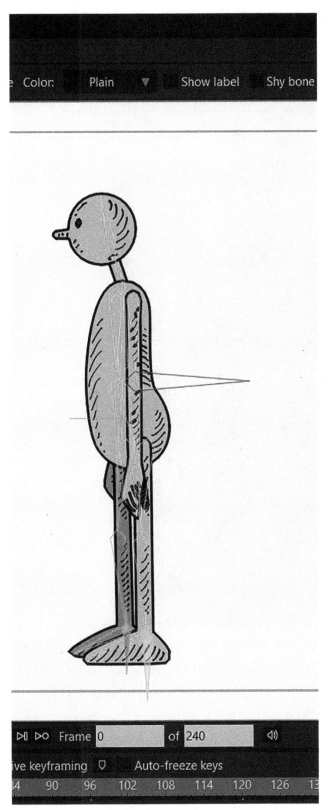

All the bones on the Arnie rig.

The only other thing I want to show you on the Moho interface is on the right. Here, we have all of our layers. These represent different "**layers**" and different "**bones**", depending on what one you select at any time.

The layers column with the bones layer highlighted.

Specifically, this layer that says *"blue text background"*. Well, that is the one that contains the background art. Here, it is switched on and off. Doing that is always useful whenever any background layer gets distracting while you're animating.

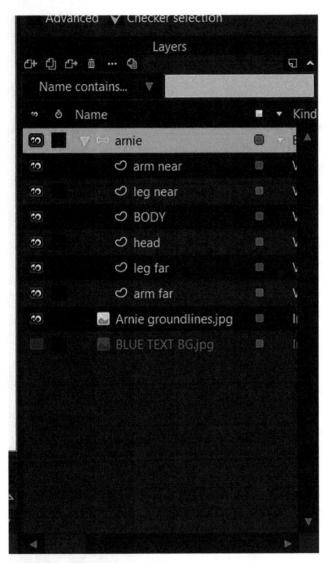

The unchecked background layer.

"**Command U**", switch on any *"tracing image"* you may have imported into this layer. Hitting *"Command U"* again will switch it off again.

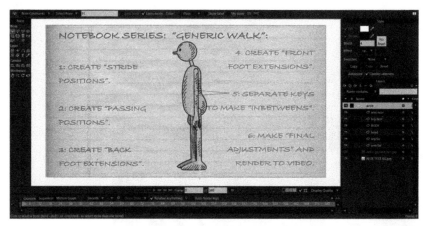

The background showing on the stage.

With the *"tracing image"* on, you'll notice that not only does the rig give you your first "**key stride position**", but it also gives you two double lines on the ground, which are the "match lines" for Arnie. (Remember: The near foot should always be on the bottom of the two lines, and the far foot on the top.) This will be a great guide to match to as you develop the leg action on your walk.

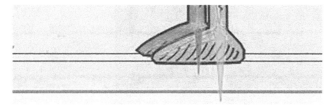

Two groundlines indicated on guide.

Now, having explained the basics of the rig, let us now start "**blocking in**" our character. The first thing we're going to do is select the "Arnie rig" level or layer.

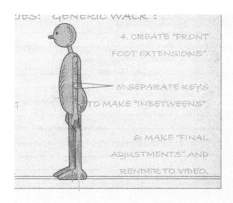

The Arnie rig layer selected.

To begin, set the line cursor on your timeline to "**frame 1**". Then, we're going to go *"Command Z"* on the keyboard, which allows us to manipulate the Arnie bones. To make life easier for you at the beginning, I want you to more or less manipulate all the bones, to get Arnie more or less into the position of the *"tracing image"*. It doesn't have to be totally precise, but make it as close as you can. Definitely be accurate in terms of the feet matching their appropriate ground-lines however. That should give you a good starting point to work with for the *"first stride position"*.

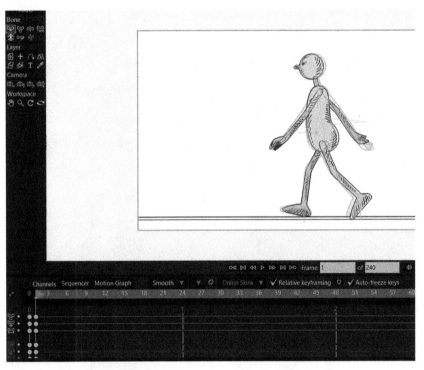

Frame 1 – the first stride position.

NOTE

Remember again that we enter into the world of Moho. It is a wonderful software program, but it will always want to do its own thing. For much of the time you will need to override it, as often it makes decisions that are logical and mechanically accurate. However, the best animation is not always that, even when doing in-betweens. So, quite often you're going to need to override logical, mathematical thinking and impose your own will on it, based on your experience. You don't have much of that for now, but trust me, I do and I'll guide you through the times when you need to take control. Sometimes, Moho's own instincts will work for what we want to do. However, if you want animation with more inherent personality, you're going to need to override the rules that Moho applies. That's what makes digital animation still a handcrafted thing at its highest level, so be prepared to do it when necessary.

Now we've posed our character in his first position, and we want to create the second, opposite stride position. To do this, need to click off the "tracing image" layer before we use a *shortcut* to create the new stride position. So, select "**frame 1**" and use "**Command C**" to copy it. Now, move the timeline cursor to "**frame 2**", to paste (Command V) the first stride position into it.

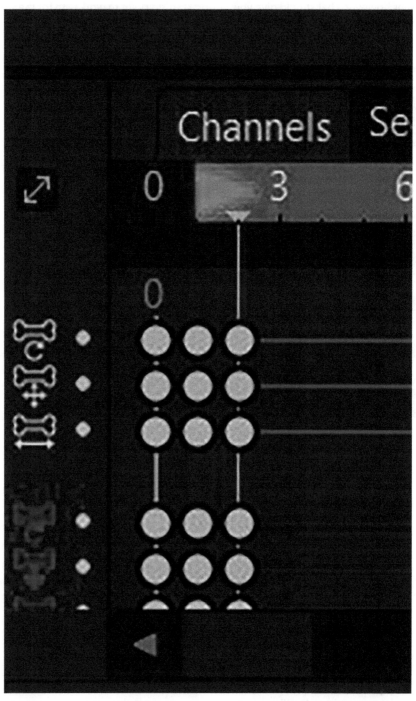

The close-up of the timeline – frames 1 and 2.

Next, in *"frame 2"*, reverse the arms and legs of the character. The rest of the body can remain the same, but the arms and legs definitely need to be reversed. Make sure the feet are on their appropriate groundlines too of course – the far foot on the top line, with the near foot on the bottom.

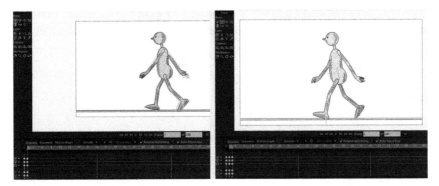

The key stride poses – 1st and 2nd.

Scrub the timeline cursor from one to the other, to make sure all the arms and legs are alternating correctly. (Note: Scrubbing the timeline like this is the equivalent of "flipping" or shooting a "pose test", in traditional hand-drawn animation.) If all is good, you have now created both "key stride positions" for your walk.

Now, we've got to create the **"passing positions"**. So, what we need to do now is highlight the *"frame 2"* and drag it one frame to the right on the timeline. This will create a **new** "frame 2", with the old "frame 2" pose becoming the new "frame 3".

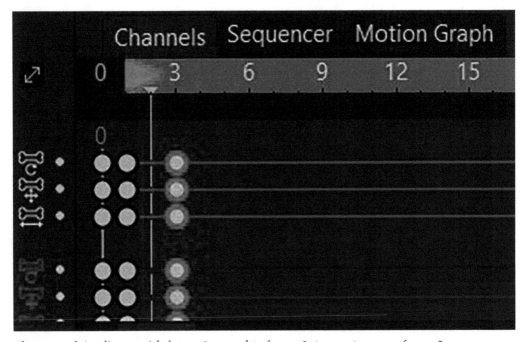

Close-up of timeline – with frame 2 moved to frame 3, to create a new frame 2.

Essentially, we have created an *"in-between"*. It's not a perfect "in-between", but it is a halfway position linking the 2 "key strides" at least. However, we need to turn it into a *"passing position"*, so we need to work on it. (Remember I mentioned above that we need to override Moho's decision-making – well this is a perfect time to do it!) Remember that a *"passing position"* has one **straight leg directly under the body**, and the "free" leg is **swinging through in a "number 4" position**, with the body **raised up**. To remind you, this is what a sketch of a *"passing position"* looks like.

The passing, "number 4", position.

To create a *"passing position"* in Moho, we need to do the following: The far (right) leg has to slide back and be a straight leg under Arnie's body, while the near (left) leg needs to be coming halfway through in a *"number 4"* position. The body has to be raised up too. So, the first thing we need to do is straighten the **right** leg, flatten the foot down and angle it directly under the body. (I would suggest you angle the left leg away for now, so you can see the right leg more clearly.) You'll notice that now the right foot is far under the groundline it should be on however.

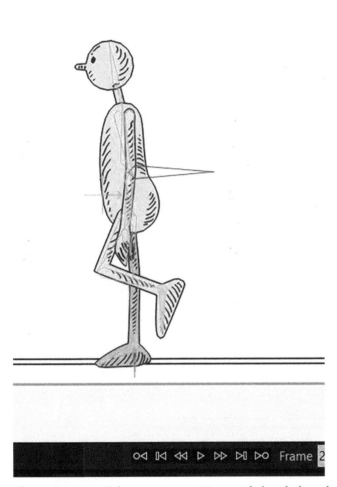

The stage view of the passing position, with foot below the groundline.

However, if you select the "**root bone**" and hold down the "**Shift**" key your move locked along a single line, you can simply drag the body up vertically until the foot on that straight leg is now sitting on the groundline. In many ways, Arnie is now in the correct body that he should be for the *"passing position"* – all that is excepting for the left leg.

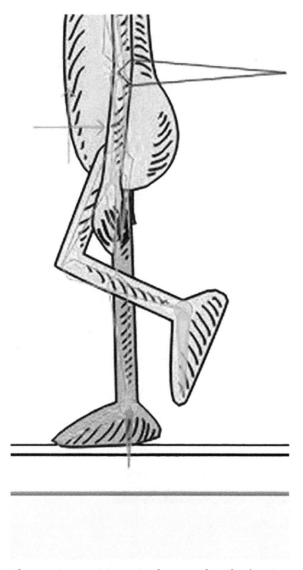

The passing position raised up, so that the foot is on the groundline.

Now, you simply need to bend the left leg into an acceptable *"number 4"* position, just as it was in the drawn sketch earlier. You won't need to worry about the arms at this time however, as Moho has actually made a good halfway decision for them. Doing all this, you will now have your first perfect *"passing position"*. If you scrub it between all three frames on the timeline, you will see the rudiments of a good walk action emerging, with a definitely "up and down" on the body.

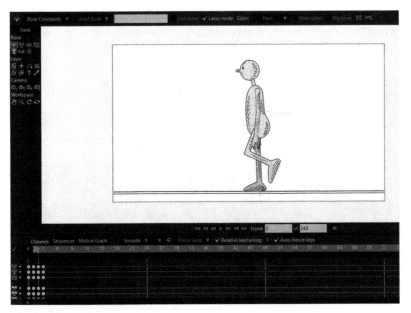

The final passing position.

Now, we have our first *"passing position"* completed, and we need to create the second one that will complete the walk cycle action back to *"frame 1"*, so it can loop over and over again infinitely. To do this, we have to replicate the *"frame 1"* position at on *"frame 4"* and then extend it out. So, move the timeline cursor to *"frame 1"* on the timeline, highlight it and then hit *"Command C"* to copy it. When you've done that, slide the timeline curser to *"frame 4"* and hit *"Command V"* to paste it into that frame.

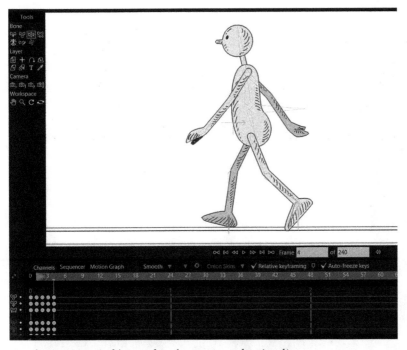

Key frame 1 copied/pasted to frame 4 on the timeline.

With that done, highlight your new "frame 4" and drag it to right along the time-line by one frame to "frame 5". That creates a new *in-between* frame, that is now *"frame 4"*.

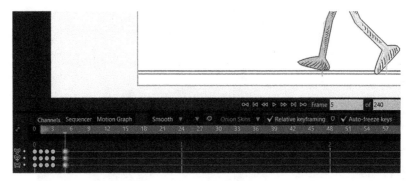

Frame 4 moved to frame 5 on the timeline.

With your new "frame 4" created, you now have to adjust it to become the second "passing position". So, just as you did before, straighten the "contact leg" under the body and flatten out the foot. Remember though that this time the "contact leg" is the left leg, as we're now working on the second stride, unlike the first one.

Second passing position adjusted, so that the foot matches the correct groundline.

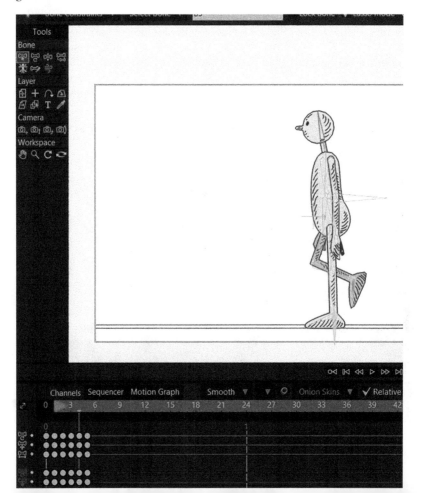

With that done, again select the "**root bone**" and, holding the "**Shift**" key down, raise the body up until the foot on the left leg matches its own lower line. That done, adjust the right leg into the *"number 4"* passing position. That creates your second *"passing position"*. So, if you scrub along the **5 frames** on the timeline now, you'll see you have the rudiments of two walking strides happening, with the body rising up and down on both passing positions. So, if we refer to our background guide list, we have created our *"stride positions"* and our *"passing positions"*.

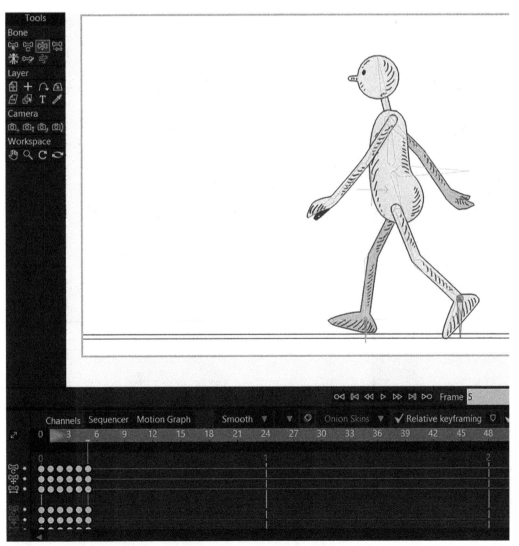

All 5 completed poses created in the timeline.

That means the next thing we need to focus on is the "**back foot extension**" on both strides. These will occur on the *in-between* frames, and we need to create between the *"key stride positions"* and the next "passing positions". So, to do the first one, we have to select frames "**2**, **3**, **4** and **5**" and slide them along to the right by **frame 1**.

Frames 2, 3, 4 and 5 slide to right by frame 1 on timeline.

If you remember from our previous, traditionally created generic walk, the *"back foot extension"* means that instead of in-betweening the back foot off the ground from the *"key stride"* to the *"passing"* position, we keep the toe on the ground and slide it back the same distance that the contact foot slides from one position to the other at the same time. And, that is exactly what we do on this first stride position, using the bones to manipulate the back leg. For the rest of the action, we can assume that Moho has in-betweened perfectly, but the back leg needs to look like this.

Final back leg extension pose.

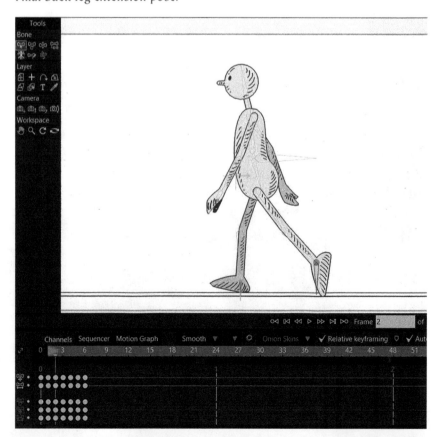

It gives us a strong push-off position on the back leg, which is what we do in real life. Now having done that on the first stride, we need to do the same for the second stride. So, this time select frames "**5 & 6**" on the timeline and slide them along to the right by **frame 1** also.

This gives us a new *in-between* position that is fine for everything but the back leg.

Frames 5 & 6 opened up by frame 1 on timeline.

So again, extend that back leg along the timeline in exactly the same distance as the contact foot on this frame moves from the contact foot on the previous frame. Doing so will give us our second "back foot extension" position.

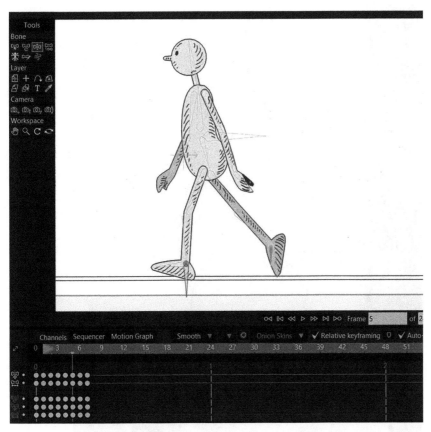

The second back leg extension.

Animating the Hips

NOTE

With the kind of rig we're working with here, the hips' positions should be a little more flexible. However, in the interests of simplicity at this stage, they are fixed. But if they weren't, you would need to move the hip back when the leg moves back, and forward when the leg goes forward. Similarly, it should do the same thing with the shoulders with the arms.

I want to make a quick diversion here. In the rig used for these illustrations, the hips are fixed in a central position in relation to the body. However, for the more advanced rig that you can download, the hips will me moveable – which is preferable, as in real life the hips do move forward and backward as the legs move. The shoulder joint at the top of the arm will move similarly. So, to animate the hips on the rig, you will have access too…

Select with the "Select bone" tool the bone of the hips. In the timeline, it will show you the animated frames of the hip bone. Select them all and delete them.

The hip bone is selected and also the corresponding frames in the timeline highlighted.

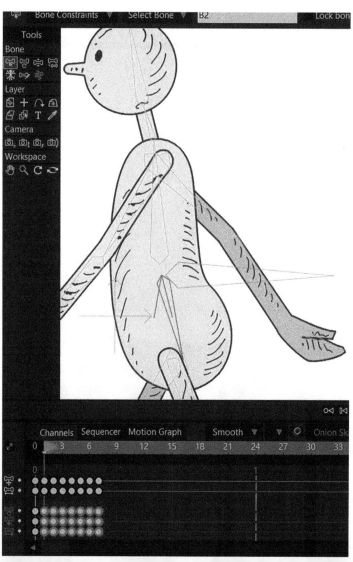

*Delete all those keys you've selected. Make sure you are on "frame 1" and move the
hip back. This will create a new key frame for the hip.*

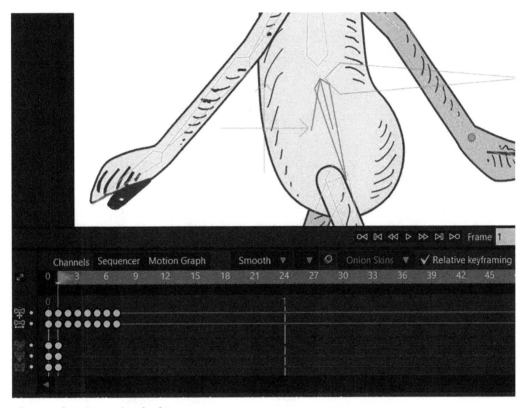

The new key frame for the hip.

Select that key and copy and paste it to frame 7.

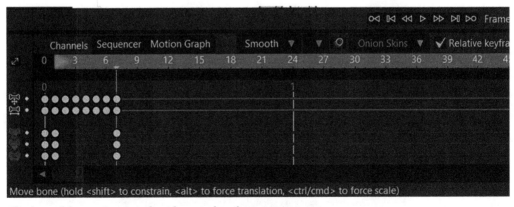

The key of frame 1, copied and pasted to frame 7.

Now move to frame 4 and move the hips forward.

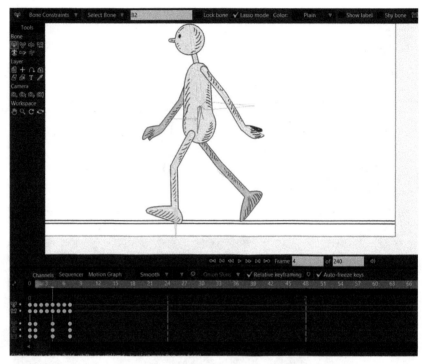

The hip moved forward.

Now let's look at the left arm. Select the upper left arm and then select/delete all the keys with the "Transform bone" tool on the timeline.

The bone arm selected and timeline keys deleted.

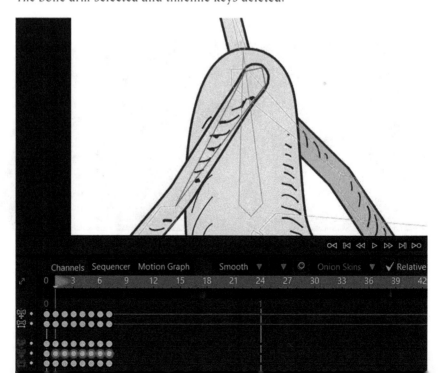

Now that you've deleted the shoulder key frames, move the bone of the left arm to the left with the transform bone tool. It should look like this…

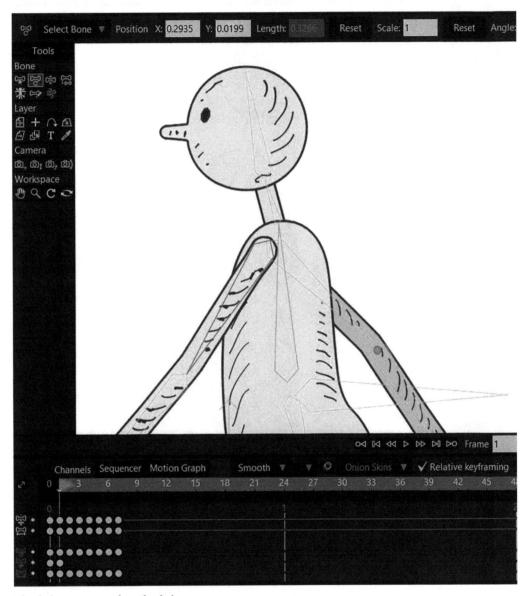

The left arm moved to the left.

Copy and paste the key of left arm to frame 7.

Now, at frame 4, move the left arm to the right.

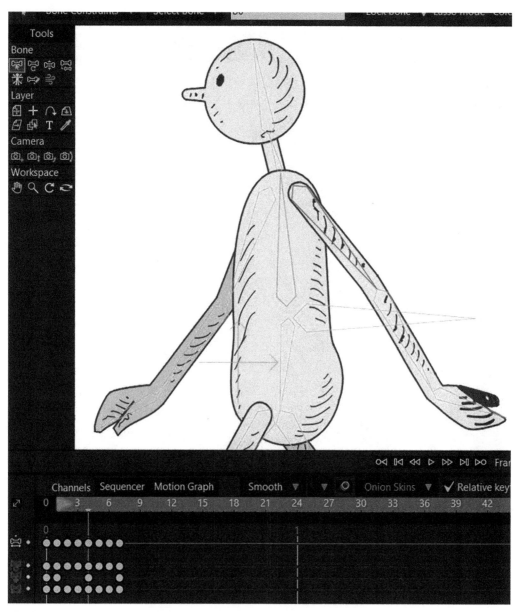

The frame 4 left arm is moved to the right.

The same can now be done for the right arm. But, at frame one, instead of moving it to the left, you move it to the right – and at frame 4 from right to the left instead.

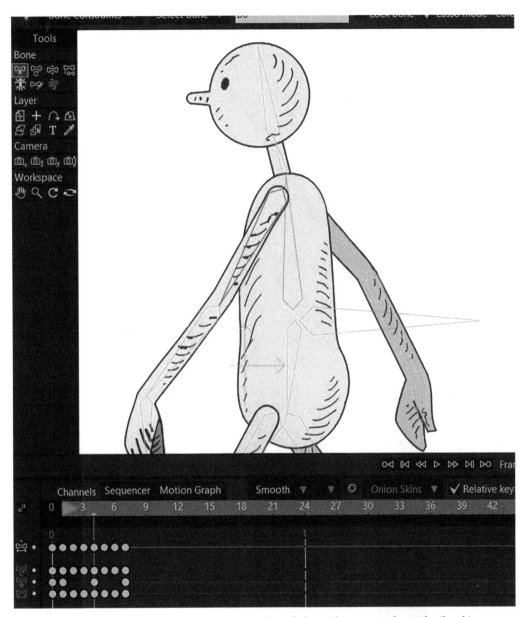

Now, the left arm is moved to the left (forward) and the right arm to the right (back).

This all should give you more flowing and fluid hips and shoulders on your walk action.

Now on our background checklist, we've done *"key stride positions"*, the *"passing positions"* and now the *"back extensions"*. To complete the major positions for each stride, prior to in-betweening, we now have to do the "**front foot extensions**". If you think back to *"Section I"*, you will remember that these required that the front foot between the *"passing position"* and the next *"key stride position"* should swing somewhat up and forward, before coming down and back to the *"contact position"* of the front leg on the next key stride.

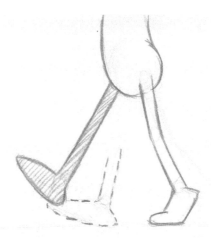

The front leg extension position is just above and ahead of the final front foot contact position.

If you let Moho do its thing here, it will have that front foot in-between down from the *"passing position"* to the next *"stride position"*, but in a straight line. This is another occasion when we have to override the software. So, select all the keys, except frames "**1**, **2** & **3**" and slide them to the right on the timeline by **frame 1**.

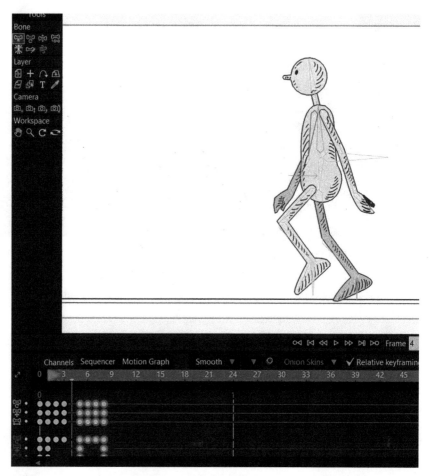

All frames except 1, 2 and 3 extended by frame 1 on timeline.

With a new "**frame 4**" created, move the front foot *"forward and up"* of the contact position on *"frame 5"*. It should look something like this.

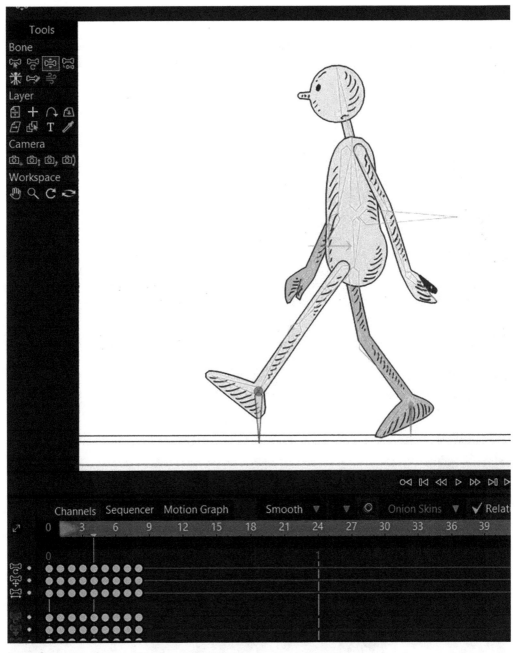

Front leg extension on stage.

If you now scrub the timeline over the first stride positions (frames 1 thru 5), you should now get a much smoother sense of a fluid stride happening, including the push-off from the back leg and the swing through and down on the front leg. If this works perfectly – as it should – you can now create the second *"front foot extension"* position. So, select the last frame only and slide it by **frame 1** to the right on the timeline. Then, with the new frame created, move the front foot forward and up in terms of the final *"contact"* position on the last frame. This should create a nice and fluid conclusion to the second frame.

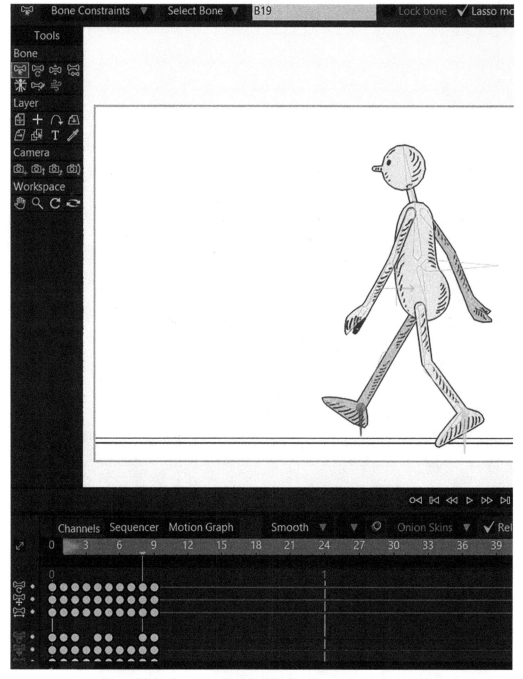

Second front leg extension on timeline.

Now, if you scrub all the way from the first frame to the last, you should get a really good sense of the two strides flowing from beginning to end. If you hit the **"Play"** button just under the *"Stage"* window, you will see the entire thing repeating – although it will be way too fast to appreciate it as a normal walk. However, before you do that, you should make sure the end frame on the second white window directly under the "Stage" is set to "8" – meaning that the action will end there before it jumps back to repeat from frame "1" and on again. (Note: This is because *"frame 9"* is actually a copy of *"frame 1",* and if we include it, there will be a slight pause in the repeat action as *"frame 1"* will effectively be on the screen for 2 frames, whereas everything else will be on for 1 frame.) Even though this action will be incredibly fast to look at, it should nevertheless show you that the legs, body and feet are moving correctly, and the body is moving up and down, as the action repeats and repeats in the *"Stage"* window.

Finally, the final thing we need to create, according to our background list, are the *"in-betweens".* Depending on how we do this, it will result in our action being somewhere between a *fast* walk and a *slow* one. But for starters, I suggest you do the following.

But, before you do anything else, I'm STRONGLY going to advise that you "Save" this version, then "Save it as" a new version, "**ANIM 03.moho**". We need to get into the habit of doing this as any software has the potential for crashing at the worst possible time – or else you will mess up so badly that it will be really difficult to retrieve what you've done! So, by saving a new version, everything you do something you like, with a new file name, means you can always go back to the previous version if something goes wrong and you don't want to lose too much of your work. I've personally been burned so many times by this that I've finally made it a habit to save as many versions of my animation as possible. So, looking again at your background list, we now have 8 frames and have to separate our key positions and create our "**in-betweens**". This will make sense of the action we've created when it's played back in real time.

If you imagine that a "generic walk" can be anything around 12 frames and upward for a single stride, it gives us a clue in terms of how we in-between it. Now I'm not going to give you hard and fast rules here, as you may like to have your walk moving faster or slower than me or anyone else. However, if I might just suggest you do the following, then it will give you a starting point to work from and you can adjust it at will. (The wonderful benefit of working with software, as opposed to drawing lots of in-betweens!) So, if we think of this walk as 12 frames per stride, we need to consider how we separate our key positions into 12 frames. At the moment, we've got just "**5**" – and really "**4**" if we don't count one of the key stride positions, as we shouldn't. Therefore, in keeping it simple, we really need to multiply everything by 3, to take our 4 frames to 12. The way to start doing that is to select everything from frame 2 onward, and I'm going to move them "**2 frames**" to the **right**. That gives me 2 in-betweens between them.

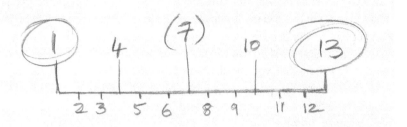

A traditional hand-drawn animation chart illustrates where the extra 2 in-betweens are positioned throughout.

Then, I'm going to select everything except our second position here, and I'm going to move all those by "**2 frames**" to the **right**. Then, go through all our key positions like that and separate them each by "**2 frames**" to the **right** as before. (And remember that you can adjust all this later, as you have complete control over how fast or slow you want to have your walk moving eventually – we are just "ball parking" it for now.)

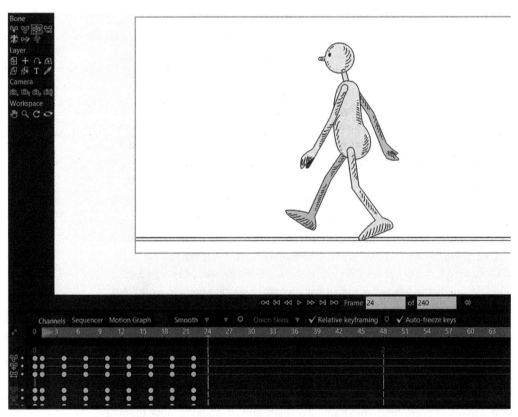

All the frames on timeline are now separated by 2 frames.

And this gives us "**24 frames**" for **2 strides** of action – that is, if we remember that frame "25" is the same as "frame 1" and we don't want to duplicate it in our final action. Now you can hit the "**Play**" button to see the difference – although you should remember to change the number in the second white window under the "Stage" to accommodate the new length.

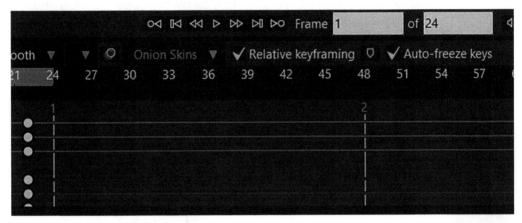

Close-up of end frame box number, showing 24.

When you play this, you'll see that we more or less have a natural "generic walk" action going on.

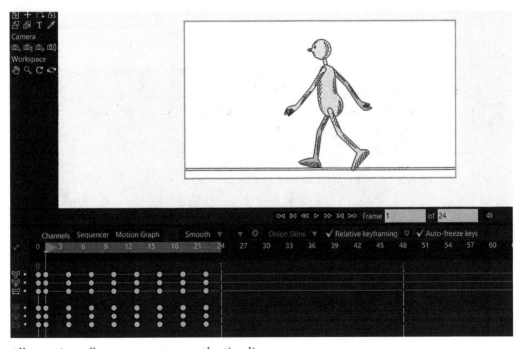

All generic walk poses, as seen on the timeline.

You will see that basically all the mechanics of the action are working fine. The body is going up and down, the back leg is pushing-off and the front leg is swinging through and back, although it has to be said that Moho doing its thing mechanically correct by saying *"You've given me key positions and you've also asked me to put in 2 in-betweens linking each one of those, so I've done it mechanically"*. However, if you look more carefully, you'll see that the feet on the ground go beneath the line for example, which is the last thing we want! This is where the sixth item on our background list comes in, "**Final adjustments and render to video**". So, we again have to override the software and finesse it manually. To do that, we have to scrub along the timeline, frame by frame, and adjust the feet each time to make sure they **don't** stray beneath the line.

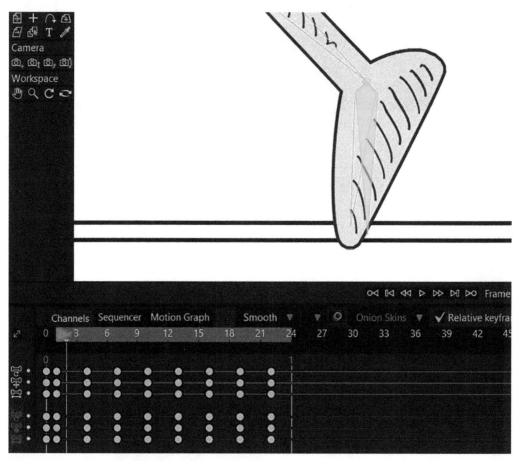

Showing feet out of alignment on the groundline.

We also have to check that after the first *"contact"* position on the front leg, the foot slaps down **flat** on the ground on each frame to the end – which doesn't right now. So again, we have to adjust it.

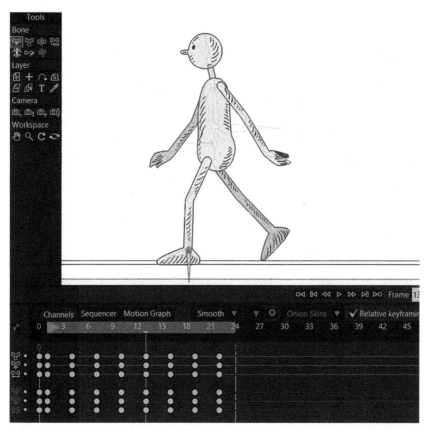

Adjusted foot flat on the groundline.

This is just one of the kinds of fine-tuning you may need to do, to ensure your animated walk will look smooth and stable. Then, when you play it back, you will see the feet are definitely sliding along the line, making a huge difference. You'll be able to see this even better if you hit "Command U", to take the "tracing image" away. It will look much more natural, as if the feet have a solid contact with the ground.

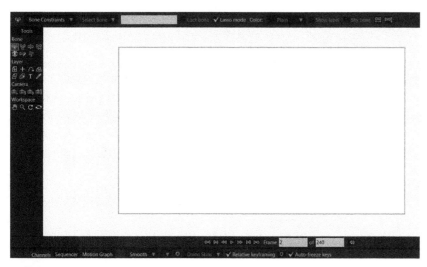

Still from stage with tracing image gone.

OK, so that's the foot tweaks down, now we need to make others – specifically the "**hands**" and the "**head**". Remember when we dealt with this when doing the traditional, hand-drawn walk? For the hands, we had them dragging behind the arms as moved forward and back – and the head moved down when the body moved up, and vice versa. Well, we need to do that to the hands and head here. First, make sure that the hands on every frame are bending back slightly, behind the moving arm – front and back arms.

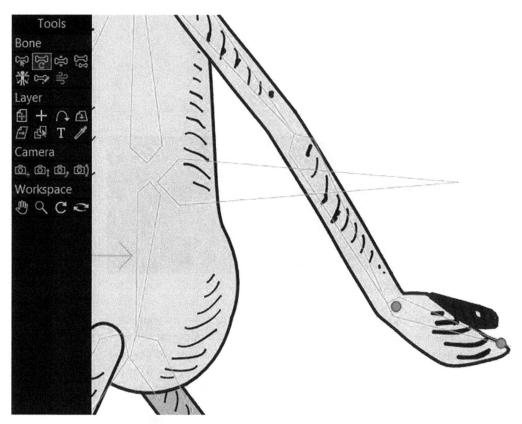

Showing the hand dragging back behind the arm.

And now do the same to the head. When the body is **up** on the *"passing positions"*, make sure the head is slightly **down**, and when the body is **down** on the *"key stride positions"*, the head is slightly **up**. With the frames between these, you need to adjust accordingly as in-betweens.

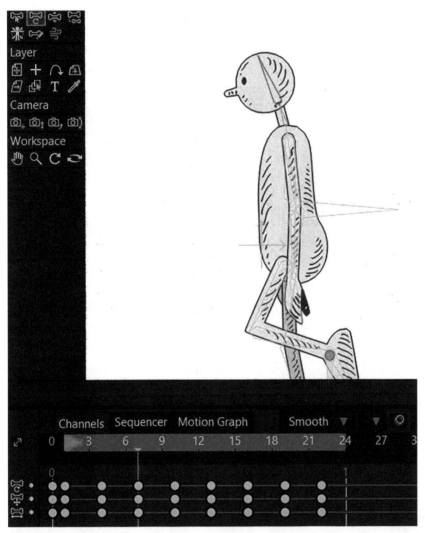

Use the head bone to have it angle up and down in opposition to the body.

If, after all this, your walk turns out to be solid and flowing, I'm sure you will be very happy. Now this is not at all a *"personality walk"* of course, but it gives you a foundation of knowledge to build on. We will be talking of variations to this later. But, for now, it is time to render your first *"generic walk"* in Moho to video. To do this, you'll need to go **"File/Export Animation"** *(or "Command E")* and choose a folder on your computer to send it to. However, before you do that,
I want to show you have to ensure it is a multiple repeating action, rather than just loop a short video of just your two strides.

It's probably a little late to tell you this now, but I want to repeat what I told you earlier about "Saving". Always save your file as a new version each time you do something that you like. Therefore, by now, you should have probably saved it several times, to save yourself work if you have a computer crash, or make an irreversible mistake. It's always better to be "safe than sorry"!

To loop your character in an extended way within Moho, select frames "1" to "24". (Remember, we don't want to use frame "25" as that is essentially a copy of "frame 1"). With the first 24 frames selected, hit "Command C" to copy them.

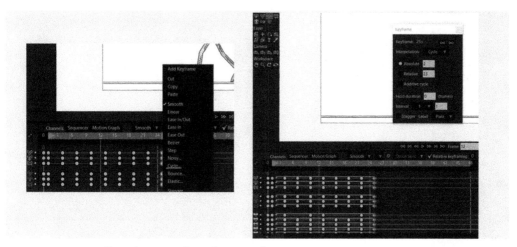

All 24 frames selected on timeline.

Then, select frame "25" only and hit "Command V". This will be that it will replace "frame 25" with the 24 frames you previously copied. This will repeat your two-stride action twice now if you hit the "Play" button.

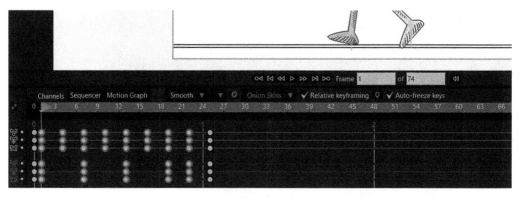

Twenty-four frames copied and pasted onto timeline from frame 25 and onward.

NOTE

There is also another way to loop the walking action here....

With this option, you need the keys of frame 25 which is a copy of frame 1. Select all the keys of frame 25, right click and select cycle. A window will pop up. Make sure to set the number of absolute to "2", as this will make it cycle back to frame 2.

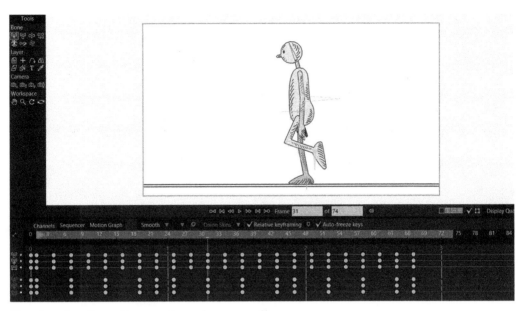

Showing the alternative way to cycle your walk.

Repeat that process for as many times as you like, so you have duplicated the repeating action for a significant amount of time. (For example, if you repeat it until it is frame 240 in the timeline, your rendered video will run for 10 seconds at 24 frames per second – and don't forget to change the second white window under the "Stage" to 240, if you want to play the whole thing in Moho before rendering!) "Save" this when completed, then render to video as discussed above. This will give you a repeating action of your *"generic walk"* for as long as you chose it to repeat, meaning you won't have to loop it when you play it.

Suggested Assignment

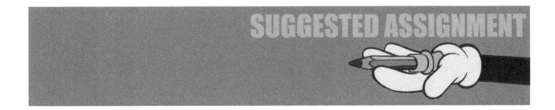

Probably you've done more than enough already to create a successful "generic walk" video. However, to teach yourself more about "in-betweens versus timing", save your file to other alternative versions and open up the frames to create different "in-between" distances between the main poses. This is a pretty quick and valuable way to learn timing via in-between spacing.

Masterclass 18/ Generic Walk Variations

With this lesson, we're going to explore some **walk variations** you can try with the Arnie rig, and now you have hopefully got the *"generic walk"* successfully done and dusted. These can be a fun exercise after all that technically demanding approach. You'll see how amazing just a slight bending of the rules can actually create something with more eccentricity or personality. But first, observational gesture drawing…

Warm-Up Drawing

I thought it might help to have a recap here – or better still, a reevaluation of how you're doing in terms of gesture drawing. So, out of interest, we are going to return to the very first assignment you did, "**Coffee drinkers**", and see how well you cope with it this second time around, and with a number of observational gesture drawing sessions under your belt. When you've completed this one, compare it with the very first one you did in your sketchbook, so see what progress you've made. You might remember that I posed the suggestion that said if you were asked to draw someone drinking coffee, what would you do from your imagination? I felt that it would be pretty generic. However, if you turn to the real world and actually look at coffee drinkers in a café or coffee bar,

DOI: 10.1201/9781003324287-20

you might find that your poses would suddenly come alive and be much more inventive. So, below are two images of coffee drinkers for you to study and draw, perhaps inspiring you to think more outside the box when creating specified poses. You should limit yourself to just **3 minutes** for pose 1 and **5 minutes** for pose 2…

Pose 1 comments: This is clearly a much more held-in and self-contained pose than what you have drawn before. This kind of pose could suggest a certain kind of introverted nature, or even shutting off from the world, so tight are the limbs to the body. However, the look in the girl's face suggests she is content with her situation – savoring the drink and enjoying the experience, which underlines the fact that expressions can override poses; otherwise, this pose could be that of a very withdrawn character indeed. This merely highlights how powerful a single storytelling pose can be, while at the same time saying that unless you think it through and adjust certain things, the poses you choose might be misconstrued in certain other circumstances. Therefore, if you conceive your poses really well, and think them through to the finest detail, you'll be surprise at how powerful they can be in communicating things, even if there is essentially no movement.

Pose 2 comments: Note this time how these two poses tell such a story. They underline again that unless you look at real-world references when working out your poses, you may miss the little subtleties that people do which can mark out a great pose from an average and generic one. Here, two people are in quite different poses; yet, they communicate their relationship beautifully. Both are entirely relaxed in each other's company, and there are no negative feelings suggested at all. Try to think things through like this when you are asked to animate a scene with two characters in it. They may not need to move excessively to tell a great story, as in this image. So train yourself always to look at everyday situations around you, then that the imagination to use them as a foundation for what you do in the animated world.

Using the real world for references like this is like you building a database on observed information in your brain. Whether you draw these out in a sketchbook, or just register them in your subconscious along the way, they will store in your brain until such a time when they will pop out as inspiration in the future when you're asked to create a particular sequence of animation that relates to them directly or indirectly. It may even bubble up like an organic "knowing" of what you need to do at any time, even though you may not necessarily remember the actual pose you drew or observed some time earlier. That part of your subconscious will enable you to translate the earlier perceived understanding into something seemingly quite unique and imaginative in your animated work. It's a very subliminal, subconscious thing, but the more you do your observational work the more it will come into play in your creative work at some moment in the longer term. So, think about the observational gesture drawings you have done so far in this book, be aware of the ones you have yet to do, and encourage yourself to do much more of this kind of thing outside the remit of what you're drawing here. I promise you it will pay off in time, as the more you put into an objective, the more you get out of it.

Instruction

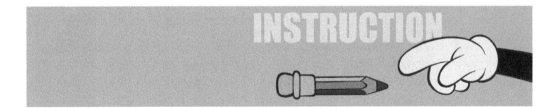

Let us now investigate some alternative variations to the *"generic walk"*. I must stress however that before you attempt these, **please ensure that you have successfully completed a "generic walk" in the first place**; otherwise, the following will not be of as much benefit to you. Animating a successful and convincing walk is indeed hard to do, so mastery of that should come before everything else. That said, if you are ready to move on to other things, then the following will be a great place for you to start – plus any other variations you created for yourself in the future. Perhaps we might call this section the *"Ministry of silly walks"* – although we'd probably get sued by the Monty Python's Flying Circus for doing so!

John Cleese-like silly walk pose.

First and foremost here, I want to give you **3 quick options** for simply changing aspects of the *"generic walk"* and getting a very different look. I'm not going to get into the complexities of working with Moho in this lesson, as I did without marathon last session. Instead, I am just going to offer you these three quick suggestions of changes will help you with some basic walking actions. There are many more you'll learn to do, but perhaps these three will get you to start thinking.

So, the first thing you need to do is set up the 2 "stride positions" and the 2 "passing positions" of the *"generic walk"* over 24 frames as we did before – plus adding a copy of the *"frame 1"* pose and pasting it on *"frame 25"*. So in other words, we've set up exactly the same as we set up for the *"generic walk"* before – except we've not done any *polishing* or *finessing* of the in-betweens linking the main positions.

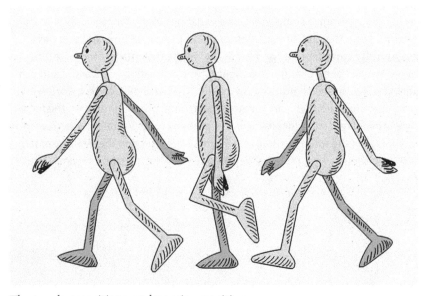

The two key positions and passing position.

Lazy walk: First, let's create what might be described as a *"lazy walk"*. We're still using the same *"generic walk"* positions, except that I suggest you hold the *"passing positions"* back and drag the feet on them on the ground at the same time.

NOTE

We will be resuming to this position every time we do an alternative walk in this section, so I strongly advise you to save more than one version of them for use each time.

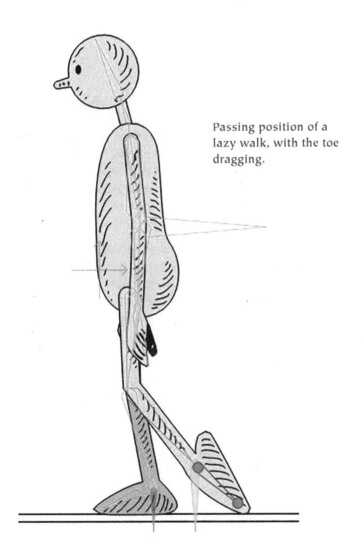

Passing position of a lazy walk, with the toe dragging.

However, this won't work unless you change the timing also. So, on the premise that the more in-betweens you have, the slower the action, we can double (or more) the in-betweens linking the first *"key stride position"* and the next *"passing position"*, which will give you a very different feel to the walk indeed.

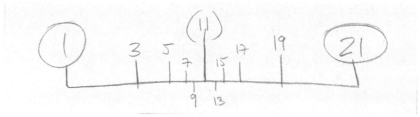

A hand-drawn animation chart shows the bunching of the inbetweens around the passing positions, giving a more lethargic timing to the walk.

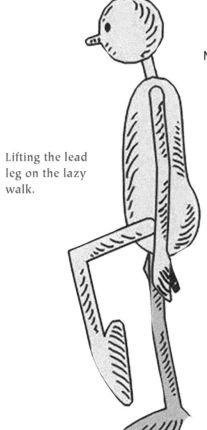

Lifting the lead leg on the lazy walk.

Now, you'll probably need to slow that action down even more to get a really lazy walk – and do a lot of finessing with the changed foot positions along the ground line, etc., if you want to take it further. Also, the action can be further improved by lifting the lead leg from the *"passing positions"* to the next *"key stride position"* up higher and more forward – giving it more of *a "slap"* as it hits the ground.

No matter how basic and simple this change may be from the original *"generic walk"* action and timing, it will nevertheless give you a stronger sense of what I'm talking about when I talk about making tweaks to the *"generic walk"* and getting another outcome.

Military march: Go back to our original five-pose *"generic walk"* sequence and let's look at how easy it is to make what we might call a *"military march"* action out of it.

NOTE

The beauty of using a digital program like Moho here is that it is easy and almost instant to make the changes on the "Stage" and "timeline" – as opposed to having to draw everything out many times, we take a traditional, hand-drawn approach to these experiments!

On the way down with a military march, you can throw the leading leg out, almost straight – like a John Cleese movement!

This time, instead of *delaying* the passing position, I want to "**advance**" it further forward, higher and with the toe pointed upward. Do this with both *"passing positions"*.

Then, if you play this one, you're going to get more of a *military-style* stomp. Now remember we haven't finessed anything here, so the *"back leg extension"* and other things need to be finessed. But as a general premise, you can see that by just moving the lead leg on the *"passing position"* forward and higher, it gives an entirely different flavor to the *"generic walk"* action. You can refine it however you need to, and you should wish to take this action further. For example, you might want to tilt the lean on the body back a little, with bigger and more dramatic, straight-arm swings to the front side of the body. These kinds of changes can only help, but improve the marching action. And if in doubt about any of this, look at footage of soldiers marching and that will supply you with more than enough references to work with.

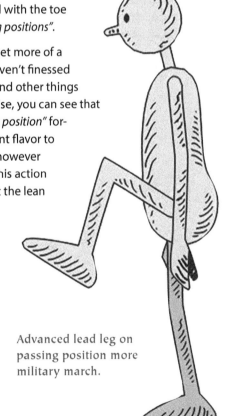

Advanced lead leg on passing position more military march.

Actual soldiers showing the passing position of a standard march.

Slothful walk: This is very similar to the *"lazy walk"* we did first – except to say that in addition to the legs doing the delayed "plod" kind of thing alone, you might also adjust the arms so that they're hardly moving and effectively hanging down to the sides of the character, limply. The head sagging downwards, staring at the ground, might also enhance this action.

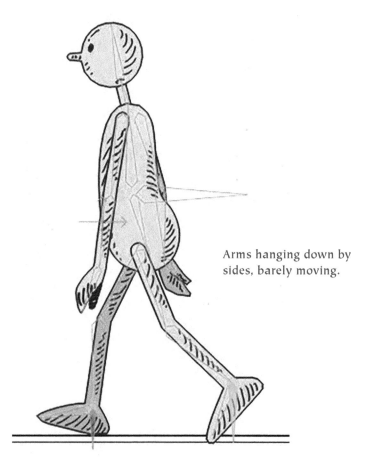

Arms hanging down by sides, barely moving.

Suggested Assignment

These brief exercises are merely to give you ideas to play with. If you want to take your own ideas forward too, you have so many options at your fingertips – such as changing the **angle of the body**, the action or angles of the arms, the movement of the head and of course the **movement on the legs** from the beginning to end of each stride. But if you try anything, I would always recommend working with the **lower half of the body first** – i.e., the *"pelvic area"* and *"legs"* – as these are the foundation of movement that everything else can be based. Once you have the lower half of the body moving as you wish it to, it's so much easier to work and adapt the top half.

*(And always remember, to "**Save as**" your files forward every time, you create something you like! When experimenting is so easy to mess up everything you've done. So if you can just open the previous stage you created – rather than having to go back to the beginning each time – you will save yourself a heck of a lot of work!)*

Masterclass 19/ New Year Greeting

This particular exercise is taken from one of the online classes that students did just prior to the western *"New Year"*. I thought it would be fun for students to animate a simple "**New Year's Greeting**" video that they could send to the family and friends. However, although this message exercise is specific for the *"New Year"* as you will see, you can easily change the text of the message to make it any greeting that you like. You can download the rig, which will contain the original message, but you just have to select the *"layer"* and *"text"* to retype it. Other than that, just follow the lesson below. But first, our observational gesture drawing exercise…

Warm-Up Drawing

Today's assignment relates to the most expressive of all the arts, "**Dance**". *"Dance"* exaggerates all the qualities in poses that we've been studying so far – i.e., *"balance"*, *"dynamic pose"* and even a little of the *"bouncing ball"* principles by being strongly affected by gravity. The following **two** poses are an excellent opportunity to study, observe and interpret all these principles in action. Give yourself **3 minutes** to draw each pose…

DOI: 10.1201/9781003324287-21

Pose 1 comments: Notice the *"balance"* here. Although the character is probably in a motion to his right, there is an essence here of the point of his contact with the ground (i.e., his toes) which is pretty much under the center of gravity of the rest of his body. In actual fact, it is not, if you eliminate his arms. But, the very fact that his arms are stretching out to the opposite side of his toes, than the body, mitigates things somewhat. Note too the powerful, curved *"dynamic lines"* that his right arm, torso and right leg make. The left arm matches that somewhat, giving so much beauty and power to the pose in the process.

Pose 2 comments: Again, there are strong *"dynamic lines"* to feature here – the one made by his left arm, shoulders and upper right arm, as well as the left hip, upper right leg, entire left leg and foot that almost parallel the first one perfectly. Almost right-angled to these are the torso and the lower right leg. These offer tensions that you might build into your drawing. Note to the eyeline that his gaze is making pretty much matching the first of those *"dynamic lines"*.

In many ways, animators have to respect the same things as dancers – in the sense that *"dynamic pose"* and *"storytelling action"* are important to the final performance they make. Dancers of course have to work hard at their bodily strength, stamina and flexibility, but animators too have to work hard at creating dynamic poses with their characters that match this. All of them have to understand that same thing, namely *"movement"*, interpretation of *"emotion"*, and certainly they need to understand and respect the nature of *"balance"* above all else. So it serves them well if animators observe and interpret the actions of dancers – even sportsmen – if they want to get the most out of their action. Dancers are especially relevant to study, as they – like animators – have to work in perfect timing with music or audio tracks also, as do animators quite often of course. So, training your *"animator's eye"* in these kinds of exercises – or just indeed watching ballet, theater or dancing expression of any kind – is really food for you to feast on. As it will help you understand how shapes float into other shapes, how timing to beats and musical impact points is best done, and certainly how *"balance"* works. Studies of these kinds are never wasted.

Instruction

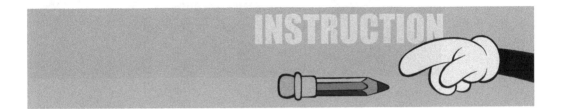

As indicated above, I wanted to have my animation students create a greetings piece for the New Year that was about to happen just a couple of weeks after I set the assignment. It is not a difficult one to do, but you will have to **download the rig file** from our dedicated web page to do it as follows. It will be called "**GREET 01.moho**" – although I strongly advise you to save a copy of it as "**GREET 01.moho**" before you start. Essentially, this is what it will look like when you finish it, unless you change the words of the greeting to match what you want it to say instead.

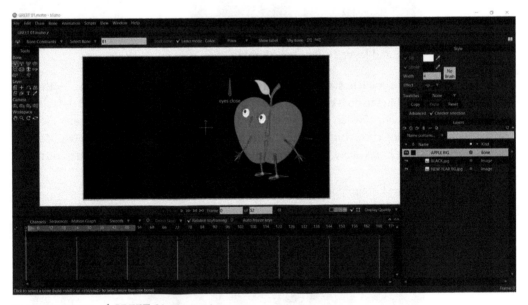

Screen capture of GREET 01 setup stage.

Basically, the screen starts black and the character magically wipes on the text by moving his arms up and down. There is a slight *"anticipation"* down as he lifts his arms up, followed by a fast swipe down of the arms to make the text appear. It is very simple, but is a good way of working with Moho or other digital software to use a basic principle of movement.

Key frames.

To *"block out"* the animation, this is what the interface will look like when you open *"GREET 02.moho"*. The named layers on the right column will read, from top to bottom… **"APPLE RIG"**, **"BLACK.jpg"** and **"NEW YEAR BG.jpg"**. The *"BLACK. jpg"* layer is used to reveal the text.

Stage and layer column highlighted.

We are going to start quite minimally, then flesh it out as we move on. So, the first thing to do is create our *"start"* position, which is where it should default to on *"frame 1"* when you open it up. However, if it doesn't, then you need to set the timeline cursor onto *"frame 1"* and create the following pose. Remember, *"Command Z"* will allow you to select and move any of the bones you need to do that.

Frame 1 stage pose.

Now move the cursor to "**frame 2**" on the timeline and create a "**down**" pose like this. To do that, "**Command Z**" then select the "root bone" and drag the character down. You can also bend the top of the apple forward a little, using the upper of the two *"body bones"* and swing the arms back to their *"anticipation"* pose also.

Frame 2 stage pose.

Scrub back and forward on the timeline to make sure everything is moving OK between the two keys, before creating the third position. This third position is going to be *"up"* with the arms swung through up and forward. Use the *"root bone"* to stretch the apple up as far as possible before the feet leave the ground. There will be a strong contact between the feet and the ground, due to them being anchored down by their own bones – although they can be pulled away if you lift the body too far. Try to keep the feet on the ground however, with the arms swung forward and high. You can also lean the upper body of the apple back too, to give a more dynamic sense of the upward stretch working. That completes our third key. Scrub all three to get a sense of how they are working.

Frame 3 stage pose.

For *"key frame"* number 4, we need to bend him down again, with the knees bending – although I would lean him forward a little, as long as he is *"balanced"* over the feet. Note that the arms will have swung back behind him too, to complete the fourth pose.

Frame 4 stage pose.

Now we need to create the final *"key pose"* frame, number "5". This is effective-ly our first key frame. So, select the keys on *"frame 1"*. Hit *"Command C"* to copy it. Then with the cursor not on *"frame 5"* of the timeline, *"Command V"* to paste it. You will now have created your fifth *"key pose"* frame, bringing the character back to where it started. Scrub through all five frames to get a sense of the ac-tion and adjust if necessary.

Frame 5 stage pose.

Now, having *"blocked out"* our five keys, we next need to thing about creating the **"passing positions"**. Most experienced animators will no doubt have their way of approaching this, but here are my suggestions. For the first one between keys *"1"* and *"2"*, select everything except *"frame 1"*. Drag them to the right along the timeline by 1 frame, which gives us an *"in-between"*. But remember, this is Moho's version of an in-between – actually but mechanically calculated. So we need to add our animator's touch to it to make it less so. My suggestion is to de-lay the arms slightly, giving us this difference between Moho's *"in-between"* and my *"passing position"*. Delaying the arms like this gives them more snap when they hit the second key position, which is what I'm going for. It also takes aspect of the action of the same keys in a sense, meaning that not everything is mov-ing the same way at the same time – a common fault with much bad, or rushed, animation.

New frame 2 in-between pose.

Next we are going to select everything to the right of the down (anticipation) *"key position"* and move them one frame to the right, giving us another in-between or "passing position" on *"frame 4"*.

New Frame 4 INITIAL in-between pose.

This time I want to keep the knees bent a little more than Moho wants them to be, and I want the arms to be up much higher. This will suggest the arms are motivating the upward action and the knees following a beat behind. I want the body slightly forward too, so it looks like it's moving on a somewhat forward arc.

New Frame 4 NEXT in-between pose – knees bent/arms up.

Now as I want the action up to be a little slower than it is, I'm going to open this section up by another frame, to give it more air.

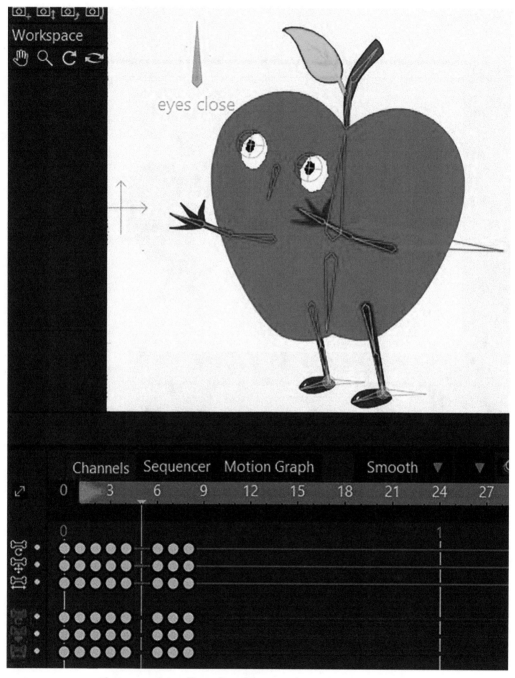

Close-up of timeline, showing extra frame.

I've added this frame, because although I want everything else to in-between normally, I want to take the arms beyond the most up position and have them go back and beyond a little.

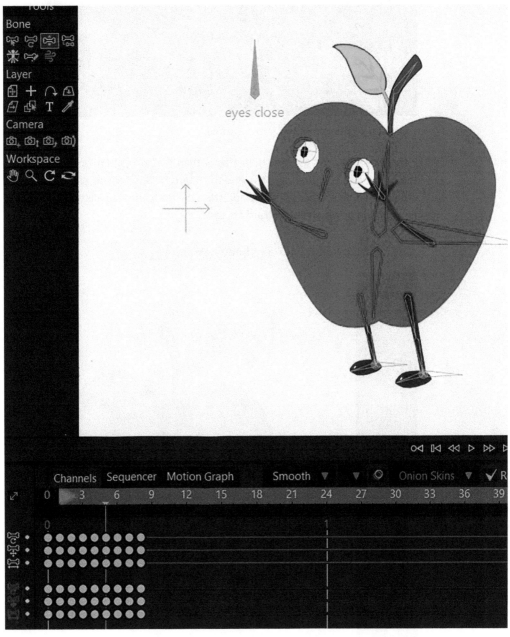

New extra frame, showing arms beyond up position and back a little.

Now I'm going to open up the last two frames by one frame to the right, to slow the down action a little.

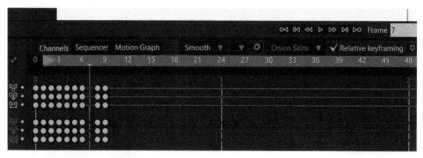

Close-up of timeline, two extra frames.

Here I want the arms to come down faster than the body, so I'm going to adjust them that way. I'm also going to bend the hands back a little bit, suggesting a little bit of drag on them. I'm also adjusting the body forward a little, to suggest him coming down on an outward arc too.

New adjusted hands back and body forward.

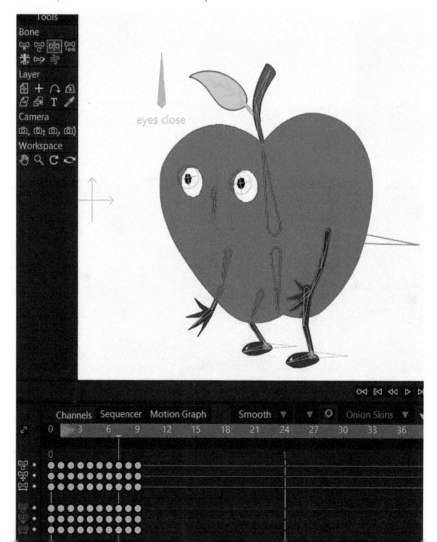

Then to create the last *"passing position"*, back to the start position, I'm going to open up the last key by 1 frame.

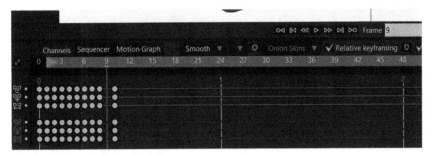

Close-up of timeline – last frame opened up by 1 frame.

Here I want to keep the arm momentum backward going further, while the rest of the body is heading back to the final position.

Arms back further and body moves toward final position.

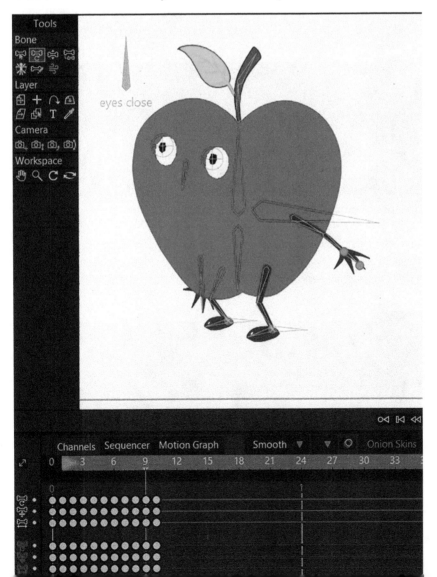

NOTE

I'm not telling you when to "Save" your work, but you should be doing it automatically as you move forward with each stage. In fact, once you saved it, you should "Save as" and create a new file to do each subsequent stage. This will prevent a lot of hurt later if you go drastically wrong at any point and can't retrieve it. If you haven't saved any of your work till now, "Save as" for the next action we take, calling it "GREET 03.moho".

Once you have that, scrub the whole action along the timeline from the very front to the very back frame to see how it works. It'll be fast but you should be able to get a sense of the flow of it by scrubbing slowly and observing carefully. If you like, you can hit *"play"* to see it repeating. Make sure you change the second white window under the *"Stage"* to *"10"*, which should be the last current frame. As I say, it will be crazy-fast, but it will also give you a feel for the flow we've created. If it looks generally OK, let's move on by adding in-betweens and finessing it further.

Now we can start moving our action on by adding some touches that will get it close to the final version. The first thing I want to do is put a *"hold"* on the first frame, so there is a delay before we see it moving. To do that, select everything except *"frame 1"* and slide it on by 1 frame, setting up a new *"frame 2"*.

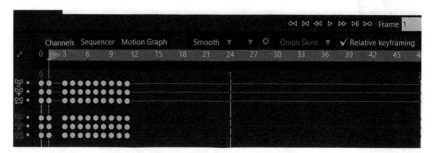

Close-up of timeline – adding new Frame 2.

Next select just *"frame 1"*, copy it using *"Command C"* and paste it into the new *"frame 2"* by using *"Command V"*. We should now have identical frames on *"1"* and *"2"*, making it a very tiny *"hold"*.

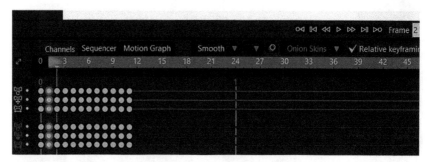

Close-up of timeline – Frame 1 copied to new Frame 2.

But because we need that front *"hold"* to be longer, we must now select everything except *"frame 1"* again, and this time slide it along the timeline by 23 frames – i.e., 1 second of screen time, running at 24 frames per second – until the old *"frame 2"* now becomes the new *"frame 24"*. Now, if you scrub along the timeline there, you'll see there's no movement at all until we hit *"frame 25"*. That is the *"hold"* we wanted.

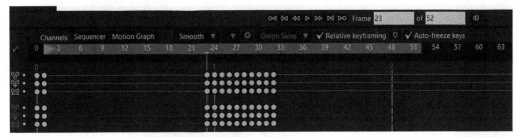

Close-up of timeline – Frame 1 extended to Frame 23.

Now select everything to the right of *"frame 24"* this time and move it 3 frames to the right.

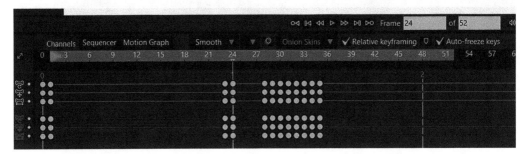

Close-up of timeline – showing extra 3 frames after Frame 24.

Then halfway among those 3 new in-between frames – i.e., *"frame 26"* – I want to make the arms a little more active by moving the elbows back and bending the arm in. This gives the arms a little *"pinching/squeezing"* action as they go up and down.

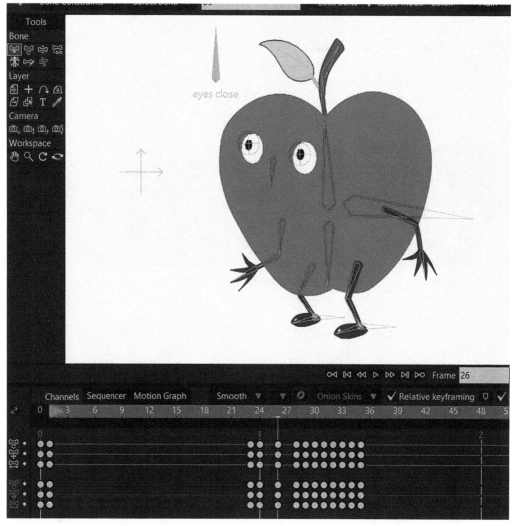

Bending arms on Frame 26.

Now to open up the next frame, select all the frames to the right of *"frame 28"* and move them to the right by **3 frames**. We don't need to touch anything here for now – Moho did a good job this time!

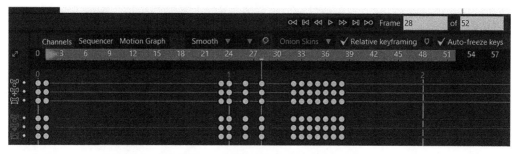

Close-up of timeline – adding 3 frames after Frame 28.

Now select all the frames to the right of *"frame 32"* and then open them up by **3 frames**.

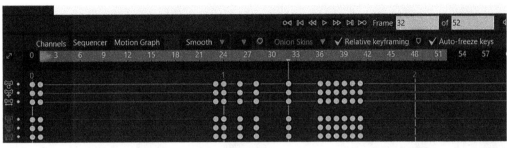

Close-up of timeline – adding 3 frames after Frame 32.

Now there are two things I would like to do with this. In the middle of the three new frames, I want to squash the body down a bit by bending the knees more, and I want to hold the arms back a little bit to change the pace of their movement upward.

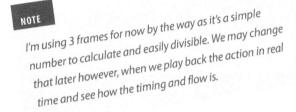

NOTE

I'm using 3 frames for now by the way as it's a simple number to calculate and easily divisible. We may change that later however, when we play back the action in real time and see how the timing and flow is.

Squash body down pose.

For the next *"passing position"*, select all the frames from *"37"* onward and open them up by **5 frames**, as we really need to slow this part down. For now, we're not going to make adjustments, just accept what Moho gives us for now.

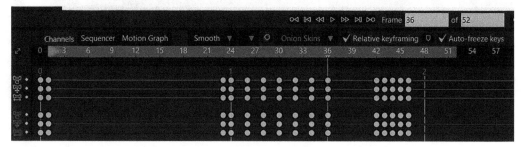

Close-up of timeline – adding 5 frames after Frame 36.

Now, select all the frames from *"42"* onward, open them up by **3 frames** and leave it as it is for now.

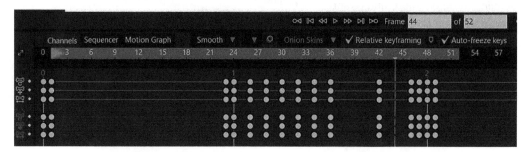

Close-up of timeline – adding 3 frames after Frame 42.

Next, select *"frame 47"* and beyond, then open it up by just **1 frame**, then hold the arms back a little – bending them a little as we do so – on that new in-between.

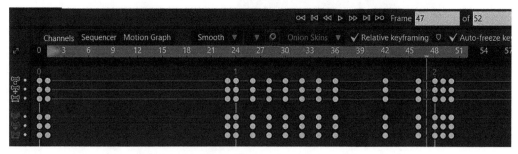

Close-up of timeline – adding 1 frame after Frame 47.

Then select *"frame 49"* and onward and just open those up by **1 frame**, then push the arms back a little further behind the body and bend them a little.

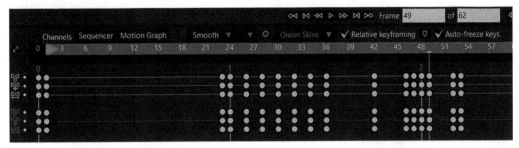

Close-up of timeline – adding 3 frames after Frame 49 + arms back on pose.

Then, as it's coming to a halt yet it shouldn't be too abrupt, select all of the last frame and open that up by **1**, making it the new *"frame 52"*. On the new in-between, bring the arms forward and bend them more, although the hands should be delayed a little by keeping them bend back a little.

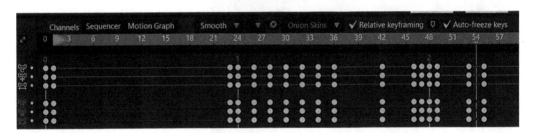

Close-up of timeline – adding 1 frame after Frame 53.

Finally, for this first pass of opening up our animation, we need to put a *"hold"* on the last frame, *"frame 54"*. So to do that, select it and hit *"Command C"*. Then move the cursor to *"frame 54"* and hit *"Command V"*. This will duplicate frames *"53"* and *"54"*.

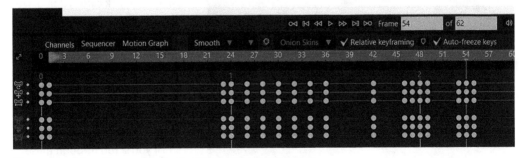

Close-up of timeline – duplicate Frame 53 on Frame 54.

With that done, select *"frame 54"* and drag it along the timeline to *"frame 65"*.

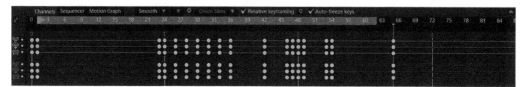

Close-up of timeline – extend Frame 54 to Frame 65.

Close-up of white end frame window showing 65 frames.

Now we have roughed out our animation, and we need to play it in Moho. So, now we know that our last frame is *"65"*, we have to write that number into the "end" white window under the *"Stage"* and hit *"Play"*.

Now this is not going to be perfect yet for me but – in the interests of saving space in the book – it's good enough to move on. Now we need to create the *"wipe"* that reveals the lettering on the left side of the screen. At the moment, it is timed out by the rig file. However, we need to adjust this, as we don't want it to be revealed until the apple's arms come down and *"wipe it on"* toward the end. At the moment, the arms are in the process of coming down approximately around the *"48 frame"* mark, and we need to make sure that the lettering *"wipe"* is happening around there too. At the moment, it's appearing far too late. So, to fix that, we need to slide that *"BLACK"* layer cover down sooner. However, to see what the black card is doing, we need to highlight the *"BLACK.jpg"* layer on the column to the right.

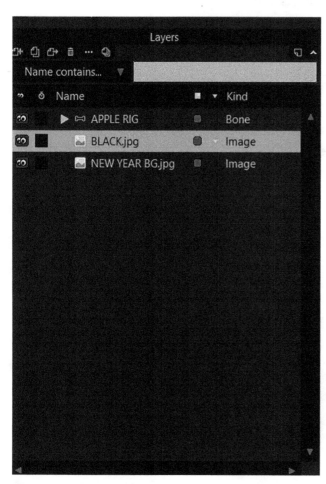

Close-up of layers with BLACK.jpg highlighted.

Now you'll see that we've got different keys on the "BLACK" layer timeline. There is one at "frame 53" and another at *"frame 58"*. If you scrub through these on the timeline, you'll see the lettering being revealed as you do so. Therefore, we simply have to change the moment on the timeline when this happens. So, as the apple's arms start coming down around *"frame 48"*, we need to drag the first *"wipe"* frame from *"53"* back to *"47"*, to anticipate the arms coming down.

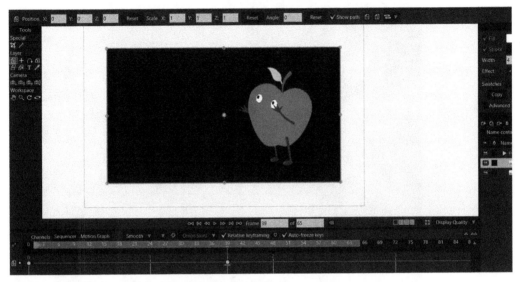

Keys on the timeline, moved from frame 53 to frame 47.

To Animate the BLACK.jpg Layer Going Down

Select the BLACK.jpg layer in your layers panel, go to frame 39 and make sure the transform layer tool is also selected to create a key for the layer left click on the black image in the stage.

Transform tool selected key on frame 39.

Go to frame 54 and move the image with the transform tool down, so that it reveals the whole text.

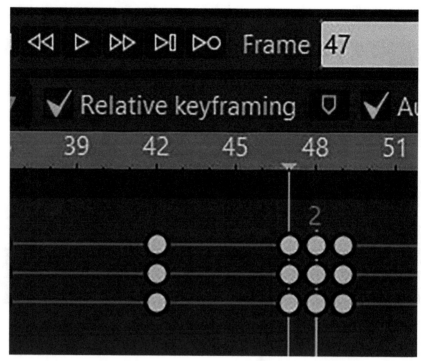

Frame 54 text revealed.

This is just a final reminder about the lettering. At the moment, it is a "Happy New Year" message. But if you want to change that, you simply have to replace this "NEW YEAR BG.jpg" file with another of your own. That way you can be revealing anything you like with the apple action.

Then, as we need the lettering to be fully revealed by *"frame 54"*, we need to drag the last *"wipe"* key to there. Now if we play the action, we'll see that the lettering reveal will be in better sync with the arms than before. You can adjust this marginally yourself, if not. At least you now know the principles of what is happening here – it will just need fine-tuning on your part to make it perfect. Then, when it is just *"Export to Video"* to make a file, you can send to family or friends.

Suggested Assignment

My suggestion here is two-fold. The first is that you might want to experiment a little on the overall apple's movement. For example, do you want to have it move slower? If so, then you'll need to add more in-betweens in places – or throughout. The choice is yours here. It's all about experimenting and finding what pace and timing you like best. (But remember, if you change the timing on the apple, you'll also have to change the timing of the text reveal *"wipe"*, so it reveals as the arm positions on the apple in sync again.) The other change you can make here is also significant. You'll notice on the rig that the stalk and leaf at the top of the apple have bones too. This is so you can add a little *"overlapping action"* to the movement, to make it all feel more natural. This is a very simple principle to the hands on a walk. Remember, when the lower arm swings forward, the hand drags back, and when the arm swings back, the hand drags forward.

Overlapping action on hands in relation to the arms.

Well, you can do the same thing with the stalk. When the apple moves forward and down, the stalk can drag back behind it. Then, when the apple moves up and back, the stalk can drag forward.

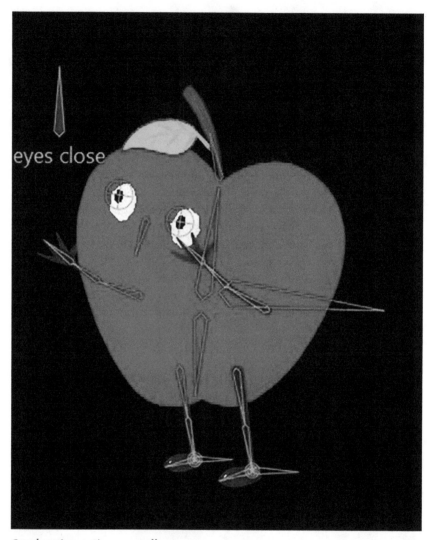

Overlapping action on stalk.

The way and the timing you use here is really down to your personal choice, but remember as some of the animation is moving on *"1s"* toward the end, you will have to adjust the stalk on *"1s"* to adjust it too. Experiment with the degree of *"overlapping action"* you put on the stalk.

Masterclass 20/ Double Jump

I think this is a good time in the Moho proceedings for you to test your knowledge. It shouldn't be a scary thing as it's not too difficult. But, before you move on, you might want to know what you retain and what you don't. If you find yourself struggling with it, however, I have given you all the right moves toward the end of this lesson. But try to do it without checking that out, as it will help you understand what you do know, and don't know, so far. But, first, let's relax to do some observational gesture drawings…

Warm-Up Drawing

I think it's time to consider drawing from movement as part of our challenge here. However, as I can't show you moving footage to draw from – as I would in a normal classroom – I will use a sequence of still images taken from a ballet studio instead. It will still be against the clock but this time I want you just to give yourself **1 minute to complete each of the images**. So, as there will be 12 images in total, this will be a 12-minute exercise. Give yourself time and space to do it without interruption, sketching all of the 12 drawings on one sheet of your sketchbook if you can. If you want to sketch them almost like matchstick figures, then this will be fine. It is the pose action that is more important than the detail of the figure.

DOI: 10.1201/9781003324287-22

Comments: Part of the skill of an animator is to observe, interpret and then communicate what has been seen, through a visual movement. So, these 1-minute poses will help you develop those skills.

Instruction

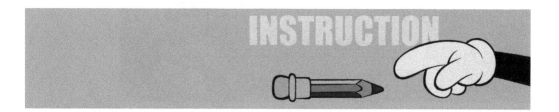

The first thing I want you to do is download the rig that is called "**JUMP 01.moho**". Once you have it, I recommend you immediately save it as *"JUMP 02.moho"*, just for safety's sake – just in case you mess up and need to go back to *"JUMP 01"* file and start again. The challenge here is for you to take the *"Apple"* character, animate him jumping forward, then animate him jumping back again. Pretty straightforward actually – and definitely something you should be able to work out on your own at this stage. But if not, then I'm including the instruction below. However, as a personal test of interest, try it on your own at first to see how it works out for you. I'm not going anywhere, but let's see how well you do this on your own…

Apple jump sequence.

Instructions

OK, I'm assuming you're not reading on to this part without having a go at it first. But just in case you didn't do it or tried but it didn't work out, here are my instructions on how to do it. Again, every time you do a new thing and it works out OK, save forward another version of it, so you can always go back one stage and start again. Another thing is before you do anything on the timeline, make sure that you're starting from **"Frame 1"**.

Close up of Timeline – Frame 1.

"Frame 0" will not show up in the video in any way of course, but as it's your construction frame, it could make your rig look weird if you start on that frame – or unresponsive to animation controls as well. However, *"Frame 1"* should be fine, so be sure to start from there.

Blocking Out

OK, so the first animation thing you need to do is to **"block out"** your action. That's where great animation can start or end. If you remember from our bouncing ball and other assignments, if the character is going to jump up, then they have to do a little squash down first. This is the *"anticipation"*. Then, when they get to the top of the jump, they need to "slow-in", then *"slow-out"* as they head downward again. Hitting the ground, their knees are going to bend, as they have to *"cushion the weight"* that is coming down. Then, they will stand up normally. These are the key positions you will need for this jump forward.

Starting pose.

Now, having established the starting position in *"Frame 1"*, move your cursor to **"Frame 2"**. Then, hitting **"Command Z"**, select the root bone and bring the Apple down until the knees bend. We're going to push it *forward* a little bit too to motivate the jump ahead of itself. The other thing you need to do here is rotate the arms back, in preparation for the jump. This is like an *"anticipation"* for the arms too, before they swing forward on the main jump forward and upward.

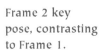

Frame 2 key
pose, contrasting
to Frame 1.

In "**Frame 3**", you need to block the character forward and high in the air. Note that his legs are bent and the toes are bent back, as a reflex action after pushing off. The arms of the other hand will have swung all way forward and up.

Frame 3 pose.

Next, we need to do the landing. To do this, we'll do a little cheat/shortcut. Select "*Frame 1*", hit "*Command C*" to copy it, then paste this onto "**Frame 4**". That way, we have the "*Frame 1*" position established, although we don't want it to end there. So, we are going to move the whole pose forward, so that it is positioned ahead of the high position on the ground where the landing needs to be.

Frame 4 pose.

That done, we have to realize, however, that this is the final position, but before that happens, he needs to bend down because of the weight of the landing. So, copy *"Frame 4"* and paste it into "**Frame 5**" also. This gives us two identical positions, although we need to return back to *"Frame 4"* to create the *"squash"* position there, in readiness for the *"Frame 5"* ending. Angle the body **backward** a little too, as his downward and arced trajectory would have him doing that. Also, keep the arms **up in the air** still before they come down to the position they're in on *"Frame 5"*.

Frames 4 and 5 – side by side.

Scrub along the timeline to make sure your blocked-in action is broadly working. Adjust as necessary until you have 5 strongly blocked-out jump-forward positions. The other thing to do now – If you remember, "overlapping action" – is to work on things that are attached to the main action. I'm thinking of the *"stalk and the leaf"* here. So, as the Apple jumps up, keep the stalk back, and when it comes down, have it coming forward somewhat. Then, as it adjusts after the squash, have the "stalk and leaf" ease into its final position – although you could have a delay to do that if you want to add more time to your action.

Improve the action on the stalk by adding overlapping action.

All that successfully done, we now need the Apple to jump backward to its original start position. This means that we're more or less reversing everything but with some small modifications. So, in **Frame 6** of our blocking-out, we need him in a *"squash"* position but leaning backward to motivate the jump. You could almost copy/paste *"Frame 4"* into *"Frame 6"* if you like and with the arms back.

Frame 6 pose.

Now, to make things easy for yourself, copy *"Frame 1"* again and paste it into
"**Frame 7**". This will give us our blocked-in end position.

Frame 1 is pasted in Frame 7.

That established, select "Frame 7" and open it up by **1 frame**. Now, take this new
"Frame 7" inbetween and raise it up high, to make it the **apex** of the backward
jump. We want the Apple to lean back somewhat at this point, as his body angle
still needs to motivate the direction he is heading in. His legs will be lifting up
too – as if he was doing one of those "bomb" jumps into a swimming pool.

Timeline and Stage – opening up Frame 7 and adjusting pose.

Finally, we need to create a *"squash"* position for the landing, before it resolves into the end position. So, I suggest you copy/paste the final frame – *"Frame 8"* – and paste it into **"Frame 9"**, making this the final frame. Then go back to *"Frame 8"* and *"squash"* the Apple down, giving it a slight lean forward at this point.

Adding Frames 8 to 9 and adding squash to 8.

Scrub along the timeline through all 9 frames to see if it is flowing nicely. If it is, then "well done" – for successfully *"blocking-out"* your action. If not, then adjust accordingly until it works.

Inbetweening

Now let's go to the next stage – which is **"inbetweening"**. Normally, we'd do the *"breakdown positions"* as a separate exercise in other animation exercises, but I think we can handle both at the same time as we **inbetween** our actions here. And… hopefully, you will have saved a new version by now? But if not, save your work as **"JUMP 03.moho"** before you do anything else. The file name will be even higher than "03" if you've been doing saving different versions already!

As it stands now, this animation is clearly going to be far too fast to work, so we've got to open these keys up by adding *"inbetweens"*. *The first thing we're going to do is open up the keys up from the "start" position to the first "squash" position. I would suggest that a couple of inbetweens here would be enough for what we want. So, select everything except "Frame 1" and drag it all to the right by* **2 frames**.

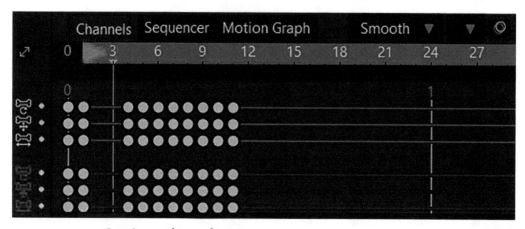

Opening up frames by 2.

So now, we have the first action with 2 inbetweens going down. This should be fast, but not too fast. Now, we're going to inbetween the action from the first *"squash"* position to the *"apex"* position. Remember from the *"bouncing-ball"* exercise we have done before that we need to **"slow-in"** to the top from the bottom. So, to do this in Moho, I'm going to select everything after the first *"squash"* position and open them up by **1 frame**.

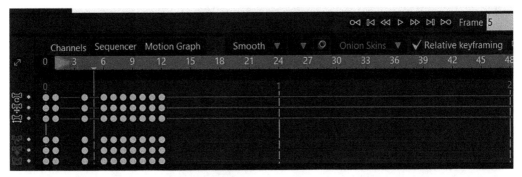

Opening up by 1 frame.

Now, we have our first inbetween going up – which is therefore a "**breakdown drawing**". And remember from the "bouncing ball" that the first *"breakdown drawing"* up is a "**stretch**" position, so we need to have our Apple as stretched as possible – in other words, its arms stretched upward and its legs straight and standing on its tiptoes. (Although the toes should still be on the ground at this point.)

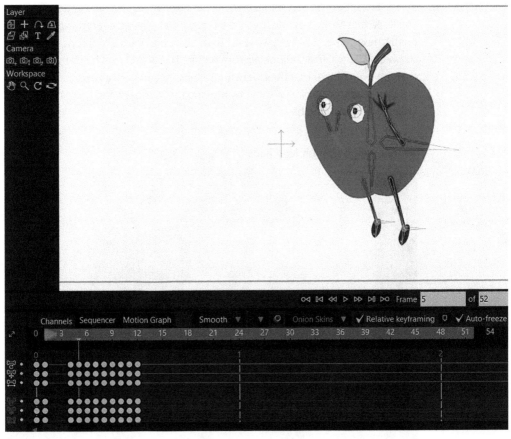

The stretched pose.

With our first *"breakdown position"* complete on the way up, we need to add perhaps another 3 inbetweens. However, as we need to *"slow-in"* to the top apex point, I suggest we open each one up **one at a time**. That way the inbetweens will get closer together as they get toward the top of the jump – rather than be spread out evenly if we just open things up by 3 frames straight away. So, select everything after the *"passing position"* we have just created and move them **1 frame** to the right.

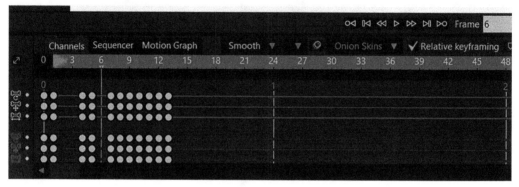

Opening up by 1 frame.

You'll see that Moho has effectively perfectly inbetweened everything naturally on this new frame. However, we want to do a couple of fixes to this perfect inbetween that will make it look more dynamic. This would require us to take the arms up even higher that they were in the *"passing position"* and further back. We also need to do a similar thing by moving the legs back and bending them a little more than Moho has.

Arms up higher, with legs back.

Now, we repeat that action again. This time, select everything after the inbetween we have just created and move that to the right by **1 frame** to create our second inbetween after the *"passing position"*. The only tweak here would be to maybe bend the legs a little more as they start to come forward.

Adding 1 frame and adjusting the pose.

Now, we follow this same procedure one more time, to add the third inbetween we need. This time, select everything after the 2nd inbetween we just created and move that forward by **1 frame**. This time, we don't need to make any more tweaks.

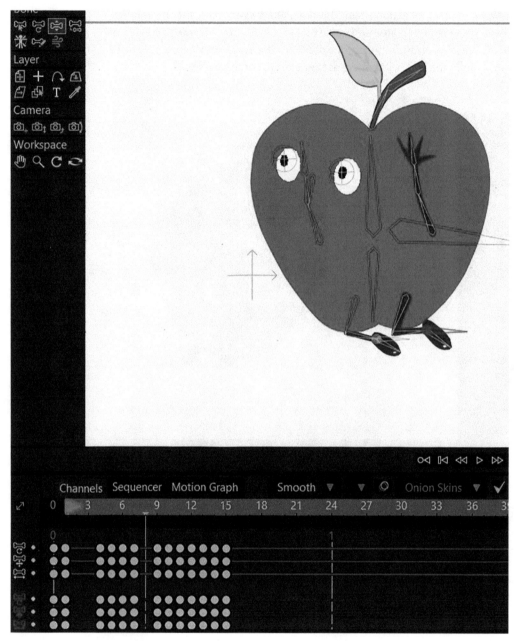

Opening up by 1 frame.

Now, having got our Apple to the top of his jump, we now have to start bringing him down. So, to do this, select everything after the *"apex"* position and move that to the right by **1 frame**. That will create the **"breakdown position"** on the way down. If you remember from our *"bouncing-ball"* exercise, this needs to be in contact with the ground but stretched out as much as possible from where it has come from. So, keep the **arms up** on the Apple, have him **lean back a little** toward the "apex" position and have his straight legs stretched as far down as possible, hitting with the **heels of the feet**.

Adding 1 frame and create a stretch pose.

Again, like going up, we should add another **3** inbetweens on the way down too. But this time, they will be "**slowing-out**" from the top, so we have to treat this slightly differently from before. Instead of selecting frames *after* the *"passing position"* on the way up and opening it up by **1 frame**, this time, we need to select the *"passing position"* and the frames after it. This will give us a new *"inbetween"* between the *"apex"* position and the *"passing position"* on the way down. This adds one *"slowing-out"* inbetween from the "apex" position.

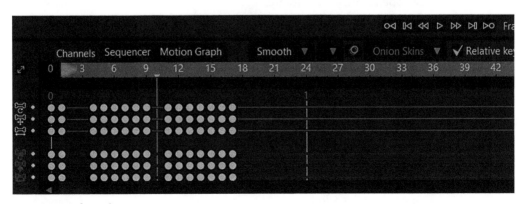

Opening up by 1 frame.

The only *tweak* I would make to the Moho inbetweening here is to have the legs angled out a little more in front of the position they've been given. That way, it will feel like they're **reaching out** before hitting the ground where they do on the next key position when it's moving at a real speed. This is a little like the front leg reaching out *"up"* and *"forward"* before contacting the ground on a *"generic-walk"* stride action.

The adjusted pose.

That done, we can open up another *"slowing-out"* frame on our downward action. So, this time, select the inbetween we've just created, plus the ones after it, and open those up by **1 frame**.

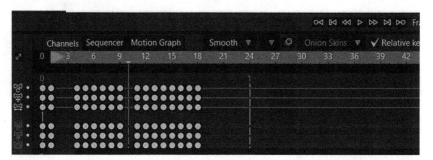

Opening up by 1 frame.

Again, you could tweak the legs a little more to help that feeling that they're reaching out and forward after the "apex" position. This should give us another successful "slowing-out" inbetween on the way down.

The adjusted pose.

Finally, we have to create our 3rd and final "slowing-out" inbetween on the way down. So, selected the last inbetween we created and the ones behind it, then open those up by **1 frame**.

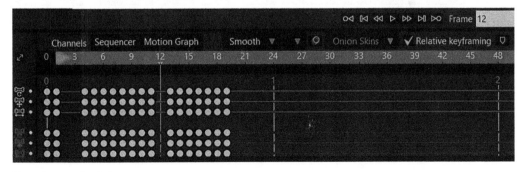

Opening up by 1 frame.

This gives us enough *"slowing-out"* inbetweens to bring him down convincingly. Remember that when he does come down, he's in a *"squash"* position, so we've got to inbetween him to the final **"stand-up"** position going forward. So, again, I'm going to suggest **3** *"slowing-in" inbetweens* here too. *That will make him return to the last pose slowly but will enable him to cushion into it at the same time. So, select the last standing-up pose and the ones after it and open it up by* **1 frame**, *which will effectively be our* **"breakdown position"**.

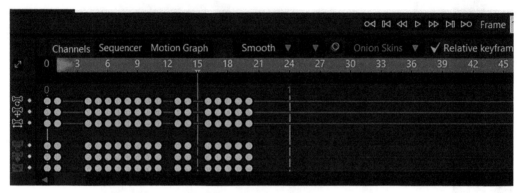

Opening up by 1 frame.

To create the next *"slowing-in"* inbetween, select the *"breakdown position"* we've just created – as well as those after it – and open that up by **1 frame**.

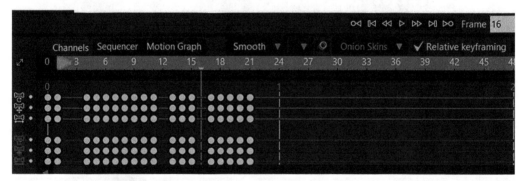

Opening up by 1 frame.

Then, to complete the final *"slowing-in"* inbetween that we need, repeat the process. Select the last inbetween and the poses after it, opening them up by **1 frame**.

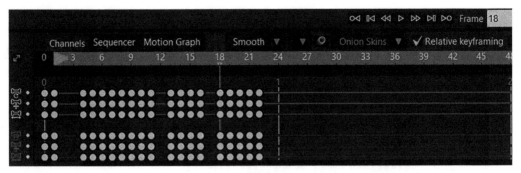

Opening up by 1 frame.

"Scrub along the timeline" to see how the entire jump forward works. It might be that it will still need adjustments, according to your own taste of wanting things faster or slower. When you've finished that though, it will help to hit the "**Play**" button to see it running on the "Stage". (Don't forget to change the end frame number on the 2nd white box beneath the *"Stage"*, so you can see it looping to whatever your last frame of the jump forward is.)

Adjusted end-frame number in the white box to 18.

When you're satisfied that the Apple's jump forward is moving as you want it, then move on to inbetween the jump **backward**. However, as this is really a *test* lesson, I am going to leave it to you to work that one out for yourself! Having just successfully completed the jump forward with my suggestions and your modifications, you should be very capable of doing that!

I have every confidence that you can do this!

Lastly, don't forget to "**Export to video**" once your entire action is complete. Viewing it in real-time video is realistically the only way of judging it for sure, as the playback on the *"Stage"* can vary in terms of the speed accuracy it gives. This can vary due to the power of your computer, then the number of layers you are working with on any scene and a number of other factors that can slow your in-software playback speed down.

Suggested Assignment

No real additional suggestions here. Suffice it to say, if your test doesn't work perfectly, try to **troubleshoot** what you've done and **adjust** your animation where necessary. The important thing here is that the action needs to be *convincing* and feel *plausible*. If you achieve that, then "**congratulations**", you have passed the test!

Masterclass 21/ Slow Sneak Animation

We're now at the penultimate Moho lesson in this section of the book. We have 12 classes in *"Section II"*, which is mainly dedicated to working with Moho. However, the last two lessons are going to be more directed at early preparation for your own project, that we will be entirely working on in *"Sections 3 & 4"*. However, we will have more than covered all the core principles of movement that we planned for a digital (Moho) approach to 2D animation, with this class focusing entirely on animating a **"Slow-Sneak"** action. However, before we talk about that, let's do our observational gesture drawing exercise…

Warm-Up Drawing

In this session, we're going to be echoing what we did in the last session and moving on with it using a different subject. As you know, in the last session, we began to develop our fast observation skills by looking at still frames of dancing movements. This time, we're going to extend this by looking at "sporting action" – specifically the throwing action of a baseball pitcher, done in a realistically illustrated way. This is specially timed for here as in the next lesson we're going to study "throwing action" in Moho. It is so valuable to observe and analyze from a real-world material, as I've said before, as it can be so informative

DOI: 10.1201/9781003324287-23

when we come to animate something. So, this exercise, coupled with the next lesson's animation assignment, is a perfect way of putting this notion into practice. What follows in the slow-motion action of a baseball pitcher. It is broken down into individual frames in this book, however, so that you can devote just **1 minute** to capture each individual pose.

Comments: Remember that you're not looking for photographic likenesses here or even detail in the clothing or props of the pitcher. What are most important here are the **angles**, **proportions** and any **dynamic lines** of movement you can emphasize with your drawings, based on this sequential action.

What we're attempting with this exercise is to give you every possible physical pose that you will encounter if you ever have to animate a pitcher – or a regular character throwing a ball, a javelin, a spear or anything that can be thrown. The thing that you're noticing most of all hopefully is that there is a slow, unwinding of the body during the throw. This has always been known in the animation world as "**successive breaking of joints**". And what this means is that now parts of the body move at the same time. For example, when any pitcher is throwing, they start in a static position, do what we know as *"anticipation"* back before coming forward and then unfold their body in stages to make the throw. This begins with the lead leg coming forward and planting down to create a solid base for the throw to happen. Then, the **hips** follow through, then the **shoulders**, then the **elbow**, then the **wrist** and finally the **fingers** as the ball is released. Even then, the action doesn't stop as there is a **follow-through** – with the throwing arm usually wrapping around the front of the body and the free leg often coming up at the back, then through to the front and planting its foot on the ground ahead of the other foot. It usually ends with the pitcher standing upright to observe where the ball has gone – although they will tend to keep their eye on the ball as much as possible throughout, except at the very beginning when he turns away during the *"anticipation"*. The whole thing is all like a coiled spring slowly unwrapping, then finally releasing, and why this kind of dynamic action has always been known as the *"successive breaking of joints"*. So, all these things are worth bearing in mind whenever you're animating a "throw", baseball-related or otherwise. It is never just a question of two main key positions – with the arm back and the arm forward – it is much more than that, which is why it is always important to reference the real world when you're working in the imaginary one. Remember too that no matter how perfectly to replicate the real-world action of anything you study, you then have to exaggerate, or caricature, it to make it really powerful in the animation world.

Hopefully, this will all give you more than enough to reflect on before you tackle an actual throwing action in the next class. But, for now, let's look at how a *"slow sneak"* can be animated…

Instruction

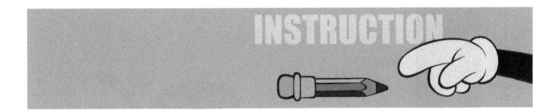

One of the key actions that have been handed down to us by our animation ancestors is the "**Slow Sneak**". So, let's analyze how that works and how we create it in a digital program like Moho. A *"sneak"* is a kind of a creeping-walk action that is very stylized. It is used to suggest a character that is either trying to stealthily sneak up on someone or a situation – or else they are trying to sneak away from someone or a situation without being seen.

Sneaking away.

I think in the interests of time and economy, we'll do a repeating *"sneak cycle"* action happening on the spot – rather than it moving across the screen, which is where it is most effective. The cycle approach will get you to understand the basic action quite quickly, so I prefer to teach it that way. You can always learn how to plot your cycle animation across the screen later, if you want it that way.

Here is our Apple rig, with the character located in the center of the screen when you open it up in Moho. The file you need to download from the dedicated website is named "**Apple sneak 01.moho**". So, the first thing you need to do before anything else is to save it as "**Apple sneak 02.moho**".

The next thing to do is *"block out"* the action. So, we're going to take our character here and adjust it to the first position. Essentially, we want **slightly bent legs** – with the **left leg back** and the **right leg forward**. In this sense, it's a bit like a walk-stride position, except that the sneak is always done on tiptoes. So, the **heels need to be up**. Also, the stride on a sneak also has a **body lean backward**, with the emphasis of the weight being on the back leg. Save that – or even as *"Apple sneak 03.moho"* if you're really cautious. (To be advised for all beginners!)

Frame 1 pose.

Now, the sneak has a peculiar way of working. It actually has two stride positions – one where it is leaning back and another where it leans forward. So, we're now going to create the second one. Therefore, move the timeline cursor to "**Frame 2**" and **angle the body forward**. The feet do not move from where they are, we just need to angle the body forward and **have the weight shifted more to the front leg** than the back.

Frame 2 pose.

To *"block out"* our 3rd key pose position, we're going to move the cursor on to **"Frame 03"** – but only after first copying *"Frame 01"* and pasting it on that 3rd frame. Although this is strictly not the correct pose we want yet, the body shape actually is. So, we're using that copy before we work with the legs. Then, with regard to the legs, we're going to take the **back leg forward** and the **front leg back**, reversing them for the next stride position. Remember to keep the character on its toes as you make these adjustments and adjust the body a little so that its weight is over the back leg.

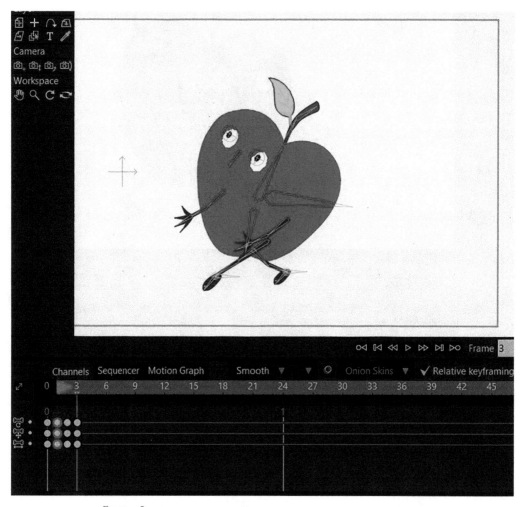

Frame 3 pose.

Next, in "**Frame 4**", we're going to angle the body and push the weight forward
with the feet remaining where they are in *"Frame 3"* – just like we did in the
2nd frame. Note too that both legs need to be bent slightly.

Frame 4 pose.

"**Scrub**" the timeline over these 4 *"key-stride"* positions to get a round idea of how the body is shifting back and forth. This is the foundational blocking for a good *"slow sneak"*. "Save" this file when you're happy and "Save As" to the next version.

First 4 positions are beside each other.

Before we do any more work on the movement, we want to adjust the arms somewhat. This means that when the body is leaning back, we want the **arms to be back** too.

Arms adjusted backward.

Then, when the body is leaning forward, we want the arms to be **forward** also. Note that here, there is a little extra **bend in the arms and hands** too. Do the same on the 2nd stride too and *"Save"* and/or "Save As" to the next version.

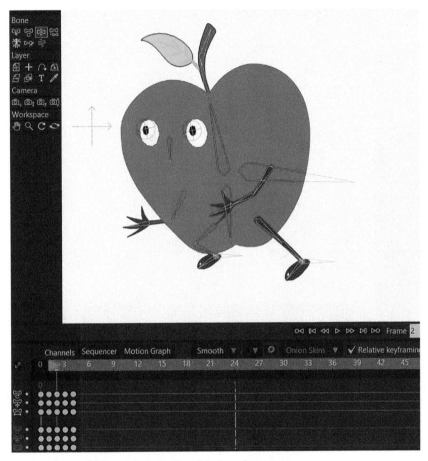

Arms adjusted forward, extra bend in hands.

Now, we need to work on the *"passing positions"*. You'll remember that they are the first inbetween we create that links two key positions together. So, the first thing to do here is select everything except *"Frame 1"* and open it up by **1 frame**.

Opening up to create a new Frame 2.

On the new *"Frame 2"*, it gives us what I call a *"Moho inbetween"* for the *"passing position"*. This means that it is technically halfway, but it is not what we want. So, we have to **override** what Moho gives us. To do this, we need to move the body position a **little more forward** and **down**, with it **leaning a little more forward** too. The arms need to be **straightened** a little as well. "Save" and/or "Save As".

Adjusted Frame 2.

Now, we move on to the next *"passing position"*. To do that, select the last two keys and open it up by **1 frame**.

Opening up 1 frame.

Again, we have a *"Moho inbetween"* that we don't want. So, this time we need to **raise the body up** much higher, and the left leg is **moving through** in what we can call a *"passing position"*. But, unlike a generic-walk *"passing position"*, we need to bring the left leg up very high, with the **toe still pointing down**. Make sure that the center of gravity on the body is right above – or even a touch forward – of the contact foot on the ground. This is our ideal *"breakdown/passing position"* here. *"Save"* and/or *"Save As"*.

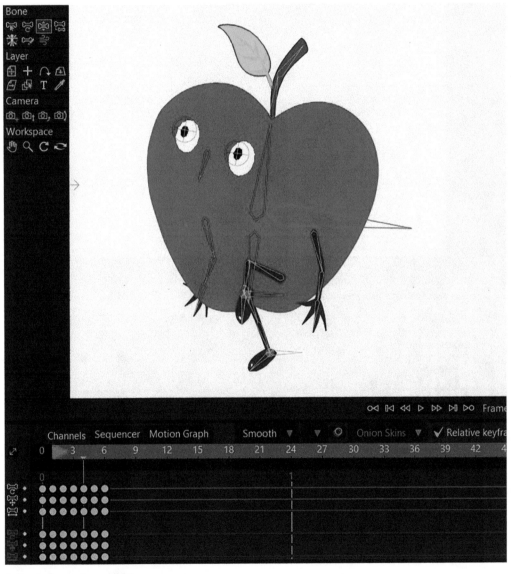

Adjusted passing position.

Now what we need to do is create the first *"breakdown position"* at the beginning of the 2nd stride. So, select the last key pose and open that up by **1 frame**.

Opening up 1 frame.

Do exactly what you did for the first *"breakdown position"* on the 1st stride – although this time the **legs will be reversed** of course. *"Save"* and/or *"Save As"*.

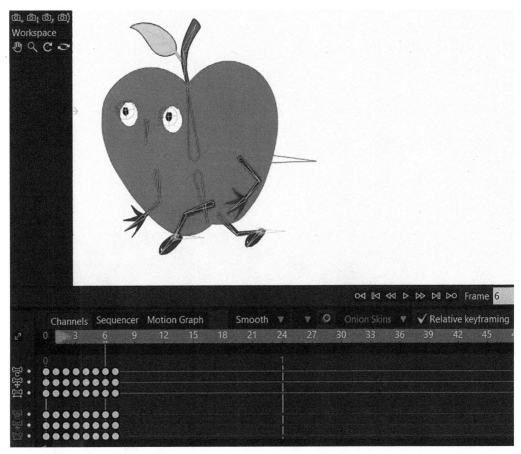

Adjusted pose in the new frame.

Lastly, we need to create the last *"breakdown position"* on the 2nd frame, which will link us back to the 1st frame on the repeat cycle. So, to do this, copy *"Frame 1"* and paste it on the frame **after** our current last frame on the timeline. When that's done, select it and open it up by **1 frame**. This will ensure that the new frame that's opened up will be the linking *"breakdown/passing position"* to where the 1st frame now is.

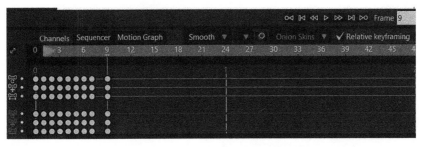

Opening up 1 frame from end to beginning of the cycle.

Finally, adjust this new *"breakdown/passing position"* as we did the one that was created for the end of the 1st stride – although again, the legs will be **reversed**. *"Save"* and/or *"Save As"* when it is done.

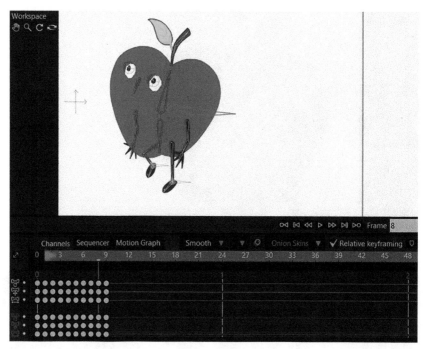

Adjusted pose of new passing position.

You have now created the *"keys"* and *"breakdowns"* for your *"slow sneak"* blocking out. *"Scrub"* the timeline to check if it moves consistently from one stride to the other. If that is OK, then it's time to start "**inbetweening**" our actions. But, first, a couple of minor adjustments.

At this stage, we should consider what to do with the *"stalk and leaf"* – which of course means we need to give them an "**overlapping action**". Essentially, what this means is that when the body comes forward, we need to take that "stalk and leaf" **back**, and when the body goes back, we need to take the *"stalk and leaf"* **forward**. Adjust them on all of the *"key"* and *"breakdown positions"*, essentially ensuring that the "stalk and leaf" move **counter** to the body positions on all these frames.

Sequence of added "overlapping action" to stalks and leaves.

The arms could be delayed a little on the *"breakdown positions"*, however, especially when moving from front to back. This means that on those two *"breakdown positions"* especially, they need to be **bent forward** a little. *"Save"* and/or *"Save As"* if all looks good.

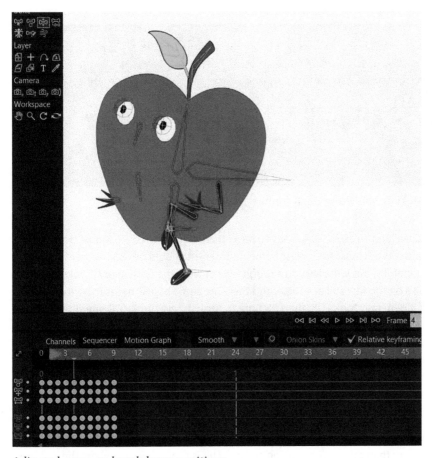

Adjusted arms on breakdown positions.

Now for the **"inbetweens"**. Let's keep it very simple to start, I'm going to select everything but "**Frame 1**", opening this up by **3 frames**.

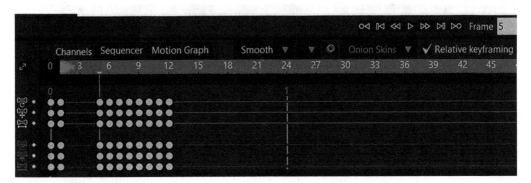

Opening up 3 frames.

Then, I'm basically going to do the **same all the way through** – i.e., selecting the next frames and opening them up by **3 frames** until every *"key"* and *"break-down position"* is separated from one another by 3 frames. Now, this is not a perfect solution for our "slow sneak", but it will at least give us a simple start to see how the basic action works at a slower speed.

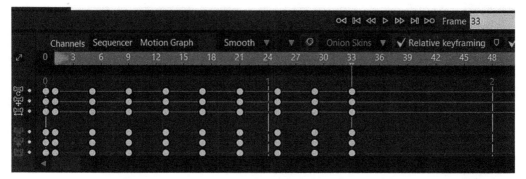

All keys opened up by 3 frames.

"Save" and/or *"Save As"* what you have, then adjust the white "**end-frame**" box under the *"Stage"* to our last frame number – it should be "**33**" – and hit "**Play**". Hopefully, this will give you a rough idea of what the *"slow sneak"* looks like. It's all a bit too fast still of course, and there are some adjustments to be made. But if it generally looks OK, then it's time to "**polish**" everything. Remember, however, that "polishing" animation may require a lot of tweaking back and forth until we get what we want. However, I have simplified things here, compared to what I would normally do on my own when animating. What follows therefore is the best shot I can share with you in a simple and direct way. It would probably take a whole book of "to-ing and fro-ing" to tell you what I normally do when polishing my animation!

With the *"slow sneak"*, what we really want to do is have it move *slowly* – much slower than this current version at least! This is especially true where the action is moving to the "**up**" position on each stride. In fact, there should be a pronounced "**slow-in**" to the *"up"* position here. So, select everything behind and including the first "up" key on the timeline and open them up for another **3 frames**.

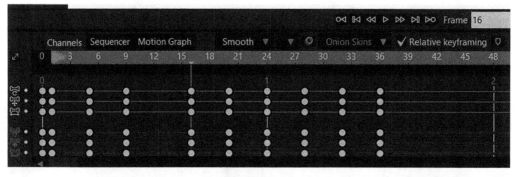

Opening up 3 more frames before the first up position on 1st stride.

Do the same thing on the *2nd stride* – i.e., opening up **3 more frames** to the "**up**" position, as before.

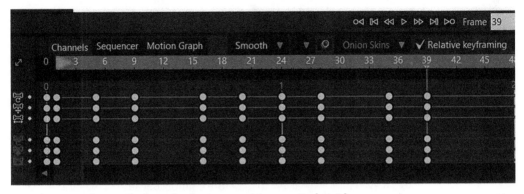

Opening up 3 frames before the first up position on 2nd stride.

"*Save*" and/or "*Save As*" and then adjust the "*end-frame*" number in the white box beneath the "*Stage*" to "**39**" and hit "**Play**". You should now see something that is more approaching a "*slow sneak*".

Now looking at it, I want the movement around the "*up*" positions to move a little slower. Not much, just a little. So, I'm going to open up the action after the "*up*" position by **1 frame** in **each case**. In other words, I'm adding a tiny, 1-frame "**slow-out**".

Opening up 1 frame after the up positions.

Adjust the "*end-frame*" box to "**41**" and "Play" again. Hopefully, this is going to give it even more of a "slow-sneak" feel to it. In fact, in looking at this, I feel we should add **1 more frame** to the "*up*" positions. We put "*3 frames*" there before, but I feel she should open it up to give it **1 extra frame** in each case.

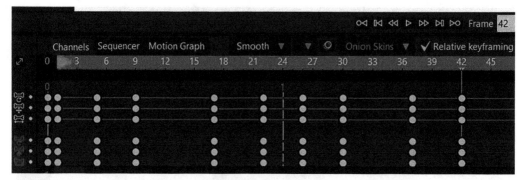

Opening up 1 frame before the up position.

Adjust the *"end-frame"* box to **"43"** and hit **"Play"** again. You'll see that this makes it even more "sneakier" than before – simply because of that appropriate 1 frame addition, making it marginally slower. You'll see that the arms are not really doing much that's essential to this kind of sneak, so we'll leave them as they are. However, I think the leg action does need a little attention.

So, halfway, when the legs start to come through from the back, I want to push the body forward a little while keeping that leg back. It's a bit like the back leg extension on a *"generic walk"*. I'm also going to straighten the leg and toe as much as possible, to underline the effect of delaying that foot. This needs to be done at the start of both stride actions of course.

Body forward and back leg stretched at the start of both strides.

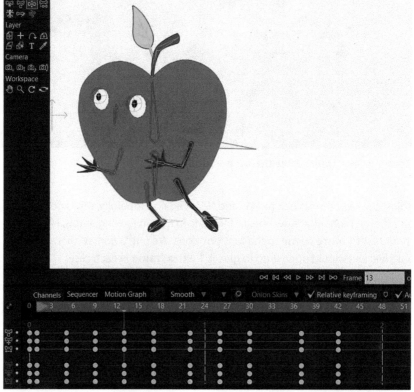

Then, when the leg is coming through from the *"up/passing position"* and down to the next *"contact/stride position"*, I want it to be **reaching out** – which is what we're trying to do with a sneak. We're trying to cover as much ground as possible, but silently and stealthily. Therefore, go to the **mid inbetween position** of the front foot as it's coming forward and down, and **point the leg and toe out** more. Do the same on the other foot also, on the next stride. "Save" and/or *"Save As"*.

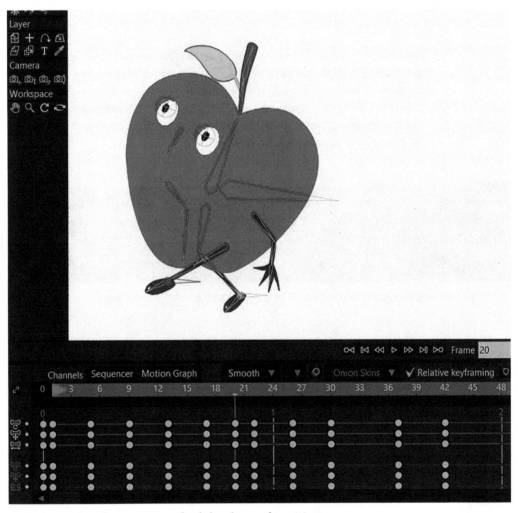

Front foot pointed out more on both leg forward positions.

So, that is basically how to create a pretty solid *"slow sneak"*. We can finesse this for hours of course. But, this lesson, I believe, takes you to a really good place for your first attempt. Therefore, with everything working fine, go to "**Export Movie**" and render it out to view it working full time. "**Loop**" the video playback to have it repeated continuously.

Suggested Assignment

Remember that the action you have rendered is for one cycle only and it is only by *"looping"* it at playback that you can watch it repeat continuously. However, if you would prefer to have it repeating in Moho continuously from the get-go, select ALL the frames, except the very last one. Then hit "**Command C**" to copy them. Then place the cursor on the last frame in the timeline and hit "**Command V**" to paste the extra cycle action frames there.

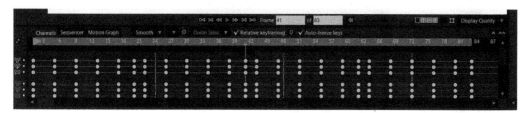

Close-up of Timeline, copy/pasting full action 1 extra time.

You can repeat this *"cut-'n-paste"* process for as long as you want the action to be repeated in Moho. Finally, render it out for a longer cycled playback on video. Additionally, you can actually experiment with your *"slow-sneak"* action beyond what we have done here. For example, change the number of inbetweens you use, to make it even slower. Or, you can delete inbetween frames, to make it faster. But, before you do any of that, don't forget to "**Save As**" every time you consider a new version, so you don't lose anything you've done already.

NOTE

*The important thing with any "sneak" action, however, is that the audience really needs to sense the **stealth** in the character's action – i.e., differentiating it from a regular "generic walk".*

Masterclass 22/ Throwing Action

We are now at the last Moho-specific exercise in Moho – not because there are not many more we could tackle, but because this one covers all the principles of movement and software you need so far in your studies. The following two lessons will deal with other options for Moho or the things that will relate to Moho. We also need to start talking about what you're going to do for your final project, although we'll only talk tentatively about it for now. Suffice it to say though, this exercise on "**Throwing Action**" will teach you a few new things. Hopefully, however, the last lesson's observational gesture drawing exercise will have given you some insights into how throws work in the real world. Here, we'll talk about how we can make a basic one work digitally, using Moho. But first, a new observational gesture drawing exercise…

Warm-Up Drawing

Here, we're going to follow on again with the fast, **3 × 1-minute** action-observation exercises on one page of your sketchbook. And in keeping with the throwing demonstration in this lesson, you're going to be working with the three crucial stages of a javelin throw, seen as silhouettes. This is not quite the same as the pitcher exercise of last time, but similar principles apply, even though the object being thrown is different. Give yourself just 1 minute to draw each of the following three poses, as that is a wonderful way to speed-train your animator's eye and brain. Although, train your imagination by putting more detail into the form and clothing of the character.

DOI: 10.1201/9781003324287-24

Comments: These are three dynamic push moments of the javelin throw, building up to a final release of the javelin. If you can replicate this action, with exaggeration, for any animation character and approach of your choice, you should end up with a great throwing action if you can apply this sequence of poses. Your drawing will be wonderful references for this if you have to create a throwing action in the future too.

I hope what you have noticed again, following the last exercise, is that when someone throws an object, it doesn't happen all at once. Remember at the back of your mind the *"successive breaking of joints"* principle we mentioned last time? Indeed, a lot of animation is like that – throwing or otherwise. An inexperienced animator will put all the key moments of action of a few poses and in between them all at once. But, a really professional, a master animator will not do that. They will analyze the action from the real world if possible – and if they can't find the actual movements to study, they'll find something close to it – and then work out how to break it down into a series of little actions where some parts of the character are moving, yet some are not. Certainly, this and the last throwing study underlines that a great deal. The real secret of this is knowing – through observation – where the real power, or intention, is applied at any moment during a movement. Even the picking up of a pen from a desk is not just two key positions inbetweened! This is why observational gesture drawing, used as a reference in a dedicate sketchbook, is so important to the master animator.

Instruction

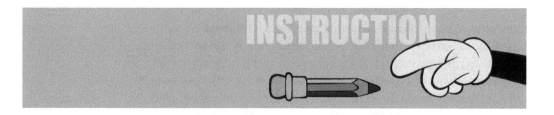

This one is another test for your Moho skills. I'm not going to leave you high and dry here but, again, I want you to look at an action and then interpret it for

yourself in Moho. This is something you will have to do as a professional animator, so it is a good exercise. Now, you're not entirely going to do this alone, as
I'm going to give you instruction on how to do it later in this lesson, but it's another one of those good exercises to get your animator's eye and brain working.
What follows are images of a pitcher throw that I've done using traditional hand-
drawn techniques. Your challenge is to study them and replicate the action in
Moho as best you can. This is really how a professional works anyway – they
study the research and then apply what they've learned to the medium they're
working with.

See the dynamic line of action and the advanced elbow position of Yankees
relief player, Luis Ayala, as he pitches the ball.

You'll note from the above action that you don't actually ever see the ball. It's all
in the action, so the ball is actually secondary to any of it. The same will be true
of your Moho "**Arnie**" rig, so you will have to make it convincing, just from the
body action alone. Another thing you'll notice above is that there's something
of a turning in three dimensions with the character. And, as he's throwing, the
body rotates around to some degree – something you can't do with Moho.

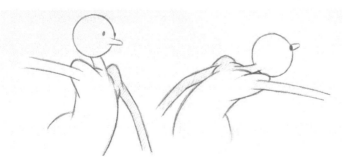

With the traditional hand-drawn animation, it is possible to put a rotation
on the body, like the shoulders especially here. In basic Moho animation,
you cannot do that, so you have to compensate in other ways.

So, you're going to be a bit creative with your animation here to make it convincing. That said, it is still a good reference material for you to refer to, in addition to your previous gesture-drawing work. Here is a Moho version of the pitcher action…

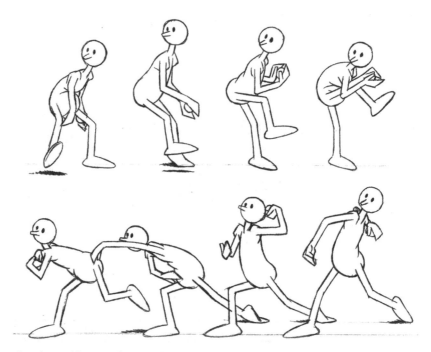

Sketches of key pitcher positions.

I'm sure you can immediately see the difference. It's obviously not so rotational, as indicated above, because Moho is not a three-dimensional program. Instead, we're dealing with flat surfaces here, being moved mechanically like a puppet on strings. But even so, when you know what to go for, it's potentially possible to get a decent throwing action. The four main things to think about are "**anticipation**", "**unfolding**", "**throw**" and "**follow-through**".

When you download the "**Arnie Pitcher.moho**" rig file for the dedicated website, you'll see that embedded behind it I have put visual aids in the background for you to work with. On the right is my original, traditionally animated version. On the left, the Moho *"key positions"* are at the top, with the *"breakdown positions"* beneath them. That should help you a lot to create the poses you need for the assignment. You'll see too that I've also suggested the frame numbers you might use. I'm not saying that you should follow these exactly, but I do think they're a good starting place for you to consider.

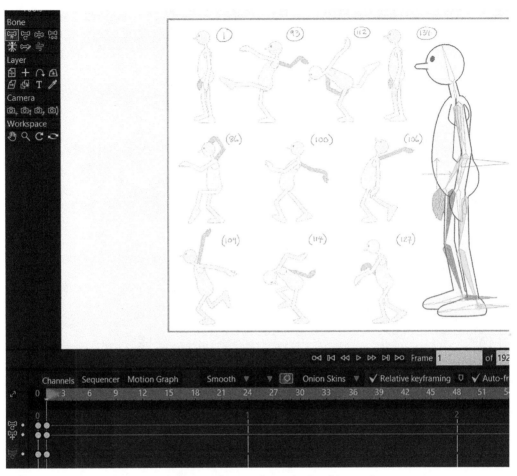

Arnie in Frame 1 position with the pitcher guide in the background.

The *"anticipation"* of the throw is clear to see, with the arm back. This is drawing number "**93**", with the *"breakdown position"* being "86".

The "Anticipation" pose, with arm back.

Following that, the throwing arm whips forward on drawing "**112**". The *"break-down position"* to this is number "**100**" – where he is still leaning back with the arm stretched far behind him.

Breakdown position, with the arm coming forward.

Finally, he moves on to the final standing position "**134**", via in-betweens "**114**" and "**127**".

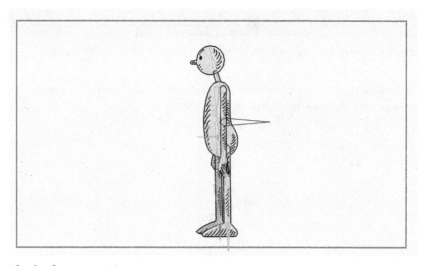

The final pose position.

So, this then is your assignment. You should have more than enough informa-tion here, and experience of Moho previously, to be able to do this one yourself. It is a bit like working with a *"key-pose animatic"*, which is a normal stage in the professional production process.

Now, just a couple of things about the "**Arnie pitcher rig 01**" file. The instructional background file should be embedded in it, but it is also available for download in the same folder. You'll also find a video of my final action there. If the background file is not embedded in the rig file, you can independently import it in yourself. Make sure it is in the same folder as the rig file, then in Moho go – "**File**"/"**Import**"/"**image**". Then click on the appropriate background file and it will put that image into the Moho file. It will be on its own layer, entitled "**background guide**". "Save" this when it's done and then "Save As" a new file, "**Arnie pitcher rig 02**", before you start animating.

Suggested Assignment

This is not connected to the above test but it is something for you to think about while you are working on it. We are drawing to a close *"Section II"* of this book, after which you will be going through the "**Pre-production**" stage of your own project in "**Section III**". So, you might give it some thought in terms of what you're going to do for your project. There's no hurry at this particular moment, as there are still two more masterclass lessons to get through in this section. However, after that, you'll definitely need to hit the ground running with your project idea.

Give yourself time for that 1% inspiration, before the 99% perspiration needs to take over!

Here are my thoughts on the project. It is so very easy for a first-time student film to throw in all kinds of bells and whistles to it and take on far too much too soon. This invariably leads to burnout, and the project never gets finished. So, here are my STRONG SUGGESTED GUIDELINES for you to consider.

 i. For a start, your film should realistically be a little more than **30-second** long.

 ii. It can be created using **hand-drawn animation** techniques or **Moho**. (Or any digital 2D program you might have instead of Moho.)

 iii. It should involve no more than **one character** and **a prop** for them to work with/react to.

 iv. Your story should be strong, with a "**beginning**", "**middle**" and an "**end**" to it.

I suggest your project should be around *"30-second"* long (i.e., the length of a standard TV commercial) because it will be just enough challenge to take on, although it doesn't sound like a lot at first. But, trust me, it will be more than enough for a first-time filmmaker. It will not require you to put too much pressure on yourself by being too ambitious. With it being like a TV commercial, imagine how much *storytelling*, *action* and *original visual ideas* can come across in the best of commercials. There's certainly enough scope to more than impress your family, friends or peers – or even a *future employer* – with what you might ultimately produce!

In terms of the **audio** content of your film, you might consider purchasing a relatively inexpensive "**royalty-free**" **track** from an **online music service** and do something *"Fantasia style"* – i.e., choreograph your animation movement to music, with no dialogue. Alternatively, you might consider recording a **custom-made voice track** for your film, by having a professional actor record it for you via a service such as **voices.com**, and for a reasonable price. Alternatively, you might just animate it in **silence**, with just a few **sound effects** thrown in at no cost from a free website like **freesound.com**.

Although you should totally focus on your final Moho project at this stage, you might begin to brainstorm your project idea as you work – jotting down **words**, **images** and **concepts** that appeal to you. But don't do anything too finished at this stage, just really rough scribbles that may or may not make the cut for your final project idea. The important thing is for you to get a **flow of ideas** going that you can build on in a more focused way later.

Masterclass 23/
Digital Coloring

Now although we are finished with formal exercises in relation to Moho, we can still explore other options that Moho offers us from a digital tool perspective. Some readers of this book, like the author, will still have a stronger passion for traditional hand-drawn animation, and Moho can have a role to play that too. So, this lesson concerns itself with what else Moho can offer the 2D-animated filmmaker, as well as other vital animation that will help make your final project something very special for a first-time (or even, not a first-time) filmmaker. But, first, we must not neglect our observational gesture-drawing session…

Warm-Up Drawing

Previously in the last few lessons, we have closely observed frozen action, taken from a live-action material. This time, I'm going to rely on your discipline and honesty here because I want you to test your memory! The following child-gymnast-themed imagery should be studied for a short while until you think you can remember everything that's there. Then, I want you to close the book and draw the **3** "**memory poses**" from recollection, taking **3-minutes to do them all** – meaning you have just *1-minute to draw each one*. Please draw all 3 on *one sheet of paper* in your sketchbook – and no cheating please, as this is a little test on how you can retain what you've observed once you've seen it.

DOI: 10.1201/9781003324287-25

Comments: Remember, you are not drawing so much from observation this time, more from memory. So, try to keep a strong memory of the poses in your mind before you close the book and sketch them out. Think of them as a sequence of action and try to "**feel**" them happening in your mind and then draw them as best you can. Again, we're not going for a photographic representation here. We're trying to put down on paper the actual bodily positions required to complete the action – as *"key positions"* in animation if you like. You should exaggerate if you like to get a better sense of animated flow in your drawings. Again, try to imprint and analyze what you're seeing before putting it down onto paper. Ultimately, you should learn to do this process in real time, as you are watching something unfold, but this is a good starting point to get your *"animator's eye"* and *"animator's brain"* working in the right direction.

This is probably a pretty exhausting exercise, considering that you've never done anything like it before! However, I wanted to really push you on this one. I wanted you to see where you're getting with both your ability to see and absorb poses you are looking at, as well as how well you're able to put them down quickly as *"gesture drawings"* of poses you might use for animation. Ultimately, it becomes quite an instinctive thing, so this is something you might develop further yourself – even to the point, as I do in my live classes, of watching a single clip of video action, three times, then recording some of the poses in it from memory. Although I am always talking about seeking out the reference material before animating a sequence, there are times when you will need to animate from memory – or at least, you won't have access to the means of getting your research material, so you will have to recall what you've seen in your mind before animating. This, therefore, is good training for that. Therefore, don't neglect exercises like this for training your memory to collect poses you have seen before and then translate them into drawings or animation later. It is an essential skill that all master animators develop over time. At the same time, don't get disheartened if you can do it well at first. It's like working a muscle if you like – *if you don't use it, you lose it*! Nothing worth having is easy to do of course and anything that is, anyone can do. It's like training yourself to be an *"animation ninja"* if you like – and animation ninjas take years and years to train!

Instruction

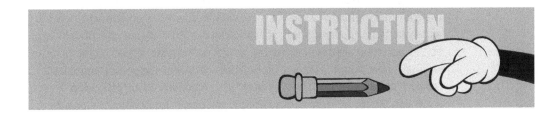

OK, so we've pretty much covered all the foundational functions of Moho that you need to be able to move on with your own animation designs and approaches now. As I've always claimed, I don't like *"teaching software"* and I've tried to honor that here. I've tried to make you think of the techniques of movement, not the technology that makes it happen. However, to get you to explore digital 2D animation, I've had to introduce you to a modicum of the software's functions to explore the principle of movement that you can quickly learn here. There are so many more amazing tools that Moho has, that go beyond anything you'll find here. Therefore, all I have been talking about is more of a *foundational* nature if you like. It by no means covers all that Moho is capable of including rotational rigging, which you should explore on your own when you become much more competent as an animator and know what you need to create from your digital rigs. But, for now, you won't need that. If you simply understand the core principles of movement, you can create some great animation from even the most minimal functions that Moho – or indeed any other digital 2D software – has. Hopefully, this section of the book has given you a good foundation, or springboard, to do that.

But, while we're on the subject of Moho, or other digital software for the 2D animator, we must mention the other opportunities it offers. So, this we will briefly do right now.

A portal to your animated imagination. © Lost Marble

If you've gone to the expense of buying software for this book and yet are still not excited by the rigged approach to animation, don't forget that Moho has *"drawing"* and *"coloring"* functions embedded into its technology too. Now, there is other digital software out there with arguably better *"brushes"*, *"textures"* and even *"virtual paper surfaces"* that you can use. But they are primarily *still-art* applications that are designed for the *"artist"* or *"illustrators"*, not *"animators"*. Having animation software, like Moho, that not only allows you to **clean up**, **color**, **composite** and then **render** your material into an **HD video** is a win-win situation. So, you are advised to not neglect that opportunity, now you have the technology at your fingertips. Moho, for example, need not be just about *"rigged characters"* from the perspective of a traditional, hand-drawn animation. So, let's very briefly explore some of those tools and potentials the software offers too. If nothing else, this will enable you to take those pencil-animated exercises you did in "Section I" of this book and bring them to a colored life on the video.

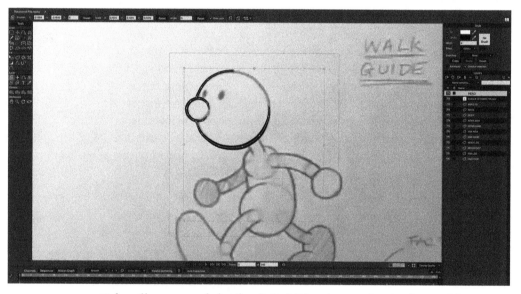

Moho offers so much for the digital 2D animator, but it also enables traditional hand-drawn animators to ink and color their pencil drawings too

If you're working as a traditional, hand-drawn animator, you will have a pile of individual drawings that you will need to convert into a color film or video ultimately. The question is how do you transition from drawings on paper to a highly finished HD video. I am very much a paper-first animator, meaning that I like to do everything on paper first, including the inking, then scanning by drawings and importing them into a software program for *"coloring"*, *"compositing"* and *"rendering"*. However, I fully recognize today that most 2D hand-drawn animators work directly into the computer, using drawing tablets or "Cintiqs", and that these old-school techniques are pretty obsolete. Yet, as I know there are traditionalists out there and individuals who love the tactile feel of pencils or pens on real paper, I am quickly going to explain my process of getting inked drawings into Moho or a similar digital animation platform.

Cleaned-up drawings: As I tend to work pretty rough, my drawings usually need to be cleaned up. Here is an example of a "before" and "after" in this process.

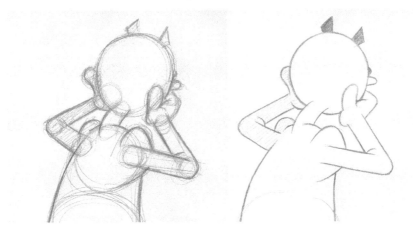

Rough drawing and cleaned-up drawing.

You can see that I really work very tight – although it's still *"rough"* in my mind – before I clean my drawings up. "**Cleanup**" to me means rubbing down the majority of the rough drawings with a "kneadable putty eraser" and then thickening up the remaining lines again with a much firmer pencil line. It is at this point that I usually do my final "**pencil test**" (or "**line test**") of the action to see if all is well before embarking on the inking process.

A QuickTime pencil test frame.

Inking: Knowing my pencil-drawn animation is complete I then proceed to ink my drawings on paper. Again, I prefer this to digital inking as I both like the "tactile" feel of pen on paper, and I also like the "organic" look that traditional pen and ink drawing provides.

A finished traditionally inked drawing of the above.

My most used style of inking is the use of "thick-'n-thin" lines with a little cross-hatching to provide a sense of shadow or form.

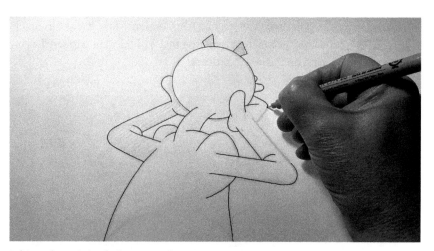

Inking the original clean-up drawing.

Now, I know that this can be replicated digitally but using a pressure-sensitive digital pen and suitable brushes in a number of art-based software, but it is almost a "therapy/meditational" thing for me, allowing me to focus entirely on the individuality of each inked drawing, knowing that my emotion, the texture of the paper and the vagaries of a pen nib can give me subtle differences in drawing each time. That is what I mean when I use the word "organic" when it comes to a traditional inking process.

Really letting go with my organic inking technique, including splats.
Concept art for my animated memoirs project – featuring my memories
of taking life drawing classes with Ralph Steadman (teacher) and Quentin
Crisp (model).

To get my "thick-'n-thin" lines, I do it in two stages. I know that this is too time
intensive for many people but for me, I love the handcrafted way it looks. It
also means that my inked animation has subtle differences from a too-smooth,
too-consistent digital approach to "thick-'n-thin" lines – although I do readily accept the fact that the digital does give a good look to the effect eventually, and
usually in half the time!

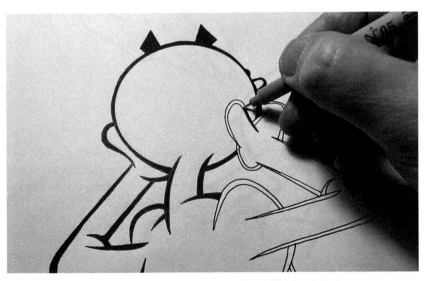

Drawing the inked "thick-'n-thin" outline, then filled in black.

"Stage 1" of my inking process is to trace my pencil lines exactly as they are drawn in the cleanup. Sometimes, I use a "dip pen" to do it, but for much of the time, I use a black "micron" fiber-tip pen. This gives me an accurate, consistent line tracing of the original art.

The micron pen I use for traditional tracing.

Next, I will then manually add the "thick-'n-thin" look to the lines by drawing a second line out of the original inked line, thickening it up in the middle, or at a junction of two lines, or in places where a thicker line is required. I then manually fill in the parts that are not yet solid black using this process.

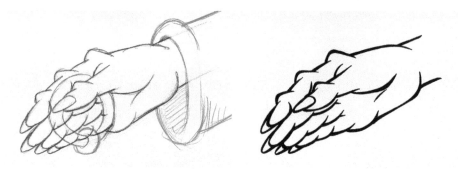

Another before and after inked image.

I do attempt to be consistent from animation drawing to animation drawing on "where" I put the thickening parts, but I don't obsess over the fact that often the degree of thickness in a specific part of the line is consistent from drawing to drawing. This all adds to the "organic" nature of the final look.

Showing the variations in line thickness that can be possible with hand tracing on paper. Usually, I will use one of these three different approaches. However, sometimes, I'll mix them up in the same sequence – when the subject matter merits it – to give the line quality an energy of its own, called "boiling".

When all the "thick-'n-thin" lines I complete, I pick an area of the character where I want to add hatching to give a shadowed or volume effect. Again, I am consistent with the area to be hatched, but not in the number of hatch lines I have. (Unlike Richard Williams in the early days of my apprenticeship with him, when he would actually count the number of cross-hatch lines from drawing to drawing when we used that style!) Again, I think consistency of area, but not of the number of hatch lines, gives a living, breathing and organic look to the action when it's seen on the screen. It may not be appreciated intellectually, but it is "felt" by the viewer on subconscious levels – assuring that the work is indeed handcrafted – and somewhat unique from drawing to drawing. This is indeed what "hand-drawn 2D animation" should be about anyway, should it not? It adds *"soul"* to the work!

NOTE

If you are using Moho for your project, there is an equivalent of digital line tracing available, where you either trace the line freehand in the program or use a series of "points" to define the line. (A traced line is defined as a "stroke".) When the character is traced in this way and you actually create a definable line (in both thickness and color), you can then select points manually and either thicken or thin the line at these points, dependent on how "thick-'n-thin" you want the lines to be. Further research via the program is recommended here for digital animators.

Cross-hatching techniques – using 1 (left), 2 (middle) or 3 (right) hatch techniques. Note though that using hatching is very time consuming, so I advise you to try it out on a free drawing at the onset to make sure that you have the need (and stamina) to carry it through on all your drawings. If you are considering it for a professional project, consider also the time involved and whether or not it will endanger your deadline by doing it.

With all my inking completed on paper, I now proceed to scan my drawings digitally, so they can be imported into the software of my choice for animating. Two things are important when you are scanning animation drawings: (i) You need to be consistent from drawing to drawing in terms of the framing you use and (ii) You have to make sure that your drawings don't move around when you scan them, so you need to tape a peg bar to the scanner surface on which each drawing needs to be placed before the scan is made.

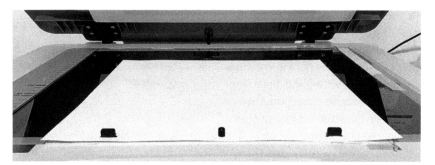

Acme peg bar taped to the scanner, with 12-Field paper on the pegs.

Scanning: Finally, scan the inked drawings in "line" mode if possible. If it doesn't have a line mode, then select "grayscale". The reason for this is that you want the scene to be as black and white and sharp as possible and the "line" mode provides for that. If you scan in "grayscale" or "color", your drawings will "pixelate" around the edges (due to the "bitmap" nature of the scanner) – especially if you size it up – which will lead to coloring edge issues later. And, if you scan in "line" mode initially, it can always be converted into an RGB color mode later, if you're working in a program like Photoshop that allows for this. Most digital animation programs will convert images automatically, however, usually into a "vector" file format for working in. *(Note: If you scan in "grayscale" and are working* *in Photoshop with your scanned files, I would recommend that before coloring them you use both the "Sharpen" and "Adjust/Brightness_Contrast" tools to harden up the edges before going into the coloring mode. It will avoid white pixels appearing between the line and the color, which can be really annoying!)*

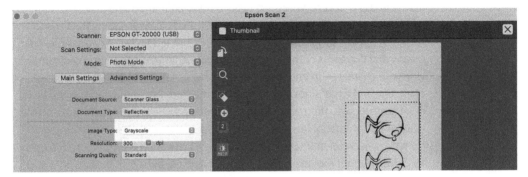

Close-up scanner settings, showing grayscale mode being selected.

Coloring: Coloring animation drawings, whether they are created traditionally on paper and scanned in, or drawn straight into the program are usually pretty quick and easy to do once you have them in Moho or other animation programs. As long as there are no breaks in the area that you're coloring, it is really a "touch-and-go" process of touching that area with the paintbrush tool on the screen and watching it instantly fill with the color you have selected.

The color palette and coloring tools in Moho.

If there are breaks in the lines containing the area you intend to color, you will either have to manually fill the gap in the lines by drawing over them and joining the gap up or else the program you'll be using will have a degree of tolerance for doing it automatically anyway.

Layers: Before we talk more about digital coloring, we might just mention the nature of using "layers" when digitally coloring animation drawings. In a digital world, it is technically possible to use hundreds of layers to create a scene. Now that may be physically impractical to do, but it is technically possible. That means that if *speed* is of the essence with your animation, then you can subdivide your character up into layers, depending on what is moving at any stage of a scene and what is not. For example, if the body is not moving but the head, or an arm alone, is, then you can put the body on one layer for coloring and the head or arm animation on another. It is what I call "cheap-'n-nasty" animation from my "character animation" perspective – but it is pretty much used in every TV or low-budget movie production these days, sadly.

A digital character, created on many layers in Moho. © Lost Marble

NOTE

"Layering" usually needs to be implemented at the animation stage, so you don't have to go through painful digital separations in the software later – which it can be if you leave it to the last minute!

Another approach to "layering" is the notion of putting the inked "line" art on a top layer and having a separate layer (or layers) behind it that contains the coloring. For most of the time, this is unnecessary. But if you're using textured or a painted look to the coloring – or if your final line style has a brush-stroke to it with many gaps in the lines containing the coloring areas – then putting the coloring on a separate layer (or layers) makes a lot of sense.

Showing the separation of layers – line and color.

Now, let's get to some more specific things related to Moho. I'm addressing this section here on the assumption that you're going to draw your animation outside of the program and import it in. Even if you're not and draw directly into the program, a lot of this will apply too. So, just take the information, as you need it. I'm assuming that you've worked out your "layer" issue already, so I won't deal with that. I'll just deal with the process of you importing drawings as drawings and then take it from there.

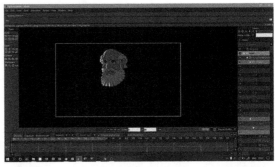

Drawing before and Moho-colored image after.

I'm also assuming that you've resized your scanned drawings to the size they're going to appear in the final film – HD1080 (1920 pixels × 1080 pixels for the best resolution. A program like "Photoshop" – using file/image size or canvas size – will do that for you. There are others that will do this too. Moho will accept the files if they have not been previously resized, but to ensure you get exactly what you want to see positioned in Moho's "stage", it's best to resize first.

NOTE

The one function I like about Photoshop specifically is "Actions". If you're resizing your artwork manually, then there is a heck of a lot to do if you're doing it to a mass of animation drawings. However, "Actions" allows you to do the resizing on one frame, which is recorded, and it enables the software to do the same thing to every other file in the sequence. As long as the images you're using up front are the same size (which they should be if you've been consistently scanning them on a peg par), then you will save yourself a whole lot of time and stress by doing it this way. Photoshop seems to be the only image manipulation software that offers this function. So, I, as a traditional hand-drawn animator, have always preferred Photoshop to all the other applications out there.

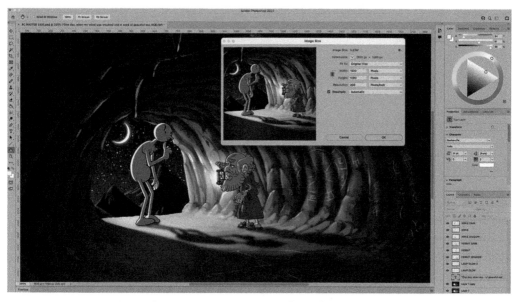

Resizing the image to HD1080 in Photoshop.

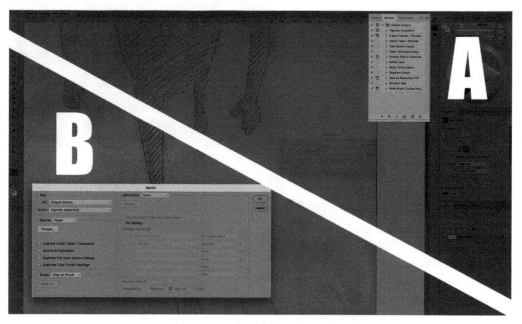

Setting up "Actions" window (A) and "Batch" processing (B) window in Photoshop.

Importing drawings into Moho: It's quite simple to import your drawings into Moho. Simply go to "**File**"/"**Import**"/"**Images**" at the top-left of your screen, then select the images you want to import. That will place them on your timeline, so you can trace and color them on another layer(s).

Inking in Moho: Inking inside Moho is pretty much like inking in any other way, except you'll almost certainly need a drawing tablet with a digital pen to do so in comfort. Drawing with a mouse is not at all the best way to do it, although if you're stuck it is technically possible – although not aesthetically desirable, needless to say! Essentially, you need to create a new layer above your imported drawing layer. To do this, go to the top of your "layers" column on the right of the screen, click the "New Layer" icon and select "Image" from the list. You have to first "name" your layer and then make sure that it is the screen size you want it to be. Now have your new layer to ink onto.

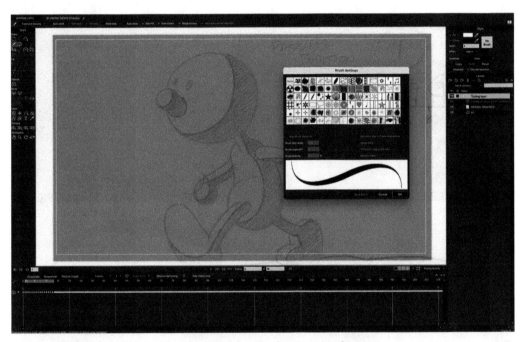

Moho "Freehand" inking tool – the "Brushes" selection window.

For inking, you need to select the "**Bitmap brush**" icon near the top of the left-hand column on the screen and select what brush you wish to use. (Note: There is a "Vector" inking option too, but as we're very much for the traditional, hand-drawn feel to animation in these masterclasses in a book, we're going "Bitmap" for the more aesthetic option it offers.) Anyway, as we're inking drawings, it makes sense to pick the "Ink" option. There are a number of alternative brushes you can use here, so try all of them and pick the one that feels most natural to you. Remember, the inking style of your animation will be unique to you and you alone. Nothing I write here should influence you in that direction as diversity in design, animation style, and indeed "life" is what makes our world rich and stimulating. So, you really do need to experiment with all the settings I'm introducing you to so that you will arrive at something that is hopefully original and unique to you alone.

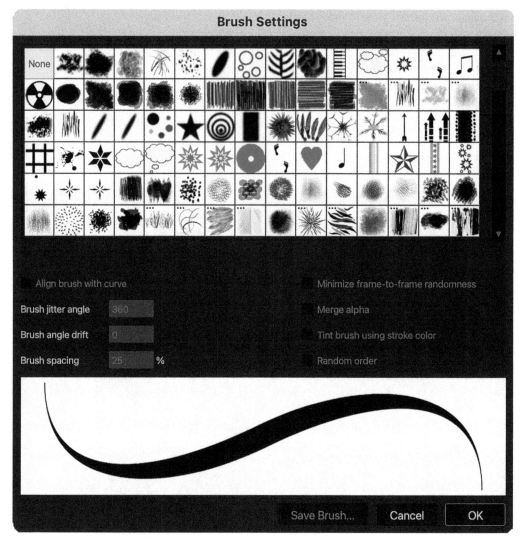

Close-up of Moho's "Brushes" palette.

You should refine your brush in terms of the thickness of the line and the visual quality of the line. For the latter, go up to the "Options" tab above the "Stage" and play with the "Spacing" and "Smoothing" control in a way that suits you. Again, this is an issue of personal taste that only you can arrive at through experiment.

Close-up of tool set options.

For the color of the line you are inking with (remember not all animation is inked black!), go up to the "Dropper" icon above the "Stage" and select the color that you want from the palette provided. You will probably want your ink line to be opaque, but there is an "Opacity" setting above the "Stage" too, just in case you wish to see through the ink line you are drawing.

Close-up of dropper selection tool.

To the left of the "Opacity" slider above the "Stage" is a "Size" slider too. Experiment with this, to see what thickness of the line you wish to ink with. When that is set, you're all ready to start inking your animation drawings on your new layer. Make sure it is selected in the "Layer" column on the right!

Close-up of opacity and size tool options.

And remember, if you are not happy with any of your inking processes, there is an "Erase" tool also to remove anything that is not how you want it.

Coloring: This is pretty simple when it comes down to it. You have your inked character on its own layer, so now click on the paint pot icon to the left and select a color for part of your character to be colored. Simply click on the area that needs to be colored if it is so, immediately. Go through all the colors of your character in this way, on all the frames of your animation. And that's it, you're done!

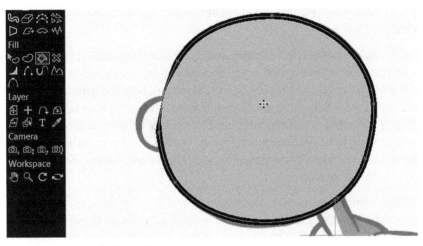

Close-up of area being colored.

When all your animation is colored, you need to add a new image layer to import your background artwork into, assuming you're going to have a background. Make sure that this layer is moved beneath your animation layer; otherwise, you won't see your animation!

Close-up of background import function.

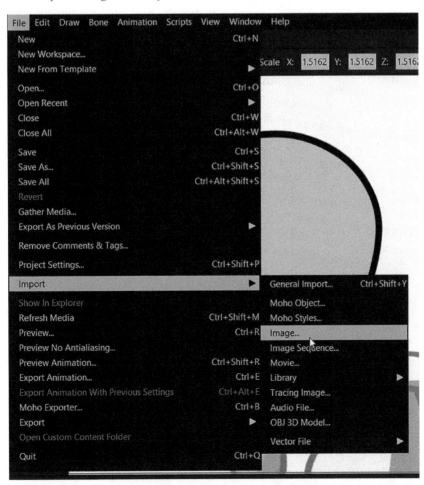

Finally, in the "File" tab, click "Export to Video" and render it out. Your animation is not completed!

Clearly, Moho's power is in its rigging and rig character capabilities. Further research on your part will pay off as you explore it all. But it's also good to know that Moho has great drawing, inking and coloring tools for the traditional 2D animator also. Hopefully, this section's introduction to these tools and capabilities will help springboard you into further explorations of what Moho can do. In the meantime, we have just one more lesson in the Moho/digital animation section of this book, dealing with the deeper aspects of color and the use of color (or not, even!) in animation.

Inking in Moho: Inking inside Moho is pretty much like inking in any other way, except you'll almost certainly need a drawing tablet with a digital pen to do so in comfort. Drawing with a mouse is not at all the best way to do it, although if you're stuck it is technically possible – although not aesthetically desirable, needless to say! Essentially, you need to create a new layer above your imported drawing layer. To do this, go to the top of your "layers" column on the right of the screen, click the "New Layer" icon and select "Image" from the list. You have to first "name" your layer and then make sure that it is the screen size you want it to be. Now have your new layer to ink onto.

AU: Please check whether the paragraph "Ink-

NOTE

For inking, you need to select the "**Freehand tool**" icon near the top of the left-hand column on the screen and select what brush you wish to use. There are a number of alternative brushes you can use here, so try all of them and pick the one that feels most natural to you. To choose which brush you want to draw with, go to the style panel. Click on no brush and this will show you different styles of brushes you can use, and don't forget to select the stroke or strokes that you have drawn with the select shape tool before going to the style panel. Then choose one of the brushes in the brush setting window. Remember too that you can play around with the settings to get the line look you are after. Select "OK" when you are done. To make some parts of the stroke thick, go to the line width tool and select the point and drag while holding the left of the mouse.

Remember, the inking style of your animation will be unique to you and you alone. Nothing I write here should influence you in that direction as diversity in design, animation style and indeed "life" is what makes our world rich and stimulating. So, you really do need to experiment with all the settings I'm introducing you to so that you will arrive at something that is hopefully original and unique to you alone.

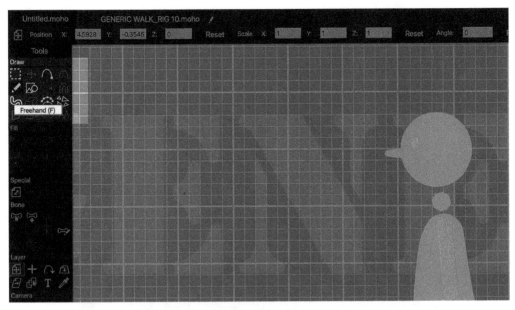

Close-up of Moho vector inking tool being selected.

Suggested Assignment

I mentioned above about adding a "**background**" to your animation.

Now, it's not my place here to tell you what your background art should be or the techniques you need to know to create it. I am assuming that the following *"Pre-production"* and *"Production"* sections of the masterclass book will give you more than enough information – hopefully inspiration – to give you an idea of how to approach all aspects of your project. All I simply suggest here, however, is how you can technically import your background artwork, whatever it is, into your Moho-based scene of colored animation. It is really simple, so this won't take long.

Go to the "**Layers**" column on the right-hand side of your screen and click on the top-left "**New layer**" icon.

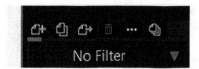

Choose "**Image**" from the dropdown menu.

Select the artwork you want to import into your scene of animation and click on the OK button.

Close-up of Image option.

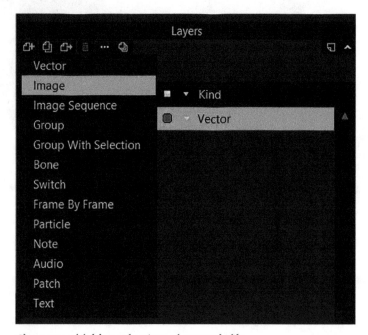

Close-up of folder selection of artwork file.

Your background artwork will simply appear on the *"Stage"* of your scene. If necessary, move it down to the lowest level, so that it doesn't cover your animation.

That done, you're all set to render your scene out to a final video version!

Masterclass 24/ Working with Color

Now we're about to cross the line on Moho, so to speak, I think it is a good time to go over some art-based essentials that are worth knowing – then some final tips on coloring in Moho. Bright color and complex design are things that seem synonymous with animation these days – especially with digital-/vector-based animation. But need it be so? This section explores that, as well as first introducing you to an observational gesture-drawing assignment that introduces you to a wonderful system of exercise that has maintained my bodily health and alertness of brain through these recent autumn years – "**Qi Gong**". So, let's not waste any further time and get drawing…

Warm-Up Drawing

Having learned by now how to approach solid observational gesture drawing, it is time to further that practice and see how you do this one. I warn you though; we're embarking on a time-challenging one! The embraced **7 × 1-minute poses** feature a *"Qi Gong instructor"* in action. *"Qi Gong"* is an ancient, incredible system of health and exercise that can bring *"wholeness"*, *"focus"*, *"vitality"* and *"relaxation"* to a person if they practice it regularly. I do and I really benefit from it – especially working in a very sedentary occupation, with the years advancing at the same time. So, I've practiced *"Qi Gong"* for 30-minutes, each day over the last 3 years and will never go back to not doing it. I feel so liberated from time and space in doing it! In addition to that though, it is also a valuable subject for

DOI: 10.1201/9781003324287-26

observational gesture drawing – in the sense that it entirely braces the notion of "**pose**", "**balance**" and "**movement**".

The big challenge for you here is not only to get all *7 images* drawn in just *1-minute* each. But I also want you to draw them all onto **one page** of your sketchbook and they should all be in perfect balance. So, let's take a deep meditative break here and jump straight in...

Comments: So, I admit that this was a long and no-doubt exhausting session. A great many of the poses are very similar, at least from the lower body point of view. This is because when you're doing any prolonged physical movement you feel need to be anchored to the ground for many of them, giving you a solid base.

Students of balance will do well to study the art of Sumo wrestling. Sumo fighters – from Jonokuchi up to Yokozuna – are masters of balance, always seeking to create a solid base upon which they can maneuver their powerful bodies surprisingly well.

The legs, feet and lower body are really a solid foundation upon which everything else is built. This means that the upper body elements – the *arms, shoulders* and *head* – are the more active factors we should focus on in this case. Tied in with deep breathing while doing these exercises, there is a very *calming* aspect to the movements – that hopefully will come through your drawings. They have certainly helped you personally with my own work.

The image I use for the Meditation Zone in my "Drawing for Animation" course, where we reflect on the purpose of each exercise after completing each one.

Living a very sedentary life – as all animators do over the short and longer term – it is essential to do something that can take the pressures off the body and enhance or enliven the mind. I'm personally not a one for the usual kind of working out in gyms – with a fitness coach barking out orders like a sadistic sergeant major – as I find at my age that this kind of more aggressive exercise does more physical damage to my body than the more passive approaches of "Yoga" or "Qi Gong". Consequently, I have learned to value these more than any other forms of exercising the mind and body.

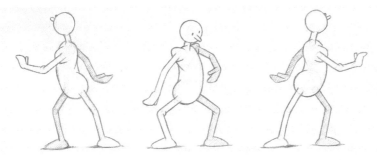

Qi Gong is not only a wonderful health and exercise technique for me, but it also helps me experience and understand good balance at the same time. It's my form of "method animation" if you like!

That said, as purely a gesture drawing exercise, it also provides you with a wonderful opportunity to witness the grace and flowing movement in action, making it a perfect subject for aspiring animators. These poses can be wonderful reference material too – especially if you're ever asked to animate a ninja fighting or any other forms of martial art combat.

Become a pencil ninja!

Also, if you're ever able to watch these forms of exercising in real time or even slow motion, you'll note that their grace comes from there being a gentle flow from pose to pose that is entirely based on *"arcs"*. This is an awareness that you can apply to all forms of animated movement, not martial arts. Indeed, whether you're animating this kind of movement – or doing it yourself physically – you'll realize that moving in arcs brings a sense of *"calmness"*, *"grace"* and *"balance"* to the movement of other; more aggressive forms of movement do not do.

Instruction

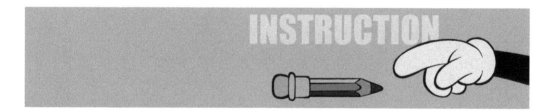

We talked about the use of color previously and it is a subject that can fill many books. Personally, I have been instinctive with the use of color – or the non-use of color – and have only really studied the subject at college way, way back and when an article of interest about the subject crosses my path. However, if you, like me, are somewhat overpowered by the often random, inappropriate or downright indelicate use of garish color in what has to be described as mass-market *"cartoon films"*, then perhaps some mention of color and its theory might be of value here. Color is a very subjective thing and of course *tastes* and *styles* in its usage change from generation to generation. Indeed, when *"The Simpsons"* first appeared with its yellow species of characters, many thought it quite outrageous or even offensive in some cases.

Once upon a time in Hollywood – the great Simpsons confrontation, with my wife, Saille!

However, time and tide wait for no man, so today the color of the skin should not offend anyone – be it in a cartoon world or indeed the real one around us! However, as this book is all about supporting the "tradition" of animation in the main, I believe it is worth making reference to the great classical, "**color**" tradition of the past and present. So, I bring to your attention here the notion of *"color theory"* and all it is said to represent. Perhaps this will help with your project's color design, or not. Maybe you might not want to use color at all – and for that notion, I'm quite sympathetic in the right circumstances.

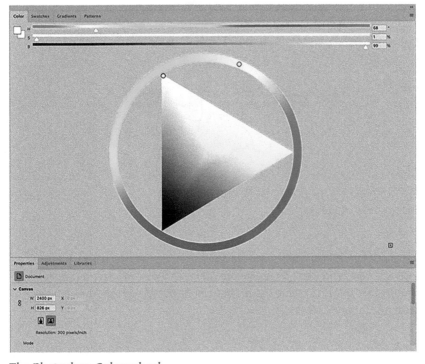

The Photoshop Color wheel.

The *"color wheel"* – or *"color circle"* as it's sometimes called – is a long-held concept that describes the arrangement of core colors and their chromatic relationship to one another. It establishes **"primary"**, **"secondary"** and **"tertiary"** colors and shows the cyclic relationship between them all. The notion is that you can choose colors, or color themes, as a result of their position and relationship to one another in the wheel. This brings us to *"color theory"*, which has traditionally given rise to a whole number of *books*, *lectures* and *opinions* on the subject in the past.

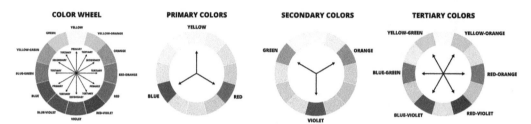

The Color Wheel, including Primary, Secondary and Tertiary colors.

The bottom line here is the theory of bringing colors together successfully, based on their relationship on the *"color wheel"*. It is a subject I don't really want to add right here, although I will share the definitions of the main players in this mystery.

The mystery of color.

Primary Colors: Primary colors are the *3 core colors* in the spectrum – namely "yellow", "blue" and "red". They are core colors, as they can't ever be created by mixing other colors to create them. They can be combined together, however, to make "secondary" colors.

The three primary colors.

Secondary Colors: *"Secondary colors"* are colors that can be made up by mixing the three main *"primary"* colors together – namely "orange", "violet" and "green". Red mixed with yellow makes *"orange"*; blue mixed with yellow makes *"green"*; and red mixed with blue makes *"violet"*.

The three primary colors + three secondary colors.

Tertiary Colors: *"Tertiary colors"* can be made by mixing equal amounts of *"primary"* and *"secondary"* colors together. Usually, they are named after the colors that are used to mix them – namely "blue-green", "orange-red", etc., but not always.

The three primary colors, three secondary colors and six tertiary colors

We can of course add more terms to the mix – I told you that many books are endlessly written about this! and here are the main 2 that might be mentioned...

Complementary Colors: *"Complementary colors"* are colors that are positioned exactly opposite to each other on the *"color wheel"*. This means that there can be a somewhat powerful effect if you use them together, as they seem to complement each other as opposites. Consequently, putting a *"complementary color"* together with a "primary color" can make a character or environment detail really stand out as a result of their diametric differences.

A Primary and a Complementary color together

Analogous Colors: *"Analogous colors"* can be aesthetically pleasing above all else, as they are colors that are next to each other on the *"color wheel"*. Therefore, there is a similarity between them. Used in this way, they can have a sympathetic or even calming effect on a design or color scheme.

Two analogous characters together.

That said, it should be stated that designing by *"theory"* and not personal feeling or intuition can be a dangerous thing – as can randomly throw colors at a design without knowing anything about color theory. I have said over and over again about animation and its fine tradition – *"The work that usually stands out above all else is the work that breaks the rules, except that you need **to know the rules first before you break them**"*! I believe it is therefore important to know about *"color theory"* and I do urge readers to do further research on the subject and view the great art and design that respects it. However, this is not an immovable goal post in my mind, as sometimes the *intuitive* use of color should be embraced – as long as there is reason and purpose, based on "color theory" behind it. Doing so can be quite liberating and often offers something quite innovative and groundbreaking.

Two incompatible colors together.

Additionally, let it not be forgotten also that the power and effect of personal emotions from day to day, month to month or year to year can have an effect on how you work with, and select, color. Also, eye and brain conditions can have a profound effect on how you see and/or express color. The amazing work of **Vincent Van Gogh** springs immediately to mind here. Arguably, the greatest painter that ever lived in the mind of some, the way he painted was apparently conditioned by the way his brain saw and interpreted the world around him.

Not Van Gogh but certainly a different way of looking at Arnie!

Similarly, in my own case. A couple of years before writing this book, I required a cataract replacement surgery. I was quite nervous about the aftereffects of it, for as an artist/animator my eyesight has always been of paramount importance to me. However, I should never have worried as, post-surgery, I was overwhelmed by the difference in the way I saw the world, as well as the colors in it. I will always remember the first time I looked at the magnets on my fridge in my kitchen, shortly after I removed my eye covering after returning home from the surgery, and was overwhelmed by the *whiteness* of the surface and the *vivid colors* of the fridge magnets that were attached to it.

Pre- and post-cataract surgery – my different views of the amazing fridge magnets my wife has drawn.

I was equally amazed when I stepped outside and encountered a different world from the one I'd seen before the surgery. The only way I could describe it to someone was that pre-surgery everything looked like a decade-old painting that had been tainted by many years of cigarette smoke tarnishing it – whereas post-surgery, it was as if the old oil painting had been restored and its original colors revealed!

The amazing restored painting effect.

In a nutshell, my poor cataracts had conditioned me over the years to see colors that were dull and **brownish** in their nature. I knew nothing else at that time and thought I had *"normal"* eyesight. However, after the cataracts were replaced, everything was so much more in the "**blue**" tones and significantly **more illuminated**. As I say, I didn't realize any of this until I had had the surgery. But suffice it to say, if I'd done a character *"color design"* before the surgery, I'm sure it would be very different from any color design I would do after it. This all goes to show of course that color choice is indeed very *"subjective"* and therefore theory alone is not enough when we're trying to express something important through our work.

Arnie colors - then and now.

This of course segues (Segways) perfectly into the next section, which considers the question of whether the animation should always be colored or not? I am so frustrated by the fact that most animation on TV, in the cinema and elsewhere is so full of colors. In some predictable areas of the industry, it is the same with *"princesses"* and *"corny songs"* – but that's another story! What I'm meaning here is that sometimes it would be so refreshing to see animation – specifically tradition-al hand-drawn animation – for what it is, "drawn", even devoid of color. Let the **drawings** domi-nate the audience, not the colors. There have been a few short film creators who have swum against this tide of course, but rarely in the mainstream world, if at all, I'm afraid to say.

Without a doubt, the finest "classically drawing" animator in the world today, is Joanna Quinn.

By way of example, I remember a time, way back in my career when I was heavy into advertising commercial productions when I had an ad that was crying out to just be in *black and white* only. I actually succeeded in convincing the advertising agency creative team, as well as the client, that this was appropriate and it would make their product stand out against all the other spots at that time. However, the suggestion was blocked when one of the "suits" from higher-up in the advertising agency refused to do it – arguing that the commercial would be played out on satellite broadcasting equipment that was tuned to enhance colors only and would *"crash"* if it only had black and white to work with! I have no idea if he was speaking the truth. But the clients bought it and we had to color everything just to appease the suit. Discussion over!

Similarly, on another occasion, I suggested to a different advertising agency creative team that we might do a similar thing and not use color in the animation but use black and white. They also agreed that *"aesthetically"*, this would be the right thing to do. But unfortunately, they were totally unprepared to stand up and argue the point with their client, as they feared that as the client was spending so much on the advertising, they would feel "shortchanged" if they didn't get color with their animation. Again, discussion over!

"Clients" – can't live with them but can't live without them!

What I'm saying here is that I am not arguing from an *anti-colorite* viewpoint, just for the sake of it. However, there are occasions where an absence of color is 100% valid – and indeed will enhance the idea an animator is trying to convey. So, I am opening up the argument here that if your project totally loans itself to the idea of *"black & white"* and the beauty and simplicity of an animated line will stand out because of it, then you shouldn't feel obliged to put color into it, just because that's always the way it's done. Ultimately, with any project, it is what comes *from your heart* that matters anyway, and if your heart (and imagination) tells you that a black line on a white background is what it should be, then that is indeed what it should be. I have seen some fabulous films that have been made without color added – just as I've seen other films ruined by the use of gratuitous color. So, listen to your heart on this, whether you choose to use color or not.

Color: To be or not to be?

Suggested Assignment

As this is the last lesson of *"Section I"* in this book and the next section deals with the "**Pre-production**" stage of your next project. Perhaps just a few words here about what that project is and what that project should contain might be of assistance. Again, I don't for one moment want to tell you what it MUST be or limit your decisions on what it is or how it should be handled. However, I do want to share my experience with you, having worked with countless students who were faced with producing their own personal projects for the very first time. A number of them attempted to bite off more than they could chew – or were so keen to impress that they threw everything at their project, including the kitchen sink – only to find they ran out of time, energy or enthusiasm – or all three – in the final analysis. So seen in this way, perhaps my suggestions here may just be of value to you.

The Hermit – small can often be beautiful!

The main thing to have at this stage is just an "**idea**". I don't mean a *script*, I don't mean *designs* and I certainly don't mean a *storyboard*. It is simply that, at the back of your mind, there needs to be a simple story you wish to tell or even a message you wish to share with the world. The *"Pre-production"* stage will put the flesh on the bones of this as we move along. But for now, at least have in your mind the glimmer of something you want to animate in your project.

That "eureka" moment when the good idea comes!

The important thing right now is that your idea is *workable* too. If you have this wonderful cinematic idea of thousands of armed trolls attacking a sacred castle, protect by the Knights of the Round Table in Avalon, then it's really a no-go as a concept. Having no doubt worked very hard so far in covering the material in the first two sections of this book, you should know by now how hard animation can be and how long it takes to do just the simplest of things. So, imagine if you have a concept that requires more than one character, with lots of props and even special effect animation to support it – ask yourself how you can possibly pull that off with the time and resources you have at your disposal.

Think smart and ask yourself honest questions about your idea at this stage.

In imagining my typical reader of this book, I see a young person – male or female – striving to learn animation for perhaps the first time. They maybe have a dream of one day working at a major studio on major projects. Or else, they may even dream of making private and personal films for themselves that uniquely express who they are and what they believe. Indeed, there is a whole universe of ideas waiting for you, if you allow your imagination to reach it.

Dare to dream big – but make your dreams be based on knowledge.

In either case, if this is you, you need to take small steps to get where you want it to be. I have deliberately made this book a series of *"small steps"* so far and intend to do so throughout. Therefore, I urge you to consider the rest of your own production process in a similar way. "**Simple**" and "**achievable**" are the keywords that spring to mind here, as you begin to form an idea of what you want to create here. "**Quality**" over "**quantity**" might be two other keywords that should dominate your thinking.

Be the creator of your own universe.

Practically speaking, I can only repeat what I've already said before. Try to make your project short film **30-seconds long** – like a TV commercial – with a simply "**beginning, middle** & **end**" storyline, involving **one character** and **one prop**. That alone will be a big undertaking for your first-ever project, but it will give you just enough scope to create something quite polished and impressive with the knowledge, experience and time you have to achieve that. There have been some knockout TV commercials in the past – classic and award-winning – so there's nothing to look down upon, in terms of something of quality that is just 30-seconds long. Trust me, you'll thank me for suggesting this restriction at the end of it all!

Thumbs up all round!

So, at this brainstorming moment in your mind, keep your ideas minimal. Do **little sketches** of various ideas in your sketchbook; write down many **keywords** of **short sentences** of ideas that come to mind. **Talk to others** about your ideas and see **which one grabs them most**. Often, in sharing with a number of people you'll find that one idea appeals to most of them. If so, that is the one you need to go with.

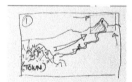

Remember, some of the greatest ideas ever have started as quick thumbnail sketches on a PostIt note or a napkin!

But first, have many ideas to mull over. Don't feel the pressure of coming up with them by the way, as sometimes the *"blank page"* is the most intimidating thing of all. Often, it can be just a *"stream of consciousness"* thing – where you start with something silly or banal and write it down, only for other ideas to start flowing in its wake – whether they are related to the first idea or not.

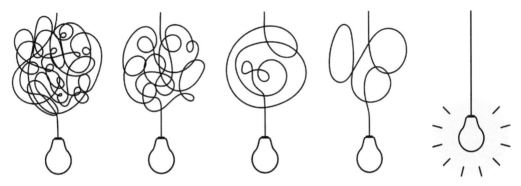

From idea, chaos can become order, eventually.

Sometimes, an idea can come from a dream you have, a piece of music you hear or a word that makes you think about something – or even an experience that you or someone else have had. In one of my animation classes, I ask students what was the strongest experience of their life – or biggest memory they have – that relates to *"animation"* in some way. Almost everyone has at least one of those – often many more – and these can be great material for building a story around. Personal experience and/or feelings can be incredibly powerful motivators!

Drawing – literally – on your own reflections of life, or those of others, can lead to some wonderful ideas and concepts.

So, in conclusion, dream well, but dream *"small"* for practicality sake. Sometimes, the least, yet the most beautifully executed, ideas can be the best of them all!

The world looks forward to meeting you, and your idea, in *"Section III"* of this book!

PERSONAL PROJECT – PRE-PRODUCTION

Bringing your imagination to life.

DOI: 10.1201/9781003324287-27

Masterclass 25/ Storytelling

So, this hopefully is where the fun starts! If you've followed through on all the lessons in this book, you should now have all the tools and techniques of your disposal to make your first film. Now, we're not saying a movie and we're not saying even an extended short film here. What I recommend to my students is to start with something really reachable – like a **30-second** piece. (I.e., The length of a standard TV commercial.) It may seem somewhat underachieving in many ways but trust me when I tell you that even a 30-second film, done well and worth showing, is still a mountain to climb for the novice. Of course, all the *Pre-production* and *Production* processes we'll be covering here can be equal-ly valuable if you're making a 10-, 20-, 30- or even a 90-minute film. But I want to set you at something that is valuable, yet definitely reachable with the skills you have available to you right now. So, keep it simple and smart. Ultimately, the most valuable skills of filmmaking are **time management** and **smart deci-sion-making**. So, I hope you'll see it that way and go for what I would suggest will be a great learning process for you. But first, we mustn't neglect our obser-vational warm-up drawing session…

Warm-Up Drawing

These observational gesture-drawing sessions are always pretty similar in nature, although the themes always change. This time, however, in honor of us entering the *"Pre-production"* stage of learning here, I'm asking you to do

DOI: 10.1201/9781003324287-28

something that's a little bit different on this occasion. So, instead of showing you pictures and asking you to draw them, I'm here going to set you a short **imaginative challenge**. More specifically, it's a **30-minute** imaginative challenge. Now, I'll need you to be quite disciplined in doing it and have to trust that you will be. But set yourself a 15-minute timer if you can and discover yourself how good, or not, you are at it.

Below is a caption, which simply means that whatever you do in your 30-minutes, it's entirely going to be yours and yours alone.

YOUR STORY!
YOU HAVE 15 MINUTES TO TELL YOUR STORY IN SKETCHES ON ONE SHEET OF PAPER - THEN POST IT INTO THE CLASSROOM!

The assignment caption I once posted for my students.

I want you to tell us a story – a simple, drawn, visual story – a story about a single incident in your life that will stick with you forever. It can be a happy story, a sad story, an inspirational story, a frightening story, an embarrassing story or even a hilariously funny story. It just needs to be real and something that was very impactful in your life. Such things are the foundations of all great filmmaking.

Now, we're not even talking about a single picture here – or maybe we are and what you're thinking of can be told in a single picture? But it will probably need to be more than that to tell it well. You simply need to put together a single sketch – or series of sketches, scribbles, whatever – that's going to communicate your story to the world. You need to explain the beginning, middle and end of your story in some way, so we probably are talking about a series of sketches here. They don't need to be highly finished sketches either. They can be quick thumbnail sketches that can share with another person just how your personal life story moment occurred.

Your story is important to the rest of this section too by the way, as what you creatively arrive at here, you will begin to carry forward through the rest of our *"Pre-production"* and *"Production"* lessons together. So, do take it seriously and do make it count. But work fast once you start. You need to get the whole thing down in just 30-minutes!

Now, in terms of how long your story needs to be told, I would suggest you actually think of a TV commercial – just 30-seconds. It shouldn't be long at this stage as I want your first production to be a *"quality"*, not a *"quantity"* one. If you take on too much at this stage, then you will ultimately find yourself compromising on so many things that you will not do justice to the skills you should have reacted to at this point in the book. Worse still – if you take on too much there is a real danger of you never even finishing it! So, many first-time animated filmmakers fall into that category, although I believe it's because if you haven't done it before you just don't know what's involved and therefore it becomes a mountain that is just too high to climb. By thinking just *"30-seconds"*, we give you something that can showcase your skills but not put too many demands on you to either finish it or finish it well. So, please be smart about this.

And do make sure that the 30-seconds you have is quite conventional from a storytelling point of view. In other words, it has a **"beginning"**, **"middle"** and an **"end"** to it. By *"beginning"*, I mean a starting position. By *"middle"*, I mean a change in circumstances from that starting position. And by *"end"*, I mean a resolution as a result of the middle phase. So, cherish your memory but creatively present it in a way that your audience will be entertained by it when they see it.

Another STRONG suggestion is that you don't get overambitious with the story you tell. For example, keep it primarily to **one character** and **one prop** if you can. A *"prop"* is something that the character is interacting with. You don't want crowds of people in your story – because with hand-drawn 2D animation you have to draw each one of that crowd individually, multiplying your challenge considerable. You don't want flowing robes, hair or an overly detailed costume either. Try to avoid dialogue or lip sync either at this stage. Keep it all simple and smart.

And finally, I don't want you to give away the entire storyline, in detail, on your sheet of paper in 30-minutes here. I simply want you to put down the gist, the broad parameters, of the idea to get the wheels turning – enough that another person looking at it can understand what's happening without you explaining it too much. If you can do that, then you'll be off to a great start. So, get to it and – please – just do it in 30-minutes. That is the main test to show that you can. Here are some examples of what some of my younger high school students previously came up with…

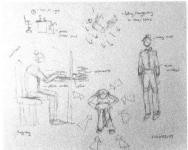

Young student, initial thumbnail, ideas by Carolin Li, Sunny Cong and Jerry Fang, from my Tuesday Night Live online class.

Instruction

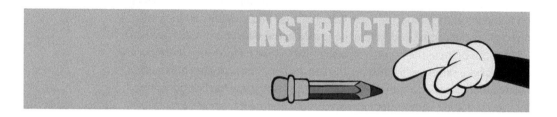

At this stage, in the proceedings, the instruction section is not so much about us doing exercises but now it's more about you exercising your *mind*, your *imagination* and your *creativity*. So, here we're going to change the pace a little. This means that I'll talk about the principles of creativity and the processes required to manifest that creativity in a practical, production environment. But more and more, you will take over your own learning processes here, biased entirely to your personal project. Sometimes, I will need to demonstrate certain things for you of course, but by and large, you must now motivate yourself to bring your imaginings to reality. In my live classes at this stage, I start to screen animation podcast videos, that I hope students can learn from, just by listening to them as they work. I have found them valuable. So, I will transcribe many of them here, incorporating into the learning material. But all that said, at the production stage, you would be your own teacher – nudged by me along the way as I show you the next step.

Idea concept sketch by student, Lucas Ribeiro.

Pre-production and Production. *"Pre-production"* and *"Production"* is what we'll be exploring in this section and the next. But what exactly are they? Well first and foremost, they're both incredibly important. The temptation for beginners is always to jump right into production and just start working on their projects. But that would be an error as if you don't prepare well, you undoubtedly will make twice as much *"busy time"* for yourself without getting very far – or even giving up entirely. So, time spent at the beginning, before any of that, is very productive time spent and all the major game, movie and TV productions repeatedly illustrate. The golden rule here is that… **"You only get out at the end in direct proportion to what you put in at the beginning"**. So, believe me, you neglect the *"Pre-production"* stage at your own peril! And at this stage especially, it's all about *"information"*.

Montage artwork from collected items for a visual concept by student, Jerry Fang.

Obviously, *"Pre-production"* means everything you are preparing for before you venture into the full production. When you make an animated film, you're confronted with two significant things. (Well, there are many things actually, when you make an animated film, but obviously *"animation"* is the main thing you're preoccupied with.) That's the main thing we're preoccupied with on the *"Production"* side. But, in order to clear your mind entirely for the animation work, you need to solve many other problems first. *"Pre-production"* involves all that. It essentially means that you're solving every single problem you're likely to encounter in making the film so that you don't have to worry about them when you're totally focused on animation. Big studios absolutely need to go through the pre-production process, as they invariably have such large teams working on the production that they daren't have anything go wrong. So, all problems, issues and creative decisions are dealt with before the big production team arrives. But it is just as important for you, a sole indie creator, to complete those things too. You're probably going to be single-handed throughout, so you don't have the time (or probably the patience or energy) or have anything go wrong or distract you when you're doing the thing you most want to do – animate.

Random concept sketches by student, Xiaofu Zhu.

So, let's look at everything that's involved in *Pre-production* and discuss it briefly. You're going to be doing pretty much all of it in the next lessons but it's good to know what's coming before you have to do it. Therefore, the stages of *Pre-production* we're talking about are…

   i. **Story Idea & Project Planning**
   ii. **Concept Art**
  iii. **Character Design**
  iv. **Storyboarding**
   v. **Audio Record & Breakdown**
  vi. **Storyboard Animatic**
 vii. **Character Rig** (2D or 3D digital animators)
viii. **Backgrounds or Environments**
  ix. **Pose Test Animatic**

In my classes, I deal with some of these over two classes, instead of one. But for this book, I'll combine them into single categories and expand the material if necessary. You see that in terms of *"Character Rig"*, we are really talking about animators who are working with software, 2D or 3D. Traditional animators may not need to worry about this lesson, although these days it definitely pays to master more than one approach. But if you are making a project here that is entirely hand-drawn traditionally, this is something you need not to worry about so much. Bottom line, if you successfully complete all these stages of pre-production, you'll be in an incredible position to essentially just focus on "making things move well" through animation. And that's where the fun really starts!

When it comes to ideas, the sky's the limit!

i. Now, we're effectively talking about "**Project Planning**" & "**Story Creation**" in this masterclass lesson, right now. Indeed, that's why I gave you a story idea assignment for the gesture-drawing assignment in the first place. Killing two tomes with one stone! "Project Planning" is really what I'm telling you here – what you need to do and when you need to do it. It stands to rea- son too that you can't start to plan your project, or Pre-production, without having a story idea in place first. So that's why you've definitely needed to come up with a story idea here. We can talk about developing it in a minute but for now, just make sure you have in mind what you want to do with your project and then commit yourself to all the required Pre-production steps to make it the best project you can possibly create.

Early color concept art for my "Hermit" project.

ii. In the next masterclass lesson, we're going to go into more depth with
"Concept Art". Indeed, I'm going to present material that I put into a
podcast I recorded for my students. I can't show the podcast content here,
but I can share the message of the podcast with readers. The bottom line of
"Concept Art" is that having got your idea with your story idea in this lesson,
in the next lesson you will need to be able to visualize your idea. You'll need
to ask yourself – I know how I want to say what I'm saying, but what exactly
is it going to look like? *"Concept Art"* works out exactly what the visual side
of it is going to be, in color or not.

The Hermit concept art further developed into a proposal for the opening
title sequence.

iii. The next stage of the Pre-production process, "**Character Design**", is sometimes done at the same time as *"Concept Art"*, but usually afterward, depending on the time pressures a studio is under. Illustrating a character and animating a character have different requirements; in other words, the character designer needs to be aware of the limitations or requirements that animation puts on the design. Additionally, a character design is not just done from one viewpoint, but needs to be designed in the round, in the form of a "**turnaround model sheet**". We'll discuss all these things in much more detail during the appropriate lesson to come.

Three-pose a turnaround model sheet of the Hermit.

iv. With the *"story"*, *"concept art"* and *"character designs"* complete, is it now time to work on a "**storyboard**". A *"storyboard"* is a visual representation of the story being told. It is not just drawing pictures that represent the scenes in a film. Indeed, a storyboard artist doesn't necessarily have to draw well – they just have to know how to communicate ideas well, filmically and creatively. The best storyboard artists know a great deal about the rules of *"filmmaking"*, *"timing"*, *"framing"*, *"acting"* and even an instinctive under-standing of *"visual theater"* too, in order that the film ultimately comes alive on the screen. Not knowing, or doing, those things can significantly damage a film and its storyline, which is why some of the *gesture-drawing* exercises in this book cover these things.

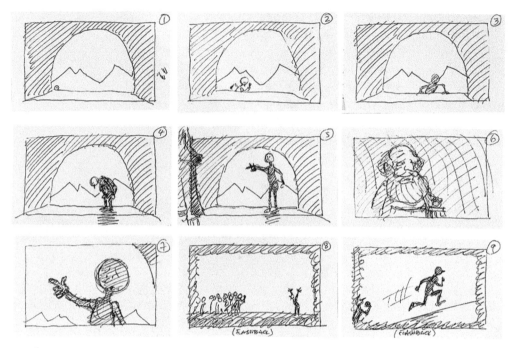

I always draw my first rough, thumbnail storyboards on yellow Sticky Notes, as they are so easy to use and interchangeable.

   v. Of course, to make most films you need to have an audio track. For my online classes, I like to supply my students with a selection of 3 or 4 tracks to work with. But you will have to record your own of course. So, in a subsequent lesson in this book, we're going to talk about recording soundtracks, and then how you can analyze ("breakdown") them to do "lip sync". Or, there are techniques to discover that will help you animate to music if you're not using a dialogue track.

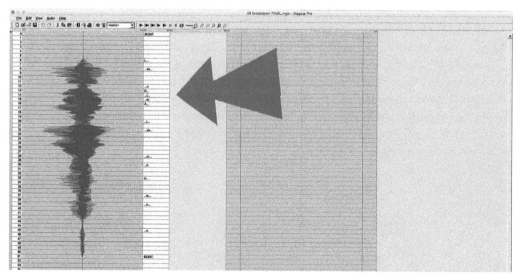

"Magpie Pro" was one of the first digital audio "breakdown" applications designed for animators to accurately time out lip sync.

vi. Beyond that, once the audio tracks are recorded and broken down, the next thing to do is combine the storyboard and the audio track to create a **"Storyboard Animatic"**. Although there is no animation created yet, this will test in real-time video your *"storytelling"*, *"visual ideas"*, *"pacing"* your *"timing"* and whether or not your sound is a perfect match to your visuals. It will be the first chance you'll see how your project stacks up on a screen, but before the expensive time and money process of animation is undertaken – and giving you a great opportunity to make changes, small or large, in the process. The *"Golden Rule"* here? Don't go any further until you are 100% happy that your *"storyboard animatic"* is as good as it could be!

"Hermit" animatic edit in Final Cut Pro.

vii. Now, if your project is Moho, this is the time to **"rig your character(s)"**. There is a lot to this, as we'll discover. Remember though, with this project, we're going to keep everything very simple. So, remember that rigged Moho characters are two-dimensional only. So, if your story requires that your characters are going to turn around anywhere up to 360-degrees – such as in a dance or dynamic sporting action or similar – then Moho is not for you. For that, you will have to take a traditional hand-drawn 2D approach. (Yes, the more advanced Moho rigs can have some dimensional turn built into them. But this is advanced rigging and not an area we intend to cover here.) Similarly, if your character needs a range of various facial expressions to communicate your storyline, then the basic Moho approach is not for you.

Basic Hermit character rig in Moho (Note: The film is a mix of traditional hand-drawn animation and rigged Moho action, depending on the scene content.)

viii. Most 2D animation – traditional or digital – will need a background environment for the animation to be set in. Therefore, now is a good time to create (and maybe even paint) your "**Background layouts**". Setting the scene, staging the action and creating a mood are all aspects of creating background layouts that can make or break your animation. So, a great deal of thought has to go into this, and the lesson on this, later in the book, will be of great value – whether you color your background layouts at this stage or not. Remember, if you have lots of *"scenes"* (or *"shots"*) in your film, you will need to have a similar number of *"layouts"* and final painted *"backgrounds"*. You may be lucky enough to have one background used all the way through your film, which would be great if you can pull it off. But if you have multiple backgrounds to do, make sure you have the time and energy to do them at a consistent level. It again could affect whether or not your film becomes a success or failure.

Layout for Hermit-related animated background sequence.

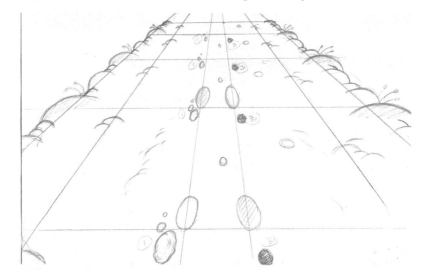

ix. And let's not forget either that if you have *"background layouts"*, then you're going to need **"character layouts"** to go with them whereas there will only be one *"background layout"* per scene, there could be several *"character layouts"*, where you draw your character in each scene, drawn in all the key *"storytelling poses"* they will be seen throughout that scene. Again, the better you plan and draw your poses, the better your animation will be – as no matter how much periphery work you overlay your animation with, if the poses are not great, then your animation will never be great either. *(Which is why I am encouraging you to do the "observational gesture-drawing" assignments at the head of each of these masterclass lessons!)*

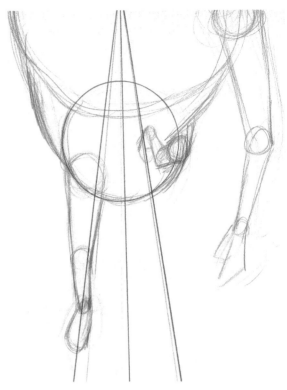

Rough character layout for Figure "Layout for Hermit-related animated background sequence".

x. Finally, when all the background and character layouts are done and/or the Moho character is rigged, the final stage is to create a new **"Key Pose Animatic"**. That is, all the layout drawings and audio tracks are edited together – as before with the "storyboard animatic", but at a higher level – so that a final, real-time version of the film can be viewed prior to the animation starting. This is the *"last chance saloon"* in terms of making changes, tweaks and adjustments to everything so that you have nothing else to worry about when you embark on making it all move well.

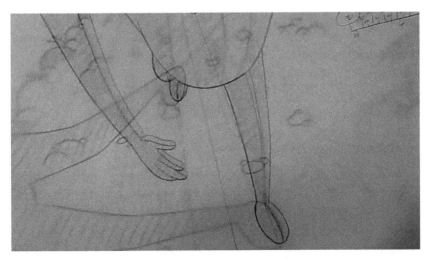

Final key pose animatic frame for Hermit scene, above.

With all that done, you've worked out all the problems, ironed out all the wrinkles and completed all the project planning you need to do. So, you're finally ready for the full "**Production**" stage, which we'll deal with in detail in *"Section IV"* of this book.

In the meantime, let's move on to the next lesson in *"Section II"* without further delay!

Suggested Assignment

Nothing extra is necessary here except to say that maybe you want to revise your story ideas from the one you have already thought about? Well, this is the moment to do it if you do. Changes further down the line could be extremely costly on your time and commitment, so really discipline yourself at this point. Either go 100% for your original idea or else think about another story or idea you want to animate for your project. But **I STRONGLY URGE YOU** to stay within the 30-second, TV-commercial length project on this one, with a single character, a single prop and as few backgrounds as possible if you don't want to fall at the first hurdle.

And if you wish to expand your idea further, by writing a formal script or screenplay for your film? well, this is the moment to do that too. There are many tutorials out there on structuring, writing and formatting a screenplay. However, you again really need to keep things very simple at this stage. Perhaps if I show you one of my own scripts, it should give you an idea of how to formally write your idea into a more structured screenplay format. This was an early promotional trailer script for my *"animated memoirs"* documentary project, **The Old Man Mad About Animating**…

THE OLD MAN MAD ABOUT ANIMATION

~ Animated Memoirs ~

CLOSE-UP COMPUTER MONITOR – NIGHT.

We see what looks like an early Fleischer Studio movie from the early days of animation. A PROFESSOR (not that unlike a Max Fleischer caricatured character) points to an early sketch of the animation process. It has the same look and style of the original "Max Fleischer Rotoscope" design. The audio track was originally recorded by Tony White for his studio's showreel opening...

> **PROFESSOR**
>
> How to make an animated film.
> Never, since the days of WALTIE
> DISSIE has animakers been so
> populode. Nowadale, everything that
> a pencilode can scribblit, or
> outlide - or even think it in the
> milode - can be, and in fact is,
> animakers!

Suddenly the monitor is switched off and the screen fades to BLACK.

FADE TO:

TONY WHITE DESKTOP – NIGHT

In the backlit light of his desktop the veteran animator, TONY WHITE, walks from the monitor he's just switched off and returns to his animation drawing desk. He proceeds to animate the title sequence for his next film, "THE OLD MAN MAD ABOUT ANIMATING". As his voice is heard as a voice over, Tony is seen to be repeatedly... i) inbetweening animation drawings, ii) switching the desk backlight off, iii) checking his drawings by flipping them, iv) switching the backlight on again and v) making necessary corrections. There's an aura of shadowy isolation and midnight loneliness about the shot. Yet Tony appears quite contented to do what he's doing.

> **TONY**
>
> (v.o.)
>
> I'm often told that animators are the loneliest people on earth - working for long hours at a time, bringing life to worlds that no-one else sees.
>
> Yet I've never actually felt alone for one moment. Truth is, I have so many strange friends in my imagination that I have all the companionship I can cope with!

CUT TO:

OVER THE SHOULDER SHOT OF TONY - SAME MOMENT.

We see what Tony is drawing. It's a pencil drawing of a simple but strange character we'll get to know as "ARNIE". On the paper, Arnie suddenly comes alive and winks at Tony, sticking his tongue out after he's done so. Tony seems not surprised at all by this. Instead, he grabs an eraser and wipes the smug smile off of Arnie's face.

TONY

(v.o.)

Sometimes my imaginary characters intrude on my life quite unexpectedly of course. Sometimes they are supportive. Sometimes they are funny. And sometimes – like this rude and self-opinionated "AR-NIE" guy here – they can be quite vexing!

Tony begins to re-draw Arnie's face. Arnie's mouthless head tries to avoid Tony's pencil. But Tony eventually pins him down and draws a new – and much more respectful – smile on him. But like a child having his face wiped by a mother who has spit on a tissue, Arnie is irritated and scrubs at his mouth disdainfully.

CUT TO:

ORIGINAL WIDE SHOT OF TONY AT DESK – SAME MOMENT.

Tony loses patience with his Arnie drawing. He tears the paper from its animation pegs, crumples it up and unceremoniously tosses it into a nearby garbage can. He replaces it with a fresh sheet of paper and begins again. But as he does so, the garbage can suddenly shake and a most disgruntled Arnie figure climbs out. He dusts himself down and jumps up beside Tony as he draws. He glares and taps his foot at the same time. Tony merely continues to do what he's doing, unmoved.

DISSOLVE TO:

SIMILAR SHOT, BUT YEARS EARLIER – DAYTIME.

A much younger Tony is drawing one of the illustrations for his first book, "THE ANIMATOR'S WORKBOOK"...

TONY

(v.o.)

"Arnie" - technical name "Animaticus Drawersaurus" – first appeared to me when I was working on my first book, "The Animator's Workbook". He'd always been somewhere at the back of my mind...

DISSOLVE TO:

CLOSE-UP OF TONY'S YOUNGER HAND, ILLUSTRATING HIS FIRST BOOK.

The hand is yellow pencil-shading an early Arnie illustration from the book.

TONY

(v.o.)

...but he only really made himself visible to me when I struggled for a simple character design that students could easily draw.

The book illustration Arnie again winks at younger Tony as he colors it. This time Tony is surprised at what happens – as this has never happened with a character he has drawn before!

DISSOLVE BACK

TO:

CLOSE-UP OF TONY AT THE DESK - NOW.

Arnie leans in to see what Tony is drawing, but Tony pushes him back without even looking up. He's seen it all before at this stage. But Arnie doesn't give up, so Tony looks at him with an irritated scowl this time.

> **TONY**
>
> (v.o.)
>
> And he has never left me since!

ORIGINAL WIDE SHOT OF TONY AT HIS DESKTOP – SAME MOMENT.

Arnie doesn't give up. He is actually quite dismissive of what Tony is drawing and gesticulates wildly, as if to tell Tony how he should be doing it. Tony ignores him and just continues to do what he was doing...

> **TONY**
>
> (v.o.)
>
> When he first arrived, Arnie was quite silent and shy. But after the book was published, and was successful, he thought it was all due to him. Indeed, it totally went to his head! Since then, he has always felt confident enough to express an opinion – or two – or three – and now I simply can't shut him up! Yet in his better moments he fills my mind with wonderful memories of time gone by. (Arnie pulls out a caricature picture of the great animator, Richard Williams, smiling and holding an award. Tony sees the picture and smiles.) For instance - the time I presented my late great teacher, RICHARD WILLIAMS, with a special "Roy E. Disney" award...

The scene suddenly transforms into the picture. Real-world Tony morphs into his own caricature and holds the "Roy E. Disney Award" up to present to caricature Richard Williams. This was 12 years earlier and the whole thing is choreographed to the actual audio track that was captured at the time...

> **ANIMATED TONY**
>
> TONY: For all these reasons I want to present to Dick the "Roy E. Disney Award".

AUDIENCE

(Applause)

ANIMATED RICHARD WILLIAMS

This is heavier than an Oscar!

(Audience laughter.) Very impressive! Ha-ha! Wanna know how to get weight! This is weird, 35 years later.

This is er, the guy with the broad shoulders in the corner.

ANIMATED TONY

(indicating his ample stomach)

And now it's a broad stomach!

ANIMATED RICHARD WILLIAMS

Weird! Well, maybe I'll take this as a longevity award. A still breathing award! (Laughs.) Oh, fantastic!

AUDIENCE

(More applause)

The action transforms back to the original real-world shot of Tony at his animation desk. He stares into space, as if lost in the thought of the memory.

DISSOLVE TO:

THE BASEMENT THEATER OF RICHARD WILLIAMS LONDON STUDIO – 1970S.

Tony has just shown Richard Williams his first ever short film, "HOKUSAI ~ AN ANIMATED SKETCHBOOK". Tony looks apprehensive as he awaits his mentor's response. Dick Williams smiles and shakes Tony's hand.

RICHARD WILLIAMS

Fantastic! You know, there is no "Tony White" in that film – it is all "Hokusai". That's a great achievement!

Tony appears almost embarrassed by the praise. He awkwardly exits the room as Dick Williams returns to viewing the dailes of his own animated project, "The Cobbler and the Thief'.

TONY

(v.o.)

Getting approval for my work from Richard Williams was always like getting approval from my father. It wasn't absolutely necessary in the greater scheme of things, but personally it sure did feel good when it happened!

FADE OUT.

ORIGINAL WIDE SHOT OF TONY AT HIS DESKTOP - NOW.

Suddenly Tony snaps out of the wayward expression as Arnie growls and paws at him, as if he were a cat about to attack. Tony's mood suddenly changes. There is now a darker, more resigned and much less positive expression on his face...

> **TONY**
>
> (v.o.)
>
> Of course, my life hasn't all been fun and roses. Long before Arnie appeared - way back during the early days of my childhood - it was a much darker and far more scary place for me.
>
> FADE TO...

YOUNG TONY'S BEDROOM AT NIGHT – 65 YEARS EARLIER.

All is dark, sinister and shadowy. In a kind of "Snow White and the Seven Dwarfs" scary-forest way, normal bedroom furniture makes frightening shadows that seem to hang over the young boy. Child Tony – in silent tears – clutches the bed covers over his face for protection. He fearfully stares out into the dark scariness of the bedroom. As he does so, the shadows shift and change. Tony looks totally terrified, as if he knows something is about to happen. Suddenly the door of his old, gothic-looking wardrobe crashes open and a powerful, realistically animated TIGER leaps out from inside. It lands heavily on Tony's chest and glares down at him - bearing its glistening teeth as it does so. After a terrifying silent moment, the Tiger's great jaws suddenly snaps down towards the cowering Tony – as if about to rip the head off his body! Tony dives under the covers...

> **YOUNG TONY**
>
> Screeeeaaaammmmmmmmm!!!

FADE TO...

FILM'S OPENING TITLE SEQUENCE. (THAT TONY HAS BEEN ANIMATING THROUGHOUT THE DOCUMENTARY MOVIE.)

FADE TO...

Masterclass 26/
Concept Art

For this one, we're going back to the previous pattern of observational gesture drawings. In fact, as you're moving more and more toward the "production" side of this book, I want you to do more timed pose work. So, although the words here may sound like a posing exercise you did before, the pictures are different. So, go with the flow of words but treat the images with a fresh eye.

Warm-Up Drawing

I want to remind you that when you are animating a character you need to understand what the circumstances in which they're moving are. For example, a walking character may have to confront wind, rain and earthquakes in a physical way – or experience fear, happiness, reluctance and excitement in an emotional way. They may be infirm or hurt in some way, or they may have superpowers. They could be young or old, male or female. All these things will affect how a character moves and how they walk. By studying the poses of others through observational gesture drawing, you get to get a sense of how different people move in different circumstances.

The following two images offer you a chance to observe other characters in other poses. You should give yourself 3-minutes to complete them…

DOI: 10.1201/9781003324287-29

Pose 1 comments: In this pose, you see a woman battling the wind and walking uphill. So, this significantly affects the way she moves, and therefore how she is posed in the key positions. You can see that with this character walking uphill and into the wind, the natural forward lean is exaggerated in order for her to overcome the incline and the wind. What leaning forward does is effectively putting more weight on the front foot, where the real push forward begins. So, the *"key stride"* here is very much modified from the *"generic walk"*, in the sense that the front and back foot position is not so evenly spread forward and back in relation to the torso. This means that the character is therefore actually out of balance compared to the generic walk, which is necessary to move forward in these circumstances.

Pose 2 comments: So, having observed a character walking uphill, this one contrasts it with a character walking downhill. *(The same pose will apply to a strong wind at their back, on flat ground, incidentally.)* Notice that the emphasis of the character's body mass is now tending to be over the back leg – and would be more so if the down gradients were steeper, or even flatter, without steps. This is because any extreme forward lean, or even regular generic walk lean possibly, would have the character falling headfirst down the steps, out of balance. So, here the character displaces the balance backward, so that his back leg is taking the weight and the front leg can cautiously edge its way forward. There would be a slight movement a little more forward onto the front leg when it makes contact with the ground, which would quickly transfer back again as the front leg becomes the back leg with the next stride. Notice too that there are no big arm swings here, with the arms actually tucked in close to the body.

I hope these two exercises have given you a little understanding of how a pose is modified by terrain or wind conditions? You will obviously need to modify it, dependent on the degree of these things in the scene you will tackle, as well as the strength and weakness of the characters themselves. Remember, the greater the incline, one way or another, the greater the body lean and leg placements in relation to the body, will be. These of course are only two of the infinite number of variations that will limit a character when walking beyond the *"generic"*. But such things should be considered with all character animation, of course, walks or otherwise. You should also consider side balance adjustments too, such as a character trying to balance their way along a fence or a tightrope walking negotiating their way along, high up in the air. Up and down terrain for a walking character would require constant adjustments of body lean and balance of course. *"Balance"* in animation – as well as in life – is something you'll soon get to appreciate the importance of as you move forward on your journey.

Instruction

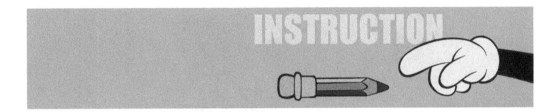

So, we're now at a stage (hopefully) where you have your idea finalized in your mind – as well as on paper – and you're ready to move forward. Now, it's quite often true that the idea is the easy part! (I know, some people take forever to come up with an idea and suffer from the "blank page syndrome" – but going with something as personal vacillation is the animator's own worst enemy!) So have the confidence to invest in your own ideas and commit to them. You'll be surprised just how creative you can be beyond this stage, taking things to the next level in a way that may even surprise you! I will personally assure you here that if you put in the work and see it right the way through to the end with your very best effort, you'll end up with something that you, and those around you – even job interviewers in the industry – will be impressed by. You just have to be single-minded and put your very best work into every stage to the best of your ability.

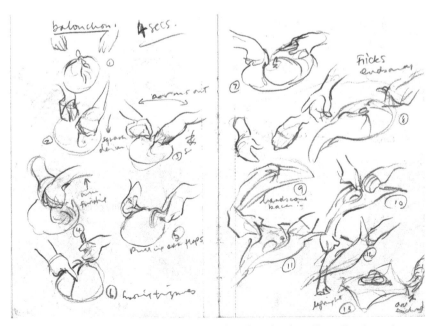

Joanna Quinn's sketchbook reference sketches for her film *Elles* (1992).

So, the next step – "**Concept Art**". To explain what "Concept Art" is, I'll quote from an audio podcast I did for my students. I'll adapt it to this book form but this is essentially what I explained to them. I advised them also that as they listened to the audio-only podcast, they might sketch out anything that comes to mind in terms of their own project. Not final work, just *thumbnail* ideas – as listening to someone can often trigger thoughts that are best put down onto a page before you lose them. Anyway, you might try it as you read the following.

Concept art for Cartoon Saloon's *Wolfwalkers* movie. © Cartoon Saloon Ltd., Melusine Productions.

We often see or hear the term *"Concept Art"*, but what is it? Well, it can be many things to many people. In terms of making a film, game or another project that relies on visual material, it is the process of creating visual imagery that defines the project before any of the full production can take place. This principally does one of two things. The first is to sell the project to potential clients, investors or distributors, to convince them that the project is the greatest looking thing since sliced bread. In that sense, it is a selling exercise. On the other hand, if the production has moved beyond that stage, it is essentially a visual statement of the look of the project that everyone in the team is working on so that they are quite literally all on the same creative page. So, in this sense, it's showing everyone something like what the final project is designed to be so that all creative decisions beyond that point can refer to it as a yardstick. Therefore, the "concept artist", or "artists", is hired to give the project a look that everyone can hopefully be inspired by and stand behind as they move forward. So, it is the "visual feel" of the project – an image starting point – although the project

More concept art for *Wolfwalkers* movie. © Cartoon Saloon Ltd., Melusine Productions.

might evolve beyond the initial concept art as various creative teams are working on the material.

Now, *"Concept Art"* doesn't have to be finished art. It doesn't have to be highly finished, polished artwork – at least not for your own personal project. If you work at a big studio like Pixar or DreamWorks, however, they will probably demand it from you and only hire you if you're capable of that. But for a first-time personal project, you are really just pleasing yourself at this stage. It doesn't have to be a final character design or background art either. But it does have to have a strong "look-'n-feel" to what the final project is going to kind of look like. This is definitely all it needs to be for a personal project – something that allows you to focus your mind on the visual direction your film will ultimately take. If it is for a personal project – a film, game, TV show, etc. – but you're looking for funding from the industry or even a creative funding site like Patreon, you'll probably have to up the quality on what you would personally be comfortable in working with. In other words, you will need to impress other people with your imaginative insights and the quality of your presentation material.

Concept art/final layout for *Wolfwalkers* movie. © Cartoon Saloon Ltd., Melusine Productions.

First and foremost, the *"Concept Art"* needs to lock you down to a specific direction – the colors, moods, vision and feel you're going after. If you can impress them, then you'll certainly be able to impress your future audiences after all the hard work of production is done. Concept art is about "conception" after all. So, depending on what your personal production needs are and where you're going with it, your Concept Art can be simple rough color sketches – indeed, it can even be pencil roughs if that will work for you. Just never forget that if you're reaching out to impress others though – "a picture is worth a thousand words, and even more in dollars if you are pitching it well to the right people"!

Color concept art for *Wolfwalkers* movie. © Cartoon Saloon Ltd., Melusine Productions.

Now, you can use watercolors, pencil shading, digital texturing or anything that will capture the imagination and choose a key scene or moment in your proposed film to encapsulate what it's going to look like. As indicated earlier, it doesn't have to be the final artwork for your project but it certainly does need to embrace that "look-'n-feel" that you're going for. You can include characters as a suggestion, but my big recommendation here is to save final decisions on that until we reach the next lesson, which deals with it more specifically. It helps though to have an understanding of what the background art and scene lighting might be like – so that when you do finally arrive at a final drawn and colored character design, it will at least fit in well with what's going behind it.

Concept art by Peter Moehrle for Drawassic's *Spirit of the Game* proposed movie project.

Technique-wise, your "Concept Art" can be simply treated, but it does have to be supportive of the idea. If you look at the production art from many different productions (don't look at "CG Hollywood alone – they all look the same in the main these days!), you'll note there's a multitude of different approaches to it. So, there's not one real thing that comprehensively defines what *"Concept Art"* looks like. It's what YOU make it to be – and please DARE to be different. The options are infinite. It's really anything that communicates your inner vision to the world at large – or more importantly, the investors or distributors of your next project!

Personally, I love to work with other concept artists and character designers as I discovered many decades ago that I am NOT a great visual artist or character designer, even though I do consider myself a master animator who can make things move in many styles and with many approaches. I proved that in the advertising world, never chose to repeat commercials if I'd worked in that style before. So, I am very inspired by other people's designs and always got incredibly excited if I had to work on a design that I didn't do. Maybe that's true of you too? Remember, no one person has the absolute vision of these things. There are people out there who can bring amazing things to your project if you're open enough to embrace their ideas too. Not every one will work but sometimes the most unexpected people can do incredible things for you and your project. So, never neglect to reach out to others if you're in a position to do so. I personally love to do that.

Concept/background art by Thomas Liera for Drawassic's *Revenge of the Fly* short film.

Anyway, within a personal project or even a big studio, *"Concept Art"* is a way of communicating a vision for a project across the board. It puts your director, producer, animators, voice actors, editors and background artists all on the same page. If it's just you, then it doesn't matter so much and you have the whole thing in your head anyway – although even with yourself, it is extremely valuable to get those abstract ideas down in some kind of concrete form on paper, adding gravity and a sense of direction to them. In a bigger studio, however, it's a pivotal point for your project, where everyone can get together through a common visual purpose – and buy into it. That is the most valuable purpose that *"Concept Art"* can have at the very beginning of a production.

Concept/background art by Tony White for Drawassic's *Pouring Clean Water* proposed movie project.

"Concept Art" can be other things too. Sometimes when you arrive at a visual styling for your film – and that can sometimes be just one single image – you or your team can start breaking it down into different definable sections. For example, if you're making a movie, then you can develop "**color palettes**" – concepts of color for characters and props that can be extended throughout your film – which will help everyone involve, knowing the kind of color spectrum they need to work with. This can evolve *later (i.e., once a "storyboard" exists)* into a "**color script**", which takes all the sequences throughout the film and applies a color theme to those too, where moods, emotions and times of day/year are represented by specific color themes. All these can come from the *"Concept Art"*. Indeed, that *"Concept Art"* can be created upfront to represent these emotional stages in the project to give diversity and depth to the entire look of the sales pitch, if investment and/or distribution are your ultimate objective. Therefore, if there is a sequence in your film that is violent, aggressive or angry in terms of a character's emotions or experience, then you will more likely use red-hot tones throughout to convey that. These will tend to fire up your audience on a subconscious level at least. Similarly, if you have a very romantic or lighthearted sequence in the unfolding storyline, then you might go to light blue or green tones to reflect that. These will tend to calm your audience down more in preparation for what might be a darker sequence that follows, which would clearly go into much darker color tones. So, a "color script", inspired by your project's "Concept Art", allows you to take a step back, look at the bigger picture and assign color themes that represent the lighter and darker shades, or more positive and negative moods, of the story arc of your film.

Tiger color model for Drawassic's *Pouring Clean Water* proposed movie project.

Now, sometimes there is confusion in people's minds when talking about *"Concept Art"* versus "**Production Art**". But they are not the same thing. The purpose of *"Concept Art"* is to conceive what the project will look like, whereas *"Production Art"* is refining and reflecting within the production stage the nature of the

"Concept Art" that has been previously established. It's a small matter, but it's worth noting here, as often people use those two terms to mean the same thing in their own minds. But they should be kept separate to avoid confusion with a production team.

Color background concept art for Drawassic's *The Hermit* film project.

Finally, just realize that from a visual perspective that *"Concept Art"* is the foundation upon which everything else is built. Your animation approaches, background styling, color decisions and the nature of the moods and emotions you put into your storytelling, all come from the establishment of good production *"Concept Art"*. In other words, inspirational *"Concept Art"* will affect the way the project is animated, the visual approach is undertaken and the assurance *(or not)* that the audience will be carried along with your storyline. Nothing should be left to chance here, so you are strongly advised to put as much effort into the creation of your "Concept Art" as you will with the animation, or other aspects of your production. *"Concept Art"* doesn't necessarily tell everyone exactly what the project must look like. But it should give strong hints in terms of the direction the visual elements of the production are going, from which each individual involved can take it further a while all the time it also reflects the visual framework that has been set up. At the same time, great *"Concept Art"* can be very simple – and should ALWAYS be established within the production resources you have available to you for your project from the outset. Great creativity can come from great limitations or restrictions of time and budget. But by creative imagination, your *"Concept Art"* can take your project to exciting new avenues, where you are a sole filmmaker or have all the resources of a big Hollywood studio behind you.

Suggested Assignment

Obviously, you have to create *"Concept Art"* for your project in one way or another. So, do your best to inspire yourself or your team with what you come up with. However, if you have several approaches on your mind and aren't clear about the direction your visual expression can take, consider doing up to **3 versions** of interpretation and show them around to others, to see what most appeals to them. Remember that you are making a film for an audience and so the more you can touch that audience with what you come up with, the more likely they're going to love your film. So, test out your alternative *"Concept Art"* options and let the market lead you, however limited your market research capability is.

NOTE

With this and all other aspects of your production work, if you are going to show your work in the hope of valuable feedback and opinion, make sure the individuals you show it to are worthy of having an opinion. In other words, ask peers and those who you respect. And if you're a youngster, working out of your parents' home, and have limited resources at your disposal, don't just rely on the opinions of parents and family to give you feedback on these things. Most family members will always try to make you feel good and are often unwilling to hurt your feelings if they, deep down, don't really like what you've come up with. So, they will not be at all representative of the audience you hope to reach with your project. So, go beyond that limited circle to friends or strangers who are both creative themselves and yet will be entirely honest with you. Honest opinions can be painful at times, but if enough of them come back with the same conclusions, then it's definitely time for you to think again about your "Concept Art" and its relevance to the audience you hope to reach!

Masterclass 27/ Character Design

In this lesson, we're going to concentrate entirely on "**Character Design**". Having hopefully established your *"Concept Art"* for your project, is it next necessary to tighten our focus on the look of what you're doing? As animation is nearly always character-driven, it is a good idea to finalize what your character looks like with the concept stylings you have arrived at. But first, observational gesture drawing…

Warm-Up Drawing

As the focus is going to be on characters here, our gesture-drawing session will apply itself to getting the most out of our characters, from an animation and pose point of view. Therefore, we are going to be looking at the nature of "**Balance**".

Now, *"Balance"* is something vitally important that all animators need to know about. For example, you can create a great sequence of movements with a character, but no matter how good it is; if the key positions are not in balance, then the action will not be convincing. Balance can work in many ways of course. But with a biped character, the important thing is that the character's *"center of gravity"* must always be over their two feet at all times, as you learned in our *"Generic Walk"* section and elsewhere. As you remember, if the character then lifts one foot, as in a stride, then the "center of gravity" must first shift over to the "contact foot" on the ground, so they can lift their foot up without falling over.

DOI: 10.1201/9781003324287-30

That's why in a well-animated walking action, there should always be a degree of "body shift" from side to side. The heavier the character is, the more that shift will be.

Of course, breaking the rules of balance can be valuable too. This would be true in the sense that if you're animating someone who is intoxicated for instance, a baby who is trying to walk for the first time or someone who is tripping over something, then the balance has to be ahead of the points of contact with the ground (foot or feet) in their direction of the fall. Below are two examples of balance in action. Give yourself **3-minutes** each to draw them…

Pose 1 comments: *"Standing on one leg"*: We are clearly focusing on a lot of weight here. But, in order for him to lift his one leg up and be in that position, he has to first shift his weight across to the right foot, which is on the ground. If he didn't do that and simply lifted his foot off the ground with his old balance position, he would fall over on the side where the leg is lifted. So, just by animating someone who is lifting their leg up, it's never going to be fully convincing unless you have the character do the leg shift first.

Pose 2 comments: *"Elephant balance"*: This is more of a fun one, although it still respects the laws of balance. As you can see, this is logically impossible. But even so, animation IS about the impossible at times, so make it plausible if you have to do something like this. *"The plausible of the implausibility"* if you like, as Walt Disney once put it. So, here we have the great heavyweight of the elephant, balancing on a tiny chair, on an unstable rope. However, it's pretty much correct in terms of the visual balance because the center of gravity of all that weight is effectively going right the way down to the point the chair touches the rope. So, it may not be possible in the real world but it does look plausible in the animation one. If we could rotate this shot around 360-degrees, we'd see a similar perfect balance like this from every angle.

OK, so that's been our short exploration of *"Balance"*. Balance is a factor of life that exists everywhere around us. The two examples you've just drawn are perhaps the most obvious exercises for this. But just imagine, everything you do and see is about balance. When you, yourself, were a baby and trying to walk, you didn't get it at first. You had to learn how to balance your body, so you didn't fall on your face. And you fell on your face because your center of gravity was ahead of your feet on the ground and you were not yet able to bring either foot forward enough to get it under the point where your center of gravity was. But you learned to do it in the end and now take it for granted with every step you take. Now, as an animator, you have to learn to do it all over again – with the characters you are responsible for animating well. Consider trying to balance your pencil on your finger. You will never be able to do it until you get both sides of the pencil in equal weight with each other, so the balance is achieved.

And so, it is with your animated characters. Unless you consider "Balance" with every pose you do, those characters will never be fully convincing for your audience≈– even if they only understand that on a subconscious level. And this in turn reflects on how your life is.

Life is all about balance too. If we go out on a limb in any one direction excessively, then we become obsessive and that brings so much disharmony to ourselves and everyone else around us. So, unless you can arrange things so that your life is all in balance and harmony, you will never be consistently stable enough to be a great animator. Richard Williams always said that he wanted animators on his team that had a stable home life – like the great Disney animators of old – because they were the ones who produced the greatest work for him. Life in the exterior animation world and life in our inner imaginative world are reflective of each other, and until we bring these into balance, as well as the balance of our personal lives, we will never be able to explore the greatness of our potential over the long term in our lives. Ultimately, in terms of animation, you need to decide whether you want your characters to be in balance, or not. So doing, you now have some understanding of what it takes to achieve that kind of thing visually, on the screen.

Instruction

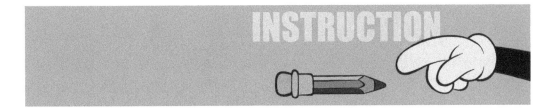

Character Design: At this point in time, in my live classes, I would now review my students' *"Concept Art"* work to make sure that everyone is on track. This is because you don't want to start character design unless your greater vision is in place first. To not do that would run the risk of you doing lots of character designs, only to find that when you do arrive at *"Concept Art"* later, they don't fit with each other and clash, unfortunately. So, reassure yourself that you are

happy with your concept work – and others are sympathetic toward it too.
This is not to say that you're slavishly doing what other people want you to do
(unless they're your director on a studio project of course) but it will confirm you
that the statement you're making with your project is finding audience approval.

Frame capture from "The Hermit" promotional film, showing character
concept art being created.

Clearly, with the proliferation of animation in the media today, we're all used to
seeing a whole range of different character designs – different shapes, sizes and
colors – using all kinds of different techniques. Some are very cute, while others
are very edgy , stylistic, traditional or even very contemporary or retro.

Some of the range of options that Joanna Quinn went through when
designing a character.

All of them though are based on certain principles of a design approach.

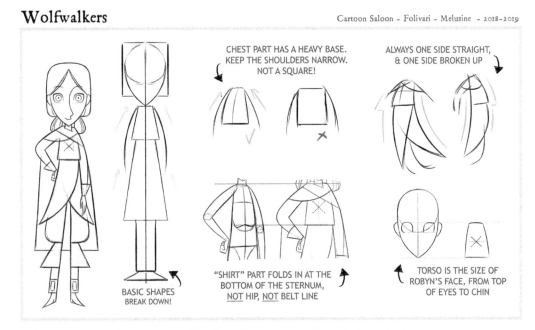

Wolfwalkers

Cartoon Saloon - Folivari - Melusine - 2018-2019

CHEST PART HAS A HEAVY BASE.
KEEP THE SHOULDERS NARROW.
NOT A SQUARE!

ALWAYS ONE SIDE STRAIGHT,
& ONE SIDE BROKEN UP

BASIC SHAPES
BREAK DOWN!

"SHIRT" PART FOLDS IN AT THE
BOTTOM OF THE STERNUM,
NOT HIP, NOT BELT LINE

TORSO IS THE SIZE OF
ROBYN'S FACE, FROM TOP
OF EYES TO CHIN

Robyn character design for *Wolfwalkers*. © Cartoon Saloon Ltd., Melusine Productions.

So where do we start? Well, the best thing to do is start with "**SHAPES**". If you look at any character designs, you'll see that they can all be broken down into basic shapes. They're either *"circles"*, *"triangles"*, *"squares"*, *"cubes"*, *"cones"*, *"cylinders"*, etc., – or whatever they are. These shapes underpin the basic design structures when you strip away all of the surface details. So, it might be good to look at those things…

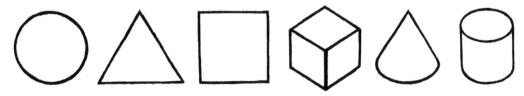

These are the core underlying shapes that make up most characters.

A "**circle**", "**triangle**" and "**square**" are perhaps THE three most important geometric shapes that are behind all character designs. I think this is a concept that most people will know. But perhaps not everyone will know that there are psychologically symbolic meanings behind each shape, which will determine whether or not they are relevant for any particular kind of character personality type. For example, a "**Circle**"…

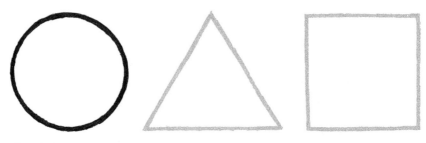

The Circle.

…represents the qualities of *"cuteness"*, *"innocence"*, *"youthfulness"*, *"playfulness"*, *"friendliness"* or anything *"comforting"*.

A "**Triangle**" on the other hand…

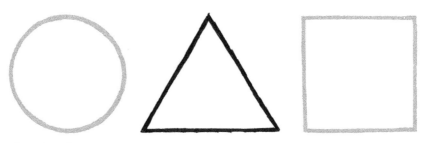

The Triangle.

…represents *"aggressiveness"*, *"sneakiness"*, *"prickliness"*, *"edginess"* or *"energy"*.

A "**Square**" on the other hand…

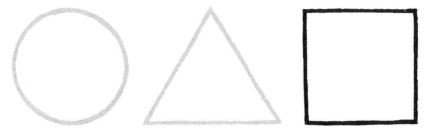

The Square.

can represent *"stability"*, *"reliability"*, *"steadfastness"*, *"trustworthiness"*, *"stubbornness"* and even *"traditionality"*.

All these are one or more qualities that you may need to have. Therefore, depending on those qualities, you might assign one (or more) of these shapes to represent the character in question. For example, here are some generic characters made up of a different collection of shapes. See how different their silhouettes feel like they are representing a different kind of emotional or psychological personality…

The three main shapes of character design.

The first is rounder, therefore more friendly or warm. The second is more triangular, therefore more edgy or nervous looking, whereas the square one suggests a character that is more robust or strong.

Then, you can expand on them and look at the various character shapes in all these recognizable character silhouettes…

Six characters that clearly differentiate silhouetted shapes.

These shapes underpin even more traditional principles of design, meaning that round shapes and corners suggest *"friendliness"* and *"femininity"*, whereas square shapes and corners represent *"masculinity"* and *"strength"*, and triangular shapes and corners represent *"villains"* and *"bad guys"*. One look at an endless range of Disney characters, past and present, will underline this.

The "sacred trinity" for animation – join the circle dots to make up the most famous and friendly cartoon character in the history of the industry!

It's all part of the *"shape language"* and mixing them together can communicate a mixture of all these qualities…

The dramatic use of core geometric shapes in design.

The bottom line here is to always design your character to suit the underlying nature of its gender or personality. In other words, if you're creating a friendly character, then you might plum for the more *"round"* and *"square"* shapes. But if you're designing an aggressive, bad or untrustworthy character, then you might use *"squares"* and *"triangles"*, making them more sharp and edgy looking. So just don't create an ideal character and then draw any design. Instead, when you think up your idea, imagine what shapes may best define it visually. This is really important, as you want to ensure that the basic shape or silhouette of your character determines how your audience interprets them – on an unconscious level if nothing else.

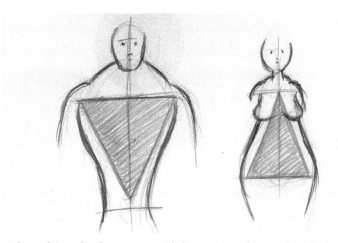

Male and female characters with basic triangles are highlighted.

Next, let's talk about "**Structure**". As once we have determined our shapes, we need to break them down or merge them into a more definable structure in order to refine the message they communicate more specifically. So, for example, if we look at **Bart** from *"The Simpsons"*, you can see this structure progression from the left. Firstly, his basic geometric structure is made up of a sphere and cylinder. This is the structural foundation of the design. Then, if we go to the next stage to develop the character further, we see that more spheres are added for the eyes and hands, with refined cylinders added for the arms. Next, more refinements are added that include a sphere for the ears and fingers. Then, lastly, the surface drawing is added, refining the details and giving us the character that we all know and love – somewhat similar to the process I recommend for your observational gesture drawing. The bottom line is that all processes should ensure that there is a solid structure for the character, based on those surface details.

A similar process can be applied to **Lisa**, who is a more sympathetic character. So, she is made up of more *"circular"* or *"spheroid"* shapes….

Homer, is essentially a big, soft lug. So, he's primarily made up of *"circles"* and *"spheres"* too…

Now, one more factor you need to know about with character designing is "**Head Heights**". Depending on the size of the head, the age of the character and the genre they are designed for, the *"head height"* of a character varies very much. Using the head as one unit of measurement for the rest of the body, we can define the age of a character for instance, by the number of head measurements that can be divided into the overall body size. So, in terms of age, If we look at the following chart, we can see that the younger a character is, the lower their head height should be.

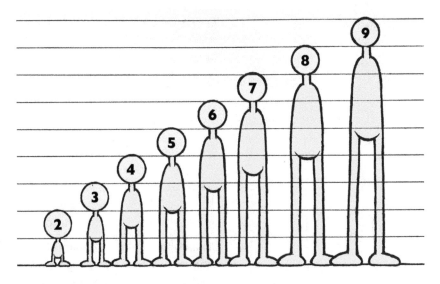

Head heights for characters – from 2 to 9.

Note that the youngest character to the left only has a *"2-head height"* design – meaning that the measurement of the head is equal to the total measurement of the body. And this is quite in keeping with our real-world development, where our body grows over the years to catch up with the proportionate size of our head.

There can always be exceptions to the rule, of course!

Pinhead character – created by Gianni Nugoli.

Therefore, a slightly older child might have a *"3- or 4-head height"* design. Then with a teenager, maybe *"5-head heights"*. Finally, a fully mature adult will normally have a *"7-head height"* design, approximately – although some Anime or science fiction characters will go up to *"8-head heights"* in some instances.

Character designs can be different from this for stylistic reasons too. For example, **Lisa Simpson**, or the **PowerPuff Girls**, are just *"2-head height"* characters, simply because they have an overall style that dictates it, not age.

Similarly too, a "**pinhead**" type of character will have a very *"high head height"* factor, simply because they are usually all brawn and no brain.

In classical times past, for example, "**Bugs Bunny**" was essentially a *"4-head height"* character, with his ears on top being an additional one and one-third measurement above the top of his head.

The head heights for a Bugs Bunny lookalike character.

A character design "**Model Sheet**" should define all these things – or even one including views of the character from an ever-possible angle, in which case it will be called a "**Turnaround Model Sheet**".

A 3-pose, turnaround model sheet of the Hermit.

Another thing to be taken into consideration too when discussing *"Model Sheets"* is **"Scaling"**. This means that if you have more than one character in a scene or project, it is advisable to have an indication of the various sizes of each character when standing next to each other. This will show the animator how big each one is, in comparison with one another, when they put them in a scene. Therefore, a *"Scaling"* model sheet can be valuable at times. For example, here is a *"Scaling Sheet"* for **The Simpsons**…

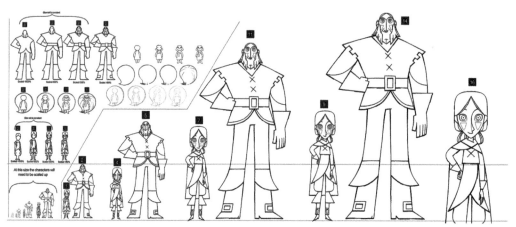

Wolfwalkers character size comparison sheet. © Cartoon Saloon Ltd., Melusine Productions.

This makes it so easy to see how large each one is when compared with another. This builds consistency of design when you are evolving your project during pre-production.

Next, we must talk about **"Silhouettes"** in terms of character design. With any project, is it fundamentally important that your audience can very quickly key in on the shape and volume of your characters, especially if they are seen in a shadow, or are obscured in any way by color, lighting and other such things? This is true for when you're creating key animation poses too, meaning that if your silhouettes are strong your animation will be strong too. I deal with this specifically in my *"Drawing for Animation"* course, as well as with at least one observational gesture drawing assignment in this book too. So, it will be good to create a silhouette model sheet of your characters, if indeed you have more than one character in your project. This is an example of the *Wolfwalkers* characters, seen only in silhouette. Note how each one can be defined solely by its silhouette, making it a good character design.

How silhouettes can define the difference in character size and personality? From *Wolfwalkers*. © Cartoon Saloon Ltd., Melusine Productions.

If your characters are very similar in their silhouettes, then I strongly advise you to think your designs through again so that each silhouetted one is distinctive in its own right. Otherwise, it is a bad character design.

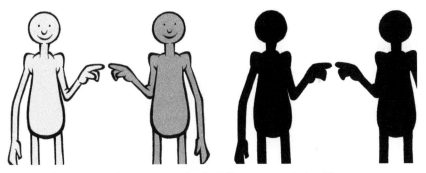

If you rely on your characters to look different, not their silhouettes, you will have problems with audience readability in some circumstances!

Without going deeply into it right now, you should make sure that the colors of your characters give separation too, wherever possible. This would be termed a **"Color Model Sheet"** although realistically, the coloring of characters can't really take place until you have the final background art against which they will appear. If they will appear against multiple background treatments, then you are advised to test your character *"color models"* against all these backgrounds.

You should only really create your color models when your characters are against the final background. From *Wolfwalkers*. © Cartoon Saloon Ltd., Melusine Productions.

Finally, on bigger productions, there is often a need for an **"Expression Model Sheet"**. **Hayao Miyazaki** is keen on doing those. What that is, is a collection of animation poses and facial expressions your characters might go through during the production. A static *"Turnaround Model Sheet"* is factually valuable but it is quite mechanically static when it comes to poses. So, some valuable time can be invested by the character designer, posing their character in all kinds of moods and

"Bill" Expression Sheet for *Wolfwalkers* © Cartoon Saloon Ltd., Melusine Productions.

states of expression, which will solve many of the visual challenges the members of the animation team might encounter as they work through a larger production.

It's probably not necessary if you're working on a small-scale, personal project, however, as usually just one person does everything and consistence is automatic.

Suggested Assignment

If nothing else, you should definitely do a *"Turnaround Model Sheet"* here, as that will be so valuable later, when you're in the *"Production"* stage. The last thing you want, when you're totally focused on movement, is to interrupt the flow by wondering what your character is going to look like, other than the single viewpoint that most people design their first character design from. So, invest some time now, working out what your character looks like from all the important angles – i.e., *"front"*, *"three-quarter front"*, *"side"*, *"three-quarter back"* and *"back"*. If you are still up for preparing yourself well for the future production stage, then may try some expressions too – relating to the known moods and experiences your character will be going through in your project. Time spent here now will definitely reward you later when animating! Of course, if your character doesn't turn in all 360-directions in your film, you don't have to do a full turnaround model sheet here!

Masterclass 28/ Storyboarding & Film Language

In this lesson, we are moving on to **"Storyboarding"**. Now you have your *"Script"*, *"Concept Art"* and *"Character Designs"* complete, and you can start to start planning your film visually. And a *"Storyboard"* is precisely a visual interpretation of your project. But not just that, *"Storyboards"* can be used for many more things than an animated film. Movies, TV shows, online videos and even websites can benefit from using them. Then, behind the actual drawing of a storyboard, there should be a significant knowledge of *"film language"* and *"film structure"* that you need to be aware of, for a *"Storyboard"* to be fully effective. So, we'll go over all this during this lesson. But first, another *observational gesture drawing* exercise is to sharpen your mind…

Warm-Up Drawing

This time we're going to do something a little different again. For my class students, I call it "Vault Sequence". Here's what that means…

Sometimes it's really good for an animator to analyze **slow-motion videos** while an action unfolds, especially if it is too fast for the human eye to see. The following sequence of slow-motion images of gymnast McKayla Maroney is said to feature the most perfect vault ever captured on camera. Taken for TV footage, each image is not entirely clear to see and probably a little small to define clearly in this book. Consequently, some guesswork on your part is required. But this is

DOI: 10.1201/9781003324287-31

a good thing, as it gets you to think with an animation mind, based on eviden-tial imagery. So, you are required to sketch down all 16 poses on a single page of your sketchbook, depicting the changing physical complexities that are being acted out. You should give yourself just **30-seconds for each drawing**, inter-preting everything as a defined sequence of bodily positions, even if they may be blurred to the human eye. This is a perfect exercise to train your hand and eye to analyze things rapidly...

Pose 1 comments: Her right leg is the nearest leg if you are unclear on that.

Pose 2 comments: Now the body is beginning to twist and unfold. Try to quick-ly understand what's going on here and anticipate where it's going. Exaggerate it if necessary.

Pose 3 comments: Now the body is almost fully twisted around and she's springing her hand/fingertips.

Pose 4 comments: Now her feet are touching the springboard and her body is fully rotated 180-degrees – so that she can spring backward onto the vaulting surface.

Pose 5 comments: Now having bounced off the springboard, she's arching out backward to the vaulting horse surface.

Pose 6 comments: Here she's on an upward trajectory, vertical to the ground. Notice too that the torso is rotating and the arms lifting up from the vaulting horse surface. Imagine what the lower legs are doing, where you cannot see them.

Pose 7 comments: Now she's clearly very high in the air and continuing to ro-tate around her own axis, traveling forward from the vaulting horse at the same time. Note how straight the head is, in relation to the torso. The arms are coming in to assist the speed of the spin.

Pose 8 comments: See here how high she still is in relation to the ground, and her torso is still rotating quickly. The arms are close to the body, hands clenched together, which assists this spinning action. Note too how straight the legs are and how pointed the toes are at the end.

Pose 9 comments: This somewhat badly blurred image forces you to use your animator's imagination. What we can tell is that her body is still spinning, ro-tating more toward horizontal. The arms are still held in. Even so, notice how straight her body remains in the air.

Pose 10 comments: Again, you are going to need to imagine the lower legs and feet here. Otherwise, she's clearly in a vertical position, with her head down. The head, however, is turning somewhat, to spot her landing in this split-second moment. The arms are still tight to the body, but beginning to open up a little, which will slow her spinning motion down somewhat.

Pose 11 comments: Coming down toward the ultimate landing here, but with her body still spinning rapidly. Again, notice how straight her body and legs remain in the air.

Pose 12 comments: Now, she's clearly on a downward trajectory toward the ground. Her body is still straight with the legs, and the toes are now slightly pointing as they approach the ground. The arms are opening up above her head, to help break her rotation.

Pose 13 comments: She is dropping fast to the ground now, her toes reaching out for contact. The arms are high above the head, slowing the forward rotation of her body. See how straight she all is, despite everything that's going on at this stage.

Pose 14 comments: Her feet are flat on the matt with her legs bending to absorb the impact of the landing. The head is very slightly bent forward to view her landing, with the arms swinging straight and down as the impact of the ground takes effect.

Pose 15 comments: Having completed the impact of the landing, she now springs up and back a touch to try to avoid herself pitching forward onto her face with the jump's extreme velocity. The arms swing down to assist her balance and she fights to keep her head up to keep everything elegant.

Pose 16 comments: And finally, she arrives at a perfectly balanced and outstretched position on the matt. She holds an upright pose, her head up, and with both arms stretched up symmetrically to indicate that she is fixed to the spot and in control.

OK, so I'm sure that was exhausting to do, especially if you did discipline yourself to just 30-seconds per pose. It was certainly exhausting for McKayla too, I'm sure! The big thing to realize here is that she did all this in just a couple of seconds – almost the blink of an eye – and yet there was so much to think about. Watching, analyzing and sketching out sequences like this are so revealing and can only illicit awe for the subjects you are looking at. This is all really valuable material for training your *"animator's eye"*. Now in outside world situations, you don't have the luxury of having sequenced images like this to help you. You simply have to assess it in real time. However, training your eye with exercises like this helps speed up your perceptions and your feel for what's going on. Ultimately, you won't really know how you're doing on this until you animate and test it. But this is a great start at least.

So, drawing a sequence like this is definitely enough to get your animator's eye and mind working. However, you might consider scanning and separating your drawings into individual files and rendering them out on **2s** (2 frames per drawing) as an animated sequence video. It won't be perfect of course, but it will give you a sense of how your drawings move in animation. To give it a little more stability, however, you might add the position of the vaulting horse to all your drawings, so that you can line these up, one over the over, when you capture your individual frames. Doing this will ensure that your drawings do not jump around the screen when you play the video back. Also experiment with the timing of the drawings, rendering them on **4s** (4 frames per drawing), **6s** (6 frames per drawing) and **8s** (8 frames per drawing) as well as on *2s*. This will give you a real sense of how animation timing works when your drawings are captured with different frame timings.

Instruction

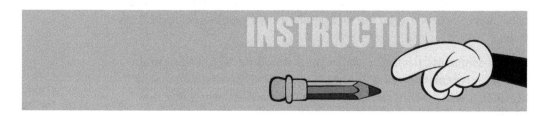

Here we're going to deal with "**Storyboarding**" and all that goes with it. Storyboards can be very rough…

Early "Sticky Note" storyboard for my animated memoirs project.

…or more formal and highly detailed, depending on the nature of the project and the budget being worked with.

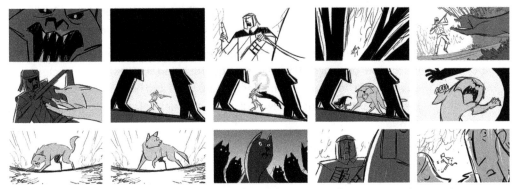

More finished production board for the *Wolfwalkers* movie – © Cartoon Saloon Ltd., Melusine Productions.

Storyboarding is not just drawing a whole series of images that show the story unfolding. It involves **"Staging"**, **"Placement"**, **"Continuity"** and many other things, especially **"Film Language"**. It's all about how you put the characters in the scenes or environments you put them in, and WHY you do it in particular ways and not others. This is effectively drawing on the vast knowledge of filmmaking, which has learned over many decades the best way to stage any shot and place the characters where they need to be. These are all the things we are going to deal with now, under the broad title of *"Storyboarding"*…

Film Staging

"Staging" is the way you show an image, or scene, designed to ensure the audience sees what you want them to see in any particular moment of the storyline. Film language in general is the knowledge, or rules, that have been built up since the industry began, making films better and ensuring the essential message they have to communicate comes across well to an audience. "Staging" is one aspect of those rules. As a filmic/theatrical technique, states how to best set shots up, so they maximize the message they are communicating.

This low horizon "up" shot from *Wolfwalkers* gives a sense of dominance or threat. © Cartoon Saloon Ltd., Melusine Productions.

What we're talking about here is all about adjusting the camera to get drama. For example, if we bring the horizon line down on a shot, as in an "**up**" shot…

…the figures in that scene will be seen high above it. Therefore, they will have much more presence, status and strength for being so. These are characters we quite literally "look up to", whether they are good and heroic, or bad and oppressive, from a story point of view. It gives them a sense of strength, dominance or power.

Now with a "**down**" shot, we effectively lift the camera up to look down on a character, with the horizon high, we get the opposite effect.

This higher horizon "down" shot from *Wolfwalkers* alternatively gives a suggestion of vulnerability or being overwhelmed by the odds. © Cartoon Saloon Ltd., Melusine Productions.

It can suggest that the vastness of the environment is dwarfing the character if they are seen small. In other words, it is making them less significant to the audience in the shot. Similarly, with this shot, we are literally "looking down" on someone – meaning that the audience, the character, or we the viewer are seeing that character as diminutive. Therefore, this shot can be used in a "fear" or "dominance" scene, where we want the character we see to be lessened, weakened or much more powerless.

This dramatic shot from *The Breadwinner* positions the camera low, offering a very scary and dominant effect with the "up" shot. © Cartoon Saloon Ltd., Aircraft Pictures Ltd, Melusine Productions.

Film Language

Film language defines what options a filmmaker has when conveying a sequence. It offers a whole pallet of shots and techniques that a filmmaker can paint a picture with, and the reasons for choosing those shots when telling a story. Let us quickly go through those shots here…

Extreme Wide Shot: This shot is more often than not the opening, "**establishing shot**", in a film or sequence. It shows the audience our location, where the sequence is taking place. In this instance, we have a tiny figure in the distance of a desert. They are so small that we don't know who they are or why they are there. In some "establishing shots", we might not even see a character at this point – so vast is the environment we are dealing with. It is the scale of the landscape, not the character or character action within that landscape, that is most important in an *"Extreme Wide Shot"*.

An extreme wide shot from *Wolfwalkers*. © Cartoon Saloon Ltd., Melusine Productions.

Wide Shot: It's quite possible that we don't want to start our film or our sequence with such a vast landscape shot. We still want the presence of a scene, but we want that scene to have meaning too. So, we go to a simple *"Wide Shot"*. This shot is effectively defined as having a full-length view of the character visible in its entirety, either small or large in the environment they are in. So, as long as we see the character as a whole figure in a particular scene, then it is a "Wide Shot". "Wide Shots" make effective establishing shots too.

Wide shot from *Wolfwalkers*. © Cartoon Saloon Ltd., Melusine Productions.

Mid- or Medium Shot: Now if we want to see more detail about the character, yet don't need to see all of that character, we can use a *"Mid-"* or *"Medium"* shot. Standard mid or medium shots usually feature the character from around the waist upward. This shot is used a lot when we need to see more visual information about a character, or else when we want to feel comfortable hearing what they are saying if they talk.

A Mid-/Medium shot from *Wolfwalkers*. © Cartoon Saloon Ltd., Melusine Productions.

Close-up Shot: Now if we want more information or see an expression or detail on their face, we will move into a *"Close-up Shot"*. Close-up shots help us see the emotion on the face, or in the eyes, of a scene – or help us make more connections to what they are saying. Close-up shots are usually framed from the neck and upward.

A Close-up shot from *Wolfwalkers*. © Cartoon Saloon Ltd., Melusine Productions.

Extreme Close-up Shot: But then, if we want even more detail of that character – perhaps focus on its eyes or their lips talking, we can move in even closer to an *"Extreme Close-up"* shot. This is a great one for seeing the eye direction of a look, a scar on the face, or even the finger on a trigger if there are guns involved. The background is almost non-existent at this point, just the object of our intention alone.

An Extreme close-up shot from *Wolfwalkers*. © Cartoon Saloon Ltd., Melusine Productions.

These then are the basic visual colors of our artist's pallet. They can be matched and mixed accordingly, depending on the filmic picture being painted. The colors you use (i.e., the shot selection) will affect the way the audience views your story and its characters. At the same time, be smart about how you use your shots and how many you use. For example, if you're making a 30-second film, you really don't want to use too many shots, otherwise it will be too distracting and defeat the object of the exercise. It is better to be thoughtful and discreet by the number of shots you use – especially in animation, where every shot will need a different piece of background art and redrawing of characters from various angles presumably. You will both distract your audience by using many shots and make a great deal of unnecessary, extra work for yourself.

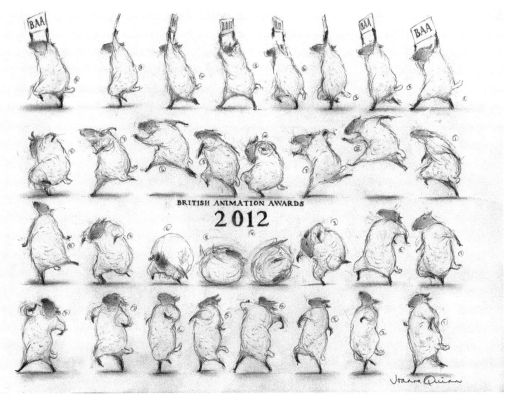

Sometimes, the beauty of animation – especially short film animation –
is by not having any scenes at all. This wonderful example of drawn
animation mastery by Joanna Quinn can be seen on the poster for the 2012
British Animation Awards.

Also, think WHY you are using a particular shot. Most films or sequences begin
with some form of "establishing shot", so unless you have a very good reason
not to do that you are advised to respect the norm. Usually, if you want to draw
the audience into your action or storytelling, start with one or other of the *"wide
shots"*, then move to a *"mid-shot"*, then a *"close-up"*.

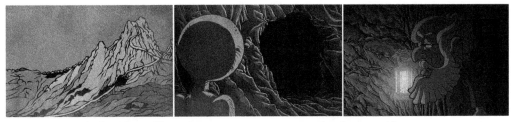

The opening of *The Hermit* film – featuring an extreme wide shot, a wide
shot of the cave and a + medium shot of the Hermit inside the cave.

This is somewhat formulaic, but it is so because it works. However, if your project gives you a very good reason to break with tradition, then do so. Just remember, if something is not broken, then don't fix it. There are so many other things that can make your film original and different, but stick to tried and tested methods of staging if you want the audience to move with you.

Wonderful use of an extreme close-up by Joanna Quinn – from the 1998 film *The Wife of Bath – The Canterbury Tales.*

These are all the things you need to think about carefully when you create your first *"Storyboard"*. Every part of your idea and script has a purpose in telling its story, so think really carefully about how you are going to frame them by the shots you will use. All this needs to be communicated in your *"Storyboard"*. And don't spend a lot of time drawing your "Storyboard" in great detail at this stage. Simple "thumbnail" sketches, roughing out your ideas are all that matter. It is unlikely that anyone else but you will see what you're doing if you're making a personal film, so just put the ideas down simply enough for you to know where you're going with it all. And if you do need to show your storyboard to another, or others, then still draw it loosely enough for them to understand it visually, while not spending too much time and *"pencil mileage"* in the process. Later on, you can do that, but you're still in the formative stage of ideas and so any changes you do, will need to be done quickly. Therefore, you don't want to have wasted a lot of your time by spending too long on something that can be communicated so much more quickly and simply at this stage.

There are more aspects of the *"film language"* to come in the next lesson on *"storyboarding"* but for now, why not take a stab at thumbnailing your ideas before you move on there.

Suggested Assignment

I would say that you will have enough on your plate in just putting together your roughed-out "Storyboard" at this stage. What I have shown you above should be everything you'll possibly need to make good creative decisions with your ideas here and now. However, before you make final commitments, I would say that you should seek out some of the big names in the industry to talk about their storyboarding work. I am thinking here of Eric Goldberg's presentation of the Donald Duck short "Trouble Shooter", or even the additional material videos on the original "Shrek" DVD, where some of the storyboard artists have been filmed making their pitches. Even though you may not be making a purely "cartoon"-styled film, there will be things in these kinds of videos that will give you ideas for your own concept, cartoon or otherwise.

Masterclass 29/ More on Storyboarding & Film Language

This lesson is a continuation of the previous one on "**Storyboarding**". Hopefully, by now you will be on your way with your thumbnail storyboarding ideas but today's information about such things as *"Transitions"* and *"Camera movements"* might help modify your initial ideas into final ones. But first, observational gesture drawing…

Warm-Up Drawing

As your time right now needs to be focused on storyboard drawing, our observational gesture-drawing session is being kept to a minimum. So, this time, we have an exercise of just 1 sequentially moving image to work from, which should last for **5-minutes** overall. The image below represents multiple positions by multiple individuals. Therefore, you should *speed-draw* each position in that action as fast and as accurate as you can. In other words, you should allow yourself only *1-minute* to capture each pose in the sequence...

DOI: 10.1201/9781003324287-32

Comments: Start with the pose on the left side of your page, rotating your sketchbook 90-degrees if it helps give you more space. Then work your way across from left to right, analyzing and drawing the actions you see. However, be fast and as accurate as you can. Note especially that the *center of gravity* of the bodies follows an arced "**path of action**" from one to the other. Generally, make sure that your *volumes* and *sizes of limbs* are consistent throughout.

Instruction

GESTURE DRAWING

Professionals from the industry have always said that the *"Storyboard"* in any production is like the *Bible* of that project. What is established at this stage should never be changed, especially in a big production pipeline where any changes later can cost huge amounts of money. Individuals making their own personal projects, however, have a little latitude here. Although, even then, **I STRONGLY ADVISE** that if you can lock your film or project down at the *"Storyboard"* stage, then you will save yourself a lot of time and grief later if you try to impose changes on yourself down the line. This is why spending time now on the *"Storyboard"* is so fundamental to the success or failure of your proposed production. Then, once you have your "bible" in place, you don't change your "bible"!

Simple but very effective storyboard by one of my students, Caroline Li.

Now although the following material may not necessarily affect the nature of your *"Storyboards"* thus far with your project, it might very much affect the way you interpret your *"Storyboards"* in the future. What this material can deal with is the timing and structure of your film – even if it's not animated – and how you can make creative decisions with regard to the material and unfolding of the storyline. So, what we're talking about here is very valuable in terms of the production side of things, beyond this stage. But it pays to know it now, as it can

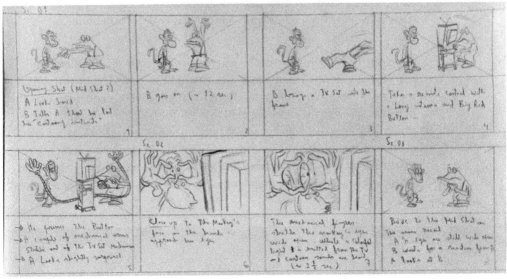

Another example of a storyboard by another student, Lucas Ribeiro.

definitely affect the way you conceive your "Storyboard" working as you draw it up. So, the following provides a storyboard overview, from the actual implantation point of view, which will hopefully help you make better decisions down the line. It is also essential knowledge if you plan to have a career in animation or anything connected to filmmaking or visual storytelling.

Using the 5-framing shots we talked about previously, you can pretty much use them to tell any story in a filmic timeline. However, the way you **transition** from one shot to another can be really effective too. So, we'll look at those options now…

Transitions

Cut: A cut is an immediate transition from one scene to another in one single frame. A "cut" is what you invariably see, from one scene to another, in most films of today. It is simple, dramatic and energetic in the effect it has on an audience. A "cut" can give a sense of suddenness, alertness or pace within the action, with audiences being confronted instantly with a change of image or action from one scene to another.

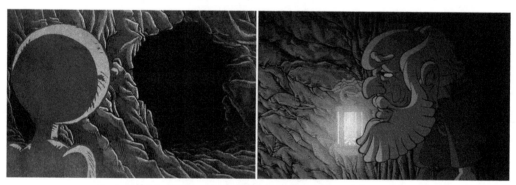

A straight "cut" from one scene to the other, with no transition.

Fade-out/Fade-in: A *"Fade-out"* is where you exit a scene over a number of frames. This is done by increasingly decreasing the image exposure throughout the frames to black. A *"Fade-in"* is where you start with black and, over a number of frames, increase the exposure until to reach 100%. "Fades" are used to give a slower and more emotionally pleasing closing to one scene and a gentle introduction to another. It gives a more reflective moment, where the audience can more easily digest what they have just seen and be introduced more slowly to what comes next. They can therefore reflect a smooth transition of *time*, *place* or *incident*.

One scene fades out to black before a second one fades in from black.

Dissolve: A *"Dissolve"* (or *"Mix"*) is a transition where the *"Fade-in/Fade-out"* of two scenes overlap over a number of frames. In other words, the image of one scene slowly disappears, while another scene, over the same number of frames, slowly appears. *"Dissolves"* can also give a sense of transition in time and space yet at a faster and urgent pace.

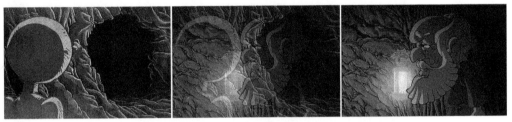

For a dissolve, one scene fades out over the same frames as the next scene fades in.

Wipe: A *"Wipe"* is where an invisible line moves from one side of the screen to the other, erasing the outgoing scene imagery and revealing the incoming scene imagery as it does. *"Wipes"* actually come in all styles, not just a straight line – *horizontal, vertical, diagonal, spiral, clockwise* and *counter clockwise* although these are not as popular today as they once were, except in very *stylized, retro, film noir* production.

A diagonal "wipe" from one scene to the other. Wipes can be created in many kinds of orientation, however.

It is unlikely that any of that will affect what you're doing at this *"Storyboard"* stage, but it's good to know as it might give you the idea of trying something different as you visualize your project. Most people just use a *"cut"*, a *"fade-in/ fade-out"* or a *"dissolve"* transition most of the time. Just remember, if you want a hard transition from one scene to another, then the standard *"cut"* is your solution, and if you want a softer transition, then a *"fade-in/fade-out"* or *"dissolve"* for a couple of seconds of screen time really is best. However, the big problem with a *"dissolve"* especially from an animation point of view is that you need to animate **double the material** for the distance of the dissolve action, covering the *outgoing* area as well as the *incoming* footage.

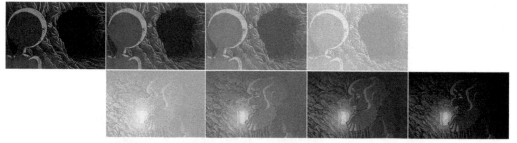

Indicating the double number of animation drawings you will have to create when one scene is fading out at the same time as the other is fading in. The number of extra frames needed is determined by the frame length of the dissolve.

Camera Moves

Now let's talk about how the camera can affect how shots are seen. There are several from the live-action world that can have an equal impact in animation too, so let's define all the main ones, so we know what options we have here…

Locked-off shot: A *"Locked-off shot"* is a standard option where the camera remains in the same position throughout the scene.

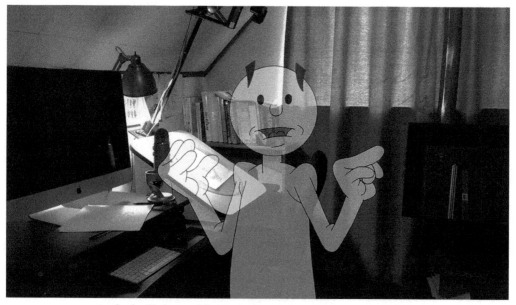

Locked-off shot, with no camera movement.

Track-in/Track-out shot: A *"Track-in/Track-out shot"* (alternatively described as a "Zoom-in/Zoom-out" shot) is where the camera moves in closer and out further from the scene being featured. For example, a scene could start with a *"wide shot"* move through a *"mid-shot"* to a *"close-up"*, or vice versa.

Track-in from a wide shot to a close-up, to catch the expression.

Pan: A "Pan" is where a camera moves along a scene, revealing more and more of it as it does so. An example would be where the camera follows a walking character through a long street scene, following the character as they go.

A panning shot, with the camera following the character as it walks.

Track/Pan: A *"Track/Pan"* is similar to a *"Pan"* shot, except that the camera moves in or out of its screen position as it does so.

A track pan has the camera move in as it pans along with the character.

Crane shot: A *"Crane shot"* is where the camera rotates around an object or character within a scene, up to and beyond a 360-degree arc. It can also be a looking-out shot from the character's point of view as they are turning around. This is great and very impactful as a circling view of the background or the character is required. (However, some caution here! In a traditional hand-drawn world, remember that the whole background will have to be drawn/animated too, in addition to any rotation on the character that may need to be created.)

360-degree "crane shot" rotation around the character – from *Bad Penguin*. Design: Dominic Sodano.

Zip pan: A *"Zip pan"* is effectively a superfast panning shot, where the camera covers the same ground as it might in a regular, slow-moving shot, but in a handful of frames. Such a shot could be used to create a sudden, immediate, reveal of another part of the environment for the audience.

A "Zip pan" can be so fast that the background can blur and there even be speed lines on the character's action.

The smart use of any of these devices is discussed in this and the previous lesson on the art of filmmaking. Do not use them just for the sake of using them. Many of them should be selected only if they add something extra to a scene that requires them. So, think very carefully before you decide on anything. As with the animation itself, "simple is often best", and any overelaboration of movement of film technique can only overwhelm or distract an audience from the essential core message that needs to be communicated. Using them just for the sake of using them, or inappropriately, will undermine your film, not enhance it. So be wise in how you use any of these things.

When I say "simple is best", I don't always take my own advice! This was a hand-drawn crane shot I animated – pre-computers – for my BAFTA-winning *HOKUSAI~An Animated Sketchbook* short film. It was primarily created with ink pen and markers on paper.

Shot Selection

Let's think through now how we might film-ically *"stage"* a sequence with, say, two characters in it…

Two-shot: A good establishing shot to introduce two characters would be a *"two-shot"*. Here, both characters would be seen together in a "wide" or "mid" shot for example. It would allow the audience to see and appreciate the differences between the two characters and their relationship with each other, as well as with the environment they're in.

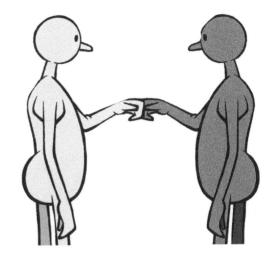

A "2-shot", featuring two characters in the shot at the same time.

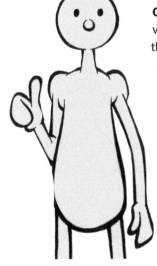

A "1 shot", featuring just a single character in the shot.

One shot: In the next shot after the "two-shot", it might be valuable to focus on one of them more intently, especially if they are speaking or doing something specific that needs to be featured. Alternatively, a "one shot" might be valuable if you want the audience to see the reaction of one character when the other (unseen) character is talking or doing something.

Over-the-shoulder shot: Like *"one shot"*, an *"over-the-shoulder shot"* focuses on one character specifically but shows a little of the back of the head, or shoulder, of the other character at the side of the screen. This is a more inclusive, intimate shot that reminds the audience of the two characters interacting with each other.

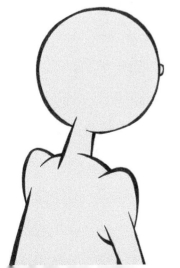

An "over-the-shoulder" shot can feature two or more characters.

Continuity

Next, we should focus on "continuity". Without good "continuity", a film can be ruined by a confusing presentation of the core action. For example, if a character is running from right to left in one scene, then running from right to left in the next scene, will be really confusing for the audience, even with a close-up of a stopwatch cut in between them. They quite literally won't know if that character is coming or going!

Note how the action continuity is broken with the scene 2 character running in the opposite direction.

It's therefore better for you to set your mind on a direction of the action – say left to right – throughout all the scenes, even if you're changing the character's size or the camera's position within those scenes.

With the character running in the same direction in all three scenes, the flow and continuity is now much more consistent.

This way the audience will follow the action in your film much better. If you should need to change the direction of the action for some reason, then think of a reason for *"cutting away from it"* in a linking shot before you change the direction. This is called a "**Cut-away shot**", which will distract the audience enough to not realize a change in direction has gone on.

The "cut-away" shot in scene 2 allows enough distraction for the character to run in a different direction than the one in the establishing shot.

Crossing the line: One really big "no-no" of filmmaking is *"crossing the line"*. This is a really important factor of continuity. Remember, that when featuring a "two-shot" of two characters or objects, there is an *invisible* line between them.

A "2-shot" with the camera on one side of the invisible line between them.

Your "establishing shot" of those two characters will establish just where that invisible line is.

The "2-shot", setup on the nearside of the line, as above.

Now, whatever side of that line your camera is, you should stay on it throughout the sequence of scenes in question.

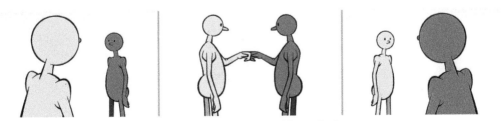

Showing just three of the many kinds of shots possible with the camera on the same side of the line.

However, if you cross that invisible line at any point in the sequence...

The camera is on the far side of the line for shot 2.

...then it will appear to the audience that the continuity of the two characters has been reversed, which will confuse them – on a subconscious level at least! This of course runs the risk of the audience not getting a point of action, or dialogue, you want them to know about during that sequence.

Note that shot 2 now appears reversed from the new (crossing the line) position – breaking the orientation continuity entirely.

The way around it, however, if you need to switch the left-to-right continuity of two characters or objects on the screen, is to throw a "cut-away shot" inbetween them.

The continuity confusion can be avoided by putting a cut-away shot in the middle of the sequence.

Although it feels very limiting on the surface, keeping the camera on one side of the "line" still gives numerous options to you as an animation director – shots that are high or low, single or two shots, etc.

All the camera views are possible within 180-degrees on one side of the line – up and down in elevation too.

As long as you don't cross the line, you can even position the camera "along the line" with successive shots 180-degrees opposite each other.

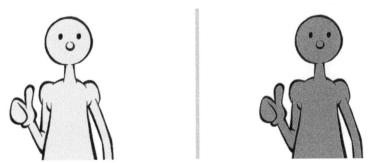

The two characters facing each other from each end of the line are also acceptable sequential camera shots.

Therefore, there is no reason whatsoever why your camera action needs to be boring or predictable when respecting the principle of "crossing the line". Once you get expert at framing, scaling, camera work and shot selection, there's no reason why you can't tell your story in the most imaginative and innovative way.

Suggested Assignment

Again, you have enough on your plate right now in terms of drawing your roughed-out *"Storyboard"*, so I don't want to add to your burden. However, if you would like to know more about creative transitions, cleaver staging, imaginative camerawork and continuity tricks, I would simply urge you to seek out online many of the excellent video tutorials out there. Many can be bad and not respect any of the above here. But if they do and give you creative options within these parameters, then definitely watch them as they might give you ideas on how you might cleverly approach your animation project. That said, never forget the golden rule that "simple is best" and an overuse, or misappropriate, use of any of these filmmaking techniques can actually undermine your film, not enhance it.

Masterclass 30/ Audio Record and Breakdown

Depending on what your project idea is, you're going to need to include an audio track. It can either be the spoken word, music or simply sound effects. But a good soundtrack can raise the bar of a project, not matter how good (or bad) the animation is in the first place. So, it pays us to focus a little on the elements of your audio creation and application here. Although most of this will not apply to you on your current project, depending on what approach to audio you're taking, it is valuable to know the various approaches that are possible as you cannot know what your animation future will hold. But first, observational gesture drawing.

Warm-Up Drawing

Another "short and sharp" session again here, just like the last one! However, to sharpen you up even more, I'm asking you to do even faster observational poses here than in the last lesson. The image below contains six different action poses of a skateboarder. Draw them in their existing order, from left to right and including the skateboard, disciplining yourself to just **30 seconds** for each drawing.

DOI: 10.1201/9781003324287-33

Comments: This is a really great exercise to give you a feel for how fast action unfolds. If you were to film these six drawings, you could consider timing them on either 1s or 2s, depending on how fast you want the action to be. Consider the shadows underneath the board and figure too, as they are a great anchoring device whenever anything leaves the ground. You don't have to put in the detail of this of course, but just having a suggestion of shadow here will give an added dynamic to the up and down nature of the action. The discipline of drawing fast like this too, if that it hones your mind and makes you see things like an animator. In the real world, you won't even have the luxury of 30 seconds, so consider being strict with yourself in getting these drawings down in the time suggested. In another time and in another place, I might even give this kind of thing as an exercise to animate – just 30 seconds to sketch out a sequence of poses from a video being observed and then capture the drawings on 2s. Student animators can learn so much in doing just that. So, don't neglect that option with your own future studies if you can find the options to do it.

Instruction

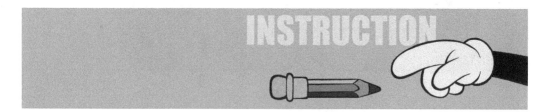

I think the best way to focus this section on "Audio record and breakdown" should be pretty much dialogue focused. This is because dialogue and animation will be the biggest challenge any animator can have when working with an audio track. However, we will briefly deal with other aspects of soundtrack creation and management later in this lesson.

Dialogue is an important part of an animator's skill set. © Lost Marble.

So, in terms of animating dialogue, I have to say right up front that this is a huge subject and could possibly take an entire book to describe all aspects of its approach. However, in this section, we will cover the core basics that any competent animator should know about when animating a speaking character. *"Dialogue"* is a specific facet of animation which can take a lifetime to learn in all its subtleties. Some animators are naturals at it, while others struggle with it. However, the following will give you a solid foundation in basic dialogue techniques, on which you can build in the future if you need to.

Animation maestro, Joanna Quinn, uses a mirror for capturing expressions and lip shapes.

As I established in my book *How to Make Animated Films (Routledge / ISBN 978-0-240–81033-1)*, the first thing we need to accept about dialogue animation is the fact that it is not just about making the lips move in perfect synchronization with the soundtrack. Ultimately, the lips do have to match the sounds they make – unless of course you're making an Anime movie, where it doesn't seem to matter anymore, as least for English-speaking audiences!

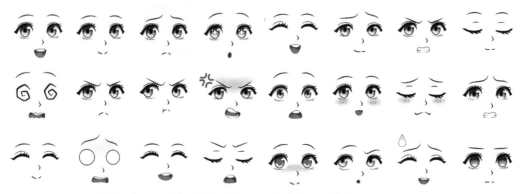

Interchangeable Anime lip and facial model sheet.

Effectively, for dialogue animation to make real impact, the animator must first understand where the underlining emotion, expression, mood and motivation are when words are being spoken. They reflect that a character's overall performance. In terms of a complete performance, it's the "**body language**" of the character that is more important than the accuracy of the lip movements. In fact, really good dialogue animation should be able to communicate the meaning of the words even if the lips are not moving at all.

Body language is often more important that the lip shape.

In live action filmmaking, the lips tend to look like a blur, or at least a percentage of them look like blurs, whenever a character is talking. The faster the character talks, the more blurring there will be. This is because a single frame of film, at 24 frames per second, is not always fast enough to capture the rapid shapes of the lips as they change.

With a fast-talking character, the mouths can often change shape on a frame-by-frame basis – less sometimes! So, being hard-edged, they can still look unreal in terms of live action film dialogue.

We are more disadvantaged in traditional animation however, because whenever we're producing it – or even in fact with CG-driven animation – we're forced to create hard-edged shapes for the mouths, giving the mouth action a harder and more staccato look at times. Twenty-four "frames per second" (fps) animation is simply not fast enough to accurately capture all the natural-looking changing mouth shapes. So, some compromise has to be made.

Standard cartoon-based mouth positions.

The process and order of producing good dialogue animation can be suggested as follows: (i) *"body language"*, (ii) *"facial expression"* and (iii) *"lip sync"*.

In this way, the body language provides the underpinning *motivation*, or objective, of what is being said. The facial expression communicates the *emotion or mood* of the speaker. Lastly, the lip sync, or the accuracy of the lips matching the sound, is the *technical connection* between mouth shape and what is being spoken. This is why I am approaching this dialogue lesson with these three crucial stages in mind. However, first you know your track.

Audio track sound waves.

Before we get down to the nitty-gritty of dialogue performance, it has to be established that we can do nothing unless and until we have understood and timed out the dialogue track first. This is in order that we are able to animate it frame by frame. Usually, the recording of any soundtrack will lie outside the realms or regular animation production. Therefore, we should first consider the "breakdown" or a soundtrack first.

Action	Fr	Dialog						Aux 2 Pegs	Aux 1 Pegs	Top Pegs	Bot Pegs	Fr	Camera Instructions
		/////											
		/////											
		H											
		OW											
		A											
		RR											
		Y											
		OO											
		/////											

Phonetic breakdown, frame by frame, on an animator's exposure sheet.

Audio Breakdown

An audio *"breakdown"* is a frame-by-frame analysis of the phonetic sounds that comprise of the audio track. I've dealt with this topic more comprehensively in my earlier book *"Animation From Pencils to Pixels"*, so I'll keep it very brief here. To do a *"breakdown"*, each frame of the dialogue sequence will need to be accurately analyzed and recorded before an animator starts. This way that animator will know exactly which sound is heard on each frame of film he or she will be working with. Knowing this enables the animator to make sure that drawn *body language*, *facial expression* and *lip sync* shape will synchronize perfectly with each frame of film to which it needs to match to. The breakdown itself can be recorded on a dedicated column down the side of the animator's *"exposure sheet"*.

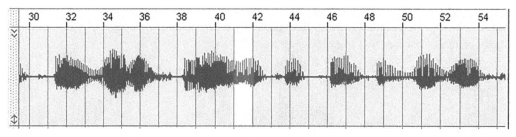

Digital animators have used programs like "Magpie Pro" to calculate their own audio breakdowns.

Body Language

With the audio breakdown completed, the first thing an animator should do is to commit time to listen to it over and over again. Doing this will give them a strong sense of where the emotion, motivation and emphasis points are within the dialogue delivery. There will be major points in the delivery that give the words spoken special emphasis. The animator has to identify those main points, as they will constitute the major "**storytelling poses**" of the animated action. These key points are moments that need to emphasize significantly, through pose and gesture.

If we're talking about drama, there is nothing more so than the theatrical performance of *Macbeth*.

Therefore, once the animator has listened to the audio track enough times to recognize these points, they should start sketching out very rough *"thumbnail pose drawings"* that represent the emphasis points the talking character is making. The big secret is **not to hold back** at this stage. We must never forget that the essence of any great animation is the *caricaturing* of real life, not just the imitating of it. Therefore, the main storytelling key poses need to be *extreme* and *exaggerated* at this stage.

I always make various thumbnail poses using my Arnie character – as he's easy to draw and therefore quick to get my pose ideas out. I will then capture them and edit them into my pose test animatic, to determine which one is the best to use in the context of the whole film.

If you're lucky enough to have had the original recording material shot on videotape, as the actor delivered their lines, you'll get further clues as to how these thumbnail key poses should look. But shouldn't preclude you from adding expression ideas of your own to the character's body language.

It's often quite valuable in observing – even recording – a voice artist delivering dialogue, as it will provide many gesture ideas for the animation.

Key Pose Animatic

What will really help at this stage is to test your key poses in the form of a "**key pose animatic**". A *"key pose animatic"* basically enables you to shoot and time out your key poses in sync with the soundtrack you are working with. When you play this back, you'll immediately get a sense to whether your thinking – and consequently the character's body language expression – is working by way of your key pose drawings. It gives an opportunity to make pose drawing changes before the inbetween drawings are subsequently created.

Make sure you get the maximum from your animation by working hard at structuring you "key pose animatic".

Final Key Poses

When you are happy with the way your roughed-out, thumbnail pose is working, you can begin to somewhat clean them up – bringing them closer to the final character design you established already. That way that there will be a continuity of *style*, *form* and *volume* throughout. These may not be the final, final cleaned up drawings of course. But they will be close to the correct styling required.

Based on my thumbnail poses, I come up with a final animation pose rough that I can work with in the final sequence.

Having completed these, you should again shoot a *"key pose animatic"*, to make sure all is working well with the new drawings. Adjust as necessary and then re-shoot the "key pose animatic" to ensure that it is exactly what you wanted. Repeat these adjustments and pose tests until is exactly what you're after.

I can't suggest enough that testing your key poses in a key pose animatic – prior to the big commitment of full animation taking place – is the only way of knowing if your poses are working in the context of the bigger picture, or not.

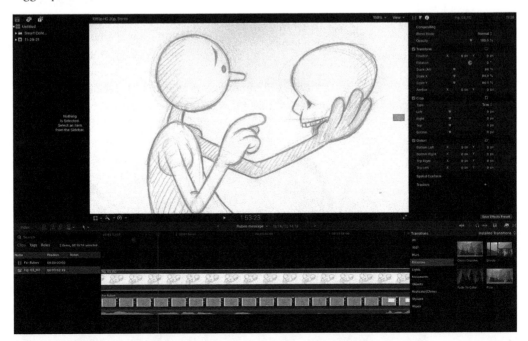

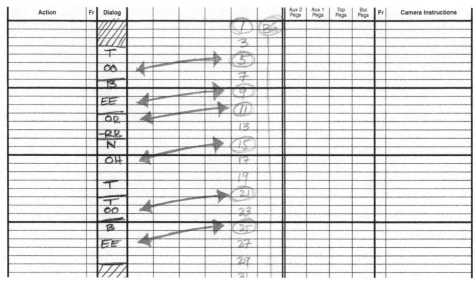

Note that the key frames containing the vowel sound mouths position keys are most effective if they are 1–2 frames ahead of the actual sound.

NOTE

*When timing out your keyframe drawings to a soundtrack you'll find that the audio-visual synchronization will work better if you position each keyframe drawing at **least one or two frames ahead** of the actual sound you're linking to – maybe more sometimes. For some reason this tends to appear more on sync than if you timed the keyframe exactly to the audio sound cue. This also applies to open-mouth positions when you're animating the mouth to strong vowel sounds. But we'll deal with that shortly.*

Facial Expressions

With your body language key frames in place, it's next time to add a little more emotion to the approach. Remember that "**body language**" gives a hint of the motivation or intention of the dialogue being delivered. But the face will better communicate the *mood* or *emotion* behind the words. This expression of emotion is especially focused around the eyes, although the overall facial expressions will communicate a great deal of feeling too. The shaping of the eyebrows can assist the visual expressions too.

Simply changing the angles of the eyebrows can alter the entire expression of a face.

It is estimated that there is something like 52 muscles in the human face, and each one of these muscles serves a purpose. The face therefore has a whole range of expressions outside the spoken word. So, it definitely pays to work hard in learning how you can communicate emotion simply through the expressions you put on the face. As stated early, the actual shaping of the mouth is the last thing you should focus on with lip sync so work on the facial expressions first and foremost. It is actually what the face is saying, rather than what the mouth is saying, that defines a great performance.

Even very simple changes of facial expression can communicate so many emotions, as we all know full well in this modern digital world!

To achieve a greater expression in the face, it is good to do a few exercises that will help your ability to deform a face to achieve certain results. A good way of doing this is the traditional "**bite 'n chew**" exercise that was once part of the now defunct Disney internship program. This required student animators to animate a character holding a candy bar in their hand. Then, the character needed to bring the candy bar to their mouth, show a certain anticipation if it tasting good as they did so. This is then followed up by the character biting of a piece from the end of the candy bar, chewing it and then swallowing it. It was a very clever exercise that was designed to explore a full range of expressions in the character's face – in addition to learn facial expression, timing and anticipation.

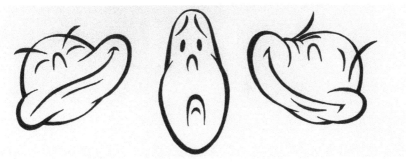

Taking an extreme, exaggerated, cartoony approach to the bite 'n chew exercise can really loosen you up in terms of facial expression.

All such elements are paramount when an animator attempts facial expression when dealing with dialogue. Of course, students we're not expected to just imagine a bite and chew action when they were attempting to animate it. They were instead required to act it out in a mirror for themselves and study every aspect of their facial expression throughout the action. They would be expected to repeat this exercise over and over again in the mirror, until they had produced a range of observational gesture drawing of the action, before attempting to animate it. Nowadays, though, videotaping the action – or even a video selfie – then playing it back over and over again is an ideal way of doing this.

Life references are always best, no matter how scary they may be at times!

Things to be most aware of when researching this kind of exercise – or something similar – are the distortions in the face specifically. But this should be done without distorting the underlying skeleton structure of the head behind the face, as was done in the more "rubber hose" form of animation that graced the early years of the industry. Other things to aim for would be the sudden snap action, when the end of the candy bar is bitten of; the circular chewing action on the jaw as the character tries to eat the candy; then finally the genuine look of anticipation and pleasure when the candy is ultimately chewed, savored and swallowed. The way that the teeth grind and slide the candy in the mouth is an important aspect to this action you should be aware of too.

Remember always that the teeth are set back in the mouth and the lips animate above them. They should NOT move with the lips!

Animating the Face

If you try it, the *"bite 'n chew"* exercise will give you a sense of how much the face can be pushed through a whole range of expressions and distortions to achieve mood, pleasure and emotion. That is the objective when working on the face when attempting dialogue animation too. So, the sooner you learn to successfully manipulate the face, the sooner your dialogue animation will begin to work well. However, none of this can be achieved successfully if you don't study the basics of facial expression first. I always advise students who want to succeed with facial expression that they should first watch a great stage, TV or film actor deliver a line of powerful dialogue. Even with TV soap operas, we can see a certain range of cliché facial expressions that can be cultivated through animation to express animated moods and emotion.

All traditions have their cliché expressions, like the Ukieo-e tradition in Japan. However, in the pursuit of originality and innovation, it still pays an animator to study different options to handling lip sync and facial expression.

The degree of facial subtlety, a good actor can achieve in a performance might not quite be possible in most animation, but the best animated dialogue will often reflect an acceptable level of core expressions and emotion nevertheless. The look in the eye; the appropriateness and timing of a blink; the hint and duration of a smile, or scorn; and the general presence of happiness, sadness, anger and humiliation in the expression are all basic facial values that an audience will understand and appreciate.

A more conventional range of cartoon-based eye expressions.

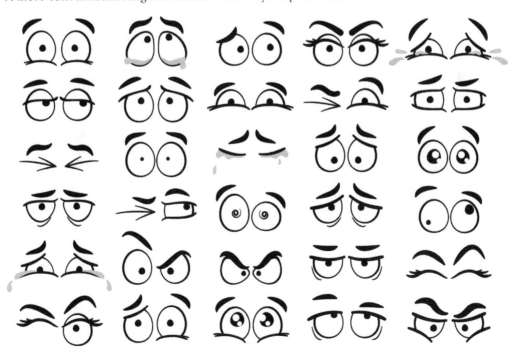

Remember, at this stage, it is nothing to do with the shape of the mouth. Just what the face is communicating as the words are heard. So, when faced with a specific piece of dialogue, having drawn up all your key body poses first, go back and listen beyond the words and try to get a sense they are seeking to express. Ask yourself "Is the character angry? Scared? Witty? Intellectual? Seductive? Or manipulative?". Once you've decided the underlining motivation, you can begin to decide the kind of facial expressions you can apply to your character.

Even pencils can talk too!

Also, if the recorded session was captured on film or videotape, you can refer to that material and see what the actor was actually doing with his face at the time of recording. This will be a huge advantage. However, if this is not possible, then listen to the words over and over again, miming in the mirror and putting your own facial expressions to them if necessary. Study what your face is doing. And again, try to capture those actions with thumbnail key pose sketches.

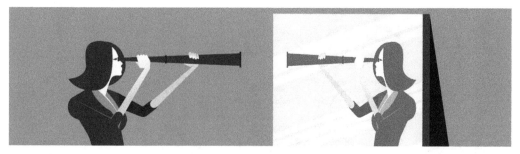

At times, the mirror is an animator's best friend.

If your dialogue has a happy quality to it, try to create happy expressions with your character's face. If there's anger, your character's face must express that emotion instead. Try to understand what particular emotion is driving your dialogue and devise your character's facial expressions accordingly. Sometimes a single line of dialogue can betray a whole range of expressions. So, you need to capture these too, all in that one sentence.

Learning to draw all kinds of facial expressions, in any style, is really valuable for an animator.

The hardest expression to capture in animation is that subtle look that is often found in the eyes of great actors. In all forms of animation, you have cruder means of achieving that same subtlety, but you must try it. For inspiration, I always refer to the work of the great Disney animators of the distant past, such as master animators Frank Thomas and Ollie Johnston. Study what they did in *Jungle Book*, *Lady and the Tramp* and other such master works of animation, and you will appreciate what can be achieved at the highest level – and always strive for the highest level if you can, although I know is desperately hard in this digital day and age to achieve anything near what they achieved. Yet excellence is possible if you prepared to put in the right work and right process.

Young high school student, Alice B, begins to define the core nature of her character through facial expressions.

Again, I can only urge you to study intently the works of the great actors as they deliver their lines. As with every other challenge in animation, if you can go to the closest source of reference for your material in the real world, you will be best informed.

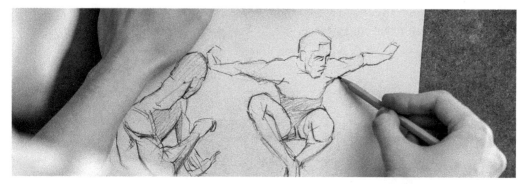

Drawing from life, not imagination, is best when animating something that has its equivalent in the real world.

That said a few, what might be considered *cliché*, tips might be useful here. Remember that when the audience watches a speaking character on the screen, they will mostly focus on the eyes and not the mouth. So, when you are animating dialogue, make sure the eyes, and more specifically the eyebrows, are delivering the emotional message you want them to deliver. For example, a simple manipulation of the eyebrows alone can communicate some basic emotion expressions.

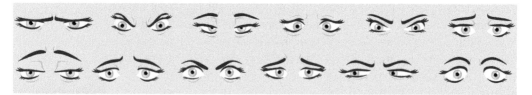

With facial or lip sync animation, always feature strongly on the eyes and eyebrows to communicate emotion.

Of course, there are approaches that are not particular subtle. However, if you adapt them to the nature of your own character design, based on your observation of actors or your own interpretations in the mirror, you will begin to capture that special quality of eye expression that your dialogue needs. Don't forget that a well-placed stare, or blink, can do wonders for punctuating the kind of emotion your dialogue action is trying to communicate. This is called a *"burn"* in acting circles.

The "Burn" look.

Lip Sync

Finally, with motivation and emotion covered, it is time to approach the cherry on the cake – the "**lip sync**". Here, we have to take special efforts to choose the correct shape of mouths, the size of the mouths opening, its timing and its overall relationship to the sounds being expressed frame by frame. This is easiest said than done, however – especially as with fast talking dialog, it is particularly difficult to fit every mouth shape that is necessary within the limitations of 24 frames per second. In such circumstances, it is often necessary to choose between one particular mouth shape and another where two phonetic sounds straddle one frame of film. Consequently, animated lip sync can rarely be perfect. Although with a slow talking character, it is much more possible to achieve. Having said all that, there are a number of key guidelines to lip sync that will help the decision-making process for every animator.

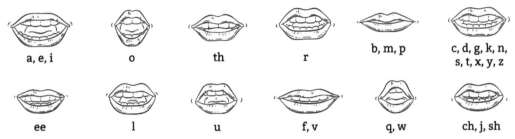

A generic range of mouth positions – although it must be stressed that with different characters, voices and design styles, these will need to be adjusted. The mirror is always your best friend, so rather than go "generic", go specific by looking at your own mouth in the mirror, speaking the words you are hearing on the soundtrack you are working with!

Vowel sounds: Vowel sounds are the single most important element of lip syncing that has to be correct. Vowel sounds are the cornerstone of all lip sync movement. The consonants are important, but not so important. The vowel sounds are **a**, **e**, **i**, **o** and **u**. Basically, all the open-mouth positions in speech.

There are different ways of opening the mouth when we speak, depending on what we are saying. So again, always refer to your mirror if in doubt and what shapes you should draw for the sounds your character is speaking.

Although there's a generic approach to all open-mouth vowel sounds, the final shapes of the mouth have to be related to the nature of the character being animated. For example, a muttering, tied lip, poker player type of character will open his mouth in a far different way than a chatty, toothy, verbally dexterous TV chat show host.

A hard open-mouth shape and a soft one. So always listen to the audio track, and reference your own mouth in a mirror for clarification on which approach to use.

Again, it requires the animator to get beneath the skin of the character who is talking and the character's mood and motivation, to interpret the way he will move his mouth. Again, make good use of your mirror. Act out the lip sync and observe how your one mouth is working when you speak the words you are animating. Even if the natural look of your mouth is different from the shape of the character's mouth, try to emulate the basic shape of your character's mouth to see the shapes making the right words. Be the poker player. Be the toothy TV host. Be whatever your character needs to be.

A mirror is not too expensive to buy but can be priceless in terms of improving your lip sync animation!

Vowel anticipation: Just as I advised you earlier to *anticipate* the sync frame with your own poses on a key pose animatic, you should also anticipate the open-mouth "vowel" positions on your animation too. I tend to advance the mouth positions around **two** to **three** frames ahead of their actual audio sync point. But sometimes the vowel shapes can be even more than that, depending on the impact the sound is making. As a general rule, the larger and more explosive the vowel sound, the more you may want to try advancing the open-mouth position ahead of its actual sound. Bottom line, it is really a trial-and-error process, so it will help if you test various options on the most important ones you are attempting.

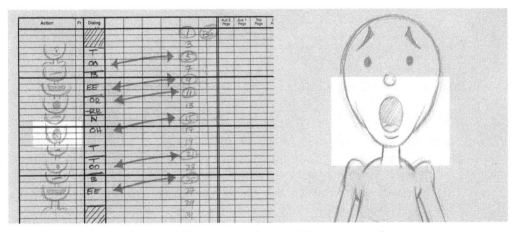

Roughing out mouth shapes in the "notes" column of the exposure sheet can help when the final key lip sync drawing is created. Don't be afraid to use Squash & Stretch on the extreme positions either!

This is also true for major other sync points, such as **coughs**, **sneezes** and **explosive laughter**. Some Disney animators in the distant past have actually anticipated these kinds of major impact points by anything up to 14 frames. But then again, this would be a big exception. Testing by trial and error is the best way forward here.

With an extreme cough key position, don't be afraid to try positioning it up to 14 frames ahead of the actual sound on exposure sheet. Obviously, this is a trial-and-error thing and must be tested on an individual basis, based on the sounds behind heard.

Tongue action: If you watch yourself in the mirror as you speak dialogue, you'll see how essential the tongue is, especially, when the letter "**L**" is spoken. The tongue always goes to the top of the mouth, when the letter *"L"* is pronounced. That said, unless your character's tongue is particularly active, try to keep it at the bottom of the mouth and as discrete as possible. Also, if you hit the upward tongue action a couple frames ahead of the actual *"L"* sound, it will always carry more impact.

Note how the tongue is pushed up toward the top of the mouth on an "L" sound.

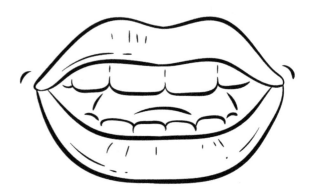

Teeth: Not all animated characters have teeth. But many do. Consequently, if your character has teeth, remember that those teeth are **fixed** to the skull within the head. Therefore, never animate the teeth as though they are rubber or they can move around the head. Many animators often draw a character's teeth appearing sometimes, then not. Remember that the teeth are fixed somewhere between the upper lip, depending on the design of the character's face and the skull. So, you have to introduce them in a logical way. That is only when the lips reveal them. To do anything else, will be misleading and distracting. Of course, if your character has buck teeth, you'll be free to introduce them more than at other times.

Whatever the mouth shape you are attempting, remember that the teeth are always fixed in the same position on the skull behind the lips.

NOTE

Some animators are natural dialogue people and others are not. So, do not despair if your dialogue animation does not go well at first. Like most things, it's all a matter of trial and error and, ultimately, experience. Dialogue animation requires fine-tuning and subtle expression. It also requires acute observation. Just as a small percentage of actors are truly wonderful at Shakespeare, so too are some animators good at dialogue. Others are not natural at it – including yours truly! However, natural good at it or not, do always strive to be better at this process. The more you do it, the better you will be at it. A really valuable thing to repeat again is – always observe great actors as they work. They'll freely offer you countless examples of how dialogue can be beautifully expressed, even with a minimum of movement. Above all else, listen to the audio track you have to animate and understand it on all its levels. Never forget that dialogue animation is not just about moving the mouth in perfect lip sync with the audio track, but communicating the essence of the character that is speaking and why that character is speaking the words in the way they're saying them.

Personally, I have a thinking problem when it comes to lip sync – I'm just not good at it unfortunately! Action is my thing.

Two-Character Dialogue

Finally, let's very briefly discuss *"two-character dialogue"*. Two-character dialogue is not just about opposing characters looking at each other and talking. More often than not, dialogue between two characters involves a certain degree of give and take – that is, one may be passive and the other one aggressive and vice versa. One may be cruel, the other one a victim. One may be provocative, the other receptive. All these factors will affect the way you stage your scene and the way you handle your characters. Always remember the *"body language"* is everything.

Listening is an acquired art!

Remember also that two-character animation is like a tennis match. One character is making the shot while the other waits to receive it. Consequently, their stands, staging and attitude should appear active and passive on a number of levels. Often a great truth can be communicated to the audience by just focusing on the listener and not featuring the character that's speaking. By focusing attention on the listener's role, the audience can often understand more about what's being said – and it's intent – than not.

Listening can be as much a focal point as talking!

Music Tracks

If you're working with music, then what you need to do is listen to the music over and over again to find the major emphasis points. It's somewhat like listening for vowel sounds in regular speech and then focusing on those with dynamic poses and major object action. So, with all music, you'll simply have to stress the key moments that occur within that music. It may be the beats, it may be a major instrument or riff, but there needs to be something you pin your major animated emphasis point on. For much of the time, the melody will take care of itself but the beats are fundamental. Then, if you watch a conductor, that conductor controls the beat and controls the pace that the orchestra must follow. You are the conductor when animating music action, so your judgment needs to be good. Bottom line though, if you accurately hit the beats, or you hit a major transition moments in the melody, then your animation is going to work so much better.

Use your pencil as would a conductor of the orchestra. You are in control of the audio, not it in control of you!

Sound Breakdown

"Sound breakdown" is a process whereby you analyze your soundtrack, frame by frame, before the animation even begins. Indeed, if dialogue, music or sound effects are crucial to your action, then you need to know what on your exposure sheet those moments occur. Trust me, for really effective animation, it's much better to work with a soundtrack up front than to add one later. It gives you **key moments** on which to hang your movement, and the *"sound breakdown"* will tell you where those moments are. Most animation is done at 24 frames per second, and usually, you're animating on 2s. So, make sure that your "sound breakdown" is based upon this, not at any other frame rate.

Action	Fr	Dialog							Aux 2 Pegs	Aux 1 Pegs	Top Pegs	Bot Pegs	Fr	Camera Instructions
		////												
		T												
		W												
		EH												
		N												
		T EE												
		E												
		OR												
		RR												
		E												
		AY												
		M												
		EH												
		SS												
		P												
		UR												
		RR												
		S												
		EH												
		K												
		OH												
		N												
		D												
		////												

Note that dialogue audio is broken down phonetically – in other words, spelled like it sounds, not how it's actually spelled.

If you have a *"sound breakdown"* of music beforehand for example, it tells you exactly where the beats are. That way, if you know you have a beat every one and a half seconds, then you know too that have to perhaps put a key frame there and inbetween 18 drawings to the next one. This should be the first thing you think about when animating music. Then, make sure that your poses on each 18 frames has strong body language and storytelling value. That way, your music animation is always going to be good and rhythmic. You just have to make sure that you hit those **beats** strongly and your poses are strong.

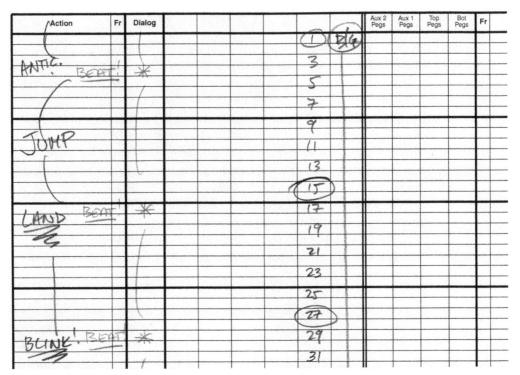

If you have a strong music beat charted out on your exposure sheet, ensure that you hit the beats with your major action keys – anticipating the beat by a couple of frames or more wherever you can for better synchronization.

Finally, the person who told me how important that hitting the vowel sounds strongly with dialogue was one of the greatest Disney animators ever, **Art Babbitt**. He was a wonderful dialogue animator, so I listened to everything he said. He even told me that you can almost ignore the consonants in speech – that is, the closed mouth positions – as long as you hit the vowel sounds well. If you do that, the audience will accept the rest of it. Indeed, he said that he had animated foreign languages that he didn't understand in the past, but as long as he hit the phonetic vowel sounds accurately, the rest of the lip sync would work.

There was no lip sync in my award-winning *HOKUSAI~An Animated Sketchbook* film, but if there was I would have been comfortable just hitting the vowel sounds of the Japanese audio track with open mouths.

Sound Effects and Foley Recording

In terms of sound effects in animation – indeed, in all filmmaking – there is a person called a "**foley artist**". A *"foley artist"* basically records the actual sound effects that need to match the action in any scene. For instance, if there's a fire burning in a grate, or you can see a fire burning away somewhere in the scene, the *"foley artist"* records those background sounds to make it look and feel real. The surprising thing about this is that good sound effects (SFX) or not necessarily a recording of the thing you are seeing moving. For example, the sound of fire crackling is often not created by recording a fire crackling! Quite often the real sound doesn't sound strong or convincing enough. So, what the *"foley artist"* will do is record something like crunchy celluloid and scrunchy it up next to a microphone. Then, when that sound is synchronized with fire animation, it looks and feels like a real fire! Consequently, foley artists are really experienced and imaginative at creating sounds that work perfectly with the things they're matching on the screen.

Foley artists use many devices to create what sounds like natural sounds – in this case, recording handheld shoes crunching on broken glass.

Another example would be the adding of footsteps to a walk. If the character is walking across on a wooden floor, then a *"foley artist"* will set up their microphone next to a wooden deck, or a piece of hardwood just one yard square. Then they'll put heavy clicky shoes on, and simply stamp up and down on the wood while watching a playback video of the animation, trying to match the steps. They'll most likely do this several times, until they eventually get the synchronization right. Even then, they may fine-tune and adjust each footstep to match the steps perfectly afterward. On the other hand, if a character is walking through leaves, they'll do the same thing in box on the ground that contains dried leaves. They'll stamp up and down in those leaves until they match perfectly the footsteps on the screen. Beyond that, *"foley artists"* will get much more creative in the way they create the SFX that go with screen action, which is why it is a very respected occupation that an animator should take full advantage off if they have the budget to do so.

Foley sounds are the equivalent of the written ones found in comic books, when trying to add impact sounds that complement the action.

Suggested Assignment

You of course should focus all your energies at this point on recording and breaking down your project's audio track. Whether it is dialogue, music or SFX, you need to be resourceful and do the best you can with the resources you have. If you don't create the sound for yourself, there are many online resources that can achieve what you need professionally, and often for minimal costs. For example, a site like **www.voices.com** had a huge stable of professional voice artists who often will offer their expert services and supply a final dialogue track for you for very little cost if they know you are a student or beginner. Similarly, there are a whole number of internet sites out there, that offer copyright free, prerecorded music for very little money. Just search for copyright free music, and you can find the one that best suits you and your project. In terms of sound effects, one great place to go would be **www.freesound.com**, where generous filmmakers and editors upload all kinds of sound effects and music that you can use for no charge. Resourcefulness is the order of the day here – especially if you have little or no money to spend on your audio track.

Masterclass 31/ Storyboard Animatic

Hopefully, by now, your project is taking shape well. You should have your *"Concept Art"* and *"Character Designs"* finalized. You should have your rough *"Storyboard"* done – and hopefully your *"Audio Track"* is ready. So, now we need to put some of these things together to see how your project looks in real time. To do that, you need to create a **"Storyboard Animatic"**, which is the subject of this lesson. But first, more observational gesture drawing.

Warm-Up Drawing

This is going to be the third of a series of sequential exercises – where you observe multiple poses within a same action and recreate them. You will again be speed-drawing against the clock, with all your drawings needing to be done on a single page of your sketchbook. So, below is a single image with **five** consecutive poses on it. For this, give yourself just **30 seconds** to draw each pose, but this time drawing them from **right to left**.

DOI: 10.1201/9781003324287-34

Comments: This time there is a prop involved, so there is a greater challenge in making your character poses not only dynamic but also with a strong interaction with the staff. Technically of course, this means that you're going to have to draw faster and with a greater emphasis on angles and relationships of limbs and tor-so to the prop supporting them. Where you can't see parts of each pose, due to another body pose blocking it, you will have to imagine it as you draw.

Instruction

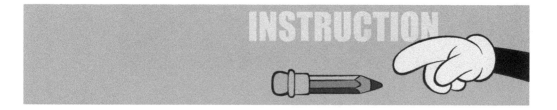

In this lesson, we're now going to explain how to put a "**Storyboard Animatic**" together.

The biggest advice I can give you is to create a *"storyboard animatic"* for your project right now. That will show you how your storytelling images will work against the soundtrack you plan to use. There is absolutely nothing better than seeing your film ideas tested out in real time on a monitor. Even when you use animation software previews of your work, the playback speed is not entire-ly accurate. So always render them out to a video format and play them back to assess them properly. And so it is with a *"storyboard animatic"* when that is play in real time. There is not hiding from that. Your approach will either be right, too fast or too slow – or a mixture of all those things. But it is better to know now, before you commit to all that animation you're going to be doing in the *"Production"* stage, than later when it is all done, and you may have to redo some or all of it.

Storyboard animatic drawing by high school student, Xiaofu Zhu.

The word "**Sync**" is short for the word *"synchronization"*. It means tying the picture and the sound to match each other in a very precise way. The most obvious way of doing this is called "**lip sync**" – meaning when a character's talking the lips move in exactly the right way to match the sounds that are being said. I'm sure you've seen it sometimes, when they mess up on tv or film they get the sync out and the lips are moving but the sounds are not happening and vice versa. So, sync is really important for animation, especially when *"syncing-up"* your storyboard drawings with the soundtrack you're using.

Even if you work very rough – such as on PostIt notes as I do – you can very quickly test your visual ideas with your audio track by creating a rough animatic.

Hopefully, prior to this, you will have numbered all your storyboard drawings clearly and accurately, so you'll know the correct order to place them in. This is because, to do a *"storyboard animatic"*, you'll need take each of those individual drawings in order, upload them to a film editing program and sync them to the words or music you'll be using in your audio track before rendering them to video. This can be a trial-and-error process, and you really need some suitable software application that will allow you to do that. The most popular software is either *"Adobe Premier"* or *"FinalCutPro"* although there are many others out there to consider too. But whatever program you use, that will need to render your edit out as a video.

Demo of creating a rough storyboard animatic in Final Cut Pro, for students.

By assigning a storyboard image to the relevant parts of your audio track, you're defining the rhythm of the film you're making. In other words, you know how long each picture – or each scene, most likely – is going to be seen on the film. What you're looking for is the big picture of everything – a series of big pictures about everything. You're linking them accurately with your soundtrack, so you can better asses your cut points from scene to scene. Remember, a *"cut"* is a transition, an instant transferal from one scene visual to the next.

Even roughly drawn out, two scenes cut together in a storyboard animatic can look quite dramatic with no transition frames between them.

Once you get a sense of how everything's working through your *"storyboard animatic"*, you can make changes in the edit if the timing is not working well. Alternatively, if all is good – or once it's good – you can move forward in the process and work out, in terms of frames and seconds, how long each scene of your animation needs to be. That will leave no guesswork for later down the pipeline, when you're handling the *"Production"* stage. Better still, when you know how long every scene is going to be, you can create a **"Production Chart"** that shows how many scenes you have, what you can title them and each stage of the animation process until completion. This is a great chart to have, as you can check off each box as you do them, giving you an immediate visual understanding of how the production process is going.

Scene:	1	2	3	4	5	6	7	8	9	10	11	12
Storyboard	X	X	X	X	X	X	X	X	X	X	X	X
Layout	X	X	X	X	X	X	X	X	X			
Background	X	X										
Rough animation	X	X	X	X								
Animation changes	X	X	X									
Clean-up	X	X										
Inking	X											
Coloring												
Composite												
Render												
Sound edit.												

Even a Word-based, simple production chart like this allows you to very quickly check off the progress of each scene as they are completed.

So, although, aesthetically, a *"storyboard animatic"* may not be your most attractive part of the project creatively, it is an invaluable opportunity to learn how your ideas are working and how much each part of the project is going to require in terms of animation footage. Remember though, it is a foundation only. Yet the beauty of it is once you have your storyboard animatic worked out, you then have a visual affirmation of what lies ahead. This will allow you to plan your animation effort better, when the time comes.

For example, you might have a very short scene that's possibly just ten frames long. (Yes, it does happen!) For example, it could be just a quick glance away – followed by a scene that's much longer. So you can plan ahead in your mind just how little the movement needs to be in the short scene, so you can better assign your time and energy to the subsequent big scene. Some filmmakers like to save the hardest scene till last, whereas others prefer the opposite. Others still will just work their way sequentially from the first scene to the last scene. But whatever method of approach you'll have, you will at least have this *"Production Chart"* scene guide to separate where the bigger effort is required and where you might even get away with a single drawing for the short scene.

Even a static image can capture the audience's attention if it's dramatic enough.

Consequently, there's many reasons why a storyboard animatic is a valuable effort to make at this stage of your *"Pre-production"*. Another reason for it is that in seeing it play in real time, you get a chance to identify where you need to put in the major *"storytelling poses"* into your future cleaned up version of the animation – which we'll talk about in greater detail in a subsequent lesson. Remember though, you're not animating yet. You're just refining what you have by developing more powerful key poses that are pivotal in the unfolding storyline you're working with.

This is a pose test of something already animated for my film, *Endangered Species* – a film about the rise, fall and hopeful rise again of traditional hand-drawn animation. Nevertheless, even if it were roughed-out, pre-animation, it would still be a valuable exercise in terms of creating a pose test animatic.

In a way, your rough "storyboard animatic" is really the first piece of an extended jigsaw puzzle you're working on. Every stage of the *"Pre-production"* and *"Production"* are further pieces you're adding to the puzzle – hopefully ending up with a very fine picture in the end. So this rough animatic first stage is an invaluable foundation of something that will grow and grow as you work further at it. This is why it is so important to get your "storyboard animatic" right at this stage!

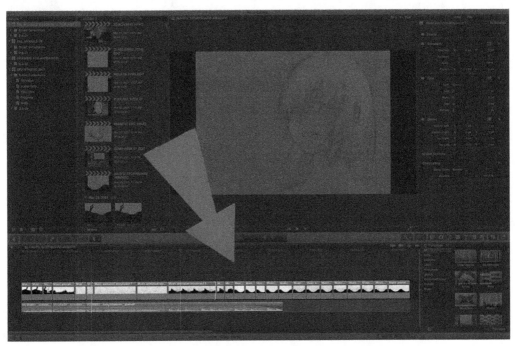

Indicating the various pose drawings arranged along the Final Cut Pro timeline for a rough pose animatic by student Xiaofu Zhu.

Remember finally that each image should be more or less drawn to the correct "screen ratio", so that although the drawings are rough, they are approximately sketch out in the right kind of "staging" for what you are trying to achieve. Most films these days are created in "**high definition**" – which means the longest side is **16 units** and the vertical or the shortest side is **9 units**. (known as "16 × 9".) The ideal *"HD1080"* framing would be measured at **1920 pixels wide and 1080 pixels high** although *"HD720"* is **1280 × 720 pixels** in size.

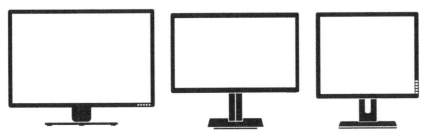

The HD1080, HD720 and Academy screen formats.

Suggested Assignment

Make sure you complete your rough "storyboard animatic" before you move on. If it is not working as you would like it with your soundtrack, modify your drawings – even your ideas at this point – as you definitely do not want to move on to the next stage, while the foundation of your project is not sound and well structured.

Masterclass 32/ Character Rigging 1

32

In this lesson, we're going to start one of two lessons devoted to polishing, preparing and rigging your character(s) in Moho. If you're not working with Moho on your project, then this is a great opportunity to polish your character design and create expression sheets for your character.

Warm-Up Drawing

GESTURE DRAWING

This is the final one of four focusing on multiple images in on picture. As you can see, there's going to be **seven poses** to analyze this time, again ranging from left to right. Again, try to draw them all on one page from your sketchbook. You need to give yourself **30 seconds** to do each one.

DOI: 10.1201/9781003324287-35

Comments: As before, start drawing from left to right and try to get the entire sequence draw across your page. (Use a landscape/horizontal view of your page to do this.) You'll notice that this sequence starts with a "down" anticipation position, before the character sketches up to the apex position – reflective a little of the upward movement of a *"Bouncing Ball"*. Note the way the arms are very active here, progressing from a very low position in relation to the torso to very high. Note the coming together of the hands around the ball in the middle and the separation over the final three poses. The torso essentially transitions from a "concave" shape at the beginning to a "convex" one at the end. Your gesture drawings should reflect all these things.

So this one was a bit more challenging but really valuable. You might not appreciate it while doing all those complete, progressive drawings, but it really will focus your observation and animation skills – which of course is the object of the exercise. If you can, separate all your drawings digitally and try to render them into a video, with each drawing on the screen for two frames each (2s). That will teach you a great deal about how your gesture drawing skills are developing, plus give you a real-time insight into how this kind of animation works.

Instruction

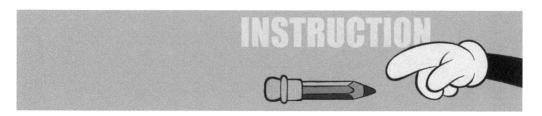

For the rest of this lesson, as well as the next one, we're going to start the process of creating your character rig in Moho. As I said above, if you're not working in Moho for your project, use this opportunity for refining and polishing you drawn character designs. Work on a color model sheet for them too.

The Hermit rig and color model in Moho.

But even if you're not using Moho, you should be aware of the following to lessons of instruction, just in case you're called to work in Moho further down the line. For everyone else, this is the time when you need to get your character(s) design finalized and rigged, ready for animation in the way your animatic suggest. With this in mind, consider this lesson as the *preparation* lesson and the next one the actual *rigging* one.

Before you begin rigging your character, make sure you have all its personality and action requirements clear in your own mind first. It will affect the way you rig and color it.

If you're not doing Moho, as we've discussed before, you're doing hand-drawn animation, either traditionally on paper or digitally on tablet. So, instead of doing this and the next character rigging assignments, I would suggest you focus on doing a highly finished turnaround model sheet – plus an expression and color model sheet reflecting all the moods and expressions your character might go through in your project. This will give you valuable drawing time with your character, prior to you actually animating it. The more you draw it, the more familiar you will be with it and the easier it will be when you have to draw it for your animation frames.

Turnaround model guide for *The Hermit.*

If you intend to work with Moho for your animation, what follows comes in two sections: (i) the preparation for Moho section and (ii) the actual rigging in Moho section.

Although you've already designed your characters previously, we now have to adjust them to the requirements of Moho. Why is it different, I hear you ask. Well, remember that in Moho, you are only going to see the character from the angle that you've drawn it. For this introductory project in Moho, you effectively can't rotate your character like you could in 3D animation or indeed hand-drawn animation. Now it's true that the latest version of Moho at the time of writing allows you to rig a partial rotational action for a character, but this is more advanced, and we won't be going into it here.

Remember, this book is not so much about teaching software, it is about teaching movement and production processes. So you can do your own research into the rotational capability of Moho rigs – or indeed the rigs any other 2D software

Moho's head turning rigs are easy to understand but very effective when used correctly © Lost Marble.

you care to work with. The tutorials of **McCoy Buck** are particularly easy to understand - although the 2D ACADEMY has it's own excellent rigging tutorial by Ruben Cabenda. In the meantime, for the purposes of our project, here and now, let's just say that you can't turn them round from the two-dimensional viewpoint they are drawn in. Effectively, you're always going to see them in that flat two-dimensional way, so we need to work with that.

Original flat and two-dimensional design, by high school student, Sunny Li.

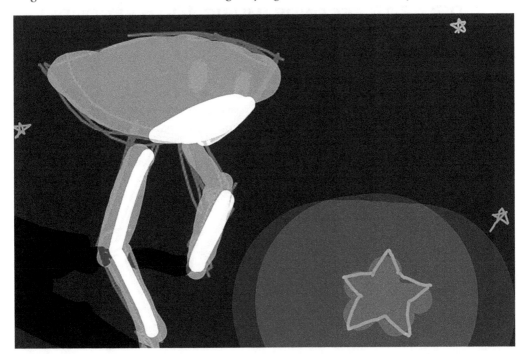

A skilled animator/director should be able to turn a stumbling block into a stepping stone and plan for that. That includes the way you rig your character. For example, if you're going to have your character walking in profile all the way through a scene, then Moho is a perfect option for that as it's easy to do and will allow your character to walk along way in terms of the background art you will provide. So plan for that and make the design of your background art fascinating and diverse, so that the further your character walks on the screen there is not risk of the audience being bored by a repetitive background.

06: 12-18 SECONDS (MUSIC 10-16 SECONDS)

"Summer" concept art for Moho project, by high school student, Chase Ferry.

Therefore, in order for your character to walk well and appear very fluid in its movement, you're actually going to have to reverse engineer you single design art into a number of separate pieces. You can still put everything onto one sheet. Eventually, each body part is going to have to be imported into Moho on its own layer, then rigged to work with the others. But to start with, put everything onto one sheet and we'll start from there.

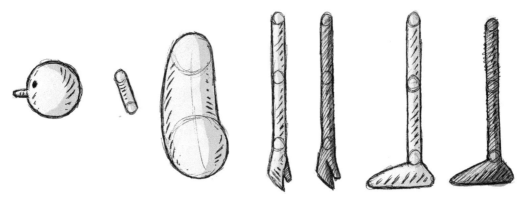

The basic separated "Arnie" body parts, in preparation for rigging in Moho. Actually, the upper and low arms and legs need to be separated, as do the hands and feet for the final prep.

Basically, we need to see these elements isolated on to the page – the **upper arm**, **lower arm** and **hand** of both arms. Although they are separate at this stage, they will have to *overlapping* at the joints when rigged together. So plan for that too.

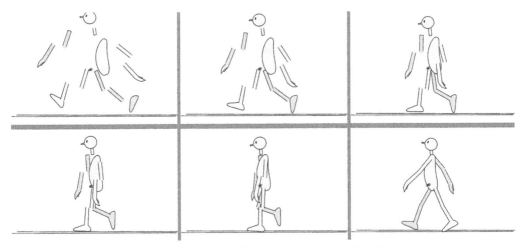

Showing how the Arnie body parts implode to become a complete figure, ready for rigging.

For both legs, you're similarly going to have to separate everything. Namely – the **upper leg**, **lower leg**, **foot** – again *overlapping* at the joints.

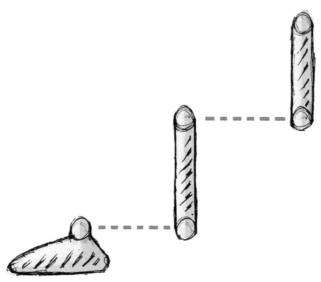

The upper leg is rigged to the lower leg at the knee joint, while the foot is rigged to the lower leg at the ankle joint.

Finally, the **body** needs to be *separate* to the **neck**, which itself has to be separate to the **head**. Again, these need to *overlap* too.

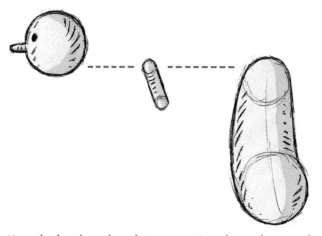

Here the head, neck and torso are rigged together, overlapped.

Now, if we implode all these separate parts, as they will be when rigged in Moho, it will ultimately all be rigged together like this.

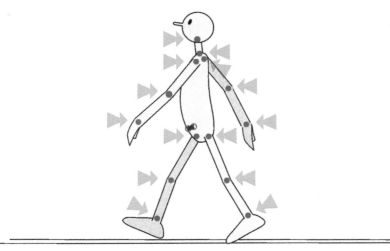

The final rigged character with the rigged joint positions that connect all the separate body parts.

Remember too that Moho gives you the facility of painting your body parts with watercolor or other textured painting technique – or, as flat colors, using its vector function. The latter will respond faster when you are working and will have smaller files sizes when implemented. But a "bitmap" version will always look more "art-based" if it has textures and feels like it is a painting or illustration coming to life.

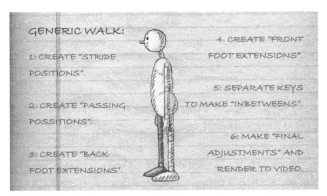
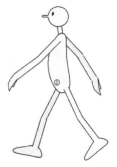

The difference between an illustrated/textured character to the left and a flat-colored, vector character to the right.

Suggested Assignment

The following are some suggestions for those non-Moho, drawn animation filmmakers.

Make sure you have a well worked out, *"turnaround model sheet"* created, which will force you to work out your character from every possible angle. Of course, if we're never going to see your character from different angles in your film idea, as with a Moho approach, then you don't need to draw different views of it at all! In your expression models sheet however, try some "up" and "down" shot views too.

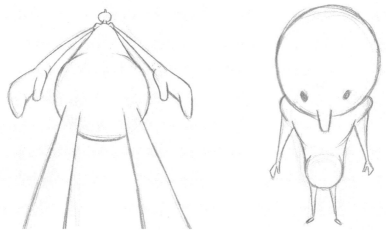

Quick exercise sketches of Arnie, looking up and down – forcing the perspective as much as possible to increase the drama.

An ideal *"turnaround model sheet"* usually contains a **front view**, a **three-quarter front view**, a **profile (side) view**, a **three-quarter back view** and a **back view**. Doing those views of your character should just about cover everything you'll likely need for your project animation.

Turnaround model sheet of the legendary soccer player, Sir Stanley
Matthews – for early Drawassic project development, *Spirit of the Game.*

The other thing you're strongly recommended to do here is an "expression sheet" of your character. In most film projects, a character is required to put on a wider range of different expressions, emotions and action poses. So it's good at this stage if you work out as many of those as you can ahead of the actual animation process. You will learn that as you start animating your character in the twists and turns of your storyline, you will be confronted by having to work out what it looks like and how it might pose in the circumstances you are planning. So, rather than slow your progress down by trying to work things out at the time, it's much better if you work the main ones out here, so there are no last-minute surprises or challenges that can affect your animation flow.

TIP

When creating your "turnaround model sheet" you'll find things easier if you draw your front view to the left of the model sheet, leaving enough room to the right of it to accommodate all the other views you plan to do. Then, when you have locked down your "front view", project across **horizontal lines** from the key points of its construction – from top to bottom. These construction lines will help you keep the size, locations and volumes of your character's features consistent from one turnaround drawing to the other.

Three-view turnaround model sheet with projection lines.

Masterclass 33/
Character Rigging 2

At this point in your *"Pre-production"* schedule, you will hopefully be inspired by what you have done so far. With a *"Storyboard animatic"* at your disposal and your final characters being worked upon, you are beginning to see light at the end of the tunnel – at least in anticipating the *"animation"* stage at last. In this lesson, you will be taking your final character work forward – either by wrapping-up your *"rigging"*, if Moho is the approach you'll be taking toward your animation, or by finalizing your *"expression model sheets"*, which should be getting you to learn how to smoothly draw your characters in all moods and all poses. But before you start that, another observation gesture drawing exercise.

Warm-Up Drawing

As you can see, we're back to our previous format for this one, in the sense that I'm going to show you two separate drawings and give you a more generous time limit to drawing them. Try to drawing them on the same page of your sketchbook however. The theme of these drawings is "**Dynamic Line**". A *"Dynamic Line"* is something that is extremely important to the creation of action poses in animation. In all very powerful poses, there is always a **strong line of action** that can define the direction of the main movement. There can even be more than one "Dynamic Line" of action in a pose. For example, observe this scene from a Disney film.

DOI: 10.1201/9781003324287-36

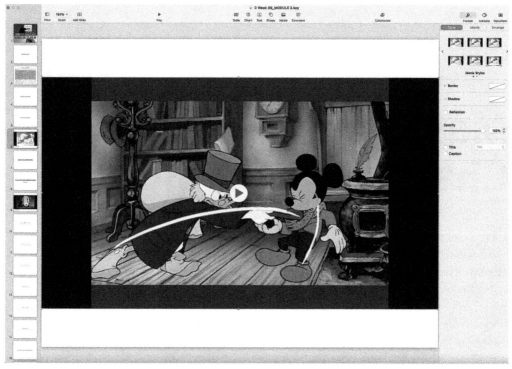

In my class presentation, I use this still from a Disney film that I found on the internet to illustrate "dynamic lines".

Notice how the main thrust of the duck character is the greater force here – which is the *"Dynamic Line"* – but the reaction and bending in of Mickey, to that driving force, is also a *"Dynamic Line"*. His curve defines the reaction to the main action. Consequently, the more defined the *"Dynamic Lines"* are in a pose, the more powerful that pose will be from a storytelling point of view.

The following two poses have one dominant *"Dynamic Line"* of action within them. You should give yourself just **2 minutes** to draw each of them. First draw the action pose, as normal, then add to your drawing where you think the *"Dynamic Line"* should go. Alternatively, draw first the *"Dynamic Line"*, then build your gesture drawing around it. Either way, you will begin to understand how powerful the *"Dynamic Line"* can be.

Pose 1 comments: I think it's pretty obvious where the *"Dynamic Line"* is in the first image. Indeed, this one is so obvious that it might help to draw the *"Dynamic Line"* first and then construct the rest of the pose around it. Quite often animators do this, so they can really take advantage of it. But ultimately, it is what you feel most comfortable doing here – as long as the *"Dynamic Line"* is as powerful in your drawing as it looks in the original picture.

Pose 2 comments: Again, I think the *"Dynamic Line"* is pretty obvious here too. So, work out what that line in is your own mind and develop it through your drawing. I would suggest that whatever approach you took in the first pose – i.e. *"DL"* first or *"DL"* second – you should do the opposite approach here, so you get an experience of both of them. Then, you can assess which one works best for you.

When I start blocking out my own animation poses, I often start with the "Dynamic Line". I don't do that every time, but I do find that in the most dramatic of action poses, it helps to get a sense of the power of the pose, around which I can build in my character or characters. Normally, I will start with a background layout drawing under my animation level, then on that upper layer I will draw in very strongly the lines of action I most want to get for the pose in question. I will bear in mind proportions and the size of the character, but the pose drawing starts with no more than a line, or lines, on the page. Then, I will convert those lines in the character on a more geometric level – meaning *spheres*, *cylinders* and *boxes, etc.* – and test that out as a *"pose test"* when the entire sequence is blocked out. This will often give a much more powerful and spontaneous feel to the key pose action.

"Dynamic Lines" really give energy and direction to everything you do. So, if you're creating *action poses*, think about what you character is doing from a *storytelling pose* and imagine where the *"Dynamic Line"* is within that pose. Just never neglect the line, as it really give a strong *spine*, *strength* and *direction* to your work.

Instruction

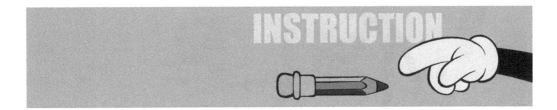

Now that we're approximately three-quarters the way through the *"Pre-production"* process. Your project should now be coming into focus nicely. We have nearly covered all the foundation material that give you the chance to create something very special. So definitely keep the pressure on yourself by either finishing your character rigging here if Moho is your production path or else polishing off those amazing *"expression sheets"* you are planning to animate your film through drawing.

Power to the pencil!

It really is very important to keep that pressure on yourself with all animation and filmmaking. If you fall back on *"Pre-production"* especially, you'll soon discover that it gets *exponentially* worse the further you move into it as time goes by. Now, if you don't have a fixed completion deadline to your project, then all is well and good, you don't need to pressurize yourself. However, if you do have a deadline in mind – real or just imagined – then you can let things slip now as animation is so time intensive that it will be very hard to catch up at the last minute.

Working against the clock! A pose test animatic frame by high school student, Caroline Li.

The ultimate objective of the *"Pre-production"* stage of any project is to put a *"***Final animatic***"* together - with your final background layouts and final **rigged** or **drawn** character key poses – which will ultimately be your "**bible**" throughout the *"Production" stage*. And if you have a real deadline to reach, then a *"***Production Schedule***"* is also something for your to aim at once the *"final animatic"* is complete. But we'll deal with that later in our *"Pre-production"* masterclasses.

All this of course is why it is so important that you don't skimp on your *"character rigging"* in any way or your drawn *"expression sheet"* that should ideally cover all the major poses and/or expressions that your character will be going through at the *"Production"* animation stage.

Animators working with rigged characters are like puppeteers.

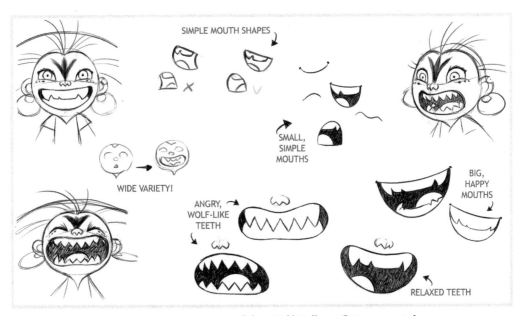

One of the many expression sheets created for *WolfWalkers*. © Cartoon Saloon Ltd., Melusine Productions.

In terms of Moho "rigging", I want to explain here the basics of how your character should be in readiness for the actual rigging process. For that actual rigging process, I would refer you to the excellent tutorials by ***McCoy Buck*** *or others* that you'll find on the **Moho website**, or the one we have at the 2D ACADEMY by Ruben Cabenda. There are other helpful tutorials out there as an alternative. However, you'll probably have to pay for those. I have rigged characters myself of course, but these online instructors are so much more experienced with the software than I. So, I would prefer to refer you on to them for *"rigging"*. The intention of this book was never to teach software anyway, just guide you through whatever you need to know to apply the things where my true teaching expertise lies – i.e. the **core principles of movement** and **production**.

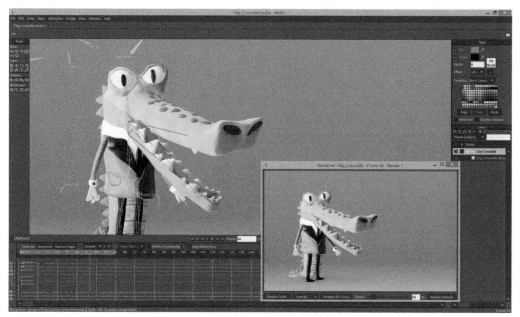

One of many great learning resources on the Moho website © Lost Marble.

In terms of correct character artwork preparation for *"rigging"* in Moho, I would suggest you need to have the following if your character is a standard "biped" character. If it is not, then again you will have to search out the best rigging tutorial that will work for your particular character design. In terms of a standard biped character, however, I want to again use my simple "**Arnie**" character here as a guideline or at least his offspring – "Arnie Jr.".

Arnie and Arnie Jr.

You can see that when broken down into his basic components, *"Arnie"* contains a "**head**", a "**neck**", a "**body**", a "**left arm**", a "**right arm**", a "**left leg**", a "**right leg**". The limbs themselves are further broken down into an *"upper arm"*, *"lower arm"* and a *"hand"* for the arms, and an *"upper leg"*, *"lower leg"* and a *"foot"* for both legs. You'll see too that the limb body parts have **curved extensions**, so they can overlap with each other at the various *joint* locations.

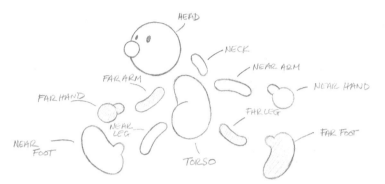

The separate body parts for Arnie Jr. note that normally the arms and legs would be broken down into upper and lower limbs too. However, for this exercise, we have avoided them to make things simple.

At this stage, they're all drawn on one sheet of paper, although to put them into Moho, they ultimately need to be broken down into separate image files that will ultimately be imported into Moho onto their own layers for rigging. You can however import this whole-page single file into Moho and then separate them into their individual layers in the program by tracing each body part onto a separate layer using the vector drawing tools.

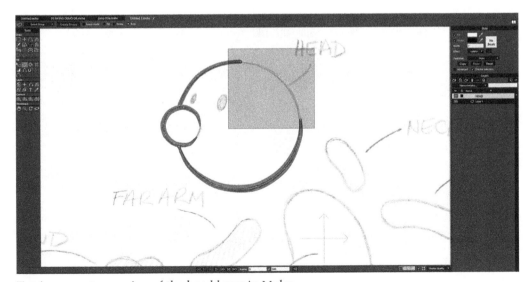

Tracing a vector version of the head layer in Moho.

Alternatively, as I usually want more of a *painted/textured* feeling to my characters, I prefer to break the body parts into separate layers outside the program, using something like *"Photoshop"*, then import those separate *bitmap/png* files into their own layers in Moho. It all depends on what kind of look you want you wany for your film's design. If you want a more *"organic"*, *"hand-crafted"*, *"texture"* feel to your project, then the Photoshop/png approach is the way to go. If you want a more *"hard line"*, *"flat color"*, *"traditional cartoon"* look, then the vector tracing approach is almost certainly a better technique for you.

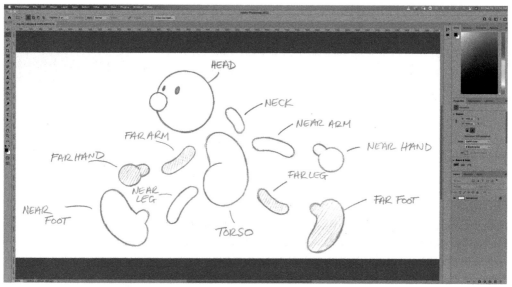

To prepare for working in Moho, start with your exploded view of Arnie Jr. in Photoshop.

If you're going with the *"Photoshop"* approach, then make sure that you keep all the body elements the same size as your full sheet design and your make the background *"clear/transparent"* before saving them as *"png"* files.

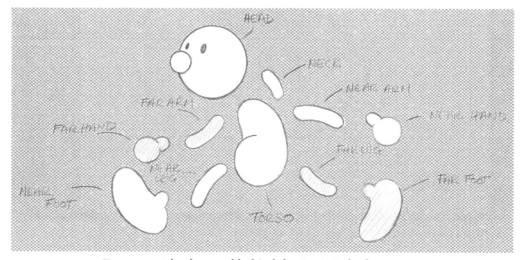

Transparent background behind the Arnie Jr. body parts.

Every *"Photoshop"* user will have their ways of creating the separate *"pngs"* or whatever other image manipulation program they prefer to use. But this is how I have always done it with my older version of *"Photoshop"*, so it might help if I share it here. I have no doubt that others may have different – maybe even better – ways of doing it in the more recent version of the program. But at least I can assure you that this way has always worked fine for me.

Let us start by saving the same body parts sheets as every induvial layer that Moho will require. So starting with the head – I go **"File/Save as"**. Then, in the folder, I allocate for my *"Arnie"* character I'm going to call it **"head"**, hit *"save"* and it's done.

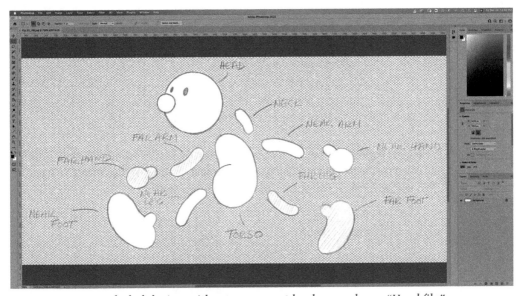

First save your exploded design with a transparent background as a "Head file".

I will now duplicate this process for ever Arnie body part, saving each full sheet as a separate body part name.

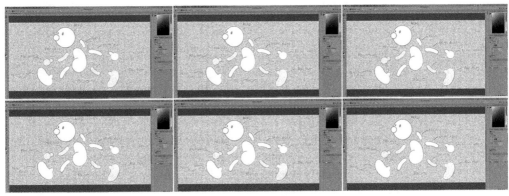

Next, save an identical version for all the other body parts – "Neck file", "Torso file", "Near Arm" file, etc., etc.

That done, I'm going to reopen my *"Head.png"* file. With the **"lasso"** selection tool, I'm going to carefully trace around just the head element on the sheet.

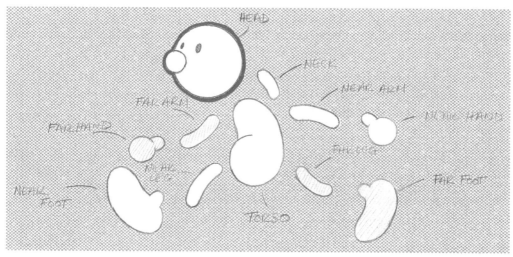

Lasso around the head alone prior to deleting.

With everything but the *"head"* selected, not go to the **"Select/Inverse"** drop-down menu, hit **"Delete"** and your file should contain just the *"Head"* image only – which is all we require for importing into Moho.

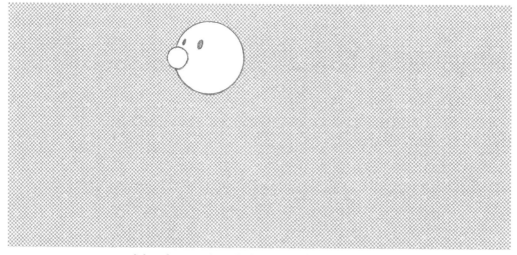

Once deleted, everything behind the object is removed, except for the body part in question – in this case, the head.

Repeat this process for all the remaining *.png files*, removing everything except the body part that the file name suggests. When complete, you should now have all your **separate color body part** images on **separate.png files**, with the backgrounds **transparent**.

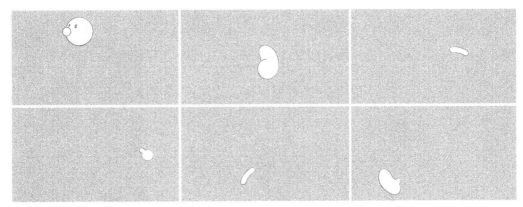

Eventually, all files will be cleared and ready to import into Moho on their own layer.

With that done, now open Moho and we'll import those separate image files into Moho layers in preparation for rigging. So, select "**Image**" on the layer menu to the right of the Moho interface.

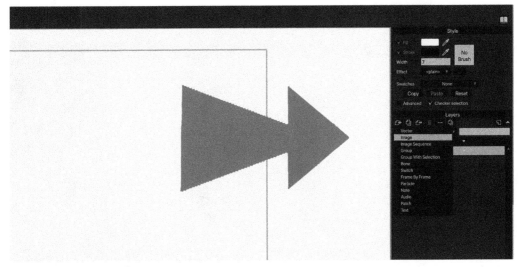

Adding a new image layer.

I'm going to call that first layer "**Head**" then browse through my saved *.png files* to find the *"Head"* one. Select it, hit "**Open**" and "**Create**". Now, with the head image imported in to Moho, on its own layer, I'm going to use the "**Transform**" tool and drag the head image to more or less the upper middle of the Moho *"stage"*.

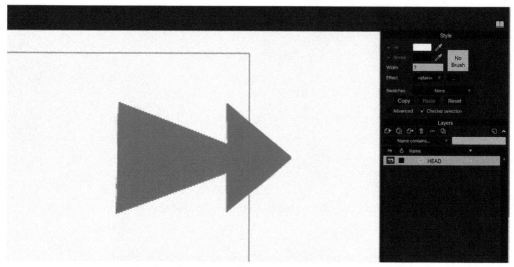

Name the first layer "Head".

Do the same thing for all the.png files, importing them into their own Moho layer, adjusting their position on the stage like this.

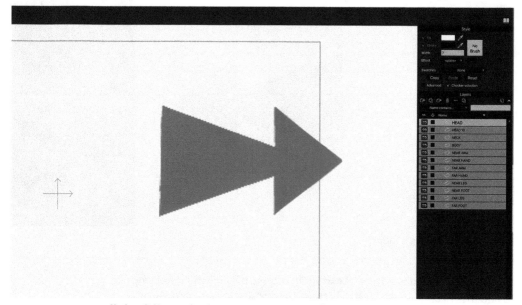

All the different body parts are now on their own layer.

You are now ready for the *"rigging"* process to begin – for which I refer you to the appropriate **online tutorials** I mentioned earlier. *(Note: Depending on which tutorial you go with for the actual "rigging", the instructor may wish you to make changes to the way you arrange your body part layers and positioning on the "stage". This is not unexpected, as every expert has their own preferred way of doing things – yours's truly included. So go along with what they say, as opposed to what I may have done differently, so that you don't get confused.)*

McCoy Buck's tutorial website at the time of writing.

The big thing about filmmaking is that it is all about **"good judgement"**, **"decision making"** and **"time management"**. Even for a personal project, you will need to make *"executive decisions"*. In other words – see what the challenge is, look at the options you have and then, at that moment decide. These things can't be taught, and I'm sure you'll make some costly bad decisions along the way. But the secret is to not panic, always save new files every time you complete something (so you can go back to the previous one later if things go wrong) and *"keep on, keeping on"*.

The latter statement may sound a little trite at first. But really, that's the only option you have when you've come this far anyway – other than giving up entirely, which none of us should ever do. The real truth of the matter is that and expert with experience only gets that way by making a million mistakes already – but perseveres and moves on regardless until they get past the challenges they face. We've all been there, so don't think that you have to be perfect from the get-go. Just keep going and have that great vision for yourself and your project in mind at all times.

Suggested Assignment

Nothing but the obvious here – get your *"rigging"* done and make sure your character does everything you need it to do for your film storyline animation. Or, complete all your *"expression model sheet"* drawings to the highest level you can. For the latter, I suggest you cover all the major *"storytelling poses"* that your project needs, so you can use them for your *"Final animatic"* soon. Moho animators will similarly pose out their rigged character(s) in all the essential project *"storytelling positions"* in their animatic too. So, just make sure you're equipped with whatever you'll need for your own project *"Final animatic"* here.

Masterclass 34/ Layout 1

We're approaching the end of the *"Pre-production"* section now, so this is a great time to follow-through and button-down what we've done so far and what we need to wrap up in preparation for the full *"Production"* stage – specifically the **animation**! For me – and hopefully for you too – that is the real fun part, when everything we have worked so far evolves into (hopefully) living, breathing characters that burst out of the screen on our production. But first we must get more specific with our *"Pre-production"* work, hopefully having covered all the bases required so far. But first, more observational gesture drawing.

Warm-Up Drawing

As this section is drawing intensive, I'm going to take pity on you and only give you one observational gesture drawing to do. It's another **"Dynamic Line"** recognition exercise. Last time, we looked at how a *"Dynamic Line"* can bring more drama and impact to an animation pose. We saw that with any powerful or dynamic pose, there is always a powerful line of action that defines the drawing and direction of the movement in that pose. So this time, we're going to take that idea one step further. The following pose contains strong dynamic lines within it. However, this time, you're required to not only observe the lines but to **EXAGGERATE** them too, as much as you can. To do this, first draw in your exaggerated *"Dynamic Lines"* and then build your character around that exaggeration – the more exaggerated the better! You should give yourself **5 minutes** to complete the drawing.

DOI: 10.1201/9781003324287-37

Comments: You will see that there's one strong and proactive *"Dynamic Line"* in this image and one secondary "Dynamic Line" in response to it. So really caricature these lines and build your poses around that. What I meant by exaggerating things – might I suggest that the guy being hit for example could have his feet much higher off the ground with the impact of the punch and the body can even be more bowed by it. The boxer inflicting the punch, however, could be pushing much further forward in their pose, with the hitting hand further pushing into the receiving boxer's face. Think old school *"Tom & Jerry"* here!

The point of doing this exercise is two-fold. One is to get you familiar with looking for those dynamic lines. These are the cornerstones, or foundations, upon which good dynamic poses are built. Therefore, if you're trying to create a strong and impactful action, you've got to fully understand the *"Dynamic Lines"* within that pose. It is only by looking at, and analyzing, the real world that you can be more effective in creating better and more impactful hidden lines within the pose. Then, the second this is that once you've identified those necessary *"Dynamic Lines"*, it is the exaggeration of what you see – not the mere photographic copying on them – that brings the real magic to your action. In that sense, we're actually **caricaturing** what we see – taking things further than they really are. That is the art of all good dynamic animation.

The evidence against the extending of live action observation can be seen with **"MoCap"** *(motion capture)* material, where actors are wired up, and their movements are recreated in a CG character environment. Unless the data are evolved by a trained animator who knows all about dynamic lines and the extending of key positions, the movement in the CG world looks wooden and dead as movement. That same was for **"Rotoscoping"** (the tracing of live action actors on film to look like 2D animation ones) when it was used in TV and movie productions in the past. The message here, of course, is that unless you push the real action beyond reality, with an animator's sensibilities, the subsequent animated action will never quite look *"real"*! So if you can learn to push your animation beyond reality, then it will definitely take your animation to the next level, hence this exercise. Try it often!

Instruction

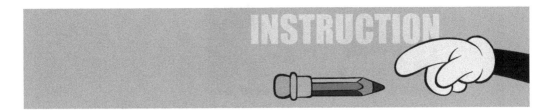

The subject of this lesson is "**Layouts**". So, what is a *"layout"*? Well, in animation production, a "layout" is a detailed, full-sized drawing that defines what each scene is visually contain and where the things in it are placed on the screen. Sometimes, a *"layout"* can be more than one drawing. For example, if parts of that scene are required to go on different layers – which is more and more common these days, then it's necessary to put all the elements on different layout drawings – including the animation and/or character, that has a *"layout"* of its own too.

Beautiful background layout drawing for *Wolfwalkers*. © Cartoon Saloon Ltd., Melusine Productions.

Layout drawings that are created, other than the bottom *"Background layout"*, are known as "**Overlay layouts**". So, a layout can be many different things for many different reasons. That said, the most common situation is to have a "**Background layout**" for everything that's behind the animation, and an "**Animation layout**" that defines where the animation is going to be seen and animated in front of the background.

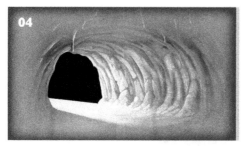

Background layout on the left and animation layout on the right.

Usually, "layouts" are highly finished drawings that reflect a storyboard drawing for any particular scene, except they are drawn full-size in terms of how large the animation is going to be created. When working with traditional hand-drawn animation, they can be drawn on two standard sizes of paper – a "**12 Field**" (i.e. 12 inches across, used many in advertising and TV productions) and a "**16 Field**" (16 inches across, used pretty much exclusively for movies).

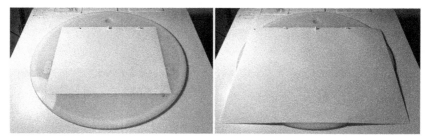

12 field paper to the left and 16 field paper to the right.

Layout drawings need to be incredibly detailed for most of the time, so that both the animator and background artist have very accurate and identical guides to work from. This will ensure that the animation, when completed, matches precisely the scale and location of the background material behind it.

Detailed city layout drawing for *Wolfwalkers*. © Cartoon Saloon Ltd., Melusine Productions.

Basically, a *"background layout"* will show what the environment behind the action is going to be like. In other words, the background painting artwork is almost certainly going to be painted precisely as the drawing is, but in color.

Another more freely drawn background layout for *Wolfwalkers*. © Cartoon Saloon Ltd., Melusine Productions.

When animated characters are going to be moving across a background, the *"animation layout"* will often show the start and end of the character' when it is moving. This informs the background artist to keep what's behind the action as simple as possible, so as not to detract from the animation by adding too much contrast or detail there in terms of painting.

Four character designs for *Wolfwalkers*. © Cartoon Saloon Ltd., Melusine Productions.

A well-trained and experienced background artist will know that the worst thing they can do is to have their background painting material clash with what's going on with the movement in front of it. So, unless otherwise directed, that background artist will keep the areas where the animation is indicated quite simple and mainly toned light or dark. They will do this as they will know the old painter's expression "**light against dark, dark against light**" – meaning that if the character is painted in light colors, the background artwork behind it needs to be tonally darker, or if the character is painted in dark colors, the background artwork behind it needs to be tonally lighter. This is why the "animation layout" has to define the action areas the character will take, so that the background artist is fully informed about it.

"Dark against light" values on a background layout on *Wolfwalkers*. © Cartoon Saloon Ltd., Melusine Productions.

Perspective

Layouts need to clarify the perspective that is needed in a shot, unless the animation is to be totally stylized with not perspective at all. There are three perspectives to consider here, "**One-point Perspective**", "**Two-point perspective**" and "**Three-point**" perspective.

One-point perspective indicates a scene where there is some perspective being used, but it only goes in one direction to a single "**vanishing point**".

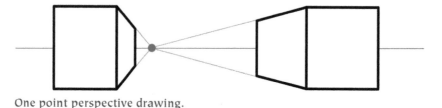

One point perspective drawing.

Two-point perspective indicates a scene where more perspective is indicated, going in two directions to two "**vanishing points**".

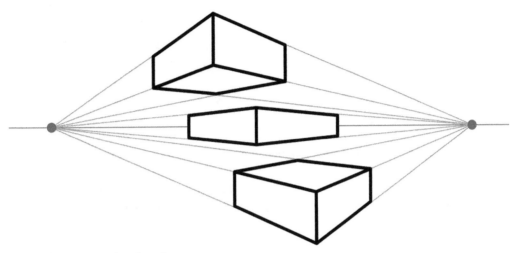

Two-point perspective drawing.

Three-point perspective indicates the most natural-looking scene of all, where the perspective is indicated in three directions, using three "**vanishing points**".

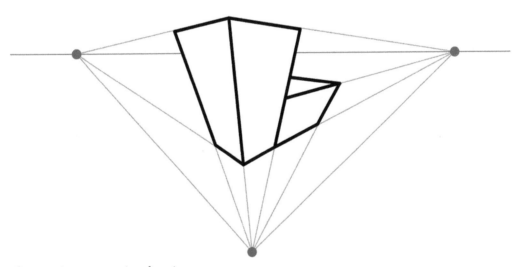

Three-point perspective drawing.

For a first production, you are advised to keep everything as simple as possible with your layouts. It's quite possible that you'll use perspective but keep the angles and details as basic as possible, as to animation in extreme perspectives is a challenge for any animator – experience or otherwise. As long as you give enough detail for yourself to know what's going on, then to animate to that with as few challenges as possible, then you will have done well!

Suggested Assignment

Before finalizing your production layouts, you are advised to research how great artists in the creative and animation world approach graphic beauty, perspective and the treatment of light in their final work. All these things should have a bearing on the way you draw your layouts and the stylistic look they have.

Masterclass 35/ Anatomy of a Sequence

Now this lesson is really a complimentary one following the lesson on *"Layouts"*. It offers an "**Anatomy of a Sequence**" from the film I am currently working on as I write this, *The Hermit*. It will take you a little bit further on from the *"Pre-production"* material you're working through right now, but it will give you an insight on a personal production that covers some of the ground we've been dealing with and some of the ground I've relied after over 50 years working as a professional. Ultimately, you will find your own way of making projects beyond this, but I still urge you to follow the standard practices we're covering in this book. But first, our observational gesture drawing exercise.

Warm-Up Drawing

As I'm sure that you're more that busy with getting all your layouts and everything else completed before the end of this section, so here is another "quickie" that will be valuable as a warm-up/learning drawing exercise, but shouldn't pre-occupy too much of your time and energies in the process. In my class, I use it as an "ab lib" assignment – where it's impact on the class time is minimal as my student push through their layouts on their project, but nevertheless, it exercises minds and drawing hands at the onset of the class. Although it is a *5-minute* exercise, it is broken down into a sequence of **five images** – each of which you should time yourself out at **1 minute each**. Also, instead of us drawing a human

DOI: 10.1201/9781003324287-38

figure for this one, I thought I'd build it around a **cat** because they're action-crazy anyway and almost everyone loves cats. (Well, at least according to their popularity on social media!)

As we did with earlier *sequential* exercises, draw from **left to right** and try to get all your poses **onto the same page** in your sketchbook.

Comments: So, start with the first position on the left and work your way across. Note how the cat's body twists in the air, with shoulders and hips counter postal for much of the time. Capture structurally the spirit of the cat's form and posture rather than a photographic representation of it. And don't forget to push, even caricature, the positions as you go! Exaggeration is always good for active animation poses!

Apart from this exercise, we are not at all dealing with the movement of animals or creatures or even fantasy characters in this book. However, remember always that the "core principles of movement" are common to all characters and objects, so you can adapt them to virtually everything – although with quadrupeds, or more, you will have to double and treble your skills of observation and interpretation as you go. Always, but always, go to Nature to research whatever you're doing. As I've said before, if you have to animate a dragon, then go to pictures and videos of similar reptiles to understand how they move. The anatomy of a dragon will – in part at least – be comparable to lizards and other critters we have on Earth. So, utilize them as your reference point – and always be "plausible in your implausibility" as you both design and animate characters we have never seen before. Innovation is always welcome in animation although it should always be underpinned by all the principles of movement we have discussed in this book.

Instruction

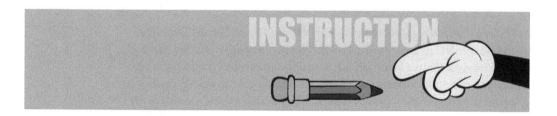

It is almost a recap of what we've covered already, but let me talk briefly about how I created this sequence for my film *"The HERMIT"*.

The first thing I started with, apart from the script of course – which was more in my head than down on paper at first – was the "**soundtrack**". We of course have to have a soundtrack for 99% of the films we make, so this one very much needed one too. This forced me to put the ideas in my head down on paper, as the voice artist had to be able to read a script of some kind. The actor in question I found on a website called *"Voices"*. There you listen to many audition tape then either approach the actors you have heard and like or else you can post it as an open audition, for anyone to contribute readings to. You don't get a final reading of your script that way, but however you approach it, you do get recorded responses that help you make decisions. You can also post a price you're willing to pay for them to record your script – as well as clarifying the word count and length of your script – and some actors might decline auditioning if you go too low, or they are just too busy. On the other hand, this really does give you economy options if you can get your recording done for less than the usual industry rate. It's a win-win situation really, as you will get a professional level recording for a lower price and the actor will get paid for something that they normally wouldn't come across. Sometimes, you can even be surprised at how an actor reads a script that your wrote and yet you didn't hear it in your head the way they deliver it. Often this is a very nice surprise – at other times, not. But, suffice it to say, with *"The HERMIT"* I got a wonderful reading from a really nice professional voice artist, *Richard Morrison*.

The Hermit title.

With my audio track recorded, I set about creating my "**thumbnail storyboard**". My usual process is to use *yellow Post-It notes* and that is what I did this time.

I find that roughly drawing out quick storyboard ideas on yellow sticky notes is the most convenience and adaptable way of blocking out story action there is.

If I were creating this project for a client I would still rough out my ideas, story-board-wise, on *yellow sticky notes* – as these are so easy and fast to work with. The beauty of them is that being tear-off sticky, I can quickly scribble down my ideas on to each sheet, stick them to a wall and juggle them around (or replace them) instantly until I got the sequence exactly as I wanted it. (Note: I'm in good company here, as this is really how storyboarding began way back when Walt Disney first invented the process at the very beginning of his animated movie journey.) Anyway, in terms of working for a client, I would then do a much bet-ter *cleaned up* version of my storyboard for presentation purposes. However, in working for myself on my own film, I was an easy client to please and the sticky note approach was all I needed!

I find that it is so easy to arrange – and rearrange – your sticky note storyboard on any convenient nearby wall to assess the bigger storytelling picture.

For the *"The HERMIT"* sequence, I had four basic scenes in it. Initially, the first scene was the opening "establishing shot". It is an "extreme wide shot" that shows down in the lower left-hand part of the screen a town. From that town, there's a long winding path that leads up to a mountain top cave.

The original mountain landscape background inked artwork.

The main character – I call him *"The Seeker"* – was originally storyboarded as walking along the path. However, I didn't like that when I saw the animation, so I dropped the animation and just let the camera move tell the story for me.

I initially had the Seeker character walking with a staff but changed it later to without a staff as I thought he looked too old for the storyline with it.

The next shot, where the seeker reaches the cave, shows that it's incredibly dark inside. So, I made sure the extreme blackness was visible inside.

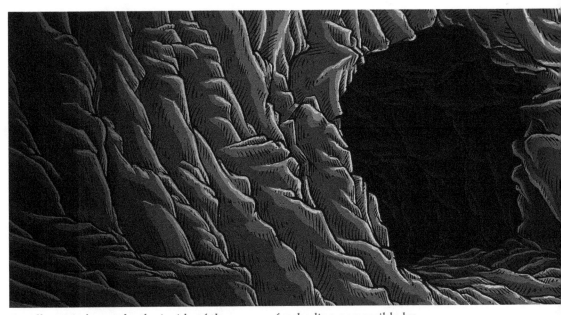

Tonally, I tried to make the inside of the cave as foreboding as possible by highlighting the contrast between the darkness inside and the light outside.

The final scene in the sequence is viewed from inside the cave, when *"The Seeker"* nervously enters. I had established that the outside of the cave was very muted and desaturated in color, when "The Seeker" fully enters the cave, it turns in to brighter and virulent colors, even though it is generally a place of darkness for him until his eyes adjust.

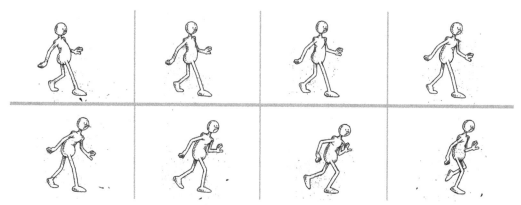

To give a sense of the Seeker nervously entering the cave, I gave the character a kind of sneak walking action – and even added random ink splats to give it a disruptive visual quality.

Next, when *"The Seeker"* meets *"The Hermit"* – a strange and unworldly figure – we are not sure if this is a good meeting or a bad one. It is almost like a Western film standoff.

I didn't have the Seeker and the Hermit meeting face-to-face initially. Instead, I had this more foreboding shot of the Hermit in profile, lifting his lantern, in the scene preceding the actual meeting.

We then see a close-up profile shot of *the Hermit*, and we hopefully get the impression that he is a good and wise figure.

The final dark and foreboding close-up shot of the Hermit looked like this.

The whole idea was to have the sequence begin as a faded, desaturated medieval woodcut print and then, as we move into the cave of *"The Hermit"* the color would intensify and change as color is brought into the world of *"The Seeker"*. As an allegory, it is somewhat reflective of the experience I have had in my own life, as my developing *graphic novel memoirs* will ultimately show.

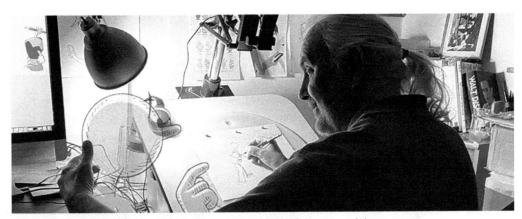

My animated memoirs project features a day in my life, as my life memories are told in that day. Set entirely around my animation lightbox, my model and muse, Arnie, interacts with me in the form of flashbacks, as I create animation for *The Hermit*.

The removal of *"The Seeker"* from the pathway to the cave is evidence that, many times, you have ideas in your mind that just don't work out on the screen when you see them playing out in real time. That is why it is **SO** necessary to do a rough *"storyboard animatic"*, or *"final animatic"* to test your ideas out. Now the truth of the matter is that I actually didn't practice what I preach – in the sense that I didn't do it myself with this sequence! Instead, I thought I knew better and stormed into the animation without testing out the idea. However, it just didn't work out when I saw it on the screen and I learned a costly lesson that I should have known better. This is precisely why I am emphasizing these things to you in the book, giving you my own bitter experience in the hope that you will avoid such errors yourself.

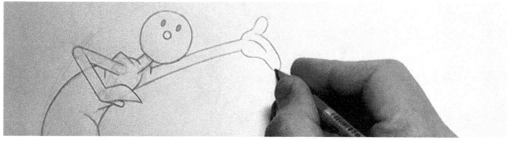

Drawing out my storyboard animatic.

In fact, as a result of my arrogant misjudgment I ended up exploring an entirely new idea that actually worked better – so all was not actually lost. I decided that it would be really cool if we had the camera looking down in a "close-up" and just focusing on the feet of "The Seeker" as he walks along the path.

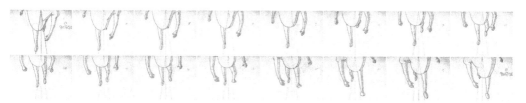

Seeker's legs, as looking down shot, shot on "1s".

In addition, I wanted to imply that time was passing on his long journey. So, I had the shadow from his legs and feet rotating around him on the path – as if 24 hours in the day were passing around him as he was walking. I even added a feeling of sunrise, midday, sunset and nighttime to the coloring, to emphasize that much time was passing.

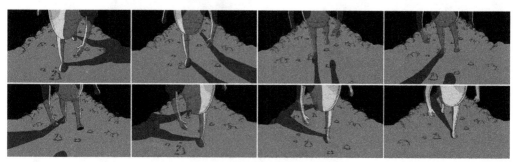

Note the rotating shadow on the legs.

Then, I even animated the ground under his fee to show that distance was being covered too.

Inking the background animation drawings with a traditional dip ink pen.

All of this of course was a huge amount of work and is some ways a bit of an indulgence. By I am never shy of taking on hard work if that is the way it needs to be to make the scene the best it can be. Needless to say, in posting it as *"work in progress"* on my social media sites, others really complemented me on it, so I knew it was the right thing to do.

👍❤️ ~~Robert Stevens~~, ~~Susan Smith~~ and 151 others   8 Comments 1 Share

👍 Like   💬 Comment   ↗ Share

It's always a good sign if the "likes" go higher than normal when you post your work!

As indicated earlier, I just used a *"extreme wide shot"* camera move to show the journey up into the mountains, toward the cave. This was no longer my *"establishing shot"*, as the preceding *"close-up"* shot of the walking feet of *"The Seeker"* became that. But it was very effecting in transiting time and space to advance us in the story in a very short amount of time.

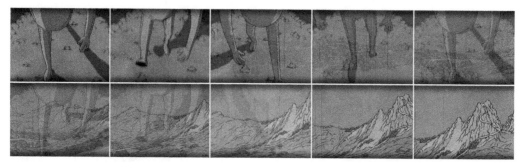

Ten frames or a much longer dissolve transition from Scene 1 to Scene 2.

Although I animated the opening walking scene for the love of it – and to specu-latively explore if the idea worked in terms of a concept – I did actually test the rest of it without animation, just as an *"storyboard animatic"*. I was relieved to find it worked and gave me a great of filmic timing, which would be valuable in knowing how much animation I would need to do for each scene.

Initial storyboard animatic version of above, connected by a rough "dissolve" symbol.

I did the final *"layouts"* for each scene as I approached them. Being my own cli-ent on this one, I had that luxury. Normally, all the final layouts would be done together and a *"final, polished animatic"* would be presented to the client.

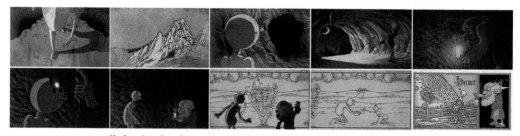

All the final color scenes of "Sequence 1" of the Hermit animatic.

From each final layout I would pencil-animate the animation roughly, then test it by capturing and rendering it out as a *"pencil test"*. The *"pencil test"* would be ed-ited in to my *"storyboard animatic"*, replacing the existing storyboard footage. That gave me a chance to test the timing and continuity of my animation, before I cleaned up and colored it.

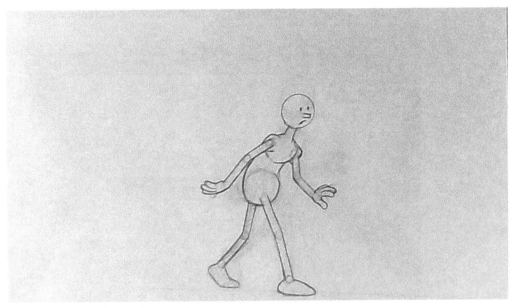

Frame from pencil test of Scene 3 animation.

Slowly, I managed to get all my pencil test scenes animated for the sequence and when they were edited in, changed and polished, they worked well. So then I committed myself to inking the animation drawings onto a fresh sheet of paper.

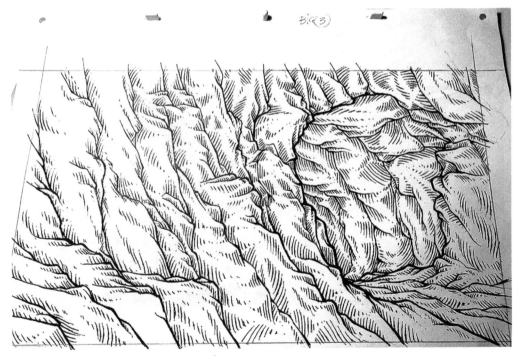

The final inked cave entrance artwork.

Then they could be scanned into my computer for coloring and compositing.

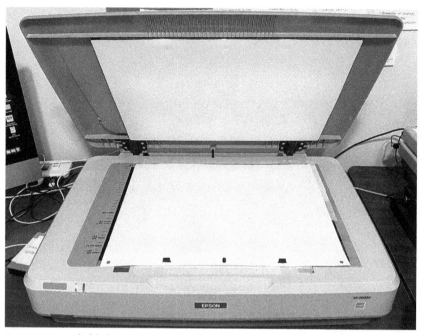

Scanning 16-field drawings on my large scanner.

For coloring and compositing, I used my old (and sadly now defunct) *"ToonBoom Studio"* software. I love that software for most of what I do in fact and very much miss it's passing, as I always loved to teach my students using it, and having them use it too! Anyway, for *"The HERMIT"*, I thought it did a great job.

"ToonBoom Studio" – gone, but never forgotten!

One point of interest in terms of the animation was something I did for the first interior cave shot – where *"The Seeker"* entered the cave and saw *"The HERMIT"* (off camera) for the first time. I wanted to imply that he was nervous. So, when he stopped walking in the cave and stared into the darkness, I animated his **knees knocking**.

The three drawings I used for the knees knocking action.

To get a *"knees knocking"* effect is quite easy. Basically it is two drawings – one with the knees bending inward and the other with the knees bending outward. The rest of the body is a **"traceback"** – which means it is not moving with the body of one leg drawn tracing perfectly the body of the other legs drawing. These were alternated on **2s** when capture onto video, giving a great (yet very simple to do) knees knocking effect.

Showing the two drawing areas being traced back from the final key inked drawing at the end.

I hope this very brief anatomy of a sequence in my film was useful to read as you approach the end of the *"Pre-production"* stage of your project? It is not a large sequence and is only a very small part of what will ultimately be a 26-minute TV Special. But I think it gives you an understanding of process and how arrogance – or the removal your eye from the ball at any stage – can create more work than you needed to do! Remember that we never stop learning as animators, not even if you've had a 50-year journey in the world of animation and are still travelling and learning!

Suggested Assignment

No big instruction here – other than to say that you must finish your layouts to the best of your ability, in preparation for your *"final animatic"* creation.

Masterclass 36/ Final Pose Test Animatic

Well, here we are, the last stage of the *"Pre-production"* process! If you followed faithfully all through stages in this section of the book and complete this final, simple lesson, you should be well placed to be about to launch into the animation *"Production"* stage of your project. It's no doubt felt like a long haul since you turned the first page of this book. But if you've followed through on everything conscientiously and to the best of your ability, then you'll now be very well equipped – using the extensive knowledge you've acquired thus far – to complete the rest of this coursework with significant skills. But first, you need to complete your "**Final Pose Test Animatic**", before which – as with all of our lessons – we need to tackle observational gesture drawing.

Warm-Up Drawing

Being that you're going to be starting the *"Production"* stage of your project in the next lesson, which inevitably means you'll be leading up to the most enjoyable part as far as I'm concerned – *"animation"* – I want to return to the gesture drawing theme we've done before, "**Pose & Silhouette**". To remind you, we said that it is fundamentally important that artists and animators create visual images or poses that are strong and readable. This is particularly true for animation keys,

DOI: 10.1201/9781003324287-39

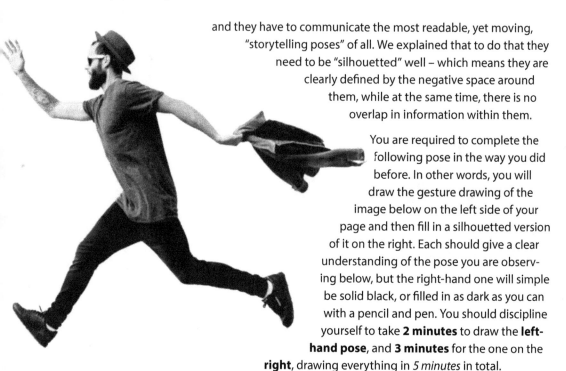

and they have to communicate the most readable, yet moving, "storytelling poses" of all. We explained that to do that they need to be "silhouetted" well – which means they are clearly defined by the negative space around them, while at the same time, there is no overlap in information within them.

You are required to complete the following pose in the way you did before. In other words, you will draw the gesture drawing of the image below on the left side of your page and then fill in a silhouetted version of it on the right. Each should give a clear understanding of the pose you are observing below, but the right-hand one will simple be solid black, or filled in as dark as you can with a pencil and pen. You should discipline yourself to take **2 minutes** to draw the **left-hand pose**, and **3 minutes** for the one on the **right**, drawing everything in *5 minutes* in total.

Comments: So, here is a good *silhouetted* pose from a profile viewpoint. Stretched out profile views are the best views of all to ensure there is a good silhouette to the pose, although of course that's not always possible with animation. Here though, you have an opportunity to recognize "Dynamic Lines" in action too. So sketch them in fast, then exaggerate or caricature the pose to make it as extreme as possible. Do likewise with the pose on the right, which should be drawn separate and is not just a tracing of the one you first drew on the left. This in some ways will give you an opportunity to exaggerate both in different ways, although the one on the right will be in black silhouette only. Nevertheless, both should read extremely well once you have completed them.

Obviously, not every pose you draw in animation can be silhouetted. If you're working in a games-based, 3D world – or even in a drawn 2D world at times – there will be many moments when your character rotates and is seen from many different angles from the pure profile view. However, you want to make sure that most of your poses, as best as you can, have a strong silhouette to them – or if you can make them entirely silhouetted, certainly the object of the action, prop or gesture, is silhouetted to the audience as much as possible. The worst thing you can do is place the prop or animate the gesture directly in front of the body when you do so. Try to rotate the body somewhat, so that the silhouette of the prop is away from it and therefore more visible whenever you can. As I say, you can't do this 100% of the time, but do so as much as you can to make your visual storytelling as strong as possible by differentiating it well from the rest of the body.

Instruction

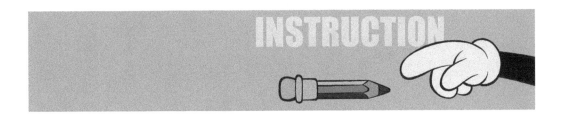

Hopefully, the following won't be too difficult if you're kept up with the pace of the "Pre-production" lessons so far. Now, as you're working on your own project, with not help and you're out of a studio situation, you can only blame yourself if you're not ready for this stage. If you are, then I'm sure that you're going to make a great job of the "Production" stage as you will have already posed and answered all the necessary production challenges you're likely to meet when animating. Hopefully you will have made good decisions with all this, although only you will know. But at least it will be you who have made the decisions and no one else!

In a studio situation, there will be many more people making decisions along the way – the bigger the studio, the more others will have a say. There's an old production saying that states, "A camel is a horse made by committee!" This means that everyone wants to have a say, and only the strongest and most powerful of directors is able to withstand the volume of opinions thrown at them. Sometimes it can be the fellow members of the production team only. But more often than not it is *clients*, *investors*, *distributors* and even *accountants* and *CEOs* who all try to chip in with their 10 cents worth, and you can often have a battle on your hands as most of them are not creatively capable of making good decisions on your behalf. Fortunately, you won't be in that position in the here and now, so take advantage of your independence because the more you work your way up the industry ladder, the less control you are likely to have over the entire project.

So for now, you need to focus on the core essentials you'll need to decide upon before you jump into *"Production"*. Compared with some of the *"Pre-production"* lessons we have had to deal with so far, the work here is reasonably simple from a practical point of view. On the other hand, it can also be somewhat deceptive under the surface, when it comes to final decision-making. I am talking about you putting together here your final "**Pose Test Animatic**". Essentially, this means editing together your *"background layouts"* with your *"animation layouts"* and timing them out to your *"final audio track"*. On the surface, this seems straightforward enough. But you'll soon see that when it is all edited together and running in real time, there might be *timing*, *action* or *continuity* issues that will need your further attention.

Decisions!
Decisions!

Rough frame from *Wolfwalkers*. © Cartoon Saloon Ltd., Melusine Productions.

As we work through the next *"Production"* section of the book, I will do a quick refresher on certain things you should bear in mind when you start to animate. But now let's go over just a few things you'll need to wrap up the *"Pre-production"* stage of your project. I'm of course referring to your *"Key Pose Animatic"*, although I would remind you that you will need to have your **turnaround module sheets**, your **"expression sheets"** and your **"audio breakdown"** material too. Alternatively, if you're working in *Moho*, you will also need to have your **character**(s) **rigged** and working. But for the here and now, you'll simply need your **"animation layout"**, your **"background layout"**, you **"audio track"** and a reliable **"film editing program"** to put everything together for your animatic.

Storyreels or Animatics?

Terminology can differ from the UK to the USA in terms of some things - Joanna Quinn.

It might help if I mention here that throughout this book I've been talking about *"animatics"* for pretty much everything. However, in certain places within the industry, such as at big studios like *Pixar*, for example, they can use the term "**Storyreels**" instead. FYI: These are both the same thing for all intents and purposes. Both are basically a storyboard captured on film and edited to the soundtrack. They both give a sense of the structure, storytelling and visual content of the film, running in real time with the sound. Traditionally, the term *"animatic"* has been used that way in the past – although the very early Disney animation studio called it the "**Leica Reel**". It has only been more recent times that the term *"Storyreel"* came into popular use. But I am very much a member of the old school – adhering to the old term, *"if it ain't broke then don't fix it"*. Consequently therefore, I will continue to use the word *"animatic" although I won't be offended if you prefer to use the name "storyreel"*.

Consensus is valuable – although it's always important to keep your own vision if you feel strongly enough.

The major thing to realize with your *"Final Pose Test Animatic"* is that you are effectively creating a fixed template upon which the rest of your film will be based. The poses you use here, the timings of the shots and the continuity of drawings – everything you decide upon here – will determine precisely how you animate and construct your film from this moment on. It is my strongest advice that this stage that once you go into production you **DON'T CHANGE ANYTHING**. So the decisions you make now will last until the end. So make sure the final version you come up with for your *"Final Pose Test Animatic"* is the very best you can make it. It really is worth the effort, although I'm sure you're chafing at the bitt to move on to your animation at this stage!

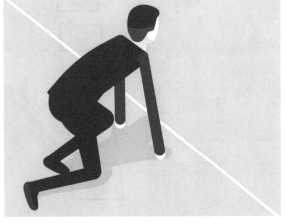

You're just about now on the starting line.

I think therefore, as you're wrapping up the "Pre-production" of your film, you should impartially ask yourself the following questions about your *"Final Pose Test Animatic"*. They are fundamental to the success, or not, of your project. So really be brave on your decision-making here. Indeed, I would urge you to be truly courageous and show it to others for their opinions too. I know you'll be scared that they'll maybe throw a whole load of objections and changes at you and that you'll have to make changes to everything we've been working through. But it honestly is better to hear the truth now than when you've gone through the far more intensive and emotionally demanding *"Production"* stage and find it all gets a poor reaction. So, dare to show your *"Final Pose Test Animatic"* to others for their honest opinions. It is your last chance after all. (And don't just send it to family and close friends – who tend to say the right thing and not hurt your feelings. Better to show it to instructors, industry professionals and complete strangers if you can manage it.)

Maybe give them a questionnaire to fill in too, so they don't have to speak their truth on your face. These kinds of things are so easy to set up on the internet these days, so you don't even have to meet them! But it is so important to the well-being of your film that I think it's at least worth the effort at this stage. Ultimately, you don't have to act on everything they say, but is a theme consistently emerges through a number of opinions, and then, there may well be something in it and you would be smart to act upon it before you animated everything.

It can be nerve-wracking to show your work to anyone!

The more objective feedback you can get at this stage, the better the final outcome will be.

Is the Timing Right?

Of course, you'll have done your very best to ensure your timing is good. You did do a *"Storyboard Animatic"* after all, and this version is no doubt based on that version. However, now, you've gone through a much more detailed version of that original storyboard, creating precise layouts that represent your ideas; it might give you're a slightly different reading on your original ideas. Timing is everything, and you might want to look at that anew; now, you're looking at precisely how your film will be seen, without the animation of course. For example, if your film is based on a music track, then consider if all the cuts from scene to scene, or all the main movements of your key pose drawings are in perfect choreographed sync? Remember that anticipating a major audio sound by anything from two to eight frames can make the difference between a scene cut being perfectly timed and feeling a little bit late. With music I like to make my scene cuts on the beat, as it seems to work best that way. So consider that for your film, if you are working with music – or even impactful sound effects at any point. Cuts on the beat feel sharp and intended, but cuts at various places between the beats feel sloppy or mistakes to me. It's a personal directorial decision of course, but one that can make or break your film.

Your animation will always look stronger if you can hit the action on the beat as much as possible.

Is the Staging Right?

Again, try to look at the way you've set your scenes up, including the way your character or characters appear in the scene. Have you made the best decisions possible? Would one shot look more impressive with a low horizon line, whereas another might deliver a better message with a higher horizon line. All good things to question before sign off on your *"Final Pose Test Animatic"*. With digital technology, it is so easy to modify images these days, so if you decide to move an horizon up and down for example, you can do that very easily in *Photoshop* or a similar software program.

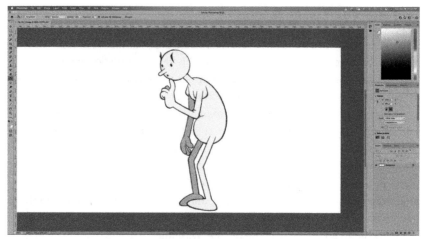

Photoshop, or other image manipulation software, is great for working out your final staging problems.

Even if you don't want to draw something and find that it's better to change an horizon line up and down, leaving a big, white blank area at the top or bottom on the scene's background.

Notice how the elevation of the horizon can give a different impression in the shot. For example, a lower horizon gives the character more strength and authority, whereas a higher horizon does not.

Try to miss anything at this stage. If you do, it will come back to bite you later!

Then, don't worry as this film is no doubt for you alone, so if you can live with it there are no repercussions. Ultimately, it means you're going to have a far better film at the end of the *"Production"* stage. So be vigilant or critical with everything you done, then be brave if you need to be!

Is the Continuity Right?

Next, check out the continuity your created. With final layouts, making up your *"Final Pose Test Animatic"* lapses in continuity can be more obvious. Clearly, *"action"* continuity will be the most apparent mistakes you might make.

For example, if a character is moving from left to right across one scene, then from right to left in the scene immediately after that, you might want to reverse one of the scene direction immediately. It will stand out more when you have more flowing animation out there, so any lapses like this right now will be even more apparent later.

Don't drop the button by not attending to the details at this point.

Double-check also that there is no *"crossing the line"* with characters in the middle of a sequence. If so, rework it – or even throw in a *"cut-away shot"* at the relevant part to distract the audience from the error. They can save the day, even when everything is animated and you notice the error for the first time!

Always make sure you understand what side of the line your character is on before you start animating it!

Is the Scaling Right?

Finally, check that if you're using more than one character, then the scaling between them is correct. For example, if you establish your characters with one being short and the other tall, make sure that those are consistently that way throughout your film. If they suddenly appear the same height, or if the "eyeline" of one character in "close-up" is not consistently looking up or down to the other character that is off-screen, then adjust that too.

Size matters – especially if the height continuity of your characters are wrong!

Check also that the volume of your characters is consistent throughout. If you have a big, bulky character, double-check that they are that way in all of the scenes they appear in, not just some. The same applies to the size and volume of the limbs in your character.

Avoid "zombie" drawings where the sizes and volumes of your character are all out of scale. The results can be monstrous!

All these things are extremely important for the well-being of your film at this final stage of the *"Pre-production"* process. Remember that there are terribly eagle-eyed – even nitpicky – critics out there who delight in jumping on the errors of others. So, it's worth nailing these things right now, before you animate, unless of course you don't mind your film being trashed across the multiple social platforms we have to embrace these days. My English grandmother used to say to me when I was a child, *"Take care of the pennies and the pounds will take care of themselves"*. Likewise I would say to you, "**Take care of the details now and your film will ultimately take care of itself**"!

I've never forgotten the wisdom of age that both my grandparents gave me!

This really is your last chance to mop up any omissions or edited errors that you may have made, so don't be remiss about it. That said, once all is done and battened down with your *"Final Key Pose Animatic"*, you stand at the starting line of the best part of the whole production – the *"animation"* stage! Bon voyage! Have a save trip! And create the finest film project you are capable of with all the knowledge and material you have got through so far!

Suggested Assignment

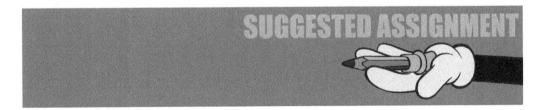

I'm sure you've done everything you can by now to ensure the *"Production"* stage of your project will be a perfect and error-free it possibly could be. So how can I ask you to do more than I have? Perhaps the only thing I can say right now is to walk away from everything for a week or so, gather your energies afresh, and they return to the "animation" stage energized and raring to go!

PERSONAL PROJECT – PRODUCTION

Making the dream a reality.

DOI: 10.1201/9781003324287-40

Masterclass 37/ Key Pose Animation 1

So here we go, the big moment, where you're about to animate your own project in your own style! (I would have a fanfare at this point, but it's not an audio book!) I call it the "fun" part, although you're still going to have to work really hard to get all your animation done – but in a different way. And I really hope that you will make a huge success of it, as I see you as the future of the industry – going into the exciting digital age with technology evolving all the time – but as well-trained and knowledgeable animators in your own right. This is not true of many colleges or courses out there, they just teach the software, and that holds their students (and the industry) back in the process. So move forward with confidence, as you are fully equipped to do some amazing work if you have kept up with all the assignments in this book so far. With a really good film under your belt, you will be ahead of most of the college or industry entry competition for sure, if that is your intention.

We're going to start this last leg of the journey – *"Lesson 1"* in *"Section IV"* of this book – by doing initial **"Animation Blocking"**. We will be continuing this theme by talking about it in *"Lesson 2"* as well. But first, we should still not neglect observational gesture drawing.

Warm-Up Drawing

This drawing assignment relates perfectly to the *"Animation Blocking"* theme we're going to deal with in a minute. It is called **"Emotional Poses"**. As a

DOI: 10.1201/9781003324287-41

professional, traditional, hand-drawn animator, you will be required to accurately draw a number of different characters throughout your career. You will then
be required to create a great number of poses and gestures with these characters, expressing their mood or the emotion nature of the scene they're in. In
this particular drawing exercise, you will be required to do both! Below, there
is the image of a single character on the left-hand side of the screen, together with four empty boxes. In your mind, divide a page of your own sketchbook
like this.

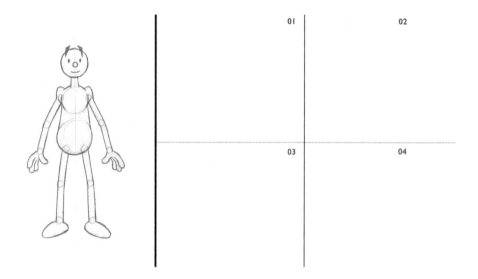

On the left, you will do the gesture drawing of the character above, as normal.
Then, you need to fill in the other four drawing areas with a different "**emotional**" pose in each imagined area. To do this, you should give yourself **3 minutes**
to draw the main character and then **2 minutes** each for the remaining emotional versions of it. The emotions you need to display with the other 4 versions
are "**happy**", "**sad**", "**excited**" and "**fearful**".

Comments: In all your drawings, try as best you can to keep the character
drawing consistent throughout. Make sure that proportions, volumes and
sizes are compatible across the board. This is the kind of thing you will need
to do when animating a character in a scene, so this really is a good warm-
up exercise for you right now. Although this is a hand-drawn exercise here,
every animator, of all styles, will need to learn how to communicate emotions in their characters, simply by attitude and body language. So, that is
why it is important for all animators to keep a sketchbook with them at all
times. You'll never know when you'll see something out of the ordinary – are
even relevant to your current project – that is worth sketching down in your
sketchbook.

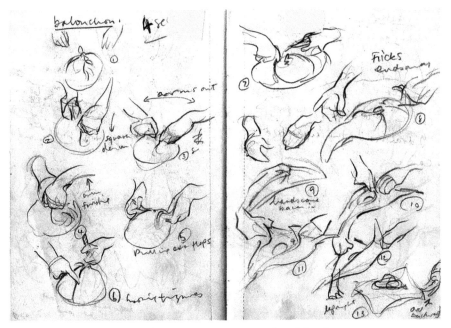

Pages of action reference from Joanna Quinn's sketchbook.

You may not need it for a long while, but there will be a time when you'll find the observational sketch you did as valuable, and you will be grateful for taking the time to do it. It's a very good exercise for getting away from the standard, predictable, cliché things that many animators do in this situation. All these are reasons why this assignment here is a good one.

Instruction

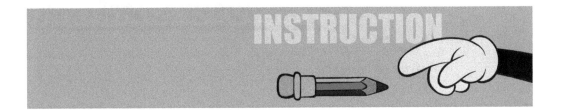

There are specific stages in this *"Production"* section that I want you to go through stage by stage. Your inclination right now is to jump straight into your first scene and animate it. However, that approach is fraught with dangers for the inexperience, so I'm going to talk you through the various *"Production"* stages, one by one, so that we're sure you're going to emerge at the end with a film we can all be proud of – and with not wasted work, which could happen if you jump right into the deep end from the get-go.

My current home-based production studio setup.

Now, let us accept up front that everyone working through this book is going to have different challenges ahead of them, at this stage. No two stories will be alike. No two characters will be alike. And no directorial decisions will be alike. So, in taking you through the following stages of *"Production"*, you will have to modify what I say into the needs of your own particular project. That said, I am **strongly recommending** that you do adhere to the stages of the process that I'm outlining for you, even though you might all interpret them differently.

Trust me on this one!

"Blocking out" your key positions is essential to ensuring your animation turns out the best it can be, without you wasting a lot of time working on inbetweens that, no matter how good and how accurate they may be, will not make your animation any better if your *"key positions"* are not right. So here and now, we're going to ensure you have the best *"key positions"* you can possible have before even thinking about inbetweens – whether you're creating them through drawing or through *Moho*, or any other digital program you may be using.

Blocked out walk poses in Moho.

References

Remember that it is OK to use reference as you create your *"key poses"*, if you can. I would 110% recommend that. Wherever you can look at research, look at reference. Work out the kind of poses you want for your character and do observational sketches of them in your sketchbook. It doesn't matter if the characters you are referencing are not exactly like your animation character, just as long as the action pose is close to what you want to do.

If you can't find the right reference, pose it yourself! Student observational drawing assignment, with myself as model.

Ideally, you should draw your reference poses from real life if you can. But if not, go to *"Google Images"* to *"YouTube"* to find picture or video references that can help you draw your poses. However, it's really important that you do your homework on this as the more you put into an effort, the more you will get out of it. I have proven this to myself over and over again in my career, so I'm very strong on animators doing as much drawn referencing as they can. The great Richard Williams used to sketch out his thumbnail pose ideas down the side of his *"exposure sheet"* and then draw them up into full-size poses using visual references. And don't neglect the great resources that your local library offers you. Quite often there are books with pictures in them that have never been scanned into Google or any other online image archive.

Never underestimate the value of books and libraries in your research!

Stages of Animation

As I said earlier, it is probably a big temptation to jump in and bulldoze through your animation, scene by scene, right now. But it would be a mistake. The best animation is created in stages, namely, "**blocking**", "**breakdown positions**", "**inbetweening**", "**clean-up**", "**inking**" and "**coloring**". Some of this can be doubled-up on, or completed more easily digitally in some cases. However, don't underestimate the amount of work that lies ahead if you want your animation to look really good. Don't forget either, the finished "**background artwork**" needs to be completed too – and before, it is finally composited with the final animation and rendered to video!

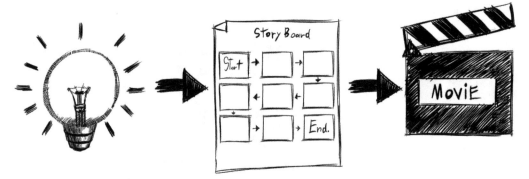

The animation production process is not quite that simple, but you should know all about it by the end of this book!

Now, let's go through all this in a little bit more detail to explain what they mean.

Animation Blocking: This is the stage of animation where you *"block out"* all your key poses. Remember that a *"key pose"* is a major establishing, or turning point, with your character's movement. "Blocking" plots out pretty much all of your intended "key pose" actions and should even involve you shooting a preliminary *"pose test animatic"* when they are done – to see whether your poses are working for each scene in question.

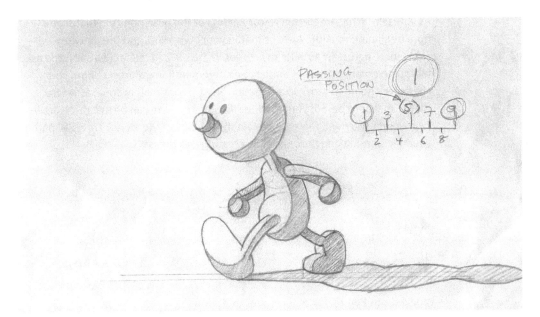

The first frame of a walking sequence, blocked out on the screen.

The most important thing here is that you work out in a scene in your head before drawing anyway. Thumbnail sketches can help.

Thumbnails of blocked out poses on 12Field paper.

As yourself, "What are the main story points or the pose points in that scene from beginning to end?" Answer that in your own mind, and the drawings will come more naturally. As with any stories, there's a *"beginning"* (we call it the establishing point), a *"middle"* and an *"end"*. From its initial starting point, your character's going to move in a direction and then ultimately arrive at where they're meant to be. So, perhaps your *"key frames"* here can be just three drawings – or do you need more to explain the journey of the scene? This is all part of your decision-making process when creating *"key poses"*.

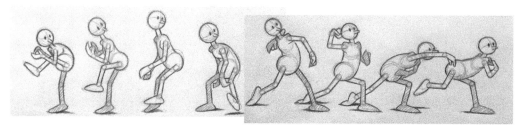

Blocked out key poses of a pitcher in action.

This thinking process is a really important exercise – not only just for each scene, but also for the entire film – and should be encouraged for everything you do. Then, once you have all your keys drawn up, you should definitely shoot a *"pose test animatic"*, placing each drawing approximately where they need to be in relation to the audio track. That way, you'll really know if your thinking is working out on the screen in real time, which it the only place it matters. It's definitely smart of you to do that, before you start the intensive or time-consuming process of inbetweening.

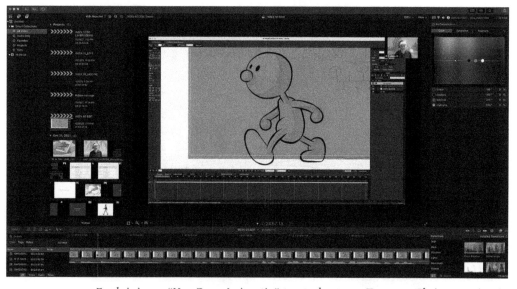

Explaining a "Key Pose Animatic" to students on Zoom at Christmas time!

Breakdown positions: Once you're sure that all your key poses are as they need to be, defining the broad storytelling intentions of the scene, you can next add in your first inbetween drawing to link them – the *"breakdown"* drawing. *"Breakdown"* drawings are not always a drawing that is in the middle position of two keys, as sometimes you need to emphasize and transitioning action in one direction or another. A *"breakdown"* position might also not be directly in the middle of two keys

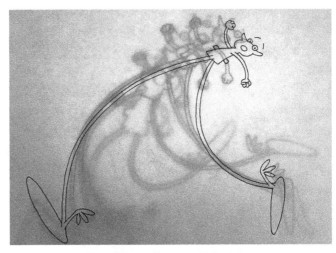

Keys, breakdowns and inbetween drawings.

in a straight line, but on a curved arc also. Everything depends on the two key drawings you're working with and the bigger picture of the scene in its entirety.

Remember, your pose positions are everything, whether they are *"keys"* or *"breakdowns"*. This is why the observation exercises are fundamental to you knowing what a "good" pose position is, and what is not. Hopefully you will have learned by now that every drawing you do is extremely important. And just to make sure that your decisions are good ones with a scene, it is advisable to shoot a further *"pose test"* of everything – to again test how your drawings are working in real time.

Carefully selecting the right key drawing is really important.

Inbetweening: When you are absolutely sure you've done everything you can to get the best out of your *"key"* and *"breakdown"* drawings, it is at last time to start working on the *"inbetweens"*. This is where you can make your action much more smooth and complete after the pose test version. It's also a time when *"timing"* becomes important – meaning that the more inbetweens you add the slower the action will be and vice versa. So, you can probably see by now that "doing animation" is not just doing animation! Everything you do needs to be thought through and planned to the finest detail. Then finally, when you've done all that, shoot a *"pencil test"* your final inbetweened action.

Carefully drawing a "superimposed" inbetween on a lightbox.

At the same time, don't settle for the first scene pencil test you do as being OK. Everything we do can be improved – the *"pencil test"* could well reveal issues with what you've done. So if you make changes, do a new pencil test each time, until you get it as you want it – then move on.

Draw the best you can and then move on!

Background art: Now with your animation complete, it is time to focus on the *"background art"*. The "background" is everything that does not move in a scene. It can even include foreground material that is layered in front of the animation. Background art can be created traditionally or digitally. Color is really important to background art too – although whatever you do should work within the color schemes you've evolved through the *"concept art"* and *"color model"* processes you completed in Pre-production.

Large-sized background art for my film, *Endangered Species*.

That said the kind of tone or color you use for your backgrounds suggests the kind of mood each scene needs to communicate? It is also the way you apply the color – that is, whether it's like flat color, textured or even pencil shading – that matters.

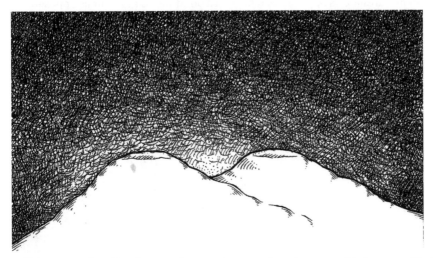

A different style of background art, using crosshatch pen and ink on my iPad.

Whatever it is, it will define the overall look of your piece. Remember also that a background usually covers **90**% of the screen in most shots, so from an audience's point of view, it can communicate as much, if not more, than the animation at times. They will often define what your audience feels about your film. So, don't neglect the quality of the artwork you use for your backgrounds.

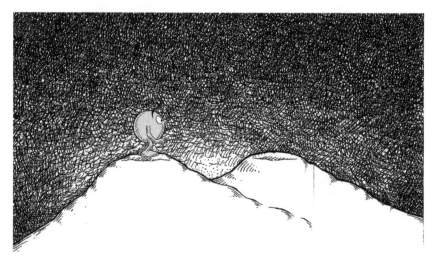

Showing the small-scale character featured in the previous background art.

Clean-up and coloring: With backgrounds completed and your pencil test working well, you now need to take your drawings to the next level. This involved *"cleaning them up"*. *"Clean-up"* usually involves tracing the rough drawings onto a new sheet of paper, using a final, neat line treatment. These line drawings are then scanned individually, imported into an animation program and colored in accordance with the earlier decisions you have made in terms of a *"color model"*. Some variation may need to be made to your original color thinking, as some scenes will use the chosen colors but others may have to have those colors adjusted if they are happening at night rather than day, in bright sunshine as opposed to rain, or in a good-mood moment as opposed to a sad one.

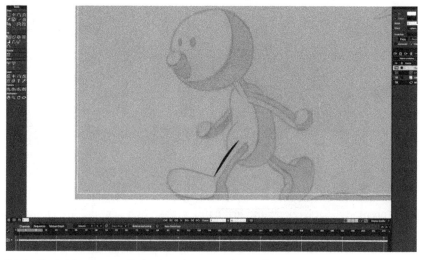

Digitally inking a pencil drawn character in Moho.

Compositing and rendering: With your animation colored and your background art completed, you now need to combine them together and render them to the required, final video format. This may again require some color adjustments, as when you have rendered a scene and edited into the full film version, you may see that the mood or flow of the film is interrupted by the overall colors being too bright or dark, warm or cold. So some color value adjustments need to be made before you sign off on a final color version of each scene as you composite them.

Working in the now (sadly) defunct "ToonBoom Studio" software on the Culpeper animatic.

Final congratulations: At this point, "congratulations" should be in order, as you have hopefully created your first masterpiece. There is some fine-tuning necessary – such as balancing the audio, adding sound effects and maybe including music that you didn't think necessary before. But essentially, this should be a moment of relieve and excitement – then nervousness when you show it to others, hoping they will think all your efforts were worth it.

Suggested Assignment

Of course, we really haven't talked about digitally created animation here, such as with you Moho animators. Essentially, the process is the same, although you of course won't be drawing your "key poses", "breakdowns" and "inbetweens". However, you should still go through the same stages of creating and testing. At the beginning of the process, block out your key poses on single frames and then scrub backward and forward to see whether the flow is right. When it is, "Save" that version as you chosen pose final.

Work in progress on a Moho walk/multiplane panning test sequence for students.

But before you move on to the "breakdown" stage, open your keys up as "holds" – so that they roughly match the timing you're planning for when the inbetweens will be added. Save this as an alternate "pose test" version and render it out to real time video. Check this and adjust your poses if necessary, as you would if you were a pencil-drawn animator.

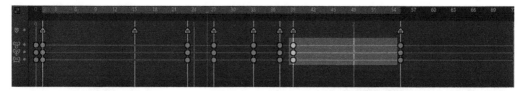

Indicating the a "hold" on key animatic drawings in Moho.

When all is good, return to your original single-frame, pose final version and open up the keys by one frame and adjust the automatic breakdown drawings that have been generated. Some of them might work as they are but, more usually, you'll need to adjust them a little to get a better transitional movement between the keys.

Reminder of opening up single-frame keys on the Moho timeline to create new in between frames.

Scrub these, adjust them where necessary and open them up to create a new pose test version as before. Check everything by playing back the real-time video and adjust if necessary.

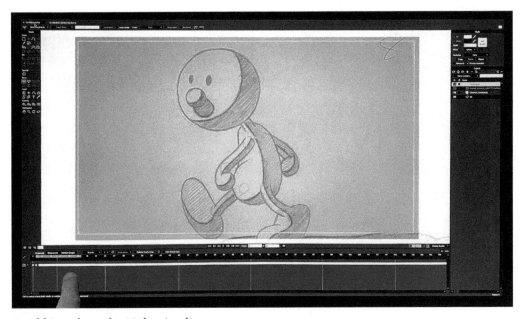

Scrubbing along the Moho timeline.

When you are certain that you have your "keys" and "breakdowns" correct, go back to the previous "single-frame" version and open those up to include the number of inbetweens you intend to put between them all. Remember always though, whatever digital animation program you use, such as Moho, it will always generate logical inbetweens, which you may not want in some instances. So it may be a question of adjust all or some part of the inbetweens generated to change the flow or the timing that will work best. Scrub along the timeline to check out everything. Then render to a final version. Hopefully this will work first time, but adjust again if necessary until it is how you would wish it.

Masterclass 38/ Key Pose Animation 2

I think we've got to the frustrating part of these masterclass lessons as far as I'm concern. With my live or online classes, I love to critique my students' work at this stage especially. Having an experienced "animator's eye", I can often pick out the weeknesses and hopefully help a student raise the level of what they're doing. Sometimes they're knocking it out of the park of course, and there's little I can add to help them. At other times I can. But sadly, I can't do that for you with this book approach unfortunately. However, I can suggest that the biggest errors the first-time animators make with their *"key pose"* work is either a "**timing**" thing, or a "**weight**" thing, or a "**balance**" thing. But as I can't be there to advise you, I strongly suggest to you that you would really benefit from another pair of seasoned eyes checking out what you're doing. Therefore, if you know of someone who is experienced at animating, then definitely seek out their thoughts with your initial *"key pose animatic"*.

Additionally, let me say also that you're beyond this stage, you should never need to change anything on your project. This stage should lock down everything, once and for all, so don't be tempted to mess with things later. If doubts should set in after you've signed off on your *"key pose animatic"* in your own mind, then brush them aside because the temptation will then be to always mess with what you're doing. Then, if that should happen, you'll either end up with a terribly compromised project or stagnate and never finish it at all as a result of your indecisiveness. So, be strong in the here and now – then stubborn and tenacious with what arrive at with your *"key pose animatic"*!

Now, that stated – let's jump straight into the observational gesture drawing exercise.

DOI: 10.1201/9781003324287-42

Warm-Up Drawing

The exercise will somewhat echo our approach to *"Emotional poses"* in the last lesson. This time though, we'll term it **"Action poses"**. Previously, you were asked to create four imaginary poses, based on an observational one on the left side of your page. This time you will be required to create four new imaginary *"action"* poses, after having drawn the observational one. As before, you should draw your observational character first, on the left. Then, you will add the four additional poses in the imaginary boxes that make up the rest of your page. Again, give yourself 3 minutes to draw the observational pose and then 2 minutes to draw each of the other four. The four *"action"* poses you need to draw will be based on a *"Generic Walk"* for the first two and then other actions for the remaining two. These will be (i) **"stride position"**, (ii) **"passing position"**, (iii) **"throw"** and (iv) **"jump"**.

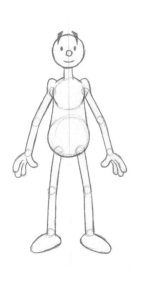

STRIDE POSITION 01	PASSING POSITION 02
THROW 03	JUMP 04

Comments: Make a good effort to draw it as it is, making sure you are accurate in the dimensions of the observational character. (i) The first action pose is a *"Generic Walk"* one, so try to remember how a full stride position looks with this character. Make sure your pose has the right relationship between the arms to the legs, and the legs are not over-striding. (ii) For the second action pose, you need to remember how the *"passing position"* looks with a walk, while all the time trying to keep your character drawing consistent with the previous two. And if you are struggling to remember what a *"passing position"* looks like, it might help if I give you the clue *"number 4 position"*. (iii) With your third imaginary pose, you can draw any throwing action you like, as long as it is dynamic and consistent in terms of the previous character drawings you have made. Think of the *"Dynamic Lines"* of force you can apply to this, to make it more powerful looking. (iv) Finally, your last action pose is a *"jump"*. Here, you are again freed to show any kind of jump you like. Essentially, your character should be in the air, but how you pose that out is up to you. Remember how effective a shadow on the ground, under the character, is to give a sense of separation to the ground.

Dynamic jump position – pencil test for simple student project.

This will have possibly been the toughest drawing challenge you have had so far, as (a) you have to focus on your character, its volumes and proportions, and (b) you had to remember elements of previous exercises we have done in the book. Even so, it will hopefully engage your mind on the essential things you will most likely need in your film project – if not them all, then certainly some of them.

Doing action poses like this is a great way of warming up too – prior to your drawing, or creating digitally, key action poses for your project. It is very rare that there are "inaction" poses with animation, so anything that peaks your thinking and trains your hand on the dynamic action side of this is extremely useful. Quite often TV animation has a lot of "inaction" and a lot of moving mouths only, but the very best of top-drawn, character animation does need you to think and create powerful action poses to tell a good story in movement.

Women's Long Jump   Heike Dreschler   GDR   **23'8"/7.21m**

Important: You should always keep your "animator's eye" open for reference. I once came across this framed long jump action by Heike Dreschler on my travels and captured it on my iPhone as I knew it would be valuable one day.

So, to do that, you need to be very expressive in the way you establish our key positions and the way you transition from one to the other using *"breakdowns"* and *"inbetweens"*. Therefore, thinking in the way we have for these two most recent drawing exercises is well in keeping with what I hope you will aspire to with your animation project work – especially as it tests your *observations* and *imaginative* skills at the same time. From your imagination, you get your ideas of course, but through observation of the real world, you can make those ideas come alive with well-observed and plausibly established poses. So never neglect these kinds of drawing exercises, even long after you have finished your project here and are (hopefully) working as a fully fledged professional in the industry.

Instruction

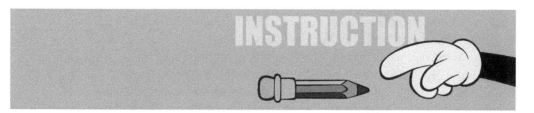

Although you have probably already started blocking in your "key poses" for your animatic, I thought I would share with here my own particular process of "blocking in". I'll keep it as visual as possible at this stage because drawings are definitely "worth a thousand words" and the briefer I can be at this stage, text-wise, the better. In the classroom, I would normally show the pencil-drawn animation footage, so students can see what I'm aiming for in the final analysis. However, as that is not possible here, check out the flipbook sequence on the dedicated website. You'll see that in The Hermit, it's essentially a "sneak" walk with the knee trembling "stagger" on the end-stopping position.

Blocked out pose 1 of a sneak.

So, in terms of blocking out a sneak sequence out, here is my first "key pose" drawing, number "1". In effect, this is the "establishing" pose for the entire scene. It represents research action for what I did for the *Seeker* character in The Hermit.

Once you have your first pose established, you need to go through and create all the various "key pose" positions that evolve from that. So, here is the second key pose position in the first stride. Remember with a "sneak", the feet stay in the same place at the beginning of a stride, whereas the body leans forward, giving us this drawing, number "9".

Blocked out pose 2 of a sneak.

And then, once before the body moves forward, the next stride is taken. So, in this case here is our next key stride position, which is effectively the reverse of the stride one position.

Blocked out pose 3 of sneak.

"Establishing pose", *"striding forward"*, next *"key stride pose"*. These are our key poses and they can be reused for the length of the sneaking sequence and repeated over each stride with the legs reversing.

All three sneak poses – stride 1.

As you can see, we can work really rough at this stage, with the basics just sketched in – although the underlying dimensions and structures are accurate nevertheless. You don't want to spend excessive amounts of time drawing in details if your key frame poses are not accurate. So work rough and work fast.

An additional key pose position added – effectively a breakdown pose between the two and three positions.

So as you can see from the next image, whatever you do for each blocked out *"key frame position"*, represents a **new change of direction** in the action. This is the process you need to take with *"blocking in"*. You have to assess on your own your personal key frame positions as they will be unique to your project. But in seeing how this is worked out, it should give you ideas for yours.

A more cleaned-up version of the above sneak, blocked out more fully.

When you have all the key poses completed in a scene, definitely do a pose test. If your pose test is working, you can go to the next stage of working out your *"breakdown positions"*. But only do that if all is working fine with your initial pose test. If it is not, then fix whatever needs to be fixed and pose test it again. Keep repeating this until your *"pose test"* scene appears how you imagined it, and then move on to the *"breakdown"* stage.

The sequence of 1-stride key and breakdown positions in Seeker's sneak.

So the *"breakdown positions"* are the first inbetweens that link between any two keys. In this case, my first two drawings are number "1" and number "9", so as I want my first inbetween to be times exactly in the middle, the breakdown drawing here will be number "(5)". (Written in parentheses, as that's how traditionally all breakdown drawings are depicted – with key positions circled.)

First breakdown position in sneak, with the body arching in a concave shape as it angles forward.

To create it, I put both key drawings on the pegs of my lightbox and placed a new sheet of paper over them. I numbered it *"(5)"* before I did anything else. Now strictly speaking, the breakdown should be pretty much halfway in the middle, but I didn't want it entirely like that. Instead, I wanted it to be a very slight "slowing-out" position and moving on an upward curve.

With the lightbox on it looked like this.

Showing the breakdown position, between two keys, on the lightbox. The drawings are inked on this occasion for greater clarity, although this is how I approached this particular scene – roughing in the drawings with a blue pencil and then inking the drawings loosely with a 0.5 micron pen.

Then, if you put the drawings in order on your lightbox, you can "flip" them to see how they're moving. Even without inbetweens in there yet, it will give you a strong impression how your key and breakdown drawings are working together in movement.

It's important for traditional animators to learn the technique of "flipping" (or "rolling") the drawings on lightbox!

Now to go beyond this, I put the next key drawing, "**25**", on the lightbox pegs, with key drawing "**9**" on top of it. Working on the idea that I need another half-way position as a "breakdown" for this, I put a new sheet of paper over the top and numbered it "**17**". (Note: The breakdown drawing isn't always numbered as the halfway number, but I'm using this as a simple example here for conve-nience.) I then drew the breakdown drawing that I needed.

The next breakdown drawing in the stride, showing the lead leg starting to reach out for the next key stride "contact" position.

You can see here that it's gone high from key *"9"* in terms of the head/torso position on number *"17"* and down to *"25"* after that. This is because it is a walk and with the majority of walks – a *"sneak"* included – the body goes up on the *"passing position"* and down on the *"keys"*.

(REMINDER: Remember that with anything in animation, the first midpoint position between two keys it is called the "breakdown" position. However, on walks, the midpoint is known as the "passing position" – hence using that term above.)

We can see that it is a *"passing position"* in this case, as on the new drawing *"17"*, the free leg is off the ground and passing the contact leg which remains on the ground.

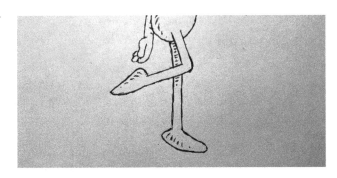

The free leg in the passing position.

Note also that as well as the head/torso going upward, the hips are coming forward as the free leg is passing from front to back.

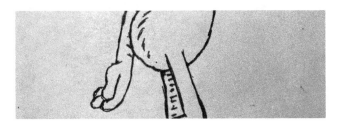

The hip forward in the passing position.

Again, I put these three drawings on the pegs – lowest number on top and highest number on the bottom – to flip the action and see how it's working. This is always the process I use when blocking out and continue onward like this until I get to the end of the scene. When I have done that and am satisfied that the sequence is working OK by flipping the drawings individually, I will shoot it on my overhead capture camera and play back the "pose test" video version, to make sure it is all working in real time too. When I see that it is, I know I can move on beyond the *"blocking"* stage.

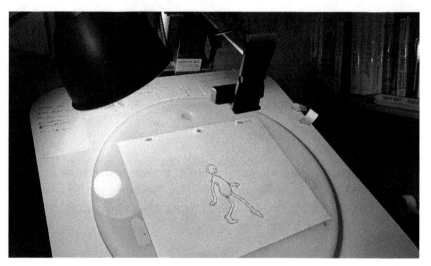

How I shoot all my drawings using an overhead webcam and editing them into an animatic or pencil test on the computer.

Now finally, I will add the *"inbetweens"*. I probably don't need to explain how to do this anymore but I will show you what one inbetween looks like with the lightbox on. In this example, it is inbetween *"3"* linking key drawings *"1"* and *"5"*.

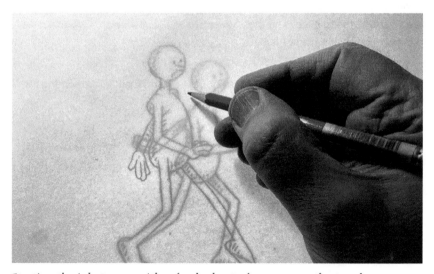

Starting the inbetween with a fresh sheet of paper over the two keys.

I did this inbetween using the *"superimposition"* technique I explained earlier in the book. However, to remind you, I will briefly say that I put the two key drawings on the pegs first and then placed the new sheet of paper over them and numbered it. Then, I marked the arc I wanted to have the head and body move through from *"1"* to *"5"* – remembering that nothing moves in a straight line, except computer-generated inbetweens!

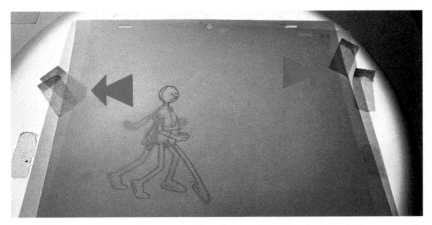

Superimposing the heads over each other and taping (arrows) the paper down to stop the drawings moving while inbetweening.

I then marked my imagined midway position of the next on the paper too, as well as where I imagined the base of the torso to be.

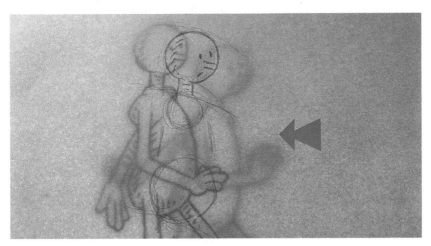

I start the superimposition process by placing the drawings on the pegs and roughing out the key midpoint positions in blue pencil. (Just the torso part in this case.)

I then took the top two drawings off the pegs, with the lightbox still on, and *"superimposed"* the torsos of them all over one another to get them as closely lined up that way as possible, tracing the new head as lightly as I could.

The torsos superimposed over each other with the papers taped down as before.

With the heads and torsos done, I do the same "superimposing" technique for inbetweening.

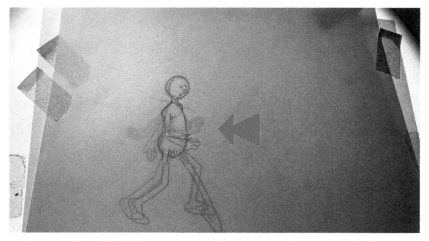

With everything taped down, it is much easier to inbetween specific areas of the body – the head and torso in this case.

When I had all that done, I turned the lightbox off and put the drawings back on the pegs with "3" on top and drew the line of the inbetween stronger, from light to dark.

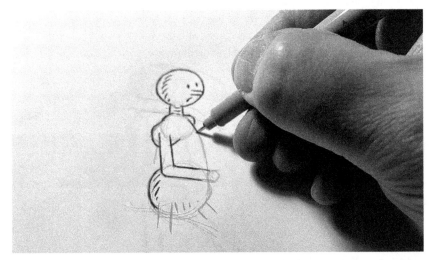

Normally, I would just strengthen up the lines with blue pencil at this stage; however, on this scene, I decided to ink my blue inbetween drawings to give more clarity here.

I then inbetweened the legs, with the lightbox on, to complete my drawing number "3".

I don't superimpose all of the characters normally, just the most significant part, such as the head and the torso separately in this case. Here, the legs are easy to inbetween with the papers on the pegs and without superimposition.

Hopefully all this will have given you a basic idea of how I approach my *"blocked out keys"*, my *"breakdowns"* and my *"inbetweens"* when I'm working on my scenes. I'm sure others will have slightly differing approaches – especially if they are working digitally – but this is a tried and trusted way of working in stages, taught to me from early on by some of the greatest Hollywood animators ever. It has served me well throughout my career, and I'm sure it gives you a solid platform to work with now and to evolve further when you get me experience yourself.

For the record, the final colored stride sequence of this action is as follows:

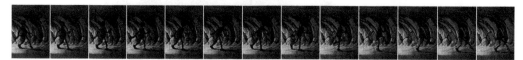

The final 1-stride action of the Seeker approaching the Hermit in the cave.

Suggested Assignment

Not really a suggested assignment hear, but just a mention that if you're work-ing differently in Moho, the process doesn't differ ultimately – in the sense that you will hopefully arrive at a similar action on the screen. But you will simply get there differently, using the techniques I have already shown you. The bottom line in all this is that what really matters is what is up there on the screen, not how you go there. But, I will say that if you're a first-time or novice animator, you are wise to follow the guidelines I have shown you in the book as it will assure you – as long as you follow it carefully and committed – of a well-produced ani-mated film at the end of it all. So my *"suggested assignment"* after all is for you to be *"careful"* and *"committed"* in following out the guidelines here!

One final comment here: When you reach the professional level in terms of traditional, paper-based animation, you'll find that you might like to disregard some of my comments in this book –the use of backlighting and lightboxes. When you have experience, you are encouraged to NOT use your lightbox un-derlight when you are keying out your animation, or even inbetweening it in some broad action circumstance. The reason is that in *"flipping"* your drawings as you do them, you should develop your animator's eye to see the flow without confirming it by switching your lightbox on. It is something we do by instinct ultimately. However, at the beginning stage of your journey, such as here, I would 100% encourage you to be accurate by using a lightbox as I indicate. As Richard Williams once said to me when I was apologitic for being slow doing his inbetweens – "You are accurate with them and that's all that matters – speed will come later!" In those earlier days, I totally relied on my lightbox to find the precise *"inbetween"* position linking two keys when I was still an apprentice. As time went by however, I began to train my eye – and my confidence – to not need the lightbox so much. And so it was with animating when I graduated to that level. For close movement, I would definitely use my lightbox to ensure the distance my keys were from one another was not too large and not too small. With broader movement however, I could dispense with the lightbox – I used just *"flipping"* to judge all my positionings. It became my *"second nature"* in the end. That said though, unless you're really experienced at inbetweening and later key creation, I still urge you to use your lightbox as much as possible, until your "animator's eye" is trained enough to not use it. I still do use a lightbox when creatings very tight and close inbetweens for myself. But if the action is broad, then I will find it limiting to use my lightbox. *"Flipping"* is a much more valuable technique to use in such circumstances, when *"feeling the flow of the movement"* is far more important in good character animation than mechanically tight *"inbetweening"* or *"superimposition"*. Only you will know when you're ready to make that kind of transition however.

Masterclass 39/
Breakdown
Position 1

By now, you should really have the sense that you're actually going to make a film by the end of all this hard work. So, well done for getting this far, although there's still a lot to do before you cross the line! But at least you will now see, through your *"key pose animatic"* that it's real, it's telling a story and you can't wait to show the world your final project! In this lesson, and the next, we're going to focus on you working on your "**breakdown drawings**" – which should bring you closer to making that first exciting project even more real. But first, observational gesture drawing.

Warm-Up Drawing

As you're no doubt beginning to be overwhelmed by drawings right now (unless you're working in Moho or another digital program using rigged characters), I thought we'd make this session of observation gesture drawing a re-assessment challenge, rather than a new one. What I mean by this is that I'm going to ask you to do once again the very first challenge you did at the very beginning of this book – "Coffee Drinkers" – to show you've progressed since then. Now, I don't want you looking back at your previous drawings right now, I just want you to jump in and complete this one before going back and comparing. But I think it will be an interesting exercise to see how your progression has evolved.

DOI: 10.1201/9781003324287-43

So, a duplicate of the first warm-up drawing exercise you did. I hope it will be fun for you to have another crack at it! (And please, no peeking at your previous drawings yet!)

Above are two poses of people drinking coffee. They are very different, emphasizing the fact that you need to think carefully about the pose you would choose if you were going to draw, or animate, someone drinking coffee for real.

If you study the poses, you will see that they are not just physically different, but they are different in terms of *visual storytelling* too. Ask yourself, what mood, emotion or attitude are they expressing? Then, decide which one best suits the scene that you are contemplating, where you animating this for a project. These two drawings are just the tip of a huge iceberg of possibilities of course. Type in *"coffee drinkers"* into Google Images, and you'll see a whole host of options popping up. Better still, go out for a coffee with your sketchbook and capture the various poses and gestures that people in the coffee shop are presenting when drinking their coffee. Be aware of how you, yourself, are drinking coffee too! The world is a huge database of information like this. So go out with your sketchbook and take full advantage of it whenever you can. Most important of all, train your eye to see all the different people, poses or personalities – not just coffee drinkers, but all of life in its infinite variety.

But for now, first look again at the two images above and **sketch them in just 3 minutes** each. Be very disciplined. The more disciplined you are, the more you'll learn and the greater the advantage you'll get from the exercise.

Student Tina Braun's revisit of the original Coffee Drinkers assignment, including her initial blocking out of the inner skeleton of the figures first (left).

Definitely an element of *"déjà vu"* about this, but a really valuable exercise to see how your *"animator's eye"* has progressed from back then the first time, till now. Of course, this will only work if you have studiously done all the exercises along the way. But if you have, look back at your first drawing then, and then the one now, and see the difference. Hopefully it will be significant and therefore give you the confidence to keep going to the finishing line with your project, knowing you're in the home straight now and that your knowledge and skill sets are so much more equipped to do it!

Instruction

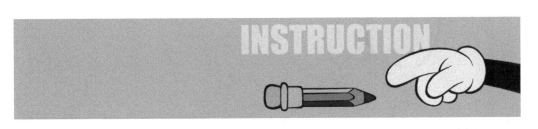

In this lesson, I want to go through two more simple examples of *"blocking out"* that I have done in the past – one for a traditional animation scene and another for one in Moho. So, before you begin your own blocking out process, I think the following will help, whether you're working traditionally or digitally.

NOTE

And even if you only work digitally only, you are strongly advised to adopt the traditional principles throughout this book and then adapt them to your own digital practices. You will benefit enormously from the kind of guidance the giants of animation's past have left us. A change in tools fundamentally doesn't change the truth of what they learned about movement and production methods and what they have passed down to us all!

Traditional Animation Blocking Out Process

To demonstrate my process, I'm first going to focus on another scene that I created for my *"Old Man Mad About Animating"* animated memoirs project. It combines live action of myself in my studio and the introduction of my animated muse, **"Arnie"**, who both disrupts and inspires my work. He's been with me now since 1978, when he first appeared in my *"The Animator's Workbook"*. As you will see, *"Arnie"* is a prankster for much of the time, so this scene highlights just one of the many ways he's inclined to let me know he's there!

Fangs for the memories, Arnie!

As you will see below, the concept is that *"Arnie"* is sneaking up behind me while I'm working and making me jump by slapping me on the shoulders. Ultimately in the scene, he steps round to the side of me and laughs. I started it all with this piece of concept art. My wife photographed me at my drawing board and then I added to the *"Arnie"* pose to it in *Photoshop*, just to get a feel of where it was all going to go. That's the core essence of the scene.

Cleaned-up drawing of Arnie, about to pounce on me.

Now, no two animated films are the same, so this process – although similar to pretty much all processes – has its own touch of individuality about it, which I want to share now. Adapt as you need to, when it comes to your project. Anyway, the very first thing before I did for this was to create a *"storyboard"*.

Rough storyboard on yellow sticky notes of my original idea.

As I don't have to satisfy a client on this one, I sketch out my storyboards really spontaneously and simply. I work quickly as I can of yellow *Post-It* sticky notes. I then stick them up on the wall in front of my desk to refer to when necessary.

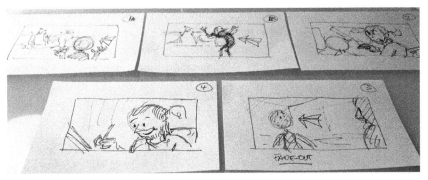

The final board rough, stuck up on the wall in front of my desk.

So here, you can see *"Arnie"* and me in the background, just drawn clearly enough for me to understand what's happening. "A" is "Arnie's" arrival, and "B" is where he slaps me on the shoulders.

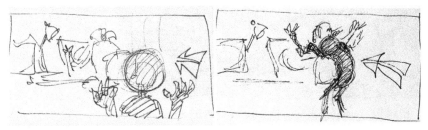

This is the main thrust of the action – Arnie sneaking up behind me and slapping me on the shoulders.

The next thing I needed to do after this was shoot the live action footage. As this is a non-financed, personal project promotional trailer sequence, I actually filmed it economically on my iPhone. I set the camera up on a tripod, got it running, then jumped into my seat and mimed out the action I needed to create for the *"Arnie"* animated action to interact with. It was fun, imagining myself drawing quietly and then suddenly jumping for nothing, as if he has slapped me on the shoulders for real!

The two most crucial positions in the live action – one of me quietly working, then me jumping as if being slapped on the shoulders. The sequence was shot in HD1080 on my iPhone.

Next, I needed a layout to match my *Arnie* animation to. Normally, you would have to draw your layouts for an animated film, but because here I was going to use the live action as my background, I printed out a key frame in a 16:9 format – as big as I could make it for the 16-field animation paper I was going to use. The specific, live action key frame I used was the frame where *Arnie's* slapping hands would hit my shoulder for the first time. I figured that this would be a perfect target for the animation action.

The frame that I printed out as a layout to animate too – showing the precise frame that Arnie's hands hit my shoulders before the reaction.

Then, I had to start the process of *"blocking out"*. As *"blocking out"* effectively means that I was needing to draw all my essential key poses that defined the sequence, I actually started with that specific *"hit"* moment with my shoulders and blocked out key positions back to the beginning of the scene and then forward to the end of it. I realized that the *"hit"* moment was the cornerstone of everything – the major "story pose" – so I worked everything out from that. Next, I filled a *"key pose animatic"* of the sequence drawings, around that single live action background image.

Key pose animatic drawings on the printed background – showing the pre-hit, hit and post-hit Arnie positions.

For the record, my cornerstone *"story pose"* ended up by being numbered *"**87**"* in the entire sequence.

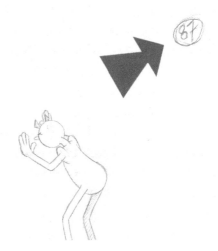

Number 87 ringed on drawing.

Now, let me show you just the *"blocked out poses"* that lead up to the actual *"slap"* moment, and you will get an idea of how I broke them down.

The blocked out poses up to and following the "hit".

Note that the one before my key *"87"* pose is a kind of *"anticipation"* position, preparing to go up and down for the slap.

The "anticipation" (center) before the hit.

And the one before that I had *"Arnie"* sneaking on a stride position, his arms up high, so you can see that he's clearly up to no good.

The end of the last stride before the anticipation, silhouetting intention.

In that way, the blocked out sequence depicts *Arnie's* arms up high, then down, then up in readiness for the slap down. This is the core action leading up to the powerful "hit" moment.

The full inbetweened sequence prior to the "hit".

Prior to that section, it was just a question of bringing *Arnie* in, arms bent upward, using a kind of *"sneak"* walk.

The final drawings or Arnie entering the scene.

Finally, I did a key pose animatic of everything, showing what all the *"key poses"* in the entire sequence would look like, in real time, on the screen.

The key poses for the full scene animatic.

Now, once the "key poses" are finalized, it is time to start thinking about the *"breakdown drawings"*. However, to create breakdown drawings, you really need to know how many inbetweens you are going to add, and quite how you're going to numerically space them out from one key to another. This involves working out the *"inbetween charts"* on each key drawing, showing how many drawings will link to the next key drawing and how they are to be spaced out. This will define just what number drawing will be a *"breakdown"* drawing in each case.

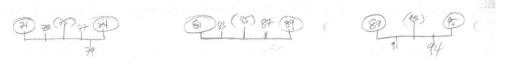

Three of the key charts, showing breakdown drawings and inbetweens.

Unfortunately, creating *"charts"* really only comes with experience over the years – and even then I still get it wrong on occasions! However, my suggestion as a starting point is to add three *"even"* inbetweens to link your keys together throughout and then adjust later when you get to see how it plays out in real time.

An "evens" chart on key drawing 81.

Remember also that when you draw up your *"even"* charts, the key drawings are always **circled** and the *"breakdown drawings"* are written in **parentheses**.

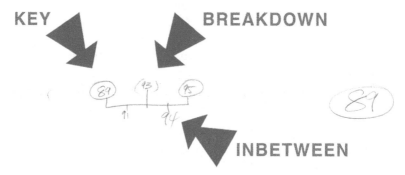

Chart showing a "Key", "Breakdown" and "Inbetween".

So let me now show you how I worked out my *"breakdown drawings"*. As an example, I'm taking it from my key pose "**45**" to my key post "**53**". In terms of charting, the "breakdown" drawing for this is "**49**". It looks like the middle drawing of *"even"* inbetweens but it wasn't drawn that way. This is where an understanding of movement and experience takes over. In this case, the *"breakdown drawing"* is definitely not a straight inbetween at all. Instead, you will see that breakdown *"49"* here is actually much closer to *"45"*, but not close to *"53"*. There's a big difference here.

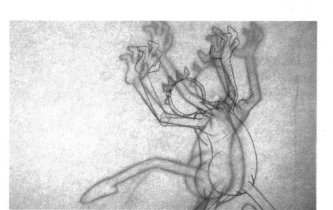

Notice how the breakdown drawing 49 is much nearer to one key position (45) than the other (53) and not a natural inbetween.

And that's why *"breakdown drawings"* are not necessarily an exact inbetween. It depends what you want to emphasize in the action. In this case, I didn't want to change from the *"45"* position much, but I did want the free leg to move through more distinctly and then the body to move back more obviously on the next inbetween position as that free leg swings forward. That's why the body at least favors key drawing *"45"*, rather than it being in a perfect inbetween position. Note also that the body on breakdown *"49"* is still concave, whereas it becomes convex on key drawing *"53"*. This gives the entire movement more of a "snap" to it when this happens. (And note also that the inbetween linking *"49"* and *"53"* is not a straight-line body position. In such cases, you need to favor slightly from the straight toward either concave or convex!)

The breakdown drawing number 49 (center) has a concave shape to the torso, like key 45 (left) – as opposed to the convex one on key 53 (right).

If we add the preceding "key" and "breakdown" drawing to the mix, we get a pose test sequence like this.

The sequence of keys and breakdown drawings used at the opening of the scene in the key pose animatic.

And this is the way you generally approach your "key pose positions" and your "breakdown positions". You need to not only understand where your keys are taking you in an action, but you also need to appreciate where to put the "breakdowns" linking those keys. This is something that comes much more natural in time, but for now, I would suggest you just keep everything in the middle and "even" on the charts to give you a safe "pose test" sequence to inbetween later.

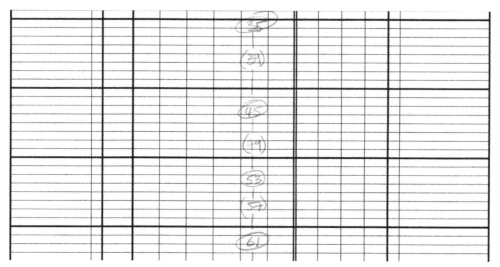

Timing of the drawings on exposure sheet of the key pose animatic.

And remember, however, you create your "keys" and "breakdowns", always but always shoot them as a real-time "key pose animatic", so that you can see how they time out on a monitor in real time, rather than imagine what they will look like on your lightbox or by flipping the drawings!

Moho Blocking Out Process

The approach you take for *Moho* "blocking out" is similar in the understanding of what you need to achieve creatively, but practically the process of "key poses" and "breakdown" positions is very different when working digitally. Let me explain using a "Bouncing Ball", repeat animation, exercise.

The first thing we're going to do is highlight "**Frame 1**" on the timeline and position the ball in its first position.

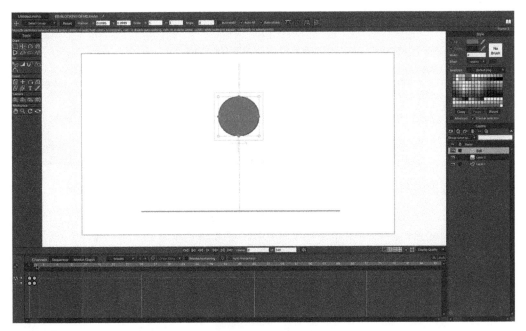

Create frame 1.

Now, I'm going to move to "**Frame 2**" on the timeline and position the ball down in its *"hit"* position – although I'm not going to do the *"squash"* immediately.

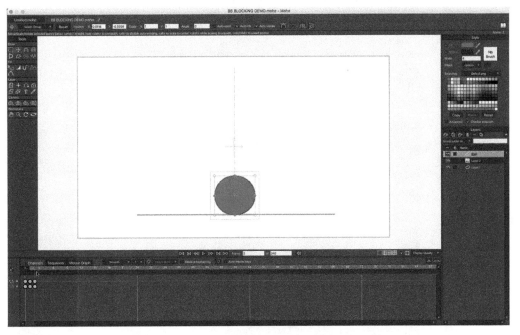

Create frame 2.

Then, I'm going to move the cursor on the timeline to "**Frame 3**" and then copy "*Frame 1*" on paste it into "*Frame 3*". (That is, "*Command C*" with the keys on "*Frame 1*" selected and then "*Command V*" when I've moved on to "*Frame 3*".)

Create frame 3.

So now, we have three "*key positions*" – up on "*1*", down on "*2*" and up on "*3*".

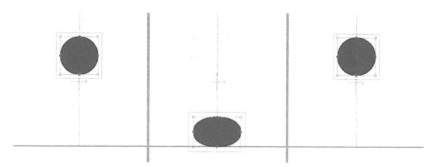

The three key frame positions – up, down and up again.

Now, let's create the "*squash*" position on number "*2*". To do that, we transform down the height at the top of the ball, but as the volume inside the ball cannot change, which have to extend out the sides to compensate.

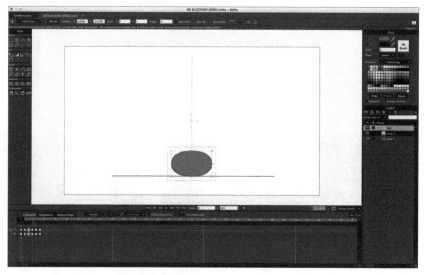

Create squash shape on frame 2.

This means we've essentially *"blocked out"* our key positions. So whatever you animation will be in Moho, you need to block out your key positions like this on **single frames**. Notice that we haven't thought about *"inbetweens"* at this stage, or the *"breakdown position"* – this is just about establishing the required *"key positions"*.

The three keys on the timeline, positions as "ones".

But now, having *"blocked out"* our *"key positions"*, we now need to work out our "**breakdown positions**". To do that with our simple example here, select the key positions for frames *"2"* and *"3"* in our timeline and with the left mouse click down, and drag them to the right by **1 frame** .

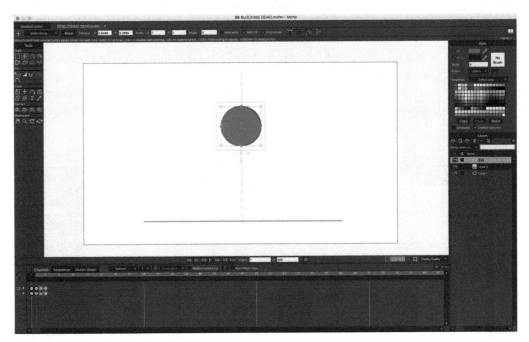

Selected frames 2 and 3 in timeline.

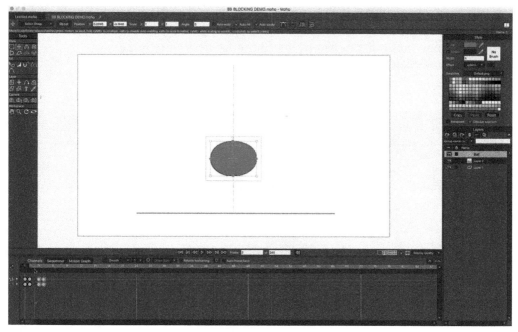

A new frame 2 is opened in the timeline.

That means we now have a new *"frame 2"*, which effectively is our *"breakdown position"*. However, as Moho has inbetweened it, it does not have the required *"stretch"* shape we need here. So, go ahead and transform the ball taller and narrower than the perfectly round position – in other words, into the correct *"stretch"* shape.

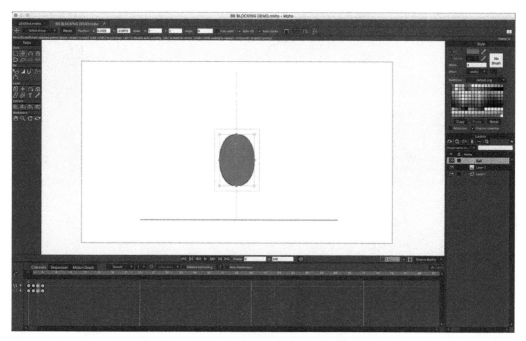

Deform the shape of the ball into a "stretch" on the new frame 2.

Now, if you "**scrub**" left and right over the first three frames on the timeline, you'll see that the action is closer to what we not it should be, based on the exercise we did earlier in this book.

Scrub back and forward over the keys on the timeline to check basic action.

So this is our first two blocked in *"keys"* and one blocked in *"breakdown"*. Now, we need to create the second *"breakdown position"* between the last two keys. So select the last key that in now on *"frame 4"* and drag it to the right by **one frame**.

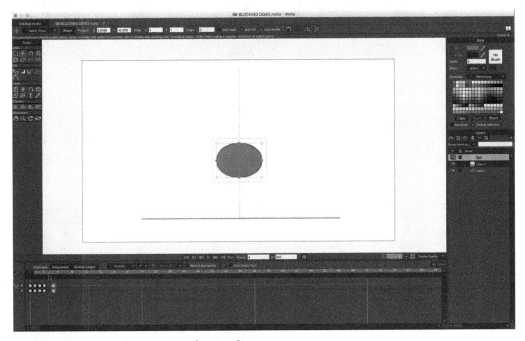

Opening up a new "frame 4" on the timeline.

Again, it will not be the shape that it should be for a bouncing ball *"breakdown"* position, which needs to be in a *"stretch"* shape rather than a regular inbetween that Moho has created for you. So, select *"frame 2"* on the timeline and paste it into the new *"frame 4"*.

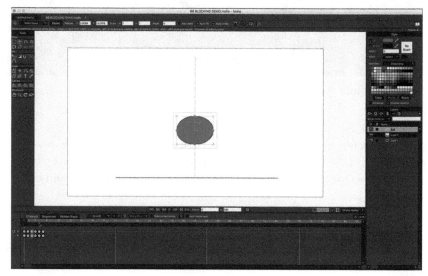

Pasting frame 2 into frame 4 on timeline.

This now gives you the five *"blocked in"* frames of a bouncing ball animation cycle. Although, if you remember the placements we did with our traditional drawn version earlier, we need to adjust the position of *"frame 2"* to overlap the *"squash"* position of *"frame 3"* to complete the sequence.

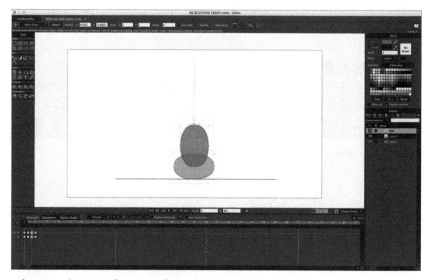

Adjusting frame 2 downward, so that there is an overlap on the ball in terms of frame 3.

Although this is a very simplistic approach to a very simplistic action, it should give you enough insights to work out how to quickly block in your *"keys"* and *"passing positions"* required for your own project. Being able to open up the frames on Moho like this saves a heck of a lot of drawing work for doing this – and will increasingly do so as you get into your **"inbetweens"**. However, we'll reserve talking about *"inbetweens"* until the following two lessons.

Suggested Assignment

No special instructions here – other than work through your *"keys"* and *"breakdowns"* diligently and don't be afraid to experiment with your *"breakdown"* options, once you have your *"keys"* finished. As I have said before, the placement of a *"breakdown"* drawing can make or break the action, so make sure you're doing the right thing. If in doubt, just make it a regular, halfway *"inbetween"* for now and adjust things later – especially in Moho, which will save you a heck of a lot of drawing work that traditional animators will have to change or throw away, if changes are made further down the line!

Masterclass 40/ Breakdown Position 2

Here, we are at lesson 40 would you believe. These current ones are critical however, because this is where actually laying the foundations upon which the rest of your project will stand or fall. Hopefully you are well on the way with your *"breakdown positions"* and almost ready to inbetween everything. But don't forget to do *"pose tests"* as you complete each scene or section, as you don't want to move into *"inbetweening"* until you are 100% sure that you're where you want to be on your keys and breakdowns. But if the heat is turning up a little too high right now, how about some observational gesture drawing to cool you down.

Warm-Up Drawing

This one is called "**turn around objects**", where we draw a single object from different positions. Remember that objects, as well as characters, are often featured in animation. As a result, animators need to learn how to draw objects consistently in size and proportion if their motion is to look that way too. The following **4 × 3-minute** skull-turning pictures constitute a single object in rotation that is analyzing. This will not only give you an opportunity to observe and draw a challenging object from all angles, but it also offers valuable underlying reference material for when you are drawing or animating a human head. This is

DOI: 10.1201/9781003324287-44

a challenging assignment, but nothing worth having is easy anyway. Whatever else it does, it will prove a valuable one to challenge in terms of your awareness regarding *"size"*, *"structure"* and *"form"* in motion. Draw all four positions, equally sized on **one page** of your sketchbook.

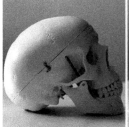   

Pose comments: Be aware of the proportions of the *"eye socket"*, the *"nose socket"*, the *"teeth"* and the *"jaw"*, as you will need to keep these consistent throughout each of the four turning drawings. In reality, this exercise is more related to scaling discipline than it is to actual drawing ability.

Student Tina Braun's gesture drawings.

Clearly, you're most likely to never be required to animate a skull. However, if they do, or if they don't, this is a really good exercise because this is where you are really challenged – not just in drawing ability – but in observational ability, in analysis, in interpreting things consistently. And even if you work in a purely cartoon world, such as "The Simpsons", or "Bugs Bunny", or *"Mickey Mouse"*, or whatever, you're always going to have the challenge of always having that character likely to be turning through several angles. This happens when any character needs to turnaround within an animated action.

A still from Ub Iwerks' "Skeleton Dance". (1929)

And so it's really going to be necessary that you need to keep aware of the sizes and proportions of a character's anatomy being consistent throughout. The better you can do that, the better your animation's going to be. So an exercise like this, although being quite fixed and static in its visual nature – and pretty *classical* in terms of an art-based drawing exercise – really does begin to develop those muscles you need to develop to keep *volumes*, *sizes* and *proportions* going in movement. So, I do recommend you doing lots of these kinds of observations drawings from time to time, not necessarily timed drawings, but ones that test your consistency of observation from many viewpoints.

Instruction

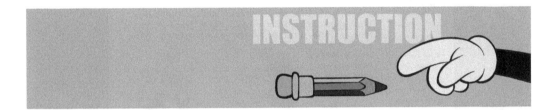

Although we know that a *"breakdown drawing"* is the first inbetween linking two key drawings, it may well be that many of them aren't that. Some will maybe not be exactly halfway between the keys, or not all of them will be hallway between the keys and I'm sure many will not be a straight linear inbetween, in the sense that they could well be positioned on an "**arc**" and not a straight line. Every project will be different of course, but at least in this and the next lesson, we'll be exploring options that you may want to consider. It might even be smart to go back to square one with our animation at this point and discuss something that is the cornerstone of all movement – namely the "**12 Principles of Animation**" – but with (and we're talking heresy here) perhaps two alternative versions at the end that will better replace a couple of the hallowed existing ones!

The 12 Principles of Animation.

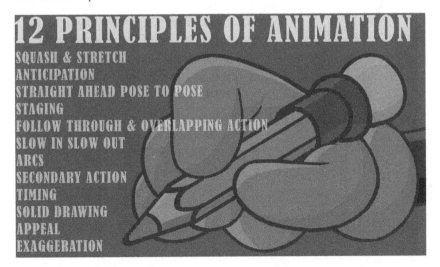

Twelve Principles of Animation

The *"12 Principles of Animation"* were first mentioned Disney legends, **Frank Thomas and Ollie Johnston**, in their classic book **The Illusion of Life**. *(Disney Editions; ISBN: 0786860707) These principles have become the foundation for all animators over the years and are taught at all good schools and colleges. It might help to go through them here, so that you are aware of them when animating your project. We have covered most of them already so far in this book but it will help to have affirmation of their value too.*

It is a testament to the respect the world has for Frank and Ollie's knowledge and talent that their website continues to exist, even though they sadly passed away many years ago!

Squash & Stretch

We have already dealt with the principles of "**Squash**" and "**Stretch**" in our "bouncing ball" exercise. But suffice it to say that it is a really important principle to draw upon if a certainly *flexibility* in an animated object or character is to be achieved. In the past, "squash" and "stretch" have been attributed to the great Disney animator, **Fred Moore**, and some research into his work will show you how effective it can be – especially his animation of the Severn Dwarfs in *Snow White and the Seven Dwarfs* movie.

Squashed and stretched Arnie.

The Disney studio evolved away from the more rubbery version of these principles eventually, preferring to use the fixed and natural anatomy of their characters to define *"squash"* and *"stretch"* in a less cartoony way. The basic principles are that when a softer character hits a harder surface, it will tend to deform into a more squashed shape – meaning that, as with a rubber ball hitting the solid ground, the ball will reduce in height and expand in width as it does so. This is *"squash"*.

Squash & Stretch – Photoshop style.

Alternatively, if an object like a rubber ball accelerates through the air or in dropping toward the ground the equivalent of *"motion blur"* in the animated world, it is extend the length of the ball along the path of action, which shrinking the width of it. This is *"stretch"*.

Anticipation

Just like Newton's third law, which states that *"for every action in nature, there is an equal and opposite reaction"*, animation's second law states that *"for every main action, there's first a less equal and small opposite action"*. Essentially, this means that if someone is going to hammer a nail in, they will not just bring the hammer down from the first position, but will lift it up first in the opposite direction before bringing it down.

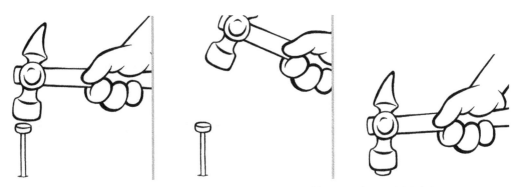

Addressing the nail (left), "anticipation" up (center) and hitting the nail (right).

Similarly, with a traditional cartoon character that is about to dash of screen in any direction, with a puff of dust following them off, there will first be a slow wind-up action in the opposite direction – like winding up a spring before releasing it.

Warner Brothers inspired "anticipation" pose.

Essentially, *"anticipation"* gives emphasis to a big movement, by easing the audience along slightly in the opposite direction. This means that when the big movement happens, they are less prepared for it and so it has more impact.

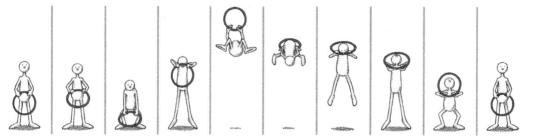

Note with this jumping through a hoop animation, there are two anticipations – the first minor one has the character and hoop rise up a little (2), and then, they sink down for the main deep anticipation (3) before the strong jump up.

Staging

We discussed *"staging"* earlier but, essentially, it is making sure that you frame your animation and everything in your scene in the best possible storytelling way. To do that, you need to understand the purpose of the scene in question, and where you most want to draw the audience's eye to as it plays out. The use of *"perspective"*, *"continuity"*, *"height of the horizon"*, the nature of the *"lighting"* and the fact that, in general, a person's eye is drawn to the place of *"greatest color and light contrast"* – all affect the nature of *"staging"* you will arrive at with each of your scenes.

The Last Supper by Leonardo da Vinci. Notice how the lines of perspective draw our eyes to the center, where the figure of Christ is located, drawing our eyes into the spot in the process. Note also that how the window frames Christ, the lighting creating the greatest contrast in the painting – which is another thing that draws our eye in to the point the artist wanted us to look.

Straight Ahead Action and Pose to Pose

Another thing we have discussed before, although I tend to use the terms *"straight ahead animation"* and *"key pose animation"*, I have rarely used the former but always use the latter, as working with keys, then inbetweens, allows you to keep control of the action, form and continuity of character so much better. The rare times I've used *"straight ahead animation"* is when, for example, a character is drumming their fingers on a tabletop. This is something that's almost impossible to do with *"key pose animation"* as the fingers tend to have an overlapping, ripple action from one to the other.

Drumming on desk – best done using "straight ahead animation".

"Straight ahead animation" can also be used when the action transports us away to a fantasy type sequence, where an existing character or object morphs before our eyes into a number of shape-shifting images that fluidly unfold before our eyes. However, these things are rarely seen, hence the fact that almost everyone works from *"key to key"*.

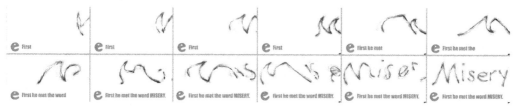

I once animated a painterly style of the word "Misery" creeping into the shot – all done using "straight ahead animation".

Follow-Through/Overlapping Action

I tend to use the term *"overlapping action"* for both of these things, although a number of purists will argue with me. Essentially, what it means is that if you have a main action within *(say)* a character moving, everything attached to that main movement will delay somewhat in the action. For example, if a girly with long hair turns her head, the hair will hold back but then continue moving when her head stops, eventually settling down it its own stop moments later.

When the head stops turning, the hair continues to move.

Similarly, if a character with a long cloak is running, then the cape will flap behind them while the run takes place but – like hair – will drag behind the action and take time to settle into place when the character comes to a halt.

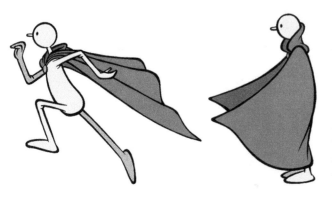

Much animation today doesn't have time or money to add *"overlapping action"* to the movement, so it is rarely seen, except for usually big budget movies of the CG kind.

Overlapping animation on cloak. When the character stops, the cloak keeps going past him and then settles down eventually.

Slow-In and Slow-Out

You will also remember this one from our *"Bouncing Ball"* exercise at the very beginning – where the force of gravity decelerates the ball as it rises up and accelerates it as it descends down. *"Slowing-in"* therefore describes any action that is slowing down and *"slowing-out"* describes any action that is speeding up. Nothing in this world moves at an even pace, it is either speeding up or slowing down. This can be achieved in animation by adding more inbetweens to slow something down, or remove them to speed it up. A traditional, hand-drawing animator will indicate *"slowing-in"* and *"slowing-out"* by the way they draw up *"inbetween charts"* on their key drawings.

Bouncing ball, showing the "slowing-in and slowing-out" by the close overlaps at the top of the bounce and the wider ones at the bottom.

Arc

Just as nothing in Nature moves at an even pace, nothing in Nature moves in a straight line – except of course, the most rigid of machines. Animators over the years soon learned that if they wanted a more dynamic and natural look to their movement, they should place their inbetweens on a slight arc, rather than in a straight line. Consequently, a *"swinging arm"*, a *"head turn"* and an *"object hurtling through space"* look so much more convincing if they move on an *"arc"*.

Animation moving on an arc – a parody of "Pinocchio", for my film *Endangered Species*.

Computer animators these days neglect this at their peril. In the interests of time and money, they tend to rely on software doing most of the work for them. *"In-betweening"* is a case in question. However, computers think in straight lines – which is why action today is to dull and static looking compared with the great animation of the past from *"volume"* studios like Fleischer, Warner Brothers and even (heaven forefend) Hanna & Barbara. Consequently, if computer animators care about what they do, they should remember the principle of *"arcs"* and force themselves out of their comfort zone by educating their software on what they need for a movement from key to key.

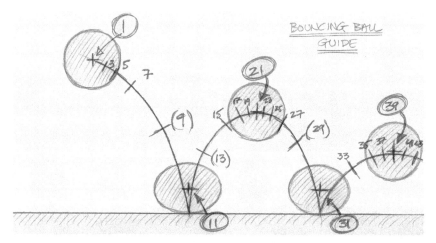

A bouncing ball guide layout, indicating the arcs.

Secondary Action

This one's a little like *"overlapping action"*. "Secondary action" is a situation where although you have a main action with a character or object, there is also something animating on its own that is somewhat dependent, or secondary, to what that main action is doing. So it could be that a character is carrying a flower in a pot as they walk along. The character walk is the main action, but possibly the cartoony flower is looking all around and enjoying the view and the main character passes along a scene. It adds value and extra interest to the scene.

I once animated a small Arnie, sitting on my desk, conducting. Note the overlapping action on the pencil when his arm reaches the top of its arc – the arm almost stops moving but the pencil continues to rotate.

Similarly, some objects are sitting on a table. However, when an angry character beats on that table, the objects are sprung up and spread around as a result of the table impact. They might go in all different directions and land in all kinds of different ways. They are not the main action but they are the *secondary* results of that main action.

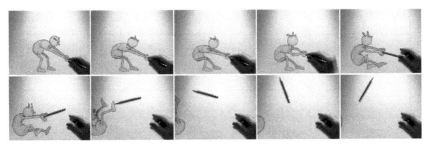

When I animated Arnie pulling a real pencil out of my hand, I had it spinning out of his hands as "secondary action" after his hand had released it.

Timing

We have dealt with *"timing"* earlier. Good animation – like comedy – demands perfect timing. If rush something too fast, or take too long with it – it can ruin a perfectly good sequence, not matter how hard it is drawn or conceived. So an animator must learn, usually by time and error over the years, how to time their action perfectly. This of course requires that they use precisely the right number of inbetweens to link to keys – with the more inbetweens there are, the **slower** the action – or the less inbetweens they are, the **faster** it will be.

Showing the different approaches to timing drawings. Column 1 is animation numbered and timed on "twos". Column 2 is the same action and timing, but with inbetweens added and shot on "ones" – the most smooth action you can achieve. Column 3 is inbetweened then shot on "twos" – doubling the length of the action in screen time.

This also brings into the equation the use of *"holds"* in animation. Meaning that sometimes – like the best of Chuck Jones' short films for Warner Brothers – a lack of movement can totally dramatize the previous or subsequent movement. This is yet another challenging use of *"timing"* for the animator – not to mention the use of *"slowing-in"* and *"slowing-out"* either!

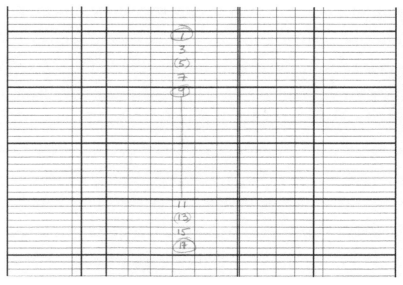

Note that drawing "9" is held for 16 frames – to give a brief pause in the action – before the movement continues.

Exaggeration

You may have remembered me talking about caricaturing reality, not copying it in animation. This is the principle of *"exaggeration"*, and it is especially important the more cartoony your animation is intended to be.

I really enjoyed channeling my mentor, Ken Harris, to achieve the extreme, Warner Brothers kind of pose for Arnie in this scene!

But even if your action is very low key and not very dynamic, you'll find that you'll get the best out of your movement if you learn to push your key positions an exaggerate what they're trying to create.

Arnie walking with a staff was based on live action reference footage I shot for a film I was trying to make at the time – William Heath Robinson's *The Adventures of Uncle Lubin*.

In our observational gesture drawing sessions, we learn to observe, but then to exaggerate where we can. If you do not do that – even if you trace off live action reference positions and inbetween them like animation – they your movement will look staid and wooden. And even if you're trying to make your animation look like real-life movement, you'll find that you have to exaggerate your key positions, then inbetween them with modified timings, before they look that way. This is why caricaturing, or extending your poses, is such an important principle.

Patrick Mate's caricatured designs of me – now and as a child – as concepts for my animated memoirs project.

Solid Drawing

In our observational gesture drawing sessions, we embrace the notion of *"solid drawing"*. However, in the days when Frank and Ollie first wrote about it, it meant so much more. Traditional hand-drawn animation is obviously based on your drawing the best keys and the most accurate inbetweens you can. To do that, you need to add you our *"animator's eye"* the skills and dexterity that will enable you to best communicate what you're seeing and what you want the audience to see. That is why our observational gesture drawing exercises are so important.

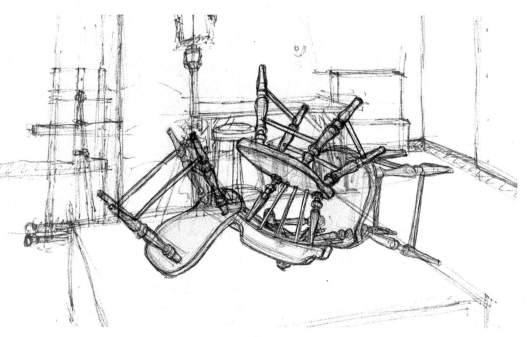

An exercise I gave students in a gesture drawing class. They were to draw a series of still life key positions that I set the chair in; then, they had to inbetween them. This is my own demonstration drawing of how an inbetween might look.

Yet even in this CG-based, 3D animation world, animators neglect their drawing skills at their own peril. Unless you can observe and translate your observations in to strongly visual sketches, you can never really appreciate what makes a good, strong pose and what does not. That's why if you look at the work of the majority of the top 3D animation animators out there, you will see a passion and a love of drawing and other aspects of artistic expression. That is why Pixar, at the very beginning, hired so many ex-Disney 2D animators to make **Toy Story** and is why that later, Pixar established their university for artists and staff – to raise their artistic skills, knowing that this will translate into superior animation technique. Their track record, and influence on the rest of the industry, speaks for itself.

And speaking of a 2D/3D crossover – it can be very useful to create a simple CG model (or physical machete) of your 2D character design. That way you have an idea how to draw it from all angles, when rotated.

Appeal

This, of all the 12 principles, is perhaps the most redundant in our modern, digital day and age. At the time, this one was written about, Disney films – as in fact today – relied on a kind of *formulaic "appeal"* that focused on a specific audience base. *"Cute"* perhaps is another word to describe it, although the animation of today has moved on to a variety of diverse styles and age appropriateness. Consequently, what was appealing back in the days of *"The Illusion of Life"* is not considered so appealing any more in the minds of the more inventive and progressive animators of today.

"Appeal" is in the eye of the beholder!

Therefore, we have to be very careful what we're talking about if we use the work appeal. *"One man's meat is another man's poison"* is a phrase that comes to mind here. For many, the formulaic *"cute"* of Disney princesses and comedic and lovable sidekicks is definitely not appealing to many emerging animators today. For some, even gothic horror can be appealing if handled well. Dark and dangerous subjects in animation can be appealing to some others too. So it is hard to exactly what *"appeal"* means anymore.

"Appeal" can be found in the most unappealing settings, if handled well.

Perhaps it is time to reconsider this and one or two other of the 12 principles to bring them more in line with our current culture?

New Thoughts on the 12 Principles

I have long thought that not all of the 12 principles stand up to modern scrutiny. I know that some purists will lynch me for this but one look at the needs of the modern world will see that most of the existing principles are 100% relevant, but not all of them are. Perhaps it would do to consider a couple of new ones they might replace the less appropriate of the old ones? This could be a bigger debate beyond this book, and there are certainly more suggestions than just the two that follow. But I definitely think these should be taught as much in schools and colleges as the existing 12 principles. They are equally relevant.

Balance

This of all my ideas is the most important. I have dealt with it already in this book, but I will restate it here, as it really is something that is missing from the 12 principles. As mentioned elsewhere, it took me many years of working in the industry before learning the importance of *"balance"* to movement. If the pose balance of your key positions is wrong, then no amount of finessing and overlaying with special effects and beautiful movement will cover up the bad movement.

In terms of biped character animation, the rule of "**balance**" is simple. The *center of gravity* must always be positioned above the point, or points, of contact with the ground if balance is to be achieved. By that, I mean that the weight of a character needs to be over one of two feet, depending on whether one or two feet are on the ground at the same time. If a char-

Although it can be a very subtle thing, good balance can make a big difference when trying to convince an audience of the credibility of your action. Left is poor balance, whereas right is correct balance.

acter needs to left one of their legs, then they have to shift the weight over the foot that is on the ground. Then, when that free comes down and the other leg needs to pick up, then the body weight must shift over to the new contact point before the second leg can be lifted. This is of course what happens with a good walking action if seen from the front – with that shift of *"balance"* being more extreme the heavier or rounder a character is.

Good balance is always achieved if the body's "center of gravity" is located directly over the key point of contact with the ground – even if the boy position has to be adjusted to accommodate it.

Of course, if the opposite visual effect is required – that is, a drunk or a child learning to walk is about to fall on their face, then their center of gravity needs to be ahead of their points of contact with the ground – leaning ahead in the direction of the fall and failing to get a free leg over fast enough to stop themselves.

We trip over because the momentum of our body – and its center of gravity – is thrown so far forward that our feet cannot move through quick enough to stop us falling on our face.

Weight

It amazes me that one of the great accomplishments of the Disney studio, when it was a great and forward-looking studio under Walt's trusteeship, is that they brought the fundamental principle of "**weight**" to their characters. Yet Frank and Ollie never listed this in their 12 principles, which it is surprising the omitted in view of them focusing on lesser principles such as very subjective things like *"Solid drawing"* and *"Appeal"*. *"Weight"* is the one thing that separated the great Disney studio way back then from their contemporaries and their rivals. Just compare their films with those of the *Fleischer* and *Sullivan* studios, and you'll see what I mean. Walt evolve the factor of weight in this character animation, and the world struggled to catch up to that.

I briefly explored the animation style of Fleischer, Disney and Warner Brothers – plus many more – in my film on the rise, fall and hopeful rise again of traditional hand-drawn animation, *Endangered Species* (2002).

"Weight" in animation demands that if a figure is heavy, or they are a normal-sized figure carrying a heave weight, then they will pose and move in a very different way than if no weight was there at all. Pose-wise, a character carrying heavy weight of any kind will need to communicate to the audience the modification their body needs to make. Their back may be more bowed, their knees

more bent, and their balance would need to adjust so that the center of gravity between their body weight and the weight being carried is above the point, or points, of contact with the ground beneath them.

The pose is everything! Each pose should tell a story and if your key poses don't, then you animation will never be fully convincing.

Equally, the movement of a character carrying some kind of weight will be affected significantly too. They will not be able to move as fast, or a sure, as that weight will require them to make a greater effort to be in control. Similarly, to lift a weight from a lower place to a higher place will be harder and slower too – and definitely need a *"slow-out"* approach to the beginning until a little momentum is achieved.

In tribute to the film, *Sisyphus*, by Jankovics Marcell – the finest example of "weight" ever animated!

Superimposition

I have dealt with *"superimposition"* elsewhere – in this book, in my classes and in some of my other books. So, I will not go into it in detail here again. Suffice it to say, although this is not a *"principle of movement"* in the *Frank and Ollie* mode, I do believe it vitally important to lump it into the discussion, as it is not dealt with anywhere else to my knowledge. And yet, at the same time, it is fundamentally important to the process of traditional hand-drawn inbetweening.

  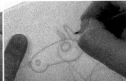 

Video demonstration of "superimposition" – marking in the key reference points (1), lining up the reference points with the superimposed keys (2), inbetweening while drawings are all "superimposed" (3) and putting drawings back on the pegs to show the final inbetween (4).

For example, where two drawings are far apart and need one (or more) inbetweens to link them, it is virtually impossible to inbetween those drawings by eye alone. But, by marking rough inbetween *"key points"* between those two drawings and then *"superimposing"* the three drawings over each other, the accuracy and the consistency of the inbetween drawing are far more guaranteed.

An example of taped down, superimposed drawings on my lightbox – lined up to work only with the torso of the body.

For this reason, I make *"superimposition"* a major principle when teaching students' animation in my traditional 2D classes.

Suggested Assignment

No special instructions here, as you've got more than enough on your plate in working through your *"Production"*. However, I just urge you to not move forward into "inbetweening" until you are absolutely satisfied that your "pose test animatic" is working well in real time.

Onward and upward!

Masterclass 41/ Inbetweening 1

This probably marks a point when the most creative work on your project is over and you just have the "grunt work" to do. Personally, I never see **"inbetweening"** as grunt work, as even now there are creative elements that come into play. As you get more experienced and have got more animation under your belt, you will begin to be quite creative with the way you do inbetweens – for example, knowing when to inbetween precisely parts of your character drawing positions, while holding back or advancing other parts to get a particular effect. However, at this stage and on your first ever animation project, I strongly recommend that you play it safe and make sure everything you draw in your inbetweens are **precisely halfway**. That way there should be no unexpected surprises when you film your final *"pencil test"*, at least unless your *"keys"* or *"breakdowns"* are not correct of course. But before we going into *"inbetweening"* further, let's warm you up with another observational gesture drawing challenge.

Warm-Up Drawing

Here, we have another of those exercises where you are required to draw multiple angles of a single object on one page. Previously, we tackled a turnaround exercise relating to a skull. This time though we're going to look at something even more challenging – in a word, **"hands"**. Hands are considered the hardest things to draw on the human body, which is all the more reason why we should spend some time on them here! Hands are a means of great expression

DOI: 10.1201/9781003324287-45

for animated characters, so we ignore them at our peril. For this exercise, you are asked to draw a hand from **six** different viewpoints. However, again you need to keep a sense of size consistency and proportion accuracy for each of the six drawings on your page. So, to help you before you draw, I suggest you divide your page into six equal size sections.

Divide your sketchbook page into six sections.

Now try to draw each of the hands below as close to the same size in each one of them as you can. Give yourself just **1 minute** to draw each one.

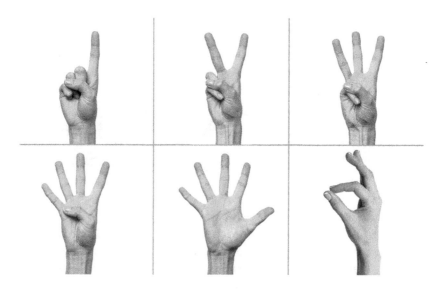

Pose comments: As you draw quickly, try to develop a formula where you first sketch in lightly the bones and joints of the hands, to get the maximum accuracy and continuity of form and proportion as you can. Then, if you have time to add to that drawing before your time is up, flesh them out as best you can.

Now, I know that this one is particularly fast and furious in its nature. However, as drawing hands is the toughest thing, it pays you greatly to do as much as you can to draw them like this. I know that you have so much work on your hands at this point in your production, so this short, sharp, shock approach is probably kinder on your energies than longer timed-out ones. But instead of backing off a tough challenge and not do it, be brave enough to take it on and do it to the best of your ability. The advantage of doing exercises like this from a book of masterclasses is that you don't have an instructor to show your finished drawings to for grading. So, what have you to lose by having a go? Remember, if something is not hard, then it's not worth doing. You need to put challenges before yourself that will take you to the next level. If I don't give you that opportunity here, then I am failing in my role too! I recommend too that you don't just do this exercise once. Take it on many times – or even draw your own hand, or a friend or partner's hand, from many directions against the clock too. And keep yourself under the same time limits too, as forcing you to rush in that way encourages you to make better decisions. Inflicting such tough challenges on yourself in this way can only but improve you as an artist and an animator. And that is what this book is all about after all.

Instruction

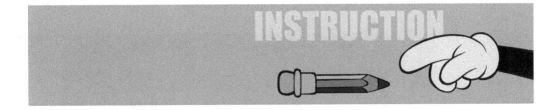

At this stage in my *"live"* classes, I usually just reprise the *"inbetweening"* and *"superimposition"* demo videos that I have shown previously. Indeed, I would recommend that this is a good time to review the things we covered for traditional, hand-drawn animation previously in the book. That said, I would just like to demonstrate my inbetweening process using another example of inbetweening, something I placed on video many years ago but which is still entirely relevant today. It will hopefully give you some additional material that you can apply to your own project.

Drawing "Arnie" – model, muse and mentor!

This is an early version of an "**Arnie**" walk that I did for a class demo. It's a *"generic walk"* so there is not unusual going on here. You can the video of it on our dedicated web page. We'll just look at doing one *"inbetween"*, so you won't e delayed in working on your own project too much. The inbetween drawing we're going to do is number "**2**", charted as being between key *"1"* and another inbetween, number *"3"*. The action is therefore planned to be filmed on "**1s**".

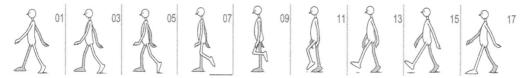

Major positions in a final, color version of an Arnie generic walk.

The first thing I did was to place down a new sheet of paper, and number it "**2**".

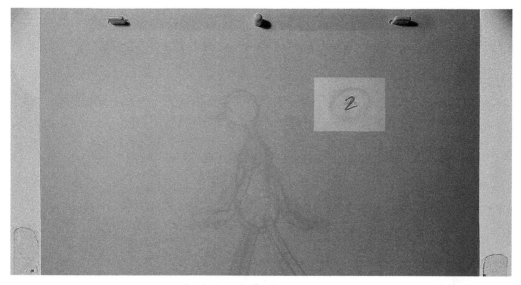

Try to get into the habit of numbering your drawings before you actually draw them – it will save you a lot of stress later!

Then with the lightbox on, with can see the difference between drawings *"1"* and *"3"*. So, the first thing to do is mark down some *"key points"* that are halfway between the two completed drawings – namely the "**head**", the "**shoulder**" and the "**pelvic area**".

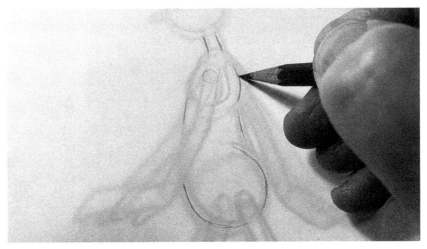

Marking key inbetween points on the torso.

So now, with the lightbox on, take the top two sheets of paper off the pegs and *"superimpose"* drawing "1" over drawing "3", lining up as best you can the "neck", "shoulders" and *"pelvic area"* over one another. Then, superimpose your *"key points"* on drawing number *"2"* over them, matching everything up as accurately as possible.

NOTE

Although we're doing this with the lightbox on behind the drawings, you should sometimes try to train your eye and hand by creating "midpoints" without the use of light at all. So just flip to and fro with the drawings and mark down where you think the midpoints are. You can always check your decisions with backlighting after of course, but it's good to get the experience of doing it without sometimes.

Lining up drawings and key inbetween points.

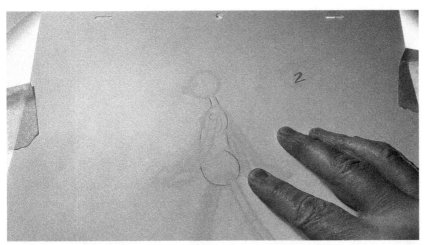

With everything lined up accurately, very lightly draw the inbetween of the *"torso"* in as accurately as you can – lightly suggesting guideline points where the arms and legs might be too. Add the "inbetween" position of the *shoulder* and *hip* circles on the pelvic area too, as this will help later. And if you're really confident, you can add the midpoints for the elbows and wrists too, bearing in mind thought that they will be moving on a very slight arc from the shoulder positions. You can also sketch in the inbetween positions of the eye and the nose too.

Lightly traced inbetween of the body, including rough positions for arms and head.

Then similarly "superimpose" the "shoulder", "elbow" and "wrist" positions over one another, lightly drawing the inbetween there too. Remember that you're superimposing each arm separately however; otherwise, there could be big discrepancies.

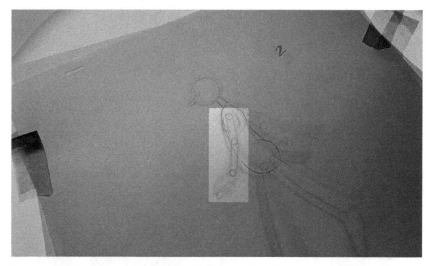

Superimposing the arms over each other, using the new guide points.

As it turned out, the hands aren't doing anything unique, so you can inbetween them when superimposing the arms individually too.

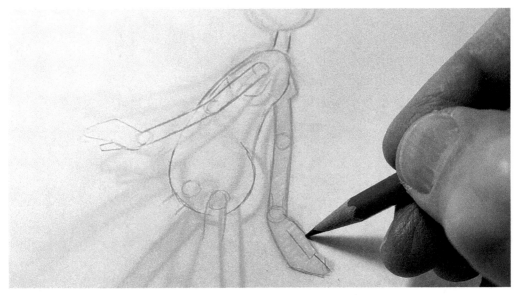

Superimposing the second arm, after having lightly drawn in the first one.

Now, if you put all three drawings back onto the pegs and turn the lightbox on, you can see we have a very accurate inbetween number "2".

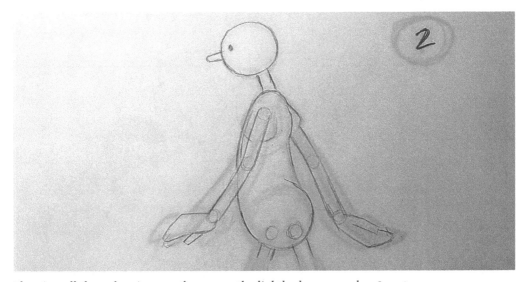

Showing all three drawings on the pegs – the lightly drawn number 2 on top.

"Flip" the pages too, with the lightbox off, so get a sense of the movement also.

Flipping all three drawings.

When you're sure that your lightly drawn "inbetween" drawing is accurate, you can go around and *"clean up"* (darken the lines) where necessary, ready for *"inking"* later.

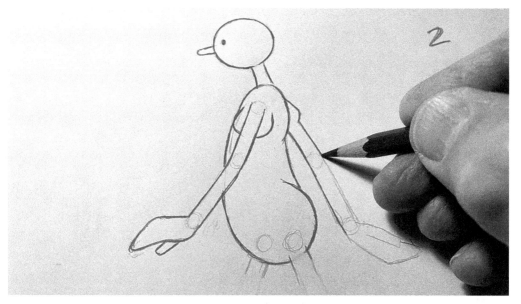

Cleaning up the drawing 2, work in progress.

And although this is a very simple and accommodating action to inbetween, just seeing the *"superimposition"* process again will help you with yours – albeit that many might be much more of a challenge to do than this one. Remember though, **you only *"superimpose"* the parts of the character that you have *"key positions"* marked down for**; otherwise, you risk some of the rest of the inbetween being significantly wrong and you'll have to erase them and draw again.

Lastly, we need to complete the *"legs"*. These are not quite as straightforward, but nowhere near impossible. So, with the drawings back on the pegs, number "2" drawing on top and the lightbox one, we roughly mark in the *"key point"* position of the **front foot** on the ground. Although you can measure this with a ruler if you like, sometimes it's possible to *"eyeball"* it (i.e., judge it by eye) to find the halfway points.

Finding the midpoint of sliding front foot.

"Superimpose" the foot of *"3"* over the foot of *"1'* and then line up the *"key points"* of drawing number *"2"* over them. Lightly draw (trace) your inbetween as before – but adding the circle for the *"ankle"* also.

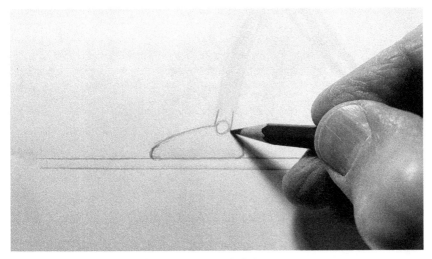

Superimposing front foot and tracing it lightly.

Now superimpose the hips and ankles as closely as you can for three drawings. You'll possibly find that the legs are not as close together on yours as mine are in this example, so you'll have to be open to a bigger challenge for drawing your inbetween. However, with mine, it's almost a simple tracing of the lead leg.

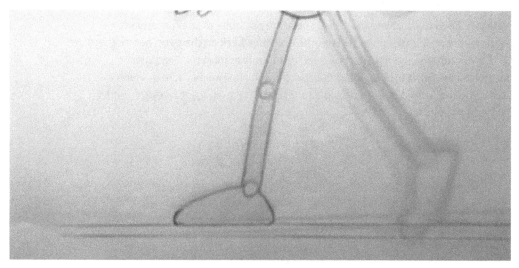

Superimposing and tracing the lead leg.

Now, the back leg is not quite as easy and although the back foot remains on the floor, the ankle is rising up more on the toes in *"3"*. But we still have common reference points for that foot, so I tried to *"eyeball"* them as best I could. That gave me a few *"key points"* to work with, including the *"ankle"*.

Roughing in the key points of the back foot position.

With those points, I *"superimposed"* the three back feet over each other as best as I could and got a very accurate inbetween in the end.

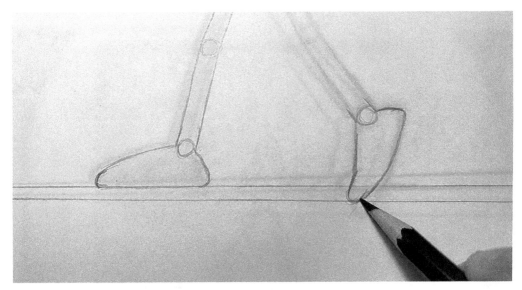

Superimposing and inbetweening the back foot.

Now, with the *"hip"* and the *"ankle"* positions marked on drawing *"2"*, I will able to line them up with the other two drawings when superimposing and then lightly inbetweening the difference between the back legs.

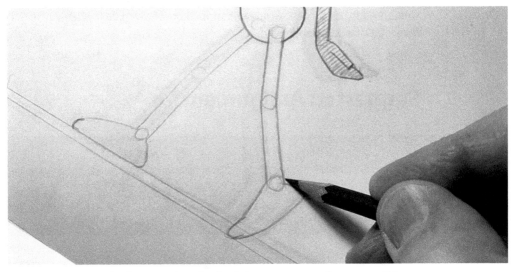

Superimposing and inbetweening the back leg as accurately as possible.

This gave me the entire new inbetween. So, I *"flipped"* it once again to double-check everything and then seeing it was fine I just cleaned up the legs by darkening the lines, completing the *"inbetweening"* exercise.

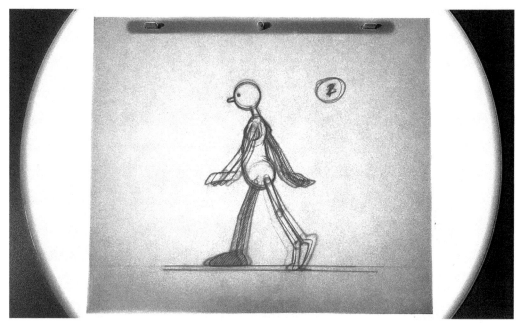

The final inbetween completed, with the back light on.

Finally, don't forget that sometimes you'll find that your inbetweens will be so close together that you don't need to do *"superimposition"* at all. However, I went through the process again here, so you know how to do it when you're not drawing just a basic inbetween.

Suggested Assignment

You'll have plenty to do in just inbetweening all your *"key"* and *"breakdown"* drawings at this stage, so I don't have to heart to give you an assignment here! Just be as accurate as you can with your "inbetweens" and learn to trust yourself when drawing without "superimposing" and when *"superimposing"*.

Moho, or other digital animators, will not have to worry about any of the *"superimposing"* techniques, although you will have to learn when to let Moho do the natural inbetweens for you, or when you have to intervene and make slight adjustments to do something that is not just mechanically halfway. But this regards judgment, based on experience. So, you might just have to settle for the mechanical inbetweening that software does for now.

Masterclass 42/
Inbetweening 2

It occurs to me to say this to your right now. If you're facing a mound of *"in-betweens"* that need to get done and are fading fast, just *keep on, keeping on*. Sometimes, the tasks we set ourselves seem just one step too far. However, by pressuring ourselves so much that we don't do them in the end, or we compromise on the quality to get it done faster, we only fall into a trap that we set ourselves. Unhappiness invariably comes from false expectations, so don't ever feel that you have to rush to achieve what you're doing. Pace yourself. Instead of seeing two weeks of non-stop work ahead of you, set different limits. Maybe two or three inbetweens a day, then get on with something else. I have met so many young students who fall at the last hurdle in this way, simply because they set themselves false expectations. I apprenticed with one of the most demanding taskmasters ever, **Richard Williams**. He would put huge expectations on himself as well as on others. But he would always say, don't waste your time and energy saying that what you're doing will never get done. Instead, he said just sit and draw, and draw, and draw, and eventually the problem will solve itself. I am personally a *workaholic*, like Dick Williams was, but I'm also a *multitasker*. So I find renewed energy by having two or three projects on the go at once. By skipping from one to the other, periodically, I find that I return to each one entirely refreshed and energized every time. Now everyone is different, and you'll need to find our own ways of climbing the mountain. But you've come so far right now it would be sad if you stop as a result of false expectations – even doubts that none of it is worthy anyway. It is. Just make sure your expectations are reasonably, and you pace yourself in a reasonable manner.

Having said that let's relax with some observational gesture drawing.

DOI: 10.1201/9781003324287-46

Warm-Up Drawing

GESTURE DRAWING

This time, to lighten your load somewhat, I'm going to suggest something different here. I want you to draw hands, but this time I want you to draw your own hands, *"live"*. What I have in mind here is really simple. In essence, I want you to draw **3 × 2-minute** poses of your own free hand. (Tape down your sketchbook if it's going to slide around without your free hand holding it.) Basically, that's all there is to it. Just place your free hand in three different positions at random – or have that hand go through a process of movement. I'm thinking here that your hand might go through three action poses like – (i) anticipating grabbing something on the desk, (ii) actually grabbing it, and (iii) holding it up to look at it. Alternatively, you could consider (i) the front of your hand, (ii) the side of your hand, and (iii) the back of your hand. Things like this will at least will get you into the spirit of observing and recording an action. But whatever you choose to do is entirely your choice here. As long as your free hand is in different positions each time and you draw all three gesture drawings on one sheet of paper, you're good.

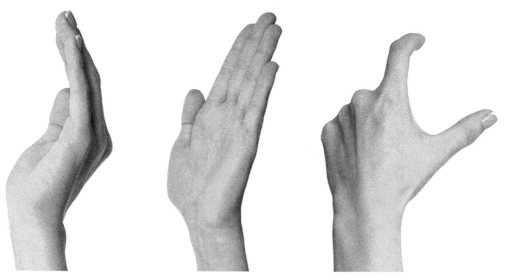

Three sample pictures of a hand – but use your own hand for the best results!

Comments: Again, we're not talking about photogenic reality here. This is all about proportions, consistency of size and structures. Work from the center out – inner skeletal lengths and angles, joints, then flesh out if you have time. More simplistically, maybe lines for the center of your finger, a box of the palm of your hand and build it up from there. Remember, it is more important that you understand how the hand works, and getting the various angles right from the joints and beyond, than making it look real. This really is the essence of *gesture drawing* as animation reference.

Instruction

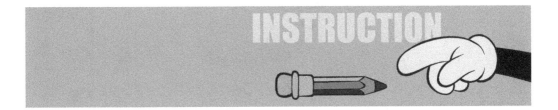

I think it would pay us to review a couple of things right now. More specifically, I want to remind you about *"timing"* and how the number of inbetweens affect the speed of the action. We dealt with the following earlier in the book, but it is so important at this stage that I think it worth repeating some basic principles – especially now, when you are doing your own inbetweens for your own project. Remember how we talked about the car movements and how they changed by the number of inbetweens we had when it went from *"A"* to *"B"*, or how it slowed down when we added more *"slow-in"* inbetweens at the end? Well, let's cover that ground again and underline a few significant facts here again. We'll use a ball rolling down a gentle hill.

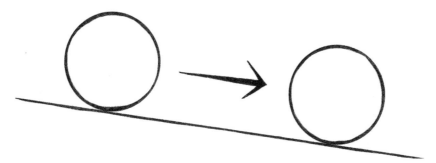

Simple action of a ball rolling down a hill.

(i) **No inbetweens**: If there are no inbetweens linking two keys, then it will be a sudden jump from one position to another. That can be quite effective if used sparingly. For example, if a golf club is swinging through to hit a static ball on a tee, that ball will cut from its first position and almost (or fully) out of the screen on the next frame – even though the golf club may still be swinging through on its own flowing, inbetweened movement.

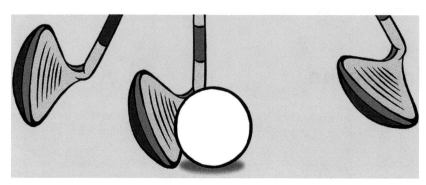

Once the ball has been hit hard it can disappear, even though the club will animate through.

Similarly, if a character is about to fire an arrow from a bow, you can do a very "slow"/"*slowing-in*" sequence of inbetweens on the pullback, but then release the bow and have the arrow placed almost – or completely – out of the screen on the very next frame. The bow maybe reacting and animating in its own right after the release but the sudden disappearance of the arrow, from one frame to another, with no inbetweens, will only serve to make the action all the more powerful.

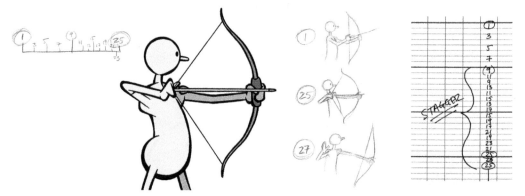

To the right, the three-key thumbnail process of firing an arrow. Address the bow (top), slow pullback to extended position (middle) and instant release (bottom). Note the chart indicating a lot of inbetweens, slowing-in significantly to the end. If a "stagger is added to the pullback, then the tension will be great when the release happens. There is no need to show the arrow leaving the bow, once the release is enacted.

(ii) **More or less inbetweens**: Remember always that the **more** inbetweens you use between two keys, the **slower** the action will be. The **less** inbetweens you use, the **faster** it will be. The following will illustrate this.

Two keys, no inbetweens.

There would be no flow to this movement, just the ball jumping from one position to another on the screen. However, if we add **three inbetweens** that overlap slightly, then there will be a sense of movement – although it will be fast.

Two keys, with three overlapping inbetweens.

Now, if we inbetween this again, we will both slow the movement down by half and have more smoothness to the movement.

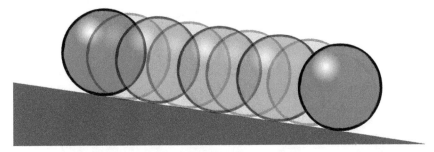

Two keys, with seven overlapping inbetweens.

Note that if there were only two inbetweens linking the two keys, and there was no overlapping, then the action would stagger or staccato, as the brain finds it hard to create the overlapping for itself.

Two keys, with two widely spaced inbetweens.

Finally, remember that speed relates to the number of frames that each drawing is on the screen for. If they are shot on "1s", then the action will be twice as fast as if they were shot on "2s".

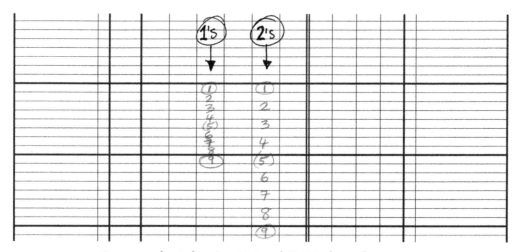

Exposure sheet showing "1s" and "2s" indicated.

(iii) **Even inbetweens**: Let us remind ourselves that the above indicates "even inbetweens" – in other words, all the inbetweens are equally spaced between the two keys as we indicated above.

Two keys and seven inbetweens, as before.

(iv) **Slow-in inbetweens**: However, if we want the action to accelerate or decelerate, we need to think again. For example, if want the action to decelerate between the two keys, we have to create "slow-in" inbetweens. This means that there are more inbetweens toward the end of the movement than at the beginning.

Two keys, with three inbetweens slowing-in toward the end.

(v) **Slow-out inbetweens**: Alternatively, if we want the action between two keys to accelerate from one to the other, we have to have extra inbetweens at the front of the action.

Two keys, with three inbetweens slowing-out from the beginning.

This is of course a very simplistic way of learning about *"timing"*. Normally, it takes a lifetime of animating to fully master what so many inbetweens mean in terms of what kind of speed you'll get between your keys. But modern technology, such as *Rough Animator* on the iPad, gives us a chance to experience this very quickly, and at first hand.

Suggested Assignment

Keep on inbetweening on your project ahead of anything else. But definitely play with the above timings if you can. Getting a sense of timing like this *rough and ready* way will help you assess how many inbetweens you'll need for your own project actions. Playing like this with software is definitely a good way of learning the principles of *"timing"*. So, maybe even have **several keys** in a sequence on your timeline and **open them up in different ways** to see how you can vary the timing throughout your *key-to-key* action. Yes, it is aimless playing, but it is always through play what all of Nature learns how to survive in the grown-up world. Similarly, playing with technology like this will help your mature in the professional world too. So, have fun – and learn!

NOTE

Don't forget to film a final *"pencil test"* of all your animation drawings when you've "inbetweened" everything! It's always good to view your work **in real time** at every stage of the process – and none is more important than at this stage. Make corrections and adjustments if necessary.

Masterclass 43/ Cleanup 1

Well, more congratulations are in order at this stage – that is, if you've kept up with the program so far. That means you've just finished your *"inbetweening"* and are about to start the "**clean up**" of your drawings. It has no doubt been a long haul doing all those inbetweens for the hand-drawn animation. But hopefully your *"pencil test"* video is brimming with excellence. So, give yourself a big slap on the back, if you can reach that far. Alternatively, animate your main character giving itself a big slap on the back – as everything is possible with animation! Anyway, perhaps the best way to celebrate is to draw some more – specifically, observational gesture drawing.

Warm-Up Drawing

Another quickie for you here – one I'm going to call "**Sequential walk**"! You're probably pretty drawn-out right now so this one is more to exercise your animator's mind and observational analysis skills than test your drawing dexterity – although drawing is required, of course. Good animation is all about understanding *"sequential action"*. To get a really convincing flow to your movement it is first necessary for you to research the action as best you can before animating it – often with exaggeration. Therefore, the following *"speed drawing"* exercise will help you understand the frame-by-frame basis better, in this case another relating to an animated walk. So, try to quickly draw each one of these

DOI: 10.1201/9781003324287-47

following positions on a single page of your sketchbook – or better still, on small and separate cards, in the same location on the cards, so that you can flip them afterwards, like a *"flipbook"*, and see the movement. You should give yourself just **1 minute** for each of the eight different poses.

Comments: As ever, it's more important for you to capture the inner action, angles and proportions here than even attempt a detailed, photography likeness. So again, sketch the *"inner stick figure"* first – ensuring you are capturing the essence of the poses – then flesh out your drawings if time permits. If you ultimately end up with a wonderfully animated stick figure flipbook action, then you have fully achieved the object of the exercise. Anything else is merely the cherry on the cake.

Gesture drawings of above by student, Tina Braun.

It has to be said that the walk you have just observed is pretty much of the "generic" variety, as we studied much earlier in this book. However, in the real world, a person's walking action is often far from generic, with each one symbolizing their mood, urgency, physical capability and sometimes even intention. So, like fingerprints, no two walks are exactly the same. Indeed, the same person can have variations of their won walk, depending on the four factors mentioned above. Our emotions, confidence, fears, excitement and celebrations will affect the way we move, and especially the way we walk. Do they cause us to walk faster, or to drag our feet? Are we happy or are we sad when walking? Are we keen to get somewhere, or reluctant? Are we walking uphill, or down – against the wind, or with the wind at our backs? Are they heavy, or are they light? Are they injured or a fit athlete?

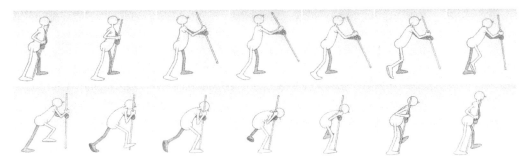

The challenge of this walk was to create a character who was both old and tired. Effectively, however, it is a basic generic walk with important pose and timing changes.

These are all questions that the astute animator will ask, prior to working on a character and their walk. Most walks look entirely generic today, even in the professional media world. Some even are really badly done. But what raises great animation from the rest is by what is communicated from the character to the audience by the way they are walking. The bottom line here is to **observe people walking** and learn from what you see! Remember too, that a walk is the hardest action to pull off as an animator. But if you can do it, and with mood or personality thrown in, then you have mastered many of the great principles of. Succeeding with a walk ensures that you'll succeed with anything else you attempt in animation because most of the secrets of animation are tied up in a walking action.

Instruction

Rough animation drawing.

Hopefully, you are now ready to "**clean up**" your rough animation drawings now? This process involves tidying up everything, so that your animation can be inked with little difficulty. Quite often *"rough"* animation means quickly drawn in shapes and rarely involves drawing a character in their final designed detail. Consequently, the *"cleanup process"* means making sense of the shapes that are working well in movement but don't necessarily look good as an individual drawing.

In a large, professional studio setting there is usually a team of *"cleanup artists"* to do that, instead of the animators. But as you've found with your own project, the load is entirely carried by you and so you'll have to do the *"clean up"* and *"inking"* stages yourself. If you're really adept as an artist and can effectively draw your character with your eyes closed, you might even risk doing the *"clean up"* and *"inking"* at the same time. But unless you are a natural artist capable of such a thing – unlike yours truly, incidentally – then you're safer to do the cleanup drawings first, then ink them from that stage afterwards.

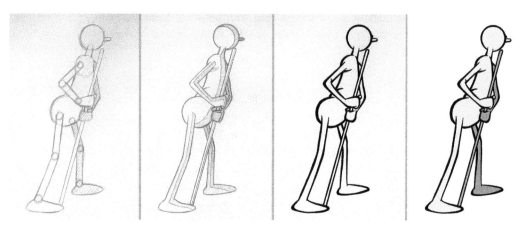

Rough drawing, cleaned up drawing, inked drawing, and final colored character.

Everyone has a different technique for *"cleaning up"* their animation. Some draw on a new sheet of paper over the top of their original drawing, while others prefer to *"clean up"* that animation drawing directly. I fall into the latter category. My process is as follows:

First, I take the animation drawing, then lightly dust over the drawing with a **"kneadable eraser"** to take the top surface of pencil line off. This leaves the original drawing visible, but much lighter than before.

Lightly erasing the heavy, rough lines with kneadable eraser.

Next, I will use my original pencil – my preference is a "**Col-erase BLUE**" pencil.

The Col-erase
BLUE pencil.

With the lead sharpened, I carefully drawing over the lightened lines with a much darker, single line.

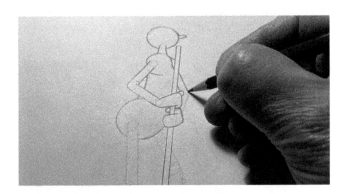

Cleaning up
the lightened
lines, making
them darker
and cleaner.

That done, I might even lightly erase the drawing again with my *"kneadable eraser"* again, to knock back everything ever further, except for the darkly drawn, most recent lines.

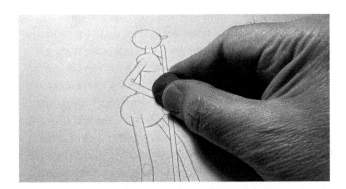

Lightly
erasing with
kneadable
eraser again,
to really
sharpen the
lines.

Finally, I will pencil test the sequence again before I move on to the *"inking"* stage.

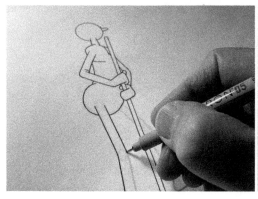 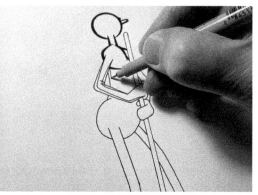

Finally inking the pencil lines. For me, I do it in two stages – the first time I trace the lines with an even width Micron pen, then draw "thick 'n thin" lines around these, finally blackening them in.

If you're confident enough, you can inbetween your key drawings directly by pen drawing, saving the pencil inbetweening stage entirely!

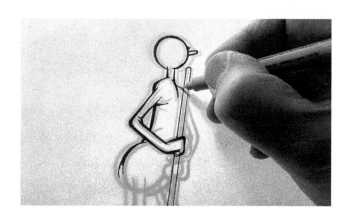

There is another option that many experienced animators take, in that they will "clean up" their "key" and "breakdown" drawings first, then inbetween them with "cleaned up" inbetweens.

This shortcuts the process somewhat, in that you don't have to do rough inbetweens then clean them up too. However, unless you are really experienced it is a risk too far – which is why in this book I am taking you through the *safe but sure* approaches to doing everything for the first time. But if you are not doing this for the first time and you have some solid animation under your belt from the past, you might consider the *"cleaned up inbetweens"* approach – maybe even drawing your *"keys"* and *"breakdowns"* cleaned up from the get-go, eliminating yet another layer of the production process. However, this really should only be undertaken when you are absolutely sure that what you're doing is going to work first time at both the *"animation"* and the *"cleaned up drawing from scratch"* levels.

Suggested Assignment

You might consider experimenting with the way you draw your *"cleanups"*. I have shared the fact that I like to use *"Col-erase BLUE"* pencils throughout my entire drawn animation process. But other animators will work somewhat differently. Even if they may use the same pencils as I do to create their rough animation, they might use a *"graphite"* pencil, or *"Blackwing"* pencil to do their *"cleanups"*, giving a much darker line than mine. So, experiment and see what works for you. Comfort is everything in animation and the more you feel confident with the tools or techniques you use, the better your work and work appreciation will be. We are all different and there is no one right way anymore. Indeed, with digital technology – which we're not focusing upon in this book, but which is increasingly more valid – the process is streamlined so much more. (For the rec ord, my next online couse is teaching iPad animation with "Rough Animator", so let it not be said that I'm a technology luddite!).

Finally, do check out how other master animators work online. I don't mean ANY other animators, but I do mean seek out only the very best and learn how they approach not only "cleanup" but other aspects of the production process too. As I say, there is not one way of approach that works for all. The principles of move-ment ARE common to all animation, but the way they are implemented is very much a personal thing. Living luminaries such as **Glen Keane** and **Aaron Blaise** especially spring to mind here. Seek out their tutorials or lectures online and learn from what they have to say too. There is one by Aaron Blaise especially, on *"cleanup"*, that might be of especial interest at this stage in your project proceed-ings. You can find it on Aaron's own personal website: *https://www.youtube.com/watch?v=hdNYfLLHIMM*. He is drawing digitally but the approach he uses applies just as much as if he were working with paper and pencils.

Masterclass 44/ Cleanup 2

You will notice I'm sure that the majority of focus over the last few lessons – and indeed, the following ones – has totally been *"traditional-centric"*. This means that I have somewhat neglected our Moho/digital animators. However, this is for good reason. Once your character is designed, colored and rigged in Moho, then you don't need to do *"clean up"* or *"inking"*. That is already established, so all you need to focus on has been the animated movement. The traditional hand-drawn animators, by comparison, need to focus long and hard on all the mid to closing *"Production"* processes. This is why I have focused solely on that work for you. It represents no favoritism, just reality. Everything about traditional animation is *handcrafted*, so at its highest level, we really need to focus on every stage in fine detail, so that you won't trip up at any stage along the way through my negligence. Thank you for hanging in there with me. But now, let's keep going with the observational gesture drawing.

Warm-Up Drawing

This is another one that I hope is a light relief from all that focused action drawing that we've been doing until now. In this lesson, I want you to kick off your artistic shoes and enjoy drawing a timeless character from my own, British artistic heritage. I spent a significant amount of time and money to try to bring William Heath Robinson's **The Adventures of Uncle Lubin** to the animated screen. Published in 1902, the story of Uncle Lubin as beautifully drawn as it is fantastic. So

DOI: 10.1201/9781003324287-48

in tribute to this timeless, classical figure from one of the great children's book illustrators of that time, I want to dispense with you drawing observationally from
the real world and have a stab at drawing this classical moment from Lubin's
illiad-like journey in time and space. So, ignoring all the detailed cross-hatching
and complex background, I would like you to draw the basic structure of Uncle Lubin and his vast hat, taking just **3 minutes** to complete it. I know there is
a huge amount of *"pencil mileage"* (amount of drawing) in the original. But I just
want you to draw Lubin as simply and as accurately as possible. Essentially, this
is an eye-judgment and scaling thing, where volumes and proportions are much
more important than the inked-in detail of Heath Robinson's beloved original.

From "The Adventures of Uncle Lubin" by William Heath Robinson.

Instruction

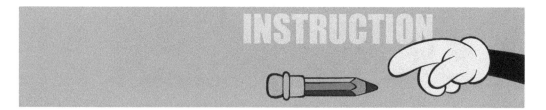

Now at this stage with my *"live & online"* classes, I give the students as much time
to work on their *"inbetweening"* and *"clean up"* as possible. One or two students
even find that they have fallen behind the class production schedule – mainly for no fault of their own in places. So, knowing that it will be impossible for
them to catch up with the other students, I allowed them a lesser challenge for

the completion of the course. Namely, the creation of a fully cleaned up and polished *"animatic"*. For those students, I created an audio podcast to show them the process I used to create an animatic for my film, *"The Hermit"*.

The **CLASSROOM PODCAST 08**
"CREATING AN ANIMATIC"

The title screen of my original podcast video.

There are sequences in the film that are inspirational text, illustrated by stylized line drawing animation. This is an adapted transcript of just part of one of those sequences, as I interpreted it as a final animatic. It was an audio podcast, so that students in the class could keep drawing on their projects while they were listening. I have added illustrations here, for the benefit of the readers of this book. But first, a finished image and the wise words of the sequence, to give it context.

> "Delight in the simple things of life, for they feed the soul. Delight in the free things of life, for they contain riches beyond value. The greatest among you are those who are humblest in spirit. The most wealthy are those who give of themselves freely through love and compassion" - from *The Hermit* by Tony White.

This is a reminder of how a *"pose test animatic"* is created. If you don't remember, I want to tell you how I create a specific sequence from my own film, *"The Hermit"*, which is a film of animated meditations for the Soul. This particular scene is about *"compassion"* and giving out what you have to share with others. For this, I wanted to create a sequence where a character is coveting all that he owns, symbolized by a food bowl. Clearly, from this pose, he's trying to keep it to himself as he walks through a barren and open environment. Here are some stills from the final color scene to give you a sense of where it's going.

The Hermit and the Seeker watch a cave wall vision of a rich man coveting his food bowl.

As he's walking along, he sees a poor person who has nothing. The stranger is squatting on the ground, with nothing, but pleading for food.

The rich man is shocked to see the poor man in front of him on the path.

The main character is shocked by what he sees and is scared that he is going to lose what he has.

The rich is moved by the sight of the poor man.

However, as he looks and the audience hear the words of the narration unfold, he finds compassion in his heart and drops to his knees.

The rich man drops to knees.

Finally, he opens his arms up and offers his bowl to the starving stranger as a gesture of compassion.

The rich man offers the poor man his bowl.

To create the animatic, I drew up all my *"key poses"*, then worked out the timing of all my key drawings. The inbetweens were not done at this point of course, so the *"key positions"* were all the ones necessary to communicate the story in the *"animatic"*.

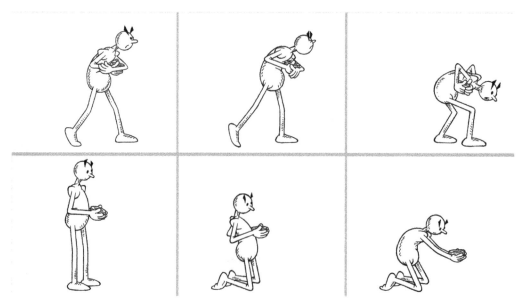

The inked-in sequence of the rich man's key poses.

Knowing the numbers of my *"key drawings"*, I was able to time out their positions in terms of frame numbers in the animatic and I shot and rendered them onto video, using those same frame timings.

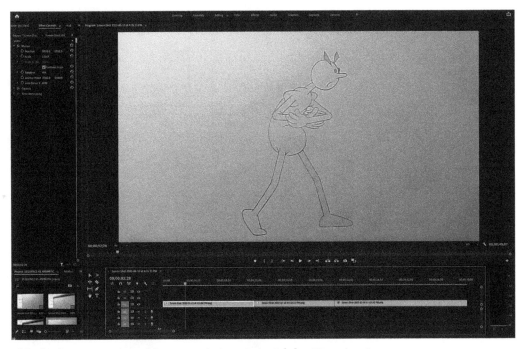

I blocked out my original key pose Animatic in Adobe "Premiere".

So, using these three drawings as a guide, my *"key positions"* were numbered "**1**", "**9**" and "**15**". Drawing *"15"* coincidentally has 15 inbetweens on *"1s"* to return it to drawing number *"1"*. (The action is a repeating, two-stride, walk cycle on the spot, with the background panning behind it to imply the character is walking forward.)

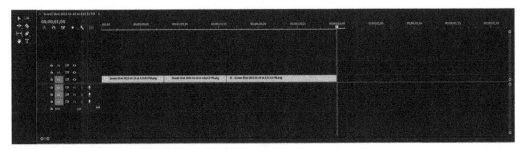

Close up of Adobe "Premiere" timeline.

Therefore, drawing "1" was held for eight frames in the animatic; Drawing "9" was also held for eight frames, and Drawing "15" was held for 14 frames. This then repeated over and over to suggest a continuous walking action. Note that is just using animation "key positions".

Action	Fr	Dialog							Aux 2 Pegs	Aux 1 Pegs	Top Pegs	Bot Pegs	Fr	Camera Instructions
							①							
							⑨							
							⑮							

The timing on the exposure chart.

These are the three pose positions I used for the animatic.

The three animatic drawings used.

And these are the pose positions beyond the walk when he notices the beggar on the ground (not drawn yet here) ahead of him and draws back in apprehension.

The three key poses when the rich man sees the beggar.

As he moves back, he pulls his bowl back with him, looking shocked and confused.

The two key poses for when the rich man pulls the bowl back.

As the moments pass, the character's shock and somewhat revulsion of the beggar gives way to a sense of compassion and a need to do the right thing. The fear he initially feels give way to sympathy. So he eases forward and falls to his knees in a newfound respect for the character. In conclusion, he reaches his bowl forward to the beggar and offers him all he has.

The three key poses for when the rich man pushes the bowl forward.

Note that he opens his fingers up as he offers the bowl, symbolizing that his offering is unconditional, and he is not attached to his possessions anymore.

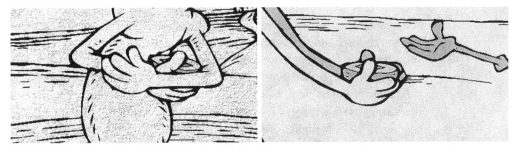

Note that the rich man's hand language goes from coveting to giving. The pose is everything, even it's often quite subliminal on the audience!

So that's basically the sequence I designed for my animation although I did have the animation mapped out and timed out in my mind already. However, in first filming, it as an *"animatic"* I was able to test the timing of the sequence, in sync with the words on the audio track. In so doing, I was aware of whether the inbetweens I'd planned were enough for the sequence and the basic timing worked in real time with the audio. If you go to my website's *"Hermit"* page, you will see how this and the other sequences look in the promotional trailer I made. *https://www.drawassic.com/thehermit.html*

'Animated Meditations for the Soul'

Sequence 01 of the film

The Hermit web page.

So, the process here is basically to create all your *"key"* drawings and *"breakdown"* drawings, approximate the timing you have in mind by way of inbetween charts on each drawing, then film the drawing according to those timings and combine it with the audio track on video. Viewing the final animatic video, you can assess your assumed timings – adjusting if necessary – before starting the lengthy process of *"inbetweening"*. In other words, you're laying down firm foundations of **"staging"**, **"framing"** and **"timing"** before the real slog work of drawing begins – hopefully saving you a great deal of time in the process.

Suggested Assignment

You might think that the previous piece on "animatics" is quite out of place on a lesson about *"cleanup"* – and you wouldn't be far wrong. But instead of giving you a further assignment to work on, I wanted to just have something for the back of your mind to mull over while you're work on your project in earnest. I find that as I work, I like to hear interviews with respected animators, artists and filmmakers, as I find it not only informative but inspirational too. So, rather than suggest an assignment here, I would just say try to absorb the above and mull it over in your mind. It will certainly have value for your future projects. I'm sure.

Masterclass 45/ Background Art

Now we get to the part of *"Production"* that I tend to call *"cosmetic"*. This means that with our animation and clean up out of the way, we can solely focus on **what the film looks like**. There are many ways of doing that and many things that influence it. Specifically, these cosmetic things will relate to the final **"background art"** your project has, the quality of **"inked line"** the characters have, and the **"coloring"** you employ to compliment that line. Each deserves a lesson in its own right, and this lesson will concern itself entirely on **"background art"**. This one will relate to Moho animators too, as their backgrounds and environments will not have been fully completed yet, but the other two have already been established by way of the final *"rigged characters"*. But before we deal with any of this, we mustn't neglect our observational gesture drawing.

Warm-Up Drawing

I think it makes sense to keep these sessions "short and sharp" to the end now as I'm sure that you have more than enough on your plate in completing your film. However, I don't want to dispense with these drawing warm-ups entirely, so we're going to do another *"copying"* exercise, like last time. It will keep your observational *"hand/brain/eye"* coordination going as well as offering a light relief from the heavy slog I'm sure your project is imposing on you. So, I'm going to suggest just **4 minutes** for you drawing the following two-character artwork. Last time we had an Uncle Lubin-based one, so this week I wanted to celebrate

DOI: 10.1201/9781003324287-49

another of my favorite films, **Wolfwalkers** from the wonderful *Cartoon Saloon*. It's possible that you will not have seen *Wolfwalkers* as it was originally only screened on Apple TV and subsequently released in a 3-movie boxed set. But if you can see it, I thoroughly recommend it! Anyway, focus specifically on the two main characters first and foremost, then add relevant aspects of the background, if your 4-minute time limit allows.

Sorry, had to use this image for a second time in this book, as it's such a great subject for you to draw at this stage! © Cartoon Saloon Ltd., Melusine Productions

Comments: I suggest you give yourself up to *2 minutes* for each character. But if you find you draw quicker than that, maybe throw in a quick sketch of the hawk and add some details of the support branch they are sitting on also. Note specifically the *"silhouette"* difference on both characters and emphasize that in your drawing. The characters are very different in the film, so the more you can illustrate that with your gesture drawing here the better.

Instruction

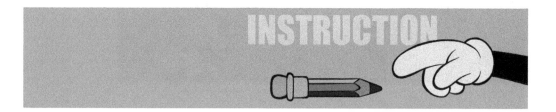

Now to offer a comprehensive coverage of "**background art**" in a single lesson is pretty much impossible. The range of styles and techniques for backgrounds in animation are as wide-reaching and diverse as the art world output in general. Some films work best with plain colored backgrounds and some work best with no background at all. The UPA movement, with its distinctly different, counter-culture approach to style and animation technique that Disney had established in the USA, was a perfect example of this in action.

The magic of UPA animation was its simplicity.

Other films need quite lavish artwork to create settings for the characters, but those can be created with a million different interpretations of style and taste in their final execution.

A more contemporary style of illustrative simplicity, from the *Wolfwalkers* movie. © Cartoon Saloon Ltd., Melusine Productions.

Watercolor, gouache, pencil shading, expressionistic poster paint, and even digital coloring in all its diversity of techniques and texturing can make up successful background art.

Although I still love to animate at any free moment I get, I believe it is also very important to keep all our art skills going in one way or another. One of my happiest moments in recent years was taking a Community College watercolor painting course, where I produced this interpretation of a Dandelion.

Consequently, it is hard to advise you on any one here – except to say that whatever your original *"concept art"* suggested, the push that style as far as you dare to make it original and entirely supportive of the character designs and coloring you ultimately come up with.

Visual inspiration can come from anywhere. I saw this watercolor sketch by Tom Sneade on Facebook once and thought it great lighting inspiration for a project I am planning. I publish it here with the artist's permission.

Even placing the subject of *"background art"* before the section of character *"inking"* and *"coloring"* could be misleading, as often the background art has to be adapted to the style and color treatment of your characters and not the other way round as I'm implying here. However, you are free to choose. You can jump to the next two lessons, then return here if you would prefer to work that way. For me – and depending on what you initially came up with for your initial *"concept art"* aside – I prefer to determine the look of the world I am in, and then adapt my characters to it. However, you may have very good reasons for not doing it that way – and you would be right if that's the way you wish to go.

I was inspired by the work of Albrecht Durer for this project development about the 17th-century herbalist/astrologer, Nicholas Culpeper. Unable to find funding for the project, I will most probably recycle the artwork for my forthcoming graphic novel memoirs project – showing how versatile concepts can be if necessary!

When all is said and done, unless you deliberately seek contrast for some specific reason, your background and your characters should feel like they **exist in the same world** and/or be seamlessly complimentary of each other.

When I made my *HOKUSAI~An Animated Sketchbook film*, I took great pains to ensure that the characters visually merged with the background, in an authentic Ukiyo-e print way – rather than it looking like a "cartoon".

All that stated, there are a few *"golden rules"* of background art – indeed all art – that are worth mentioning here. They should apply to almost all the styles and techniques you might employ with your *"background art"*, so it is worth mentioning them here.

Light and Shade

The use of *"light and shade"* can have a very dramatic effect on the way your "background art" looks and feels. There is an age-old saying that always should be considered here – *"Light over dark/dark over light!"* I will clarify what this means below but you should basically remember that when conceiving a scene or a sequence in a production you need to ensure that the featured character will stand out a little from the background – although, as confirmed above, that character will still need to feel seamlessly integrated with the background world too. Having the characters stand out, a little will ensure that they will appear visually stronger, and therefore, their action more powerful. It of course maximizes the *"silhouette"* effect of them too. Another thing to remember also is that the audience's eye will always draw to the part of an image that has the strongest tonal contrast. So you should always exploit this fact when painting and coloring your scene material.

In this centenary tribute to the late, great soccer player, Sir Stanley Matthews, it was important to have his ghost stand out in the stadium where his legend was established. Note the perspective lines of the bricks on the wall also draw the audience's attention to him as the focal point of the scene too.

Light over dark: With this option, you need to make sure that your foreground character or element stands out in contrast to the rendered background coloring, especially if that background tends to be dark in its nature. Therefore, the colors of your character for this approach need to be selected lighter in tone and value to the colors on the background behind them. This will effectively have them standing out more strongly as they move.

A light character against a dark background.

Dark over light: Alternatively, if your background is much lighter, then you should ensure that the colors you select for the characters or objects in front of them are darker in tone and value. Again, this will ensure your animation will stand out more strongly from the audience's point of view.

A dark character against a light background.

Stronger contrast: If you really want your characters or objects to stand out in a very dramatic way, pump up the contrast between the character colors in the foreground and the colors in the background. Strong contrasts like this immediately will draw the audience's eyes to that part of the screen. For example, a darkly silhouetted character against a lit doorward or window at night will immediately stand out from everything else.

Another clear example of strong contrast in a background – from my film *Endangered Species*.

Color Script

When professionals make a full-length movie, they will invariably create a "**color script**" to help establish moods and events along the storyline. Essentially, this is breaking down the entire film into individual screens and representing each scene like an extended storyboard.

When planning out your projects, it's really important to consider how different colors evoke different moods and feelings.

Then each scene will be color coded to represent the color *themes* they represent. This means that there is a sequence depicting anger, aggression, or fighting in the scenes, then the coloring for those overall scenes will tend to be in the *"red"* range.

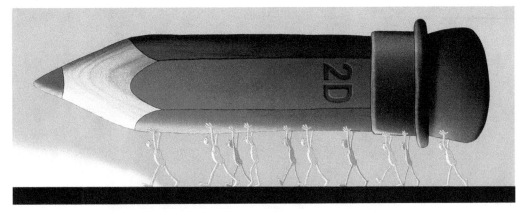

The color red evokes action, anger, passion, and intense emotion for me, that is, why I colored this pencil in that color for this scene – as opposed to the blue pencils that I actually draw with!

Alternatively, if a sequence is to look cold, or isolating or need to generate a sense of loneliness for a character or characters, then *"blue"* will be the theme.

In this scene, concerning my own life journey, I wanted to invoke a sense of isolation, loneliness, and a certain degree of coldness – which is why I made blue the predominant color.

Obviously, day and night will be represented by *"bright"* and *"dark"* colors, respectively.

A cold winter's night in a cave – it doesn't get any darker, or bluer, than that! Note too that the strong rim lights around the characters give them extra definition.

Sunrise or spring could be bright *"yellows"*, *"oranges"* or *"greens"*.

I loved directing/animating this short film project - of a bright, spring-like day in the city – although there inevitably has to be a fly in the ointment somewhere! Design: Thomas Liera.

Midday or summer might be strong "golden yellows", sunset or fall could be *"light browns"*, *"dark greens"* or *"fading oranges"*, and night or winter could be *"dark blues"* or *"purples"* in their nature.

I tried to invoke a sense of blistering hot summer, high in the mountains with the colors in this animated graphic novel frame.

These are not hard and fast rules to this of course – except to say that by selecting overall color themes for sequences like this, you underly for the audience the kinds of moods and emotions you want them to see or feel at any point in the story. The background artists therefore will take their cue for their *"background art"* from the *"color script"* and will work with a suitable color palette accordingly.

I have always loved this gorgeous piece of background art- for my *Thank You Stan* tribute film! Artist: Peter Moehrle.

Of course, for your own initial project, you will not need a *"color script"* to guide you. However, you should bear in mind the kind of color palette you choose for your background art – and subsequently your characters to match. For example, if your project is up and light in its nature, then use up and light colors to support that. If you project on the other hand is dark and reflective, then you should select dark and reflective colors for your coloring. It is all about setting the scene, quite literally, so that your audience is taken along the emotional path you want them to do. The selection of colors – or no colors at all – is all part of this supportive process you need to consider when establishing our *"background art"* and subsequence character coloring.

Light and Shadow

One last comment here must be devoted to *"light"* and *"shadow"*. Within any of the options above you should remember that within the world you are creating – unless it is deliberately flat or abstract in its nature – the elements of *"light"* and *"shadow"* should be playing out. In other words, think where the *"light source"* is in any of your scenes, what is the nature of that *"light source"* and how is that *"light source"* affecting your characters or action? Now it could be that none of this is necessary for the film you are making – and of course it would involve a lot more work on your part if you decide it is of value to you! However, giving a presence to our characters and the world they are existing in can add a lot of value to some stories being told.

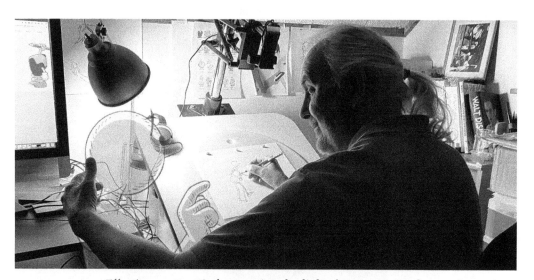

Effective – yet entirely unscripted – light, for my personal memoirs project with Arnie.

Now some *"light"* and *"shadow"* can be added to the background elements only, which can work very well as long as you carefully color your characters to feel compatible with that.

Flat-colored characters on highly realistic, shadowed backgrounds can be very effective if you color your characters well. A concept still for my animated memoirs project - portaying my guided climb to the top of the Great Pyramid in Egypt!

However, the big dramatic effects can come from having light and shadow on your characters too – and not only on your characters but from your characters in the form of ground shadows, etc.

The use of matching shadows and watercolored textures can be very effective – as this still from "The Hermit" illustrates.

Adding light and shade to a background is relatively easy. But adding light and shade to your characters can be a huge amount of extra work for you. Essentially, you'd have to go back to the *"clean up"* drawing stage and add shadows to those drawings before *"inking"* and *"coloring"* them later.

However, this is a possibility to consider, if your project is crying out for such an effect.

Depth Layering

Sometimes you can get greater depth to your artwork by "depth layering". This means that if you can break your scene up into several background layers, you can treat those various layers differently in terms of tonal value to imply depth. The wonderful movie "Klaus" used this technique to great effect.

Notice that the shadow areas are indicated in RED on this cleaned-up key drawing.

Breaking a background down into (four, in this case) layers with different tonal values to get a sense of depth. If it is a panning scene, the layer nearest us will pan the fastest and the layer furthest us will pan the slowest.

Essentially, it means that in order to imply depth to a scene, you can always create background layers that appear to be going back into the distance by either each layer getting tonally lighter the further way it appears to be or else getting progressively darker. A lot will depend on the nature of the scene, the time of day, the state of the weather and other factors to determine whether you go light or dark into the distance. But whatever way you go, it can me immensely effective.

Notice the dramatic, scary effect of having the far layer very dark, the mid-distant trees in mid tones and the foreground grass very light. It is framed nicely with the darkened stumps of trees, low, to the left and right. From *Wolfwalkers*. © Cartoon Saloon Ltd., Melusine Productions.

Suggested Assignment

Not so much an assignment here, more a recommendation. Before deciding on your background art and coloring immerse yourself in art and illustrations from other artists, illustrators and filmmakers. This is an infinite world to explore of course and you could do it forever and never get round to finishing your film!

However, it is really valuable to see how various respected artists have treated their subject and to be aware of the various light, shade and color decisions they have made. Filmmakers especially have a whole range of lighting and coloring tricks at their fingertips, so when you watch films or movies, try to look past the storyline and see how they manipulate and audience into seeing or feeling certain things as the films unfold.

Simply by the use of shadow and composition, horror filmmakers can communicate a story without there being any actors in the shot at all!

And don't just go to YouTube for your references. It will have some good ones for you of course, but in the main, you would be better going directly to the source of the material – namely entire movies of the genre you are most interested in – or even to the art section of your local library, where there will be far more valuable material that has never been posted on YouTube or Google Images. Saturating yourself in this way with the high art of others can only benefit you when creating your own!

Masterclass 46/ Inking

Now we're very much in the home straight with the project now, it's time to return to your character(s) and define exactly what they look like in the final version. Remember, unless you have a very strong reason for not doing so, they have to be in the same visual ballpark that your final *"background art"* is in. So let us explore the various options you have for "**inking**" them before we move on to color. But first, let's warm up again with another observational gesture drawing exercise.

Warm-Up Drawing

Extending on from the last two *"copying"* exercise, taking major classic pieces and redrawing them in the interests of understanding their style and construction, we're going to venture into something very cool and contemporary: **The Saga of Rex**, by industry maestro, Michel Gagne. Inspired by his successful graphic novel of the same name, the film is currently in production. What I have seen of it so far, this one-person feature is going to be fantastic. So, in tribute of what's to come after the publication of this book, I want you to have fun drawing the main character, Rex. I recommend that you give yourself **3 minutes** to draw this really charming story from a much darker and challenging science fiction/fantasy world.

DOI: 10.1201/9781003324287-50

From "Rex" by Michel Gagne.

Comments: What we're looking for, first and foremost, with this exercise is the accuracy of the relevant geometric shapes and volumes the character is constructed with. Try to stick to just the size proportions at first, working fast to sketch out the basic inner structure of the character – making sure you get the angles of the body right. Then, when you're sure you have the proportions right, flesh out the fuller character details as necessary.

Instruction

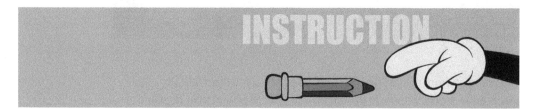

OK, so for the benefit of those working on a drawn version of their project, as opposed to Moho, I want to go through the process of "**inking**" in your drawings prior to coloring. So many traditional animators work digitally these days, so much of the following will be redundant for them. However, many others like to work traditionally – i.e. pencil on paper – so I just want to record the process I and other traditionalists use, so we can preserve the process for future animators.

However, before that I just want to discuss the line qualities you should consider when inking. Mostly, filmmakers tend to use a thin, consistent ink line to "*ink*" their drawings, but there are many to choose from. So, let us here list the options you might want to consider when taking on *"inking"* for your project. I am talking about traditionally, hand-drawn inking here of course, as digital inking has a myriad of options, depending on what brushes or textures you use.

The major inking line techniques. From left to right – "thin even", "thick even", "thick 'n thin", "boiling" and "scratchy".

Even line: *"Even line"* inking is very much as it suggests. It is essentially taking your original cleaned up drawing and *"inking in"* all the relevant lines that define the action, using a thin black line that is consistent all the time. The thickness of your even line is dependent on your overall design style, but the essence is that whatever thickness of line you choose, it is consistently that throughout.

Even line inking, thin and thick.

Thick 'n thin line: Again, a *"thick 'n thin"* line is pretty much as it suggests. Unlike the previous approach, this one uses the strength of a more brush-like application of the line – where the line might start thin, get thicker in the middle, then taper off to thin again at the end. This can be a common approach used in *"digital inking"* although not always.

"Thick 'n Thin" line inking.

NOTE

The thicker aspects of the line can suggest the strong parts of the line, whereas the thinner parts suggest softness or even a controlled weakness implied in the drawing. Foreshortened, overlapping perspective can be implied using a *"thick 'n thin"* line too.

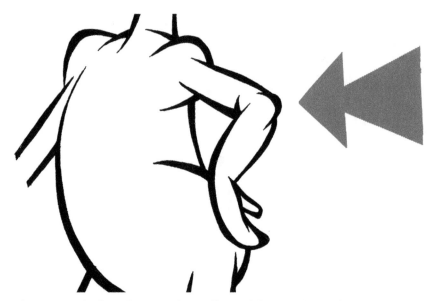

The use of "thick 'n thin" can be really useful to imply overlapping volumes in a shape or character.

Boiling or scratchy line: These approaches have a much more energetic or *"artistic"* look to them. Rather than be slick or smooth, they give an energy to the line quality of the animation. A "boiling" inking approach is almost random in its nature. You follow the original pencil line of the animation of course, but the line is not straight but shaky. Consequently, when played back, the line has a "boiling" (wobbly) quality to it. This can be particularly effective when the action hits a "hold", but the line stays active because it is traced back many times over the number of frames the hold lasts. The scratchy line is similar, in the sense that the line is made up of a series of random, thin scratchy line, rather than a continuously traced one. It gives a simple "boiling" effect to the quality of animation.

The "boiling" and "scratchy" line styles.

Other Line Styles and Techniques

Color line: Although most animation uses black lines or whatever complexion above is used, you might also consider a *"color line"* instead. Color lines, depending on what colors are selected", can give the drawing feel a softer or more integrated feel with the background. Sometimes a combination of color and black lines is used – i.e. with the main body inked in color and the features of the face being inked in black. Numerous variations along these ideas can be used, giving a more unique feel to the whole thing.

Invisible line: Today, with the advent of vector-based animation, it is not unusual to see *"invisible lines"* being use to define the character. However, this gives a less hand-crafted feel to the animation although that may be the intention. *"Invisible line"* inking can make very strong graphic statements with the animation, which may suit some projects better.

Color inked line style, for the *Bad Penguin* movie project development.

The "invisible line" style which is basically flat color with not outlines. Featuring characters I designed for a children's TV project.

Pencil drawn: One approach that requires a great artist to pull off is the "pencil-drawn" style. Basically, instead of cleaning up animation and inking it, you just go with finished drawings and color those. It does take a great artist to pull this style off convincingly, but it looks terrific when they do. Richard Williams springs to mind with this although the current maestro of the art form is Joanna Quinn, whose films in this style are incredible.

Joanna Quinn's latest, award-winning masterwork, *Affairs of the Art*.

Thickened outline: Another technique for "inking" might well be mentioned here. A *"thickened outline"* to a character or object can ensure that this character or object will stand out more from the background than would normally be anticipated. For example, if a character is inked with an *"even line"*, then the entire outline of the character drawing has a thicker black line applied to its circumference, it can make a bold statement on the screen. However, this does involve a second pass of inking work, but some projects could well benefit from that extra work in the final analysis.

Note how, by thickening the outline of a character, you make it's silhouette stronger.

Strong foreground line: Similar to the *"thickened outline"* discussed above, you might also consider having the character that is nearest to the viewer have a thicker line than anything behind it – such as other characters or even a line-based background design. Indeed, you could work out a process whereby the further a layer is from the observer, the thinner the line is that you use to trace it.

I've used this example elsewhere, but it perfectly illustrates the process that by thickening the line, and making it colored, on the character it stands out more.

My Traditional, Hand-Drawn Inking Process

OK, let me now give you a *"making of"* approach to how I treat *"inking"*. In this example, I am using my simple *"Arnie"* character and showing how I prefer to use a "**thick 'n thin**" approach to *"inking"* him rather than a *"even line"*, which might be more obvious for such a simplistic and cartoony design. In doing this, I don't want to give you the impression that this is how you must do it, or this is the way the industry does it. There are so many variables in this process – depending on the design and intention of the project – but it might just help if you eavesdrop on my thinking as I "clean up" and "ink" a character drawing. The sequence is of Arnie bowing. I didn't actually use this animation for a production, as planned. However, it seems a fitting illustration to use – in view of the fact that this entire book course is close to it drawing to a close, and therefore, it seems a suitable time for Arnie to take a bow!

Note that when I animate, I tend to do so in a **rough**, **blue-pencil line** way to begin with, leaving geometric construction lines and points visible. Construction lines never bother me at any preparatory stage, as I know that ultimately, they won't be visible.

Original key pose test animation drawings.

Next comes testing and adjusting of the key pose test animatic, as well as the animation. Once these work, it's time to move forward with the cleanup and inking.

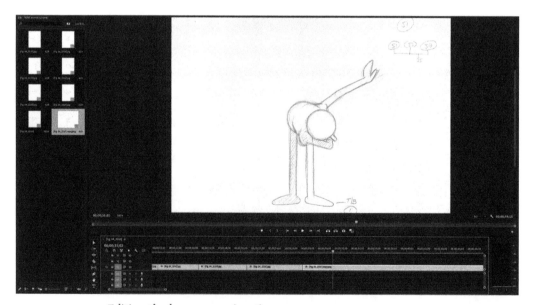

Editing the key pose animatic.

Once I have my pencil animation working, I got into *"cleanup"* mode. Remember, the *"cleanup"* process is making the whole thing more presentable, ready for final *"inking"*. Ultimately, this means a drawing that looks like this. It needs to be nice and clean and defining all the action as clearly and as concisely as I can.

Before and after clean up.

This can be done in two ways – either by cleaning up the rough drawing on the original sheet of paper I used or else by adding a fresh sheet of paper over the top and tracing the drawing underneath neatly. I have already explained that for the former, I tend to erase the original drawing down to a pale line with a kneadable eraser, then do my clean-up drawing over the top of that. This is what I did here.

NOTE

As the feet are not moving from where they are on the first drawing, they need to be "traced" back from drawing 1 on each occasion. We show this on the pencil drawings by using a red pencil to indicate the trace back, adding a note next to it, "T/B 1". (Or whatever other drawing it may be traced back to in other sections on in other scenes.) It is important to remember that if you use tracebacks in any way, you should always trace them back from the original drawings and not the last traceback you did – especially at the inking stage. This will prevent any slippage or boiling that may occur if you traceback from a traceback, etc.

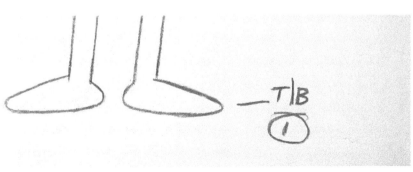

How to show the traceback information on a drawing.

Occasionally, I'll do the cleanup drawing on a fresh sheet of paper. In this case, I will put the original rough drawing on the pegs of my lightbox, place a new sheet of paper over that one and number it identically. Then, with the lightbox switched on, I'll use the backlight to clearly see the original drawing beneath as I trace my cleanup. You'll note though that as the head of *"Arnie"* is in fact a circle, I'll use a circle guide to trace it accurately, drawing it very lightly at first, rather than make is a heavy, solid line.

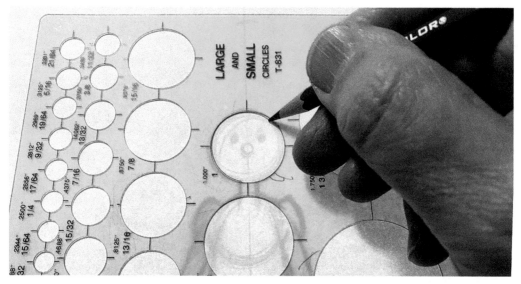

I prefer to use a circle guide to draw Arnie's head, at least at the cleanup stage.

Next, I trace the rest of the character with a light touch too – until the who character is completed. I leave out all construction lines of course, and just tidy up what lines I need so that I have the best lightly drawn cleanup drawing I can do.

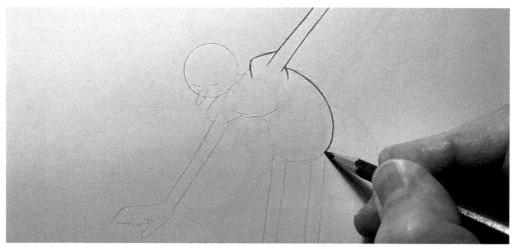

I tend to work light with the lightbox on for my initial cleanup drawing, then switch the lights of and strengthen the lines afterward, as seen here.

Now I've actually cleaned up very lightly the entire character, I have the option of either inking over it on this sheet of paper or strengthening up this drawing in pencil, then adding another sheet of paper over the top of that for final inking. The risk in the former of course is that if you mess up the inking on the lightly cleaned up version, you will have to clean it all up again on a new sheet of paper! But that said, I'm going to start inking on the cleanup drawing with an *"even line"*. I usually quickly use the kneadable eraser to take the edge of the blue cleanup lines before inking by the way, ensuring that the ink line is the strongest.

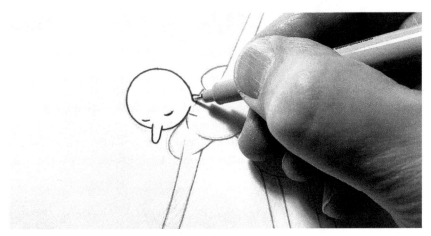

Tracing the head with even ink line.

I hand trace the head without a circle guide at the *"inking"* stage as I still want my final drawing to have a more organic, hand-drawn feel to it – rather than it being a perfect, computer-drawn, digital approach. So, any small shakes or imperfections in the line are fine by me. In other words, if we're working in a traditional, hand-drawn world, why not celebrate that fact and do your inking with a less-than-perfect hand-drawn approach too. I call that approach *"soul drawing"* – in the sense that they have a little of your imperfect, human personality to them.

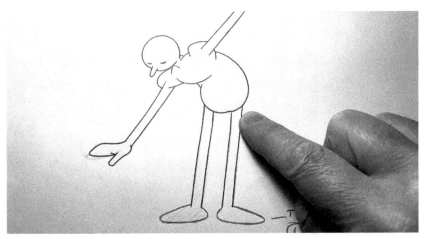

There are always little imperfections that make each drawing different although I tend to smooth them out a little more at the "thick 'n thin" stage.

The way I trace my line when inking is to use a *"feathering"* approach. This means that I go back and forth over the line, building up the layers as I do so. This is unlike a lot of people who just trace an *"even line"* with a continuous flow from beginning to end. *"Feathering"* adds a little more of that *"soul"* to the line, being that it's impossible to make the line *"even"* that way.

Feathered line technique.

Then, once I have all my character traced, I then go back and add *"thick 'n thins"* to my lines using a similar feathering approach. Generally, I will make the center of the line much thicker, reserving the original *"even"* style of the lines to the end. Sometimes I'll use the *"thick"* part to emphasis an overlapping section however, such as with the crease of the inner elbow or back of the knee.

Adding "thick 'n thins" to lines.

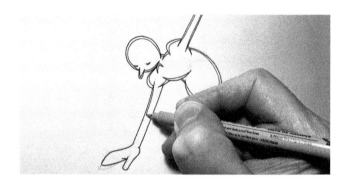

I will also use the *"thick 'n thin"* technique to elegantly stylize a defining line such as the curve of Arnie's fat abdomen.

The "thick 'n thin" approach around the stomach.

Then, in something like the neck, I prefer to have the thickness of the line pronounced when it joins the head, but tapering off to thin at the other end.

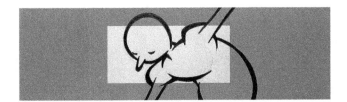

The "thick 'n thin" technique on the neck.

I'll continue to use these same inking techniques on all the body, emphasizing certain parts with *"thick 'n thin"* lines where appropriate. *"Thick 'n thin"* lines can bring really strength to aspects of your inked drawing and in time you'll learn how to do that for yourself, if this is a technique that appeals to you for your project. Consistency with your application of *"thick 'n thin"* lines throughout the body is really important however.

Finally with my Arnie character, when all the *"thick 'n thin"* lines are complete on the drawing, I might sometimes choose to add selective "hatch" lines to define a little form and shadow. As long as you keep these consistent in broad areas from drawing to drawing, they can be very effective. Note at the same time, they will never be perfectly the same as you're working more spontaneously (rather than inbetweening the hatching from *"key"* to *"key"*) but that's OK as it simply amplifies the handdrawn, *"soul"* nature of inking your drawings this way.

Final thick 'n thin inked character.

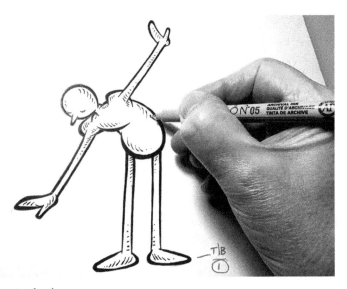

Adding hatching to Arnie.

And don't forget to hatch a little suggestion of shadow on the ground to emphasize the character's contact with it. This can make a world of difference!

Hatching around feet, simulating contact shadows.

Inked Arnie on wheels, rocking it!

So there you go. Below is my final *"inked"* character, done the *"Arnie"* way. As I say, I don't use this approach with everything I animate and I'm sure that this will probably only apply to a few people and their projects. But at least sharing my process for *"Arnie"*, it might give some of you ideas how to approach the *"inking"* of your own characters.

Finally, for the record, as my *"inking"* here is done traditionally on paper, the next stage would be to scan these drawings to a high-definition level and import them into a suitable computer-based animation program where the coloring will be handled quickly and digitally. This can even be done in Moho even though this animation approach is far removed from the more popular Moho "rigged character" approach. However, the BIG advantage of working on paper like this in my estimation is that if your project becomes a huge hit, you can attract additional revenue (i.e., funding for your next project maybe?) by selling signed original drawing from your film – something you can't do if you work digitally!

Suggested Assignment

No additional assignment here, as I'm sure you got your hands more than full already with all this inking and scanning to do. However, I would urge you to experiment a little with the *"inking"* approach to your film. Try several inking options, using one animation drawing, and see what turns out best. You may find an approach that no-one has thought of before, which will make your film totally original looking. Remember the saying I've used before in this book – *"You only get out of a project at the end in direct proportion to what you put in at the beginning!"*

Masterclass 47/ Coloring

Hopefully, you're still with us on the plan and just have to color your animation to finish your project. It's been a long, hard haul no doubt, but if you're completed everything this far, it's pretty much downhill in terms of effort from now on – especially with the *"digital coloring"* options that are open to filmmakers today. As mentioned in the previous masterclass, if you scan your inked paper drawings, you will soon be ready to take advantage of the speedy way that computer animation software can handle the coloring. There's one small chore to prepare your scanned files before that perhaps, but little else. However, before we talk about that and do anything specific to "**coloring**" let us once more embark on another observational gesture drawing challenge.

Warm-Up Drawing

As promise previously, this is another of those *"copying"* challenges, where you need to draw a still from a famous film production. But just to raise the bar a little, this reference material is of a 3D animation nature, not 2D. Below you will see a still from the original ***Kung Fu Panda*** movie. That film contains some wonderful character animation and really broke through in my estimation in terms of that for the CG approach. Yes, Pixar have come out with some fabulous character animation movies themselves – indeed, so high is their bar that it is expected of them. But *Kung Fu Panda* showed that great animation and great storytelling could also come for other studios, which ironically started a trend that arguably started a

DOI: 10.1201/9781003324287-51

trend downward from the once marvelous Pixar. Anyway, give yourself 4 minutes to draw this Panda pose. Being 3-dimensional, it doesn't give you the easy lines to copy. Instead, it challenges you to create your own lines that define the character and define the pose. Good practice for the traditional 2D animator I might add!

Comments: Because of the 3-dimensional nature of this pose, of the CG nature of this pose, you particularly have to make sure that with your gesture drawing the "**proportions**" are good, the "**volumes**" are good and the "**angles**" are good. Work again with the inner skeleton and build out from there. This is a strong dynamic pose, and your drawing should reflect that. Pay special attention to the "**balance**" in your drawing too, as well as the "**dynamic lines**" – all good reasons why this pose is so valuable to draw.

Instruction

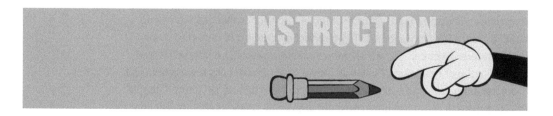

OK, let's start from square one with your final drawings. Let's assume that you have *"cleaned up"* and *"inked"* them all, and they are therefore ready for scanning. This now is the process I would recommend.

Scanning

If you have your drawings on traditional animation paper, make sure that you tape a compatible peg bar to your scanner before starting. You need to do this as it is just as important to register your drawings, one to the other, as it is when you draw them. So if you worked on pegs to do that, you have to use pegs to scan them. Scanners are different in design but you need to find a convenient place on the outside the scanning area where you can tape your peg bar, while allowing the scanner lid to be dropped down each time.

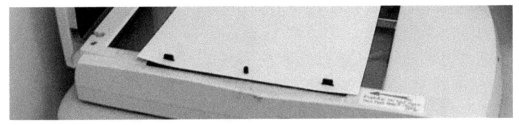

Even small scanners, with peg bars attached, will work for most traditional, hand-drawn animation projects.

A lot of the software that comes with scanners allows you to select a scanning area and (hopefully) save it for current and future use. So, on the assumption that you have a *"Field guide"* for your animation, place it face down on the pegs, drawing side down toward the scanning glass, and do a test scan.

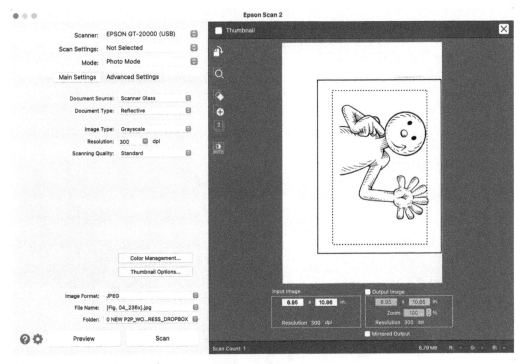

Adjusting the framing on the scanner.

This will enable you to select the area that you want to scan consistently for all your drawings, essentially the outer edges of your field on your *"Field guide"*. Save it on the scanner software if you can, so that if you even need to come back and scan your drawings again – or if you have more than one scene of drawings to scan and they're all draw to the same *"Field guide"* size – then you can do so without setting up each time.

An animation field guide to animate to and line the scanner up with.

With all your scanning drawings saved onto a folder on your computer, you will need to adjust and resize them to match the final resolution of your final film. These days it will either be "**HD720**" *(1280 × 720 pixels)* or "**HD1080**" *(1920 × 1080 pixels)*. There are different ways in doing this, depending on the software you have on your computer. But I tend to use the "**Actions**" function on Photoshop.

The traditional animator's most undervalued resource in Photoshop – the "Actions" function!

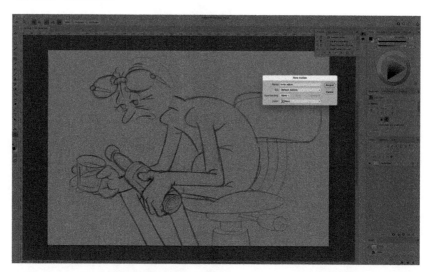

To set up my *"Actions"* in Photoshop, I save one of my scanned drawings with a new name. It can be anything you like but I tend to use the word *"sample"*. Using that file, I open actions and then adjust that file visually to suit the definition I'm going to be working too. Scanning varies, but with my scanner, all the drawings tend to be upside down when they are scanned, so I have to rotate mine 180 degrees as the first stage of the actions I take. Next, I will resize my drawings to match either the *HD720* or the *HD1080* field size. Sometimes I need to sharpen up the image or increase the contrast of the scans, so I'll do that too while my *"Actions"* function is still recording. When I have fully adjusted and resized my *"sample"* file, I will close down the *"Actions"* recording and prepare to apply it to all my final scan files in the folder.

The before and after of "Actions" – resizing, recoloring and sharpening of an image as a multiple drawing process.

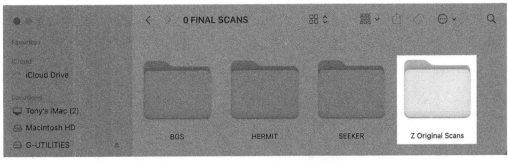

Always store your backup scans in an "Original scans" folder before using Actions or doing anything significant to your animation files!

In Photoshop, I now go to the **"File/Automate/Batch"** link and select the main folder where your scans are held. Hit **"OK"** and *"Actions"* you recorded should not be applied to all the drawing files you have scanned. When it is complete, open them up to check that all is good with them.

NOTE

*I STRONGLY suggest that before you take on the "Actions" recording, you duplicate all your scans and place them in a new "**Original scans**" folder. This gives you a fallback position if something goes wrong with your initial "Actions" process – which has happened to me more than once, hence I now automatically making a scans backup folder!*

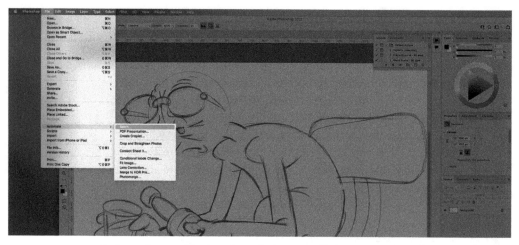

To launch your "Actions" rendering… "File/Automate/Batch".

Now you are ready to import your scans into whatever software you are using to color your animation. I have said earlier that I still love most my own "**Toon-Boom Studio**" software, which is sadly no longer available but will always be on my computer as I like using it so much. It has a number of functions that cover everything I will ever need for my traditional 2D animated film – including combining animation with live action footage. I am sad that I cannot recommend it to all students, and it is a wonderfully simple learning app for beginners. Of course, you probably won't have access to *"ToonBoom Studio"*, so you'll have to learn how to do the following in whatever software you're using to color your animation and render it to video – Moho included. However, as far as this demo is concerned, I will use ToonBoom Studio, and you will have to find ways of replicating it in the software you have – whether it is Moho or otherwise.

The "ToonBoom Studio" interface.

In ToonBoom Studio, I can define what resolution I want my film to be *(HD1080 for most of mine)*; then import all my scans into the timeline on their own animation layer. I will also import the **"background art"** into a lower layer, so I can see the animation character on top of it as it is being colored.

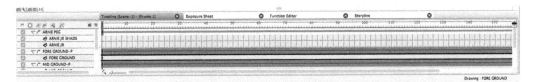

The ToonBoom Studio "timeline", including the Arnie layer, the Arnie shadows layer and various background layers. The animation is on "two's" – in other words, each drawing is on for two frames of film.

In that timeline, I can decide whether my scanned frames are on **"1s"**, **"2s"** or indexed any other number of frames per drawing I like. I usually keep them as *"1s"* for the coloring process and open them up to their final **"FPS"** (frames per second) later.

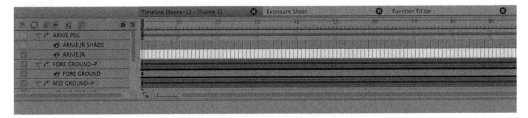

The timeline showing that the Arnie animation layer has been changed from 2s to 1s at the click of a button. Compare to the shadow layer above, which is still on 2s.

I then highlight **"Frame 1"** on the timeline and proceed to color it.

Frame 1 highlighted on the timeline.

To choose a color, there is usually a palette of colors to choose from in each software package, as well as a color disk for custom mixing and saving any color that is not in the main palette.

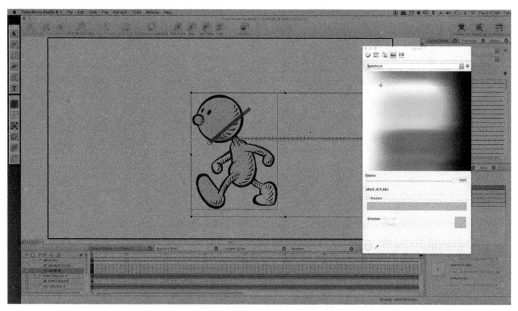

Just one of the color palette options that ToonBoom Studio had.

With the first color selected, I then just touch the screen in the area I want to be colored and the *"fill"* is instant.

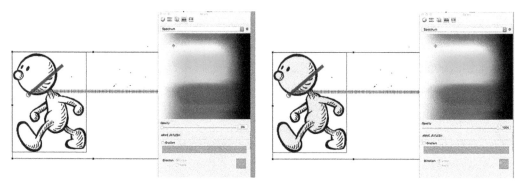

Just like any other program since, you just selected a color and touched the screen with a Paintpot tool to color animation in ToonBoom Studio.

I will then select a second color for another part of the character and so the same thing.

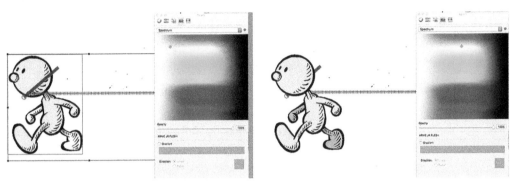

Selecting and painting another color on your character is instant too.

Eventually, I will work my way through the entire range of colors that my character needs, then move on to "**Frame 2**" and color that one likewise. I will of course save all the colors I have selected for the character, so I can access them instantly for all the remaining animation frames.

When you've finished coloring Frame 1, you move on to Frame 2 and do the same thing again – and so on, until the entire scene is completed.

With all the coloring done, you might want to make slight color adjustments to your character in relation to your background. Sometimes when a character is moving across the screen, it passes colors on the background that is similar to it, and therefore, it is not so clear or well-defined colorwise. Most programs – including ToonBoom Studio – allow you to adjust your saved colors in the selection palette, automatically changing the corresponding colors in your animation timeline too. This is a wonderfully efficient what of making changes to your colors without having to physically go through everything and repaint all the frames, one by one.

NOTE

Some people choose to color the entire character on the first frame, then move on to the second frame and fully color that, then onto the next, and so on, until all the animation frames are done. Other people take just one color and apply it to all the frame consecutively, then return to "Frame 1" and start coloring another part of the character all the way through. Keep doing this until all the colors are filled in on all the frame eventually. Neither way is right or wrong. It is just down to personal preference.

Once you allocated and saved specific colors for your character in ToonBoom Studio, it was so easy to modify them instantly by moving the cursor around on the color palette!

With all your colors selected and working well against your background art, it is time to do a final render of your scene. Remember though, if you colored your frames as *"1s"* but your animation is planned for *"2s"*, you need to change your frame lengths before you render your video out. Again, this is very easy to do in a well-designed software program like *ToonBoom Studio*.

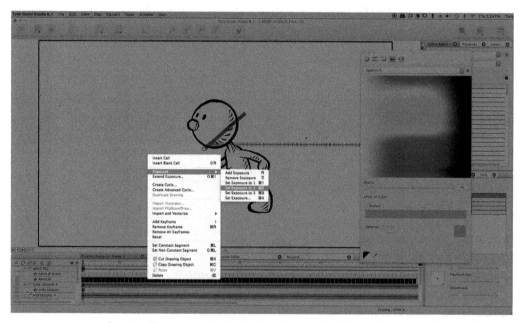

Showing how easy it was in ToonBoom Studio to change a selected layer of animation frames from 2s to 1s – or indeed to any number of frames you want them to be held for!

When it's rendered, playback your video in real time and make sure all is good. There are normally not surprises at this stage, if you have followed all the procedures I have suggested in these lessons and so all will be good. Complete any other scenes that make up your film, coloring, rendering and checking them as you complete them.

Suggested Assignment

At this stage, you should have no further assignments to do as, when the coloring is complete, you have effectively finished your film. Maybe crack open a bottle of Champagne to celebrate if that is to your taste – or natural fruit juice is you would prefer. Now there is just a little "**Post Production**" to do, which shouldn't be much if you've followed all these lessons throughout.

Masterclass 48/ Post Production and Distribution

If you were a big studio making a big production, then there would still be a great deal to do on your project. Things such as "**special effects**", "**editing**", "**Foley effects**", "**sound and music mixing**", "**color grading**" and "**publicity and marketing**" come to mind here – and I'm sure there are more. However, for your first film – or even for any personal film you are likely to make – there is not so much work involved. So, if you've kept with the program up to here as advised then it's almost a hearty "**congratulations**" for pretty much finishing your project! I would however recommend a few lose ends that you could do – termed "**Post production**" – and we'll talk about them in this final lesson. However, for all intents and purposes, you've made it and so we should celebrate by one more observational gesture drawing challenge.

Warm-Up Drawing

As our final warm-up drawing session, I want to conclude with another *"copying"* session – but this time focusing on one of the most *triumphant* and *iconic* drawn images forever – featuring my person tribute to the finest traditional, hand-crafted animation ever created – **Fantasia**. However, instead of using images from the original film, I want you to use my own recreation of the Mickey Mouse

DOI: 10.1201/9781003324287-52

sequence in *"The Sorcerer's Apprentice"*. These frames are from my homage to the great achievements of the Disney studio and others, "Endangered Species". I drew the animation in this way as I was not able to animate the original characters, due to legal challenges. However, my *Arnie-fication* of Mickey is not a sign of disrespect or lack of reverence for the original. Indeed, it was my humble effort to study and recreate the amazing animation of the original sequence by **Preston Blair**, using my character. It reflects entirely the wonderful key positions of the original animation, so I ask you to draw these three frames for your final observational gesture drawing assignment. Give yourself **3 minutes** to draw each pose.

Comments: For me, *Fantasia* is the finest animated film ever made. If the truth were known, we probably don't have the talent or know-how to replicate it today despite all the gizmos and technology we have at our disposal. Although somewhat dated and limited in its overall look and story structure, the character animation in the film's individual sequences has never been bettered – and is unlikely to be bettered in this digital day and age. The imaginative use of animation with classical music was a truly breakthrough moment for the industry and the Disney studio – a studio that was never short of animation magic already.

I didn't end my brief *Sorcerer's Apprentice* sequence like the film. Instead, I wanted to celebrate the humble pencil, the masses of animation drawings and the desktop that enabled all that Disney magic to happen. I made the film with absolutely no budget – just my students to help me, and a whole lot of love for the man and the legacy that showed us what great traditional, hand-drawn animation magic could be, all those years ago!

The Sorcerer's Apprentice is all about a character becoming arrogant, over confident and ultimately getting carried away with themselves. The humility they finally learn is in discovering that such an overinflated view of themselves can only lead to disaster. This I believe is how society tends to view the modern animation world. We have all the gizmos, technology; tricks and marketing that money can buy; yet there's no one alive who could hold a candle to what the master animators in Disney "golden age" could do.

Walt died on December 5, 1966. The studio was making the *The Jungle Book* at the time. So, I thought it only right that I mark the poignancy of that moment in *Endangered Species*. I did this by showing the reluctant spirt of Walt rising up from the body of my King Louis style ape while it was dancing – reflecting one of the high spots from the film, while at the same time marking one of the saddest moments for the entire animation industry. The studio was never the same again after Walt had left us – neither was traditional, hand-drawn animation!

Therefore, I have selected this image as a tribute – and as a reminder – that no matter how good we think we are today, we are but a pale imitation of what the Disney greats did back then. Their work humbles us, in the sense that it shows us that there is always another mountain to climb and another level of artistic ability we need yet to achieve. So, as you draw this image above, think of the mastery that created the pose in the first place and be inspired by the remarkable drawing quality that portrays it. It should remind us all that there is yet still a long way to go before we all reach true mastery – although it is within the reach of all of us if we never neglect the fine fundamentals and principles of movement the master animators gave us all those many decades ago. Use them wisely, grasshopper!

Instruction

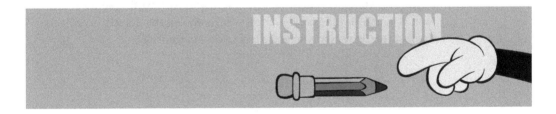

In terms of wrapping up your film now, the minimum you need to do is take all the separate scenes of color animation you have created and edit them together with the final audio track you used for your *"final pose test animatic"* at the end of "Section III". Software programs such as **"Final Cut Pro"** (for Mac users) or Adobe **"Premiere"** (for Windows users) are probably the main ones to turn to, for this. Although, any film editing program that allows you to put together various video clips and render them out with an audio track to a HD master copy is all you need. Indeed, the process is a very simple one in terms of what digital film editing programs can do these days.

A quality program like "Final Cut Pro" is great for editing showreels, event recordings and anything else beyond just animation of course - however, if you're strapped for cash, the FREE "HitFilm Express" video editing program can be an answer to a dream!

Other things you might look at if you have the time or inclination to do it is polish and/or add to your audio track in some way. Although what you had for your *"final pose test animatic"* is no doubt more than suitable, you might consider adding additional sound effects or music to it to give it another level of professionalism. That said, adding music especially to your film could be quite complex – and even expensive if you want to use copyright material. On the other hand, you may know a band or musician who could record something for you that is original and would just sit well with your existing audio track. Music can make a world of difference, even for the most mediocre of projects. (Not that I'm suggesting that yours is mediocre of course!)

If you need music for your project, I'm sure there's a local band, musician or singer who would be keen to do something for you if you give them a credit.

Adding "**SFX**" (sound effects) or "**Atmos**" (atmospheric sounds) might be something you could consider. There may be actions in your film that could be highlighted by a sound effect here or there. For example, a character hammering might be all the more powerful if you "**sync**" (synchronize) a suitable sound effect to go with the hammer hitting.

If you don't have the sound effect you want, you have to record it!

There are a million other things that you might find valuable in your own project idea that could do with a sound effect added here and there although it is not mandatory. If you should feel that *SFX* in your film is appealing, you might go to the *www.freesound.com* website, where there are thousands of donated and free sound effects you can download. You may even get clips of music there too, if you're lucky.

Freesound website home page. https://freesound.org.

"*Atmos*" can be very supportive to a film is you choose the right now and use it discretely. For example, if you have a scene that is set in a busy city, then it makes sense to have the low hum of city life in the background of your audio track. Again, the *"freesound"* website should have a number of options you can choose from, no matter what *"Atmos"* effect you want.

Looking for hammering SFX on Freesound.

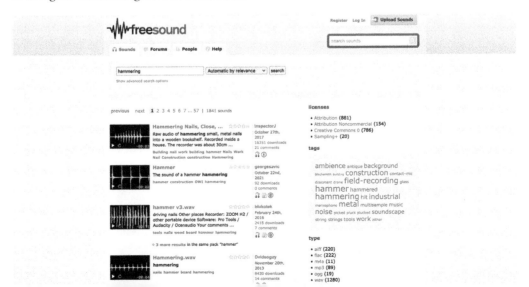

"**Foley**" is a thing that most big-time professional filmmakers will use to fill out their audio track at the *"post production"* stage. *"Foley artists"* are people who specialize in creating original sound effects that need to go with certain aspects of action or atmospherics in a film. They have their own recording studio for such tasks or may even go out on location to capture the right sound for the right image. It is unlikely you will have access to such services however, so focus more on the resources on the *"freesound"* website, unless you have money to burn in hiring a specialist foley artist to create the sounds for you. If you have access to a good sound recording studio however, you might be able to create your foley sounds yourself.

The secrets of recording footsteps in a Foley studio.

Distribution and Marketing

Again, if you were a big studio making a big movie, video game or TV project, you'll probably have a big *"distribution and marketing"* operation behind you. It is one thing to take months or years to produce an animated film, but once the investment in that has been made and its ready to go, it is essential to promote it and make sure it is seen by as many paying customers as possible. Filmmaking at that level is a "business" after all, so recouping production costs and making as much profit as possible is a priority. I'm sure we're all familiar with the film *"trailers"* and *"promos"* we see across the various media just before a film or similar project is about to launch. Well, there is invariably a huge team of strategists and marketing people behind those kinds of campaigns, and sometimes these advertising campaigns can cost as much as the film's budget itself! One of the finest and most respected of independent animation distribution companies in the USA is "GKIDS". If you've done something special in independent animated movie production, you are definitely going to want a conversation with these guys.

Wolfwalkers

A FILM BY TOMM MOORE, ROSS STEWART
IRELAND, LUXEMBOURG, UNITED STATES, UNITED KINGDOM, 2020, 100 MIN   PG

() 91st Academy Awards Nominee   Best Animated Film
() Golden Globe Awards Nominee   Best Motion Picture - Animated
() Annie Awards Nominee   Best Independent Feature Animation

"GKIDS" website. https://gkids.com.

You on the other hand will probably have no such marketing resources at your fingertips although it will be really important to you that as many others will see your work as possible. So you need to consider a scaled-down campaign to promote your film. It is of course unlikely that anyone will actually pay to see your film, as short films traditionally never make money – not even the big budget ones that the big studios put out around **"Oscar"** times to win themselves a cheap **"Academy Award"**.

That said, there are a few things that will help you get your project out there and see. It is unlikely that your first film will win accolades or make you any money, as we've noted. But you do want it seen. Also now it exists, you should consider it as a *"call-*

NOTE

It used to be that the short film categories at the "Oscars" and other similar award-winning events were reserved for young, up-and-coming filmmakers, looking for a break in the industry with their short films. But now, sadly, the big studios see this category as an opportunity for them to buy themselves a cheap "Oscar" by throwing money at a short film that, although a lot to us is not very much for them, will hopefully dazzle the judges with the technological bells and whistles they can throw at it. This makes it so much harder for the young, up-and-coming, animated filmmakers to compete with such powerful production and marketing resources – and therefore is very unfair.

ing card" for bigger and better things for you in your future. For example, your film could lead you to a new job or support for the next new project you want to make. And it certainly doesn't hurt if you will an award or two with it along the way. So it's really important for you to get your film seen out there and your name attached to it. With that in mind, here are some low-cost options that should well be in the reach or any in-dependent short filmmaker.

Website: The first thing you might do is build a dedicated "**website**" around your film. You don't necessarily have to show the film in its entirety if you don't want to. But having a site with "**stills**" from your film, a "**bio**" about you, some "**making of**" material behind the scenes about how you made the film will all give you a *"footprint presence"* in the world that will act as a focus and founda-tion for all the other promotional things you might take on. Platforms such as *"Weebly"* or *"Wix"* offer free website space for folks to use – and there are many others – so take advantage of that while you can.

My ArtStation home page. https://www.artstation.com/tonymation.

Blog: Closely allied to your website might be a "**blog**" page. This is where you can not only talk about your film and other aspects of it creation – maybe even mentioning this book in helping you make it! – but also give yourself a platform to have an opinion in the world of animation and filmmaking. Remember, your film now has to be a *"sprat to catch a mackerel"* – in the sense that now you've made it you want to venture on to bigger and better things beyond it. This would be a perfect platform for you to express your thoughts and share your ambitions with the world if you have them.

ANIMAKERS blog page.

Email list: In this day and age, "**email list**" is golden. It is your means of reaching "your people" with a *"newsletter"* or other promotional material for this or your next project. *"Email lists"* are invariably created by folks writing to you about what you're done or hope to do – or else you can solicit folks sending you their email address from your website or blog site, so they can keep up on the latest news about you and your latest project.

My Mailchimp account newsletter home page.

YouTube, Instagram or Vimeo: If you have the right kind of personality, you might even consider starting a "**YouTube channel**" as a platform for your work and your project(s). If you don't have that kind of personality, "**YouTube**"-, "**Instagram**" or "**Vimeo**" might be a place where folks can view your film in its entirety - or at least in part. And, if you find you have a real *"hit"* on your hands, then you might even charge a small streaming fee that could go toward funding your next project, should you have one.

My YouTube channel.

Social media: It goes without saying that the best way of promoting your project, or your blog, or your website, or whatever, is to develop a "**social media**" presence. However, you may find that to compete on this level in terms of self and project promotion, it will take as many hours and as much sweat on your part as you needed to make your film in the first place! But if you can pull this off and build a presence, there's no reason why a social media campaign for you or your film could not be a scaled-down equivalent of a big studio marketing and promotional machine. In fact, I just created my own Facebook page for the "2D Academy" and will be building other social media sites soon.

The 2D Academy Facebook page.

Newsletter: If you feel that you have more to say about your film, your future work or indeed the animation world at large, then consider even publishing a "**newsletter**" from time to time. This is where having an *"email list"* comes in really handy. Indeed, there are some great newsletter creation platforms out there – such as *"Mailchimp"* and its ilk – that make such a venture very possible. A few individuals can build up quite a following for their opinions and their work but have a great and original *"newsletter"* behind them.

My "Drawing the Line" newsletter.

Festivals: And of course, the finest way of getting your film out there and seen is by entering it into various "**film festivals**". There are many platforms – like "*filmfreeway.com*" for example – where you can have access to all the festivals around the world. As long as you possess a small fund to pay for entry fees, there's no reason why you can't enter your film into many festivals, large or small. Nothing attracts attention like winning an award or two at a number of festival. So this is definitely something to consider.

My "DRAWTASTIC Animation Festival" home page on FilmFreeway. https://filmfreeway.com/DRAWTASTIC2023

Remember though, entering a festival – such as my own online "*DRAWTASTIC Animation Festival*" – doesn't guarantee your film will be accepted for screening. But if it does accept your film, most festivals will give you a "*laurel*" digital logo that you can add to the title page of your film and wear it like a badge of honor. "Laurels" confirm that your film is worthy of being watched by audiences. If you get enough laurels from a number of festivals, you might even get other festivals (and sometimes TV channels) calling you to screen it at their event!

Our coveted "Golden Pencil Award".

So, hopefully the above suggestions will give you some ideas of what you can do to promote your film once you have made it? I'm sure others will occur to you too. However, just remember that you have conquered a mountain in making this first film – in terms of your career you have just passed the first foothill. Hopefully, you'll go on to even more amazing things in time and you should begin to consider the future you might now have before you. If your film is good enough, the what you have just completed could be a perfect calling card for a future position in the mainstream animation industry or as a launchpad for further "indie-based" films you want to make outside of the industry. You could always set up a "**Patreon**" page, of something similar, so that supporters can help fund you to do what you love to do.

My *The Hermit* Patreon page. https://www.patreon.com/Muse2D.

Either way, this first film will be something you should be proud of, as well as something you can use to leave a path forward for yourself in the future. And don't forget support platforms like "Kickstarter", "Indiegogo", "Patreon", and their like. If you have something worth showing and something beyond that you want to do, then platforms such as these can open you to people who will fund our future dreams and ambitions. To anyone who has made a successful film on their one – and it is no mean achievement that you have done so by the way – a path may well now open up to you for an incredible future in animation. You just have to make these opportunities work for you and grasp new ones firmly when they appear! Making this film is your first step, but it is a really glorious step and one you should be justly proud of.

Congratulations, you are now a full-fledged **animated filmmaker**!

Suggested Assignment

Have a BIG party! You just completed an amazing achievement. Bravo!

NOT AN END – BUT A BEGINNING!

In writing this book, I find myself in the autumn years of my career. Indeed, I have announced for some time now that I'm in the exit line – but I just don't know how near to the door I am right now! The one thing that I do know, however, is that this is definitely the most creatively stimulating time of my life. I am grateful for being able to publish this book at such a time, knowing that what is offered here will far long outlive me. I therefore hope it will be judged a suitable legacy. After all, we are talking about a long tradition of animation knowledge that is in great danger of being lost in this digital age. Yet many traditions are worth fighting for, and I believe that traditional, hand-drawn animation is one of them. My heart bleeds for the great legacy we have been left, and yet which is being lost in the interest of speed and cost-cutting through new technology. We need to preserve the knowledge we have been given, as does the Japanese culture to some great extent – with some companies there, passed down through the generations, lasting anything from a few hundred years to one temple building organization that has existed for over 1,500 years! This proves that it is still possible to take the best of the past and move it forward with the tools of today

DOI: 10.1201/9781003324287-53

into a bright and ever more inventive future. The two are not mutually exclusive, which is what I believe this book will show.

Over the 10-month period I have been writing this book, it has become clear to me that there has been a slow evolution of even my own thought and methods in terms of animation. For my entire life, I have work traditionally, with pencils and paper, and probably will continue to do so until I depart for that great lightbox in the sky. However, in researching and exploring the "pixels" aspect of this book – as opposed to the "pencils" part – I have had revealed to me an entirely new avenue of creative discovery and expression. I have not entirely gone over the "the dark side" of technology, as things such as 3D animation, VR and even video games just don't grab me, despite my respect for what they can do. However, it might just surprise readers to know that a certain amount of the artwork and illustrations found in this book were actually created digitally. As a result, I am currently planning with great excitement the possibilities of digitally drawn iPad-based animation using *"RoughAnimator"* software among others. I still adore the tactile pleasure of pencil on paper of course – and process that is much more expressive and far more accurate from an inbetweening point of view I might add – but I can definitely see the advantages of "going digital" too. I still fundamentally believe that learning the core principles of movement through traditional methods is still the finest way of learning animation – even knowing that there is almost a 100% likelihood that the student will be forced into to a digital animation career ultimately. All this is why I still maintain that hand-crafted animation traditions need to be respected, protected and preserved. However, do not be surprised to see a course on iPad animation coming out from me in the foreseeable future!

My very first experiments with a "jump" action, using "RoughAnimator" in the iPad.

The Best Is Yet to Come – For You Too!

I don't believe that traditional, hand-drawn animation is the ONLY way of learning animation in this digital day and age. But I do absolutely believe it is the BEST way of learning, especially in the hands of an experienced teacher who can demonstrate what they say! For me, the kind o eye/brain/hand coordination that an animator needs to develop early on in their journey is best done by "observational sketching. Later, this can be extended through the core principles of movement. Technology is a wonderful thing and I truly celebrate it every day for the innovation and range of expression it offers the emerging artist. But technology for technology's sake, offering time savings and shortcuts, is not an advantage but a stumbling block for the emerging student animator. There is an underlying obsession that anything that makes things easier and faster has to be preferable. Yet this is a corporate myth that is singularly designed to sell more product – not improve the quality and effectiveness of character-based, animated movement. In the wake of such "progress", we lose observation, tactile experience, thinking outside the box and, in many cases, imagination or innovation. Algorithms provide us with codes and formulas, where the "same old, same old" seems to be lauded and originality is challenged or dumbed-down. But remember that the mainstream media corporations have one objective and one objective only – to get the maximum buck for the minimum of risk. That inevitably means catering to the lowest common denominator in the main – cutting out innovation, cutting out risk and cutting out opportunity for those with a new vision. Yet these things are what moves the world forward, so they should be encouraged not blocked. That is why I respect so much the indie animators of this world – the ones who don't succumb to the whims of corporate mentality and who strike out on new paths, on their own if necessary. The indies – as was the iconic Walt Disney in his early years – seek to create "art" first, then ally that to commerce and not the other way round. I hope therefore that this book speaks most loudly to the groundbreaking indie spirits in this world.

Wolfwalkers, the third of a Celtic trilogy of Oscar-nominated movies created by the incredible "Cartoon Saloon" studio in Ireland – undoubtedly the most creative and imaginative of indie animation stables anywhere in the world right now! ©Cartoon Saloon Ltd., Melusine Productions

Define Your Purpose

Ultimately, the success of this book will lie in the "intention" of its reader. If you are seeking ways of doing things that are "cheap and fast", then this book is probably not for you. However, if you admire the great tradition in animation that has evolved at the highest pioneering and expressive levels over the past century or so, then perhaps this will be the best route for you to obtain animation mastery. With my students, I don't so much tell them what to do with the knowledge I pass on to them. Far from it, I want them to show me what is within THEM – to amaze me and inspire me with their own inner spirit coming out. However, to do that and do it well, they need first to have the right skills, tools and techniques at their disposal to express themselves well. That is what I hope this book is – an all-embracing tool kit, or encyclopedia of knowledge – that will enable to confidently move forward in ways you never thought possible. Technology is not the enemy. But it can stifle knowledge at the very beginning of your journey and will restrict you later along the way too, if you don't have enough foundational skills to cut it when thinking outside the box. There is no bigger thrill than seeing what you have created – from concept to final execution – come alive, knowing that you have told your story, visually and expressively, through the highest means of character you can muster. But unless you discipline yourself to be a master animator first, and software technician second, you will never realize the potential that your future projects can have.

I was born a generation late to have made it to the Disney animation building during its Golden Age. But I now feel confident that everything I have learned and shared with you in this book can take you to that level, in the indie industry if nothing else!

Riding the Wave

I will never, ever forget the incredible advantages, opportunities and experiences I uniquely had in my early days in the industry. To apprentice with my hero, the incredible Richard Williams, and through his studio to meet and learn from some of the great masters of the golden era of Hollywood animation, was a dream come true. Then, to apply that knowledge with a life well spent in animation, and still doing so, with love, today is the kind of stuff that dreams are made of. The big regret of my life is that I have never been given that one opportunity to make a movie and show the world what I too can offer. But I have been close several times and have done pretty much everything else that was possible to do – from short films to TV specials, from advertising to award-winning productions. When seeing the admiration that others have certain master animators of the past and realizing that I actually knew them and studied and even apprenticed with some of them, I have to pinch myself at times to make sure it is real.

It doesn't come any better than this! Spending the day with my hero, mentor and teacher, Richard Williams, decades later at the Aardman Studio in Bristol, England. It was the last time I was to see him too, which makes this a bittersweet picture for me at the same time!

Improving with Age!

I am still as passionate about animating and teaching animation today as I ever was. I have never lost that special enthusiasm for what I believe is (can be, at least) the premiere art form in our present era – at least at its highest and most creatively liberated expression. My early training still governs everything I do and seek to do beyond here. Indeed, I still imagine the ghosts of my great teachers looking over my shoulder and correcting everything I do! And long may it ever be, as I only want to get better and better at what I do! My only regret today is that my body is fighting me now and cannot do everything my excited mind and imagination wants me to do. Most of all, my eyes strain more readily and my neck aches from prolonged hours at the drawing board. However, to compensate, I do a 30-minute session of Qi Gong every morning – a kind of moving meditation activity – which really does help and genuinely is the best thing ever. I have no idea if these exercises will prolong my life, but I can totally endorse that they bring more quality to the time I am having, both in health and in efficiency. Without a doubt, I find that I am still able to work as hard, if not harder, at what I do than most individuals half my age! But most important of all is the excitement and adrenalin for animation that has never left me. I still dream of making that one elusive movie – or at least working on one in some form or other – and my teaching keeps me young and informed on how the emerging generations can take what I share with them to the next level. I may not be around to see it ultimately, but I know that they will be well prepared for the potential that lies ahead of them.

My high school-level animation class students keep me young and on my toes at all times!

Paying It Forward – 2D Academy

In the face of those illusive feature projects I want to make, teaching is my biggest passion today. I love nothing more than sharing what I know with those who want to learn. Indeed, that is the biggest motivation behind this book – it certainly isn't money. Most of all, I want readers of this book to realize that it is the nearest equivalent I can offer in terms of the defining apprenticeship training I had at the hands of some of the greatest animators ever seen. So, I urge you to embrace it with all your heart – as it can only make you a much better animator in terms of the knowledge you can bring to the digital tools and technologies you'll be confronted with in the future. Nothing worth having is easily won – if it was, then everyone could do it and you would not stand out in the crowd. Beyond this book however, I am proud and honored to offer more personal teaching through my 2D Academy. At the time of writing, the COVID pandemic is dominating our lives and preventing in-classroom work from taking place. But I have tried to make the online teaching experience we offer as close to a personal, one-on-one mentoring experience as I can in a digital classroom situation. It is to facilitate the master animators of the future, based on my knowledge of the present and the great learning I had in the past. At the same time, the 2D Academy will offer on-demand video courses that share the teaching from my live classes, so that students can learn in their own time and in their own way. Further courses will be offered as time goes by – and I am indeed planning a 2D ACADEMY self-teaching campus app as we speak. This is all part of my commitment to doing everything I can - for as long as I can - to preserve the very best of animation training for anyone who wants it – and at a level they can afford. Check out our website at **http://www.2dacademy.com** for news of future offerings and developments, when and as they happen.

Graduation "Diplomas", "T-shirts" and "Golden Pencil Awards" are what the 2D Academy can offer students, in addition to top-of-the-line tuition in animation of course!

2D Animakers – Our Traditional Animator's Network

In addition to education, the 2D ACADEMY is also trying to develop a worldwide social network for traditional animators. "**2D ANIMAKERS**" is an online platform where students can study, communicate, share work and enjoy the best of submissions at the annual "**DRAWTASTIC Animation Festival**" that we sponsor too. Currently, our private online animation classes are held live via the 2D Animakers platform – as is our monthly *"Animator's Sketchclub"* drawing and/or animation challenge, also hosted on our private Facebook group that has over 11.2k members at the time of writing. However, plans for more expansion on our network are currently in progress. My vision is to not only have a center for teaching. It will also hopefully become one that celebrates current animation through our DRAWTASTIC festival, celebrates traditional 2D animation of the past through a dedicated museum, and takes everyone involved with traditional 2D animation forward into the future by way of full-scale production. At least, that is the dream! Needless to say, I strongly advise you to visit our website at **www.animakers.club** to learn of our future developments in time.

My author's page on Amazon – still dreaming of making 2D animated films out of some of them – with still more to come!

Back to the Future

But what of my own personal creative journey? Well, in an ideal world I would love to make an animated docudrama of my memoirs – with special emphasis on my journey with the animated muse, mentor and model, "Arnie", in my life. But such is the way of things these days (and the pattern of my past life efforts) that it is very unlikely that I will find funding for such a project. Yet I believe that my journey – both in and out of animation – might inspire others, just like learning the life journeys of others has inspired me. So, for the time being, my focus will be on creating a graphic novel version of my memoirs, entitled *Pouring Clean Water*, plus bringing to life one of my original movie screenplays, *MADA and the Magic Tree*, as a mystical hero's journey "graphic novel". (The significance and explanation of the title is to be revealed in the first part of my journey.) Then, if my graphic novels succeed, as I hope they might, then perhaps the funding for the animated movie versions will be forthcoming. If nothing else though, the graphic novels will enable me to share some of the truly amazing experiences and lessons I have learned thus far and is something that I can guarantee will get made, as long as I am given the time and energy to complete it. But all that is in the lap of the Gods – all I can do is *"keep on keeping on"* with everything that is in my heart and mind.

"Arnie" and I have come a long way together – and I suspect we still have a long way to go yet before our story draws to a close!

So, in conclusion (for now), I do encourage students and teachers of the various animation schools around the world to approach this book with an open mind and a willing heart. I really do think that everything I have included here will form the finest foundation of knowledge and effort that any animator of the future will need – even if their future will be entirely computer based, as I suspect it will in the vast majority of cases. And even if the whole thing cannot be implemented in it's entirely by the schools and colleges of animation out there. Even small aspects of it will lift a student's capability beyond their graduation. Students of any kind – formal or self-taught – who embrace all the challenges and assignments thrown at them here will be so far ahead of many of those already succeeding in the industry. I am thinking that TV-, Web-, app- and games-based animation will benefit especially here. Ultimately, animation has to be a "moving experience" for both animators and animation audiences. So, venture forth all you master animators of the future, and show us where this kind of knowledge, plus your own vision for the present and the future, can take the ever-evolving art form of animation. I sincerely hope that this book will enable you to do that!

Tony

July 26, 2022

My entire life and knowledge in animation, reduced to this almost 600-page manuscript. But what is yet to come, I ask myself!

Index

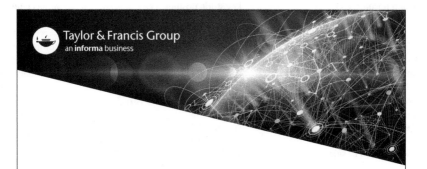

Printed in the USA
CPSIA information can be obtained
at www.ICGtesting.com
LVHW082340150324
774517LV00005B/700